FOURTH EDITION
A HISTORY
OF THE
AFRICAN PEOPLE

FOURTH EDITION
A HISTORY OF THE AFRICAN PEOPLE

ROBERT W. JULY

Professor Emeritus
Hunter College and Graduate Center
The City University of New York

WAVELAND
PRESS, INC.
Prospect Heights, Illinois

For information about this book, write or call:

Waveland Press, Inc.
P.O. Box 400
Prospect Heights, Illinois 60070
(708) 634-0081

Photo Credits
Cover: United Nations
Title page: United Nations
Part One: United Nations
Part Two (lower right): Church Missionary Society, London
Part Four: United Nations

ISBN 0-88133-631-9

Printed in the United States of America

7 6 5 4 3

Preface to the Fourth Edition

A decade and more has passed since the last edition of *A History of the African People*, an interval crowded with events in Africa's turbulent history. It has also witnessed an outpouring of research by a host of scholars whose work has appeared in book and journal, at scholarly meeting and in the lecture hall. Innumerable monographs, articles, and theses have shed light on previously obscure matters. At the same time more general histories have introduced this latest scholarship to a larger audience—for example, new or updated histories of West, Central, and South Africa, as well as the two major historical surveys of the continent sponsored by UNESCO and the Cambridge University Press.

All this profusion can be daunting to those seeking an understanding of Africa, past and present. Even the multivolumed histories from Cambridge and UNESCO are sometimes impressive more for their scholarly detail than for their clarity; the latter perhaps traceable to the former. Such an abundance of data has also been daunting in the production of this fourth edition, but simultaneously I feel it has surely dictated the necessity.

As I embarked on my labors I was struck once again with the conviction I had expressed years ago in the preface to the first edition; that is, the need for a history that illuminates and clarifies events otherwise dimly seen. Thus I have tried to make this a history which not only brings new data to light but one which also gives coherence to fact and hypothesis, thereby providing a balanced and intelligible account of the past. This history, therefore, though basically chronological, deals with themes that cut across time and place to furnish their own unity and consistency. There is, for example, migration— the vast movements of peoples, most notably the Nilotes and the Bantu. There is the power of religion, particularly in those upheavals that have periodically convulsed savanna populations ever since the advent of Islam. There is the 500-year interval of that uncertain romance between Africa and Europe that has so greatly influenced events in both continents and in the Americas.

These and other motifs appear and reappear throughout the text, but there are two in particular that have struck me with renewed emphasis from my reading of recent scholarship. The first is the intimate relationship between the African climate and Africa's history. This observation may come as no surprise to even casual readers of the daily press with its continual tidings of drought and famine, plague and mortality. What may surprise them, however, is the fact that these conditions are millennia old and have placed their mark on African societies many times over, past as well as present.

The second motif involves Africa and the wider world. Here is a relationship that has had much to say about Africa's history, an invasion of peoples, of ideas, of institutions that has often taken the initiative from Africa to favor the outsider. Such incursions, beginning in antiquity, have come down to us in the present, and have been a pervasive influence in shaping African political, economic, and social life.

I have retained the textual organization introduced in the third edition, dividing the volume into four parts. Part One, Ancient Africa, is concerned primarily with traditional African societies. Part Two appears under the title Revolutionary Africa, to emphasize those important developments across the continent that characterized the nineteenth century. Part Three, Colonial Africa, covers the brief but pivotal era of colonial control, leading to Part Four, Independent Africa, now a history in its own right, fully a generation old.

Each chapter provides suggestions for additional reading for those who wish to explore further. I have tried to keep these recommendations as brief and simple as possible. Those who wish to delve deeper may resort to the many excellent bibliographical aids currently available—the annotated bibliographies of the Cambridge African history, to name but one.

Finally, I have attempted to do what surely distinguishes history from chronicle, that is to explain through the past how Africa's present came to be as it is.

Contents

PART ONE Ancient Africa

1 The Beginnings of African History 3

The Geographic Base, 3
The Genesis of Humankind in Africa, 8
Africa and the Origins of Agriculture, 12
The Agricultural Revolution in Egypt, 16
The Distribution of African Populations, 19
Suggestions for Further Reading, 23

2 Africa in the Ancient World 24

Egypt and Kush, 24
Mediterranean Africa, 33
The Ancient Land of Axum, 36
Suggestions for Further Reading, 41

3 The States of the Western and Central Sudan 42

The World of the Desert, 42
The Ecology of Sahel and Savanna, 44
Traders in the Sahara and Sudan, 47
The Golden Commerce, 50
The Mercantile Civilization, 52
Sudanic State Systems, 56
The Kingdom of Ghana, 58
The Rise and Fall of Mali, 59
The Empire of Songhai, 61
Kanem-Bornu and the Hausa States, 64
Suggestions for Further Reading, 69

4 The Cosmopolitan World of East Africa 70

The Rise of the City-States, 70
The Portuguese on the East African Coast, 74
The Omani Suzerainty, 78
Ethiopia—The Trials of Isolation, 82
Christians and Muslims in the Eastern Sudan, 88
Suggestions for Further Reading, 90

5   The West African Forest Civilization   92

The Land and the People, 92
The Daily Life, 98
Ife, Oyo, and the Rise of the Yoruba, 103
The People of Benin, 104
The Kingdom of Dahomey, 106
The Akan States of Asante and Fante, 108
Suggestions for Further Reading, 112

6   The Great Migrations   113

The Civilization of Zimbabwe, 113
The Bantu Speakers, 116
Bantu Cultures, 119
Cushitic and Nilotic Movements, 122
Some Bantu and Nilotic Communities, 124
   Central African Bantu, 124
   Bunyoro and Buganda, 125
   The Kikuyu, 127
   Turkana Pastoralists, 128
Suggestions for Further Reading, 129

7   The Coming of Europe   131

The Roots of European Expansion, 131
The Imperial Design of Portugal, 132
The Portuguese in Kongo and Angola, 134
The Arrival of the Dutch, 137
The British and French in West Africa, 143
The Nature of the European Impact, 144
European Commerce, 149
Africa and the Atlantic Slave Trade, 151
Suggestions for Further Reading, 154

PART TWO Revolutionary Africa

8   The Genesis of Modern Africa   157

The Age of Revolution, 157
Muhammad Ali and the Modernization of Egypt, 160
Suggestions for Further Reading, 164

9   Religion and Empire in Western and Central Sudan 165

Prelude to the Great Jihads of the Nineteenth Century, 165
Usuman dan Fodio and the Sokoto Jihad, 167
Seku Ahmadu in Masina, 172
The Jihad of *al-Hajj* Umar, 174
Al-Kanemi and His Successors in Bornu, 176

Samori and Rabih, 179
Suggestions for Further Reading, 183

**10   The Eastern Sudan—Egyptian Expansionism
      and the Mahdist Revolution   185**

Invasion from the North, 185
The Ecology of Poverty, 187
Egypt in the Sudan, 191
The Southern Sudan and the Slave Trade, 193
Backdrop to the Mahdi, 195
The Mahdist Revolution, 197
Epilogue—The Khalifa Abdallahi, 200
Suggestions for Further Reading, 201

11   Population Explosions in Southern Africa   202

Mfecane—The Road from Zululand, 202
Central Africa and the Great Ngoni Trek, 207
The Search for Security—Sebetwane and Mzilikazi, 210
Moshoeshoe and the Diplomacy of Self-Defense, 212
The Boer Trekkers, 214
The Shape of Things to Come—South Africa at Mid-Century, 218
Suggestions for Further Reading, 223

12   West Africa and Europe's Humanitarian Revolution 224

The Enlightenment in West Africa, 224
Colonization, Christianity, and Commerce, 226
Senegal—The Jacobin Heritage, 229
The Bible and the Plough, 231
West African Kingdoms in the Nineteenth Century, 235
The Vanishing Dream, 239
Suggestions for Further Reading, 244

**13   Commerce and Statecraft in Eastern
      and Central Africa   245**

The Rise of International Trade, 245
The Economic Imperialism of Sayyid Said, 249
Firearms and the Shifting Ecology of the Interior, 252
Mirambo, Tippu Tip, and the Demise of Merchant Imperialism, 255
Buganda and the International Trade, 258
Suggestions for Further Reading, 260

PART THREE   Colonial Africa
14   The Partition of Africa   263

The Berlin Conference, 263
Partition—The Causes, 265

Partition—The Process, 270
Partition—The African Response, 277
Modernization and Independence in Ethiopia, 281
Suggestions for Further Reading, 286

15   Early Nationalist Stirrings in West Africa   288
Adaptation and Survival, 288
Politics and Commerce in Senegal, 290
Sierra Leone and African Nationalist Self-Consciousness, 294
Edward Blyden Creates a Philosophy of African Nationalism, 297
Liberia and the Tribulations of Independence, 300
The Demise of the Forest Kingdoms, 302
Abortive Alliance—The Westernized Africans and the
  Traditional Authorities, 304
Suggestions for Further Reading, 308

**16   The Foundations of Progress and Poverty
       in Southern Africa   310**
The Birth of a New Society, 310
Britain and Complexities of Colonial Stewardship, 311
The Revolution of Diamonds and Gold, 312
The Road to Union, 316
The Other Union, 321
Beyond the Limpopo—, 327
—And Across the Zambezi, 331
Suggestions for Further Reading, 336

17   Colonialism and Nation Making in East Africa   338
The Logic of European Imperialism, 338
British Paternalism in Uganda, 339
Kenya—Racialism in a Colonial Society, 343
Kenya—Alien Rule and African Response, 346
Kenya—The Onset of African Political and Social Aspirations, 348
The Tanganyikan Colony and Mandate, 351
Multiple Colonialism in Zanzibar, 354
British Rule and Nationalist Stirrings in the Nile Valley, 356
Suggestions for Further Reading, 359

**18   Between Two World Wars—Nationalist
       Frustrations in West Africa   361**
West Africa and the First World War, 361
The Theory and Practice of Colonial Administration, 362
Nationalist Politics in West Africa Between the
  Two World Wars, 365
The National Congress of British West Africa, 374

The Pan-African Movement, 376
Liberia and African Nationalism, 379
Suggestions for Further Reading, 381

19   In the Heart of Darkness   **383**
The Unity of Diversity, 383
The Belgian Congo, 384
French Equatorial Africa, 391
Portuguese Angola and Mozambique, 396
Suggestions for Further Reading, 400

20   The Two Societies of Southern Africa   **401**
Apartheid—Colonialism in South Africa, 401
Apartheid and the Republic of South Africa, 407
African Nationalism in South Africa, 409
South-West Africa and the High Commission Territories, 414
The Theory and Practice of Partnership in Central Africa, 416
The Rise and Fall of Federation in Central Africa, 419
Suggestions for Further Reading, 424

PART FOUR   Independent Africa

21   Toward Independence   **429**
The Foundations of Freedom, 429
The Changing World, 434
Independence Movements in the Northeast, 437
The West African Catalyst, 439
Independence—The French-African Variant, 446
The Crisis of Independence in the Congo, 450
East African *Uhuru,*   453
Black and White Independence in Central Africa, 461
The Haves and the Have-Nots, 465
Suggestions for Further Reading, 466

22   Independence Economics   **468**
The Meaning of Freedom, 468
Alternatives of Economic Development, 469
The Problems of Modernization, 473
   Agriculture, 473
   Mining, 476
   Industry, 477
The Vagaries of Economic Growth, 481
The Debt Repayment Crisis, 487
The New Pragmatism, 489
Suggestions for Further Reading, 490

23 States and Nations   **491**

The Indispensable Unity, 491
Decline of the Parties, 492
The Soldiers, 499
Civil War, 504
Suggestions for Further Reading, 512

24 Disintegrating Citadels in the South   **513**

Portugal Bows Out, 513
From Rhodesia to Zimbabwe, 516
Namibia—The Last African Colony, 520
The Afrikaner Laager, 522
"Freedom in Our Lifetime," 526
A Turning Point, 529
Suggestions for Further Reading, 531

**25 African Cultural Independence—
Ideals and Complexities**   **533**

Negritude, 533
An Independent African Civilization, 536
Europe and the African Personality, 539
The Victims, 543
The African Woman—A Quest for Social Justice, 546
Ecological Imperatives, 547
Free Markets and Democratic Politics, 550
Suggestions for Further Reading, 551

Index 553

Maps

Africa: Physical Features 6
Africa: Vegetation and Rainfall 7
Africa: Peoples and Language Groupings, c. 1800 21
Egypt, Kush, and Axum 27
Mediterranean and Saharan Africa in Ancient Times 34
The Western and Central Sudan, c. Eighth to
  Seventeenth Century 46
The East African Coast before 1800 75
Ethiopia and the Eastern Sudan, c. Fourth to
  Eighteenth Century 87
The West African Forest 95
Bantu Africa 117
European Exploration and Trade along the West African
  Coast, 1400-1800 136
Early Dutch Settlements in Cape Province 141
The Western and Central Sudan in the Nineteenth Century 168
The Eastern Sudan in the Nineteenth Century 190
Bantu and Boer Migrations, c. 1820-1850 208
Southern Africa, c. 1850 219
West African Kingdoms in the Nineteenth Century 237
East and Central Africa in the Nineteenth Century 247
The Partition of Africa, c. 1880 274
The Partition of Africa by 1914 275
South Africa at Unification, 1910 320
The Rhodesias and Nyasaland, c. 1890-1925 335
East Africa, c. 1940 342
French, Belgian, and Portuguese Equatorial Colonies
  before the Second World War 393
Independent Africa 457

PART ONE
Ancient Africa

1

The Beginnings of African History

The Geographic Base

History begins with geography. The history of humanity has always shown the deep mark of environment; put another way, the development of humankind can be seen as a struggle for freedom from the limitations of the surroundings, as an effort to control environment rather than suffer its restraints. To understand the great movements of African history, therefore, it is necessary to grasp the essentials of Africa's geography.

Though Africa is the second largest of the continents, comprising 11.7 million square miles, its size is not its most significant characteristic. More important is its equatorial location, its northern and southern extremes almost equidistant from the equator at 37° 21' North and 34° 51' South respectively. More than nine million square miles of Africa, or four-fifths of its area, lie between the two tropics of Cancer and Capricorn.

The equatorial position of Africa has contributed to its tropical climate which is warm but extreme only in certain locations and which lacks the violent temperature fluctuations found, for example, in North America. More significantly, Africa's location athwart the equator determines the pattern of continental rainfall which in turn has had a profound influence on African ecology and history. Latitudes close to the equator are continually covered by a blanket of low pressure air, that line of contact between the hemispheric air masses called the *Intertropical Convergence Zone* (ITC). As the equatorial air rises from the hot land, it cools, its burden of moisture condensing and falling in the form of heavy tropical rains. This region of heavy rainfall— chiefly in the Zaire (Congo) River basin and the Guinea coast of West Africa— gives rise to a verdant rain forest, but across the continent in East Africa, wind, sea, and topographical conditions along the equator limit precipitation, and hence vegetation, in that area.

Moving northward and southward away from the equator, the rainfall gradually diminishes through the zone of the trade winds until the subtropical high-pressure belt is reached with a precipitation of less than ten inches a year falling on its vast desert regions, the Sahara in the north and the Kalahari and Namib in the south. Once again elevation on the eastern side of the continent causes variations. In the north, the Ethiopian highlands usually receive ample rain from the spring and summer monsoons, whereas in South Africa the Drakensberg Mountains on the east coast cause updrafts and abundant rainfall locally within a narrow coastal corridor, a condition that serves to accentuate the dryness of the steppe and Kalahari regions to the west. In the extreme northwest and southwest sections of the continent a Mediterranean climate prevails, more extensively in the north where it is shielded from the Sahara by the Atlas Mountain barrier.

Because of the gradual decrease in precipitation as one draws away from the equator, the rain forest quickly gives away to a savanna grassland which in its various forms is the characteristic vegetation of Africa. Approximately one-half of the continent is covered by varieties of grass in occasional combination with forest stands, a fact that accounts both for the abundance of wild game and the importance of Africa's pastoral societies. Even the so-called desert consists primarily of arid shrub and grass areas suitable for limited grazing; indeed, although Africa's deserts cover an additional forty percent of the continental surface, only eight percent is occupied by desiccated sand and rock wastes incapable of supporting vegetation. Similarly, scarcely another eight percent of the total continent is given over to the equatorial rain forest.

The progressive gradations in precipitation must be understood in terms of long-range averages, for a major characteristic of Africa's weather pattern is in fact the erratic fluctuation in amount and timing of the rains from year to year. This fluctuation is caused by the unpredictable behavior of the Intertropical Convergence Zone which moves north and south with the seasons, following the sun in an irregular drift that finds it sometimes well beyond the equator by the time of the June and December solstices, but on other occasions lagging behind by hundreds of miles. Hence the rains may vary markedly from year to year, both in quantity and in the moment of arrival and departure. In marginal areas, those bordering the Sahara, for example, the ITC can fail to arrive at all in any given year, retreating as autumn approaches, not to return for another twelve months. Even in regions of adequate precipitation, the rains typically come in the form of violent downpours that leach the soil or run off too quickly to be absorbed into the soil. Such a capricious weather pattern has long forced low agricultural productivity and chronic food shortages, limiting population to what can be sustained in the worst years only.

Mauritanian desert

Tropical rain forest

East African plains
fronting Mt. Kilimanjaro

*Neg. No. 324778, photo by Dugmore, courtesy Department
of Library Services, American Museum of Natural History*

Victoria Falls

Highland farming in Burundi

Africa's equatorial location is based upon a geological record that hypothesizes a continent of ancient rock floating on a viscous substratum, having drifted slowly northward from a position near the South Pole to reach its present latitude about 20 million years ago. Much earlier still, this block had been subjected to extensive folding, faulting, and erosion, then about 200 million years ago it entered a benign period of periodic uplift and erosion, yielding a continental land mass of largely metamorphic character with a varying cover of sedimentary formations, and occasional igneous intrusions. Tilting slightly upward to the east and south, the continent rises from sea level in such West African points as Senegal and the Niger Delta to the several thousand foot elevations of eastern and southern Africa.

Uplift has also caused extensive internal faulting, like cracks in a sidewalk pavement, thereby forming a series of regional basins usually occupied by major rivers such as the Niger, Nile, Zambezi, or Zaire. These streams pursue leisurely, meandering courses through much of their long passage, occasionally spreading out into broad, shallow basins that once held inland seas, and finally spilling over the continental edge of the plateau in waterfalls and courses of rapids before emptying into the sea. The most celebrated of these cataracts is Victoria Falls on the Zambezi, but most other rivers have their falls—for example, the cataracts of the Nile, the rapids of the Zaire just below the city of Kinshasa (formerly Leopoldville), or the interior rapids and falls on the Niger and Senegal rivers. These rivers are navigable for long stretches in the continental interior, but their falls have greatly impeded penetration of the continent from the outside. Despite early and continuing contacts that go back to the times of Homer and Herodotus, it was not until the nineteenth century that Europe came to know anything substantial about the African interior, while only the occasional traveler from the Middle East was able to advance into black Africa beyond the Sahara. For their part, the Africans have rarely attempted to travel beyond their own continent to explore other parts of the world and to spread knowledge of Africa's people.

Africa's interior basins appear as undulating plateaus of varying altitudes, but faulting or volcanic action has created occasional highlands such as the Tibesti and Ahaggar massifs of the Sahara, the mountains of Ethiopia, the Futa Jalon in Guinea, Nigeria's Jos Plateau, or the volcanic peak of Mount Cameroon. By far the most spectacular example of faulting is found in the Rift Valley system. This gigantic four thousand-mile displacement begins in the Middle East, moves down the Red Sea, then cuts through Ethiopia before forming the long line of finger lakes in its western prong—Turkana, Tanganyika, Malawi, and others—as well as the celebrated Rift Valley of Kenya and Tanzania to the east, thus flanking the great basin containing Lake Victoria. The Rift system has been marked by spectacular volcanic action, witness the peaks of Kilimanjaro, Kenya, or Elgon, as well as the highlands of Ethiopia.

Interior basins characterized by navigable rivers and widespread savanna

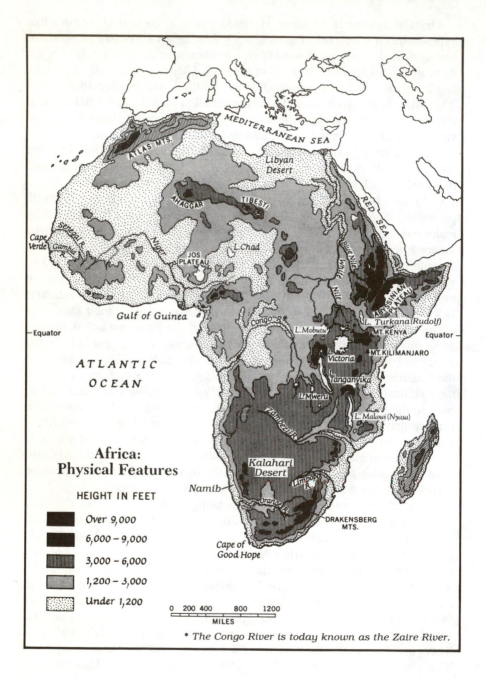

MEDITERRANEAN SEA

Libyan
Desert

ATLAS MTS.

RED SEA

AHAGGAR   TIBESTI

Cape
Verde

Senegal R.

Gambia R.

Niger R.

JOS
PLATEAU

L.Chad

Blue Nile

White Nile

Nile

ABYSSINIAN
PLATEAU

Gulf of Guinea

Congo R.*

L. Turkana (Rudolf)

—Equator

L.Mobutu

MT. KENYA

Equator—

ATLANTIC
OCEAN

L.
Victoria

MT. KILIMANJARO

L.
Tanganyika

L.Mweru

L. Malawi (Nyasa)

Zambezi R.

**Africa:
Physical Features**

HEIGHT IN FEET

Kalahari
Desert

Namib—

Limpopo R.

Orange R.

Over 9,000

6,000 – 9,000

DRAKENSBERG
MTS.

3,000 – 6,000

1,200 – 3,000

Cape of
Good Hope

Under 1,200

0   200 400   800   1200
MILES

The Congo River is today known as the Zaire River.

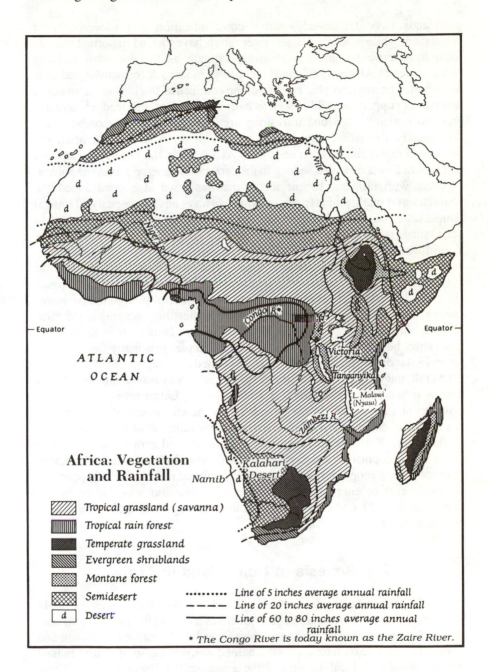

ATLANTIC
OCEAN

— Equator   Equator —

Victoria

Tanganyika

L. Malawi
(Nyasu)

Zambezi R.

Africa: Vegetation
and Rainfall   Namib   Kalahari
                                   Desert

▨	Tropical grassland (savanna)
▥	Tropical rain forest
■	Temperate grassland
▧	Evergreen shrublands
▦	Montane forest
▨	Semidesert
d	Desert

············· Line of 5 inches average annual rainfall
– – – – Line of 20 inches average annual rainfall
——— Line of 60 to 80 inches average annual
                    rainfall
* The Congo River is today known as the Zaire River.

grasslands have facilitated interior communication and movements of population, while in modern times, river rapids have yielded important sources of hydroelectric power; nevertheless, climate aside, the most striking consequence of Africa's geological record lies in its rock formations and their soil cover. The metamorphic systems of the continental shield contain immense deposits of copper and gold as well as bauxite, uranium, tin, lead, chromium, and other metals. Igneous intrusions are the source of diamonds, while sedimentary formations are responsible for South Africa's coal beds, the petroleum reservoirs of West and North Africa, even the famed salt deposits of Taghaza that contributed so long to the caravan commerce across the Sahara.

Along with climate, subsurface formations have also conditioned the character and quality of African soils, not always advantageously. Tropical temperatures in air and soil cause minerals to dissolve quickly, later to accumulate as salts after evaporation. In the case of iron, this action creates a hardpan known as *laterite*, covering about one-third of the continent, especially in the wetter savanna lands, and notoriously inhospitable to agriculture. In other areas excessive erosion following heavy rains has a similarly depressing effect on cultivation. More generally, high temperatures cause rapid decomposition of organic matter, its fertility escaping in the form of gases instead of contributing to a buildup of humus. It is difficult to generalize, however; in other regions—for example, seasonally flooded river valleys—lands of good fertility have prevailed.

Overall, the geography of Africa has produced an environment more difficult than a tropical location might at first suggest. Large areas suffer from insufficient rainfall which, combined with a mixed pattern of soil fertility, has tended to encourage a subsistence economy rather than high agricultural productivity. Until recently, shifting cultivation and erratic harvests have restricted the population and forced political decentralization. Before the advent of modern technology, large states usually emerged only with the appearance of resourceful or energetic chieftains; social cohesion was limited by the particularities of tribal differences and the difficulties of maintaining lines of communication over long distances.

The Genesis of Humankind in Africa

It was Charles Darwin who early suggested that the human species might have originated in Africa, and subsequent research seems to bear him out. The higher primates were present in the Nile valley 40 million years ago and some 20 million years later a creature named *Kenyapithecus* appeared in East Africa, possibly a local version of the genus called *Ramapithecus*. While coexisting with true apes, *Ramapithecus* possessed certain characteristics of facial bone structure and dental arrangement similar in some respects to those of modern humans, thereby prompting the discoverer of *Kenyapithecus*, the distinguished archaeologist and paleontologist Dr. Louis Leakey, to suggest that his find was a hominid, or human-type, distinct from the ape line of pongids. For Leakey, therefore, it followed that the hominid family had already split from the pongids as long ago as twenty million years, and a common ancestor for humans and apes must have lived in Africa in an even more remote past.

Leakey's conclusions, based solely upon fossil evidence, have been sharply contested in recent years by molecular biologists studying the genetic makeup of present-day organisms. In examining the genetic structure that is present in each cell, these scientists have found that the difference between humans and certain higher apes is very slight, in the case of the chimpanzee a difference of approximately 1 percent. When this variance is calibrated on a time scale, it suggests an antiquity of only about five million years, and only at that much later time were the hominids forming into a family separate and distinct from the apes. While the dispute between archaeologist and biologist continues, the more recent dating seems to be gaining ever-widening acceptance.

Whatever its age, *Ramapithecus* has been accepted by some authorities as the earliest known hominid, the remote ancestor not only of the *Homo* line leading to the modern human species but also of related parallel genuses collectively called *Australopithecines*, their fossil remains slowly coming to light through archaeological excavations. There was, for example, the Taung skull found in South Africa in 1924, a creature thought to have lived between one and two million years ago. There were the Ethiopian fossils unearthed in 1974, collectively termed *Australopithecus afarensis* and including an almost complete skull dated at more than three million years of age. There were the footprints discovered by Mary Leakey in 1978 six years after her husband's death, prints of hominid origin and fully 500,000 years older than the *afarensis* fossils. Finally there was *Homo habilis*, the "skillful man," first discovered by Louis Leakey in 1961 at Olduvai Gorge in modern Tanzania with subsequent finds by Leakey's son, Richard, in the Lake Turkana region, particularly the skull identified as "1470" which came to light in 1972.

Louis Leakey claimed *Homo habilis* as humankind's true ancestor, basing his contention on the evidence of a larger brain, meat-eating dental equipment, facile hands, and other anatomical distinctions. Like many, if not all, of the *Australopithecines*, *H. habilis* was a biped, and also a toolmaker, with a cranial capacity of up to 800 cubic centimeters (considerably larger than the 500 cc. cranial volumes averaged by *Australopithecus*). Leakey concluded that *H. habilis* had fashioned the flaked stone tools found near the remains, using them probably for butchering meat.

There continues to be much dispute as to the place of these various creatures in the line of descent. Richard Leakey, for example, argues that *Ramapithecus*, as the earliest hominid, gave rise to several lines of descent, the *Australopithecines* as well as *Homo*, all flourishing several million years ago. Eventually the *Australopithecines* became extinct, leaving only *Homo* in the form of *Homo habilis* who thrived between one and three million years ago. Others say *Rama* was antecedent to both pongids and hominids, that it was *Australopithecus afarensis* who was progenitor to *Homo* and the later *Australopithecines*. For Leakey, however, *afarensis* is probably a late surviving form of *Ramapithecus*. At the moment there seems to be agreement only in that *Homo habilis*, including the 1470 skull of Richard Leakey, is the first indisputable *Homo* and therefore the direct forebear of modern humans.

Whatever the particular antecedents, the emergence of humankind appears to have resulted from interaction between physical form and physiological function responding through the process of natural selection to the pressures of environment. Thus, reduction of forest cover might have forced certain smaller apes out of the trees in search of food, the survivors being those able to thrive on a varied animal and vegetable diet, while developing a bipedal carriage for purposes of hunting and defense. Upright carriage freed the forelimbs for carrying and for toolmaking; tools in turn led to greater facility and precision in use of the apposable thumb, at the same time necessitating the development of a larger brain to give effectiveness to newly acquired skills; a bigger more complex brain heightened perception of environment and increased inventiveness of adjustment to its limitations; and so the interaction of form, function, and surroundings brought forth the human species, its most notable distinction from other animal types being the shift in capacity from susceptibility toward adaptability to environment.

Over time, more advanced types appeared, the earliest dated at about 1.5 million years and classified as *Homo erectus*, with capabilities well beyond those of *Homo habilis*. Though its place in the line of descent has been disputed, *Homo erectus* possessed a much larger cranial capacity than *habilis*, reaching 1225 cubic centimeters as compared with the 1500 cc. volume of modern humans. The anatomy of *Homo erectus* also featured a narrowed pelvis, legs designed for striding, hands capable of refined manipulation, and better crafted tools. The most characteristic implement of this species came to be a large, pear-shaped, chipped-stone instrument with a heavy base and a pointed or edged blade, which was used as a general-purpose tool in food gathering and preparation. This so-called hand ax reached its peak of development about a half-million years ago by which time *Homo erectus* had migrated throughout the African continent and far into Europe and Asia. This widespread presence, extending over several hundred thousand years, demonstrated an ability to thrive under conditions as varied as the chilly uplands of northern China and the equatorial savanna of the East African plains. Such adaptability was due to a growing inventiveness reflected in such major steps as the inauguration of conscious vocal communication, hunting in groups, and the utilization of fire.

Since it has been demonstrated that some animals use primitive tools, the control of fire has become the quintessential human condition. Until lately the earliest use of fire had been identified at sites in modern China dating about 500,000 years ago. *Homo erectus* was thought to be the fire innovator and also regarded as the fire user at a recently discovered excavation near Lake Baringo in Kenya that has greatly extended the earliest utilization of fire to an antiquity of 1.4 million years.

Despite this resourcefulness, *Homo erectus* had shown a limited ability to specialize, as evidenced by the widespread and long-lived use of the all-purpose hand ax. In Africa as elsewhere, environmental shifts induced new and rapid responses that led to the eventual extinction of the *H. erectus*, who was replaced by newer, more adaptive types. The expanding polar ice caps pushed temperate zone climate and vegetation into the Saharan and Kalahari desert areas, enabling such types to extend their range and to multiply; coincidentally, the systematic use of fire permitted occupation of the forest while generating a dramatic advance in living standards across the ancient savanna preserves. Fire was used to drive game, to cook foods, and to prepare poisons for spear tips and glues for hafting weapons and tools. Fire also permitted the utilization of rock shelters and caves for greater comfort and safety; more than that, these semipermanent campsites introduced the possibility of division of labor, perhaps between the sexes.

Once the idea of specialization had taken hold, it suggested its own development to a human species whose rapidly expanding intellectual capacity permitted advantageous exploitation of otherwise potentially dangerous environmental changes. New techniques yielded smaller, more efficient stone tools—chisels, gouges, awls, knives, scrapers, spearheads, and eventually arrows—each tool designed to perform but a limited task that each executed, however, with much-enhanced efficiency. These improvements indicate that these people also understood the use of animal and vegetable products such as hides, bone, horn, ivory, bark, and resin, all capable of heightening their domestic comfort or their effectiveness as hunters and gatherers of food.

With greater specialization of implements and an incipient division of labor came the growing ability to adjust to regional environmental differences. For example, tool design began to vary from place to place, depending upon local needs; thus by twenty-five thousand years ago tool design in forested areas favored woodworking and rooting while in the open plains it centered upon small blades employed in the hunt. In all areas, however, an expanding population and greater social complexity led to the need for improved communication and thereby to the introduction of articulate spoken language. Communication by spoken word lay profoundly at the base of these peoples' subsequent success in creating stable societies, diversifying cultures, developing artistic and mechanical skills, and formulating aesthetic judgments and ethical standards. One notable effect of the technological revolution was that it enabled them for the first time to deal with the sheer necessity of survival on a part-time basis, thus providing leisure that they could and did begin to devote to other pursuits, chiefly artistic activity, including personal adornment, as well as reflections of a religious nature. Here was the beginning of a self-conscious preoccupation with their place in the world.

These rapid developments appear to have begun with earlier versions of *Homo sapiens*, whose inventiveness in adjusting to their surroundings was matched by a capacity for genetic change leading to the emergence of the modern human species, as we know it, *Homo sapiens sapiens*, approximately fifty thousand years ago. Various geographic conditions stimulated biological as well as cultural adaptation, causing selection and encouragement of desirable genetic characteristics to meet the exigencies of particular environments, while broadcasting widely those genetic traits that assisted these populations in successfully adapting in all parts of their expanding world. Within another twenty-five to thirty thousand years, further genetic variations had appeared from which the present racial patterns of the world are derived.

Africa and the Origins of Agriculture

The change in human economy from food gathering to food production has rightly been regarded as a shift of monumental importance in human history, its implications as profound for humankind as the previous revolution of specialization and division of labor. First, it brought a vast increase in population, for it was now possible greatly to multiply and localize the supply of food. Even more significant was the shift from a nomadic to a settled form of social life. Hunting communities obliged to move with the game and subject to seasonal water shortages, could never establish themselves long in one place and consequently could never produce and accumulate wealth above the bare necessities, which they were obliged to carry with them. As cultivation was introduced, however, these early human beings could look beyond immediate toward ultimate objectives. They could accumulate and preserve food for future consumption, utilizing the time freed for some other purpose than subsistence. They could continue the process of specialization, exempting certain individuals from the task of food production to follow other pursuits — war-making and statecraft, artistic endeavors, the practice of religion, the development of writing, the improvement of technology, and, in general, the acquisition of knowledge. Greater population density and a sedentary existence made possible for the first time an urban culture wherein exchange of goods and services and the communication of ideas became the natural order of things. Some argue that these developments could also have marked the genesis of warfare; the necessity to protect or to attack accumulated wealth.

For a long time it was widely accepted that this food-producing revolution had its beginnings in the Fertile Crescent of the Middle East, more particularly at hillside sites in ancient Palestine and Babylonia. There, as far back as ten thousand years before Christ, a people known as *Natufian* began to cultivate barley and wheat, utilizing serrated stone sickles for harvesting and, incidentally, inaugurating urban settlements of which the best known is Jericho with its brick dwellings and its massive walls, celebrated in Biblical annals.

The origin of plant cultivation in Africa apparently occurred much later, during the middle of the fifth millennium before Christ in Egypt and at analogous or later times in other areas such as Ethiopia and the West African savanna.

It seemed reasonable to infer that cultivation spread from the Middle East to other continents; in Africa to Egypt, where wheat and barley came to flourish in the rich soils of the Nile floodplain, as hunting and fishing peoples gathered, driven to the river by the growing desiccation of the surrounding Sahara region. For Ethiopia an independent invention of agriculture was often suggested for the crops were different and indigenous; even here, however, there was a widely held belief that cultivation might have arrived with Semitic immigrants coming from southern Arabia during the first millennium before Christ. In West Africa there were also local crops including millet, sorghum, rice, and yams. Many authorities contended that agricultural methods probably reached this region from the east, filtering across the desert or spreading up the Nile valley from Lower Egypt, thence across the southern savanna fringe below the desert, the technology of cultivation adapting itself to the local West African cereals and tubers.

At first much of the evidence of agricultural origins came from archaeological findings and their radiocarbon dates which unequivocally established the early start of cereal farming in the Middle East. At the same time, the advantages of farming in supporting complex civilizations argued that the seemingly less efficient hunter-gatherer societies were quick to take advantage of a more efficient food-producing economy. It appeared, therefore, that agriculture had been invented during a short interval at a single point from which it spread quickly and widely across the world.

Increasingly this concept of rapid revolutionary change has come into question. To begin with, there were many crops and agricultural methods that clearly did not have a Middle East origin. In Africa, hoe and digging stick cultivation has always predominated while the use of mounds and ridges remains characteristic of the wetter zones. Many local African crops have been identified, for example, the cereal, teff, and the bananalike ensete in Ethiopia; or the West African millet known as fonio. Conceivably the methods of cultivation for cereals like millet and sorghum might have spread from the Middle East via Egypt, but this hardly takes account of techniques for growing rice or yams, both indigenous to the regions below the Sahara, both raised by methods far removed from the plow and draft animal of the Middle East.

Further, there is the growing suspicion that cultivation was long in developing; that much time was needed to evolve the crops, the competence, and the customs to support an effective agricultural system. By 3000 B.C. most of the world's major cultigens were already in use, some in highly evolved forms and many geographically far removed from their points of origin as wild plants. The case of cotton seems particularly illustrative. In the form of woven cloth cotton appeared first about 3000 B.C. at Mohenjo-Daro, centered in the ancient civilization of the Indus River valley. The cotton of Mohenjo-Daro came from a cultivated plant that had undergone much genetic and structural change but was nonetheless identifiable as the descendant of a wild ancestor still growing today along the edges of the Kalahari Desert in southern Africa. Historical botanists have speculated at great length about the formidable questions of how, where, and by whom the cotton was domesticated, and what means were employed for transporting it thousands of miles by land and sea from its homeland to a far-off civilization apparently unconnected with Africa. Whatever may be the answers to these difficulties, it seems clear that a very long history of travel and cultivation must have preceded the fact of a flourishing cotton cloth industry in the Indus Valley fully five thousand years ago.

Finally, the tendency to view agriculture in its present-day capabilities, feeding massive populations and sustaining the complexities of modern life, tends to obscure the fact that the first domesticated plants would have shown no clear advantage over food gathering, for primitive crops initially differed little from their wild progenitors. A stable environment needs no altering. Hunter-gatherers living in reasonable sufficiency would have had no reason to change their ways. Only the pressure of necessity—a growing population or dangerous environmental changes, for example—could have forced a shift to new systems of food production. When cereal cultivation suddenly appeared in the Nile Valley, its quick adoption probably indicated a long prior familiarity with the manipulation of plant and animal resources, combining incipient domestication with the collection of wild species.

Thus, for Africa, as for other continents, the origin of agriculture appears as more evolution than revolution, a process rather than an event, the domestication of crops coming at different times with different species at different places. Humans developed a symbiotic relationship with certain plants, beginning with simple gathering, graduating to intermediate stages of mutual dependence and assistance, and culminating in certain cases with full-sale cultivation. In Africa even today there are wild grasses that are collected for food, sometimes growing in close proximity to cultivated plants. Other plants, such as the oil palm or shea butter tree, are not planted but are encouraged through clearing and burning of surrounding brush; thus their yield is harvested as their growth is aided. With cultivated crops like yams there has been genetic alteration through selective harvesting, thus making the plant fully dependent upon cultivation for survival. People protect and cultivate; in return they gain nutrition, convenience in cropping and storage, and predictability for future harvests.

Advanced hunting societies possessed pottery, sickles, and mortars employed for food gathering and processing, and these implements were easily adapted to plant domestication. Between the tenth and third millennia before Christ an aquatic fishing society appeared widely across the Saharan latitudes which were then marked by an environment of lakes, swamps, and streams. These fisherfolk manufactured harpoons, designed pottery, and spoke related languages, but there is no evidence that they practiced agriculture; nevertheless at Saharan sites there may have been domesticated goats or sheep as early as the late sixth millennium, that is, before the appearance of herding in the Nile Valley. It can be argued, therefore, that some preagricultural societies of the Saharan region were already familiar with aspects of domestication and that they gradually evolved a broad area of agricultural activity from West Africa through the Niger bend and Lake Chad to the Nile and the lakes of East Africa, responding perhaps to population increase, to the growing desiccation that reached its full extent by the mid-third millennium, to the arrival of Middle East crops, or to a combination of all these factors. It was not until the third millennium B.C. that food production and pastoralism appeared widely throughout sub-Saharan Africa, but it is difficult to escape the notion that there was a long anterior knowledge, if not practice, of agriculture.

Perhaps the Saharan pastoralists were a separate people and not the harpoon-throwing fisherfolk; in any case, recent research in linguistics has introduced a new conjecture over agricultural origins. Those involved, it has been suggested, were Cushitic speakers, that is, ancestors of present day East African peoples like the Beja of the Red Sea Hills or the Ethiopian Agau. As long ago as 7000-5000 B.C. they spoke a common language that can be located geographically in a homeland along the upper Nile Valley in Nubia north of the Ethiopian highlands. For its part, archaeological research has established that the practice of grass collecting preceding systematic agriculture had its earliest known manifestations by 13,000 B.C. in the Nubian Nile Valley, with later appearances extending across North Africa and into the Middle East. The particular grasses utilized varied from region to region, as did the harvesting implements, but the basic impact of the evidence points to an invention of grass collecting in Lower Nubia between the Nile and the Red Sea Hills.

Here is a thesis that specifically contests and contradicts the orthodoxy that cultivation began from a nuclear location in the ancient Middle East. The Afro-Asiatic languages include Berber, Egyptian, and Semitic branches as well as Cushitic and others. Reconstruction from modern grammars and vocabularies makes it possible to determine that an ancestral Afro-Asiatic language of great antiquity, perhaps fifteen thousand years old, led to divisions exemplified by modern languages now spread from North Africa to the Middle East. The original homeland was in the northeast Africa of Nubia. Thus there is a remarkable correlation between the origin and spread of grass gathering and the linguistic diversification of the Afro-Asiatic language family. In the words of a recent authority, "It is difficult to escape the overall import of the evidence that grass collection was invented first in or near Lower Nubia, perhaps in the region between the Nile and the Red Sea, and spread from there to its other areas of occurrence."

Such an hypothesis supports the notion of a long period of experimental plant cultivation prior to the advent of full-time farming. It accounts for the appearance of agriculture at different times in scattered discrete points with different crops and local tool design. In Africa it fits the eventual demise of the Saharan harpoon fishing civilization, and it explains the appearance of new methods and sources of food production. It sheds light on the relationship between agriculture in the Nile Valley and the Middle East. And, as with the origins of humankind, it offers Africa as a possible source for the invention of plant cultivation.

The Agricultural Revolution in Egypt

The fisherfolk of the Sahara are thought to have been primarily negroid and present linguistic kinship hints at a common ancestral language. The harpoon fishing civilization stretched from the rivers and swamps of West Africa through the Niger River floodplain and Lake Chad, on to the Nile and thence to the great lakes of East Africa. Characteristic bone harpoons and clay pots decorated with a distinctive wavy line are found throughout as are linguistic connections such as those between Songhai spoken along the Niger bend and the Nilotic tongues of East African peoples like the Luo or Maasai. Increasing desiccation gradually destroyed this aquatic civilization, leaving only a few remnant peoples clinging to the shores of shrinking lakes and streams; others may have migrated to more friendly environments like the West African savanna or the Nile Valley. In any case, pre-dynastic Egypt came to be peopled by hunters and gatherers who gradually developed a sedentary existence on the edge of the river valley where they engaged in fishing and where they began to grow cereal crops. A number of independent groups occupied several river points stretching from the delta (Lower Egypt) south to Upper Egypt, but though there were differences in the details of their culture, the essentials were much the same. Hunting, fishing, and foraging provided the basic support of the economy, but all communities cultivated both wheat and barley. Most possessed domesticated animals including cattle and sheep or goats. Flax was grown on which a textile industry subsisted. Silos were used for grain storage, pottery dishes were common, and serrated stone sickles were employed for harvesting. Housing was primitive, consisting of reed-mat windscreens, and the communities were small and in some cases temporary. Being food producers, the people now had leisure time which they devoted to the refinement and elaboration of local arts and crafts. Economic self-sufficiency was still the standard and there were only the beginnings of an exchange economy between the settlements. There was as yet no thought of public works or the capital improvement of the land. Such an idea as controlled irrigation, for example, seems to have been unknown.

Gradually a changing environment forced more sophisticated responses.

As the Sahara wet phase drew to a close, and desert tributaries dried out, settlements on the edge of the Nile Valley could no longer be maintained and by the fourth millennium the communities were moving down the sides of the valley to the naturally irrigated floodplain of the Nile. The result was a dramatic increase in food production followed by a similar expansion in population. The older semipermanent villages gave way to completely settled communities which grew in size and complexity. By the middle of the fourth millennium the culture of Egypt's Nile Valley had evolved in several important respects. First of all, the economy had shifted once and for all from a combination of farming and food gathering to a major reliance on agriculture, which was now aided by a certain amount of artificial irrigation. Secondly, the earlier near-isolation had been replaced by a lively long-distance trade with centers in the Aegean and the Middle East. Obsidian from Abyssinia, juniper berries and timber from Palestine, copper from Sinai, and lapis lazuli from Afghanistan were exchanged for flint, stone vases, and other local products. Papyrus boats turned the Nile into a highway and the domestication of the ass made possible caravan transport to the Red Sea.

The establishment of agriculture and the expansion of commerce led in turn to further specialization within the economy, for increased production meant that merchants and craftworkers could be supported, and trade with distant places demanded the manufacture of local products for exchange. Flint was mined systematically, metalwork was introduced, first with nonsmelted ores and later through casting, stone tools were further refined, the production of elegantly worked stone vases increased, and new artificial substances were manufactured such as glazed pottery suitable for ornaments. Finally, a changing economy meant a rising level of personal prosperity. The old windscreens and round huts came to be replaced by substantial mud structures, rectangular in form and generous in size, with framed doors and windows. Graves, too, became larger and more lavishly furnished. Here was evidence of incipient inequalities in wealth which reflected the rise of a class structure.

The record was not one of unbroken progress and expansion, however, for with the development of settled, stable communities came competition for land, trade, and livestock. Towns were early fortified and local warfare became part of existence. Wars with outsiders also had to be endured. Hence there arose very early in the Nile Valley a condition that has characterized life in Egypt ever since—the search for political stability to insure economic prosperity. By the third millennium B.C. Egyptian peasants from the fertile river floodplain could produce approximately three times as much food as they needed, but they required freedom from unrest to achieve this output. Consequently, they were always willing to concede a substantial degree of authority to whatever political establishment could guarantee protection from internecine warfare and invasion, submitting to the confiscation, through taxation, of their surplus production in return for peace in the land.

When the pharaohs of the First Dynasty unified Upper and Lower Egypt and installed themselves as absolute temporal and religious rulers, they introduced for the first time this idea of a strong power at the center so necessary to the economic health of the river valley. With their rule, a divine kingship was imposed on the population with all its extravagances of royal prerogative. Princely palaces reflected great wealth but were nevertheless exceeded in their grandeur by the great tombs which contained not only the lavish accouterments necessary for the needs of their royal inhabitants but also large numbers of human victims who were obliged to accompany their royal master to the grave.

Nevertheless, the social and economic growth made possible by unification led to revolutionary changes which established ancient Egyptian civilization as one of the great cultural flowerings in the world's history. Not only did the population rise dramatically from the thousands to the millions, but further specialization introduced by the state was the basis of a growing class structure in a society of increasing complexity capable of producing and consuming a broadening variety of artistic and utilitarian goods. Making use of the surplus production of the peasantry, the kings supported a priestly and ministerial class, a professional army, large numbers of artists and craftworkers, laborers for the mines, quarries, and irrigation projects, as well as the hordes of engineers, artists, and workers who built the great palaces and monumental tombs of the pharaohs. The social structure became in essence a static hierarchy with a large serf population serving a ruling nobility and a king-god.

This social structure was the basis for Egypt's cultural revolution. The monumental architecture of royal palaces and royal tombs was supplemented by decorative arts of great beauty. Though pottery was widely used, it was largely utilitarian, but the Egyptian stone vessels of the day have yet to be equaled by later civilizations in their technical and aesthetic perfection. The manufacture of linen had already so advanced by the First Dynasty that there has been little improvement ever since, and Egyptian jewelry is justly celebrated for its intricacy and variety of materials. Bone and ivory carving along with woodwork and leatherwork produced articles of everyday utility, but these crafts also yielded their share of artistic achievement in carved statuettes or engraved household articles.

Great steps were taken by scribes in the development of writing, which began with simple pictograms for the keeping of records but which soon advanced to more complex, stylized hieroglyphs and a cursive script. Writing in turn led to systematic accumulation of knowledge and assisted in the development of precise scientific calculations necessary for the vital business of agriculture. A calendar was early invented as an aid in anticipating the annual inundation of the Nile, and this device was supplemented by other astronomical observations. The floodwaters were controlled by a network of banked fields and canals, and there was a system for raising water to higher ground above the floodplain. Farming implements were made of both stone and metal, for copper had become a common material in the manufacture of tools, weapons, and vessels. Indeed, copper woodworking tools effected a remarkable advance in cabinetry that involved not only a thorough knowledge of techniques such as joining but also a refined use of carving and the inlay of mixed woods with ivory or ceramics.

An expanding economy and a society of increased sophistication required the constant import of raw materials for manufacture. Copper, malachite, and turquoise were brought in from Sinai; quantities of cedar and cypress from Lebanon; ebony, ivory, and resin from the south; and semiprecious stones from western Asia. Exports consisted of raw materials and manufactured goods, especially the celebrated Egyptian stone urns that have been located in Palestine, Crete, and as far off as the Greek mainland. Internal trade was also brisk judging from the extensive distribution of hallmarked pottery and the use of natural materials from widely scattered centers.

No doubt the daily life of the peasants remained simple, their possessions crude, but the more prosperous members of the community lived in comfort and, in the case of the nobility, in luxury. Rectangular houses with brick- or wood-vaulted roofs often contained well-appointed, separate living and sleeping quarters along with baths and toilets. Wooden beds and chairs were usually built low to the ground and upholstered in leather or cloth. Small stone tables served individual diners while alabaster chinaware alternated with rough pottery in presenting a wide variety of poultry, meat, fish, cereals, fruit, and drink, including wine and beer. Clothing was appropriately light, while cosmetics were much fancied as a complement to the jewelry of which the ancient Egyptians were unusually fond.

The Distribution of African Populations

Whatever the genesis of agriculture in Africa, it seems clear that regionally distinctive populations were emerging across the continent during the later Paleolithic age. One major early-evolving form appears to have been a proto-Bush, or Khoisan, type who ranged widely through an Africa of woodland and grassland areas sustained by moderate Mediterranean climate. About ten or twelve thousand years ago rising temperatures and a varying distribution of moisture gradually brought about the configuration of desert, savanna, and rain forest which has continued to exist across Africa to the present day. These changing conditions induced genetic shifts within localized segments of the proto-Bush population, thereby promoting the racial specialization that now exists.

On the southern and eastern plains, for example, small-statured ''Bushmen'' made an appearance and thrived for a time, though today they survive only in minute numbers in southern Africa as the San (''Bushmen'') hunters and the Khoikhoi (''Hottentot'') cattle herders. Within the heavy Congo forests, the Khoisan forebear developed into the diminutive pygmoid hunter; in each case, smallness of stature was the adaptive response to a hunting environment where one's survival depended upon quick reflexes and muscular agility.

In a broad band across the continent extending northward into the steadily drying Saharan regions, the proto-Bush Khoisans evolved as the negroids, whereas in northern Africa, it seems probable that they formed the ancestral body to the caucasoid Berbers and the Egyptians of historical times. Much later, West African negroids gave rise to a vast migration that spilled across subequatorial Africa during approximately the first fifteen centuries of the Christian era, filling the southern part of the continent with the variety of peoples known as Bantu. Beyond these divisions, hybrid populations attest to intermixing among basic African groups as well as with outsiders from other continents.

During recent years uncertainties have developed concerning the most effective means for describing this distribution of African populations, more specifically whether an accurate assessment is best achieved by racial or by linguistic classification. While at first racial groupings might seem superior, this method presents ambiguities which have led to growing reliance upon language, a technique that indeed eliminates certain complications, but unfortunately introduces others.

The traditional approach employing racial classification defines large blocks of fixed racial types, taking little account of internal variations or of groups that fit none of the major classifications. For example, southern Bantu living in close contact with Khoikhoi or San are much different in appearance and culture from the Arabicized Swahili Bantu of the East African coast; again, East African Nilotic herders and West African farmers, both negroids, are infrequently classed together by observers who tend to emphasize other quite substantial differences in appearance and culture. It was at one time even suggested that the Nilotes were a mysterious branch of the white race.

Description of African populations by language grouping has offered a plausible alternative to racial categories, both in view of the relative precision of linguistic classification and its total independence of racial considerations. Thus, the linguistic configuration in Africa finds the language family known as Afro-Asiatic occupying, with its Cushitic variant, much of the northern continent from the Sahara to the Mediterranean and Red seas; the Niger-Congo groups in West Africa but probing eastward almost to the Nile in the form of Kordofanian; the Nilo-Saharan languages in north central Africa following a line from the Niger bend to Lake Victoria; the Bantu speakers throughout the subequatorial portions of the continent; and the click Khoisan languages in the extreme south.

Such an arrangement tells much about the movement and placement of African peoples. The homogeneity of Bantu languages permits the bold hypothesis that small groups from the Benue River valley began a migration about the time of Christ which spread across the southern third of the African continent in less than the two millennia of the Christian era. Substantial differences among the Niger-Congo (or Niger-Kordofanian) languages suggest

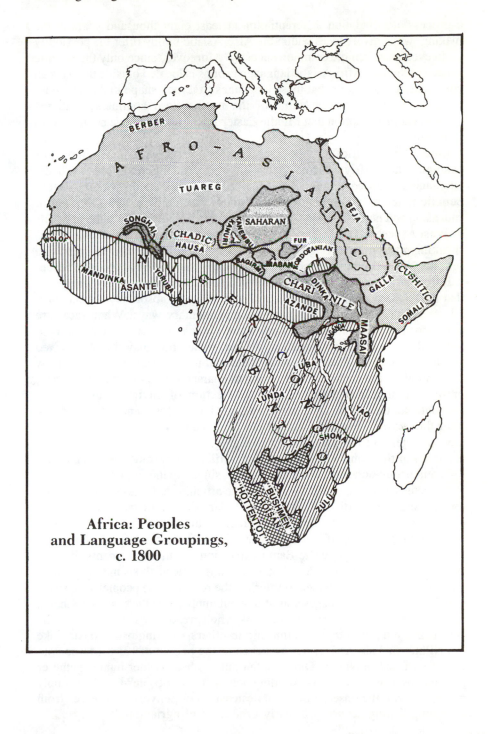

Africa: Peoples
and Language Groupings,
c. 1800

a process of population differentiation at least eight thousand years in the making, while divergences within the Afro-Asiatic family offer the possibility of an even more remote common ancestry. Moreover, since only the Semitic branch of the five Afro-Asiatic language groups is located outside the African continent, it is arguable that these languages first took shape in Africa, more particularly in the lower Nubia of the northeastern continent, with the consequent presumption that Middle Eastern Semites may have been African in origin.

Linguistic classification, however, is also beset with difficulties. For example, the clearly negroid Hausa of northern Nigeria speak a Chadic language associated through the Afro-Asiatic family with Middle Eastern Semitic tongues, while neighboring Fulani, seemingly a hybrid fusion of caucasoid and negroid strains, are firmly linked linguistically to the negroids of West Africa. In East Africa, the Nilotic Luo have become part of a Bantu-speaking population in Buganda and adjacent regions, but on the other side of Lake Victoria other Luo continue to employ their original Nilotic speech.

If there is a lesson to be drawn from such complications, surely it suggests that no single system of classification is absolute or absolutely satisfactory; all can help to illuminate the past in complementary ways. When races are understood not as homogeneous population blocks but as concentrations of physical or genetic characteristics, a racial population may then be viewed as a higher density of these characteristics within a time and space flux. New concentrations are continuously forming as characteristics multiply, hybridize, or die off in response to the natural selection of environmental forces. Populations, therefore, need not be regarded as uniform and static; indeed, quite the contrary, for many and various combinations of racial characteristics are possible, and they are always changing.

Acting in the same way, linguistic classification permits assessment of a different population flux, also branching, fusing, expanding, or fading away. If this confuses, it also clarifies—the Semitic affinities of Hausa suggest cultural connections with north and east, just as Fulani skin color indicates a similar genetic connection. Already, where other methods are wanting, linguistic analyses are providing African historians with stunning reassessments of major historical events. Beyond the Bantu expansion are the movements of other African migrants, notably the Nilotes, and linguistic analysis may yet clarify still another of Africa's ancient mysteries, the role of those peoples who speak the Central Sudanic languages now strung out thinly along the southern Saharan edge. Were these the harpoon fisherfolk who spread across the width of the continent? What was their relationship to others—to linguistic cousins like the Nilotes of East Africa, perhaps even to the people of Kush-Meroe who later flourished in Nubia? Did they fan out to absorb older hunter-gatherer populations or was theirs an expanding homogeneous people? Did they simply disappear with the onset of Saharan desiccation or convert themselves from a hunting-fishing economy to early producers of agriculture?

Suggestions for Further Reading

For African geography and geology see J. F. A. Ajayi and Michael Crowder, eds., *Historical Atlas of Africa* (Essex, England: Longman, 1985) along with an older general geography of the continent like L. D. Stamp and W. T. W. Morgan, *Africa: A Study in Tropical Development*, 3rd ed., (New York and London: Wiley, 1972).

Knowledge of early humans in Africa changes so rapidly that up-to-date assessments are likely to be found in journals. See, for example, Jeremy Cherfas and John Gribbin, "Updating Man's Ancestry," *New York Times Magazine*, August 29, 1982, or the excellent *National Geographic* articles, "The Search for Our Ancestors" and "Homo Erectus Unearthed," vol. 168, no. 5, 1985. For the dispute over *Homo* origins see Richard Leakey and Roger Lewin, *Origins* (New York: Dutton, 1977), and *Lucy's Child* by Donald Johnson and James Shreave (New York: William Morrow, 1989). See also the recent survey, D. W. Phillipson, *African Archeology* (Cambridge: University Press, 1985).

Hypotheses concerning agricultural origins and dispersals are discussed in J.D. Clark and S. A. Brandt, eds., *From Hunters to Farmers* (Berkeley: University of California Press, 1984) and in the older but stimulating C. O. Sauer, *Agricultural Origins and Dispersals*, 2nd ed., (Cambridge, MA and London: M.I.T. Press, 1969). Two important articles on early African food production are Christopher Ehret, "On the Antiquity of Agriculture in Ethiopia," *Journal of African History*, vol. 20, no. 2, (1979) and J. E. G. Sutton, "The Aquatic Civilization of Middle Africa," *Journal of African History*, vol. XV, no. 4 (1974).

For predynastic Egypt there is J. D. Clark, ed. *Cambridge History of Africa, From Earliest Times to c. 500 B.C.* (Cambridge: University Press, 1982), or an earlier work: *Archaic Egypt* by W. B. Emery (Harmondsworth, Middlesex and Baltimore: Penguin, 1961).

The evidence offered by African linguistics is to be found in J. H. Greenberg, *The Languages of Africa* (Bloomington, IN: University Press, 1966). See also R. Oliver, "The Problem of the Bantu Expansion," *Journal of African History*, vol. 7, no. 3, (1966) and Greenberg's "Historical Inferences from Linguistic Research in Sub-Saharan Africa," J. Butler, ed., *Boston University Papers in African History*, vol. I (Boston: University Press, 1964). The older G. P. Murdock, *Africa: Its Peoples and their Culture History* (New York: McGraw Hill, 1959) offers a comprehensive survey of Africa's peoples and cultures but a number of its conclusions have been challenged by specialists.

2

Africa in the Ancient World

Egypt and Kush

During the third millennium B.C. Egypt established her position as one of the preeminent powers of the ancient world. A strong and absolute monarchy made possible full exploitation of the rich soil of the Nile floodplain, and a rising national wealth led to some of humanity's greatest cultural and artistic achievements. For more than two thousand years Egypt held her place as a major seat of ancient civilization in the West. Facing outward from Africa, she placed her imprint on the Mediterranean world, but she also faced inward to exert the authority of her ideas and institutions on the people of Africa.

The main line of Egyptian penetration to the south was along the great highway of the Nile, and the impetus was trade which only gradually led to conquest and occupation. Egypt's natural boundary on the south was the First Cataract of the Nile near the modern site of Aswan; below lay Nubia, inhabited by peoples of unknown and quite possibly varied origin, sedentary groups presumably engaged in farming and herding. Egypt had little interest in Nubian foodstuffs, however; rather she sought other products—gold from the Red Sea hills, hardwood and ivory to supplement her own dwindling supplies, granite for the massive tombs that Egyptian architects of the Old Kingdom were producing for her divine monarchs.

Egyptian influence in Nubia appeared early in dynastic times. The records of the First and Second Dynasties at the beginning of the third millennium refer to successful military expeditions to the south based on superior organization and weaponry, and graves of the Nubian people dating from this time contain copper tools that were of Egyptian design and origin. By the time of the great pyramid builders of the Fourth Dynasty (c. 2700-

24

c. 2550 B.C.) Egypt was quarrying quantities of Nubian diorite for her mortuary sculpture without encountering local resistance, while during the Sixth Dynasty (c. 2420- c. 2260 B.C.) the pharaohs received homage from tribes south of the First Cataract despite the fact that no attempt had been made to occupy the country on a permanent basis.

Nevertheless, during the Sixth Dynasty which closed out Egypt's Old Kingdom, there was a record of increasing interest in the south. Canals were built through the First Cataract to enable boats made of Nubian timber to bring Nubian granite blocks north for the royal pyramids. Soldiers from the south were recruited into Egyptian armies engaged in campaigns against Bedouin tribes to the east. Finally, there were a number of expeditions made deep into what later came to be called the Sudan to explore and to trade. The name of one of these caravan leaders has survived, and thus we know of Harkhuf who undertook four journeys, each well over six months in duration, returning with quantities of ebony, ivory, frankincense, skins, and on one occasion a dwarf with which the pharaoh, Pepi II, was much impressed.

Harkhuf went south, not by boat, but across country with three hundred donkeys to the "Land of Yam." Perhaps the dwarf was in fact a Pygmy, thus implying a deep penetration to the south. More likely, however, Harkhuf journeyed only as far as Kerma just beyond the Third Cataract, an important market even in those ancient days where caravans from the south or from the El Fasher region of Darfur would have arrived with the goods that Harkhuf obtained. Hence whatever the extent of Harkhuf's own travels, there clearly were trade contacts with people far in the interior. These contacts did not necessarily imply peaceful relations for Harkhuf reported hostility toward his expedition on at least one occasion, and eventually punitive campaigns were required to subdue the southerners. With the death of Pepi II, however, the central authority in Egypt collapsed. Not only did this bring an end to the Old Kingdom, but for a time it also terminated Egyptian interference with the peoples to the south who were now left free, sometimes to prey on their former overlords.

Egyptian interest in the Sudan, somewhat tentatively expressed under the Old Kingdom, became much more pronounced with the revival of strength during the dynasties of the Middle Kingdom. Coincident with the demise of the Old Kingdom and possibly caused by the withdrawal of Egyptian power north of the First Cataract, Nubia had been occupied by a race of pastoralists whose origins are obscure but who may have been either indigenous or migrants from the steppe country west of the Nile. These so-called C Group people spread as far east as the Red Sea hills and were in possession of the Nile Valley south of the First Cataract when Egypt was united once again by the princes of Thebes who founded the Middle Kingdom about 2150 B.C. Egyptian unity led quickly to a revived interest in trade to the south which in turn brought conquest and occupation. Several military expeditions led to the establishment of a series of forts along the Nile as far as Semna, a strong point about twenty-five miles south of the Second Cataract where a permanent frontier was fixed.

The existence of fortifications certainly indicated that the local people did not take kindly to the Egyptian presence, but from the Egyptian point of view military strength was a necessary step in a carefully executed plan to develop a major trading center far down the river where ivory and gold could be obtained. The forts, which were fourteen in number, were of sturdy mud-brick construction reinforced with timber and were designed with multiple walls, towers, and revetments which made them virtually impregnable. Some were evidently sited to maintain peace-keeping garrisons while others were placed along the river at points where the traffic was vulnerable to attack. Clearly they were an important and successful device insuring a free flow of commerce through the Nubian province between the First and Second Cataracts in the face of a potentially hostile local population.

The object of this commerce was the land known as Kush with its center at Kerma about one hundred fifty miles due south of the frontier post of Semna. Here, beyond the Third Cataract, the river opens up for a long stretch of navigable water known as the Dongola Reach. At Kerma the Egyptians of the Middle Kingdom built a trading post on what was at that time an island in the river. This trading station, which was probably the work of the Pharaoh Amenemet II (c. 1938- c. 1904 B.C.), was of typical reinforced mud-brick construction with the main building approximately one hundred fifty feet long and seventy-five feet in width. A second floor contained storage rooms as well as living quarters for guards and the community of Egyptian artisans who worked there. Nearby on the mainland a large cemetery with remains of both Egyptians and local residents suggests that the Egyptian post at Kerma, while fortified, was essentially a trading center and that the Egyptians lived peaceably over long periods among the local people on a basis of mutual commercial advantage.

Within the Egyptian compound were workshops where a variety of goods were produced, judging from the raw materials such as graphite, resin, mica, and rock crystal, which have survived along with supplies of partly manu-factured glazed pottery and beads. What the remains at Kerma indicate is the beginning of a Nubian culture of local origin with an Egyptian overlay. Burial customs and practice appear to have remained Nubian, but the funerary chambers contained Egyptian statuary, and there is evidence that the local population favored a certain style of Egyptian jar long after it had gone out of fashion in the north. The artisans working at Kerma produced a wide variety of pottery, cabinetwork, jewelry, metalware, and ornamental objects that showed both Egyptian influences and local motifs. Surprisingly few goods were imported directly from Egypt, a fact that would indicate that the people of Kush by and large preferred the adaptations of the craftworkers based in Kerma. It is possible that the virility of the local culture reflected the fact that only a small number of Egyptians were ever permanently resident in Kush.

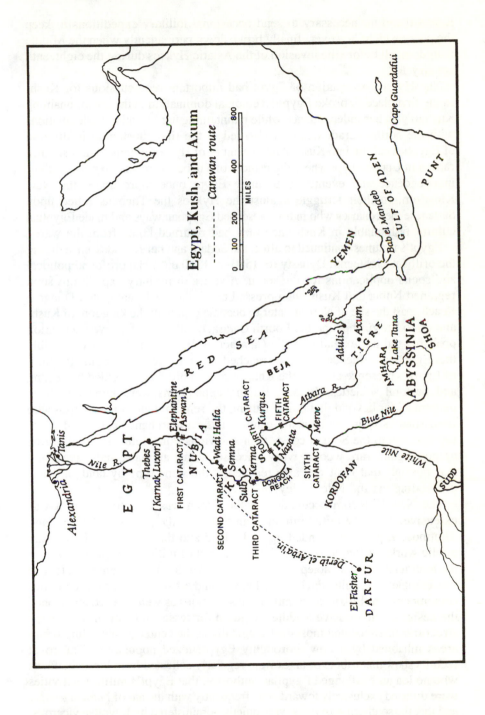

Egypt, Kush, and Axum

--- *Caravan route*

MILES

0   100   200   400   800

It was therefore necessary to send occasional military expeditions to keep the peace which, however, finally broke down permanently when the Middle Kingdom fell before the invasion of the Asiatic Hyksos during the eighteenth century B.C.

The Hyksos occupation of Egypt had important repercussions for Kush. In the first place, it broke Egyptian colonial domination in the south, enabling Kush to gain her independence while maintaining her lucrative trade relations with the north. Paradoxically it also led to the first substantial infiltration of Egyptian culture into Kush. After a century of Hyksos domination, resistance rallied in Upper Egypt where the princes of Thebes were able to reassert their independence and eventually to unite Egypt once more under the New Kingdom. In their struggle against the Hyksos the Thebans relied upon Sudanese mercenaries who in time absorbed Egyptian ways and made Egyptian culture fashionable in Kush once they had returned home from the wars.

Egypt's fortunes continued to affect the Sudan, and her recrudescence during the brilliant Eighteenth Dynasty (c. 1580- c. 1340 B.C.) had profound political and social implications for the south. A series of military expeditions soon regained Nubia and Kush, then pressed along the easily navigated Dongola Reach, past the site of Napata, later to become capital of the kingdom of Kush, and on to Kurgus beyond the Fourth Cataract, although effective occupation probably did not extend past the Cataract itself. Nonetheless, it is possible that Egyptian influence may have reached as far as Meroe, bringing the limit of Egypt's presence close to the Khartoum area previously settled by fishing and pastoral societies. Indeed, trading expeditions were known to have penetrated far beyond that point. During the reign of Queen Hatshepsut who flourished early in the fifteenth century B.C., a merchant fleet sailed down the Red Sea to the Somali coast, then known as Punt, returning with a rich cargo of gold, rare woods, ivory, incense, skins, animals, and slaves, and it is possible that Punt was also reached at the same time by land caravans proceeding via the Nile Valley.

The New Kingdom occupation of the Sudan was as complete as it was extensive. After the initial military campaigns of the pharaohs Ahmose and Thutmose I, peace descended upon the land and the emphasis of Egyptian public works shifted to serve religious instead of military purposes. During the long reign of Amenhotep III (c. 1405- c. 1370 B.C.), for example, a temple was completed at Sulb which rivaled in size and artistic merit its more famous contemporary at Luxor. Such military installations as were erected abandoned the design of the massive Middle Kingdom fortresses in favor of formalized structures often located most unstrategically at the center of sprawling urban areas inhabited by a now thoroughly Egyptianized population. The royal records show that tribute or taxes were regularly collected from local chieftains who no longer challenged Egyptian authority, that Egypt's military activities were directed exclusively toward Asia frequently with the aid of Nubian troops, and that the southern provinces were quietly administered by Egyptian viceroys.

It is difficult to estimate how many Egyptians actually lived in the Sudan during the New Kingdom era, but the number was probably not great. At no time did the Egyptians develop a taste for emigration, and as the Sudanese became absorbed into Egyptian culture, the need for outside control was correspondingly reduced. Apparently the many temples helped maintain Egyptian ascendancy, and not only in religious affairs for surviving records suggest that a range of economic monopolies were granted to the priests by the pharaoh. One of these was the trade in gold which continued to be a major export to Egypt, being widely mined in Nubia and Kush as well as obtained from peoples dwelling further south. Other exports included the always popular ivory and ebony along with ostrich feathers, animal hides, perfumes and oils, and some grain and cattle. Slaves were also brought up from Nubia and Kush although the large numbers claimed in the Egyptian records may be exaggerated.

The rhythm of Egypt's history led once more to decline, this time to provide Kush with the opportunity to turn the tables on her former master. It was now more than five hundred years since the armies of Thutmose had moved irresistibly up the Nile, and a virile royal line had long since been replaced by a weak and corrupt administration divided by intrigue in which Nubian troops and officials played an increasingly important role. By the close of the Twenty-second Dynasty, which came to power during the tenth century B.C., Egyptian authority had become so weakened as to enable Kush to exercise actual if not nominal independence. A royal line of Kush emerged which ruled from the capital established at Napata, which practiced many local customs such as Nubian burial rites, but which presumably considered itself the protector of an Egyptian civilization now in danger of corruption in the land of its genesis. The royal tombs at Napata grew steadily more imposing, and the rulers more wealthy and powerful. Substantial numbers of Egyptian scribes, priests, and artisans now lived and worked in the southern cities and the Egyptianized kings of Kush practiced traditional pharaonic religious and dynastic customs, for example, the marriage of royal brother and sister.

By the middle of the eighth century, the kings at Napata had extended their authority to include Upper Egypt; then under Piankhy (751-716 B.C.), the Kushite armies conquered the rest of Egypt, and the ancient country astride the Nile fell under the control of its Twenty-fifth Dynasty made up of the kings of Kush. Piankhy's successors consolidated their control over Egypt but almost immediately came into conflict with another expanding power. From the rugged Assyrian hills of Nineveh emerged tough, disciplined armies equipped with iron-tipped weapons that soon proved irresistible. By the end of the eighth century, Assyria was master of the ancient Near East and was thwarted in an attempt to invade Egypt only when her troops were cut down by plague in Palestine in 701 B.C.

The Assyrian attack was merely postponed. In 671 B.C. Esarhaddon led his armies to Egypt and defeated the energetic and resourceful Kushite King Taharqa (688-663 B.C.) whose forces could not stand up to the Assyrian iron weaponry and fighting tactics. Taharqa was defeated but not conquered, however. Retreating to his capital at Thebes, he raised another army and reoccupied Lower Egypt as soon as the Assyrian forces had withdrawn. It proved to be only a temporary success. The Assyrians soon returned, defeated Taharqa a second time, reoccupied Memphis and other centers in Lower Egypt, then took Thebes in 666 B.C. forcing Taharqa to flee southward. A few years later an ill-conceived effort to retake Egypt by Taharqa's successor resulted in the devastation of Thebes by the troops of Asurbanipal, and the Kushite reign in Egypt came to a permanent conclusion after its brief hundred-year ascendancy.

The military and political exploits of Egypt's Kushite kings were paralleled by a sensitive regard for cultural development. King Taharqa was particularly active in this respect. He erected monuments at Karnak, Thebes, and Tanis in Egypt proper, and raised or rebuilt a number of important temples in Kush. The description of one of these has survived—how it was constructed of sandstone with the help of Egyptian architects and craftworkers, how some of it was faced with gold leaf and how the landscaping included an artificial lake and gardens, how gold, silver, and bronze altars adorned its interior, and how the mighty king was able to dispatch the wives of defeated princes from Lower Egypt to serve in his temple far up the Nile.

This preoccupation with Egyptian civilization survived long after Kush had lost her political control over Egypt. The kings continued to use their Egyptian royal titles and represented themselves wearing the double crown of Upper and Lower Egypt. Court ceremony and religious practice remained Egyptian as did the official written language. The burial chambers of the royal pyramids were laid out in the classical manner with the traditional granite sarcophagi, the full complement of pots, tools, jewelry, and other articles needed in the spirit world, and the religious texts drawn from the Book of the Dead or the tombs of earlier Egyptian dynasties. Yet, at the same time, parochial influences were at work that were ultimately to convert Kush from an outpost of Egyptian civilization to a self-contained Sudanic kingdom, gradually replacing reliance on its northern neighbor with an intrinsically domestic culture tinged with Egyptian and other foreign influences.

At first it was military and political considerations that contributed to isolation. In 591 B.C. an Egyptian army from the delta defeated Kush and sacked Napata, sealing off the south with a garrison at the Second Cataract and ending once and for all any lingering ambitions that the Kushite kings may have had to reoccupy Egypt. One direct result of this defeat was the transfer of the capital farther southward at Meroe, long a thriving river port located upstream from the Atbara confluence and only about one hundred fifty miles north of the site of present-day Khartoum. Though the immediate cause of the move was strategic, it was invited by other considerations. The kingdom of Kush now reached well beyond the junction of the Blue and White Nile and may even have extended to the great papyrus marshes of the Nile known as the Sudd, as well as west into Kordofan. Hence Meroe with its central location and southern orientation was a more appropriate capital than Napata. Not only was Meroe a good port, but it also had easy access by caravan to the Red Sea trade, while its location within fine grazing land made it logical for the country to rest the basic economy on its herds of cattle, goats, and sheep. Finally, it was at Meroe that an early African iron industry developed. A plentiful supply of ore and wood for fuel was available locally, thus enabling Meroe to become one of Africa's first iron-producing centers from which knowledge of ironworking is presumed by some authorities to have spread broadly throughout the African continent.

Not surprisingly in view of its economic assets, the kingdom of Kush continued to thrive from its new capital. Meroe was well known to the ancients with its walled palace on the river's edge, its great temples with their massive masonry platforms, its rows of pyramids in which generations of kings and queens were buried, its furnaces and forges and the great slag heaps still visible today, and its sprawling urban clutter. For some time the culture remained uncompromisingly Egyptian, for example during the reign of the great King Aspelta (593-568 B.C.), despite the fact that he had probably been responsible for transferring the capital from Napata to Meroe. Gradually, however, isolation from the north began to leave its mark, and a century later the knowledge of Egyptian hieroglyphs was clearly declining. Egyptian of an increasingly corrupt style continued as the court language, but early in the second century inscriptions in the local Meroitic tongue first appeared, initially as hieroglyphs in the Egyptian manner and then in an idiomatic phonetic form. Although Meroitic writing has been deciphered, its words, as with Etruscan, cannot yet be understood, an impediment both to a proper grasp of Kushite history and civilization and to identification of the linguistic sources of the Meroitic tongue itself. The relationship of Meroitic to the main body of African languages still remains a matter for present-day speculation, although it has recently been linked tentatively to the eastern Sudanic branch of the Nilo-Saharan family. Such uncertainties are related to others—for example, the origins of the inhabitants of Kush and the identity among those peoples of modern Africa who are their descendants.

Along with the establishment of its own vernacular language, Kush steadily developed an indigenous culture, particularly after the third century B.C. While Egyptian influences persisted, they were joined by Hellenistic and certain Asian art forms arriving via the caravan routes from the Red Sea, all synthesized into an identifiable Meroitic style. This eclecticism manifested itself in various ways—the locally inspired preoccupation with lion and elephant motifs, the utilization of Greek architectural elements, or the presence of sculpture showing possible Indian influences. Typical in this respect are the temples at Naga—the low, ungainly Lion Temple, its hulking strength of distinctively Meroitic character, standing near the so-called "Kiosk" with its Hellenistic style and Egyptian embellishments.

If somewhat derivative, Kushite civilization was scarcely the result of political weakness, at least until the first century after Christ. Those few inscriptions that have survived tell of active kings such as Ergamenes, or Arqamani (c. 220 B.C.), whose power extended north to the First Cataract of the Nile; Netekamani and his queen, Amanitare (c. 12 B.C.- c. 12 A.D.), who built the temples at Naga; and Sherkarer, the son of Netekamani, who celebrated a military victory over an unknown foe with an unusual carved relief depicting his triumph. To be sure, a Roman army sacked Napata in 23 B.C. in retaliation for a raid on Aswan, but the defeat need not have been overwhelming and no occupation ensued. In fact, the last known contact that Meroe had with the Mediterranean world came in the form of expeditions sent by the Roman emperor Nero in pursuit of interests that may have been as much mercantile as military.

Fresh contacts such as this might have sustained the cultural and political virility of Kush, but from this point it followed a steady decline in power and wealth. It was not an age of growth, however, either in the Sudan or in the Mediterranean. Rome was uninterested in a decaying kingdom far off in the sandy wastes of Africa, and as atrophy slowly spread throughout imperial Rome during the early centuries of the Christian era, poverty, depopulation, and stagnation became more and more general. Shut off from a dying world, Kush expired alone. While to the north Egypt slowly collapsed under the weight of famine, brigandage, nomadic attack, and urban unrest, Kush left no record of its final agony. It is necessary to turn to the kingdom of Axum to learn that Kush apparently fell to a local people called Noba who in turn were subdued by the Axumites during the early fourth century A.D. Some years later King Ezana of Axum dispatched a punitive expedition that overran and destroyed Meroe and its surrounding territories:

> I made war on them [the Noba]. . . . They fled without making a stand, and I pursued them . . . killing some and capturing others. . . I burnt their towns, both those built of bricks and those built of reeds, and my army carried off their food and copper and iron . . . and destroyed the statues in their temples, their granaries, and cotton trees and cast them into the [Nile]. . . . I planted a throne in that country at the place where the rivers [Nile] and [Atbara] join.

The sack of Meroe put an end to the thousand year hegemony of Kush, yet the ultimate fate of its surviving people has remained a mystery. It was at one time suggested that they might have retreated westward into Kordofan and Darfur, perhaps even as far as West Africa where many peoples have traditions of eastern and northern origins, and where certain artistic motifs or ideas like divine kingship or centralized government might have come from Egypt and Meroe. Such speculations seem now to have been abandoned for lack of concrete evidence. No Meroitic materials have been unearthed west of the Nile, while West African traditions of eastern origin can easily be accommodated by later arrivals connected with the spread of Islam and the growing activity of the trans-Saharan trade.

There is also the question of Meroe's position as the source from which knowledge of ironworking spread throughout the African continent, presumably moving to West Africa in the hands of the fleeing Meroitic refugees after their defeat by Ezana. Probably Meroe was the first iron-manufacturing center in eastern Africa, but whether it was the earliest for the sub-Saharan continent as a whole, or even the most important point of dispersion, is open to serious question. Iron artifacts have been found in Kush dating from the fourth century or earlier; nevertheless the habitual refining of iron at Meroe does not seem long to have preceded the first century B.C., by which time the mining and smelting of iron had already appeared among the Nok people of West Africa. However the Nok may have gained this knowledge, either by independent invention or outside influence, it does appear open to argument, considering the dating, that the necessary techniques first arrived by way of Meroe.

Mediterranean Africa

If knowledge of ironworking did not arrive in West Africa from the east, it may have come from the north, across the desert trade routes from Carthage which was founded by iron-using Phoenicians, probably late in the ninth century B.C. At first, the Phoenician interest in Africa was tangential, for her merchants were concerned with the east-west trade in the Mediterranean, and African ports were but way stations where ships could put in for provisions and goods could be transshipped. Carthage was only one of many such entrepôts, but it was extremely well situated at the narrow waist of the mid-Mediterranean, and with the decline of the Phoenician cities, the African colony emerged as the center of a trading empire of Punic settlements that stretched to the Pillars of Hercules at Gibraltar and beyond. The city of Gades on the Atlantic side of the Iberian peninsula was a Carthaginian outpost leading to trade farther north in Cornwall and Brittany. How far south the Carthaginian ships penetrated is uncertain. Carthage had inherited a number of Phoenician trading posts on the Moroccan coast beyond the Pillars of Hercules, and Herodotus reported active Carthaginian trading down the west coast of Africa. Moreover, there survives an account from the fifth century B.C. which tells of a Carthaginian admiral, Hanno, undertaking a long journey that may have led him to Sherbro Island on the Sierra Leone coast and possibly as far as Mount Cameroon.

The credibility of Hanno's account has been frequently called into question, but it does seem probable that Carthage attempted a certain amount of exploratory travel down the West African coast, and it is also reasonable to

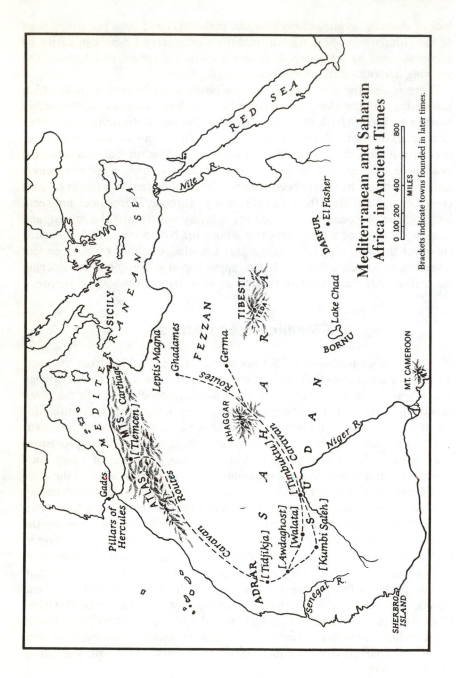

Mediterranean and Saharan
Africa in Ancient Times

0 100 200   400   800
MILES

Brackets indicate towns founded in later times.

speculate that she might have had some commercial interest in overland routes south across the Sahara. On the whole, however, the small amount of evidence available is negative. While the main items of trans-Saharan trade—gold, slaves, ivory, ostrich feathers, skins, and carbuncles—were to be found in the Punic markets, these items could also have been obtained in Mediterranean Africa. There survives a report of at least one Carthaginian said to have crossed the desert, but the report is secondhand and suspect. Though circumstantial, the fact might also be noted that no coins from the Mediterranean world have yet been found in the western Sudan, whereas many have been located in East Africa as far south as Natal. It would appear, therefore, that Carthage's African preoccupations were essentially agricultural, not commercial—that is, she was interested primarily in the Mediterranean coast and its Berber population as a source of food for her maritime establishments, and these ports were oriented northward, not southward.

Much the same judgment can be made of Rome after she had defeated Carthage and established herself as the chief power along the North African coast. Roman interest in Africa was even more exclusively limited to food production, and her administrative and military policies were keyed to this objective. African trade never bulked large for Rome. Her demand for gold, slaves, wild animals, and ivory was considerable, but these items were in good supply without the necessity of turning to trans-Saharan sources. Some Roman legions probably marched south to Tibesti and others may have crossed the desert to reach the Sudan, but these would have been isolated instances, discrete military operations rather than part of an effort to establish definite relations southward. Yet relations there were between the Sudan and North Africa; indeed, there had always been contact dating back to the prehistoric era when the Sahara enjoyed a moister climate and supported, first a widespread fishing economy along her water-courses, and later pastoralists on her slowly desiccating surface.

By historic times a regular connection between the sub-Saharan Sudan and Mediterranean Africa was being maintained and, Egypt and Kush aside, the contact followed two well-defined caravan routes. The first was in the east running from Germa and Ghadames in the Fezzan southwest to the Niger near the top of the great bend. The other was western, beginning in Morocco, descending southwestward along the Sahara side of the Atlas Mountains to the district of Adrar in modern Mauritania, then east to the trading centers in the region of the Niger bend. Writing in the fifth century B.C., Herodotus had spoken of the Garamantian people of the Fezzan proceeding south into the desert where they used four-horse chariots to chase "Troglodyte Ethiopians." Presumably the troglodytes were the Teda, or Tubu, people of Tibesti, but the story of Herodotus had been discounted as improbable until the recent discovery of numbers of cave paintings in the Sahara representing horse-drawn chariots. At the time Herodotus composed his history, conditions in the desert may have been only slightly less severe than they are today.

In any case they permitted the use of horses during historic times to maintain contact across the desert. It was probably the Hyksos who first introduced horses to Africa. By the beginning of the first millennium B.C. they were being used in the Fezzan and gradually they spread throughout all of North Africa and into the desert. Before this, it is likely that oxen were extensively employed for transport. Hence by the time the camel came into general use in the desert during the third and fourth century A.D., trans-Saharan communication had long been a reality.

Trans-Saharan communication should not imply a substantial trans-Saharan commerce, at least not at this early stage. It is true that the Carthaginians regularly obtained carbuncles from the Garamantians whose attacks on the Teda, moreover, may have been for purposes of commercial slaving. Nevertheless, both Carthage and Rome seem to have been primarily interested in products commonly available in North Africa, and neither appears to have been particularly sensitive to the potential gold resources of West Africa. Such indifference argues ignorance, which in turn suggests that the trade was modest and intermittent, conducted probably by Berber pastoralists for North African markets with little reference to wider international exchanges. The large-scale trans-Saharan trade that finally emerged rested upon two essential but later developments—the establishment of the camel to revolutionize desert transport, and the appearance after the eighth century of the Arabo-Berber merchant to organize the great trans-Saharan caravans.

The importance of the early Berber pastoralists should not be ignored, however. It was these nomadic people who traversed the Sahara first by oxen, then later by horse-drawn chariot, and finally by camel. They discovered and cultivated the oases, dug the wells, and pursued a trans-Saharan trade along with their pastoral activities. The exchange of goods was accompanied by an exchange of ideas and an intermingling of blood. Thus, if the knowledge of ironworking and the use of certain plants came to West Africa from elsewhere, it may well have been the Berber who brought them south from the Mediterranean world.

The Ancient Land of Axum

To the south and east of the valley of the upper Nile, the land rises in a series of giant terraces to the heights of the Abyssinian plateau, a massive block of mountains which extends from the Nile to the Red Sea. Here, in this rolling upland, the Blue Nile traces its course in a great loop, racing from its source in Lake Tana in a five-thousand-foot descent through the cascades of its deep-cut gorge finally to join the more sedate White Nile at Khartoum. This mountainous country, with its peaks so easily converted into fortresses and its river canyons impeding communication, has found internal cohesion difficult but freedom from invasion relatively easy to achieve. Its history has therefore tended to unfold in isolation from outside interference and influence, but often in a pattern of parochial dissension and division, a pattern that has frequently meant economic and political unrest as well as social stagnation.

Such isolation was not always the case, and to the ancient world the land of Ethiopia was regarded as an important outpost of the ancient civilization of the Middle East and Mediterranean basin. Much further back in time the Ethiopian plateau had been occupied by peoples now thought to have been Cushitic speakers, who developed one of the earliest centers of agriculture in Africa. In the southern highlands, hoe cultivation of ensete predominated, while to the north the Cushites concentrated on grain culture. These northern highlanders apparently utilized plow cultivation, both with their indigenous cereal, teff, and with imported grains such as wheat, barley, and millet. Whether their plows were developed locally or adapted from Middle Eastern designs is presently unknown.

It seems probable that early relations with Egypt existed and that Egypt was the source of Ethiopian wheat and barley and possibly of ensete as well. In any event, plow cultivation by indigenous farmers appears to have preceded a major intrusion of Semites from the Yemen who began to cross the Red Sea and occupy the northern Ethiopian plateau early in the first millennium before Christ. The Semites were traders and their crossing of the Bab el Mandeb from Arabia to Ethiopia was a logical step toward commercial control of both Red Sea coastlines. Their mercantile pursuits led them up onto the plateau in search of trade, but here the mountain climate encouraged them to settle among the local Cushitic speakers as farmers. Though the migrants were few in number, their movement to Africa was continuous over a thousand years and more, and gradually they joined with the local Cushites in a genetic and cultural fusion that formed the nucleus of the Ethiopian people.

Compared with the much larger body of resident Cushites, the newcomers were not numerically significant, but they arrived with important cultural baggage that was to contribute profoundly to the Ethiopian civilization as it subsequently emerged. To begin with, they introduced many technical achievements including a written language, advanced architectural forms, systems of irrigation, and a number of agricultural skills. The language of the Yemeni immigrants was Sabaean, a Semitic tongue that combined with local Cushitic forms eventually to produce Ge'ez, the classical language of Ethiopia. Indeed, the very word, Ge'ez, derives from the southern Arabian tribal name, Agaziyan, just as the geographic term Abyssinia follows from Habeshat, another Semitic group from the Yemen.

If influences from southern Arabia could be expected, more surprising were the numerous Hebraic elements that also crossed the Red Sea to become integrated into the literary and religious traditions of Ethiopia. The source appears to have been an expanding Hebrew kingdom in the days of Solomon and his successors, a development that introduced Jewish immigrants to southern Arabia and eventually to Ethiopia. The result was contained in a broad range of Jewish cultural influences—the tradition of the Ethiopian royal line stemming from Solomon and the Queen of Sheba; the legend of the Ark of the Covenant brought to Ethiopia by Menelik, Solomon's son and Ethiopia's first king; the Judaic beliefs and ceremonies of the Cushitic Falashas and other Ethiopian peoples long resistant to Christianity; and finally the many Hebraic practices—dietary requirements and observance of the Jewish Sabbath, for example—to be found in Ethiopian Christianity itself.

During the initial stages of their Ethiopian residence, the Yemeni Semites remained a Sabaean colony, but distance and assimilation into Cushitic strains led to independence and the eventual emergence of the sovereign state of Axum. Establishing their kingdom on the northeastern Abyssinian plateau which descends in an abrupt scarp to the Red Sea, the Axumites traded with their ancient Arabian homeland, and from their position on the shore of the Red Sea they became part of the commercial system that linked the eastern Mediterranean, the Middle East, and the East African coast with the thriving markets of India. This was an ancient commerce based upon the demands of pharaonic Egypt for the spices, the precious stones, and the incense of India needed to satisfy the king-gods on the Nile. East Africa, too, was an early supplier for the Egyptian market; even under the Old Kingdom there had been expeditions to the land of Punt in search of gold, ivory, ebony, and myrrh. That this trade continued to be important to Egypt was evidenced by the successful expedition of Queen Hatshepsut during the ascendancy of the New Kingdom one thousand years later.

The exact role of Axum in this early trade rests on supposition, for no direct evidence survives, but by the time the Ptolemies succeeded to the Egyptian throne during the third century B.C., there were close relations between Egypt and Axum. Occupying the site of Adulis which later became the chief port for Axum, the Ptolemies added elephants to their other imports from the south, for these beasts were in great demand to support military campaigns against the Seleucids. Adulis became a possession of Egypt which colonized it and drafted the local people into the Egyptian army, and Axum, though remaining independent, came under strong Egyptian influence.

By the time Egypt fell before the armies of Rome, Axum had become a major element in the trading complex of the Red Sea and the East African coast, and her commerce and authority steadily increased. The capital city of Axum was a wealthy, cosmopolitan center where the interior trade routes converged and caravans arrived regularly from the south and west with ivory and rhinoceros horn, animal hides and gold dust; these were sent on for export to Adulis, now the port for Axum, along with locally produced spices and gum, as well as tortoiseshell gathered along the coast. By the first centuries of the Christian era, Axum was said to control large areas of the African coast, ranging from the northern extremity of the Abyssinian plateau to the beginning of the East African "horn." This expanding state resulted from energetic campaigning such as was evidenced by one Axumite king, the account of whose exploits has survived to the present. In a series of engagements he consolidated his control over the Tigre region of northeastern Abyssinia, extended the hegemony of Axum north and northwest as far as Egypt and south to the straits of Bab el Mandeb, and crossed to Arabia where he subdued tribes that had been plundering ships and caravans, thus securing trade routes by both sea and land.

It was in the middle of the fourth century A.D. that Axum achieved its greatest development both as the leading entrepôt and strongest military and political power in East Africa. King Ezana, who reigned long and successfully during this period, busied himself making safe the caravan tracks within his realm and extending his control to areas of chronic unrest where the ambush of traders was the chief occupation. In this way he subdued the Beja in the deserts north of Ethiopia and forced them to live within the Axumite kingdom, then proceeded with other campaigns aimed at chastising those who preyed on his commerce. His last expedition was also his greatest—the campaign against the people of Kush in response to their revolt against Axumite overlordship. Ezana's success was complete, driving his adversaries before him, sacking their cities, taking many prisoners, destroying their crops, and confiscating large quantities of livestock.

In commemorating his exploits Ezana had always spoken of his debt to the pagan gods of Axum, but in the case of Kush he ascribed his good fortune to the "Lord of Heaven, Who has helped me and given me sovereignty . . . and . . . has this day conquered for me my enemy." This was a significant change for it meant that the king had been converted to the Christian faith which had been making some headway in his realm since the early years of his reign. Ethiopian tradition states that the kings of Ethiopia are of Judaic stock in direct descent from Solomon and the Queen of Sheba, and goes on to offer a somewhat fanciful account of the country's Christian conversion, completely ignoring the role of Ezana. In fact, Christianity had been early introduced into Axum through mercantile relations with Byzantium, but it became the official religion of the state as a result of Ezana's conversion. This resulted from the devoted missionary work of a Syrian Christian named Frumentius who had been Ezana's tutor and who eventually became bishop at Axum on appointment by the bishop of Alexandria. However, Ezana's conversion seemingly had political as well as religious implications for it cemented good relations with the Roman emperor, Constantine, and ratified Axum's position as the commercial and cultural outpost of Hellenic civilization in East Africa.

Outside the court the conversion had little immediate influence for the majority of the people still worshiped their ancient gods. Nevertheless, by the sixth century after Christ, Christian influence had become well advanced and, because of the historical connection with Alexandria, the Ethiopian church followed the Egyptian Copts in their adherence to the Monophysite doctrine. This doctrinal divergence had no effect on relations with the Mediterranean world, for Byzantium, though it persecuted Monophysites in its own land, regarded Axum as a friendly Christian power. Ethiopian merchandise continued to play a major part in the international trade complex, and there is evidence that Axum's far-ranging commercial activities may have penetrated well inland, possibly tapping gold-bearing areas of the interior.

Nevertheless, signs of decay were already apparent. The Mediterranean world, its strength spent, was slowly disintegrating. By the end of the fifth century A.D., the power of Rome lay destroyed in the West, the victim of successive waves of invasion combined with internal decay. In the East the old Greco-Roman trade with India dwindled and died, and knowledge of East Africa's ports was lost. The agricultural population of Axum had always been dependent on outsiders to maintain its contacts with Mediterranean civilization; hence, when the Muslim conquests of the mid-seventh century engulfed Egypt and North Africa, Axum was suddenly cut off and thrown in upon itself. Arabs occupied Adulis, and other Red Sea ports fell to the rejuvenated Beja who scattered the Yemeni, Jewish, and Greek merchants and severed the trade routes. Economic stagnation led to cultural decline and political chaos. Greek was no longer spoken, minted currency became rare, church construction ceased, and pagan worship was revived. Gradually the Christian faith was naturalized and adapted to local conditions, producing the particular brand of Christianity that developed in Ethiopia with its amalgam of Coptic doctrine, indigenous pagan survivals, and Jewish practices imported from Arabia before the rise of Islam. At the same time the central power declined and the local nobility began to indulge in civil strife. The pressure of the Beja forced the Axumites to turn their attention inward, first to the hills of their native Tigre and then by degrees to the less accessible parts of the Abyssinian plateau in the Amhara and Shoa country to the south. Here the Axumites found a population to whom they brought their Semitic language of Ge'ez and their Monophysite Christianity, and gradually there emerged an Ethiopian people born of the fusion of the Semitized Axumites with the Cushitic highland peasant farmers.

Although the strength of Axum declined, its culture survived to become part of another Ethiopian civilization that was to live in isolation for a thousand years. Unfortunately the substance and source of the ancient culture of Axum is little known. Certainly there was influence from southern Arabia and from Greece—the earliest known king of Axum had a Greek education and later kings issued their public documents in Greek as well as Ge'ez. Essentially, however, these early Ethiopians developed their own civilization; witness, for example, the pronounced artistic sophistication of local inspiration exemplified by the celebrated stone monuments of Axum. The purpose of these monoliths is not certain—some say they marked grave sites—but clear to see is their lightness and grace and the architectural motifs that indicate a secure knowledge of stone and wood construction of a post-and-lintel design. Indeed, some of Axum's ruins suggest that at one time she was the site of multistoried castles with stepped walls and battlements. Such seems likely, for travelers reported that during the sixth century the king of Axum lived in a formidable palace with corner towers, bespeaking a power and elegance appropriate to the importance of its royal inhabitant:

> The king . . . was naked, wearing only a garment of linen embroidered with gold from which hung four fillets on either side; around his neck was a golden collar. He stood on a four-wheeled chariot drawn by four elephants; the body of the chariot was high and covered with gold plates. The king stood on top carrying a small gilded shield and holding in his hands two small gilded spears. His council stood around similarly armed and flutes played.

Suggestions for Further Reading

The rise and fall of Kush and its relations with ancient Egypt are dealt with exhaustively in William Y. Adams, *Nubia—Corridor to Africa* (Princeton: University Press, 1984). See also P.L. Shinnie's chapters in the *Cambridge History of Africa*, vol. II, J.D. Fage, ed., (Cambridge: University Press, 1978.)

Recent scholarship dealing with the Sahara and Sahel of West Africa is summarized in the chapter by R. Mauny in vol. II of the *Cambridge History of Africa* listed above, but the standard work on the subject remains E.W. Bovill's *Golden Trade of the Moors* in the revised edition by Robin Hallett (London: Oxford University Press, 1970). For North Africa see J.M. Abun-Nasr, *A History of the Maghrib*, 2nd ed., (Cambridge: University Press, 1975)

There are no recent histories dealing with the Axum period of Ethiopian history, although there are chapters in the *UNESCO General History of Africa*, vol. II, G. Mokhtar, ed. (London: Heinemann and Berkeley: University of California Press, 1981). An older history is Ernest Budge, *A History of Ethiopia* vol. I (Oosterhout, Netherlands: Anthropological Publications, 1966). Information on the role of Axum in the Indian Ocean trade is contained in *The Periplus of the Erythraean Sea*, an early guide book to the Indian Ocean commerce, often dated about late first century A.D. There are two editions—G.W.B Huntingford (London: Hakluyt Society, 1980) and the earlier W.H. Schoff (London: Longmans, 1912).

3

The States of the Western and Central Sudan

The World of the Desert

When the Sahara began drying up about six thousand years before the time of Christ, it necessarily brought profound changes in the ecology of the region. Life did not end, however; it merely altered to meet the new conditions. Like a receding tide, the water left the desert, taking with it much of the animal and vegetable world it had supported. During its wet phase, the Sahara had been a meadowland where trees and shrubs complemented its prairie grasses, an open terrain crossed by streams and dotted with lakes or swamps, a genial countryside wherein dwelt much of Africa's traditional wildlife—lion, giraffe, elephant, antelope, and ostrich.

Humans, too, had found this an attractive abode, its many waters at first offering a good living to fishing populations, its ample pastures later attracting the attention of herding peoples. These early inhabitants appear to have been primarily negroids who may have migrated up from West Africa in search of new lands until they had spread broadly across the Saharan area from the Atlantic to the Nile. Their farthest advance north took them beyond the Tibesti and Ahaggar uplands and into contact with caucasoid hunters from Mediterranean Africa, and with these groups they doubtless mingled, mixing blood and culture as the foundation for a later desert civilization.

Over time the land grew slowly more arid, approximating its present condition about mid-third millennium B.C. Where once savanna grass had flourished, subdesert bush took hold, while deep in the interior even this type of scrub gave way to the desolate wastes of bare rock and drifting sand that mark the fully desiccated desert. Game still existed on a reduced scale, for there were some animals capable of surviving for long periods solely on the moisture of their forage, while others limited their range to highland areas where water was available. Some districts like Ahaggar contained permanent pools or intermittent streams within their lofty heights where crocodiles still thrived and air-breathing catfish managed to endure drought periods for months or even years at a time.

The human population also retreated with the receding waters, but some remained, like the wildlife able to adapt themselves to the rigors of desert life. This they accomplished by withdrawing into steadily shrinking islands of fertility where they could find water and marginal land to sustain a modest agriculture. To the north these oases were inhabited by Berber farmers, while the southern centers became the home of negroid cultivators known collectively as Haratin. It was an uncertain existence marked by decreasing resources and growing isolation; nevertheless, those small communities that survived were able to develop a type of agriculture well suited to desert conditions. Gardens were carefully cultivated by hoe and watered by hand, the supply coming from oasis wells and raised to the surface by means of a balancing mechanism still used in some districts today. Such staple grains as wheat, barley, and millet were widely grown along with vegetables and melons, but fig trees and grapevines were also planted; most of all the date palm was a staple in every desert oasis.

These sedentary farmers were not the only inhabitants of the desert, for the Sahara attracted a variety of nomads. Some were hunters but mostly they herded sheep, goats, donkeys, and, eventually, camels, moving their animals in a constant search for pasture and water, and dominating the people of the oases with their martial belligerence. In the southern and eastern desert surrounding the Tibesti massif, it was the Teda nomads who predominated, a negroid people who nonetheless are thought to have had Berber antecedents as well. Their pastoral economy was supplemented by stock raiding and caravan trading as well as by controlling palm groves, the gardens of which were tended by Haratin sharecroppers.

Much the same living pattern was manifested by the Berber nomads who filtered down from the north eventually to dominate the western and central Sahara. Their most celebrated representatives were the colorful Tuareg whose imposing appearance commanded equal respect with their warlike habits. For the Tuareg, as for other desert nomads, warfare was a necessary aspect of ecological balance. Raiding helped replenish dwindling herds; more than that, it enabled each group to maintain control over its own range in a parlous land where incursions of belligerent neighbors might threaten limited forage and water, and unchecked population expansion could eventually bring disaster to all.

The Tuareg warrior was a striking figure enfolded in his loose garments, his face masked by the *litham*, a length of dark blue cotton that wound about the head to form a combined turban and veil. Arranged to allow only a narrow slit for the eyes, the litham created an image at once enigmatic and terrifying, a highly useful aspect for this silent marauder who swooped down on his prey atop his swift-riding camel, bristling with javelins as he and his companions drove off a rival herd or made away with the wealth of a camel train before the victim fairly knew he had been struck. The Tuareg raider was as elusive in retreat as he had been stealthy in approach, riding great distances across difficult terrain, doubling on his tracks, setting up false trails, all designed to throw off pursuit, however determined.

The aggressiveness and mobility of nomadic Teda and Tuareg—as with the Bedouin Arabs who spread across the northern desert after the eleventh century A.D.—rested squarely on the competent humped back of the Arabian dromedary introduced into the Sahara early in the Christian era. Before his time, oasis communities were constrained by chronic isolation, and trans-Saharan traffic was an intermittent affair, limited by the daily need for ample water and forage to sustain the horses that provided its main motive power. The advent of the dromedary, or Arabian camel, liberated the oases from their seclusion, enabled pastoralists to penetrate the desert and survive within its environment, and eventually helped alter the trans-Saharan lines of communication from a modest traffic to a major avenue of commerce and cultural exchange.

To be sure, camels had their limitations. They were fragile and needed careful, knowledgeable handling. They were ill tempered and stubborn, unattractive even to those who needed them most. Their ability to survive and work in the desert, however, far outweighed these irritations and made them a major support of the desert ecology. Unlike other transport animals, the camel could work at normal efficiency without water or nourishment for several days in succession, a performance that rested on a very low rate of liquid elimination. Camels could, moreover, travel over protracted periods at speeds well beyond the capabilities of other desert animals such as the horse, the donkey, or the bullock. These qualities greatly extended the mobility and range of desert pastoralists who also made good use of camel by-products such as milk, butter, and cheese, or hides from which the Tuareg made their tents. In time it was to be the trading caravan, organized by Arabo-Berber merchants from North Africa, but sustained by the broad back of the desert camel, which built the trans-Saharan commerce into an important mercantile exchange influencing the economies of three continents.

The Ecology of Sahel and Savanna

The Arabs looked on the Sahara as an ocean, a metaphor reflected in their use of the term Sahel, or shore, to describe the desert borders both south and north. Thus, towns on the Saharan littoral like Sijilmasa in the north and Timbuktu to the south were Sahelian ports of call which desert caravans reached after their long journey across the ocean of sand. There was no sharp line to separate Sahel from desert for the terrain altered gradually, reflecting the gradual change in precipitation. While the full desert received only occasional cloudbursts and fixed locations might endure years without a storm, the Sahel annual rainfall was normally about 10 to 15 inches, enough to sustain a pastoral economy with marginal sedentary agriculture.

South of the Sahel of West Africa was the *Bilad-al Sudan*, the "land of the blacks," another Arabic term defining the West African savanna. Here rainfall, though highly variable, averaged about 25 inches annually in support of a predominantly agricultural economy which also contained a livestock component. Further to the south the rain forest stretched along the West African tropical coast in a relatively narrow band of varying width. Into these territories the Saharan negroids retreated before the force of the expanding drought. Settling there among the indigenous, presumably negroid, populations, they helped evolve local variations on a common cultural and linguistic heritage over a period of several millennia. Rivers like the Niger and the Senegal combined with the open country to facilitate movement, and even the forest was not impervious to migrating groups moving slowly in search of food or retreating to a shelter to avoid pursuit by some enemy.

Throughout West Africa, then, the basic economy rested upon agriculture; in the savanna it was the small farming village which ultimately sustained commerce, both internal and external, and formed the main building blocks from which were fashioned such great empires as Ghana, Mali, Songhai, and Kanem-Bornu. Whether the knowledge of crop cultivation developed locally or was imported, it had established itself in the western Sudan by at least the second millennium before Christ, and toward the close of the pre-Christian era it was followed by the introduction of ironworking. The two skills joined to produce the savanna cereals, millet and sorghum, raised on small family farms with the aid of the shorthandled iron hoe. On the whole, the lands were of indifferent quality, and farmers were obliged to endure a minimal and eccentric rainfall; hence, poor harvest and crop failures were common while soil exhaustion caused frequent removal to new fields cleared through traditional slash-and-burn techniques.

Besides millet and sorghum, savanna farmers grew varieties of beans and peas, okra, squash and melons, rice in the moister river valleys, oranges, lemons and limes, and yams in the southern regions near the rain forest belt. Indian corn, or maize, did not enter the area until after the discovery of the Americas, but cotton was introduced from East Africa, probably by way of the trans-Saharan trade, the manufacture of cotton cloth becoming an important industry in such districts as Nupe and Hausaland. Heavy reliance on basic grains necessarily produced a monotonous cuisine, the basic food a porridge made of millet or sorghum flour stirred into boiling water. Varying in consistency from a doughy loaf to a soupy gruel, it appeared in diverse forms at different meals, embellished with greens, spiced with herbs when available, and very occasionally served with the meat of hunted or trapped animals.

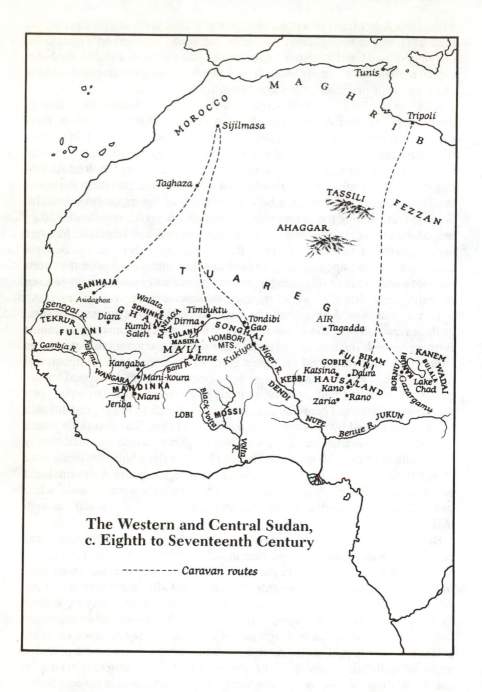

The Western and Central Sudan, c. Eighth to Seventeenth Century

---------- *Caravan routes*

Subsistence cultivation was achieved with a simple technology which, however, given the limitations of environment, was well adapted to savanna conditions. Fields were largely cleared by fire, the ash serving as fertilizer along with decaying vegetable matter, for animal droppings were not generally used, probably because of scarcity. Planting began with the first rains and continued at intervals, thus permitting the simultaneous growth of several crops in a single field, while a judicious rotation schedule varied the annual plantings and helped conserve soil fertility. Interplanting individual plots made possible an even distribution of crops over a period of several years and produced staggered harvest times which insured that the soil would be protected against water and wind erosion throughout the full growing season.

In some communities the women assumed the important work of weeding and transplanting; in others, it was the job of the men, who were also charged with the heavy work of clearing new land or preparing fields for the first seeding. Harvesting was a community affair shared by all in a headlong rush to bring in the crops before they were damaged by the attacks of predatory birds, monkeys, and insects. The grain was stored in straw-lined pits or great urns made of dried mud, elevated to protect their contents from termites. Women did the threshing, winnowing, and milling; they also prepared the meals and raised the green vegetables in small family gardens.

Though limited in important respects, the savanna crops were well chosen. Both millet and sorghum were unsatisfactory calorie producers and required a considerable expenditure of labor proportionate to yields. Nevertheless, they demanded little nourishment from infertile savanna soils, while their short growing season was vital in a region where the rains were brief and slight. Equally important, they produced a high proportion of proteins, vitamins, and mineral salts, an essential for savanna farmers whose diet rarely included animal foods. The chief dietary problem, therefore, was undernutrition rather than malnutrition. The vagaries of the weather raised a constant threat of harvest failure and famine, but even with normal conditions the chronic insufficiency of energy-producing foods threatened farming effectiveness and was especially acute during the growing season when people frequently faced intensive activity in the fields with exhausted granaries and empty stomachs.

Traders in the Sahara and Sudan

Villagers in the savanna were compelled by the conditions under which they lived to endure the rigors of a subsistence economy, yet they managed to produce occasional surpluses which they were eager to trade whenever the opportunity presented itself. In his extended journey through Mali and adjacent territory, the well-travelled North African, Ibn Battuta, reported no difficulty obtaining local foodstuffs at stopping points along the route, farming wives greeting the travelers with millet and rice which they sought to exchange for such treasures as salt, glass ornaments, and perfumes.

This was but particular evidence of a trading complex that spread its network throughout the West African savanna and forest, accounting for a lively and continuous exchange at local and regional markets, and eventually channeling goods into the main commercial arteries that bound West Africa to the Mediterranean and Middle East. At the village level, the markets were held weekly or at some other regular interval, each day at a different hamlet, the goods restricted for the most part to locally grown foodstuffs, the merchants those hard-working farm wives hopeful of adding to their limited resources through the sale of a chicken, some eggs, a portion of surplus grain, or even a hot snack produced expertly in a tiny portable kitchen.

From time to time the itinerant merchant appeared at the village market but more often he was to be found in the larger regional centers that grew up at important intersections or near the seat of government. Here were located mercantile clans like the Mandinka-speaking Wangara or Dyula for whom trade was a full-time occupation which they pursued with such skill and determination that their very name came to be synonymous with "trader" throughout West Africa. Making full use of family connections, Dyula merchants shipped goods across West Africa, moving them along forest paths on the heads of slave porters, across the savanna in donkey trains, and down the rivers in fleets of dugout canoes.

The movement of goods involved many items in a complex exchange marked by a shrewd sense of profit and the patience to postpone immediate for ultimate gain. Rice, for example, might be sold at a loss in a forest market in order quickly to obtain kola nuts for sale at high prices in the north. Rarely, however, was the transaction a simple exchange of two commodities. More typical was a commerce involving numerous shipments, purchases, and sales, with consignments making several journeys to centers where they were divided, some sold, some retained for further shipment, some combined with new lots and sent off to still other markets. Such complexities required that merchants fill many roles, acting variously as exporter and importer, as broker, as shipper, as wholesaler, and as retailer.

Much of this local and regional traffic eventually found its way to the principal Sahel entrepôts perched near the edge of the desert, for it was, in fact, part of the great movement of goods that formed the trans-Saharan trade. At towns like Awdaghost, Walata, or Gao, the caravans arrived and departed, negotiating the difficult desert passage in a two-month march during which they often fought both storm and brigand, ever mindful of the need for haste to the next oasis before supplies of water were exhausted. Given competent guides, protection purchased from the desert peoples through whose territory they passed, and wells unspoiled by drifting sand, the travelers found the Sahara passage more uncomfortable than dangerous, its chief irritants those desert lice and scorpions encountered at each oasis. Buffeted by storms or attacks, however, a train might lose its way in the wasteland, perhaps slaughtering its camels for the moisture in their craws, a desperate measure that sometimes saved those for whom rescue was near, but more likely merely postponed for a few miserable days the ultimate loss of men, beasts, and cargo.

The earliest known desert crossings date from the first millennium before Christ and were undertaken by horse-drawn chariots, evidence of which occurs in cave drawings from the Fezzan to the Niger. Herodotus reported these vehicles in the fifth century B.C., but, once the camel made its appearance, use of the horse declined except along the desert edge. It seems probable that a certain amount of commerce was transacted across the Sahara in these early times; however, the lack of Mediterranean artifacts in the savanna and the paucity of references in ancient texts suggest that such trade must have been slight and intermittent.

The camel greatly eased the desert passage, but it remained for the Arab and Berber merchant from North Africa to organize and direct the great caravans that maintained the trade for over a thousand years until the last decades of the nineteenth century. Following the rise of Islam in the mid-seventh century, Arab armies conquered North Africa and Arab settlers were soon established in Egypt and in the Maghrib, those regions of Mediterranean Africa lying to the west. From centers along the northern desert such as Sijilmasa or Wargla, North African merchants began to organize and dispatch caravans to the south laden with rich cloths and tempered steel, with cowries from the Indian Ocean and glass beads from Venice, with copper for the bronze-casting industries of Ife and Benin, with dates, figs, and other oasis foods, with a few slaves for the courts of savanna kings, and with vast numbers of Barbary horses to sustain the royal cavalries and endow the king's officers with a prestigious transport appropriate to their elevated station. By about 1000 A.D. there were four main routes. Two in the west started from Sijilmasa in Morocco, one descending through Taghaza to Awdaghost and the other proceeding straight south to Timbuktu and Gao. The other routes began in Tunis and Tripoli, moving across the desert to Hausaland and Bornu respectively via the Fezzan. Still other tracks, less frequently travelled, connected West and Central Africa with the Nile Valley.

The caravans also brought south quantities of salt quarried from Saharan mines; in return West Africa sent north its celebrated malaguetta pepper, acacia gum used in Europe as fabric sizing, kola nuts for the North African market, leather goods and cotton cloths particularly from Hausaland, and many slaves destined eventually for the Mediterranean basin and the East. Far more than all these other goods, however, it was gold that was shipped north to the hungry markets of North Africa and Europe.

Like the Dyula, the Arabo-Berber merchants maintained agents at numerous points north and south to keep check on the competition, to follow the market trends, and to observe, perhaps to influence, important political developments. Such elaborate organization was essential, for expenses were high and decisions based upon faulty or inadequate information could prove fatal. The cargoes were taxed at both northern and southern terminals as well as en route, and to these costs were added expenses of transport—camels rented or bought, guides, outriders, and drivers, food and forage for the journey—as well as the price of the cargo itself. All these factors greatly heightened anxieties over the desert journey, yet the profits were great indeed for those who adventured and overcame its hazards. Personal fortunes may be reckoned by an individual promissory note of six thousand gold ounces recorded in the tenth century, or the seventy-five hundred ounces of gold exported annually by merchants from Jenne in the sixteenth century. While overall estimates are difficult, it seems reasonable to value the total volume of business crossing the desert both ways each year at several hundred thousand ounces of gold.

The Golden Commerce

Two major components of the trans-Saharan trade were northbound slaves and horses headed for the Sudan. Indeed, the two streams were interconnected, for slaves, utilized as concubines, enunchs, and servants in North Africa and the Middle East, helped to pay for the cavalry which Sudanic monarchs regularly employed in slave raiding. Such cyclical economic activity was more prevalent among Central Sudanic states like Bornu where there probably was less gold for export than in the west, but all across the Sudan the Saharan slave caravan was an ancient and lucrative institution. The volume, and therefore the value, of the slave traffic are very open questions for there are no statistics, only occasional traveler accounts such as Ibn Battuta's observation that he crossed the desert in a caravan containing 600 slaves.

Whatever the importance of the Saharan horse and slave trade, however, these were much less valuable than two other commodities—salt and gold—that drove the Saharan trade over the centuries. In tropical West Africa, salt was both in heavy demand and short supply, while local mines produced quantities of gold much needed by the commercially minded societies of Europe and the Middle East.

Salt for the West African markets was readily available at several mid-Saharan sites, particularly at Taghaza, a miserable village located in fully desiccated wastes about a three-week journey below Sijilmasa and a like distance north of the major emporia of the Sahel. At Taghaza the salt lay in thick beds about ten or fifteen feet below the surface where it was easily quarried in large two-hundred-pound blocks. These were loaded two blocks to the camel and hurried five hundred miles to Timbuktu or to other centers where the salt was sold, transshipped, and gradually disseminated throughout the hungry West African regions. Taghaza village was a cheerless place controlled by the Messufa Berbers and inhabited only by the slaves who worked the mines for the profit of their masters and whose very lives depended upon the uncertain supplies of food brought in by the caravans that visited the site.

At Taghaza salt was so common that it was used to build the houses and the mosque of its wretched inhabitants, but in the savanna, several hundred miles and a perilous journey distant, it was held in such esteem that it was said to command a market exchange of equal weight in gold.

If such an estimate appears exaggerated, it only sharpens the importance of the Taghaza salt that was especially prized by the people of the gold-producing district known as Wangara, an Arab corruption of the Senegal River region of Gangara. There has always been some mystery as to the exact location of Wangara, but in fact it was probably several places, their identity carefully hidden by the miners who controlled them. Initially Wangara probably referred to the Bambuk (Bambuhu) and Bure districts along the Falémé-Senegal and upper Niger watersheds respectively. Later the gold centers came to include the Lobi region of the upper Black Volta River and other scattered sites extending as far south as the fields of Asante.

It was in the gold-producing regions that the celebrated silent trade was commonly practiced, an ancient exchange frequently remarked by historians from Herodotus onward. Under this arrangement each side simply alternated in matching piles of gold and salt until a satisfactory exchange had been consummated, and during the whole transaction no word was spoken and none was necessary. Indeed, the miners were seen no more than heard since they typically retired after depositing their gold, returning to accept or reject each subsequent offer, usually under cover of darkness, until they finally departed, their demands satisfied. Such precautions were no caprice, for the miners were determined to allow no one, neither savanna king nor Maghrib trader, to discover and to capture their fields.

The gold was mined in pits and along underground passages that were cut through loose alluvial earth laid down originally by stream action. The alluvium, formed by the breakdown of an earlier gold-bearing quartzite, was dug out by miners crouching in the narrow darkness. Waist high in water, they loaded the pay dirt into large calabash trays which were then floated to the mine head for processing. At the surface the earth was washed by women who extracted the few precious grains of gold dust contained in each load. Stored in hollow feather quills, the gold was thus transported to the major centers by Dyula merchants, where much of it was purchased for the long trip across the desert.

The kings of Ghana and Mali appropriated all nuggets passing through their domains, partly as tribute but partly to control the supply and maintain the market value of their precious export. Estimates vary greatly from about two up to a maximum of nine tons of refined gold produced each year, a small fraction of today's annual yield of African gold but an important engine at the time for the economies of Europe and North Africa. Approximately two-thirds of this was exported; what remained, among other things, served to highlight the power and wealth of West African princes. In Ghana, the kings surrounded themselves with gold-bedecked functionaries, and one possessed a nugget large enough to be used as a tether for his horse. A similar opulence characterized the court of Mali where gold trim was a common feature of the ceremonial weapons, while in Songhai the royal dogs were held on leashes of finest wrought gold links. When Musa, the *mansa* or king of Mali, made a pilgrimage to Mecca in 1324-1325, his splendid entourage and lavish generosity spread the knowledge of Sudanic wealth throughout the Mediterranean world, and quite literally established Mali on the medieval maps of Europe. One hundred fifty years later, a second pilgrimage by the ruling *askia* of Songhai, Muhammad Toure, once again impressed upon Europe and the Middle East the wealth and power that West African mines had bestowed upon the great savanna states.

The Mercantile Civilization

Living in the savanna over countless centuries, West African blacks governed their communities through indigenous custom and law which adapted well to foreign people and ideas. The geography of the Sudan favored absorption and accommodation, for its easy lines of communication made it a natural meeting place where ideas, institutions, and blood strains could touch, fuse, and strengthen one another. Somehow, the fusion of local and exotic strains terminated in a hybrid more characteristically Sudanic than otherwise. For example, many savanna peoples possessed traditions involving immigration of ruling dynasties from the north and east, but whatever the basis for such traditions these rulers were soon absorbed and black kings held the reins of government during the apogee of Sudanic states like Ghana, Mali, and Songhai. The bulk of the savanna population came from intermixture among diverse groups, and it was commonplace for villages of completely different tribal and cultural entities to coexist peaceably. Perhaps most illustrative of this process of blending and adaptation in the Sudan have been the Fulani with their hybrid background of caucasoid and negroid blood, their history of migration, and their intimate involvement in the affairs of Sudanic communities from the Senegal to the Benue.

The ability of the Sudanic civilization to adopt, absorb, and utilize outside influences was well exemplified by its early reaction to Islam. Islam arrived in the savanna via the trade routes, brought both by nomadic desert people and Arab merchants from the north. These latter established Muslim communities in the cities at the southern end of the caravan trails where mosques were raised, written Arabic introduced, and the wealth of Islamic learning laid open for all comers. Muslim interpreters were pressed into service in Ghana by its pagan Soninke kings and most of the state ministers were Muslim. In Mali the ruling dynasty numbered several practicing Muslims whose effective government was aided by Muslim officials and administrative practice. A similar pattern developed later in Songhai as well as in the Hausa states and the kingdom of Kanem to the east, aided perhaps by the Fulani who had begun to move through the savanna by the thirteenth century A.D., eventually spreading Muslim law and theology as a by-product of their wanderings.

Yet this Islamic impact was uneven. The vast majority of the people were untouched by the new faith and even the royal dynasties seemed to regard the teachings of the Prophet as an aid to more efficient administration rather than a divinely inspired way of life. The kings of Ghana remained pagan almost to the end, and the great Muslim rulers of Mali and her successors constantly shocked devout observers by their casual religious ritual or their continued accommodation of pagan institutions. In Mali the mansa gave scrupulous observance to Islamic practice but combined this with a tolerance for traditional customs at court and in the community at large, for example, certain accepted forms of public nudity or the practice of covering the head with dust when prostrating oneself before the ruler. In Songhai, the renowned conqueror King Ali of the Sunni dynasty, was a professed Muslim who nevertheless permitted himself to persecute the Muslims of Timbuktu. His successor, Askia Muhammad Toure, though encouraging Islamic institutions and relying heavily on Muslim advisers, failed to establish Islam as a state religion or to introduce it widely among his people.

The fact is there was no genuinely popular response to Islam among the people of the savanna until the religious upheavals of the nineteenth century. The Muslim way was able to make only slow progress over the centuries in the face of traditional customs. As for the rulers of the medieval kingdoms, they were glad enough to have the assistance of literate, educated advisers, and Islam greatly extended their power, but they were also well aware that their political strength frequently rested not on an alien system, but upon their mystical and spiritual powers as king, priest, and clan head under traditional African religious practice. Thus can be understood the double standard of the kings of Mali or the apparent paradox of Sunni Ali's hostility toward the religion he embraced as his own. Thus too may be explained Muhammad Toure's devoted encouragement of Islamic law and culture alongside his long-standing indifference to *jihads*, or holy wars, against pagan neighbors and his deference to traditional institutions as an important element in his celebrated imperial administration.

If Islam did take hold in any particular environment, it was in the great cities of the Sudan-Walata, Awdaghost, Kumbi Saleh, Gao, Kano, Timbuktu, and others—whose commercial preoccupations made them receptive toward outside influences and new ideas to an extent not to be found in the simpler bucolic world that surrounded them. If trade was the basis of their existence, a bourgeois culture and a cosmopolitan population was the hallmark of their character. Local farmers driving their produce-laden donkeys to market fought for space in the crowded streets with caravans from far to the north led by sharp-eyed Arab merchants. The king's horsemen, for all their military impressiveness, competed for the attention of passersby with squadrons of blue-clad

Tuareg beating and cursing their furiously protesting camels. Naked servant girls hurrying along on some errand brushed past Muslim scholars quick to express a sense of puritan outrage at what they regarded as pagan indecorum. The cities were the places where the royal court sat with its galaxy of ministers, scribes, petty functionaries, and attendants, but they also abounded in artisans, students, slaves, scholars, and representatives of far-flung commercial enterprises. The African sections were marked by the characteristic round huts topped with thatched roofs, but large foreign quarters had also grown up to accommodate an expanding population of Muslims from the desert and beyond. Here were the mosques and the rectangular stone or mud houses with their interior courtyards, their heavy windowless walls on which were traced obscure symbols in geometric pattern, and their comfortable quarters where good food was prized along with good conversation, and a life of contemplation was aided by well-stocked libraries.

One feature of the Sudanic cities was the honored place that was given to women. In Kumbi Saleh they wore collars and bracelets, a form of adornment that was otherwise reserved for the king himself. In Walata they were renowned for their beauty and, though devout, were free to have lovers as they desired. The social position and personal liberty enjoyed by women never ceased to astonish Muslim travelers, nor yet did the widespread custom of uterine descent whereby the heir apparent to the throne was not the king's son but the son of his sister. The important position of women, in addition to the bourgeois — mercantile quality of urban society, was reminiscent of the cities of the European Renaissance, and like the European cities, those of the savanna maintained a quasi-independent status despite their location within a series of powerful empires.

Though similar in many basic respects, each metropolis had its particular character and period of greatness. Awdaghost, lying a two-week journey west of Kumbi, was a wealthy town where personal comfort and luxury held sway along with cultivation of the arts. Perched on the edge of the desert, it nevertheless had an abundant water supply which sustained fine herds of cattle and sheep and made possible a wide range of agricultural produce including wheat, millet, figs, dates, and grapes. Kumbi, the chief trading center during the ascendancy of the kingdom of Ghana, was in fact two cities combining the Muslim quarter of Berber merchants with its mosques and stone dwellings and the African town that featured traditional clay and thatch houses as well as the king's palace celebrated for its golden trappings. Kumbi finally collapsed when seized by the Soso in 1203 and was replaced during the thirteenth century by Walata, a hundred miles to the north, as the new terminus for the Saharan trade of the western desert.

Eventually Walata gave way to Timbuktu and Gao as the political center of gravity shifted eastward, first from Ghana to Mali, and then to Songhai. Gao, on the Niger bend, was reportedly a large and beautiful metropolis with an active trading life and abundant crops, including a special kind of cucumber which delighted Ibn Battuta when he visited the Sudan in the middle of the fourteenth century. Further up the Niger from Gao, Ibn Battuta identified Yufi [Nupe ?], a city of blacks where white men were not welcome and which he did not visit, but his own travels took him eastward from Gao to Tagadda, another wealthy market town that imported fabrics and other goods from Egypt, and reportedly mined copper which, according to Ibn Battuta, was cast locally and shipped south and east to Hausaland and Bornu. The Hausa cities, Kano, Katsina, Zaria, and others, were thriving caravan centers especially after the sixteenth-century decline of Songhai. They were located in combined woodland and farming country that produced abundant citrus fruit and cereal crops raised by the tall, black-skinned, broad-faced people of the region. Eventually Kano would become the leading market of the central Sudan with its houses of sun-baked mud, its vast market, its mosques, its great walls, and its complement of cultivated and prosperous merchants.

The most celebrated of these savanna cities, at least outside the Sudan, was Timbuktu, founded about 1100 A.D. by Tuareg nomads as a communications outpost just north of the Niger near the top of the river's great bend. Timbuktu had grown with the fortunes of Mali and had survived the persecutions of Songhai's empire builder, Sunni Ali, to become an important center of commerce and scholarship by the early sixteenth century. It was visited at that time by another renowned traveler, Leo Africanus, who set down a faithful description of its appearance and the life of its people just as it was being developed by the great askia, Muhammad Toure, as a regional capital where the Islamic civilization of the Sudan might thrive.

Leo noted the fine Sankore mosque and palace erected in the time of Mansa Musa (1312-1337), and spoke glowingly of the wealth and power of Muhammad Toure. He also commented on the many shops owned by merchants and craftworkers, growing rich on the lively trade in fabrics, spices, copper, gold, ivory, ostrich feathers, and slaves. An ample supply of water was available from wells and sluices that brought the overflow from the Niger, and this supply was sufficient to sustain a thriving agriculture. The population, probably exceeding twenty-five thousand, was friendly and hospitable and given to celebrations that went far into the night with much singing and dancing in the streets. Most of all, Leo was impressed by the city's intellectual activities, for the king, Muhammad Toure, had attracted many learned and professional men to Timbuktu and supported their studies from his own treasury. Libraries were large and numerous and the Sankore mosque was doing double duty as a university as well as a place of worship. Located strategically at the end of trade routes that stretched as far as Venice, Genoa, and Cairo, Timbuktu flourished as long as the civilization it represented was able to provide peace and political stability for its trade. With the collapse of the Songhai empire, however, the fortunes of Timbuktu took a permanent turn as the once thriving city eventually declined, an isolated, dusty town and a handful of unimpressive mud buildings housing a listless population which time had finally passed by.

Sudanic State Systems

The great empires of the medieval Sudan have sometimes been regarded as ephemeral political entities without great intrinsic unity and lacking even frontiers to delineate the extent of their authority. In a purely temporal sense it seems unreasonable to impute weakness to states that lasted as long as Ghana's minimum four centuries, Mali's effective existence from the advent of Sundiata in 1230 A.D. until the capture of Jenne by Sunni Ali over two hundred years later, the unbroken thousand-year reign of the ruling *mais* of Kanem-Bornu, or the long-lived stability of the Mossi states. Furthermore, the test of political vitality in these African kingdoms must be in terms of Africa's own traditional social institutions which made for an administration and political structure rather different from modern concepts of national entity.

"Ghana, the golden land," remarks the Arab astronomer, al-Fazari, saying little but suggesting much in wealth, and by implication, in power. This first external notice of the state of Ghana dates from the late eighth century; what came before the rise of Ghana can be reconstructed only indirectly from archaeology, linguistic analysis, and surviving bits of tradition.

It seems reasonable to suppose that African peoples moving generally southward from the encroaching desert lived simply in small groups — herders whose social and political organization centered on family-owned cattle, farmers inhabiting village communities made up of lineage groups related by blood to a common ancestor. Supplementary ties, no doubt, emerged to neutralize lineage competition, in some cases a central structure of government culminating in a ruler and his council drawn from heads of lineages; in others, age groupings made of successive generations, or hierarchies of titles, that cut clearly across lineage loyalties. On occasion quasi-religious secret societies imposed a further check on the governance of a ruler who in any case probably based his own authority on a supernatural sanction as magician and priest.

Government was simple among these modest populations of farmers and pastoralists, for they were content to invent devices sufficient to their needs and no more. What characterized them all, however, was their firm basis, not so much in law as in a web of personal relationships like the feudal societies that emerged in Europe over much the same period of time. Land occupation and utilization was the ultimate objective of political organization among people whose survival depended upon control of a territory and its products. Nonetheless there were no such things as national boundaries; even the kingdom had no name, and visitors from the Arab and European worlds typically misused the name and title of the ruler to identify his domain.

The large kingdoms of the savanna seem to have developed naturally from these smaller, simpler states, in effect a petty kingdom writ large. In time some communities grew complex, developing clans that divided along social or economic lines. A vigorous head of a warrior or royal clan, or perhaps the leader of an age set might have succeeded in imposing his fiat on a growing number of neighboring villages, partly relying on interconnecting loyalties but also utilizing military force. Such authority varied inversely with distance, but communication was relatively easy across the open savanna, and after the introduction of North African horses, an energetic conqueror like the Songhai ruler Sunni Ali could and did maintain his hegemony, though it necessitated an almost ceaseless regimen of military conquest. Such activity eventually posed problems of administration and of succession. Remote districts, difficult to control, were often left in the hands of tribute-paying local chieftains. Alternatively, rulers assigned members of the royal clan to positions as regional viceroys, a dangerous device that invited revolt and led to the alternative institution of non-royal provincial governors, especially chosen because they had no legitimate claim to princely succession.

After the rise of Islam the arrival of Arab and Berber merchants from North Africa introduced a new element that greatly strengthened the large savanna states. Along with their commerce the northern traders brought their religion and their literacy, both of which helped consolidate imperial administration. Muslim scribes and advisors were widely employed while the religion of the Prophet, slowly adopted by the savanna nobility, introduced administrative standards for such activities of scale as the policing of markets or the levying and collecting of taxes.

It was, however, the trans-Saharan trade and the wasteland it traversed that were the main engines responsible for the emergence of the great states that bordered the desert. The peoples of the Sahel and savanna, both north and south, had long been in contact with the desert dwellers, sometimes peacefully, sometimes in contention. Possessing the camel, the nomads of the desert were not always content to confine their raids to one another's herds or to prey only upon passing trans-Saharan caravans. Tuareg and Teda, for example, recruited their domestic slaves through regular forays upon savanna farming villages; more generally, the desert people maintained a symbiosis with the more settled areas, varying from peaceful seasonal migration to large-scale warfare and conquest. During cycles when the rains were normal and water holes remained productive, the pastoralists abandoned the desert only for the dry months, the Bedouins moving into the Atlas highlands to graze their flocks on the mountain pasture, the southern nomads conducting a similar infiltration of the Niger River valley. In difficult times, however, when the rains failed and the wells ran dry, these pacific movements converted to armed invasion, sometimes in the form of hit-and-run raids and sometimes as more permanent conquest and occupation.

Indeed, the desert nomads were bound up in a vast rhythm of history with the peoples who lived to the north and to the south of them. At moments of stress when conditions became severe and the savanna or Mediterranean regions were weakened, the desert encroached on the settled areas and the desert people predominated. Conversely, when the savanna organized and unified itself under a strong central regime, the settled area extended farther into the desert, and it was the nomadic peoples who were forced back and obliged to pay allegiance to the more powerful authority.

More important still was the impact of the trans-Saharan trade. The great value of the West African gold mines was easily recognized; more generally, it was apparent that those who controlled the trade to the north commanded great wealth, but control implied political organization to insure the peaceful passage of caravans and the orderly conduct of business in the marketplace. While the sovereigns of the savanna states failed in their attempts to seize the mines of Wangara, they did succeed in taxing the trade both through the appropriation of all gold nuggets and with tariffs levied on caravans arriving at the major savanna entrepôts. In return they provided their celebrated "pax savanna" which, at its best, insured honest dealings in the markets and enabled strangers and local people alike to travel throughout the realm without fear of molestation. When the savanna states could no longer provide protection, the trade moved elsewhere as their strength atrophied; thus it was with the eventual demise of Ghana or the desert march of the Moroccans that later settled the fate of Songhai.

The Kingdom of Ghana

The earliest known kingdom of the Sudan was Ghana, and its history well exemplified the ancient conflict between the Sahara and the savanna, involving both the religious asceticism of the desert and the desire for gold that has infected all peoples. Its origins have been lost, but by the time it had come to the notice of Arab commentators in the eighth century, Ghana was already a thriving state headed by black African Soninke kings and renowned for its wealth in gold. Traditions speak of various founding dynasties, including non-black northerners, doubtless a reflection both of Ghana's close contact with neighboring Berbers and of later attempts by West African Muslims to associate Sudanic states with Islamic and Arabic antecedents. By the ninth century Ghana was approaching the fullest extent of its power and influence with territory extending to the south as far as the upper reaches of the Niger and Senegal, to the north into the desert and eastward to the Niger bend.

Control over the gold commerce assured the prosperity of Ghana's kings, but Ghana suffered from the competition of Awdaghost lying to the west, which was held by Sanhaja Berbers and which was pressing its own claim to become the major terminus for the commerce across the western Sahara. The vexation of the Awdaghost competition was temporarily laid to rest in 990 A.D., however, when the Soninke of Ghana captured the rival city during a period of internal dissension among the Sanhaja. This was the peak moment of glory. The market city of Kumbi Saleh became the chief mercantile and intellectual center in the Sudan and its king was renowned for his wealth and the splendor of his court. When he held audience, he appeared resplendent in garments of fine cloth and ornaments of gold, while his retainers and even the royal animals were similarly bedecked. His tariffs filled the royal treasury, his armies kept the peace across his vast domain, and his fame spread far to the north where people spoke of "the king of Ghana . . . the richest monarch in the world."

Such prosperity was difficult to maintain. During the eleventh century, the Sanhaja experienced a profound religious revival led by a particularly puritanical Muslim sect, the Almoravids, and the white heat of religious fervor was soon converted into a jihad with repercussions as far as Morocco and the states of Andalusia. In the Sahel, this holy war took the shape of a campaign against Ghana. Authorities differ over the consequences. Some say Kumbi fell to the Almoravid jihad as Ghana was forcibly converted to Islam. Others contend that the conversion was voluntary. In either case the Almoravids extended their control of the desert trade at Ghana's expense, and the Soninke kingdom, though subsequently cooperating with the Almoravids, gradually declined in power and wealth. The ensuing power vacuum was soon occupied by the Soso chieftaincy of Kaniaga, a former vassal state which had already revolted successfully, and now moved to capture Ghana under the leadership of Sumaguru Kante. In 1203 Kumbi was sacked and the independent kingdom of Ghana ceased to exist. The merchants of Kumbi, no longer able to pursue their affairs at the old site, moved north toward the desert to the rising commercial center of Walata.

The Rise and Fall of Mali

The exploits of Sumaguru seemed to be the beginning of a new power centering on the Soso, but in fact the heir to Ghana's authority lay in another quarter. South of Kaniaga along the upper reaches of the Niger, were Mandinka blacks occupying fertile farm land near the source of West Africa's gold supply, and these people were subdued by Sumaguru after his victory over Ghana. According to one tradition, Sumaguru put all the sons of the Mandinka ruler to death save one who was spared as an inconsequential cripple. This sole survivor, Sundiata, overcame his weakness, rallied local support, and fashioning a guerrilla army, eventually defeated and killed Sumaguru in 1235. The Soso were quickly absorbed, whereupon Sundiata advanced northward, sacked and annexed the remnants of Ghana in 1240, at the same time taking control of the gold trade routes and the port cities of the Saharan commerce. This was the genesis of the empire of Mali which, in a few short years, had established itself, extending its hegemony to include all of the former sphere of influence of Ghana.

Although the early Mandinka princes were said to be Muslims, it seems likely that Sundiata was a pagan, and it was on the traditional relationships within clans and lineage groups that he built his administration. Securing these relationships by force and persuasion before confronting the Soso, Sundiata established his capital, possibly at his ancestral village of Niani, from where he and his successors ruled their extensive empire. Mali was an agricultural community but this by no means meant a neglect of the commercial possibilities of the trans-desert traffic. In addition to the gold supplies in the south, Mali reached out to control the salt trade of Taghaza as well as Saharan copper, and it was during the period of Mali's growth during the thirteenth century that Timbuktu began its development within the new kingdom as an entrepôt for desert caravans.

The precise extent of the empire under Sundiata is not known, but after his death in 1255 additional conquests were made by Mansa Uli and by Sakura, a freed slave of the royal household who seized power during a period of weakness within the ruling dynasty. Either Sundiata or Uli first brought Songhai under Mali suzerainty and Sakura was apparently responsible for campaigns against Tekrur in the west as well as for the capture of Gao in the east. Nevertheless, until recently many of these conquests had been attributed to Mansa Musa (1312-1337), partly because Musa's devotion to Islam attracted the praise of Muslim historians and partly because of the fame of his glittering pilgrimage to Mecca.

The progress of Musa's caravan has been recorded and savored by historians—the five hundred slaves bearing golden staffs, the hundred camels each loaded with three hundred pounds of gold, the spending spree in the bazaars of Cairo, and the scattering of bounty with such a lavish hand as to force a serious depreciation of gold on the Cairo exchange. So too has his sponsorship of as-Sahili, a poet and architect from Andalusia, who returned from Mecca with Musa's entourage to introduce an Arabian style to the religious and secular architecture of the Sudan. These events, along with the number of Muslim scholars he brought back from the Middle East, emphasized Musa's Islamic persuasion and doubtless pleased Muslim historians who thereby may have tended to underestimate the accomplishments of Musa's royal predecessors. Moreover, they may have overlooked the degree to which the king, for all his devotion to Islamic religion and civilization, continued to rely upon traditional institutions for the administration of his realm. For example, when the propagation of the true faith threatened gold production in pagan Wangara, proselytizing was quickly abandoned. Moreover, despite the might and glory of Mali's great rulers, the integrity of local chieftaincies was scrupulously observed, and no attempt was made to eliminate traditional ritual at the royal court. Describing the audiences of the mansa a few years after Musa's death, Ibn Battuta approvingly commented on evidence of Islamic practice, but he was also obliged to observe the importance of customary usage—the mansa seated amid the many traditional articles symbolic of royal authority, the elaborate ceremony with its liberal reliance on ritual magic, the rigid demands on time-honored protocol tendering homage to the ruler through prostration and dusting, and the royal Mandinka decorations for distinguished service which took the form of trousers of exceptional width.

The splendor of Mali reached during the reign of Musa continued for several decades, but by the late years of the fourteenth century the problem of dynastic succession had intruded a fatal weakness into the government. Palace quarrels encouraged outside attack. As the fifteenth century opened, the Mossi were raiding the middle Niger having earlier sacked Timbuktu. This luckless entrepôt was occupied by Tuareg in 1433-1434, and in 1468 Sunni Ali of the growing power of Songhai captured the city with great loss of life, five years later reducing the supposedly impregnable town of Jenne. The rise of Songhai put an effective end to Mali's hegemony in the eastern Niger region, but her power lingered on fitfully in the west. Gradually deteriorating, however, it was finally snuffed out in the middle of the seventeenth century with the appearance of the Bambara states of Kaarta and Segu. Thus, after four hundred years, the great Mali empire had finally returned to the original status of a small chieftaincy on the upper Niger.

The Empire of Songhai

By the time of Mali's final demise, Songhai, her imperial successor in the Sudan, had experienced her own brief moment of ascendancy—a century and a half that saw a rapid expansion across the western savanna, a short period of stability, and then an equally rapid decline into extinction. All this came as a climax to a long era of much more modest development.

The point of origin for the Sonhgai people seems to have been those reaches of the Niger River downstream from the great bend, centering on the town of Kukiya. Here the Za dynasty presided over an agricultural community, giving way to the Sunni line at a time when Mali was still ascendant throughout the Niger country. North of Kukiya lay Gao, a market town on the Sahel edge, like Timbuktu under Malian control, and attracting traders from south and west as well as from North African points. Toward the end of the fourteenth century, as Mali began to suffer internal decay, the Sunnis of Kukiya sensed their opportunity to share in the lucrative trade of the Gao area, probably occupying the river port about the time Timbuktu fell to the Tuareg.

It was a step that initiated the transformation from insignificant principality to major Sudanic empire. First, Songhai began to enjoy the riches of its improved trading position, an expanding wealth that meant growing influence and widening authority. Next, control of Gao placed Songhai astride the east-west route of the Niger bend, a strategic position that offered the possibility of a thrust westward toward Timbuktu and beyond. It was Gao, moreover, that moved the Songhai into close contact with Islamic civilization, bringing at least a measure of conversion to the royal house if not to the general population.

In the days of Mansa Musa, Songhai had been subject to Mali; now during the fifteenth century an independent Songhai began to acquire territory at the expense of her former master, at first pushing westward into Mema and adjacent Sahelian provinces beyond the Niger bend. The main imperial expansion came, however, with the long reign of Sunni Ali which began in 1464. With furious energy he overran the whole Niger country, capturing Jenne after his occupation of Timbuktu, pushing back the Tuareg to the north and punishing the Mossi states on the south after they had sacked Timbuktu and besieged Walata. During twenty-eight years of almost incessant campaigning, Ali created, then protected, an empire along the Niger that dominated the trade routes and the great grain producing region of the Niger's inland delta.

Under Ali, the administration of the Songhai state seems to have been delegated largely to military commanders backed by Ali's own mobility and martial energy. He maintained a fleet on the river, controlled the overland route through the Hombori Mountains south of the Niger bend, established several "capitals" the better to control his domains, and placed distant provinces in the hands of local rulers responsible to him for maintaining order and collecting taxes. His armies apparently consisted of a core unit of troops under his personal command along with special levees raised for particular campaigns.

Much of the information concerning Sunni Ali and his activities comes from Muslim accounts which have pictured him as a ruthless, bloodthirsty conqueror, as well as an unbeliever, a reaction to his savage persecution of Timbuktu Muslims, particularly those associated with the Sankore mosque. Ali argued that his persecution of the Sankore adherents was purely political, occasioned by their support for his Tuareg foes. After his occupation of Timbuktu, Ali did not molest other Muslims in the town and in general maintained good relations with the Islamic community throughout his lands. It is true that Ali bore his Islamic faith lightly, and local tradition emphasizes his position as a great magician who followed many indigenous practices, for example, worshipping idols and consulting diviners and sorcerers. It would seem that Sunni Ali's actions were indeed largely political and economic. The Songhai state was created through conquest and sustained primarily through force, but there was necessarily an element of persuasion. At least nominally Muslim, Ali could command the loyalty of most true believers, while concurrently he remained an African priest-king sensitive to the spiritual interest of his pagan people.

Sunni Ali died in a drowning accident in 1492, and the following year the throne was usurped by Muhammad Toure, governor of the Hombori region and founder of the succeeding Askia dynasty. Sunni Ali had established the basis for the Songhai empire. Under Askia Muhammad it was greatly expanded and institutionalized.

As with Sunni Ali, Askia Muhammad's objectives were strategic and economic, although his tactics were far different, at once more comprehensive and more subtle. Concerned that Ali's war making had disrupted the Saharan gold trade, Muhammad moved to stabilize the western empire, campaigning against the Mossi in 1498-1499, and soon thereafter probing westward to Diara in ancient Ghana. His conquest of Air in 1501-1502 secured the trade routes to Tripoli and Egypt while his absorption of the Taghaza mines brought control of the salt and gold trade of the western Sudan.

Military action, however, was balanced with diplomacy. Only three years after taking power, Muhammad undertook a pilgrimage to Mecca, the purpose certainly involving religious piety, but it was also a move to cement relations with important Muslim commercial circles in both North and South Africa. Again, Askia Muhammad placated the Muslims of Timbuktu and cultivated the celebrated North African cleric, al-Maghili, achieving the double objective of gaining Muslim support, at the same time obtaining al-Maghili's verdict that Sunni Ali had been a pagan and therefore an appropriate objective for legitimate military takeover.

Muhammad also effected basic administrative reforms. He created a professional army of slave soldiers, ruling over his domains, partly through tribute-paying local chieftains, partly through hereditary royal title holders, and partly with the help of Muslim advisers and officials, relying often on Islamic sanctions regarding such matters as taxation and trade. Nonetheless these changes were less than fundamental. Askia Muhammad conducted no jihads against infidel neighbors, retained numerous traditional customs at court, and acknowledged indigenous authorities at the village level. Staunch Muslim though he was, he realized like Sunni Ali that much of his authority stemmed from Songhai tradition from which he could stray too far only at his peril.

One element of effective administration that eluded Askia Muhammad was the matter of orderly succession. After a long reign the Askia had declined in health and energy when in 1528 he was deposed in a rebellion engineered by his sons. This was the first of a series of coups that ensued over a sixty-year period, undermining the state, almost invariably bringing disunity and weakness, and leading to its final disintegration which came abruptly at the end of the sixteenth century. Over this period no less than eight askias reigned in Songhai. One of these, Daud (1549-1582), was an able and successful ruler, but his success only underscored the shortcomings of the others.

During the second half of the sixteenth century, Songhai came under increasing pressure from the Sadian kingdom of Morocco, intent upon gaining access to the rich trans-Saharan traffic, particularly through control over the salt mines of Taghaza. The move may have been occasioned by the new sea routes around Africa that diverted European commerce away from the Mediterranean; in any event Morocco saw opportunity to the south. Taghaza and other desert oases were periodically attacked and plans were made for an advance on Songhai in the hopes of gaining control of its gold supply.

Although these Moroccan threats were well known in Songhai, her rulers felt secure in the protection of the desert; indeed, for all its belligerency,

Morocco had not been able to hold Taghaza, let alone march on the Niger. Nevertheless, in 1591 a column of four thousand soldiers led by an Andalusian, Judar Pasha, succeeded in crossing the desert and appeared at Tondibi on the Niger above Gao. It was a much smaller force than the Songhai army but it contained a large proportion of European Muslim converts equipped with muskets, which, in addition to superior discipline, were decisive against the bows and spears of the ill-organized enemy. Songhai, already weakened by civil war, was easily defeated, its army put into full retreat, and the Niger country rendered defenseless against the invaders.

Military defeat was quickly followed by political collapse. Morocco gained small recompense from her adventure, for she found little of the wealth she sought and was unable to occupy and exploit Songhai. Nevertheless the invasion spelled the end of the Songhai empire. Gao and Timbuktu were occupied, the latter permanently, for the Moroccan soldiers eventually settled along the Niger bend ruling the region first as a protectorate, and then as they gradually became absorbed into the local population, establishing an independent, albeit politically feeble, state. Elsewhere Songhai split into its components. The Songhai themselves retreated down river to the Dendi home whence they had originally come and where they succeeded in eluding the Moroccans. In Masina and Dirma, the Fulani raided the local farming people, the Jenne region was attacked by the Bambara, while Tuareg visited their usual devastation all along the Niger bend.

Political disintegration was followed by famine, and famine by plague. When some semblance of stability finally returned, political cohesion had been reduced to a much more modest scale than that which had characterized the apogee of the great Sudanic kingdoms. Raiding by nomadic and warrior groups combined with internecine struggles to keep states small, weakened, and defensive; hence, larger units did not reappear until the emergence in the eighteenth century of the Bambara kingdoms of Segu and Kaarta. Trade, too, suffered from the political fragmentation, although in general merchants managed to keep the trans-Saharan traffic moving at its former levels despite the vigorous interference of desert raiders. As for the civilization that Islam had introduced by way of the northern trade routes, these were not years of growth, and the indifference that the true faith encountered both at court and in the countryside was to build frustrations leading to the religious upheavals that engulfed the western and central Sudan during the early nineteenth century.

Kanem-Bornu and the Hausa States

The pattern of population movements, economic growth, and political centralization that had characterized the western Sudan was repeated with variations in Kanem-Bornu and Hausaland. Here, too, the drying out of the Sahara forced ancient negroid hunting and fishing societies south into the more congenial latitudes of the savanna, where they turned gradually to a sedentary farming life, leaving the increasingly arid desert to nomadic herders. In its time, the trans-Saharan commerce arose to bind the central Sudan to the markets of North Africa, and to stimulate the appearance of Sudanic states concerned in part to protect that commerce. Finally, Islamic theology and culture spread its influence in the central Sudan, as it had in the west, coming across the desert to gain the allegiance of royalty, but failing by and large to extend its sway beyond the limited populations of the market cities.

Judging from the present-day linguistic configuration, those migrants who descended into the regions directly west of Lake Chad spoke languages comprising the Chadic subdivision of the Afro-Asiatic linguistic classification, those to the east belonged to the quite different Saharan branch of the Nilo-Saharan grouping, while south of the lake were Benue-Congo speakers of the Niger-Congo family. These migrations very likely involved a variety of folk filtering into an indigenous population, a process that gave rise during the first millennium after Christ to a heterogeneous mixure of herders, farmers, and fisherfolk. Traders visiting the region introduced their own names and these eventually became permanent—Zagawa to identify the people and Kanem for the loose collection of local states bordering the lake.

Kanuri tradition credits an Arab leader, Saif ibn Dhi Yazan, with unifying these diverse peoples and establishing the ruling Saifawa dynasty of the Kanuri mais or kings, a probable myth designed to gain legitimacy for the Kanem rulers by linking them with the name of a great Arab hero. In any event, the Saifawa dynasty, probably founded in the ninth century, was to survive for a thousand years, an unusual longevity during which the state of Kanem emerged and endured, developing other qualities that added an idiomatic flavor to its basic vitality. To begin with, the mai was regarded as divine, and as a god remained aloof from the profane gaze of his people, speaking from behind a screen and always taking his meals in solitude. The institution of a divine, ritually secluded monarch, widely practiced among traditional African societies, was joined by characteristics more typically Kanuric—an elaborate, highly centralized palace hierarchy, royal descent in the male line combined with important and powerful positions for the queen mother and other female members of the mai's household, and a minutely regulated provincial administration and military organization based upon feudal rights and obligations.

It was trade that stimulated the centralizing efforts of the Saifawas, responding to the growing number of merchants from North Africa who sought to organize and control the Saharan commerce after the rise of Islam in the seventh and eighth centuries. The northerners were primarily interested in slaves for soldiering and domestic service in the Middle East and these they purchased with fabrics and metals, chiefly copper and bronze. Though merchants, they were also active proselytizers for Islam, and toward the end of the eleventh century the Saifawa royal house was converted in the person of Mai Hume. Succeeding mais built upon this beginning by establishing closer relations with Muslim states to the north and east and encouraging the *hajj*, or pilgrimage, to Mecca, a policy that presumably had commercial as well as religious objectives.

These political and institutional developments were accompanied by the gradual expansion of Kanem beyond its homeland just east of Lake Chad to form an empire that spread as far west as Kano, its eastern territories taking in the region of Wadai but not reaching as far as Darfur. By the middle of the thirteenth century, under Mai Dunama Dibalami, Kanem had also extended its control northward into the Fezzan, thereby securing its position as a major African state dominating the central Sudanic regions. Even at this moment of maximum strength, however, Kanem began to feel the effect of disruptive forces which eventually brought about the disintegration of this first Kanuri empire.

Partly, the trouble was internal, involving wasting dynastic struggles within the expanding Saifawa family. Beyond this, throughout the fourteenth century, there were difficult wars, first with the So people located south of Lake Chad, and then during the second half of the century with the Bulala, these formidable antagonists attacking the Kanuri so successfully that they finally precipitated the evacuation of Kanem.

There was probably another, largely economic, reason. As Kanem expanded, reaching out for a growing share of the Saharan trade, her pastoralism and oasis farming could not sustain the military cost of defending her desert commerce. The long distance trade began to bypass Kanem, moving directly from Bornu to the Sahara, a potential disaster for the state which could only be averted by moving the court to occupy its Bornu province on the western side of Lake Chad. Late in the fourteenth century, under the leadership of Mai Umar ibn Idris, the ruling house abandoned its old territory and reestablished itself in Bornu, parts of which had previously fallen under Kanuri control. For about a hundred years the state remained weak, its armies faring poorly, its mais following one another in quick succession, victims both of assassination and of enforced exile. Toward the end of the fifteenth century, a measure of stability at last returned, and with this renaissance came the beginning of the second Kanuri empire.

The individual responsible for the upturn in Kanuri fortunes was Ali Ghaji who, as mai during the last quarter of the century, put an end to the power struggles within the palace, checked the aggressions of the Bulala, and founded a new capital in Bornu, the walled city of Gazargamu, which became the first fixed seat of government since the remove from Kanem a century earlier. Ali's son and successor, Idris Katakarmabi, temporarily liberated Kanem through two successful campaigns against the Bulala, and later mais extended Bornu domination to the Saharan region of Air, possibly in connection with diplomatic and commercial relations that were concurrently established with the Ottoman rulers of Tripoli.

Such successes, however, were but a prelude to the reign of Mai Idris Aloma (1571-1603) under whom Kanem-Bornu reached the height of its power. During much of his long tenure Idris was preoccupied with military campaigns through which he both consolidated the triumphs of his predecessors and added fresh conquests of his own. Thus, he subdued dissidents in Bornu and secured a long-lived peace with the Bulala who remained a quasi-autonomous people in Kanem. His campaigns as far as Kano assured his suzerainty in Hausaland, while with the aid of camel-mounted cavalry he routed the Tuareg and Teda on his northern frontiers, thus protecting his commercial ties with North Africa. Indeed, much of Idris Aloma's military success was due to his introduction of new weapons and tactics—greater mobility through improved transport, an effectively drilled standing army to supplement the traditional feudal levies, flexibility of battle plans altered to suit the idiosyncrasies of terrain and foe, and, perhaps most of all, the introduction of firearms against adversaries limited to their traditional bowmen and lancers.

Idris was by no means exclusively preoccupied with conquest, however. A devout Muslim, he made his pilgrimage to Mecca and established hostels in that holy city for the shelter of Bornu pilgrims, built brick mosques in the capital city of Gazargamu in lieu of the older reed structures, and began to replace customary law and traditional tribunals with courts under Muslim magistrates following the dictates of Quranic law. His reforms extended to moral as well as juridical questions for he took a strong stand against adultery and obscenity. ''So he wiped away the disgrace,'' observed a contemporary, ''and the face of the age was blank with astonishment.''

Military conquest and the encouragement of Muslim law seems to have been accompanied by no great change in the traditional political administration of the empire. The same complex hierarchy of officials aided the mai in governing; if anything, the system was more rigid than ever, based upon a pattern of fiefs granted to nobility and royal servants in return for both their loyalty and material assistance to the crown. The economy, moreover, had changed little from earlier days. The basic productivity of the land was agricultural, and the basic labor force was the peasantry supplemented by substantial numbers of slaves. Slaves were also an important commodity in the lively trans-Saharan trade, the Kanuri continuing their time-honored custom of raiding to the south for slaves to be shipped to North Africa—eunuchs and young girls were a specialty—in return for the horses of Barbary.

By the end of the eighteenth century, the Kanem-Bornu empire had declined from the greatness of the Aloma era. Succeeding mais became less aggressive, preoccupying themselves with Muslim piety as subject neighbors gathered strength and slipped away one by one. When a new crisis arose early in the nineteenth century, the Saifawa were no longer equal to the need for vigorous leadership. The Fulani armies that had already overrun Hausaland attacked Bornu and compelled the ancient kingdom to embark on a new period of reform and reconstruction in order to forestall disintegration and annexation by the new power that threatened her. As for the Hausa, the Fulani occupation brought revolutionary changes to a way of life that in many ways had been typical of the civilization of the savanna.

For long centuries the Hausa had occupied the area between Songhai and Kanem-Bornu. Their tradition postulated the familiar theme of a ruler who came from the north—in this case, Bayajidda, son of the king of Baghdad, who slew the serpent harassing the people and married the local queen, and whose grandsons became the kings of the major Hausa states of Gobir and Daura, Katsina and Zazzau (Zaria), Kano and Rano, and finally Biram. Such a tradition seems to suggest southward migrations of Saharan hunters and fisherfolk who filtered into the savanna with the onset of desiccation. Indeed, although Hausaland undoubtedly absorbed such migrations, the Bayajidda legend appears to have been a later development, antedated by early population movements and the emergence of the Hausa city-states.

Like their neighbors, the Hausa were agriculturalists. The broad, flat plains of their countryside were well suited for the cultivation of corn, barley, rice, and cotton, while livestock fatted on the rich grass and citrus fruit grew wild in the low, wooded hills. Most of the people lived in small farming villages but in time walled towns like Kano and Katsina had established themselves as centers of trade and of religious and secular thought. Like Kanem-Bornu, the Hausa states engaged in a brisk exchange with North Africa across the Sahara, the chief southern products being slaves and kola nuts, the latter always in great demand as one of the few stimulants permitted Muslims. Katsina and Kano rose to be the major Hausa entrepôts, but the other states also contributed to the trade in a well-conceived division of labor—Zaria to the south served as the slave raider, Rano was a center for industry, and Gobir on the edge of the desert protected Hausaland against the raids of the desert nomads.

Islamic culture and religion entered Hausaland gradually via the urban centers, probably having been first introduced through contacts with Bornu. Kano and Katsina were under Islamic influence by the late fourteenth century, but the degree of commitment was modest both among the general population and within the ruling class. Other states were even more lightly touched. Gobir was still pagan in the sixteenth century and Zaria was not converted until the nineteenth century jihad of Usuman dan Fodio. Indeed, dan Fodio's religious war was precipitated by his perception of a general laxness in Islamic practice, both at court and on the countryside. Theology aside, the impact of Islamic civilization was considerable, especially in the cities. When Timbuktu was enjoying a peak in the fifteenth and sixteenth centuries, a number of its scholars visited Hausaland, living and working in Kano and Katsina— for example, al-Hajj Ahmad who taught theology in Kano; Muhammad ibn Ahmad, a Sankore scholar who became a magistrate in Katsina; and al-Maghili who wrote an essay on the art of governing, advising Muhammad Rimfa (1463-1499), the king of Kano, that, "the eagle can only win his realm by firm resolve. . . . Kingdoms are held by the sword, not by delays.''

Until the Fulani achieved unity in Hausaland good advice and firm resolve had never been sufficient to bring together the Hausa states under a single ruler. This is surprising because the Hausa during much of their history were under pressure from powerful states—Mali and Songhai in the west and Kanem-Bornu to the east—and from time to time put forward resourceful local rulers like Queen Amina of Zaria or Sarkin Kanajeji who reportedly introduced iron helmets and chain mail to the armies of Kano. Outside pressure, however, usually meant periodic Hausa vassalage, now to Songhai at the time of Askia Muhammad, now to Kebbi during its sixteenth century ascendancy under the *kanta* or king, Kotal, or from time to time to Kanem-Bornu, whereas regional leaders were generally unable to achieve more than the strengthening of their own state in relation to the others in the Hausa complex. Intramural rivalry dominated Hausa affairs over the years. Kano and Katsina were chronically at war with each other over which would dominate the southern end of the Sahara trade, and during the eighteenth century Gobir enjoyed a period of strength which she put to use largely in attacking her fellow Hausa states. It was in Gobir, on whose kings Islam had made little impression, that Usuman dan Fodio served as tutor to the royal princes, and eventually set in motion the forces of the Fulani jihad that was to bring ultimate political unity to Hausaland at the beginning of the nineteenth century.

Suggestions for Further Reading

The prime sources of information for the medieval Sudanic kingdoms are the accounts of contemporaries like Ibn Battuta, Leo Africanus, and others. Their writings are mostly available in complete editions—for example, H. A. R. Gibb, tr. and ed., *Ibn Battuta: Travels in Asia and Africa* (New York: Cambridge University Press, vol. 1, 1958, vol. 2, 1962)—but for one coming to African history for the first time the substantial excerpts contained in E. W. Bovill's *Golden Trade of the Moors*, (2nd ed. London: Oxford University Press, 1968) may be more palatable. Bovill should be supplemented for more recent scholarship by chapters 4 and 5 of the *Cambridge History of Africa*, vol. III (Cambridge: University Press, 1977) and the appropriate sections in J. F. A. Ajayi and Michael Crowder, eds., *History of West Africa*, 3rd ed., vol. I (Burnt Mill: Longman, 1985). Both sources point to substantial additional literature—see, for example, the interesting controversy concerning the relations of ancient Ghana and the Almoravids in D. C. Conrad and H. J, Fisher, ''Ghana and the Almoravids,'' *History in Africa*, vol. 9 (1982) and vol. 10 (1983), or Fisher's review essay, *Journal of African History*, vol. 23, no. 4 (1982).

4

The Cosmopolitan World of East Africa

The Rise of the City-States

Sometime toward the close of the first century after Christ a traveler from Alexandria, possibly an official of the imperial government of Rome, was cruising along the East African coast taking note of the terrain, of the people in the various ports of call, and of the types of merchandise that his ship was engaged in exchanging. In itself this event was nothing extraordinary. The "horn" of Somalia had been known to the Mediterranean world at least as far back as the expeditions that Egypt's Queen Hatshepsut had sent to Punt over fifteen centuries earlier, and since that time a lively trade had developed across the Indian Ocean involving the Mediterranean, Arabia and Persia, India, and the islands of the Indonesian archipelago as well as the Abyssinian kingdom of Axum and a series of East African entrepôts facing the Gulf of Aden and the Indian Ocean. What made the voyage of this particular witness noteworthy was the fact that he had recorded and compiled his observations in the form of a guide to the ports and trade of the Indian Ocean, a guide known as the *Periplus of the Erythraean Sea* which has survived as the only testimony from ancient times giving a firsthand account of the East African coast.

The voyage began in the familiar waters of the Red Sea. Fitted out and stocked in an Egyptian port like Berenice, the ship first stopped at the busy emporium of Adulis, port city of Axum, where a wide range of goods — linen and cotton, unworked copper, brass, and iron, cooking utensils and tools, wine and olive oil — were exchanged for the local ivory, tortoiseshell, and rhinoceros horn. Proceeding southward, the ship passed through the straits of Bab el Mandeb into the Gulf of Aden where a number of stops added to the stores of ivory and tortoiseshell accumulating in the hold, but where incense, slaves, and Indian cinnamon could also be obtained. At last the rocks of Cape Guardafui were sighted and passed, and the travelers turned south into the Indian Ocean, cruising down the Somali coast.

This cheerless land, its low cliffs and sandy wastes shimmering in the blazing heat, seemed to deny the possibility of human habitation, and indeed, after Opone, located a moderate distance beyond Cape Guardafui, there was no sign of life for hundreds of miles as the shoreline sloped southward and slightly to the west. Gradually the aspect began to change. South of the Juba River, the monotony of sand and stone was replaced increasingly by a flat coastal plain covered with tangled wild growth. Occasionally the terrain was punctuated by stretches of mangrove swamp; in some places, as at the site of Lamu, it was broken into island groupings by the action of rivers, inlets, and tidal creeks. The air was warm, but the fierce sun of Somalia was gone and the evenings were often freshly bathed with an onshore breeze.

This more genial coast with its milder climate and its many anchorages beckoned to the traveler who found not only water and shelter but human settlements as well, for example, the large offshore island which may have been Zanzibar where the crocodile was the only wildlife and the people fished with wicker baskets placed to trap the outgoing tide. A further sail of two days brought the ship to Rhapta, in those ancient days the farthest removed of the East African ports. Here the people were reported to be of great stature and given to piracy. They lived under what must have been regarded as primitive conditions in the eyes of Alexandrine sophisticates, for they exchanged their ivory and tortoiseshell for manufactured iron tools and weapons unobtainable locally, and were pleased to receive in the bargain small gifts of wheat and wine. They seem to have been neither Bantu nor Bushman and they were ruled, at least nominally, by Arab kings living far off in the Yemen whose representatives had long come to Rhapta for its ivory and who had in many cases married and settled in the land. This was the extent of Mediterranean knowledge of East Africa. Beyond, reported the *Periplus*, "the ocean curves westwards . . . stretching out from the south and mingling with the western sea." Catching the summer monsoon, the visiting mariners turned from the mystery of the unknown and were soon headed toward the markets of India and Malaysia far to the east, where their ivory would bring a good price and a cargo of cotton, sugar, grain, and oil could be obtained for the return trip to Egypt.

These ancient contacts with East Africa, at once so extensive and so limited, implied no knowledge of the interior or communication with any people resident therein. It seems unlikely that the Bantu in their vast migration across central Africa had as yet reached the East African coast and, in any case, the forbidding terrain did little to invite exploration of the interior. The harborless shore of Somalia with its heat and its sand offered no temptation to linger, and even to the south along the tropical belt from Lamu to the Zambezi there were natural obstacles in the way of adventurers who might wish to push inland.

Of the numerous East African rivers, only the Zambezi was of inviting dimension and it suffered from rapids, that chronic impediment of Africa's waterways. Overland travel was even less feasible. North of the Tana River lay the scrub and sand of Somalia, but to the south stretched the formidable Nyika, a belt of rising ground back of the coast averaging one hundred miles in depth and covered with a jungle of thorn bushes and trees, a daunting barrier across the path of those seeking the highland plateaus beyond.

The years passed, the traders kept coming, and the coastal entrepôts developed in size and number. By the end of the fourth century A.D. there were several settlements on the southern coast of Somalia, and Rhapta had grown in importance. It was apparently located on a river which might have been the Pangani or an arm of the Rufiji Delta on the Tanzanian coast. From Rhapta some contact had now been made with the interior, for the snowy peak of Kilimanjaro was known to visiting seafarers. South along the coast there had also been some exploration, since cannibals were reported living there as well as "Fish-Eating Ethiopians," these groups possibly being early Bantu arrivals on the coast. But that was all. "South of these," reported Claudius Ptolemy in his *Geography*, "is the unknown land," where it was suspected but not known that other Ethiopians might dwell.

No physical record of these ancient settlements remains. Roman and other coins of the early Christian era have been found along the coast, but whether they came there at the time or later is uncertain. It is probable, however, that few Alexandrine Greeks visited East Africa after the collapse of Rome in the fifth century A.D., and that Persian and Arab seafarers monopolized the carrying trade thereafter, bringing quantities of the ever-popular African ivory to India and farther east where it was variously in demand for palanquin litters and incense in China, as dagger handles, sword scabbards, jewelry, and ornaments in India. By the tenth century the East African entrepôts had added gold and iron to their range of exports, the iron coming from coastal deposits in the Mombasa-Malindi area, the gold brought down from the far interior to the southern ports located along the Mozambique coast. Leopard skins were another popular export, and faraway China also received black slaves, rhinoceros horn, ambergris, and tortoise shell, transshipped in India and south Asia.

If the *Periplus* was ambiguous as to the kinds of people living in Rhapta, later commentators were unanimous that the coastal inhabitants were negroids. Black slaves were being exported to Persia as early as the seventh century, and from the tenth century onward black people were consistently reported to be the inhabitants of the coastal towns. They were variously described as hunters, as fisherfolk, as cannibals, and as traders, as well as cultivators of a variety of tropical products including rice, millet, sorghum, cucumber, coconuts, sugar, camphor and the ubiquitous banana. Although Arab Muslims lived in small colonies along the coast, the local people were as yet pagan worshipers of nature and practitioners of magic, ruled by kings whom they regarded as divine but who were nevertheless vulnerable to assassination if found tyrannical or unjust.

It is not clear what type of relationship was maintained between the Arab immigrants and the indigenous inhabitants of the East African coast—the Land of Zanj, or blacks, as the Arabs called it. The traditional coastal chronicles, transcribed at a much later time, speak of early Arab settlements and Islamic conversion of the local population during the seventh century with consequent allegiance to the Caliphate, but such a development seems very unlikely. For example, the migration of the Shirazi from Persia, assigned in the traditional accounts to the tenth century, now seems to have taken place two hundred years later and to have come not directly from Persia, but south from Somalia. Similarly, the allegiance to Islam was probably a development of the thirteenth century paralleling the establishment of Muslim states in Indonesia, India, and Persia. It was also at the end of the thirteenth century that a Yemeni dynasty was established at Kilwa. These external influences, however, were limited to the coastal towns and their immediate environs. The African hinterland remained unaffected.

The pattern of outside influence, therefore, possibly followed a sequence beginning with Arab trading posts at or near local African towns and in time becoming a series of Arab-Muslim kingdoms established over a gradually Islamicized population. Alternatively, African trading centers may have developed in response to outside commercial demands with African royal houses slowly becoming Islamicized through the influence of Arab merchants living in these communities. In any event, Arab settlers, arriving in increasing numbers from the twelfth century onward, were continually being absorbed into a Bantu majority. According to a Portuguese account of the early sixteenth century, the people of Sofala were either black or mulatto; those of Mombasa, black, tawny, or white. The island of Kanbalu—probably Pemba—was reportedly part Muslim by the tenth century but in this case the process of assimilation worked both ways, for those converted nonetheless spoke the local language. Mogadishu possessed a mosque in the thirteenth century, and by mid-fourteenth century the population of both Mombasa and Kilwa was staunchly Muslim. External contacts were by no means limited to Muslim Arabs, however. Waves of immigrants had crossed from Indonesia as early as the beginning of the Christian era, the evidence of this is to be found in the Malagasy language and people of Madagascar and the presence in Africa of Malaysian plants such as the banana. There is, moreover, the visit to Malin—the elusive Malindi of former times—by Chinese junks in 1417.

If there is some uncertainty as to whether these cities were governed by indigenous dynasties or Arab immigrants, there is little doubt that the prevailing culture, like the coastal people themselves, evolved essentially through a mixture of African and Middle Eastern characteristics. The basic language came to be Swahili with its Bantu base and its strong Arabic influences. The initial lack of currency and paucity of funerary inscriptions and the importance of African customs among the population and rulers of such towns as Kilwa and Mogadishu argue for African cultural development in combination with the Muslim. In one respect, however—in the domestic and state architecture that has survived—the inspiration is clearly of Arab, Persian, and perhaps Indian derivation with no discernible African character.

The earliest of surviving structures is the Kizimkazi mosque on Zanzibar, a part dating from the beginning of the twelfth century, but Kilwa on the Tanzanian coast has a thirteenth-century Arab palace and another ancient building that bears close stylistic similarities—though surely not equal antiquity—to the architecture of the Umayyad and early Abbasid caliphates of the seventh and eighth centuries A.D. The Kilwa palace occupies about two acres along a cliff overlooking the sea and is a complex of courtyards surrounded by rooms, sometimes with barrel vaulting, sometimes in double stories. The building material was coral rag set in lime mortar, but cut stone was used for roofing, decorative slabs, and architectural features such as doorways and stairs.

Many other coastal towns display architectural remains of Middle Eastern inspiration, particularly noteworthy in this respect being the Arab colony at Gedi on the Kenya coast which flourished between the fourteenth and sixteenth centuries. The town contained a mosque and a palace with a labyrinth of rooms designed for everything from state audiences to private quarters for the women of the harem, and salesrooms for the commercial activities of the merchant-king. More modest domestic architecture consisted of houses of coral and mortar, singled storied and flat roofed, usually with four and five rooms comprising living and sleeping quarters, storage, bath, and kitchen facilities, in front of which was a courtyard employed for both recreation and commerce. These were moderate-sized towns, much like today's older coastal cities. Populations from about ten thousand, inhabiting a hodge-podge of buildings separated by narrow pedestrian lanes with few public edifices save the mosque and perhaps a ruler's residence. It was a comfortable if not luxurious existence. There was none of the sophistication of the great cities of Arabia and India, but these coastal communities, though culturally provincial, were reasonably prosperous.

The Portuguese on the East African Coast

The international trade on which the prosperity of the East African coastal markets rested reached its climax in the late fifteenth century. In addition to the traditional exchange with Arabia and the Persian Gulf, there were now substantial exports from East Africa to China, Indonesia, and India. During the twelfth and thirteenth centuries, moreover, a new element was added when Europe, reestablishing through the Crusades her ancient contacts with the Middle East, began to demand increasing quantities of Africa's gold and ivory.

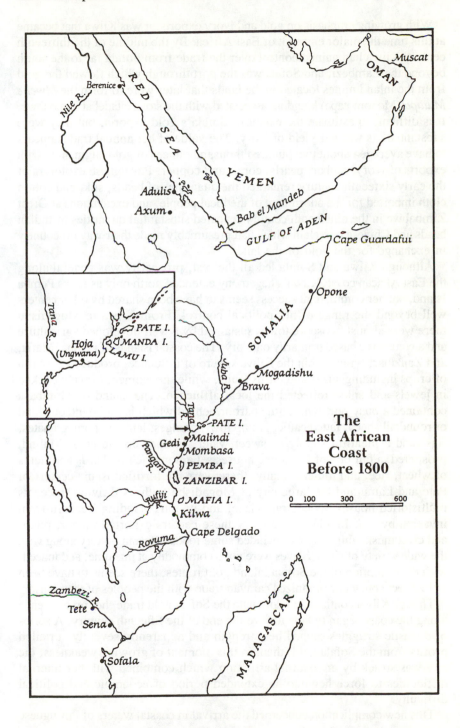

The East African Coast Before 1800

OMAN

Muscat

RED SEA

Berenice

Nile R.

YEMEN

Adulis

Axum

Bab el Mandeb

GULF OF ADEN

Cape Guardafui

Opone

SOMALIA

Juba R.

Tana R.

Mogadishu

Brava

PATE I.

Gedi
Malindi
Mombasa
Pangani
PEMBA I.
ZANZIBAR I.
Rufiji R.
MAFIA I.
Kilwa
Cape Delgado
Rovuma R.

Zambezi R.
Tete
Sena

Sofala

MADAGASCAR

0   100   300   600

Tana R.

PATE I.
MANDA I.
Hoja
(Ungwana)
LAMU I.

With growing emphasis on gold and ivory exports, it was Kilwa that became at this time the major entrepôt of East Africa. By the middle of the thirteenth century Kilwa had gained control over the trade from Sofala far to the south beyond the Zambezi, and Sofala was the port through which flowed the gold from the inland mines located in the lands that later were to form the *Mwene Mutapa* (Monomotapa) kingdom associated with the stone citadel at Zimbabwe. It is difficult to estimate the extent of Sofala's gold exports, but they were substantial, as was her yield of ivory. The value of her annual trade appears to have averaged about two hundred thousand ounces of gold augmented with exports of ivory, amber, pearls, coral, and copper. Portuguese explorers of the early sixteenth century remarked the quantities of beads, silk, and cotton cloth imported for the adornment of the local people, and excavations at Great Zimbabwe in the nineteenth century revealed substantial quantities of Indian beads and Chinese porcelain which had presumably made their way up-country in exchange for the gold of the land.

Although Kilwa and Sofala led all the rest, prosperity was general along the East African coast. Kilwa's hegemony extended north only as far as Pemba Island, but her commercial success seems to have been shared by other centers well beyond the range of her political control. From Kilwa to Mogadishu there were almost twoscore towns sustained by a well-developed agriculture and a commerce based primarily on ivory. The coastal islands of Pemba, Mafia, and Zanzibar, lying within the Kilwa sphere of influence, produced a wealth of crops including sugar and citrus fruits, while the women, bravely decked in jewels and silks, reflected the local affluence. The island of Mombasa contained a busy port with a fine harbor behind which lay a bounteous land of roundtail sheep, fatted cattle, plump fowl, oranges, lemons, pomegranates, figs, and a plentiful supply of sweet water. Farther up the coast Malindi prospered, a fair city of fine stone houses set among rich orchards and fields of wheat, rice, and millet. Finally, there were the fortified island centers of Pate and Lamu and the large city of Mogadishu with its thriving trade, its multistoried houses, its central palace, and its long-standing freedom from invasion by sea. In addition to ivory these centers exported timber, pitch, and civet musk while imports included some foodstuffs and pottery along with the wide variety of cloth. Slaves were not a commodity at this time, and indeed, with the exception of the Sofala inland gold routes, there seems to have been little direct contact or organized caravan trade with the peoples of the interior.

Though Kilwa continued to dominate the Sofala gold trade, her preeminence along the coast began to fade toward the end of the fifteenth century. A series of dynastic struggles sapped her strength and apparently severely curtailed profits from the Sofala gold; then, in this moment of growing weakness, the city was struck by an external affliction which combined with her internal difficulties to force her into an extended period of economic and political difficulty.

This new complication concerned the arrival in coastal waters of Portuguese naval expeditions, intruders who soon developed into a major constituent of the local scene, menacing East African commerce and threatening the independence of the trading states. Portugal, pursuing the expansionist dreams of Prince Henry the Navigator, had sought the double objective during the fifteenth century of throwing back Islam on behalf of Christ while achieving economic ascendancy through control of both African gold and a sea route to the markets of the East. Decades of exploration along the western coast of Africa culminated in 1487 when Bartolomeu Dias rounded the Cape of Good Hope and Pero da Covilhã set out to explore the Indian Ocean ports by an overland route. Ten years later Vasco da Gama conducted his portentous reconnaissance of East Africa and western India, an exploration that suggested the possibility of a maritime empire in the Indian Ocean were Portugal able to gain control of a number of strategic points, including a foothold on the East African coast.

It required only a few brief campaigns for Portugal to achieve her design of empire. In 1509, a combined fleet of Egyptians, Arabs, and Persians was destroyed and with it went the ability of Middle Eastern powers to offer effective resistance to Portuguese expansionism. Already commercial and military posts were being established on the Arabian, Persian, and Indian coasts, while East Africa was systematically brought under control—Kilwa made tributary in 1502 and Zanzibar the following year; Sofala occupied in 1505 by a fleet which then sailed on to sack and garrison Kilwa; and Mozambique annexed in 1507, eventually to become the central point of Portuguese authority in East Africa. The northern towns escaped occupation but not attack, the Portuguese contenting themselves with the plunder of Mombasa in 1505, laying waste to both Hoja and Brava the following year in response to a show of defiance there. Lamu and Pate avoided conquest through submission, and Malindi willingly became a faithful ally of the Portuguese, her dislike of Mombasa presumably outweighing any sense of local solidarity. Only Mogadishu managed to maintain her independence, because the Portuguese captains were reluctant to attempt an assault against this large and well-defended citadel.

Within a short decade of da Gama's first appearance, Portugal had become nominal master of the coast, but her conquest, so quickly and easily achieved, proved much more difficult to exploit. To begin with, the occupation of the southern ports miscarried, for the newcomers soon found themselves presiding over deserted towns and stagnant commerce, their aggressive conduct countered by the passive resistance of the local population. Once her Sofala connection had been severed, Kilwa quickly atrophied. Her trade collapsed in the face of Portuguese mercantile restrictions, while large numbers of her people removed to the northern cities rather than submit to the inequities and abuses of alien administration.

By 1512 the Portuguese had written off Kilwa and evacuated their garrison, but they were soon disappointed by a parallel decline in the fortunes of Sofala, the golden port and key to the wealth of the interior. To their dismay the flow of gold soon declined to a trickle, while overall commerce reportedly did not even meet the expenses of the Sofala trading factory. Subsequent attempts to effect an occupation of the interior by way of the Zambezi valley were also unsuccessful, insofar as the Portuguese were unable to exploit the chief mining sites and were eventually ousted from the Zimbabwe plateau by the state of Changamire.

Along the northern coast, Portugal encountered other complications. Here the ports were more powerful and the trade better sustained; hence, Portuguese attacks, though often irresistible in a military sense, resulted only in destruction of towns quickly rebuilt and in occasional payments of tribute. The cargoes of cotton and other goods continued to arrive from India to be transshipped at Mogadishu, Pate, Mombasa, and other centers for dispersion along the coast. Despite her military vigor, by the middle of the sixteenth century Portugal had not yet succeeded in monopolizing the coastal trade.

To be sure, the main Portuguese thrust was directed toward India and farther east in a successful effort to gain control of the spice trade, but the need for a major East African station remained, a need that Mombasa seemed best able to fill because of its size, location, and mercantile importance. In 1528 the Portuguese had again plundered Mombasa without occupying the town, but the arrival of Turkish warships in East African waters during the 1580s finally precipitated more definitive action. Rallying the coastal ports, the Turks established themselves at Mombasa in 1589, thereby provoking a successful Portuguese attack that eventually led to permanent annexation of the city and the construction of Fort Jesus as a stronghold and administrative center. Now at last Portugal was able to dominate the coastal states and maintain closer surveillance over their trade.

Portugal's predominance, when it was finally achieved, survived for a hundred years, but it brought little satisfaction, for elsewhere Portuguese power was already in decline, and her position on the East African coast thereby foredoomed. Held by the Spanish crown between 1580 and 1640, her far-flung possessions under increasing attack by Europe's rising mercantile powers, Portugal gradually lost control of her empire, East and West. By the middle of the seventeenth century, the Omani sultans had dislodged the Portuguese from Muscat and were raiding the East African entrepôts. A long period of strife ensued marked by local rebellion and growing attacks from the outside against a declining Portuguese power. In 1698 Fort Jesus fell to the Omani and thus for all practical purposes ended the period of Portugal's ascendancy in East Africa.

The Omani Suzerainty

Two hundred years of Portuguese presence had contributed much to the decline of the coastal civilization. Portugal had sought economic exploitation through military control, but this policy, poorly conceived and weakly administered, had ended only in undermining commerce, denying its benefits with an even hand both to the exploited and to the exploiter.

Nevertheless, during this period the Portuguese were not the only calamity to visit the coast. In approximately the year 1580 there appeared before the Portuguese trading posts of Tete and Sena on the Zambezi a Bantu group, the Zimba, who had abandoned their normal peaceful existence and embarked on an extended campaign of militant migration. In this respect they resembled the Jaga people who were invading the kingdom of Kongo during much the same years, or the Nguni and Sotho Bantu in their vast and desperate spasms of death and destruction during the migrations that were to follow the rise of Shaka early in the nineteenth century. The Zimba were no simple marauders but, according to a contemporary observer, practicing cannibals whose sudden warlike impulse may have been related to unrest in the Malawi (Maravi) federation located between Lake Malawi and the Zambezi River.

What prompted the Zimba incursion has been disputed among historians; it may have been the jostling of Bantu groups on the move or alternatively a desire within the Malawi federation to participate in the gold and ivory trade. The Zimba were apparently disaffected subsections of the Malawi, and, when their economic or political objectives were frustrated, they abruptly attacked the Portuguese and subsequently moved up the coast into Swahili territory.

The impact of the Zimba on the coastal towns was clearly devastating. First Sena and Tete were overwhelmed and their inhabitants consumed; then, a band of five thousand Zimba broke away from the main body and moved up the coast in the direction of Kilwa, "killing and eating every living thing, men, women, children, dogs, cats, rats, snakes, lizards," sparing only those who joined them in their insane orgy. Kilwa, already weakened by Portuguese attack and subsequent emigration, could not resist this additional onslaught. In 1587 some three thousand of her people were slain and eaten; the few survivors who had fled to the forest returned to find their city in ruins, a shattered remnant of its former wealth and vitality.

Proceeding northward, the Zimba arrived at Mombasa in 1589 in time to witness its reduction by the Portuguese punitive expedition sent from Goa to subdue the inhabitants who had chosen to defy Portugal's power on the coast with the assistance of Turkish allies. The Portuguese systematically reduced the defenses, then permitted the Zimba to hunt down the local population, many of whom dashed into the sea, preferring to take their chances with the Portuguese and the elements than with the ravenous hordes at their rear.

Their appetite yet unsatisfied, the Zimba pressed on to Malindi which they soon brought under siege. This time the defenders were more fortunate. On the point of breaching the defenses, the Zimba were surprised by the warlike Segeju people moving down the coast, who "came suddenly on their backes when they had gotten up the wall . . . and chased them with such a furie, that only the Captaine with above one hundred others escaped. . . . And thus much of the Zimbas.''

Apparently the Zimba abruptly abandoned their war making and returned to a peaceful existence in their Malawi homeland. As for the Segeju, here was another example of interior peoples affecting the affairs of the coastal states. Probably they originated in the district of Shungwaya lying back from the Somali coast north of the Tana River to which, according to tradition, various Bantu groups had migrated as part of their extensive movement across the southern and eastern stretches of Africa. Later, the Shungwaya Bantu began a complex series of secondary migrations, which, among others, brought the Segeju to Malindi in time to thwart the Zimba, and then, scarcely two years later, to defeat the quickly rejuvenated Mombasans, taking their city as prize and presenting it to Malindi and her Portuguese ally.

With a garrison at Fort Jesus, Portugal emerged at last the supreme power on the coast, not so much out of her own wasting strength as from the continued weakness and division of the coastal principalities. Periodic uprisings continued, ever hopeful, always unsuccessful, but toward the end of the seventeenth century hope found greater substance in the growing power of Oman and her developing interest in the affairs of the East African trading ports. When, in 1650, Sultan bin Seif dislodged the Portuguese from Muscat and the Arabian coast, this event was applauded in East Africa's trading cities where the image of a Muslim-Arab kinship with the Omani led to dreams of a similar emancipation in Africa from Western rule. An appeal to the Omani by Mombasa precipitated a series of raids in combination with local revolt, and although Portugal counterattacked by subduing the rebellious islands of Pate, Lamu, and Manda, she could do nothing to forestall the vast Omani fleet that lay siege to Fort Jesus for thirty-three months during 1696-1698. The Omani pressed their attack with no great vigor, yet eventually succeeded in reducing the fort despite a number of Portuguese relief expeditions. Only a faint spark still remained. Aided by internal divisions among the Arabs, Portugal once more took control of Mombasa in 1728, but this quickly proved to be a dying gesture, for the following year the garrison was easily ousted by the Mombasans without even the necessity of Omani naval assistance. From that time forward, the Portuguese presence was effectively restricted to her coastal and inland posts in Mozambique south of Cape Delgado.

It was not long, however, before the East African coastal cities began to regret the encouragement they had lent the Arabs of Muscat, for the Omani soon proved no better masters than the Portuguese—an Asian overlord where once the Europeans had held sway. Civil war in Oman during the early eighteenth century led a number of trading centers to renounce their allegiance to Muscat, and thereafter Omani suzerainty was maintained only with difficulty. During the Omani civil war, Pate, Malindi, Pemba, Mafia, and Kilwa were at various times in revolt. At mid-century both Mombasa and Kilwa were at war with Oman, and each regarded herself at the time as an independent state. Indeed Mombasa succeeded in sustaining her independence under the leadership of the Mazrui family from the time the first Mazrui became deputy governor in 1727 until the days of Sayyid Said one hundred years later. For a time Zanzibar displayed an unenthusiastic loyalty to Oman, but in 1784, when the Omani attempted a direct occupation of their African possessions, Zanzibar resisted and had to be subdued by force. Pate and Kilwa also submitted at this time, but Oman's control continued uncertain, leaving the coastal states substantially free to indulge their taste for local quarrels and to ignore the vexations of nominal rule from afar.

During the latter part of the eighteenth century there was one preoccupation in which all merchants, those of Oman and of the East African emporia alike, could agree. Slaving had never been an important part of the coastal trade during the Portuguese era and before, but in the middle of the eighteenth century French traders had begun to take slaves from Madagascar and Mozambique, and this activity was gradually expanded to other coastal points in a search for labor to work the plantations of the Indian Ocean colonies, Île de France (Mauritius) and Bourbon (later Réunion). Soon slaving had become a major economic factor on the coast, and the foundation had been laid for the slave trade of the nineteenth century.

The activities of the French were decisive in this respect. A French trader, Captain Morice, visited the coast and concluded a treaty with the sultan of Kilwa in 1776 whereby Morice was to be supplied with one thousand slaves a year. He also urged the extension of French power to the Kilwa area which he regarded as suitable for the establishment of a slave market as well as the development of plantations such as existed at Île de France. Morice looked on Zanzibar as another likely site for a slave depot and recommended its absorption into the French empire, arguing that three hundred Omani defenders among a population of forty thousand would offer no serious deterrent. France, however, made no move against either Kilwa or Zanzibar, for she was unwilling to risk alienating Oman in a move that would have complicated her struggle with the British in the Indian Ocean. Moreover, she already was receiving substantial supplies of slaves from East Africa. By 1790 the French were averaging approximately fourteen hundred slaves a year from Kilwa and upwards of four thousand more from Portuguese sources in Mozambique, while others were available in quantity at Zanzibar where a large and profitable slave trade had developed by the early nineteenth century. Slaving made an enormous difference in the ecology of the French islands. Île de France, which contained only six hundred black Africans in 1735, possessed a slave population of forty-nine thousand in 1807, and Bourbon had changed over the years in similar fashion, numbering almost thirty thousand slaves by 1787.

Although the sale of slaves to the French was profitable, it was only a part of the total developing trade. The French captains who called at Zanzibar complained of discrimination in favor of Arab slavers bound for Muscat and other ports in the Red Sea and Persian Gulf, and a similar discrimination was practiced at Kilwa. By 1811, Zanzibar had become the chief center of the coastal trade and was exporting between six and ten thousand slaves annually to Îe de France, Muscat, and India, as well as quantities of ivory, rhinoceros horn, and other products from which the authorities realized a large revenue through customs. Though the Omani sultan received better than half of Zanzibar's annual tariff revenue, his fiat had little practical authority on the island and even less along the coast. Nevertheless, the booming trade was bound to attract the attention of the reigning sultan, Sayyid Said, who had fought his way to the Omani throne in 1806. At a later time, when circumstances were to permit such a move, this resourceful monarch would reassert an active control over his East African possessions and even move his seat of government to Zanzibar, thus establishing a new political configuration in East Africa.

Ethiopia—The Trials of Isolation

In the spring of 1520 a Portuguese mission arrived at Massawa on the Red Sea, an expression of Portugal's expanding interests in the Indian Ocean and its bordering complex of territories and waterways. The immediate objective was the establishment of relations with what was thought to be the land of Prester John, but perhaps the most enduring result was the narrative penned by one of the mission's members, Father Francisco Alvarez, the first foreign description of the remote highland kingdom of Ethiopia, and one of the few glimpses granted the outside world of a land that had grown in myth and mystery even as its true character had vanished into legend. "The Ethiopians slept near a thousand years," Gibbon was to note, and forgetful they were of the world about them, but by others they had not been forgotten so much as lost, particularly in the West whose civilization they had shared in ancient times.

If the mountainous inaccessibility of the Abyssinian highlands made for potential isolation, it was the rise of Islam that divorced the Ethiopians from their Mediterranean connections, turning their gaze southward and forcing them in upon themselves. Although no holy war was directed against Ethiopia, the seventh-century expansion of Islam saw the fall of Egypt, the collapse of the Persian and Byzantine empires, and the beginning of Arab occupation of Red Sea bases. Beyond this, the Beja nomads of the Red Sea hills, in one of their periodic eruptions, overran the Eritrean plateau late in the seventh century, cutting off the people of Axum from their northern and eastern contacts. Thus isolated, Axum lost complete touch with its earlier Hellenistic and Semitic influences, and apparently suffered political fragmentation and cultural decline as well. During the ensuing centuries, Ethiopia disappeared from the view of the West and, even in her own land, her history for a time gave way to legend.

Despite a ninth-century commercial relationship with Muslims in the regions bordering the Red Sea, Ethiopia maintained her prevailing southern orientation. The Axumites gradually migrated to the mountain districts of Amhara, Gojjam, and Shoa where they reestablished their kingdom in the face of hostile pagans, particularly the Agau people. At first the Axumites were successful, partially subduing and converting the Agau. Late in the tenth century, however, there ensued a confused period of invasions and of revolt by the Agau who ravaged the country, slaughtering the clergy and virtually obliterating the Christianity of the Axumites. At last the monarchy prevailed, but the nation that emerged from the ordeal was the result of fusion, not of conquest. Thenceforward the Christian Axumites formed the Abyssinian aristocracy while Ge'ez and Amharic came to be the dominant national languages. Slowly the Agau yielded to Christianity but only as their own religious practices were absorbed into church ritual, while they themselves emerged as the major ethnic element in the Abyssinian population. This cultural, political, and religious fusion was far enough advanced by the middle of the twelfth century for the Agau to gain control of the monarchy in the form of the Christianized Zagwe dynasty that ruled the Ethiopian state for approximately one hundred fifty years and presided over a religio-cultural flowering that was to be of great importance in shaping the character of Ethiopian civilization.

The physical expression of this flowering was projected most eloquently by the monolithic churches built in the highland fastness of Lasta during the reign of King Lalibela (c. 1181- c. 1221). These astonishing architectural monuments were cut directly from their mountain of volcanic stone, hollowed out and shaped into arcades, chapels, naves, and sanctuaries, pierced with windows, supported by columns and arches, and embellished with reliefs and architectural ornamentation-all carved from the living rock like a series of gigantic sculptures. Eleven churches in all, they were no mere eccentricity, for they followed in the long tradition of religious architecture already widely practiced in Ethiopia, and utilized ancient motifs such as the shaped arches inspired by the summit of the great stele at Axum.

The churches of Lalibela were more than an architectural triumph, however; they represented the emergence of the unique Christianity of Ethiopia and the close relationship of church and state that has come to characterize Ethiopian society. The Christianity of the Axumites had been drawn from the Coptic persuasion and their bishop consecrated by the patriarch at Alexandria, but ethnically and culturally they were Semites from Arabia, and much of their ideology came to reflect a growing identity with ancient Israel. For their part the Agau exhibited Judaic as well as pagan characteristics, perhaps because of influences derived from Yemeni Jews before the advent of Islam. The resultant clash of these two strains almost brought the end of Christianity in Ethiopia, but when at last the Axumites had prevailed, Ethiopians saw themselves as God's chosen people maintaining Christian purity in their "second Israel," imitating religious and cultural institutions drawn from certain pagan practices but also in great measure from the Old Testament. There is, for example, circumcision and polygamy, dietary prohibitions and ritual cleanliness, strict Sabbath observance and certain forms of church music and dance, as well as the claim to possess the original Ark of the Covenant taken from Jerusalem by Menelik I, Ethiopia's first king. In the end the Ethiopians came to identify themselves with the lost twelve tribes of Israel, their royal line stemming from the union of Solomon and the Queen of Sheba.

The Zagwe dynasty of the Agau, of which Lalibela was the most illustrious representative, gave way to the restored Solomonid line about 1270, and Solomonid monarchs ruled Ethiopia continuously thereafter until the emperor, Haile Selassie, was deposed by military coup in 1974. Under the early kings of this dynasty, Christian conversion was pursued as before, but increasingly it shared the royal attention with military campaigns against the numerous Muslim states—Ifat, Hadya, Bali, Doaro, Adal, and others—established by local Cushitic speakers like the Sidama along the southern and eastern edges of the Ethiopian plateau. These kingdoms, absorbing Islam from coastal Arabs, had emerged between the tenth and twelfth centuries while the Axumites and Agau were mutually preoccupied, and they now pressed in upon the Ethiopians only to be repulsed and, for a time, reduced to vassalage.

Unlike the Zagwe period for which little historical information survives, the era of the restored Solomonid kings was marked by chronicles that provided at least an outline of events. Yekuno Amlak (c. 1270- c. 1285), the first of the "king of kings," shifted his base of operations from Lasta to his native Amhara and began to move against Muslim neighbors, but major expansion at the expense of these states was not achieved until the reign of the militant Amda Seyon (1314-1344). The dynasty reached an early peak under Zara Yakob (1434-1468), who not only consolidated the gains of his predecessors, but also greatly stimulated local religious activity and established relations with Rome in an effort to stave off both the external influence of Islam and the continuing effects of indigenous paganism. Zara Yakob's methods were often harsh. Aside from his commentaries on church doctrine and his program of church construction, he instituted a much feared inquisition designed to stamp out heresy. Consequently, records his chronicle, "there was great terror . . . on account of the severity of his justice and of his authoritarian rule and above all because of the denunciations of those who, after having confessed that they had worshipped . . . the devil, caused to perish many innocent people by accusing them falsely."

The Ethiopian gesture toward the church of Rome coincided with Europe's own developing interest in Africa and Asia which brought the Portuguese to East Africa at the beginning of the sixteenth century, seeking both to dominate the material wealth of the East and to destroy the spiritual world of Islam. An attempted liaison with the Christian kingdom of Ethiopia therefore was a natural outgrowth of Portugal's search for allies in a hostile land as well as the quest for that mythical Christian king, Prester John, whose existence had been rumored since the twelfth century, first in Asia and finally in Ethiopia. Thus it was that the Portuguese explorer Pero da Covilhã had made his way to Ethiopia in 1494 at the conclusion of his travels to India, the Middle East, and East Africa, while a quarter-century later the diplomatic mission that included Father Alvarez arrived to pursue closer relations between the two countries.

Although nothing came of the mission, the need for cooperation soon became apparent. The kingdom of Ethiopia was powerful and extensive as the sixteenth century dawned, stretching from Massawa in the north to the tributary states of Ifat, Fatajar, Doaro, and Bali in the south, but the Muslims were tireless in their opposition and needed only the unifying strength of effective leadership to shift the balance of power in their favor. Population pressure possibly originating in Somalia, a renewed sense of religious mission, and a developing Ottoman interest in East Africa finally came to a focus in the Muslim state of Adal during the early sixteenth century, and when Adal shortly produced a gifted general in the person of Ahmad ibn Ghazi (1506-1543), the Ethiopians soon found themselves facing a crisis of survival.

Ahmad, called Gran, or left-handed, organized a powerful army, instilled it with the spirit of the jihad against the infidel, and in 1529 scored a decisive victory over the Ethiopian emperor, Lebna Dengel (1508-1540). This engagement was followed by a systematic devastation and occupation of Ethiopia which brought most of the country under Muslim control, laid waste to large areas, destroyed much of the intellectual and artistic heritage of the land, brought the forcible conversion of large numbers of people, and reduced the emperor to a hunted fugitive in the remote mountain districts of Tigre, Begemder, and Gojjam. In desperation, Lebna Dengel appealed to the Portuguese for help and in 1541, after the emperor had been succeeded by his son, Galawdewos (1540-1559), a contingent of four hundred musketeers arrived at Massawa and helped defeat the Muslims in an engagement near Lake Tana during which Gran himself was slain. Resting largely on the shoulders of one man, the Muslim menace was removed, suddenly, dramatically, and indeed, permanently.

The problems of the upland empire were by no means ended, however. The Muslim forces retiring to their capital at Harar were almost at once replaced by a new threat in the form of the pastoral Galla, Cushitic speakers who, in the middle of the sixteenth century, began to move northward from their nucleus in southern Ethiopia. They occupied the emirate of Harar, scaled the mountains on the east and south of the Abyssinian plateau, and flooded Shoa, moving on to infiltrate Amhara and Lasta. Military action had no effect on this vast movement, nor were the Galla susceptible to assimilation into the more developed Ethiopian culture. Before their relentless advance, the Ethiopians were forced to withdraw and to share their country with the invaders with whom they lived side by side over the ensuing centuries, but always as strangers and potential enemies.

Coincident with the beginning of the Galla migrations there was a Turkish occupation of Massawa and other coastal points which the emperor, Sarsa Dengel (1563-1597), succeeded in neutralizing though not eliminating in 1589. Staggered and depressed by incessant invasion, the Ethiopian nation now faced yet another intrusion of a different sort. Portuguese aid against Ahmad Gran had caused renewed interest at Rome in converting the Ethiopians, and a Jesuit mission was soon dispatched with this end in view. At first success was slow in coming, but through the patient tact of Pedro Paez, the mission ultimately gained the conversion of the emperors Za Dengel (1603-1604) and Susenyos (1607-1632).

Unfortunately for the cause of Roman Catholicism, Paez died in 1626 and was replaced by a zealot, Alphonso Mendez, who sought at once to impose the Roman church on the whole country, forcing the emperor to do him public homage, rebaptizing the population, remodeling the liturgy, forbidding many ancient practices, and introducing others anathema to local custom. Such a move led straight to bloody rebellion, anarchy, and eventually to the deportation of the Jesuit mission. For a time Susenyos stoutly supported the Latin reforms as his country sank in self destruction, but finally he could endure the spectacle no longer. In 1632, the emperor reestablished the Ethiopian church. "Hear ye! Hear ye!" read his proclamation. "We first gave you this faith believing that it was good. But innumerable people have been slain. . . . For which reason we restore to you the faith of your forefathers. Let the former clergy return to their churches. And do ye rejoice." Susenyos then abdicated in favor of his son, Fasiladas (1632-1667), and soon after died despondent, still embracing the faith his people had rejected.

Contrary to some accounts, Fasiladas apparently maintained open and friendly relations with Europe and his Muslim neighbors, but he and his successors could do little to offset the country's internal regionalism and doctrinal differences that had developed within the Ethiopian church. Along with the ceaseless pressure of the Galla, these forces led to internal decay, political fragmentation, and ultimate collapse of the central authority. Fasiladas established a fixed capital at Gondar, an inaccessible retreat in the mountains of Amhara, and this move effectively divorced the emperors from their people. The royal line in its growing weakness appealed for Galla support which further discounted imperial authority in the eyes of each local prince, or *ras*, only too ready to exercise independent rule. Galla mercenaries came to dominate the monarchy, and in 1755 a half-Galla king mounted the throne. The Galla were too divided among themselves, however, to impose national unity through their own rule, while the Ethiopians found themselves pressed into isolated islands by the expanding sea of Galla intruders.

By the middle of the eighteenth century, the throne had lost all authority, maintaining its existence only through the tradition of its sacred origin while *de facto* government rested in the hands of the Galla leaders and provincial chiefs. Civil war was continuous, and separatism steadily gained strength.

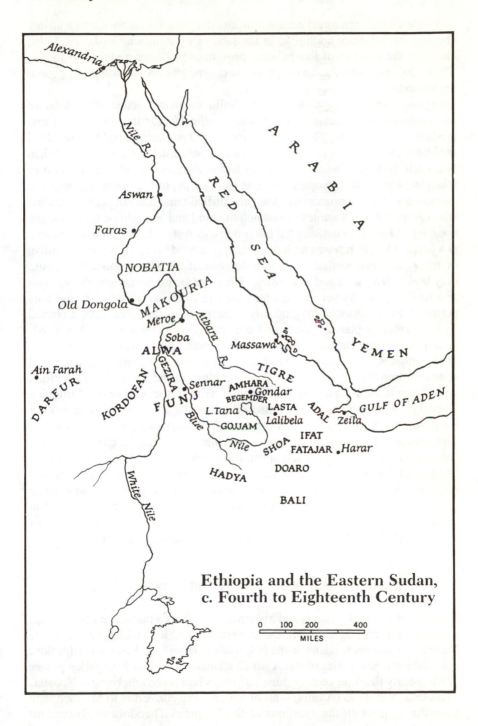

**Ethiopia and the Eastern Sudan,
c. Fourth to Eighteenth Century**

0   100   200   400
MILES

Only the church remained national in identity, but its authority was at low ebb and its influence negligible in the face of militant war lords. By 1840, although the number of independent provinces had been reduced to four— Shoa, Gojjam, Amhara, and Tigre—the disintegration of Ethiopia appeared permanent.

Beyond the divisive thrust of the Galla intrusion acting on a land of mountainous inaccessibility, there was another factor that both aided and hindered national unity. The Ethiopian character had been shaped by a highland environment in which remoteness spawned parochialism and conservatism in a static society. The difficult years following the seventh-century rise of Islam had forced the Ethiopians to come together in political unity and religious communion, but the process was long and difficult and had not been completed when Ahmad Gran's armies devastated the land and brought on the awesome apostasy to Islam. Eventually the old order was restored, but restoration came at a price. The church was no longer receptive to ideas from without, Roman or otherwise, and settled down to a defense of the status quo which could only lead to ignorance and inbreeding. The royal house abandoned the strength and flexibility of its peripatetic court for the isolation of Gondar, and thus permitted each provincial ras gradually to establish his own local rule, protected by his mountain inaccessibility and the apathy of effete kings. Introverted, Ethiopian society languished and the Ethiopian spirit atrophied.

Nevertheless, the fusion of Agau and Axumite had brought forth a national state consummated in the glory of the great kings of the Solomonid restoration while providing a spiritual brotherhood within the shelter of Ethiopian Christianity. During the most critical days of the Muslim invasion neither the monarchy nor the church ever lost faith in its traditions and responsibilities. The invaders were driven out and a new national strength emerged which reached full force in the uncompromising rejection of the Jesuit effort to Westernize the Ethiopian church. Later, as the nation split into warring factions, both church and royal dynasty still retained enough prestige to survive in name if not in authority. When, during the nineteenth century, forces were set in motion in the direction of political unity, it was found that the Ethiopian spirit had not yet expired nor had the vision of an Ethiopian nation.

Christians and Muslims in the Eastern Sudan

The sack of Meroe by Ezana and his armies cut short a particular civilization; it did not put an end to life in the eastern Sudan. It would appear that the Nubians, as ancient residents in the Nile Valley, rebuilt the Sudanic civilization, establishing a new series of states which ultimately replaced the fallen power of Meroe. By the sixth century three kingdoms had come into being—Nobatia, Makouria, and Alwa (Alodia)—all of which were converted to Monophysite Christianity through the exertions of the Empress Theodora of Byzantium and the Egyptian Coptic Church. For a time, however, it seemed that the Arab invasion of North Africa might engulf these states. Following the conquest of Egypt, a campaign was launched that brought a Muslim army to the gates of Old Dongola, now the capital of the single kingdom of Makouria that had embraced Nobatia. Undaunted, the Nubian archers stood off the attackers and Makouria secured a treaty, the celebrated *Baqt* of 652, which established a peace that endured for six hundred years, guaranteeing the faith of the Christians and promising annual imports of northern fabrics and foodstuffs in return for a yearly payment of 360 slaves. To the south, Alwa (Alodia) stretched her hegemony from the site of ancient Meroe to take in most of the Gezira lying between the White and Blue Nile, her capital of Soba located just below the confluence. Much more than Makouria, Alwa was oriented southward toward the heart of Africa, and her greater remove from the Mediterranean world meant much less knowledge in the north of her affairs, religious or secular.

For many centuries the Christian Nubian civilization prospered. Along the Nile numerous villages and good-sized towns contained attractive churches and monasteries within their urban clutter, set among gardens, vineyards, and pastures rich in produce. The strength of Nubian Christianity may be seen in the distinctive religious art of the period. Only recently a buried cathedral unearthed at the Nobatian capital of Faras has yielded an abundance of murals, often brilliant in color, combining Coptic and other foreign influences with local characteristics, depicting Biblical and other religious subjects with portraits of Nubian kings and bishops. As with the northern territories, Alwa was described by contemporaries as a rich and fertile land, primarily devoted to stock breeding. According to one tenth-century account, the king of Alwa was wealthier than Makouria's monarch, possessing large numbers of horses and soldiers. Soba was said to contain numerous churches embellished with gold, and many beautiful gardens, but archaeological remains do not bear out these seemingly fanciful claims.

Following several centuries of peace, prosperity, and cordial relations with Egypt, a change set in midway in the thirteenth century. The arrival of the Mamluk rulers in Egypt touched off a series of military campaigns into Makouria which, though abortive, weakened the regime and destroyed much of the country's wealth. These expeditions led in turn to large scale Arab immigration from Egypt, hitherto rigorously forbidden, which resulted finally in the political collapse of Makouria early in the fourteenth century. More remote, Alwa lingered on, but by the fifteenth century her people had been overrun by pastoral Arabs infiltrating from Egypt. Resultant civil war and political chaos created a vacuum of authority that was filled early in the sixteenth century by a new power, the Funj sultanate.

The final disintegration of the Christian kingdoms of Makouria and Alwa opened the way for the spread of Islamic religion and civilization throughout the eastern Sudan. Arabs from the north continued to filter into the land, driving their flocks before them, and gradually there arose a new strain made up of the local population combined with an Arab infusion. At the same time indigenous institutions tended to give way before Arab political organization and language, while Christianity and paganism were replaced by Islamic culture and religion. The fall of Makouria and Alwa, therefore, represented a turning point in the history of the eastern Sudan, for thenceforward it was Islam and the Near East rather than Nubian Christianity that came to shape the lives of the people.

The Funj were a good case in point. Of obscure origin—possibly an offshoot of the White Nile Shilluk, possibly from a black nation of the upper Blue Nile—they appeared suddenly and dramatically in 1504-1505 to found their capital of Sennar on the Blue Nile and to establish their hegemony over the Sudan until the days of Muhammad Ali three hundred years later. They quickly subdued the Abdallabi Arabs who had taken over the collapsing state of Alwa, but were themselves just as quickly converted by Islam and brought into a close economic and cultural association with Egypt.

By mid-seventeenth century, the Funj were at the height of their power, exercising suzerainty over a series of vassals as far north as the Third Cataract, and controlling directly the Gezira plain between the White and Blue Nile. A century later, however, Funj power began to decline as civil strife robbed the regime of its strength. By the time the armies of Muhammad Ali advanced on Sennar in 1821, not only the power but the will to resist had departed, and the Sudan fell to the invaders uncontested.

Suggestions for Further Reading

For the East African coast see the chapter by N. Chittick in the *Cambridge History of Africa*, vol. III, ed. Roland Oliver (Cambridge: University Press, 1977), and that by E. A. Alpers and C. Ehret, *ibid.*, vol. IV, ed. Richard Gray (Cambridge: University Press, 1975), along with the older but rather more accessible *Oxford History of East Africa*, vol. I, R. Oliver and G. Mathews, eds. (Oxford: Clarendon: 1963). An entertaining supplement is J. S. Kirkman's *Men and Monuments on the East African Coast* (London: Lutterworth Press, 1964). Primary materials are sampled in G. S. P. Freeman-Grenville, ed., *The East African Coast* (Oxford: Clarendon, 1962). A discussion of the Zimba incident is found in M. D. D. Newitt, "The Early History of the Maravi," *Journal of African History*, vol. 23, no. 2 (1982) and M. Schoffeleers, "The Zimba and the Lunda State . . ." *ibid.*, vol. 28, no. 3 (1987).

Ethiopia's complex history in the post-Axum period up to the mid-eighteenth century is detailed in the relevant chapters of the *Cambridge History of Africa*, vols. III and IV (cited above) and vol. V (John E. Flint ed. Cambridge: University Press, 1976), although some may prefer the older but more articulate account in J. S. Trimingham, *Islam in Ethiopia* (London: Franck Cass, New York: Barnes and Noble, 1965). M. Abir, *Ethiopia: The Era of the Princes* (London: Longmans, New York: Praeger, 1968) is fine for the period, 1750-1850. For Galla origins see H. S. Lewis, "The

Origins of the Galla and Somali,'' *Journal of African History*, vol. VII, no. 1 (1966).

By far the most complete work on the Christian period in Nubia is William Y. Adams' splendid *Nubia: Corridor to Africa* (Princeton: University Press, 1984). For the Funj, R. S. O'Fahey and J. L. Spaulding, *Kingdoms of the Sudan* (London: Methuesn, 1974) may also be consulted.

For a general survey of economic and social factors in precolonial Africa see R. W. July, *Precolonial Africa: An Economic and Social History* (New York: Scribners, 1975).

5

The West African Forest Civilization

The Land and the People

The West African coastal area, stretching along two thousand miles from Senegambia to present-day Cameroun, contains people whose languages and customs suggest a common ancestry far in the remote past. Much less uniform is the land in which they live; even the rain forest which characterizes so much of the region along the coast varies greatly in nature and extent, between the Gambia tidewater and the hills of present-day Sierra Leone or from the dry slope of the Accra plains to the humid jungle swampland of the Niger Delta.

When European mariners first began to explore the West African coast during the fifteenth century, they divided it into the western or windward district extending from Cape Verde to Cape Palmas (Upper Guinea), and the eastern, or leeward, coast which comprised the sheltered shoreline of the Gulf of Guinea (Lower Guinea). Such divisions had little meaning for the West African inhabitants. More significant were the varying stretches of forest, the pattern of river drainage, or the elevation of the terrain. To the west in what is today Senegal, the Gambia, and Guinea-Bissau, the land is open and well watered by navigable streams that quickly abandon the mangrove swamps near the sea to range through fertile flatlands whose sandy soil is now employed in the cultivation of rice, millet, and groundnuts, and whose rivers give easy access to the interior.

The Senegambia is in fact not a true part of the West African forest for its latitude betrays a closer kinship to the savanna, but farther to the southeast the windward coast undergoes a marked change in character. In this region of modern Guinea, Sierra Leone, and Liberia a thick expanse of forest covers the coastal areas and at one time penetrated far inland before the advent of widespread bush farming. Here the rivers rush down from interior iron-bearing hills like the Futa Jalon only to lapse into sluggishness as they approach the coast, finally creeping to the sea through delta marshes. Unlike the Gambia, this country defies easy communication. Not only are the rivers difficult to navigate but in places the hills come right to a shoreline that offers no harbor save the excellent bay at modern Freetown, while overland travel must contend with a forest encouraged by an annual rainfall frequently well in excess of one hundred inches.

East of Cape Palmas the wooded area is less extensive and the terrain less severe. Gently rolling hills are covered by a relatively narrow band of forest which disappears entirely as the savanna reaches the coast from a point in western Ghana through Togo and most of the modern state of Benin, reflecting the lower precipitation in those areas. In the region of the Niger Delta, however, both rainfall and vegetation are abundant in a country that is both connected and divided by a network of waterways—a means of communication for the native of the land but a labyrinth to befuddle the stranger. Elsewhere the coast is somewhat more hospitable with lagoons and inland waterways and occasional rivers like the Ogun and the Volta that permit some access to the interior.

Linguistic, anthropological, and archaeological evidence has yielded a number of hints about the origins of West Africa's forest dwellers, but this evidence is largely circumstantial, more suggestive than conclusive. Stone Age tools, for example, have been found in abundance throughout the West African forest indicating human residence covering thousands of years. More specifically, near Akure in the southwestern Nigerian forest archaeologists have unearthed a skeleton amidst materials dating from the tenth millennium B.C. Whence came any original forest population—at first, hunters without a doubt—is an open question but a secondary penetration seems also to have occurred, coming in connection with the desiccation of the Sahara during the last few millennia of the pre-Christian era.

This later dispersion, covering the savanna as well as the forest, is supported both by historical traditions of many West Africans and by analysis of languages spoken throughout West Africa today. It is known that most West Africans speak variations belonging to the Niger-Congo branch of African languages, and that these languages stem from a single ancestral tongue with an antiquity of at least eight thousand years. More than that, this ancient proto-Niger-Congo language contained terms for domestic animals, thus implying an early knowledge of agricultural techniques. If this is so, groups of Niger-Congo speakers might have at some time moved into the forest as cultivators to supplement and perhaps to absorb the resident hunter-gatherer population.

Such possibilities are firmly backed by traditional accounts of origins. A number of West African peoples such as the Yoruba retain founding traditions that postulate immigrant princes arriving from north and east, often from points outside Africa, to establish the first kingdoms on which subsequent nations were built. Whatever their particular details these foundation legends give strength to the concept of a southward movement of savanna peoples into the forest, yet they are strongly contradicted by the obvious fact that West Africans are blacks indigenous to their current location with no apparent connections outside the African continent.

By and large historians have rejected these ancestral traditions as much later accounts established primarily to authenticate latter-day Islamic connections and influences. What seems more probable is that there were indeed early migrations, not from far-off Egypt or Arabia but only from a short distance as certain savanna dwellers moved into the forest. Moreover, while these migrants may well have practiced farming, there is further skepticism among historians regarding a major early shift from hunting to farming within the forest itself.

The reasons relate to the forest environment. Savanna grains like millet and sorghum cannot be cultivated in forest land and even yams are best suited to the forest fringes. More than that, given the rudimentary character of Stone Age tools, or even later iron technology, it would have been extremely difficult for these migrants to clear virgin forest land. To prepare a single acre of forest requires removal of several hundred tons of vegetation; put otherwise, a small family farm would have entailed the removal of thousands of tons of vegetable matter, a task well beyond both the labor and mechanical means of these early settlers. It therefore seems probable that the full-scale shift from hunting to farming did not take place in the forest until quite recently, in some locations perhaps as late as the fifteenth and sixteenth centuries A.D., by which time southern migration had become more persistent, adequate labor was available, and the demands of commerce had forced advances beyond the limitations of small hunting or fishing economies with only a modest agricultural accessory.

A forest environment had two other characteristics — it provided protection against invasion and attack, but protection came at the price of isolation. Communication was difficult and early communities were small, their political organization simple, their economies meager.

Yet generalization invites distortion, for not all the forest dwellers were isolated nor all the states small or politically and economically undeveloped. Benin was already a strong and extensive kingdom when the Portuguese discovered it in 1485, and subsequently the Yoruba of Oyo, the Asante, and Dahomey established stable, centralized states with extensive political authority, widespread economic interests, and a highly sophisticated culture. It was the Yoruba of Ife who cast bronze portraits of their sovereigns, beginning as early as the eleventh century A.D., which are among the world's finest examples of naturalistic sculpture, which may have derived from the celebrated Nok terra-cottas of an earlier era, and which were forerunners of the superb bronzes that Benin began to produce in the fifteenth century. Artistic output of a high order was never the monopoly of a few, however; witness the imagination and humor of the gold weights of Asante, the subtle music of the talking drums in what is today Ghana and Nigeria, the delicate Bulom ivory carvings so

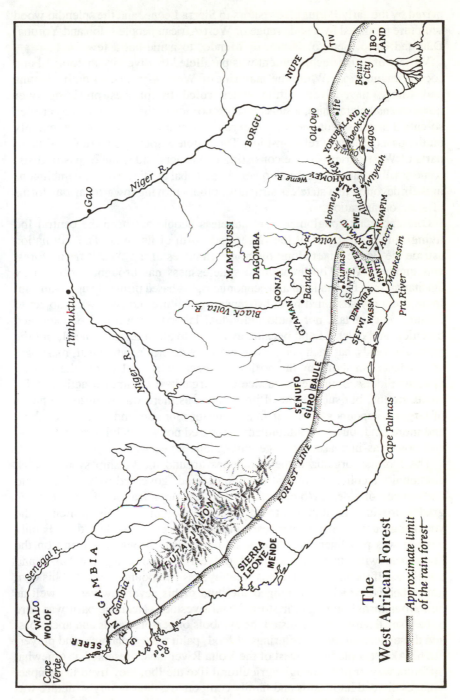

The
West African Forest

—— Approximate limit
of the rain forest

prized by the early Portuguese visitors to Sierra Leone, and the splendid wood sculpture produced by a wide range of West African people—Ibo and Yoruba, Dan and Guro, Senufo, Baule, or Mende, to name but a few.

Variety of artistic achievement was paralleled by diversity in political and social organization. While the majority of West Africans, in both savanna and forest, have lived within states ruled by princes presiding over governmental hierarchies, a substantial proportion of the population has created so-called stateless communities wherein government proceeded essentially on the basis of family relationships. The stateless societies were found in all parts of West Africa—some consisting of farmers and some of pastoralists; some small isolated groups and others large tribal entities; some unambiguous in their devotion to a stateless structure; others moving toward various forms of state organization.

One important conglomerate of stateless people has been the central Ibo living in the forest east of the Niger and north of its delta. The Tiv nation astride the Benue River along the northern edges of the West African forest was another. The Tiv devotion to statelessness has brought forth a truly egalitarian society with legal and economic rights based primarily upon kinship. In an economy sustained by subsistence agriculture, no crop was subject to tribute, rent, or tax, nor could individual labor be controlled or exploited by chiefs and elders. Land became available to all in terms of need, but the particular fields that each person worked were determined by birth, marriage, or residence, in short, by the position of each individual within the kinship system. Elders administered justice and organized communal activities for small groups, but such political importance as there was went to the heads of larger compounds; a bigger family meant more dependents, more labor, and more land, but these attainments reflected not so much increased wealth and power as increased prestige among one's peers.

The Ibo also organized their societies around the kinship system, each community a collection of scattered homesteads governed by a village head and council of elders. No centralized political organization existed, but age grades provided an important and vigorous system of public policing, the younger groupings charged with carrying out the decisions of the elders. Family descent was patrilineal and family solidarity was strong, centering on the homestead with its heavy walls of red earth surrounding the barns and dwellings. If the householder was wealthy, his compound contained his own house behind which were ranged the huts of his several wives as well as numerous farm buildings for storage and livestock. Near the barn was sure to be a small shrine where rested the symbols of personal gods and ancestors, and these received regular offerings of food, palm wine, kola nuts, and prayer.

The Akan people living west of the Volta River have presented a somewhat different way of life. Though agricultural like the Ibo, they lived in compact villages divided into wards and family compounds; their family structure was essentially matrilineal, and they typically organized themselves into complex states with a ruler and attendant ministers. Royalty in the West African forest was a precarious profession, hemmed in by many limitations, however. The *alafin*, or king of Oyo, always stood the risk of a no-confidence vote by his council of state, which according to the dictates of custom compelled him to commit suicide. Among a number of peoples it was the rare king who died of natural causes, but this may have reflected not customary regicide so much as the natural uneasiness of crowned heads. Even in his prime, a king was limited by his advisers. An early Portuguese account records how a Sierra Leone king was obliged to consult his elders before initiating warfare, ''and if it appears to them that the war is unjust, or that the enemy is very strong, they tell the king that they cannot help him, and give orders for peace despite the king.''

Among the Wolof and Serer of Senegambia, royalty, if vigorously sustained, fared better. The Wolof king was elected by the nobility, but once chosen he quickly consolidated his power and was surrounded by taboos and certain attributes of divinity. A warrior-chief, he protected his authority by a retinue of soldier-slaves, dependents, and praise singers, he appointed local rulers who were obliged to repay him with a share of their tax revenues, although in practice they were often virtually autonomous. The Serer kings presided over a similarly centralized organization, and both Wolof and Serer political systems conceded important powers to the women of the royal clans. The king's mother, for example, controlled certain villages which paid her tribute, and presided in judgment over cases involving adultery.

Both the Wolof and Serer societies were rigidly hierarchical. Among the Serer there were clearly defined classes of royalty, nobility, warriors, peasants, and crown servants, as well as special low castes including smiths, butchers, leatherworkers, and praise singers. Slavery was widespread but it too was carefully divided into such groupings as slaves pawned for debt, hereditary house servants who could not be sold, and true slaves acquired through war or purchase. Slaves represented a large portion of the population and in certain instances they enjoyed great power and privileges—for example, those who dwelt in the royal household and served as advisers to the king.

Political cohesion within forest societies was, as elsewhere, a balance of potentially antagonistic forces. Among the stateless communities, the emphasis on kinship and lineage had none of the countervailing centripetal pull provided by an articulated governmental hierarchy; hence, emphasis upon lineage was frequently set off against a powerful age-grade system. Age grades created community-wide loyalties that crossed the grain of family ties, providing within the village a coherence of decision making and law enforcement otherwise denied. Among themselves the age grades created their own balance, setting pragmatic, conservative, experienced elders against impatient, idealistic, inexperienced but vigorous youth. Each needed the strengths of the other, and together they established unity where the family could not.

The age grades performed a similar service for the centralized states, strengthening the princely power by countering lineage rivalries; otherwise this support at the center was sometimes provided by the secret societies that flourished across West Africa, particularly in the region lying between Portuguese Guinea and the Ivory Coast. Like the age grade, the secret society replaced clan loyalties with broader affiliations; like the age grade, its functions included the enforcement of mores and standards of behavior, its mystery and its secrecy ensuring acceptance of frequently harsh sanctions because they were expressions of the general public good.

Such activities did not always come to the aid of the chiefly authority, their powerful influence in the shaping of local customs and the imposition of taboos constituting for practical purposes a very real check on the powers of the established government. Many societies existed, but the most widespread among a number of peoples were the *Poro* for the men and the *Sande* for the women, each concerned principally with sexual education and the metamorphosis from adolescence to adulthood, but associated in the popular mind with supernatural powers, which enabled the societies to wield great authority in temporal affairs.

The *Poro* practiced rites that claimed death and resurrection for its candidates who emerged from initiation with a deeper spiritual strength as well as the authority to indict individuals in their villages for alleged breaches of the law or even to forbid others the performance of certain normal actions such as planting a crop or making a journey. Noncompliance generally resulted in the offender being carried off into the bush by spirits, never to be seen again, a dreadful supernatural process that rarely failed to impress a people already convinced of the awful power of the society.

Among the Mende of Sierra Leone the secret societies were the *de facto* guardians of the ethical and moral standards of the people. They were concerned specifically with sexual values and practices, but the ultimate goal was the propagation of socially accepted behavior—womanly character and virtue, codes of male honor, or rules of public conduct on which there was common agreement as the ethical foundations for a healthy society. Hence these societies claimed a wide-ranging prerogative to dictate in such matters as public health, agricultural production, education, or political succession relying on their close liaison with the spirit world as a basis for their authority. In this respect they were not unlike the medieval church in Europe, which also prescribed rules of conduct and codes of behavior based on spiritual authority, and which frequently compelled the temporal power to compliance.

The Daily Life

Once agriculture entered the rain forest, the typical forest dwellers became full-time farmers, living in small villages, their neighbors including numerous near or distant relatives, their lives a repetitious, if not especially taxing, round of tasks related to subsistence farm management. Houses were usually set along the one or possibly two streets of the village, mud-brick rectangular structures with a raffia palm or grass roof and perhaps an inside veranda surrounding an interior court. Set in a small clearing, the village was sometimes encircled by an earthen wall beyond which a narrow band of forest gave way to the farming area. The village fields had been cut from the high forest, a continuing process that added new clearings every few seasons while other tracts, their fertility temporarily exhausted, were permitted to revert to bush.

The farms were not large; limited by the labor capacity and nutritional needs of individual families, they expanded or contracted as required. A farm of six or eight acres was average, such a tract capable of supporting a moderate-sized family, with each able-bodied male maintaining the equivalent of two or three acres under cultivation. The farm family usually worked cooperatively for a common harvest, but it was not unusual for individual members to have their own private fields, an important consideration in the case of young men of marriageable age seeking the necessary assets to obtain a bride and begin a family of their own.

The heavy work of clearing new land was performed by the men, usually during the dry season when the sky was smudged with the swelling columns of smoke that marked burning stumps and brush fires preceding the actual turning of the soil. The larger trees were left standing; not only were they difficult to fell but they would later provide oases of welcome shade for field workers. Turning the soil was an especially arduous task, for sun-hardened, dehydrated land combined with matted root systems to complicate the most persistent efforts; yet the careful farmer knew that his fields must not be too thoroughly plowed for fear of losing precious topsoil to winds or tropical cloud bursts.

If the typical savanna crop was millet, in the forest it was the yam that formed the principal staple, yam fields characteristically prepared by hoeing the soil into large two-foot-high mounds in which were placed the seed yams, in some areas the mounds capped with a heavy layer of grass or weeds to prevent erosion. The yams required considerable moisture and a good deal of attention—maintaining the mounds and staking the vines, for example—but given proper care, they afforded rich harvests of far greater caloric yield per acre than the savanna grains. The chief nutritional deficiency of the yam was its poverty of proteins, minerals, and vitamins; hence, the forest diet required substantial supplementary support from leafy vegetables and animal foods to obviate the malnutrition that too often impaired the health of the typical forest villager.

Dietary balance, when properly achieved, was readily apparent in the cooking pot. Mature yam tubers, dug out of the ground and cut into pieces, were soaked, then pounded or ground into a paste, placed in bags, and allowed to ferment in the sun for a day. Mixed with water, boiled, and strained, the yam paste would serve as a porridge in the morning and reappear later in various guises, most typically as the main ingredient in an evening stew. In this case, a loaf of dough was placed in a highly peppered sauce of palm oil that had been mixed with greens and seeds, both cultivated and wild, and augmented with bits of meat or fish, when these delicacies were available. As the family gathered around the main calabash dish, each member would take a piece of the yam dough, later widely known as fufu, deftly roll it into a ball, dip it into the stew, and then consume it.

There were many varieties of yams under cultivation, including imports from Asia that had arrived with the cocoyam (taro) and the banana, and were eventually supplemented by new world cassava (manioc). Nevertheless, it was palm oil, perhaps more than any other ingredient, that lent special character to the forest meal. Nothing could have been more appropriate, for the forest abounded with palms, both in number and variety, and their contributions to the comfort and well-being of the forest population were almost without measure. One rhapsodic observer described the oil extracted from the palm kernels as combining the odor of violets, the flavor of olives, and the color of purest saffron. The oil also served as lighting fuel and cosmetic body ointment, while the kernels, if not eaten directly, were retained as livestock feed.

Palm trees and their products were considered private property in most communities, even when growing on another person's farm, and in some cases they were thought to possess mystical significance to accompany their elevated economic status. Throughout the rain forest, in the Congo (Zaire) basin as well as in West Africa, the palm gave a distinctive profile to the civilization of the forest people. Its fibers provided some with the walls of their houses, others with cloth, and still others with currency, fish traps, or animal snares. From one species came a yellow plumlike fruit excellent in the eating, while others provided the celebrated palm wine with powers to quench the thirst and soothe the temper. The tall palm groves bestowed a welcome shade on villagers who employed other palms as a living hedge around their compounds to ward off attack.

Next to the palm, the kola tree was most prized, for chewing its rosy nut provided a mild, reputedly therapeutic stimulant much prized throughout West Africa, where this nut, presented to traveler or guest, was a sure sign of hospitality freely bestowed. The kola nut was frequently the monopoly of particular growers, a jealously guarded monopoly with important economic benefits reflected in the widespread commerce in kolas throughout West Africa and, indeed, across the desert to the Maghrib. In most areas it had as much ceremonial as medicinal significance; it was the conventional means of inviting guests to important kinship ceremonies; it marked a pledge of political allegiance and personal loyalty; it was the universal expression of friendship; and it served widely as token payment for small services rendered.

Such gestures were normal within small village societies requiring much communal effort and mutual assistance in the everyday affairs of life. In Africa as elsewhere, farm management necessitated much cooperation within each family, and there were complex arrangements whereby a family could draw upon extraordinary sources of labor in moments of need. A farmer could normally expect the assistance of the healthy adult males in his compound, but many communities specifically required field work from the women as well, and even children had their assigned duties—the important task of chasing animal pests from ripening harvests constituting a chief responsibility. Beyond these arrangements, other kin or friends were available for assistance according to time-honored rules of privilege and obligation, and when a major undertaking exceeded the capacity of an individual household, villages had recourse to systems of mutual aid through large-scale collective labor.

In Africa, labor was rarely performed in isolation; cooperation, companionship, and friendly competition were concomitants that frequently added social and sportive aspects to work tasks, transforming potential drudgery into festive as well as productive occasions. Such qualities characterized the work party, summoned by the needy farmer for extraordinary labors beyond his capacity—constructing a wall, roofing a building, or clearing fields— and frequently organized through an age grade of young men in the village. Assembling early on the appointed day, and invariably accompanied by a band of musicians, the workers divided into competing teams, their prevailing frame of mind a combination of anticipated pleasure for the contest to come and pride in the skills and strengths to be displayed.

If a roof were to be built, the groups assembled the necessary materials on either side of the building, then began the work, some preparing poles, others stripping palm fronds, still others sewing thatch and making rope, while a special group mounted the eaves to install the supporting framework and lay the thatch. As the work went forward, the pace quickened in response to the rising excitement, the workers urged on by the shouts of a growing body of spectators, the rhythm of the work songs, and their own sense of achievement. Skillful performers were singled out for encouragement and the clumsy were targets of jibes, but all strained to capacity until the contest suddenly rose to a climax, both teams ranged along the ridgepole, sweating and gasping in hot dispute about which side had carried the day.

The job completed, attention turned next to the festivities, the dancing and feasting wherein the participants converted their intense but good-natured contention to postmortem analysis, emphasizing their arguments with illustrative gestures and graphic dance steps. Much comparison was made between the achievements of this day and those of other memorable contests, and much pleasure was gathered from the occasion through the sense of accomplishment, the companionship, and the merrymaking. Withal, a difficult and necessary job had been well done, one that lay outside the capacity of the individual farmer who, in this instance, was obliged only to supply the requisite food and drink in recompense.

Cooperation of another sort was to be seen in the organization of regional trade that moved through the West African forest, connecting it to the savanna and ultimately to the traffic across the Sahara to North Africa. Communication within the West African forest had none of the ease that characterized the movement of people in the savanna, but isolation was not absolute, and trade was an important part of life in the forest belt. Village markets existed for the exchange of commodities produced locally, but there was also a long-distance trade, which dealt in specialty goods that were distributed widely along well-established trade routes. Salt manufactured on the seacoast was exchanged for iron or gold mined in the interior. Leather products of pastoralists living on the edge of the savanna were shipped south where they might find a market in cotton-growing, cloth-producing communities. Slaves and gold found ready purchasers in the kingdoms of the Sudan, and later, when the Europeans began to visit the West African coast from the fifteenth century onward, gold, and then slaves, became major exports of the forest region south to the Atlantic trade.

The antiquity of this commerce is open to conjecture, but surely it was already in place as the demand for slaves grew; indeed, there is at least one suggestion of much earlier mercantile activity. At Igbo Ukwa in Iboland excavations have revealed a variety of sophisticated bronze and copper artifacts crafted by the lost wax method and probably dating from the ninth century after Christ. These works may well have been created locally but the copper must have been imported, for the nearest source was several hundred miles to the north in the Sahel district of Air, and most West Africa copper came from Europe in any case. Hence the people of Igbo Ukwu were part of a long distance trading system and that system probably involved a number of other products such as foodstuffs, salt, or kola nuts.

Commerce of this sort led to a certain amount of economic specialization. Most people were farmers but some clans came in time to be associated with such occupations as mining, weaving, or smithing, while trading was the part-time occupation of many, especially women. Indeed, commerce became the specialty of certain groups like the Dyula who had their representatives located strategically along trade routes and who devoted their full time to merchandising, leaving cultivation of their lands in the hands of domestic slaves. On these routes towns developed whose main function was the exchange of goods, and here were to be found the large markets with a wide variety of products—gold dust, fabrics, kola nuts, shea butter, and salt, along with food and other consumer goods to sustain the people whose main work was the conduct of business in the market. These centers engaged in more than economic exchange, however. They were also places for relaxation and the enjoyment of friendship, for the exchange of gossip, for romance, or for intrigue. It was there that news of the outside world could be obtained, where fresh ideas first made their entry into the circumscribed universe of the forest villager.

Ife, Oyo, and the Rise of the Yoruba

Tradition credits Oduduwa, son of the supreme being, as the founding father of the Yoruba nation. There are two genesis versions. Arriving at the site of Ife, either from the heavens or as a refugee from Mecca, Oduduwa established several Yoruba principalities as well as the state of Benin, his sons serving as their first kings. Linguistic analysis suggests a prosaic but more plausible alternative. The Yoruba, the Edo speakers of Benin, the Nupe nation, and other West African peoples belong today to a Niger-Congo subgroup speaking languages that probably originated in the savanna near the Niger-Benue confluence. Slowly over several thousand years these peoples separated culturally and linguistically, probably reaching their present locations many centuries ago. The Nupe, for example, came to occupy savanna lands along the Niger while the Edo settled in the forest above the Niger Delta and west of the river. In the case of the Yoruba, they colonized a large area of both savanna and forest in the western region of present-day Nigeria.

The Yoruba apparently comprised small discrete and mutually independent groups, including the Oyo who were later to create a large and powerful empire. The shrine city of Ife remained influential, the founthead of Yoruba royalty and a source of spiritual inspiration and cultural expression. That Ife was an important center by the eleventh century may be inferred from its splendid art of that period, but in no way was it given political primacy by other Yoruba communities. This unity among the Yoruba was expressed mainly through cultural singularity, for example, a central language and common religious beliefs. Not even the name, "Yoruba," was a shared identity, having originated during the nineteenth century, created by outsiders to designate the Oyo people.

It was Oyo, however, that eventually imposed some measure of Yoruba political unity. After a period of uncertainty, the Oyo state began to develop during the seventeenth century, pressing against Nupe and Benin and gaining varying measures of control over a number of Yoruba principalities. In the eighteenth century Oyo expansion was even more rapid, reaching its greatest extent under Alafin Abiodun (1774-1789). Most of Yorubaland was overrun, Dahomey defeated on several occasions and finally made tributary by 1748, while outlets were secured on the coast in the region of Porto Novo.

The coastal emporiums were important, for much of Oyo's expansionism was connected to the Atlantic slave trade which by the eighteenth century had become extremely profitable and highly competitive. The strength of the Oyo armies lay principally in their cavalry, and horses were purchased through the Saharan trade either with slaves captured in campaigns or with European goods obtained on the coast, also in exchange for slaves. Hence Oyo imperial growth was achieved largely by military means, a major objective control over local trade as well as the international Saharan and Atlantic commerce with its attendant national and royal wealth.

The alafin not only levied trade tariffs, he also gained much revenue from tribute and war booty. In theory he was an absolute despot controlling the administration of the empire through his provincial governors, but in fact his powers were circumscribed by custom and condition. His primary limitation lay in the *Oyo Mesi*, the lineage heads of the seven Oyo wards who formed a council of state, their main function to advise the alafin in his governance. Though the alafin was not in any formal sense obliged to heed the Oyo Mesi, prudence argued cooperation for the Oyo Mesi were responsible for choosing each succeeding alafin and, if they felt the need, to force abdication and suicide. Moreover, the Oyo army was controlled by the Oyo Mesi whose leader, the *Basorun*, normally served as commander in chief.

To counter the authority of the Oyo Mesi, the alafins made direct appointments of provincial governors, tax collectors, and military commanders, thereby creating an essentially unstable condition by counterpoising two competing sources of power. Late in the eighteenth century this fateful instability climaxed when falling income from trade brought general disaffection and eventual civil war that led to the ultimate breakup of the Oyo state.

The initial blow came with a severe drop in slave exports in the 1790s caused by the naval wars between England and France. To compensate, taxes and tribute were increased thereby intensifying already simmering disaffection at the capital and in the provinces. During the century a number of kings had met violent ends as a result of the growing power struggle; now, with the death of Abiodun, his successor was deposed in a coup which created permanent schisms within the ruling cliques of Oyo. Such disaffection led by stages to the civil wars that dominated Yoruba history in the nineteenth century and were not to end until the British occupation of Yorubaland in 1893.

The People of Benin

Benin lies in the West African forest east of Yorubaland. Not only was its territory adjacent, but it shared many close cultural contacts with the Yoruba including elements of a common heritage. The traditions of both the Bini and Yoruba people describe how an early Benin state, lacking effective royal leadership, invited Oduduwa, the king of Ife, to send a prince to rule, and how the choice finally fell on Oranmiyan, who was later to found the state of Oyo. Oranmiyan reportedly decided that only a prince of Benin blood would suffice, and so he fathered a son through the daughter of a Bini chief, and this son, Eweka, became the founder of the future Benin empire. This myth suggests that migrations into Yorubaland at the time of the establishment of Ife might also have affected the Bini, or Edo, who were either conquered by a wave of Yoruba immigrants, or possibly admired the efficiency of their neighbors sufficiently to invite a member of the royal line of Ife to rule as *oba* in Benin.

Whatever the cause, the royal infusion introduced a new cycle into Benin history, an era that was to culminate in the emergence of Benin as one of the great West African forest kingdoms. The process, developing slowly, had both internal and external manifestations. Internally, it took the form of a chronic struggle for power between the king and the *Uzama*, or ancient hereditary chiefs. Subsequently town and palace chiefs were added, appointed by the oba in a complex and formalized system of government and elaborate court ceremony, which, despite intermittent difficulties, gave stability to the monarchy and, through it, to the state.

The reign of Eweka may be dated very tentatively at the early thirteenth century, but the obas do not seem to have asserted themselves over their chiefs until Ewedo, fourth in Oranmiyan's line, succeeded in reorganizing the hierarchy and ceremonial functions of the palace chiefs in ways that emphasized his primacy. During the mid-fifteenth century, the great ruler Ewuare set the Uzama off against the town chiefs, thereby allowing him to manipulate a new power balance, at the same time introducing the principle of primogeniture for determining the royal succession. Primogeniture did not become firmly established, however, until the late seventeenth or early eighteenth century, but by that time the office of oba had been transformed, and a tradition of warrior-kings replaced with the institution of spiritual leaders confined to the seclusion of the palace. While the occasional strong ruler found himself equal to this new situation, most were dominated by their chiefs, while, despite primogeniture, the problem of orderly succession continued to defy solution as political confusion and bitter, bloody conflict marked virtually every new transfer of power.

Such intramural skirmishing appears to have had surprisingly little effect on the external expansion of Benin. The reforms of Ewedo included reorganization of the army, thereby laying the basis for later conquest, which reached its climax during the reign of Ewuare. This energetic and resourceful commander and his successors campaigned regularly to push Benin's frontiers to the Niger in the east and southward to the sea, while pressing westward into Yoruba country to gain suzerainty over several states and to establish a colony on the site of Lagos. By the middle of the seventeenth century, the kingdom had reached its maximum territorial expansion; from that point onward there was a slow erosion, marked in part by a drifting away of tributary states, and partly by the loss of terrain through conquest by aggressive neighbors. During the centuries of expansion, the strength and stability of the kingdom was manifest in many ways, not least by the artistic output of cast bronzes and carved ivory that were used not only for ornamental effect but to set forth the accomplishments of the Benin kings and state.

With its location near the seacoast, Benin was one of the earliest West African states to come into contact with the European explorers who were making their way down the West African coast during the fifteenth century. It was in 1485 that the Portuguese appeared at Benin in search of trade, which was quickly instituted with pepper and slaves as the chief exports. At this time, however, Benin was a stable and established state, and the appearance of the Portuguese had little effect on her Edo-speaking population. In the first place, the slave trade never achieved important proportions in Benin, whose indifference to such a commerce forced the traders to look elsewhere on the coast where better markets existed. Moreover, the Portuguese were careful to keep firearms from falling into Edo hands so that guns never played a major part in Benin's armament and expansionist policy. Finally, Portuguese efforts at Christian conversion were a pronounced failure in the face of a vigorous and complex state religion.

Though the importance of Europe may have been minimal, the early presence in Benin of Western traders and voyagers offered an unparalleled insight into the life of a West African community before there had been any infiltration of alien influence. The image of a virile society emerges. During its sixteenth-century apogee, Benin City was a stronghold twenty-five miles in circumference, protected by walls and natural defenses, containing an elaborate royal palace and neatly laid-out houses with verandas and balustrades, and divided by broad avenues and smaller intersecting streets. The power of the oba was apparent in his wealth, his divinity, his domination over commercial transactions, and his large and lavish court. In this prosperous society, the wealthier classes dressed and dined very well. Beef, mutton, chicken, and yams were staples, while the less well-off made do with yams, dried fish, beans, and bananas. No beggars existed in Benin, where those unable to keep themselves were normally supported by the king and lesser officials.

As with the source of Benin's growth, her gradual decline during the seventeenth, eighteenth, and nineteenth centuries is equally difficult to diagnose. Perhaps it was the custom of secluding the oba, which developed during the reign of Ehengbuda late in the sixteenth century and which tended to place military and political power in the hands of the chiefs, the oba limited to the exercise of religious authority. Perhaps it was the struggle over royal succession which often preoccupied rival groups of chiefs, for most chiefly positions were not hereditary and had to be protected, frequently by dominating weak obas. Perhaps it was an administrative complexity grown unwieldy. Perhaps, during the nineteenth century, it was Fulani pressure in the north and European commerce in the south. In any event, internal disputes proliferated and were accompanied by breakaway movements of subject people until the last decades of the nineteenth century found Benin in full decline ready to be toppled by the British occupation of 1897.

The Kingdom of Dahomey

The Yoruba had also maintained intimate connections with another powerful state, the kingdom of Dahomey, which arose at a later time on their western flank. During the eighteenth century, although a vassal of Oyo, Dahomey had become one of the chief intermediaries of procurement and supply for the West African slave trade.

Dahomey first appeared in the seventeenth century, one of a number of Aja states occupying the territory from the Volta River on the west to the frontiers of Yorubaland. At the time the major Aja kingdom was Allada, located on the coast along with others like Whydah and increasingly concerned with the burgeoning Atlantic slave trade. These states sold off captives and criminals, but they also served as intermediaries for slaves coming from interior points such as Oyo, their considerable profits giving them access to European goods, particularly firearms. Growing competition for the Atlantic commerce led to chronic warfare and unrest which was a chief reason for an attack on Allada in 1698 by Oyo, intent upon keeping open its direct contacts with coastal trading centers.

By the end of the seventeenth century a new Aja polity had emerged inland at Abomey, presumably in response to the Atlantic traffic, and soon this state of Dahomey was expanding its territory and challenging the coastal principalities for primacy in the region. During the early years of the seventeenth century, Dahomey was able to conquer Allada and Whydah, thus establishing itself on the coast while expanding in other directions to form a powerful kingdom in its own right, an heir to Allada as the dominant slaving community in the Aja region. At the same time Dahomey's success brought her into conflict with Oyo, the outcome of which was twofold—Dahomean ascendancy in her own area while at the same time she was forced to concede overlordship and tribute to Oyo.

There has been dispute among historians as to the motive for the Dahomean conquest of Allada and Whydah. Some experts have argued that the Dahomean king, Agaja, wished to shut down the slave trade to insure greater political stability in the region. Others feel the move aimed primarily at obtaining a greater share of the Atlantic traffic. At all events Agaja soon became actively engaged in the slave trade and Dahomey emerged as a major slaving power, dominant over all save Oyo. During the eighteenth century, although Dahomey remained basically an agricultural community, slaving came to represent a sizeable portion of the economy, especially lending wealth and power to the royal line.

Much more than the alafin of Oyo, the Dahomean king was an absolute monarch. The highest offices of state were hereditary but many others were appointed by the king, and the very multiplicity of titles diffused authority among many with the king manifestly supreme. Moreover, directly or indirectly, the Dahomean monarch controlled much of the profits from the slave trade as well as state taxes and tribute. Further, while the army was under command of special officers, the *Migan* and the *Mehu*, the king also had his private guard including the celebrated female contingent of "Amazons." Finally, the king's exalted position was signaled by the "Annual

Customs'' involving large numbers of human sacrifices that were designed to honor former monarchs but more particularly to establish through terror the omnipotence of the royal line.

No doubt the Customs frightened many neighboring peoples into submission as Dahomean armies campaigned annually in slave catching exercises. Nonetheless, by the close of the eighteenth century a number of factors had brought a steadily declining prosperity. Slaves from Oyo were being diverted from Dahomey's ports, and her own expeditions were no longer able to bring back sizable catches from the now-empty country north of Abomey. At the same time European demands were dwindling, first as a result of the commercial uncertainties caused by the long-lived eighteenth-century wars, and then in response to the abolition of the slave trade instituted by Britain in 1808. Depressed trade led to political unrest, which found outlet in abortive attempts to throw off the Oyo yoke and to replace the ruling dynasty at home. King Kpengla (1774-1789) tried in vain to break the Oyo hold and to replenish his barracoons by raiding the Yoruba kingdom of Ketu. His successor, King Agonglo, was the victim of a palace assassination in 1797, but the revolt failed to unseat the royal line. Finally, in 1818, Gezo seized power from Agonglo's son, Adandozan, and during the long reign lasting until 1858 he began to regain a measure of Dahomey's former prestige and wealth. After freedom had been secured from the failing Oyo kingdom in 1823, Gezo turned next to the problem of rehabilitating the Dahomean economy. His search for new sources of slaves as well as opportunities for legitimate trade soon resulted in a series of raids on the Egba stronghold of Abeokuta, and thus brought Dahomey squarely into the nineteenth-century Yoruba civil wars.

The Akan States of Asante and Fante

West of Dahomey in the forest area contained between the coast and the lower reaches of the Volta River and its Black Volta tributary lies the country of the Akan states. Akan traditions speak of early societies that came into existence in the forestland, made up of resident hunters who were brought together into clans and then small states about the same time that a major shift took place from hunting and gathering to agricultural production. The traditions seem to locate these political and economic developments at about the sixteenth century, a surprisingly late date that is, however, more or less borne out by archaeological findings that record surviving Stone Age technology well into historical times.

Although firm evidence is scanty, circumstance suggests that these early Akan people made the shift to agriculture in response to the growing international demand for gold, obtainable in quantity within the Akan forests. Dyula traders from the savanna exchanged slaves for gold with those who operated the mines and these individuals utilized their newly acquired slave labor to clear land for agriculture. Land was then distributed to settlers who controlled their own farms but accepted the fiat of the ruler in an arrangement that obliged them to provide goods and services in return for use of the land. Thus petty feudal states were born. Later, Europeans arriving on the coast exchanged manufactured goods, including firearms, for Akan gold, and the growing military efficiency that followed made possible political expansion by the more aggressive communities. In the seventeenth century, when slaving began to replace the gold trade, these nascent Akan states were ready to participate in the new commerce.

Commerce, then, not land, was the economic engine of Akan growth. By the close of the seventeenth century there were two major commercial preoccupations within the gold regions—a series of older interior routes heading north to Jenne, Timbuktu, or the cities of Hausaland, and the newer southern traffic to the coast. There, along the Gold Coast, a whole range of stations represented, among others, Dutch, British, and Danish interests, while Portuguese and French ships sailed Gold Coast waters, though neither nation maintained permanent bases in the area.

Such conditions laid the basis for the rise of the Asante kingdom which was to give the most dramatic and formative expression to the political and economic character of the Akan people. A modest beginning brought small numbers of Akan to an area in the northern forest where, led by the Oyoko clan, they founded several centers including the town of Kumasi. It was a region rich in gold and kola nuts and a junction for converging trade routes. For a time, however, the Asante were unable to exploit their advantage, since, about the middle of the seventeenth century, they fell under the control of neighboring Denkyira. In response, the Oyoko consolidated their control around Kumasi, then threw off the Denkyira yoke, and began to develop a major military and commercial power in the Gold Coast region from the sea to the savanna.

The achievements of the Oyoko kings were of the greatest importance to the growth of Asante. Under Obiri Yeboa, who was killed in battle during the 1670s, the supremacy of the Oyoko clan was acknowledged by all in the Kumasi area and the other ruling lineages were taken into the Oyoko line, which established the nuclear states of Asante—Mampon, Kumasi, Bekwai, Juaben, Kokofu, and Nsuta. Osei Tutu solidified this beginning by establishing the spiritual unity of Asante in the sacred symbol of the golden stool; then he chose Kumasi as the nation's capital, and instituted a constitution that acknowledged the supremacy of the *kumasihene*, or king of Kumasi, who would henceforth be known as the *asantehene*, or head of the Asante state. The kings of the member states were integrated into the new political union in various ways—they became commanders of the national army and formed a council of advisers to the asantehene, they were obliged to supply the army with requisitions of troops and were expected to preside at the annual national festival. Nevertheless, in local affairs their authority continued unchallenged.

Thus a fine balance was struck between loyalty to the center and freedom for the parts.

Once his reforms were complete, Osei Tutu began the expansion that claimed Denkyira and extended suzerainty to the coast. Most of the new territories were incorporated into the Asante union, which had reached substantial proportions by the time Osei Tutu fell during a campaign against the Akyem in 1717. His great-nephew and successor, Opoku Ware, followed these accomplishments with further conquests deep into the northern gold-producing regions of Banda and Gyaman, then south to subdue Akyem, Akwapim, and Akwamu, entering Accra in 1744. Further campaigns followed, and with Opoku Ware's death in 1750 Asante was unchallenged among the Gold Coast states.

National cohesion and military organization therefore served commercial appetite, for like other Akan, the Asante were bent on exploiting the gold and slave trade, in the process acquiring firearms to augment their imperial purpose. Few could mount effective opposition; perhaps most successful in this respect were the coastal Fante, who because of their geographic location, stood squarely in the path of Asante expansionism during the eighteenth and nineteenth centuries.

The Fante claim their origin in the savanna whence they migrated in small groups, penetrating the forest and arriving near the coast where they established their capital at Mankessim. By the late fifteenth century the Portuguese knew of their existence as a small city-state a short distance inland from the coast. Toward the end of the seventeenth century, however, there was a rapid expansion along the coast, which was soon filled with a series of independent Fante states stretching from the Pra River to the Ga state in the west.

The Fante expansion was probably related both to population increase and to a desire to act as intermediaries between the European trade and the interior markets. Nevertheless, such commercial ambitions would surely have been stillborn had not the Fante managed to combine their dispersion with a political union, apparently in response to the rising power of Asante. Emulating Asante, the Fante states formed a league with a parliament composed of national representatives headed by the *braffo*, or ruler, of Mankessim who became the head of state. Like the Asante federation, the Fante union brought into being another large state among the Akan, but there was an important difference between the two. The Fante union was essentially pragmatic—a specific counter to the Asante threat—and lacked the sense of brotherhood and the symbols of national unity that brought the Asante into such long-lived cohesion. Fante unity therefore tended to rise and fall with the immediacy of an Asante move to the south, and at its best never approached the effectiveness displayed by the northerners. Nevertheless it did represent a concrete response to Asante expansionism within the balance of power of the Akan states.

Indeed, for a long time there was no Asante challenge to the Fante. Up to 1750 the Asante were preoccupied in the north and then until the beginning of the nineteenth century constitutional upheavals and civil strife at Kumasi kept them engaged at home. Early in the nineteenth century, however, there was a series of Asante invasions of the south, but by this time wars among the Akan were no longer largely intramural affairs, for they had come to involve increasingly the European commercial and military establishments along the coast. Thus the later history of Asante and Fante became part of the history of nineteenth-century European penetration in West Africa.

During the early nineteenth century the Asante administered a series of defeats to the Fante, which eventually brought British intervention in the dispute. Partly these defeats were the result of Fante disunity, but they also represented Asante success in creating a strong state with an effective central administration. Under Opoku Ware, Asante power had extended rapidly into regions that were not acceptable within the definition of the original Asante union; hence those who followed him as asantehene were faced with a critical problem of consolidation and imperial administration, a problem that was brilliantly solved by Osei Kwadwo (1764-1777) and augmented by his successors, Osei Kwame (1777-c. 1801) and Osei Bonsu (c. 1801-1824).

The Asante empire of the late eighteenth century sprawled over some one hundred fifty thousand square miles of forest and savanna, from Sefwi and Gyaman in the west to Dahomey, and from the coast north to Dagomba and Mamprussi. Administering this vast region with a population of three to five million called for radical measures, which were soon introduced by Osei Kwadwo. In the first place, the hereditary chiefs of Kumasi were systematically eliminated and replaced by a bureaucracy which, although it in time became hereditary itself, was subject to royal appointment and control. Thus the imperial financial and political affairs were directed by ministers solely responsible to the throne, while the provinces were ruled by proconsuls similarly under royal surveillance. A national treasury was established in charge of tolls and other taxes, a state trading company and state-controlled mines drew financial power closer to the asantehene, while special political officers represented the king's will at home and abroad.

Beyond this, the asantehene moved to circumscribe the powers of the original nuclear states, which were exempt from imperial reforms and still possessed a large degree of local autonomy as well as power within the Asante army. In part he attempted to limit their kings, or *henes*, by developing new military formations of foreign mercenaries directly controlled by the crown. In part, pressure on the henes developed from the steady accretion of power at the center—the replacement of a king-in-council with ad hoc advisers, the cultural assimilation of subject people, and the imposition of an ideological uniformity throughout the state. Although the chiefs managed to salvage some of their declining powers, the authority of the asantehene grew steadily during the nineteenth century, giving rise to a complex, centralized, bureaucratic state unusual among West African societies.

Suggestions for Further Reading

Of a rich body of material covering this chapter, the latest and most complete coverage is contained in the third edition of *History of West Africa*, J. F. A. Ajayi and M. Crowder, eds. (New York: Longman, 1985). This volume is densely packed with information but also well footnoted for further reference. There are relevant chapters as well in the *Cambridge History of Africa*, Vols. III and IV (Cambridge: University Press, 1977 and 1975 respectively). For discussion of daily life as well as social and economic factors in precolonial Africa see R. W. July, *Precolonial Africa* (New York: Scribners, 1975). There are convenient collections of primary sources, for example Thomas Hodgkin, ed., *Nigerian Perspectives*, 2nd ed. (London: Oxford, 1975); Freda Wolfson, *Pageant of Ghana* (London: Oxford, 1958); and C. Fyfe, ed., *Sierra Leone Inheritance* (London: Oxford, 1964). For secret societies, see Daryll Forde, eds., *African Worlds* (London: Oxford, 1954).

There are numerous specialized studies of particular kingdoms or regions. See, for example, Robin Law, *The Oyo Empire c. 1600-c.1836* (Oxford: Clarendon, 1977); Samuel Johnson, *History of the Yorubas* (Lagos: C.M.S., 1921); J. U. Egharevba, *A Short History of Benin*, 3rd ed. (Ibadan: University Press, 1960); A. F. C. Ryder, *Benin and the Europeans* (New York: Humanities Press, 1969); R.E. Bradbury, "The Kingdom of Benin," in D. Forde and P. M. Kaberry eds., *West African Kingdoms in the Nineteenth Century* (London: Oxford, 1967) which contains a number of other studies of value on Yoruba, Wolof, Dahomey, Asante, and others. Asante is otherwise particularly well served in two works by R. S. Rattray, *Ashanti* (Oxford: Clarendon: 1969) and *Ashanti Law and Constitution* (New York: Negro Universities Press, 1969); and Ivor Wilks, *Asante in the Nineteenth Century* (Cambridge: University Press, 1975).

For Dahomey see I. A. Akinjogbin, *Dahomey and its Neighbors 1708-1818* (Cambridge: University Press, 1967); and M. J. Herskovits, *Dahomey: An Ancient African Kingdom*, 2 Vols. (Evanston: Northwestern University Press, 1967). The coastal regions are represented by C. Newbury, *The Western Slave Coast and its Rulers* (Oxford: Clarendon, 1961); Walter Rodney, *A History of the Upper Guinea Coast, 1545-1800* (Oxford: Clarendon, 1970); K. Y. Daaku, *Trade and Politics on the Gold Coast* (London: Oxford, 1970).

6

The Great Migrations

The Civilization of Zimbabwe

The modern state of Zimbabwe lies athwart a high plateau that forms the watershed between the Zambezi and Limpopo rivers. On the southern scarp of this gently rolling upland is located one of Africa's most notable monuments — the stony ruins known as Great Zimbabwe, whence the recently independent nation derives its name. There are a number of structures of which two predominate. Perched on a granite ridge is the so-called Hill Ruin overlooking the adjacent valley that contains a cluster of additional sites, most particularly the great enclosure, some eight hundred feet in circumference, which archaeologists have named the Elliptical Building.

Stone monuments are not common in areas of Africa untouched by outside influence. Thus, although Great Zimbabwe existed along with some one hundred fifty similar, albeit smaller, ruins spread across the plateau, ethnocentric Europeans who examined the site consistently ascribed its origins to alien activities, sometimes with highly romantic, improbable, associations like Solomon and Sheba. What visitors saw offered no support to such fanciful hypotheses, for both in appearance and probable function the Zimbabwe buildings in no way resembled any known architectural styles in other parts of the world. Basically the structures consist of a series of enclosure walls, either abutting or incorporating granite outcrops as in the Hill Ruin or standing in the free form of the Elliptical Building. In all cases the walls are made of dressed stone blocks, shaped from the local granite and laid in horizontal courses without cement binder. Varying in height and in construction from rough to fine finish, the walls rise to a maximum of about thirty feet, tapering slightly, their thickness at the base usually about half their height. These structures, which conform to no geometric pattern, seem to have been erected solely by eye measurement, a series of gently curving ellipses, apparently designed to encircle and protect village residences. The Elliptical Building, for example, contains a number of smaller complexes whose walls at one time abutted clay and gravel structures now long gone, while the Hill Ruin seems to have been used for residence and possibly religious or ceremonial purposes.

The word *zimbabwe* comes from the local Shona language, probably a corruption of phrases meaning "houses of stone," or "venerated houses." Such a connotation is well supported by recent archaeological study. The lightly wooded plateau and adjacent lowlands were ideally suited to cattle-keeping which seems to have been practiced in the area from the ninth or tenth century A.D., probably by newly-arrived immigrants thought to be the ancestors of today's Shona population. As cattle culture spread and combined with farming, it was also joined by commerce with the Indian Ocean emporiums, chiefly in gold that had been discovered in local reefs on the plateau. Such diverse activities called for fixed residences and social controls practiced through some form of political authority. In time economic specialization and class distinctions developed along with a ruling dynasty that exercised its governance through religious sanctions and built zimbabwe sites from which its kings directed their affairs.

The stonework ruins extend from the Leopard's Kopje region near modern Bulawayo to sites close to the Indian Ocean, the earliest dating from about the eleventh century, probably beginning with hillside terracing to improve agricultural productivity and evolving to include the walled communities of which Great Zimbabwe was the largest and most complex. The enclosures, resembling cattle kraals, could have been for both protection and prestige, the stone walls encircling the palace while lesser folk resided outside in simpler mud and wattle dwellings. At Great Zimbabwe the royal enclosure likely included the residences for the king's wives as well as his ministers, while a conical tower on the site may have marked the location of the palace itself.

Clearly, then, Great Zimbabwe was the capital of a kingdom or cluster of principalities that dominated the central plateau, primarily from the thirteenth to the fifteenth centuries, controlling land and its resources through a royal lineage and monopolizing the armed forces of the state. Though the economy was rooted in cattle, much of the king's wealth derived from the busy trade in gold that passed on its way to the coast, chiefly from the mines of Leopard's Kopje. In return Zimbabwe imported large quantities of textiles, along with beads and dishware, the growing prosperity of the state reflected in its expanding capital. Eventually, however, the state and its city grew too large for the resources of its environment, and by 1450 Great Zimbabwe had collapsed of its own weight. Nevertheless, earlier success bred imitation as new successor states arose, particularly Torwa and Changamire in the southwest, and Mutapa to the north bordering the Zambezi River.

The Mutapa state flourished from 1450 into the seventeenth century, and was well known to the Portuguese who named it Monomotapa, a corruption of *Mwene Mutapa*, or Master Pillager, the praise name given its *mambo*, or king. According to Shona tradition the first monarch was Mutota who left Zimbabwe to establish the northern kingdom, his work extended and solidified by his son and successor, Matope. Mutapa waxed powerful, like Great Zimbabwe its economy based on cattle with much additional wealth accruing from the local gold trade in the Zambezi River valley, its domains greatly expanded by military conquest. It was the commerce that first attracted the attention of the Portuguese on the East African coast. Gradually they effected a penetration of the interior during the latter part of the sixteenth century, establishing trading posts at the Zambezi towns of Sena and Tete, developing a network of inland stations and missions, acquiring large tracts of land and mining concessions, and eventually circumscribing the authority of the Mutapa state. By 1629 they had succeeded in making its monarch a vassal of the Portuguese crown, a situation that endured until the Changamire kingdom emerged and drove the Portuguese off the plateau at the end of the seventeenth century.

Changamire, originally a subject of the Mutapa king, conquered and occupied Torwa about 1685, creating the state in its place which came to bear his name. Having subsequently disposed of the Portuguese, it was the Changamire kingdom, led by its Rozvi dynasty, that dominated the plateau during the eighteenth century, reducing Mutapa to a minor principality and taking control of the international gold trade. Mining techniques were simple, either washing of riverside alluvial deposits or open pit extraction that was exploited only down to the level of the water table since pumps were not used. By the nineteenth century the upper level deposits had been removed and gold production fell, but by this time Changamire was also in decline. During the 1830s it fell victim to both the Ngoni and Ndebele when these invaders ravaged the Shona countryside during their northward flight from the Bantu upheavals in South Africa.

The Shona monarchs were revered as gods and lived on a most lavish scale with their wives, concubines, and officials. Audiences were held in public but the king remained aloof, removed by elaborate ritual from suppliants who came creeping and clapping their hands to show proper homage. When the king died his queens and some of his ministers were dispatched to keep him company in the spirit world, while all the fires in the land were extinguished, for fire was associated with the royal authority and new fires could be kindled only with the flame of the new king. Yet this seemingly omnipotent personality was also the creature of powerful customary limitations. As a god, the king had to be of flawless aspect; hence if he became seriously ill or deformed he was expected to commit suicide. The royal compound, situated behind a high fence, tended to isolate the monarch and make him dependent upon his deputies, the legion of officials, courtiers, and queens into whose hands much actual power devolved. The royal office was therefore powerful but its power lay as much in its symbolic strength as in the authority wielded by the royal incumbent.

Beyond the court, life was simple. Peasant farmers, living in mud huts behind stockades, cultivated their fields and tended their cattle in a timeless round. Local production of cloth and ornamentation must have been minimal in view of the constant demand for the textiles and ceramics of the East, but the wealth of Mutapa and her sister kingdoms was such that these things could be afforded at least by the wealthier classes. The Portuguese were impressed both by the trading and fighting ability of the people, and indeed their weapons were varied and well made. There being no written language, historical tradition was entrusted to a class of mediums whose accuracy was exceptional. To Portuguese ears the language had much appeal, particularly in comparison with what they regarded as the guttural harshness of Arabic. "[They] pronounce their words with the end of the tongue and the lips, that they speake many words in a whistling accent, wherein they place great elegance. . . . Their stile of speaking is by Metaphors: and Similitudes very proper, and fitted to their purpose."

The Bantu Speakers

The civilization that produced Great Zimbabwe and the states of Changamire and Mutapa was related to a massive migration that originated in western Africa long before the time of Christ, a movement of peoples that continued into the nineteenth century of the Christian era with profound effects on the ecology and history of subequatorial Africa. The start of this great dispersion moreover was roughly concurrent with the beginnings of agriculture in Africa, and was accompanied in most of its later passage by the knowledge and utilization of iron. It was also the consequence of a major change in the pattern of Africa's weather.

The environment of the Sahara began to change from a region of lakes, streams, and swamps about eight thousand years ago. As desiccation spread, it drove Saharan dwellers to more favorable climes, some moving east to help establish the civilization that ensued in the Nile valley, some no doubt moving northward, and still others drifting south to the moister latitudes of west and central Africa. There, in the savanna and on the forest edge south of the Sahara, they began to add farming to their fishing and hunting activities, converting from the gathering of wild plants to their active cultivation. In the savanna it was local sorghums and millets that were domesticated, whereas along the forest edge, root crops, yams in particular, predominated. It is possible that these migrants came with domestic animals as well, for there is evidence of herding in parts of the Sahara about 6000 B.C.

The forest dwellers also harvested the palm tree, their penetration of the forest along with their agriculture enhanced by the practice, lately adopted,

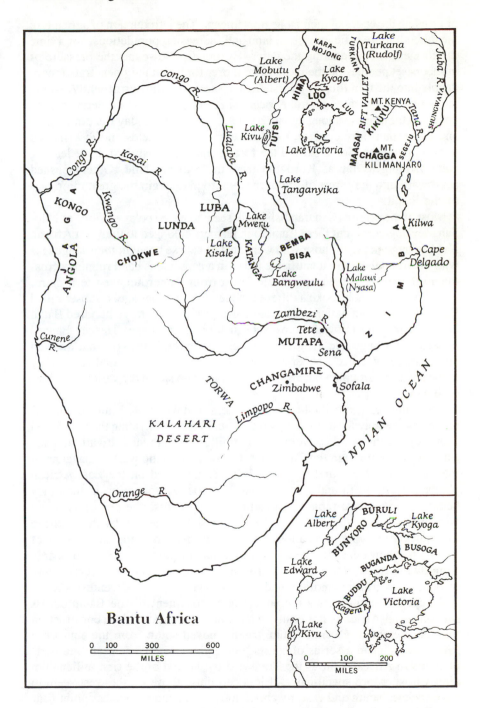

Bantu Africa

0 100   300   600
MILES

of grinding the edges of their stone implements. The introduction of agriculture meant both more efficient use of land and increasing populations, for a time the former accommodating the latter. Eventually, however, the pressure of numbers set peoples on the move once more. Bit by bit they penetrated more deeply into the rain forest of West Africa, there to settle permanently. Along the northern edge of the central African rain forest, however, a different pattern developed. Perhaps as long ago as 2000 B.C., in what is today eastern Nigeria and Cameroun, farmers struck out in search of new fields and they moved in two directions. Some skirted the forest, traveling eastward, their leading edge arriving as far as Kordofan near the Sudanic Nile. Others pushed southward into the forest of southern Cameroun to begin the great migration of the Bantu.

Most of the original Saharan fisherfolk seem to have spoke versions of Nilo-Saharan languages, but these Cameroun farmers belonged to the West African Niger-Congo family. Those who went east of course brought their languages with them and these are identifiable today in a continuous band running across the northern side of the tropical rain forest from Cameroun to eastern Zaire. The southern branch spoke a different Niger-Congo language, a subset called Benue-Congo from which descended the approximately three hundred Bantu languages spread so broadly across subequatorial Africa today. Hence "Bantu" is basically a linguistic identification describing the languages that evolved among these migrants. The term "Bantu," however, is often applied not only to the language grouping but also to the peoples who spoke the various versions of Bantu.

These pre- or proto-Bantu speakers seem to have moved into the forest, remaining possibly for as long as two thousand years, cultivating their preferred root crops, although they were not unfamiliar with cereal cultivation. They filtered slowly through the Cameroun-Gabon area to the western savanna of the Zaire watershed, and by about 300 B.C. appeared on the East African plains as well, north and west of Lake Victoria. At this point in time they began to move more rapidly, spreading swiftly across the open plains and woodland south of the equatorial forest, possibly egged on by the pressure of a quickly growing population. Versatile farmers speaking early forms of Bantu, they now began to make use of iron, having gained that skill, probably from two sources—the state of Meroe and the Jos plateau of Nigeria where in both cases iron technology had been known for several centuries.

Except in general terms the subsequent movement of the Bantu across subequatorial Africa is not easily determined, but a possible reconstruction may be attempted. Overall Bantu groups moved south from the equatorial forest, possibly in a series of spurts, occupying eastern, central, and parts of southern Africa as far as the Transvaal by the end of the first millennium after Christ. More specifically, if less certainly, those on the west seem to have traveled south and east, by about 400 A.D. gaining a nuclear point near Lake Kisale in the upper Zaire basin whence they spread in many directions, north and east as well as south. Some authorities feel the eastern Bantu followed two routes, one south into central Africa toward the Zambezi and the other moving rapidly to the Tanzanian coast to spread both north and south. During the eleventh century there was another quick expansion, seemingly by the eastern Bantu who colonized the Zimbabwean plateau to establish their "stone house" culture with its large-scale kingdoms and gold mining. By the fifteenth century the Bantu had extinguished or absorbed resident Stone Age bushmanoid hunters in all areas save the far southwest where the Kalahari and Namib deserts held up their advance. When the Dutch colonists moved out of their Cape Town settlement in the seventeenth and eighteenth centuries, they found Bantu-speaking groups along the Orange River and in the Natal corridor as far as the southeast corner of the continent.

By and large the movement appears to have been peaceful, small bodies of farmers breaking away in search of new land and pasture. There is evidence, however, of occasional strife among the Bantu themselves, some exceedingly bitter and destructive. There are, for example, the Zimbabwe kingdoms, resulting from territorial and economic competition, as well as the lust for power in leadership. There is, moreover, the devastating march of the Zimba and a roughly contemporaneous explosion in Kongo and Angola by the people whom Portuguese observers called Jaga. Finally there are the convulsive population movements in southern Africa in the early nineteenth century associated with the military conquests of the Zulu monarch, Shaka. Authorities still dispute the causes of these aberrations, but a recurring argument centers on the paucity of land in relation to growing numbers of people.

Bantu Cultures

Not the least interesting aspect of the Bantu expansion is the manner in which it has been identified and described. Preliterate, the Bantu speakers left no written records, possessed oral traditions often difficult to interpret, and were observed by very few, intermittent, outside witnesses. Yet the broad outlines of the Bantu movement are accepted today, largely without dispute. That we know as much as we do about the history of the Bantu peoples is a tribute to the work not of historians but of archaeologists and, particularly, of linguists.

The key to the reconstruction of Bantu history is a linguistic technique called *glottochronology*, simply stated, the history of language or of language change. It is well understood that languages evolve over time, altering in form and content and moving apart as they descend from a common ancestor. Students of African languages have long known that there was a great similarity within the family of Bantu languages, and that they began to split into their many variants very recently, that is, about two thousand years ago. Linguists also determined that the Bantu languages had definite kinship with the Niger-Congo subdivision called Benue-Congo and spoken today in the eastern Nigeria-

Cameroun area. It was therefore possible to conclude that the ancestors of present-day Bantu originated in eastern Nigeria and Cameroun whence they began their massive migration about the time of Christ.

In recent years archaeologists have excavated numerous sites in Bantu Africa that determine the establishment of an iron-working culture in subequatorial Africa from about the third century A.D., along with pottery remains that bespeak a common culture. Since the arrival of iron-working and characteristic pottery appeared coincident with the spread of Bantu languages, historians have reasoned that the iron-users were in fact Bantu speakers while the carbon dating of sites gave indication of the direction and timing of the Bantu movements. Scholars have also checked archaeological and linguistic evidence against oral traditions, at least for the more recent centuries, and, where possible, the testimony of outsiders has also been utilized. For example, the *Periplus of the Erythrean Sea*, dated in the late first century A.D., makes no mention of black people on the East African coast, whereas the fourth century edition of Claudius Ptolemy's *Geography* speaks of "Ethiopians" living on what is today the Tanzanian coast. It is a slender piece of evidence but it tends to support the linguistic and archaeological arguments. In the same way the hypothetical arrival of Bantu groups in southern Africa receives corroboration from eyewitness accounts of European mariners who visited the southeastern African coast in the sixteenth and later centuries.

A society of Bantu-speaking, iron-using farmers suggests a homogeneous culture, but in time important differences appeared in Bantu Africa, brought about largely by the imperatives of environment. Bantu farmers in the equatorial rain forest lived in compact villages, for group effort was needed in clearing fields or conducting cooperative hunting and fishing enterprises. On the savanna isolated homesteads were more common; in open country the clearing of land was less of a problem. Across the high plains of eastern Africa, a cattle economy predominated, causing daily and seasonal movement and a scattered population, although the need for water and an adequate range were magnets that brought cattle-raising people together in temporary, seasonal communities. Along the East African coast a characteristic Swahili civilization emerged that combined Bantu and Arab strains, in population, in culture, and in language. In time the southern Bantu-speakers came to adopt some of the linguistic traits of the resident Khoisan peoples they encountered. In the forest, Pygmoid hunters lost their language in favor of Bantu speech even as they instructed immigrant farmers in the refinements of the hunt.

There were regional differences of diet as well, also shaped by circumstance. In the forest and woodlands, the yam and palm continued to predominate, eventually to be joined by Asian imports such as the taro and banana. The savanna millets and sorghum in time made room for maize once New World crops became available, while manioc from the Americas ultimately gained a secure place alongside the yam.

Initially there must have been little occupational differentiation within communities as all performed the various chores of the farming household. In an early Iron Age, however, smithing would have been an exception, and in many Bantu societies the blacksmiths stood apart, their special craft making them honored members of the communities. Potters may also have comprised a separate class, perhaps hunters as well, especially those whose skill later contributed to the international trade in ivory. Villages located near salt pans would also have developed specialties in the refining and exchange of that precious commodity, always in short supply throughout large areas of Africa.

An undifferentiated economy was reflected in political and social institutions. Despite a large increase in numbers over earlier hunting peoples, the Bantu population remained low; even as late as the nineteenth century, for example, the Zaire watershed contained only an estimated 10 to 15 persons per square mile. The basic political unit was the village cluster of individual family homesteads presided over by a chief and council of household heads. Small-scale, simple political structures were usually sufficient to meet the needs of these communities, although a lack of political machinery did not necessarily mean an absence of social distinction. Households had their hierarchy, consisting of clan and lineage relations, but also often involving outsiders such as more distant kin, clients, pawns, and even slaves. It was therefore not a democratic society. The important citizen was one who owned property and commanded people, controlling the distribution of women, and determining the utilization of land.

The spread of the Bantu peoples has been described in two stages. During the eleventh century A.D. the initial expansion appears to have been replaced by a second wave, the later Iron Age, initiated principally by the eastern Bantu. It was this movement that was responsible for the Zimbabwean culture, but its influence went well beyond geographical movements. A new style of pottery appeared coincident with greater sophistication in economic activity and in statecraft. A more refined division of labor reflected growing specialization in regional economies and individual activity. The basic economy remained agricultural and pastoral, but there were important adjuncts. In the lakes region of the upper Katanga, for example, a fishing industry arose encouraging trade with copper miners from the lower Katanga and with the guardians of the salt pans in southern Tanzania and other regions. Ingombe Ilede on the Zambezi River became an emporium for trade in copper and ivory, much of it destined for the East African coastal markets along with gold mined in the Mutapa kingdom, all in payment for imports of textiles and the ever popular glass beads.

Iron, too, figured in the growing trade complex and served, along with copper, as currency, both metals shaped into characteristic crosses which the Portuguese said resembled the vanes of windmills. Such multifarious activity strained the simple structure of village organization and led to a more clearly defined ruling class marked first by shrines and priests and then by administrators, judges, and finally, monarchs. Large-scale kingdoms like Mutapa were rare, but occasionally an energetic clan head, wealthy householder, or trader could gather retainers and set out on a career of armed conquest to fashion a large state capable of organizing and profiting from such complex activities as the mining, transport, and marketing of gold. In such a case force and clan or other loyalties were the cement that bound the state together, but these characteristics were usually more personal than institutional, thereby rendering such large-scale enterprises intrinsically unstable. Offsetting these centrifugal factors, however, was the importance of religious doctrine and practice among the Bantu.

Both state and society were deeply involved. The firm belief in a supernatural world, in the efficacy of sorcery and magic, in the need for ritual to propitiate the spirits, and in the existence of a metaphysical continuum between the living and the ancestors all contributed important sanctions to reinforce basic social values. Hence the institution of divine kingship drew authority from belief in the royal power over fertility, while the prominence given to the ancestor helped strengthen the essential unity of the group in a perilous world.

Cushitic and Nilotic Movements

It should be noted that in East Africa the Bantu occupied the moister regions, avoiding a north-south band beginning at the southwestern foothills of Ethiopia, running through the Kenya highlands and down the Rift Valley into Tanzania. This was no accident. Although they possessed cattle, the Bantu were farmers, not herders, and they sought out high rainfall areas like the Rwanda highlands or the western shores of Lake Victoria. There may have been another reason, however. The drier Rift had already been occupied by others, Cushitic speakers from the Ethiopian highlands who practiced a pastoral, and possibly a farming economy. Later these dry ranges were the target of other southward moving pastoralists, those peoples who spoke related Nilotic and Central Sudanic languages of the Nilo-Saharan family.

The presence of the so-called Southern Cushites may go back two thousand years before Christ; certainly they were in East Africa in the first pre-Christian millennium. A Stone Age people, they could also have cultivated cereals to supplement their animal diet. Widely dispersed, they were apparently few in number, and their ignorance of an iron technology might have assisted the various Nilotic intruders who encumbered the ranges of the Cushites, and eventually squeezed them into a few small surviving pockets.

As with the Bantu, the testimony for Cushitic and Nilotic movements is provided by linguists and archaeologists, their vastly different forms of information yielding rather different conclusions as to the arrival of peoples in East Africa. The linguistic evidence indicates that the ancestral Nilotes had mastered iron technology before they embarked on their migrations and split into their numerous components. Linguists tend to hypothesize an early Nilotic arrival in East Africa, perhaps even contemporaneous with the

Benin bronze: warrior and attendant

Bambara antelope headdress

Bakongo ancestral figure

Asante gold weight

Ife bronzes

St. Mary of Sion—Axum

AP/Wide World Photos

Conical tower, Great Zimbabwe

N. "Bud" Lazarus

Urban skyline, Western Sudan

appearance of the Bantu. Archaeologists, however, can find no material proof
for this dating and prefer to place the Nilotic advent at a much later time,
after 1000 A.D. with the onset of the later Iron Age. In either event the Nilotes
came southward in a series of incursions, though much more slowly and far
less widely dispersed than the Bantu. In the west the movement consisted
of probable Central Sudanic speakers, who settled in southwestern Uganda
and the Rwanda highlands, the likely ancestors of today's Hima and Tutsi.
Further east the Nilotes crossed the Kenya highlands into Uganda and the
Rift Valley, arriving in intervals like successive waves of an encroaching tide.
The advance took place over several centuries, in some cases with related
peoples strung out over vast distances, in others, bunched closely together.
Thus, for example, the Kalenjin family containing such peoples as Nandi,
Kipsigis, and Pokot all came to rest in the Kenya hills east of Lake Victoria,
whereas the Bari, Turkana, and Maasai, linguistically akin, ran from the
southern Sudan through the deserts of northern Kenya to the Rift Valley of
central Tanzania. Still another section of the Nilotes moved only a short distance
into the upper Nile valley where they remain today in the form of the Dinka,
Nuer, and Shilluk of southern Sudan. Their related Luo speakers, by contrast,
engaged in a complex series of movements north and south that ultimately
brought the main body of Luo to the northern shores of Lake Victoria where
they came to play an important and continuing role in the political and cultural
life of the region.

The Maasai appear to have been the last of the migrants, reaching the
Tanzanian Rift by the early nineteenth century as the people of East Africa
came to approximate their present geographic placement. Bushmanoid remnants
lingered in isolated points as did scattered Cushitic communities like the Iraqw
and Gorowa of Tanzania. The rest was Bantu country pierced by the great
Nilotic wedge, but this configuration did not mean cultural exclusiveness.

The Cushitic speakers had largely disappeared, but Cushitic influences were
apparent everywhere throughout the highlands, manifest, for example, in the
strong Cushitic elements in the vocabularies of some Bantu languages, or in
the adoption of Cushite food taboos and circumcision rites by certain Nilotes.
For their part, there were Cushites who abandoned their agricultural economies
for the hunting way of life of the bushmanoids, while others took over
characteristically Nilotic customs such as systems of age grades. Indeed, what
slowly emerged in the East African highlands was a complex interpenetration
of Bantu, Nilote, Cushite, and Bushmanoid genetic strains along with a similar
fusion of cultural and linguistic influences leading to the hybridization of
populations so apparent today.

Few peoples remained untouched. Nilotic languages were superseded in
some areas by Bantu, while many Bantu societies absorbed the Nilote love
of cattle, and possibly the technique of milking as well. Within a confined
area of central Tanzania, Cushitic, Bantu, Nilotic, and Khoisan languages
all exist today alongside one another in a complex balance reflecting much

earlier expansion, differentiation, and fusion. The highlands of Kenya were occupied by Kikuyu and Meru, who came in part because of Cushitic population pressures, and who since have caused numbers of pastoral Maasai to abandon their cattle culture for a sedentary farming life. In the Lake Victoria region Nilotic Luo of Bunyoro embraced a Bantu tongue; by contrast, Luo settlers at Kavirondo Gulf abandoned their traditional pastoralism for the farming culture of the Bantu but retained their Nilotic language.

Some Bantu and Nilotic Communities

Central African Bantu

As they entered the forest and savanna of the Zaire watershed, the early Bantu were trailblazers in more than one sense. New lands made strange and difficult demands on their resources. Resident hunting societies contested their presence. Land had to be cleared, old crops adapted to new conditions, new crops domesticated, new methods of cultivation and new crafts invented, new ways devised for living among themselves. By and large they succeeded and multiplied, preparing the ground for later, more sophisticated societies, like those that produced Great Zimbabwe. These developments have sometimes tempted observers to talk of kingdoms, of states, even of "empires," but for the Bantu of the early Iron Age such grandiose concepts are surely premature.

A more pertinent theme would be the endless struggle for mere survival in the face of a hostile environment. Soil fertility varied greatly from place to place, but the determining factor was the African climate, ever capricious, as it is today, periodically choking harvests in dusty drought, in flood converting fields into swampland, through plague and famine, blotting out herds and herders with an even hand, forcing the colonists to turn against each other in their want, then driving them to move on in hope of better pasture, richer land, sweeter water beyond the next hill.

There were no empires among this scattered population, but there were attempts at unity and cooperation; these were the imperatives of survival. Populations congregated where food could be produced—a fertile valley, a lake shore, a well watered pasture. People came together in mutual protection—a woodland village defending fields hacked out from the surrounding forest, a savanna community holding a strategic high point against interlopers. In time specialties developed that called for cooperation and protection. There were salt pans and iron-rich soils, seams of copper, streams and lakes where the fishing was good, regions where elephants and their ivory abounded. Here were desirable sites well worth fighting for.

The need for collaboration, therefore, was early recognized but its achievement was slow. The family was a natural unit, then the village. Families or villages, even ambitious, vigorous, or talented individuals, reached out to fashion larger unities designed to protect or gain efficiency, or merely to create power, to provide greater leisure, more luxurious living for their inventor. Where these centripetal forces succeeded, a form of tyranny generally ensued, the early Bantu communities in no sense egalitarian. A family head, a village chief, a clan leader, the community elders tended to exploit lesser folk, engrossing authority and wealth for their own use. The weaker were the victims—women, young men in need of land and wives, strangers, debtors, distant relatives, and slaves conquered in battle. What made these tyrannies bearable was the possibility of new lands. The disaffected could always move on, and they did. The unknown was dangerous but also hopeful.

Thus the Bantu spread. In time the centripetal forces became more pronounced as populations waxed and the growing complexity of societies demanded more centralization and more sophisticated social organization. By that time, however, a thousand years had passed, and the Bantu had progressed to a new level that was indeed marked by greater evidence of states, kingdoms, even "empires." By that time, moreover, new forces had come to Bantu Africa, requiring even greater attention to political organization and unity. These were the forces of the wider world, arriving forever to shatter the isolation of Bantu Africa.

Bunyoro and Buganda

In the area around the Great Lakes the development of large-scale political units came about by a process involving Nilotes as well as Bantu. Bantu farmers in the region were apparently organized in loosely connected clans or tiny chieftaincies, their relative affluence and rising population resting on the easily raised plantain and banana. Into the area came cattle pastoralists, the Hima, who settled in Uganda to the north and west of Lake Victoria, and the Tutsi who came to rest farther south near Lake Kivu. During the fifteenth century there arose a ruling clan or dynasty called Chwezi, once thought to be the creation of these herding peoples but now regarded as serving equally both pastoral and farming communities. The Chwezi overrule, though extensive, was short-lived and by the end of the fifteenth century was supplanted by an invasion of Nilotic Luo who took over much or most of the Chwezi territory while establishing their own Bito dynasty of the newly formed kingdom of Bunyoro. The Hima moved southward, perhaps voluntarily, perhaps pressed by the Luo, establishing a new ruling clan, the Hinda, that was responsible for a number of kingdoms and principalities stretching from the region of the Nkore people on the western side of Lake Victoria as far as Burundi at the northern tip of Lake Tanganyika. Like the Chwezi these were symbiotic societies, the royal court coordinating for mutual profit the complementary productivity of the farmers and the herders.

For their part, the Luo eventually established a ring of tributary states around Bunyoro—Buddu, Buganda, Buruli, the Busoga principalities, and others—which were ruled in most cases by subdynasties of the Bito clan more or less subject to Bunyoro control. Hence, with the arrival of the Hima and Luo, the Bantu area of the Great Lakes was converted into a series of kingdoms in which loyalty to the crown rather than to kinship ties was the basis for new and more centralized systems of political enterprise.

In Bunyoro this new loyalty was hard earned. The basic orientation of the people continued toward community and clan; furthermore, poor communications and a rudimentary military technology invited separatism under ambitious local leaders. Nevertheless, numerous devices were introduced which strengthened the idea and the fact of a central authority. First of all, the institution of the monarchy was related as closely as possible to the people as a whole—by divorcing the king from his connection with the Bito clan, by stressing the divinity of the ruler and identifying him with the prosperity of the nation, by making him the source of a vast political patronage surrounding the palace, and by concentrating a large share of the national economy in the form of an exchange of gifts between the king and his subjects. At the same time the chiefs were subordinated to the crown through nonhereditary appointment, through royal sanction of chiefly investiture, and through elaborate ceremony. Finally, the king's authority was strengthened by the system of royal tours whereby the court changed headquarters constantly, requiring that the local population maintain the royal entourage in royal fashion, and enabling the king to gain a firsthand view of affairs throughout his realm.

This growing sense of national unity evolved even more successfully in Buganda despite her modest origins. While Bunyoro held the stage during the sixteenth and early seventeenth centuries, Buganda quietly gathered strength, its very smallness an asset. The Bantu, Hima, and Luo strains were merged into a homogeneous population securely fixed in a structure of Baganda clans which were in turn closely linked to the monarchy. Hereditary chieftaincies within these clans therefore added to national unity, but even more significant was the process, instituted in the seventeenth century by the *kabaka*, or king, Kateregga, who installed war leaders as provincial chiefs over conquered territories. Thus new peoples were thoroughly incorporated into Baganda society, ruled directly under a highly autocratic royal power. In the seventeenth and eighteenth centuries a series of able Baganda rulers pursued an aggressive expansionism that made Buganda master of the northwestern shoreline and hinterland of Victoria from the Nile to the Kagera River.

In the nineteenth century the Baganda people continued to expand northwestward at the expense of a declining Bunyoro, and as her domains increased her imperial administration took on additional refinements. For example, new territory, such as the southern province of Buddu, was governed by royal administrators, bureaucratic appointees who held office at the kabaka's pleasure and did not become hereditary. Moreover, during the eighteenth century the kings of Buganda began to encourage large-scale external trade which remained a royal monopoly designed to augment the king's wealth and power. Royal wealth bought increasing loyalty to the crown and made possible the military strength to extend and to protect commercial enterprise. In Buganda the idea of centralization and economic growth had become firmly fixed by the middle of the nineteenth century.

The Kikuyu

If the trend toward centralization and territorial acquisition was the hallmark of some peoples, it was by no means the choice of the majority who remained members of small village societies regulated by lineage or age groupings. Nevertheless, decentralization did not necessarily mean a lack of political and social cohesion, a fact that the Kikuyu nation amply illustrated. The Kikuyu Bantu eventually formed a large and active agricultural community situated in the highlands south and west of Mount Kenya, having finally settled there after migrating from the plains to the east. Beginning with small groups, possibly of hunters and herders, they colonized the hill country, cleared the forest, and grew rapidly as successful farmers. Despite the increase in their population, which today numbers in the millions, the Kikuyu endured no local chiefs nor centralized state, and generally eschewed village life in favor of individual homesteads scattered about the countryside. Yet Kikuyu society was far from disorganized and a highly articulated coherence was in fact characteristic of the Kikuyu nation.

This essential unity was maintained through the family, the sub-clan, or *mbari*, and the age group, called *mariika*. Consanguinity and common ancestors were bonds that were strongly felt and led to cooperation among individuals who might otherwise have been unresponsive to authority. Within the family the father was the head, and the law of the homestead lay in his hands. Beyond this an elaborate system of relationships was maintained among family and clan members which defined and governed their actions as individuals and established mutual obligations and rights. Indeed, among the Kikuyu the idea of individual initiative was discouraged as self-seeking, whereas the concepts of corporate effort and group responsibility were regarded as the cardinal virtues.

Each family had its own council with the father as the head and it was he who represented the family in the government. If there was a village council, it consisted of the heads of the several families in the village. Similarly, there were regional councils, but more important were the *riika* councils representing successive age grades from the younger, warrior groups to the *kiama* or council of elders. There were also the *muthamaki*, leading citizens who served as council leaders and spokesmen, but their authority was limited. These positions were elective and the group had the power to dismiss or suspend those officeholders who had transcended the established rules of conduct. Hence a system of government developed which was egalitarian within the range of accepted practice, relying heavily on group discussion and the power of public opinion to bring about efficient but responsible government.

The Kikuyu, therefore, despite their aversion to centralized, structured government, conducted their affairs through two well understood institutions. There was the mbari that united clan members and the age grade that provided layers of responsible generations who dealt successively with issues from matters of defense (the obligation of the young warrior riikas), to questions of law (the province of the elders). Thus the individual was guided through life's several stages with security, a security that became the endowment of the Kikuyu community at large.

Turkana Pastoralists

In East Africa, social and political organization by extended family, the so-called stateless society, was especially characteristic of the Nilote pastoralist. This was a natural outgrowth of the seasonal migrations demanded of herders in search of adequate water and forage. As cattle keepers, the pastoralists tended to inhabit the more arid ranges; hence, their normally nomadic existence militated against the type of formal state structure found more readily in sedentary farming societies. Even blood ties were attenuated among people whose survival rested with the ability of each individual to sustain his herds. Cooperation was likely to be a temporary expedient, fashioned to meet the vagaries of each season's weather, permitting no narrow containment within rigid institutions, and avoiding excessive deference to formalized kinship relations.

Such a splendidly unfettered existence reached near-classic proportions among the Turkana, a branch of the Nilotes, who came to occupy the parched steppe lands lying west of Lake Turkana. In this difficult country where an annual rainfall of over fifteen inches is an event to be remembered, the Turkana long tended their herds of cattle, goats, sheep, and camels, their daily lives organized around the homestead, their society and economy rooted to the ownership and maintenance of livestock. Each family—a man, his wives, and their children—was an independent unit, its property, except for minimal personal belongings, residing in its herds, its livelihood drawn almost exclusively from the products of its livestock.

The Turkana homestead was a roughly fashioned, thorn-fenced kraal containing huts and cattle pens, designed solely for temporary occupancy, no single site surviving more than a few months. Homesteads were usually found in neighborhood clusters of three or four, such assemblages loosely congregating about some recognizable point, usually a water source near a serviceable range. Families came and went at will; the choice of any particular neighborhood was individual and unrelated to family ties. Moreover, the makeup of one season's settlements was not likely to be repeated in the next.

Among the Turkana law and polity had their own parochial definition, for, strictly speaking, there was no body of law, and no state existed to enforce its strictures. Legal sanction was only what custom permitted, and enforcement lay in public approbation or the strength of each individual hand. Age grades survived primarily as a means for organizing war parties. The essential political and social unit was the family, its sovereign the head of the household; authority springing from his stewardship, if not ownership, of the family livestock. Not only was he the source of support for the women of the household; his sons, too, were largely dependent upon his goodwill. Unmarried sons could not obtain wives without the payment of a heavy bridewealth in stock supplied by or through their father, while married sons were unable to establish their own households until they had developed their personal herds of a size sufficient to ensure economic viability.

Livestock, then, was the essential commodity of Turkana life. It provided clothing and food, weapons and utensils. It governed daily routine and kinship relations, its ownership a measure of family prosperity and individual security. More than that, livestock held the Turkana together as an organized society. Theoretically, it might have been possible for each household to sustain itself through its own herds, but practical experience demanded cooperation for survival, and among the Turkana, as with most pastoral people, cooperation was effected through a widespread system of livestock exchange.

By custom, stock changed hands through loans freely begged and granted, sometimes for a bridewealth, sometimes only for the sake of the loan itself. In this way each family herd came to be widely dispersed among many friends and relatives living often in far-removed corners of the Turkana country, and the benefits redounded both to the individual and to society as a whole. Through the broad dispersal of his cattle, each man reduced the dangers of catastrophe— the destruction of his herds through disease, an enemy raid, or drought. By freely giving his stock he widened the number of those friends, relatives, or mere acquaintances on whose assistance he could rely in future moments of need. More generally, such a system of exchange acted as a form of social insurance in the redistribution of wealth especially to the places where it was most needed at given moments. Finally, the borrowing and lending of cattle created bonds of mutual obligation and friendship that gave shape and purpose to Turkana society while ensuring individual self-respect and psychic satisfaction. Little wonder that the pastoralist has been moved to say, "If you don't have cattle, you won't be a person."

Suggestions for Further Reading

The standard work on Great Zimbabwe is P. S. Garlake, *Great Zimbabwe* (London: Thames & Hudson, 1973), but a detailed history of the Shona people is available in David N. Beach, *The Shona and Zimbabwe, 900-1850* (London: Heinemann, 1980).

A great deal has been written in recent years on the Bantu expansion based upon linguistic, archaeological, oral, and other sources. Despite much research and analysis, Bantu history remains speculative except in broad outline. For further information, begin with the good overall introductory summary by David Birmingham in *History of Central Africa*, Vol. I, Birmingham and Phyllis M. Martin, eds., (London: Longman, 1983), which also provides several regional analyses in much greater detail. See also Roland Oliver, "The Problem of the Bantu Expansion," *Journal of African History*, Vol. VII, No. 3, 1966, as well as his more recent assessments in both volume II (1977) and III (1978) of the *Cambridge History of Africa* (Cambridge: University Press). Many additional references are available in the excellent bibliographical notes of the *Cambridge History of Africa*, not only lists but bibliographical essays as well. See also Jan Vansina's "Western Bantu Expansion," *Journal of African History*, Vol. 25, No. 2, 1984. For the linguistic evidence, refer to J. Greenberg, *The Languages of Africa* (Bloomington: Indiana University Press, 1966) and his "Linguistic Evidence Regarding Bantu Origins," *Journal of African History*, Vol. XIII, No. 2, 1972, along with J. Hiernaux, "Bantu Expansion. . .," *ibid.*, Vol. IX, No. 4, 1968.

The quality of Bantu culture may be gleaned from numerous sources. The works by Oliver, and Birmingham and Martin, cited above, are a good starting point, but see also G. P. Murdock, *Africa: Its Peoples and Their Culture History* (New York: McGraw-Hill, 1959), J. Vansina, *Kingdoms of the Savanna* (Madison: Wisconsin University Press, 1966), J. C. Miller, *Kings and Kinsmen: Early Mbundu States in Angola* (London: Oxford University Press, 1976), Garlake on Zimbabwe cited above, L. S. B. Leakey, *The Southern Kikuyu before 1900*, 3v. (London: Academic Press, 1977-78), and R. Gray and David Birmingham, eds., *Pre-Colonial African Trade* (London: Oxford University Press, 1970), among others.

For Nilotes and Cushites one may turn to Christopher Ehret's linguistic analysis contained in *Southern Nilotic History* (Evanston: Northwestern University Press, 1971). See also the relevant chapters in B. A. Ogot and J. A. Kieran, eds., *Zamani* (Nairobi: East African Publishing House and Longmans, 1968), and Oliver's discussion in volumes II and III of the *Cambridge History of Africa*, cited above. Oliver's "The Nilotic Contribution to Bantu Africa," *Journal of African History*, Vol. 23, No. 4, 1982 should also be consulted along with his chapter in the *Oxford History of East Africa*, Vol. I, R. Oliver and Gervaise Matthew, eds., (London: Oxford University Press, 1963). To these may be added B. A. Ogot, *History of the Southern Luo* (Nairobi: East African Publishing House, 1967).

Further information on Bunyoro may be had from J. H. M. Beatty, *Bunyoro: An African Kingdom* (New York: Holt, Rinehart & Winston, 1960) and his "Bunyoro: An African Feudality," *Journal of African History*, Vol. V, No. 1, 1964. The basic work on Buganda is S. Kiwanuka, *A History of the Buganda to 1900* (London: Longman, 1971). For the Kikuyu see Godfrey Muriuki, *A History of the Kikuyu, 1500-1900* (Nairobi: Oxford University Press, 1974). For the Turkana, there is G.H. Gulliver, *The Family Herds* (London: Routledge and Kegan Paul, 1955) as well as John Lamphear, "The People of the Gray Bull," *Journal of African History*, Vol. 29, No 1, 1988.

A general survey dealing with economic and social factors in precolonial Africa is R. W. July, *Precolonial Africa: An Economic and Social History* (New York: Scribners, 1975).

7

The Coming of Europe

The Roots of European Expansion

As the fifteenth century dawned, few Europeans could foresee a future in which Western ideas and institutions would sweep across the seas and Europe would take possession of large areas on all the world's continents. Within Europe herself plague, famine, and warfare had dominated the preceding hundred years, filling minds with confusion and hearts with despair. The great flowering of Italy's Renaissance was only just beginning; what was more immediately apparent was the enfeebled, corrupt leadership within the Church as two rival popes presided in Avignon and Rome. Beyond Europe, moreover, the prospect offered little encouragement for it had become increasingly clear that the Crusades were failing in their attempt to wrest the Holy Land from the grasp of Islam. By the end of the thirteenth century, Palestine had been retaken by Mamluk armies, thus permanently ending Christian control of Jerusalem. In the decades that followed, Ottoman Turks had overrun Asia Minor and driven into the Balkan peninsula, a move that would lead to the capture of Constantinople and the fall of Christian Byzantium in the middle of the fifteenth century and open the way to eventual Ottoman domination of eastern Europe.

Nevertheless the foundations were already taking shape for Europe's subsequent global ascendancy. For several hundred years there had been a steady recovery from the chaos following the collapse of the great empire which Charlemagne had left at his death in 814 A.D. The slow revival of trade and industry, the expansion of agriculture, the rise of towns, and the growth in population combined to produce economic strength and political stability reflected in the social order of the feudal system and the first steps toward

131

national monarchies. Progress was particularly apparent in the vigorous assaults on Islam which by mid-twelfth century had recaptured control of the Mediterranean, which rolled back the Muslims in southern Italy and the Iberian peninsula, and which took control of important territories in North Africa and the Middle East through the lusty war making of the early Crusaders.

The Crusades helped create an appetite in Europe for the goods of the East and brought further wealth to Italian shipping centers already engaged in transporting the exotic products of Asia to Europe's expanding markets. By the early fourteenth century these international movements, which tended to break down parochial isolation, were being paralleled with far-reaching developments in Europe herself. Commerce and urbanism had begun to turn the countryside away from manorial self-sufficiency toward a growing involvement in an exchange, profit-oriented economy. Slowly, serfdom started its conversion to tenancy or freehold tenure, and, as the traditional interdependence between lord and peasant dissolved, it was the monarch who assumed the responsibilities and loyalties no longer exercised by the feudal nobility.

The setbacks of the fourteenth century thus proved to be but a temporary hesitation, for the essential thrust of Europe's growth remained undiminished, stimulated by her energetic acquisitiveness and crusading fervor. There was the continued demand for the luxuries and spices of the East and the lure of enormous profits to be gained from that traffic. There was the intensified search for precious metals, always scarce in Europe and now critically so as bullion drained away to pay for the products arriving from Asia. Finally there was the white heat of Christian faith, undimmed by adversity and eager to regain the initiative in the holy war against Islam.

In the Iberian peninsula were people with both the experience and the determination to combine a search for commercial profit with a renewed assault on Islam. For centuries they had slowly pushed back the Moorish invaders from Africa, restricting them finally to the southern enclave of Granada where their unhappy remnants would eventually be absorbed or expelled. In the liberated area, small Christian states gradually took shape and by the early fifteenth century had combined into three kingdoms, Castile, Aragon, and Portugal. It was these states—first Portugal, and later Castile and Aragon joined to form the kingdom of Spain—that were to take the lead in initiating Europe's great imperial expansion into the world beyond.

The Imperial Design of Portugal

Portugal possessed modest but important advantages for the imperial adventures on which she was about to embark. Her position in Iberia athwart the path of the Islamic thrust into Europe had given her a firsthand knowledge of the Muslim world, an essential tool for both Crusader and merchant adventurer.

Moreover, Portugal was a nation of sailors; hence her people possessed the practical experience necessary for the marine reconnaissance of the East which would eventually turn the African continent and outflank the established trade routes through the Mediterranean and across Asia. Finally, Portugal produced at this moment a royal leadership that combined ingenuity with stability, thus enabling an essentially poor and weak state to achieve successes seemingly beyond her reach. Of most importance in this connection was Prince Henry the Navigator, the youngest son of the Portuguese king, John I.

Portugal's first move was direct—the conquest of Ceuta on the Moroccan coast in 1415. While this was a psychological blow and military defeat for Islam, it nevertheless did nothing to loosen the Moorish hold on the trans-Saharan gold trade. Clearly, if Muslim-controlled trade routes in Africa and Asia were to be captured, more resourceful and far-reaching means would be needed. Urged on by Prince Henry, Portugal experimented with ship design, map making, and systems of navigation, and gradually Portuguese exploration brought the West African coast into view. The first halting moves were made in familiar waters as Madeira was occupied in 1419; then, overriding the fear of the unknown, Henry's captains pressed on—Cape Bojador was passed in 1434, the Azores sighted in 1439, Cape Blanco reached in 1442, and the following year Arguin Island was discovered. By 1460, the year of Prince Henry's death, Portuguese caravels were moving along the Guinea coast beyond Cape Verde approximately as far as Sierra Leone.

Concurrently with exploration went the search for trade. In 1441, one ship returned to Portugal with some gold dust and captive blacks, and other captives soon followed, victims of slave raids but indicative of the possibilities for a more systematic commerce. In 1448 Arguin was fortified in the vain hope that the Saharan gold trade might be diverted to that coastal point. As the Portuguese moved down the coast, they probed inland up the Senegal and Gambia rivers seeking contact respectively with Tekrur and one of the Mandinka chiefdoms, but they were never able in this fashion to gain access to West Africa's gold. Much more successful were the ventures of Fernao Gomes, a Lisbon merchant who between 1469 and 1475 explored the coast under royal charter, reaching beyond Fernando Po and south of the equator. In 1471 the ships of Gomes located an area where abundant supplies of gold were to be had, a region they named Costa da Mina and which subsequently came to be known as the Gold Coast.

The gold of the Costa da Mina joined with other products, including pepper and modest numbers of slaves, to insure substantial Portuguese profits in West Africa, and they encouraged the crown to organize the trade in a series of state monopolies. Forts and factories were established intermittently along the coast as far as Benin, but the Portuguese kings were not the sort to rest content with their West African gains. The route to India still eluded detection, and when the energetic John II came to the throne in 1481 he determined to press forward with the business of exploration. In 1483, Diogo Cão discovered the Congo (Zaire) River and established relations with the kingdom of Kongo. Five years later Bartolomeu Dias rounded the Cape of Good Hope and the way to India was at last open to Portugal's mariners. Deterred by an exhausted and timorous crew, Dias got no farther, but word concerning the wealth of India eventually trickled back to Portugal from Pero da Covilhā who had left home at the same time as Dias and had finally reached Calicut by overland route. In 1497, therefore, a fleet under Vasco da Gama was dispatched which proceeded to Calicut via East Africa, collecting a variety of spices in India and establishing the tone of acquisitive aggressiveness which came to characterize Portugal's long-lived presence on the East African coast. During the early sixteenth century successive naval expeditions occupied the major coastal towns of East Africa, established Portuguese power in India, defeated a number of Arab fleets in naval battles, and thus took direct control of the trade of the Indian Ocean. One hundred years after Ceuta, Portugal had achieved her grand design of a commercial and Christian empire in the East.

The Portuguese in Kongo and Angola

At first Portugal showed more than passing interest in the Kongo state perched on the shores of the Zaire River. To be sure her basic concerns lay elsewhere — in the East, in her crusading responsibilities, and in the search for a sea route to the riches of India and China. Nevertheless the great Zaire estuary seemed a likely avenue that could lead to the kingdom of Prester John and eventual reconquest of the Holy Land. Concurrently, Kongo offered fertile ground for Christian conversion of a heathen people, a work worthy of the Crusader. And if profit were to accrue, through mining and commerce, so much the better for Christ's soldiers. Portugal thus sought an alliance with an equal and sovereign sister state.

There was more romance than realism in this view. The uplands of west-central Africa, lying between the Congo River and the Kalahari Desert, contained a Bantu population long limited to a struggle for survival. Parts of this essentially savanna plateau contained fertile land, but rains were irregular, often inadequate; hence those living close to the soil were forced to endure periodic drought with its attendant malnutrition, plague, and sometime famine. Populations remained scattered, communities small and isolated, warfare a chronic condition in defense of usable land or the search for better.

This was the baseline of Bantu existence, but some peoples were more favored. There were those whose good fortune lay in a fertile valley, nearby salt pan, iron-bearing hills, or a fish-filled river. Such riches could be converted into a higher living standard; an accumulation of capital in land, clients, or wives; development of a prosperous trade; and thus eventually, a community of numbers and prestige. Such had been the case with the kingdom of Kongo.

Kongo was fortunate to lie at the hub of intersecting trade routes. Her rulers were able to control interregional commerce involving shells, salt, and foodstuffs, to develop thereby both wealth and followers, and finally to extend their control over neighboring communities through political alliance and marriage contract. By the late fifteenth century, with the arrival of the first Portuguese, the *manikongo*, or king, presided over an extensive state, but its size was illusory for it was in fact loosely federated, the king's authority often more formal than actual.

Initial Portuguese overtures were well received, and in 1491 a mission arrived at the court of Manikongo Mzinga Mkuwu, a complement of artisans and missionaries with tools and gifts that greatly pleased the king and soon led to his Christian conversion. The motivation of the Portuguese appears to have been modest and straightforward—an alliance between equals by which Christianity and Western technology would be exchanged for prospecting and trading rights while the passage to Prester John was explored; indeed, an early version of what later came to be called "technical assistance" and "modernization."

It was a flawed vision. To begin with, a transplant of European religious and cultural institutions on a distant African shore far outreached the realities of two thoroughly divergent ways of life. More than that, the Portuguese crown gave relatively low priority to Kongo, for its main imperial objectives lay in India and beyond. After a few years only a handful of functionaries remained to advise the manikongo and his son, Afonso I, who succeeded to the throne in 1506. Worse still, other Portuguese gravitated to Kongo, undesirables and adventurers for the most part, who cared little for Lusitanian-African relations, who intermarried and settled down as permanent residents and busied themselves with plans for personal fortune. Many moved to nearby São Tomé island, there to raise sugar on plantations that were soon operated with gangs of slave labor drawn from the mainland.

The reign of Afonso lasted until 1543 and throughout he seems to have taken seriously the grand design of an African kingdom in European guise, a vain objective that was resisted both by his own people and by those resident Eurafricans whose fortunes rested on independence from Portuguese restraints. The Portuguese government assisted Afonso in his efforts to administer his federated principalities and extend his domains, but assistance was intermittent and ultimately insufficient. At the end of his reign, Afonso had begun to lose control over provincial chiefs whose resistance was supported by Portuguese-African mulattoes in alliances that bred still greater unrest as they fed a burgeoning traffic in slaves. In 1568 collapse became complete when Kongo was overrun by cannibalistic Jaga (Imbangala) raiders, possibly driven by famine conditions in the interior. The Jaga were finally expelled with Portuguese military assistance, but when order was restored Kongo had ceased to be a sovereign state in an alliance of equals and had become a virtual client

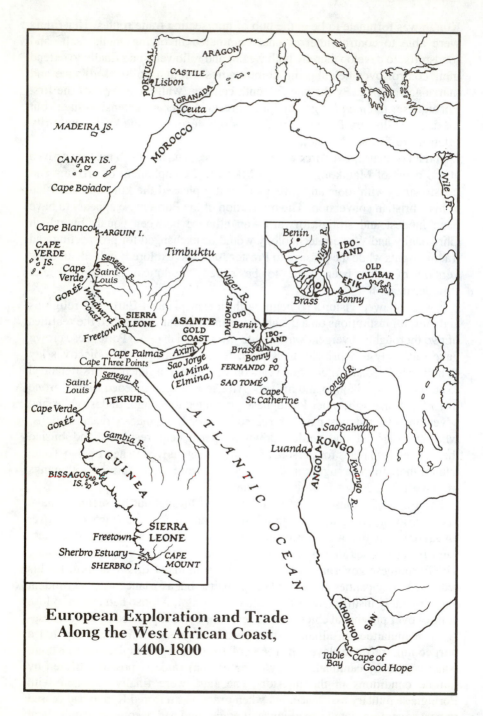

**European Exploration and Trade
Along the West African Coast,
1400-1800**

of Portuguese traders, its function primarily the procurement of slaves for the island planters and the Atlantic slave markets.

The slaving and political instability that Portuguese presence brought to Kongo was repeated to the south where the hinterland of what became the port of Luanda was occupied by Mbundu people living under rulers holding the title of *ngola*. Gradually in the sixteenth century the ngolas extended their local authority and in 1556 gained their independence from Kongo to which they had previously been subject. Nevertheless in Angola, as the Portuguese called the region, the same centrifugal forces came into play, bringing the same social disintegration and the same trafficking in slaves that had taken place in Kongo. The ngolas could not maintain control over subject chiefs, and the chronic civil war that ensued was intensified both by Jaga invasions and Portuguese intrigue, all of which cultivated chaos and produced growing numbers of uprooted to feed the demands of the Atlantic slave system.

In Angola Portugal dropped all pretense of cordial alliances between equals. In 1571 the Portuguese king granted Angola as a proprietary colony to one of his followers. Although a system of royal governors was later instituted, faraway Portuguese authority failed to exercise control as its own representatives, the resident Eurafrican trading and slaving community, and local African princes contended with one another in intermittent skirmishing. Despite occasional efforts at political consolidation, as with Queen Anna Nzinga during the first half of the seventeenth century, centrifugal forces generally prevailed. The Jaga invaded Angola after their Kongo adventure and a Dutch squadron captured Luanda in 1641, but the main disability was the chronic chaos caused by the expanding slave trade in which all participated. Even during the late nineteenth century after slaving had been abolished in Portuguese territories, Angola's unhappy experience with the traffic was to continue virtually without stint until the eve of the First World War.

The Arrival of the Dutch

As with the Portuguese, the Dutch appearance in Africa was but part of a grander geopolitical design. Portuguese expansionism did not go long unchallenged within Europe. Even as Portugal was laying the basis for her Indian Ocean empire through the voyages of Dias and da Gama, Spain was underwriting the explorations of Columbus which were to lead, among many other things, to her own New World empire based on gold and, particularly, on silver. The success of these Portuguese and Spanish enterprises, combined in 1580 under the rule of Philip II of Spain, led, however, not to monopoly but to greater competition. For the Portuguese, the long-range effect of Spanish control was disastrous for it encouraged Spain's enemies to mount a successful attack against the overextended network of possessions which Portugal had established with much effort in the East.

In the case of the Netherlands, also ruled by Philip as part of his initial inheritance, the situation was quite different. Within the Low Countries, antipathy toward Spanish rule on political, religious, and economic grounds erupted in a revolt by the northern Netherlands provinces which, after a long struggle, brought virtual independence in 1609. In the course of the conflict, the Dutch found themselves cut off from supplies of Asian goods arriving in Europe at Lisbon. Their natural response was to seek these goods directly, an effort that soon led to sharp mercantile-military competition with both Portugal and Spain.

In the East, Dutch industry and thoroughness combined with imaginative merchandising and superior seamanship to rout the Portuguese and hold off British mercantile pretensions while establishing a highly successful commercial empire centered on the Dutch East Indies and administered by the East India Company founded in 1602. Rising Dutch power struck with equal force in the Atlantic where the Dutch West India Company chartered in 1621 visited heavy damages on both the Spanish and Portuguese. Portuguese Brazil was occupied for a time during the first half of the seventeenth century while Spanish settlements in the Caribbean were repeatedly ravaged. Dutch merchant ships dominated the European carrying trade while her fighting ships were everywhere, convoying and protecting her efficient and numerous fleets of cargo vessels.

The reflection of these global operations was soon apparent in Africa. Dutch ships were prowling West African waters before the close of the sixteenth century, and initial reconnaissance was closely followed by stronger measures—at first raids on São Tomé and São Jorge da Mina, then the occupation of the island of Gorée in 1617 and the capture of Arguin in 1633. Four years later came the crowning indignity to Portugal's authority when São Jorge on the Costa da Mina was plucked from her defenders and converted into the Gold Coast stronghold of Elmina. These operations were designed to capture the Guinea trade from the Portuguese, and by the first quarter of the seventeenth century Dutch ships had blanketed the West African coast, dealing in gold and ivory and then increasingly in slaves for the plantations of America. It was the slave trade, for example, that accounted for the capture of Luanda, for Angolan slaves were much prized in Brazil where Dutch slavers were active suppliers. Nevertheless, it was not these lucrative commercial activities that were to account for the most fateful of the Dutch enterprises in Africa.

In the spring of 1652 a small fleet of three Dutch ships dropped anchor in Table Bay at the bottom of the African continent and established the tiny community that was the beginning of European presence in South Africa. Initially there was no thought of African colonization, for these ships contained only a modest number of employees of the East India Company charged with developing a station midway between Europe and the East where merchant ships on the long journey to and from the Indies could put in for water and fresh food. The pragmatic Dutch were not concerned with local conquest or exploration. The empire to which they aspired lay far to the east, and the commander, Jan van Riebeeck, was given explicit instructions — establish a truck farm and barter for cattle with the local people, build a small fort but avoid trouble with the Khoikhoi (Hottentot) inhabitants of the region.

At first these instructions were followed with reasonable fidelity, but in time circumstances altered the nature and the activities of the community. In 1657, in a move to increase production, nine of the company employees were given the status of free burghers and allocated small individual farms, and the following year slaves were imported from Java and Madagascar to augment the labor supply. Hindsight views these as momentous developments for at once they converted the settlement from a temporary expedient to a permanent colony, and established the institution of servile labor. Soon another fateful decision was taken when company herds were formed in order to supplement the unsteady Khoikhoi meat supply. This move led to disputes with the Khoikhoi over grazing rights and to eventual armed conflict which drove the Khoikhoi off their lands, and began the process of disintegration of their social and political institutions. At the same time the authorities made the first move in South Africa toward apartheid — an abortive attempt to avoid trouble between the settlers and the Khoikhoi by means of physical separation.

In time came other innovations. Strategic considerations argued for a strong and populous community at this South African station standing athwart the sea route between Europe and the riches of the East; consequently, an active immigration policy was instituted during the administrations of Simon van der Stel and his son Willem who directed the colony between 1679 and 1707. Dutch and German settlers were recruited as was a body of French Huguenots, but unlike company employees, these settlers brought their wives, thereby foreclosing any possibility of mixed marriages and an eventual Afro-European community. Simon van der Stel founded the village of Stellenbosch, and other centers followed based upon farm holdings granted in full ownership. Despite these measures the population rose but slowly, and by 1708 there were only seventeen hundred free burghers and about an equal number of slaves. Nevertheless the pattern for the colony had been established — a permanent agricultural settlement in which labor was performed by a servile group under the direction of a privileged landowning class. This was a far remove from the original concept of a refreshment station sustained by hired employees of the Dutch East India Company.

Immigration was not encouraged after the era of the van der Stels but by that time the company had begun to lose control of its venture. Henceforward the destinies of the colony lay increasingly in the hands of its body of permanent settlers acted upon by the exigencies of their adopted land. In the area of initial settlement which was well suited to the truck-, cereal-, and viniculture required by the company, a society emerged, based on agriculture and commerce, closely regulated by the rules of a paternalistic regime but accustomed to evading those rules through such devices as smuggling and bribery, living a leisurely life in which slaves performed physical labor. The leisure that resulted, however, did not cause greater intellectual activity or increased appetite for a cultivated life. Schools were few and existed only at the elementary level. The first theater did not appear until the nineteenth century, and there were so few readers that this provincial community did not support a single bookshop. The main recreations were weddings, occasional dances, funerals, and endless gossip, either at home or in the town's numerous taverns.

Beyond the hills encircling the Cape region, however, there slowly took shape another community which was to form the basis of the Boer people. Slave labor and land shortage in the settled districts encouraged young people to move along to an area where land was available in quantity, and if the land were suitable mainly for grazing, this neatly fitted the increasing demand at Cape Town for supplies of fresh meat. Thus the *trekboer*, or frontier farmer, came into being. Moving eastward with his herds, he occupied territory over which the Dutch East India Company exercised only nominal control and he occupied it in great six-thousand acre lease holds that amounted to outright ownership. In typical farming fashion, he had large families and each of his many sons in turn came to require his own six-thousand-acre homestead; hence, in only a few generations a vast region had been swallowed up as the *trekboers* probed far to the east, well beyond the practical limits of the company's government. A vast region, it was thinly held. Of 14,000 Europeans in the colony at the end of the eighteenth century, no more than 5,000 were spread across 450 miles of arid trackless land running eastward from the Cape Town settlement.

On the frontier, life was more monotonous than difficult, and durability was the essence of survival. In the trekboer, self-esteem joined with self-reliance, and physical toughness was matched by tenacity and endurance. With self-reliance, however there emerged a deepening antipathy toward official authority and a tendency to confuse land occupation and land ownership. The isolation that shaped self-sufficiency also bred an individualism that was suspicious of innovation and hostile toward the stranger, yet egalitarian to a much greater degree than that found in the stratified society of the Cape Town area. At the same time intermarriage and a sense of common destiny bound the frontier trekkers together in a cohesion that was ultimately to emerge in Afrikaner nationalism.

Both on the frontier and in the more established areas the settlers early developed the racial attitudes that came to characterize the apartheid philosophy. First of all, the Europeans brought with them their unshatterable conviction of white racial superiority. Although an initial shortage of European women led quickly to miscegenation, few children of mixed marriages achieved citizenship status, most joining the population blend of slaves, freed slaves, and Khoikhoi that eventually gave rise to the Cape Coloured people. Khoikhoi

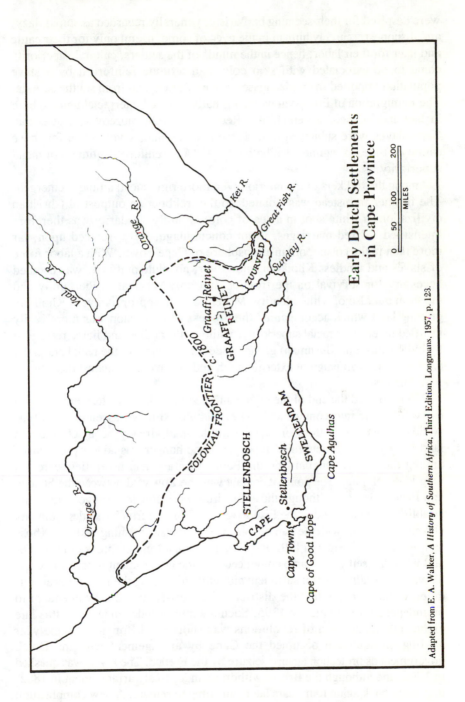

Early Dutch Settlements in Cape Province

Adapted from E. A. Walker, *A History of Southern Africa*, Third Edition, Longmans, 1957, p. 123.

were despised for their seeming barbarism, generally regarded as stupid, lazy, and dishonest, scarcely human in the eyes of some, useful only for their cattle and later for their labor; hence in the minds of the settlers, cultural superiority came to be associated with skin color, an attitude reinforced by a slave population imported from Madagascar, from Africa, and from southeast Asia. The immigration of European women greatly reduced interracial unions, both in fact and in social acceptability. Recent research, moreover, argues that Cape slaves were subjected to a rigorous discipline, severe even for those calloused times, a regimen that both reflected and reinforced attitudes of racial superiority.

Among the trekkers of the interior even more rigid racial attitudes emerged. The frontier farmstead was isolated, to the trekboer an outpost of Christian civilization, a white spot in a sea of color. Family solidarity was therefore intensified. Mixed marriages, if not concubinage, were frowned upon, far more than in the cosmopolitan atmosphere of Cape Town. With a labor force of slaves and landless Khoikhoi, moreover, absolute authority was deemed necessary for survival on the frontier, not only survival of the family and the farm but also of white identity. Moreover, the appropriation of Khoikhoi grazing land which accompanied the process of expansion was more easily justified in terms of racial superiority, while cattle raiding and fierce resistance by indigenous San (Bushman) groups added its measure to the racial antipathy expressed in a campaign of extermination and enslavement against these Stone Age hunters.

When, toward the end of the eighteenth century, the Boer farmers trekking eastward came into contact with Bantu peoples slowly descending the East African coast, the pattern of racial attitudes had already been set among a land-hungry, independent-minded people. Land hunger was no less pronounced among the Xhosa vanguard on the Bantu frontier, and hostilities were not long in developing. The point of contact was the Zuurveld between the Sunday and Fish rivers, and although the authorities were able to arrange a truce and establish a boundary along the Fish River in 1778, the frontier settlers, already chronically at war with the San people, were soon skirmishing with the Xhosa as well. Severe drought in 1791 and 1792 brought a fresh outbreak of hostilities and when the settlers became convinced that the government in faraway Cape Town was lending them insufficient aid while hindering their attempts at self-defense, they proclaimed the districts of Graaff-Reinet and Swellendam to be independent republics in 1795. Such a show of independence in this late eighteenth-century era of revolutions was short-lived, for in the same year an English squadron occupied the Cape by arrangement with the Dutch government as protection against seizure by the French. The revolt was quashed in 1796, and although the British withdrew under treaty arrangement in 1802, they were back again four years later, this time to remain. A new complication had been added to the complexities of South Africa's intramural affairs.

The British and French in West Africa

Both England and France were relative latecomers to the imperial adventures begun by Portugal, but having arrived last they also were to exercise the most pervasive influence as colonial powers. Nowhere was this more true than in Africa.

It was the slave trade that first brought British and French merchants in force to the West African coast. The Portuguese had traded for slaves as early as the fifteenth century and Spain's New World possession had provided a ready market in the sixteenth century. The interest of England and France, however, was linked to the growth of their own plantation colonies in America, and these did not become important producers much before the middle of the seventeenth century. As these colonies developed at a time when mercantilist theory proclaimed the necessity of a closed economic system embracing colony and mother country, official policy in both England and France required that the growing demand for slaves be satisfied exclusively through national resources. Hence this was the era of the British navigation acts and similar mercantilist restrictions by France, the period when the Dutch were ousted from New Amsterdam and their naval power steadily eroded by the competition from France and particularly from England.

In West Africa British and French mercantile activity took the form of national trading monopolies like the Royal African Company chartered by Charles II in 1660 or the French West Indies Company created by Colbert in 1664. These interlopers, who were quickly joined by commercial interests representing Sweden, Denmark, and Brandenburg, successfully challenged the Dutch in West Africa and by the opening of the eighteenth century had taken over much of the slaving on the West African coast, exclusive of the Portuguese in Angola. The French early established themselves in the region of the Senegal River, occupying Saint-Louis Island at the mouth of the Senegal in 1659 and capturing the slave depot of Gorée from the Dutch in 1677. British establishments were concentrated on the Gold Coast where a series of fortified posts brought a direct confrontation with the Dutch bases such as Elmina and Axim. Elsewhere along the coast either the natural deterrents of poor anchorages and difficult navigation or the determination of the local people kept the traders at arm's length, forced to remain in their ships or to maintain unfortified trading posts under the watchful eye of African princes. This did not mean a lack of sympathy among Africans for the slave traffic but rather a desire to share in its control, and the volume of trade rose steadily through the eighteenth century, by which time the British commercial effort had far outstripped all competitors. Paradoxically, it was in England during the late eighteenth century that the first steps were taken leading to the eventual abolition of the slave trade.

The Nature of the European Impact

Descriptions of Africa by outsiders have tended toward the exotic and mysterious, often uninformed and not infrequently with pejorative connotations. Africa was the "dark continent," remote, inscrutable, primitive. Africans were said to have no language; they squeaked and jibbered. They did not think and could not dream. Some had tails, others were dogfaced, still others headless with eyes in their chests. This last was reported by none other than Herodotus, who at least admitted he was speaking at second hand. Even as informed a reporter as Ibn Battuta was capable of remarking that he had been safe from cannibalism while traveling in Africa because he was white and therefore considered unripe by pagan blacks.

Such superstitious comments were the product of prejudice as much as ignorance, for foreigners had in fact managed to penetrate the continent from very early times, if only intermittently, and there were periodic accounts of travelers providing authentic information to offset the tall tales. Mariners from Arabia had visited the East African coast, surely as far back as Herodotus. North Africa and its interior were known to the ancients by reason of Carthaginian and Roman occupation, and later the spread of Islam brought regular and intimate contact between North and West Africa and the Middle East.

One remarkable feature of Africa's long-lived relations with the wider world is the fact that in virtually all cases the initiative has come from outside Africa. Aside from the obvious dispersion of the Homo species from its African origin, there are no recorded instances of Africans visiting other shores. There is an isolated account of ships that sailed into the Atlantic from West Africa during the heyday of the Mali empire, and there are the intriguing similarities between Egyptian and Precolombian architecture in the Americas, but that is all. The flow of traffic has been overwhelmingly from the outside in.

The coming of Europe to Africa, an event so intimately connected with Europe's worldwide economic expansion, affected African communities in different ways and varying degrees. In xenophobic Ethiopia, Portuguese Jesuits struggled in vain for a foothold, but Portuguese soldiers may well have saved Ethiopian Christianity from annihilation at the hands of Ahmad Gran and his Muslim armies. On the East African coast, the Portuguese quickly subdued the ancient trading states: but made little impression on the local society and culture which remained staunchly Muslim, Arab, and African. In South Africa the Dutch overwhelmed the fragile cultures of the San and the Khoikhoi, destroying and displacing the former in a war of extermination, and transforming the latter from a loosely knit nation of pastoralist to landless rural laborers and uprooted urban dwellers, and ultimately causing them to become lost in the Cape Coloured community. The inland kingdoms of Mutapa and Changamire were able in the long run to neutralize Portuguese intrusion, but across the continent in the west, the people of Kongo and Angola were devastated by these same Portuguese, the Kongo kingdom disintegrating before the ravages of the slave trade which likewise decimated the population and depressed the economy of her Angolan neighbors. Indeed, disintegration in the Kongo and Angola areas in time became the basis of a new sociopolitical system in which perpetual unrest, warfare, and slaving predominated. The Portuguese, although numerically and politically weak, remained rapacious and slave mongering, while prestige and power among independent chieftaincies rested upon the number of slaves each regional principality controlled.

In West Africa, where Europe came early and remained late, the Western impact was also various, but nowhere did it lead to the disintegration that befell the indigenous people of South Africa or the Kongo kingdom. The Portuguese presence, for example, had but a minor influence in Benin where the intruders traded and proselytized with their usual vigor for some twenty years after their arrival in 1485, but where the slave trade was disappointingly limited as was the interest of Benin's oba in Christianity—an interest, moreover, prodded not by a yearning for spiritual elevation as much as by a desire for firearms. There was another reason. The oba was religious as well as temporal leader of his people, and had no enthusiasm for any limitation on his authority.

Along the Upper Guinea coast between the Gambia River and Cape Mount, Portuguese influence was somewhat more pervasive, but primarily in social and economic matters for the local rulers were jealous of their sovereignty and guarded it tenaciously. Here and there forts were built in small-scale replica of the Gold Coast castles, but it was impossible to practice mercantilist restrictions in the face of chiefly independence and this unrestricted coast came to be the favorite base of operations for numbers of private traders, drawn from various European nationalities.

In their economic and cultural impact, however, the Europeans caused some fundamental changes on this Upper Guinea coast. In the first place, there seems to have been no distinct slave class in this part of West Africa before the rise of the transatlantic trade; yet by the late eighteenth century there had developed an indigenous population variously designated as clients, household slaves, serfs, servants, or subjects. Many of these were the property of mulatto chiefs like the Caulkers and the Clevelands who maintained slave labor in the form of sailors, porters, farm workers, and artisans, and who sold off these chattels in the international market if the occasion demanded. The slave trade, moreover, caused basic changes in law and criminal punishment. Under traditional law, fines, not imprisonment, had been the usual penalty for transgressors, but with the rise of slaving many misdemeanors came to be punishable by sale to Europeans. Finally, and most significantly, these early European contacts were the means through which a wide range of plants were introduced to West Africa. The Portuguese brought sugar from Madeira, corn, cassava, sweet potatoes, pineapple, and pawpaw from the Americas—all with profound implications for population growth and density.

European traders on the upper windward coast encouraged a local taste for European goods and also led to the rise of a small but important mulatto population, largely of English antecedents in the area of the Sherbro estuary, and Portuguese farther up the coast. Taking local wives, many of these traders tended to settle down within the compass of local custom, some even wearing tribal tattoos. The process was reciprocal, however, for there were Africans educated in Europe who clung tenaciously to the symbols, such as clothes or furnishings, of their European experience. Those who could afford a European education usually availed themselves of it, although the motive was often no more than the mastery of mercantile techniques. The cultural amalgam was often complex. Some individuals gave every outward sign of a European way of life but could not always change habits of mind or morals with their dress. Others broke under the impact of a foreign education and were unable to maintain themselves in either their old or new world. Still others were able to be thoroughly African or European, faithfully changing in response to circumstance. Many exhibited latent attraction to charms, witchcraft, and other superstitions, but this was only what was observed among many Europeans as well.

Farther up the coast in the French settlements of Saint-Louis and Gorée, a *métis* or mulatto community had arisen which was on the way to a much more thoroughgoing Westernization. Formed through the union of African—chiefly Wolof—women, and officials, artisans, and others, the mulattoes of Gorée and Saint-Louis quickly assumed important social and economic functions. The women, called *signares*, contracted common-law marriages with visiting Europeans which were defined with precise formality and which guaranteed the social status and economic independence of each signare upon the eventual return of her husband to Europe. Many signares therefore became respected and wealthy matrons while mulatto men, called *habitants*, had ample opportunities for careers in commerce or government service. These people were practicing Christians, and by the opening of the nineteenth century were on the way to adopting French speech and dress to match their French names and Gallic orientation. There were *métis* mayors of Saint-Louis and Gorée by the late eighteenth century, and when French citizenship was extended to the colonies during the French Revolution, the Senegalese sent their list of grievances to the Estates General just as did French citizens from the home country.

There were a few pure-blood Africans in Saint-Louis and Gorée who, like the mulattoes, identified themselves with Europe, but the overwhelming proportion of the population of the French communities of Senegal, to say nothing of the hinterland, contained Africans almost totally unaffected by European language, religion, or custom. Moreover, French political authority was limited to her two urban centers in addition to a few trading posts along the coast and up the Senegal River. This was typical of the European presence throughout West Africa. Rarely did it penetrate beyond the coast, for the seaboard states took pains to keep it out in order to maintain their status as intermediaries between the European visitors and the markets of the interior. Nowhere was this development better illustrated than among the trading city-states of the Niger Delta.

These states had existed long before the coming of the Europeans, arising from a mutual need for exchange between the delta fisherfolk and the people of the interior—the latter in quest of protein and salt, the former eager to offset their lack of bulk foodstuffs, clothing, tools, and household goods. In addition, the overpopulated Ibo of the hinterland exported labor for agriculture, while various skilled artisans from up-country were also much in demand among the delta people. The whole system worked through a complicated web of markets operated by part-time petty traders and full-time merchants. When the Portuguese first arrived, the trade structure had therefore already been well established and the changes occasioned by the newcomers were in terms of products, rather than patterns of trade. The Europeans demanded and received ivory and slaves, and it was easy to alter the status of contract laborer to that of slave and to obtain slaves by other means in the overpopulated centers of the interior.

One of the chief vehicles of the slave trade in Iboland came to be the *Aro Chuku* oracle. The oracle was widely recognized as the voice of Chuku, the supreme deity, and the representatives of the oracle, therefore, exercised great power throughout Iboland. Scattered colonies of Aro, an Ibo subgroup, not only provided access to the oracle but, as one rare, centralized organization in normally decentralized Iboland, it acted as a mercantile network along which goods and travelers could pass with safety. Thus the Aro became the commercial agents of Iboland, and as the demand for slaves arose, they utilized their special position to monopolize the slave trade as well. Universal belief in the power of the oracle established it as a final court of appeal in the settlement of disputes. The Aro who controlled the oracle passed sentence in terms of fines to be paid in slaves and soon they were the dominant force in the slave trade from which they gained great wealth and power.

Although the essential nature and function of the Niger Delta trading states had predated the arrival of Europeans, their eventual size, political structure, and social makeup were certainly a direct result of the European presence. Traditional African societies usually revolved around the extended family bound together by blood ties. In the delta states, by contrast, economic needs and European contacts led to another type of social structure, the House System. In order to meet the international demand for slaves, the original Ijo, Efik, or other people of Bonny, Brass, Old Calabar, and their sister states imported large numbers of slaves from the populous Ibo interior, retaining some of these as household chattels. In this way powerful trading houses arose consisting of a family of freeborn and its complement of slaves. Since all members of a house, slave or free, and their progeny remained members of that house, it was possible for families to grow in size and influence while the original small fishing and trading village developed a cosmopolitan quality and scale. Each house was ruled arbitrarily by its head, and the government, whether royal or republican, was in fact an oligarchy controlled by the most prominent traders. A rough-and-ready democracy existed, however, for heads of houses were elected by all house members, and it was possible for slaves to rise in the hierarchy through merit and succeed, as some did, to the headship of the house.

These burgeoning delta states were an effective screen against direct European penetration to the interior, but they were also in part a response to European demands for strong and stable trading outlets. On the Gold Coast stability was sought through the construction of fortified posts but these castles gained no more than a minimal foothold, for their garrisons remained by sufferance, unable either to exert political authority outside their walls or to enforce their desired trade monopoly. Indeed, local rulers characteristically exacted the payment of tariffs, fines, and rents, while refusing the traders access to the interior, always seeking to maintain their own control over the inland trade. Typical was the situation reported by one seventeenth-century European agent in taking note of the authority of the Fante: "The blacks . . . drive a great trade with all interlopers without regarding the English and Dutch factors. . . . Neither of those European nations dare oppose the natives . . . for fear of being ruin'd themselves."

Perhaps the degree of tenacity in opposition to European penetration was best exemplified by the stubborn defense of John Conny, a Gold Coast chief of the early eighteenth century. Conny was a man of obscure background, a commoner representing no established royal house, who took charge of the Brandenburg trading stations at Cape Three Points, reviving their commercial vitality after their Prussian directors had faltered. In this way he gained control over a major route leading inland to Asante, holding his seacoast terminals for almost fifteen years despite the growing opposition of European, chiefly Dutch, competitors. He stood off the Dutch when they tried to land an armed party and take his fort, succumbing only after seven years of combined diplomatic and military pressure by his attackers who were convinced of the necessity for eliminating a powerful and successful rival.

Hemmed in the Europeans may have been, but in their trade they came to exert a pervasive if indirect influence throughout Gold Coast territories. In the first place, the commerce changed the character of many coastal communities, converting sleepy fishing villages to lively commercial centers, and introducing a novel breed of African trader. There were cosmopolitan entrepreneurs free from the dictates of traditional life, who built a new kind of commercial, and sometimes political, dominion. In the example of Conny, among others, the Atlantic trade produced an African merchant prince, creator of his own coastal power which presented a direct challenge to European shippers seeking the patronage of the forest states of the interior.

In like fashion, the Atlantic trade touched the destinies of inland peoples, turning their attention southward away from the trans-Saharan commerce, encouraging, if not originating, the rise of those large-scale forest states that culminated with the dramatic appearance of the Asante kingdom at the beginning of the eighteenth century. First, there was Akwamu, its militant expansionism during the late seventeenth century overrunning, among others, the coastal principality of Accra whereby the former secured for a time her preeminence as a prominent commercial as well as military power. During much the same years, the state of Denkyira had embarked upon her own territorial aggrandizement, initially directing her efforts northward to take control of trade routes and gold mines, then turning to the south toward the attractions of the maritime commerce. At the height of its power as the seventeenth century drew to a close, Denkyira fell into mortal conflict with its Asante dependent, the latter intent upon political independence as well as control of the profitable trade routes north and south. Asante came to be the last and most successful of the new forest kingdoms, but all appear to have been stimulated by mercantile designs, particularly after the arrival of the first Europeans brought a new dimension to the age-old commerce within the West African savanna and forest.

European Commerce

Whatever the indirect consequences of Europe's arrival on the West African coast, it was commerce that brought the strangers in their ships and commerce that attracted the Africans to Europe. Sometimes this mercantile preoccupation showed itself in colorful, if superficial, fashion—the silver buckles or satin waistcoats of local kings, for example, or the institution of "dash," a gift that supplemented and consummated each commercial transaction and came in time to be a characteristic aspect of West African life. More typically, however, the mutual interest lay simply in the exchange of goods, articles possessed by one and coveted by the other.

The Europeans brought crafted and processed merchandise designed to appeal to agricultural communities of a relatively limited technology. Indigenous African industries produced salt and cotton cloth as well as iron ore and utensils manufactured therefrom, but European cloth became at once a popular commodity, iron bars were imported to supplement African supplies, and European shippers even succeeded in competing with the local salt trade in some areas. Varieties of jewelry, particularly glass beads, were steady favorites, while tobacco and alcoholic spirits were also in demand. In exchange the traders sought ivory, animal skins, spices such as malaguetta pepper and, most of all, gold, that West African staple which had long fed the Saharan trade and which was always in short supply within bullion-hungry Europe.

Various figures for the gold trade indicate exports at the coast ranging between one and two tons a year toward the end of the seventeenth century. In time, however, it was the slave trade that grew to be the major traffic of West Africa, eclipsing all others including gold as Africans in rising numbers were shipped across the Atlantic to serve as labor for the plantations of the New World.

Wherever trading occurred, it exhibited a characteristic blend of African and European merchandising techniques. The European traders came with goods to be sold at a profit which they calculated in currency, but the African importers were concerned only with the equal exchange of their own goods for items they did not possess. What emerged was a system linked both to barter and to monetary exchange. Goods were grouped together in what was called the sorting, a collection of individual items, each of which was valued according to its worth as expressed in a medium of exchange—bronze "manilla" bracelets along the Niger Delta, the gold trade ounce on the Gold Coast, iron bars, salt cakes, bags of cowries, and slaves. The sorting was then traded against a similar combination of goods calculated to be of equal value. Hence, a sorting of textiles, alcohol, firearms, tobacco, and hardware might have been exchanged as a unit for an individual slave or a quantity of gold. In determining valuation, the European merchants added a markup for profit, a concept, though lacking from the African system of equal exchange, that soon resulted in a corresponding rise in the price of the goods offered by the African dealers. By and large the currencies utilized were rarely employed in actual payment, their major function being to act as a convenient standard of value and method for keeping accounts.

By the middle of the seventeenth century, European firearms had become much in demand, their influence in West African affairs rising steadily with their increasing importation. The traders, with some exceptions, were quick to supply the market. An early Portuguese regulation forbade the sale of guns to non-Christians, thus limiting the distribution of arms in Benin, and the first Dutch stations on the Gold Coast also withheld guns from their list of trade goods. Such restrictions quickly broke down, however, as competitive Europeans vied with each other to satisfy the local demand. While overall statistics are difficult to gather, individual transactions are sufficiently eloquent—for example, the sixty-six thousand firearms shipped to West Africa by the British Royal African Company between 1673 and 1704, the inventories of the Dutch Gold Coast stations during the last years of the seventeenth century showing thousands of weapons in stock and thousands more on order, or the eighteenth- and nineteenth- century reports of growing armies of musketeers serving such military states as Asante and Dahomey.

The interest in firearms was understandable among those West African states bent upon conquest or defense. Beyond that, however, state making in the seventeenth and eighteenth centuries often arose as a device for controlling trade routes, gold production, or the growing industry of slaving; hence, a share in the gun trade became essential policy for those African powers that sought to dominate commerce more generally. States such as Denkyira and Asante apparently prospered and expanded as a result of their mercantile aspirations, in the process refining their military technology away from close-quarter thrusting weapons to the bow and arrow, then accelerating the shift to missile armament by adding musketeers to supplement their batteries of archers. The repercussions of such developments soon affected widening areas of the state structure. Changing armament led to new battlefield tactics, which in turn brought the formation of military units headed by commanders who tended to assume political and administrative functions as well. In Asante the army leadership possessed formidable political authority as was the case in Dahomey, a state whose more or less permanent military footing was characterized by its famed corps of "Amazons," a policy of universal military service, and well-trained regiments of musketeers.

The connection between firearms and warfare can be overstressed, however. Muzzle loaders were cumbersome and slow in reloading, often far too slow in competition with quick-firing archers. Maintenance was difficult, moreover, powder and ammunition expensive and of doubtful quality. Musketeers needed to be trained and competent instructors were in short supply. The older forms of warfare hung on, therefore, well into the nineteenth century, especially in the savanna interior where lance-bearing cavalry remained a superior armament. Indeed, guns seem to have been used most widely not for arms but for ceremonial functions, for hunting, and for keeping animals at bay during harvest time.

Africa and the Atlantic Slave Trade

Discussion of the Atlantic slave trade begins with numbers, a most difficult debut since it attempts to answer a question of great emotional intensity with data that are scattered and incomplete. Until recently the subject was examined more through bias than fact, and even serious estimates varied from five to twenty-five million slaves landed in the Americas over a four-hundred-year period ending in the late nineteenth century. About twenty years ago, however, historians began to analyze, first, data in published accounts, and then, further materials in archives the world over, subjecting these figures to sophisticated statistical analysis to achieve newer and more viable totals.

At present there is some agreement on a figure of approximately 11.7 million slaves exported between 1450 and 1900, departure points extending from Senegal as far as southeastern Africa. With some 9.8 million landed in the Americas, the estimated shipboard losses of 1.9 million amount to 16 percent of all who left Africa. There are those, nonetheless, who argue that these estimates are too low, in one case by as much as 4.4 million, a shortfall of slightly over 30 percent. If the 11.7 million total may be accepted, however, further refinements are possible, both by century and by region.

Slave Exports from Africa: the Atlantic Trade

Period	Volume	Percent
1450-1600	367,000	3.1
1601-1700	1,868,000	16.0
1701-1800	6,133,000	52.4
1801-1900	3,330,000*	28.5
Total	11,698,000	100.0

*Includes 55,889 slaves exported from Angola to African coastal islands, chiefly São Tomé, between 1876 and 1892.

The 9.46 million slaves exported during the eighteenth and nineteenth centuries represent four-fifths of the overall total, two areas being hardest hit. The so-called Slave Coast running from the Volta River east to the Niger Delta yielded 23 percent of the total during the eighteenth century and 17.5 percent from 1801-1867. Even more severe was the attrition in the Kongo-Angola region—37 percent for the eighteenth century and fully 48 percent in the nineteenth century up to 1867. Not included in this last figure are the slaves sent from Angola to the offshore islands between 1876 and 1892.

The transatlantic traffic was intimately connected with a plantation economy that arose in the Americas during the seventeenth and eighteenth centuries, particularly in Brazil and the Caribbean islands. Producing sugar for the European market, New World plantations purchased slaves offered for sale in West Africa, for this was found to be the cheapest form of labor recruitment. Both American Indian and European workers succumbed to unfamiliar diseases, and the expense of rearing slave children in the New World for ultimate employment outweighed the cost of purchase and transport of fresh slave cargoes from Africa. Hence the traffic continued and, indeed, increased, particularly during the eighteenth century. By the early nineteenth century, however, slave prices in Africa had risen to a point where slave breeding in the Americas became a preferable economic alternative. After 1807, when England outlawed the slave trade, there ensued a modest decline in the Atlantic traffic although Portuguese activity, particularly in the Kongo-Angola area, continued well into the nineteenth century.

When Europeans first arrived on the West African coast during the fifteenth century, they were offered slaves in exchange for their trade goods. This has caused historians to speculate that the institution of slavery was indigenous and not a result of the subsequent slave trade. Certainly there were in West Africa social and economic inequalities, even castes, that relegated segments of the population to inferior status. Under certain circumstances such individuals were liable to sale into bondage or even sacrifice in a religious rite, but there does not seem to have been a generally recognized class of bond slaves. Those who were fated for sacrifice or sale were more than likely war captives, new arrivals, and strangers who had not yet been absorbed into the community through attachment, however lowly, to a resident family. Once assimilated, such individuals were not normally offered for sale; hence as the Atlantic traffic expanded, its numbers were recruited primarily from prisoners of war whose disposal was an economic windfall through hostilities otherwise generated. There were indeed slave catching expeditions and warfare was no doubt influenced by the potential profits of slaving, but these developments seem to have been accelerated by the slave trade as it expanded rather than created directly by the trade to feed its own purpose.

The effect of the slave trade on West African societies has long been a hotly debated subject, often for want of concrete information, frequently because of the great variety of circumstances among different African communities. Largely abstaining from the trade, Benin, for example, was lightly touched. So too were the Yoruba until civil war during the nineteenth century produced great numbers of captives who became the dominant group in the traffic to Brazil and Cuba. For its part, Dahomey developed into an active procurer and its economy became captive to the trade. Again, the enormous exports from Kongo and Angola had much to do with the political instability and social unrest in those territories. By contrast, Asante, another vigorous provider of slaves, maintained its political strength up to the colonial era, but contemporary observers have testified that many neighboring communities were wiped out by the continual slaving of Asante and others.

These are examples in detail. If one generalization may be risked, it could be said that, despite unexampled individual misery, despite devastation and depopulation in certain areas, the slave trade had relatively little impact on West African society taken as a whole. Certainly, although those affected by the trade were numbered in the millions, their loss to West African communities does not appear to have been significant. The attrition was spread over four hundred years and covered vast areas; much more concentrated by comparison was Europe's massive emigration to the Americas during a few short decades preceding the First World War. Moreover, though losses in West Africa were unevenly distributed in time and place and bore most heavily on the healthiest sections of society, major states such as Asante and Oyo remained virile, while centers like Iboland from which many slaves were drawn seemingly suffered no important loss in population. No doubt an economy based on slaving was based insecurely, while nations devoted to slave mongering became brutalized and unproductive. Yet the conviction cannot be escaped that, by and large, Europe's initial impact on Africa was minimal, in no way comparable with the influence she was to exert when she returned again during the early nineteenth century, this time with humanitarian as well as predatory motives.

Suggestions for Further Reading

For the era of European expansion see J. H. Parry, *The Age of Reconnaissance* (Berkeley, CA: University of California Press, 1981); Charles R. Boxer, *The Portuguese Seaborne Empire, 1415-1825* (London: Hutchinson, 1969); and Fernand Braudel, *The Perspective of the World* (London: Collins, 1984).

The activities of Portugal in Kongo and Angola are reviewed in the relevant chapters of David Birmingham and Phyllis M. Martin, eds., *History of Central Africa*, Vol. I (London and New York: Longman, 1983), but see also Birmingham's *Trade and Conflict in Angola . . . 1483-1790* (Oxford: Clarendon, 1966), and Jan Vansina, *Kingdoms of the Savanna* (Madison: University of Wisconsin Press, 1966).

For early South African history there is Richard Elphick and Hermann Gileomee, eds., *The Shaping of South African Society, 1652-1820* (Middletown: Wesleyan University Press, 1989), which may be supplemented by two fine overall surveys: Leonard Thompson's *A History of South Africa* (New Haven: Yale University Press, 1990) and *South Africa: A Modern History* by T. R. H. Davenport, 3rd ed. (Toronto: University Press, 1987). South African slavery is dealt with in Robert Ross, *Cape of Torments: Slavery and Resistance in South Africa* (London: Routledge and Kegan Paul, 1983), and Nigel Worden, *Slavery in Dutch South Africa* (Cambridge: University Press, 1985).

During the past twenty years much historical work has been done on the slave trade. One may begin with Philip D. Curtin, *The Atlantic Slave Trade, A Census* (Madison: University of Wisconsin Press, 1969), but see also Paul E. Lovejoy, "The Volume of the Atlantic Slave Trade: A Synthesis," *Journal of African History*, vol. 23, no. 4, 1982 as well as Curtin's chapter in J. F. A. Ajayi and M. Crowder, eds., *History of West Africa*, vol. I, 3rd ed. (New York: Longman, 1985). For dissenting views consult J. E. Inikori, ed., *Forced Migration: The Impact of the Export Slave Trade on African Societies* (London: Hutchinson, 1982), and Inikori's "Measuring the Atlantic Slave Trade . . .," *Journal of African History*, vol. XVII, no. 2, 1976. J. D. Fage discusses the origins of slavery in West Africa in "Slaves and Society in West Africa," *Journal of African History*, vol. 21, no. 3, 1980, and Curtin offers an evocative collection of personal accounts dealing with the impact of the trade in *Africa Remembered* (Madison: University of Wisconsin Press, 1968). For an antidote to the slave trade numbers game see David Henige, "Measuring the Immeasurable: The Atlantic Slave Trade . . .," *Journal of African History*, vol. 27, no. 2, 1986. A recent attempt at synthesis is Lovejoy's *Transformations in Slavery* (Cambridge: University Press, 1983), with further refinements to be found in the *Journal of African History*, vol. 30, no. 1, 1989.

PART TWO
Revolutionary Africa

8

The Genesis of Modern Africa

The Age of Revolution

Mid-twentieth-century Africa was marked by great political, economic, and social change. A revolution of political freedom transformed colonial status into national sovereignty for some twoscore African states. Economic development, long demanded by subject peoples of their colonial masters, became a prime objective of independent African governments. At the same time, a major social revolution gained momentum, challenging an older way of life, questioning traditional values and customary relationships, and presenting Africa with many of the same advantages and the same problems which the process of modernization had already brought to other parts of the world.

Modern Africa—the Africa of national patriotism and national independence, of economic planning and aspirations for material prosperity—had its genesis during another revolutionary epoch in Africa's history. In the early decades of the nineteenth century, the peoples of Africa were also subjected to great and rapid change. Across much of the continent, the rhythm of more leisurely development was interrupted and altered, events were piled upon events in accelerated tempo, new directions were opened to African societies, and long-standing isolation from outside influences was irrevocably shattered. The thrust of new forces introduced Africa to its modern era, an era of which the present-day revolution of political independence and economic development is but the latest manifestation.

These new influences were various—in place, in substance, and in impact—but they tended to be related to events outside Africa, particularly events connected with the explosive expansion of a European presence into all corners

157

of the earth's continents. In most instances the early nineteenth-century European involvement in Africa was indirect, albeit important, but in West Africa it was immediate and portentous, introducing a new way of looking at the world which was greatly to influence the shaping of modern African societies.

In the early nineteenth century, at recently established coastal centers like Freetown or expanding older establishments such as Saint-Louis, there dwelt small numbers of Africans dedicated in greater or lesser degree to the metamorphosis of traditional African communities and institutions toward closer conformity with concepts and practices they had learned from the West. Their ideas had been influenced by Europeans—in part by English missionaries seeking to end the traffic in slaves, in part by the French extolling the democratic principles of their great Revolution of 1789—and they had become convinced of the wisdom for redesigning West African societies along the lines of the European cultures they had grown to admire. They absorbed and accepted Christianity along with the profit motive, and Western education hand in hand with Western dress. Though they often remained sympathetic toward certain elements of traditional African society, they were far more than casual adherents to European cultures. They saw their duty as West African leaders—clergy, merchants, and public officials—to encourage the spread of Christian-European ideals and institutions among neighbors and relatives and thereby to introduce revolutionary social and economic concepts which would bring about the modernization of West Africa. Although their drive for national independence was thwarted by late nineteenth-century European colonial occupation of Africa, their advocacy of modernization slowly spread its influence and led to a growing assimilation throughout West African societies of Western ideas and standards. These beliefs in turn provided the basis for the eventual surge toward independence and the determination to secure a better life that reached a climax in the two decades following the end of the Second World War.

Concurrent with these developments in West Africa, and far to the south, another revolutionary change was taking shape, partly caused by immigrants from Europe but mainly affected by basic mutations within indigenous African society. During the late eighteenth century, Boer farmers spreading out from the Dutch enclave at Cape Town had come into contact with the Xhosa vanguard of the Nguni-speaking people, and the hostility that was generated from this early confrontation of Boer and Bantu was to lead to the racial separation, exploitation, and antipathy that has characterized South African society down to the present day. The early Boer trekker had already developed racial antipathies based upon color during their relationship in the seventeenth and eighteenth centuries with Khoikhoi pastoralists and San hunters. Such attitudes were easily transferred to the Bantu. Utilizing their mastery of European technology the Boers extended their dominance over all black peoples in South Africa and by the opening of the twentieth century were on their way to converting the African from an independent pastoralist to a largely landless laborer, in the countryside as well as in town.

Prior to this eventuality, however, Bantu society had already begun to change radically, setting in motion political and ecological forces that profoundly affected African populations over vast areas in the southern, central, and eastern portions of the continent. The driving force was probably land hunger caused by population pressure among migrating cattle keepers, and the vehicle was the military outburst known as the Zulu *Mfecane*. The loosely knit Bantu societies, spread across the southern end of the African continent, were suddenly overturned and scattered by the concentrated onslaught of the disciplined, martial Zulu. Many groups were destroyed and many others absorbed by those nations that survived by adopting the centralized state and military tactics of the Zulu conquerors. The shock waves of the Mfecane spread outward from its nucleus on the eastern coast of South Africa, propelling group after group in a frenzied flight from extermination. Long-lived migrations drove people thousands of miles from their homelands, reorganized state systems, and established new nations of many diverse tribal remnants as far to the north as the swamps of the upper Zambezi or the plains south of Lake Tanganyika.

Indeed, the great migrations from the south were not the only elements of change that touched the high Tanganyikan plains during the first half of the nineteenth century. Before the arrival of these militant Ngoni invaders, the East African plateau had been slowly shedding an introspective preoccupation with village stock- and crop-raising through a growing trade with the Swahili entrepôts along the coast. By the opening of the nineteenth century, slaving had joined the traffic in ivory, and the expanding international demand for this merchandise had tempted groups of coastal Swahili and Arabs to adventure inland where they competed or cooperated with inland African traders. Over the years, increasing emphasis on slaving brought raiding and warfare which was further intensified by the introduction of firearms by the coastal traders. When the Ngoni appeared with their highly organized military state, they added their considerable measure to the spreading chaos of the interior plains. As in the south, the strong survived and the weak were annihilated, while new political and social configurations made their appearance. Some nations endured by adopting Ngoni military centralization, others by arming themselves with muskets. At the same time entirely novel groupings emerged, made up of adventurers and refugees torn loose by the troubled times from their more stable existence, and devoted to warfare and brigandage. Slaving visited death, destruction, and moral breakdown as did the great ivory hunts conducted by armed gangs led by Arab, Swahili, or African freebooters. Only in the northern plains and the region of the Great Lakes, politically stable and beyond the Ngoni reach, was the breakdown of order avoided.

If the nineteenth century put an end to East Africa's isolation from the outside world, it did little to prepare her people for the colonial occupation that was to follow. European influences were initially minor and indirect, the faintest indication of what was later to develop. Similarly, across the broad savanna of the sub-Saharan Sudan, Europe was a remote phenomenon to the farmers and herders caught in the great upheavals that altered their lives during this same era of change. Early in the nineteenth century accumulated social, political, economic, and ideological frustrations burst forth in Hausaland in the form of a jihad which created unity from diversity and placed the indelible mark of Islam on a vast area roughly coincident with the northern regions of Nigeria. It seems likely that this jihad was part of a spreading expression of malaise throughout a Muslim world dismayed by the pretensions of a renascent West; in any event, it was followed by other similar risings to the west and the east which brought religious ferment and political revolution to the vast savanna from the Senegal to the Nile. New states came into existence at the urging of new leaders, a millennial figure of great influence arose in the Egyptian Sudan, and the Islamic faith, civilization, and way of life at last gained the allegiance of the vast savanna it had been seeking for centuries.

One other area of early nineteenth-century ferment remains—the Nile Valley of Egypt. Here too the Muslim world was under pressure from Christian Europe, and here Africa made dramatic and effective response.

Muhammad Ali and the Modernization of Egypt

In Egypt, since the mid-thirteenth century, the Nile Valley *fellahin*, or peasants, had forfeited liberty in exchange for the doubtful security and the certain tyranny provided by their Mamluk overlords. The Mamluks, a special caste of Turkish and other Asian slaves, had long formed an important element within the armies of the Muslim Caliphate, their growing strength culminating in the middle of the thirteenth century when the Mamluks in Cairo seized power, and thus established themselves as Egypt's *de facto* rulers for the next five centuries. For the Egyptian farmer the long-lived Mamluk regime was an agony compounded of plague, famine, civil war, and the tax collector's whip. In 1517 Egypt became part of the Ottoman Empire, but this event had little long-range effect on Mamluk rule which eventually reasserted its oppressive ways much as before. The Mamluks held the land under a feudal system designed for maximum exploitation, and as their hold on the country became progressively more corrupt and inefficient, the lot of the peasant grew correspondingly critical. By the latter part of the eighteenth century great tracts of land were going out of cultivation for lack of proper irrigation as two and one-half million people incongruously scratched for the barest subsistence in this potentially rich earth.

In July 1798, Napoleon landed an army in Egypt in a move designed to sever Britain's link to India. As imperial strategy it was well conceived but the execution was faulty, and the French were gone in less than three years, forced out by British arms and the complexities of governing a prostrate and blighted people. For France and Britain it was but an incident in their protracted struggle for domination of the seas. For Egypt it was the cannon shot that ended her weary centuries of stagnation and torpor. To be sure, it did not put an end to Egypt's ordeal of tyranny and oppression at the hands of foreign masters, for practical independence was not to come for another century and a half. It did, however, introduce an age of political stability during which peasant productivity was reestablished; more than that, it forced the Egyptians out of the medieval into the modern world.

The instrument of this revolution was Muhammad Ali. A professional soldier who arrived in Egypt with a troop of Albanian cavalry in support of the resistance mounted by the Ottomans against the Napoleonic invasion, Muhammad Ali remained after the French had departed, eventually to become the founder of yet another dynasty of foreign princes. By 1805 he had survived a complex power struggle involving several Turkish factions and the Mamluks, to emerge as the most powerful leader in the land. The following year the reluctant sultan in Istanbul was obliged to name Muhammad Ali Pasha as his viceroy or governor in Egypt. In 1811 Ali eliminated the Mamluks forever, slaughtering them in an ambush which left him without challenge to his plans to revive Egypt's economy and rebuild her political fortunes.

Personal power as a road to personal wealth was the goal of Muhammad Ali, who has been characterized essentially as a merchant. The elimination of the Mamluks brought him control over Egypt, and a strong renascent Egypt was a stepping stone to riches and preeminence in the Middle East. The French occupation, though brief and uncertain, had amply demonstrated Western technological superiority, particularly in its military manifestations; hence, Muhammad Ali set about with the aid of French technicians and military experts to reorganize his army and to create an officer corps on Western lines. Military instruction, moreover, suggested reforms of a broader educational perspective and led severally to the dispatching of young Egyptians for study abroad, the establishment of technical institutes in Egypt, and a massive program of translation into Arabic of the many essential European texts.

These were expensive innovations, but they were an investment essential to enhanced public revenue. In turn, revenue compelled a thorough rehabilitation of Egypt's obsolete economy, replacing subsistence cultivation with a modernized system based upon cash crop production and local industry. Egypt's traditional agriculture relied upon the periodic overflow of the Nile into her floodplain where the precious water was captured through an arrangement of dikes, and the fields revitalized with annual deposits of rich alluvial soil. Nevertheless, frequent floods and drought could not be controlled by such archaic techniques which, in addition, supported only one annual crop during the high-water period.

By the early nineteenth century the expanding industry of Europe was already consuming vast quantities of cotton—between 1800 and 1830 Britain's yearly imports rose from fifty million to three hundred million pounds—and Egyptian soil with proper irrigation was ideally suited to cotton culture. With the assistance of European hydraulic engineers, Muhammad Ali installed a network of deep-cut canals, adding steam-driven pumps to bring the river water to the fields during the dry summer months. The result was two annual crops and a vast increase of cultivable acreage. High-quality long-staple cotton came in time to dominate Egyptian exports while other cash crops, notably sugar, tobacco, and indigo, were produced, as well as summer rice and corn to supplement the traditional yields of winter wheat and barley.

Increasing food and cash crop production was not to be wasted on the Egyptian peasant, however, for all increases in revenue were earmarked for economic and military development. A surprisingly modern system of state capitalism emerged. First of all, land was nationalized with the understanding that peasants, though nominally tenants, would be virtual owners of their tracts as long as they kept up their tax payments. This was no mean task, for taxes were heavy and were supplemented by other burdens—forced labor requisitions for public works such as canals and dams, and a system of government monopolies for basic crops like cotton, tobacco, or sugar, whereby the state bought each year's output at a minimum rate and sold it on the world market for a substantial profit. Moreover, vast areas were brought back into cultivation and large tracts were parceled out to influential citizens including numerous members of Ali's own family.

Muhammad Ali's techniques brought a dramatic increase in national resources. Between 1800 and 1850 the population almost doubled while acreage increased from 3.2 to 4.15 million. Over the same period government revenue rose almost four times with exports and imports increasing tenfold. Muhammad Ali used these funds to pay for his increasingly efficient army and his extensive educational and industrial reforms—schools, textile mills, shipyards, an iron foundry, and other manufacturing establishments created and operated by government, as well as the large numbers of foreign technicians imported to manage the complex machinery of Egypt's new economy. It was an expensive but important principle, for the absence of foreign loans and concessions also meant the absence of foreign economic and political interference; failure to grasp this essential fact was later to plague the reign of Ismail, Muhammad Ali's grandson, and lead to eventual European occupation and loss of independence for Egypt.

The long-suffering, hard-working fellahin contributed to Muhammad Ali's success in another important respect when converted into line soldiers for the renascent Egyptian armies. An early experiment with Sudanese slaves proving impracticable, the governor turned to his peasants, and soon his French instructors had trained a modern army along Western lines which was the most powerful in the Middle East. For a time this force was deployed in support of Muhammad Ali's Ottoman masters, but eventually Turk and Egyptian came into conflict, and it soon became evident that the decaying power at Istanbul was no match for the Egyptian pasha who appeared ready and able to take the Caliphate and establish himself as sultan of the Ottoman Empire.

Muhammad Ali's very success had now become an embarrassment. His rising predominance in the Middle East troubled the British who preferred a weak and responsive Turkish power in control of the routes to India and the Far East. At home his growing industrial establishment protected by tariffs and sustained by a stable currency and up-to-date marketing methods vexed European merchants who sought free access to the Egyptian market for their own manufactured products. In the end it was the West, the source of Muhammad Ali's strength, that destroyed him. In 1838 Britain obtained the right of virtual free trade within the Ottoman dominions, and three years later the Treaty of London forced Muhammad Ali to conform—to abolish his protective tariffs and sharply reduce the size of his army. His nascent industrialization thus scuttled and his military force emasculated, the aging viceroy could no longer maintain his interest in economic reform, and most of his programs, particularly in education and industry, were permitted to lapse during the years preceding his death in 1848. Indeed, it is probable that some relaxation would have been necessary in any case for, after centuries of stagnation, the burdens of a rapid, forced modernization—a costly army, an initially inefficient industry, and an agricultural revolution that yet denied its benefits to the farmer—were probably more than the peasantry and the ancient land could have endured indefinitely.

Whatever its deficiencies, Muhammad Ali's program effected vast and permanent changes in Egypt. There was a fundamental shift away from subsistence farming to the much more productive cash crop agriculture which so greatly shaped the country's economic future. Although early industrialization failed and the educational innovations for the most part did not survive their founder, the ideas they engendered remained and grew. Egyptian students returning from Europe as well as Western teachers and technicians in Egypt stressed the virtues of Western civilization, while Muhammad Ali's extensive translation program not only introduced Western scientific and technical knowledge to the Muslim world but also enriched Arabic literature with new approaches to law, politics, history, and literary expression. Equally important was the emergence of the Egyptian civil servant, a European-educated bureaucrat whose stake in the survival of an Egyptian nation contained the seed of nationalism, yet who maintained the conviction that Egypt's progress was closely linked with Westernization. Perhaps Muhammad Ali's greatest shortcoming was his failure to see need for a modernized, revitalized Islam to accompany and guide technical and economic modernization along lines acceptable in the Muslim world. Traditional Islamic thought and practice was left to continue, unchanged, resentful, and suspicious, and its reconciliation with Western technical superiority still remains a major problem of Muslim leadership in the Middle East today.

Muhammad Ali's revolution of modernization cast a long shadow forward. No less important to the shaping of modern Africa were those other early nineteenth-century phenomena—the jihads of the sub-Saharan Sudan, the population explosions in South Africa, the intrusion and dissemination of the tenets of Western civilization in West Africa, and the opening of East Africa to international commerce. It is now necessary that each of these developments be examined in detail through the chapters that follow.

Suggestions for Further Reading

For Muhammad Ali and his modernization program the most recent studies are Afaf L. Marsot, *Egypt in the Reign of Muhammad Ali* (Cambridge: University Press, 1984), and F. Robert Hunter, *Egypt Under the Khedives, 1805-1879* (Pittsburgh: University Press, 1984). See also P. J. Vatikiotis, *The History of Egypt*, 3rd ed. (Baltimore: Johns Hopkins Press, 1986), as well as the older Helen A. B. Rivlin, *The Agricultural Policy of Muhammad Ali in Egypt* (Cambridge, MA: Harvard University Press, 1961; reprinted 1967).

9

Religion and Empire in Western and Central Sudan

Prelude to the Great Jihads of the Nineteenth Century

The collapse of Songhai at the close of the sixteenth century marked the end of an era in the western Sudan. For the next two hundred years political centralization bowed before particularism, while Islam appeared to be in check, both on the countryside and in the courts of kings. The invading Moroccans had strength only to destroy Songhai, and the state they substituted soon found itself defending a shrinking sovereignty along the Niger. By the eighteenth century their center of Timbuktu had come under attack by groups of Berber and Tuareg, the latter eventually occupying the city and subjecting the *arma*, as were called the descendants of the original Moroccan invaders. To the east the Hausa states continued divided and discordant while Bornu was in decline, the victim of external pressure and the dry rot of ineffective leadership. Only along the upper Niger did a degree of stability emerge during the eighteenth century in the military oligarchies of the Bambara states, Segu and Kaarta, while to the southeast in the Volta watershed, the Mossi kingdoms— Wagadugu, Yatenga, and others—still flourished in their traditional strength.

Political uncertainty does not appear to have greatly impeded commerce, either trans-Saharan or regional, but its effect on the development of Islam is more difficult to assess. It has been said that Islam suffered a positive decline after the breakup of Songhai. Recent research does not sustain such a generalization, however. Across the plains, the tillers of the soil and the herders of their stock still worshipped the old gods, while rulers, as always, kept close ties with those practices and traditions that were so often the sources of their legitimacy. At the same time there were many converts to Islam in the towns where a commerce of ideas accompanied the trade of material merchandise. In new states like Segu or Masina, moreover, chiefly clans came under Muslim influence, and kings everywhere continued to find practical assistance in the advice and support of Muslim clerics and merchants as had been the case since the days of ancient Ghana.

Thus an ambivalence developed over the presence of Islam with factors that both encouraged and combatted proselytization. Examples abound. The founder of Segu built his kingdom with the aid of both traditional Bambara custom and Muslim adviser. Despite the authority of indigenous religion, an eighteenth century Mossi ruler of Mamprussi is said to have encouraged Muslim settlement in his realm. Hausa monarchs were well known advocates of traditional as well as Islamic practice, and by the seventeenth century Islam had made important advances within a general Hausa population still devoted to old time worship. Even the long-lived Muslim state of Bornu countenanced certain indigenous customs unsanctioned by Islamic law, a transgression that would eventually be utilized to justify the nineteenth century Fulani jihad against Bornu.

By the eighteenth century, therefore, Islam was making headway, but in a slow and unspectacular fashion that gave little hint of the great religious upheavals that were to follow in the next century. Yet the movement held explosive elements within itself, forces that were to combine with changing social and economic conditions to bring the jihads and mass conversions that ensued.

The reasons were various. First of all, there was a variety of conflicting clerical groups and individuals, some in the cities, others living on the countryside. Generally, the religious scholars of the towns were advisers to kings and thus defenders of the political status quo. Those living in the country, however, led lives, either as self-contained religious communities or as itinerant reformers intent upon conversion or the correction of apparently improper, inexact Muslim practice.

The protestations of these reforming clerics fell upon receptive ears among a general population of pastoralists and farmers. In Hausaland the cattle keepers were for the most part Fulani who chafed over what they regarded as repressive taxation while growing restive as their grazing grounds were hemmed in by competing Tuareg and other herders. The basic cause was ecological, that is, Africa's chronic tribulation of insufficient or capricious rainfall. Severe droughts are known to have taken place during the eighteenth century, especially between 1738 and 1756. This recurrent African affliction of water shortage had predictable results. Militant pastoralists, moving down from the desert and sahel, invaded already occupied grasslands and farming areas, destroying their economies and disrupting trade. Some authorities suggest that Fulani religious unrest in Bornu at the end of the eighteenth century was due as much to land shortage as theological scruples, a condition that might equally have applied to Hausaland. Thus the jihads, for all their clearly religious impulse, may be seen in a larger context of economic dislocation.

There was comparable discontent among the predominantly Hausa farmers. Subsistence cultivation was giving way to cash crop production with consequent economic dislocation, and the traditional family unit had grown unstable as sons departed the households of their fathers and began to strike out on their own. In town, moreover, there were also unsettling influences, largely between Muslims and the Hausa nobility over the exact role of religion in governance. These factors created ferment, not so much an expression of despair as a desire for clear guidelines to direct a new and changing society.

The main upheavals began in Hausaland as the nineteenth century dawned, but other, less far-reaching, jihads had already taken place, particularly in the Futa Jalon highlands of modern Guinea and the Futa Toro that bordered south along the Senegal River. Small in scale compared with what was to follow, these jihads were also limited essentially to disputes among ruling groups of Fulani, but the net result in each case was the establishment of the theocratic Muslim state, hence the successful fulfillment of the principle of jihad.

In Hausaland the holy war was played out on a much larger stage with more profound sociological as well as religious consequences; yet despite its scale, the Sokoto jihad, as it came to be called, was largely the creation of a single individual, the *Shehu*, or sheikh, Usuman dan Fodio.

Usuman dan Fodio and the Sokoto Jihad*

Usuman dan Fodio was by birth, education, and temperament the embodiment of a Muslim teacher and scholar. Born in the Hausa kingdom of Gobir in 1754, he was a member of the Fulani Torodbe clan of professional clerics and an adherent of the Qadiriyya brotherhood, one of the number of religious orders that practiced the cult of *sufism*, or saint worship. The Qadiriyya, as with similar orders, followed the precepts of a *sufi*, observing a *tariqa*, or

*Sudanese States and the Nineteenth-century Jihads

Sokoto	Kanem-Bornu	Masina
Shehu Usuman dan Fodio	*Shehu* al-Kanemi	*Seku* Ahmadu Lobbo
b. 1754, d. 1817	d. 1837	b.c. 1775, d. 1844
Muhammad Bello	*Shehu* Umar (1837-1881)	*Seku* Ahmadu II d. 1852
Sultan of Sokoto		*Seku* Ahmadu III d. 1862
(1817-1837)		

Mandinka Empire	*Tokolor Empire*	
Samori b.c. 1830, d. 1900	*al-Hajj* Umar b.c. 1794,	
	d. 1864	
	Ahmadu b.c. 1835,	
	d. 1898	

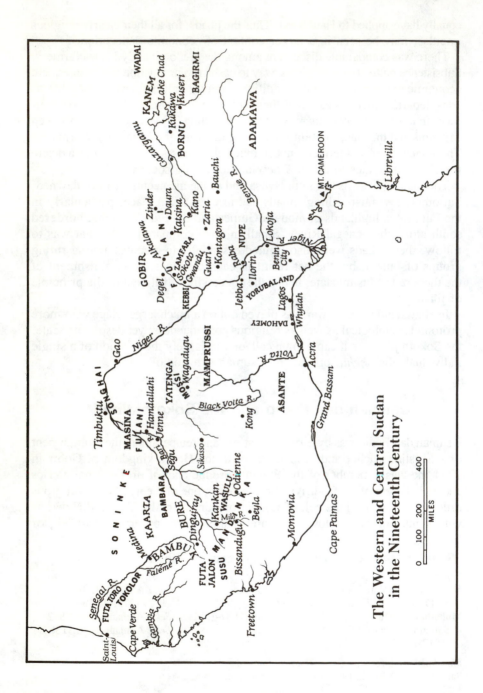

The Western and Central Sudan in the Nineteenth Century

path, of special litanies and other activities prescribed by the saint himself. There were many Qadiriyya followers in the western Sudan, including the Kunta Arabo-Berbers, pastoralists who dwelt north of the Niger, and the ubiquitous Dyula, Mandinka merchants presiding over their far-flung trading networks. Usuman's Qadiriyya connections were conventional enough, therefore, but he differed from many other scholars both in his erudition and his determination to travel widely in the countryside in order to spread not only knowledge of Islam but the precise manner in which the holy path was to be followed.

Throughout a long apprenticeship, Usuman had gained close acquaintance with Quranic knowledge and Muslim law. He came to understand that the Quranic injunction, "enjoining the right and forbidding the wrong" could be achieved only through an intimate awareness of the precise requirement of Islam; hence his emphasis on travel and teaching and his use of vernacular verse to ease the learning process for illiterate Fulani herders and Hausa farmers.

By the time he was twenty Usuman dan Fodio had begun to teach at Degel, his home in Gobir, and soon he was traveling and preaching extensively, the burden of his message being the need to end misgovernment and unsanctioned religious practice and to be guided by the *Sharia*, the law of Islam. In addition to licentiousness and lust, Usuman declared, the rulers of Hausaland were corrupt and sacrilegious, persecuting the true believers and debasing Muslim rites with pagan ceremonies. Over the years Usuman's persuasiveness brought a growing number of followers to Degel and finally gained him access to Bawa, the sultan of Gobir, whom he attempted to instruct in the true path of God. "None was his equal," his son, Muhammad Bello, was later to attest. "People trusted him and flocked to him. . . . He instructed the *ulama* [learned men], and raised the banner of religion . . . He spread knowledge and dispelled perplexity. . . . Revered by both great and small, he was a reformer at the head of this generation."

Fame brought power which in turn engendered fear. Usuman's demand for reform added to his adherents in Gobir as well as in adjacent Zamfara and Kebbi, and his copious writings enhanced his reputation still further. Religious reform, however, meant social reform and a direct threat to the established authorities, for their rule was based in no small part on their support of traditional Hausa social custom and religious practice. Sultan Bawa of Gobir allegedly planned to assassinate the Shehu in 1789, but instead of carrying out the threat, granted important religious and economic concessions at Usuman's insistence, thereby creating a semi-autonomous Muslim "state" within Gobir. Slowly circumstances moved on to extremity. By 1795 the idea of jihad had formed in the Shehu's mind and that same year the reigning sultan, Nafata, repealed many of Bawa's concessions, for example, further conversions to Islam and the wearing of turban and veil, those distinctive symbols of Usuman's people. Usuman countered by urging his followers to arm themselves, a virtual declaration of independence. When Yunfa succeeded his father, Nafata, in 1802, the final break came quickly, for the new sultan, though a former pupil of the Shehu, was determined to break the latter's power. In 1804, Yunfa attacked Abd al-Salam, a non-Fulani supporter of Usuman, killing and capturing many of his followers. To this aggression, the Shehu responded by ordering his people to emigrate from Gobir, and with this *hijra* the ultimate break had come. Only jihad could follow—war against the infidel.

After some initial setbacks, the forces of Usuman proceeded to conquer the Hausa states within a few short years. The Shehu provided the prestige of his spiritual leadership but left military affairs in the hands of his brother, Abdullahi, and his son, Muhammad Bello, while numerous Fulani leaders from points in Hausaland received flags from Usuman as army commanders charged with military activities in their several areas. Much of Kebbi was occupied in 1805 and the Fulani war camp was established at Gwandu. A year later Zaria was taken without a struggle and in 1807 both Kano and Katsina fell. In 1808 several armies converged on Alkalawa, capital of Gobir, and in the ensuing battle Yunfa was defeated and killed. This ended effective resistance in Hausaland which eventually was divided into two regions— Gwandu under the administration of Abdullahi and Sokoto under Bello.

By this time, although the jihad was far from finished, its character had already been substantially altered. Usuman and his pious followers were motivated from the first by a desire to achieve purity of religious devotion, a thoroughgoing social reform, and the renascence of Islamic culture in the Sudan. In this respect their purpose lay close to the substance of other roughly contemporary reformist movements in the Muslim world, for example, the Mahdiyya in the eastern Sudan and the Sanusiyya of Cyrenaica. The Sokoto jihad, however, required soldiers as well as scholars and in any event tended to attract individuals with something less than the Shehu's religious zeal. Fulani solidarity rallied many Fulani pagans to the cause, and others came, attracted by the prospect of personal gain. Gradually the jihad assumed a more secular character in which a Fulani aristocracy replaced Hausa kings and courts and the idea of a Fulani empire eclipsed the universalist concept of a better world under Islam. Needless slaughter and plunder attending most Fulani victories, persecution of Hausa by Fulani forces, and the appointment of Fulani to virtually all important posts alienated the Hausa population and sharpened the point of Fulani imperialism.

With the collapse of Hausa resistance the force of the jihad swung eastward to Bornu where some small territorial gains were made but where the Fulani were effectively checked by 1812 through the energy and ability of al-Kanemi, the leader of the Kanembu nomads from the Lake Chad area. In 1812 the Shehu retired from all active participation in government and when he died five years later, the leadership of the empire devolved on Muhammad Bello, Abdullahi somewhat reluctantly stepping aside. Conquest continued, now moving southward and eastward, and eventually extended as far as Adamawa in the east, and Nupe and Yorubaland to the south where, in the last instance, diplomacy rather than force of arms effected an occupation of the Yoruba town of Ilorin. When Muhammad Bello died in 1837 he was ruler of a territory roughly equivalent to what later became the northern region of Nigeria—a Fulani empire of Muslim emirates, or provinces, in Hausaland and beyond.

To a considerable extent the empire was the work of Bello. During the early years of the jihad he had supported his father's spiritual leadership with essential military persuasion, and when he succeeded to power as sultan of Sokoto, he continued active campaigning, dispatching almost fifty expeditions during his reign to subdue dissidents or to extend the realm of Islam farther into pagan territory. Yet Muhammad Bello ruled by persuasion as well as by force. A Muslim scholar scarcely less brilliant than Usuman, he found time to produce numerous tracts on science, law, morals, history, or Islamic doctrine in which he sought to explain the objectives and tactics of the revolution. As an administrator he attempted to introduce government according to the precepts of the Sharia, frequently taking a personal hand in provincial affairs, checking the excesses of his troops in conquered territory, restraining corruption, and intervening in the decisions of his magistrates in the interests of justice. Sokoto became a center where Islamic scholars flourished, and the precepts of the jihad were from there broadcast throughout the Sudan.

Muhammad Bello's many campaigns reflected a degree of restiveness with Fulani rule which continued after his death; nonetheless, the empire did not collapse and was intact when occupied by the British at the beginning of the twentieth century. This cohesiveness is remarkable not only in view of the traditional divisiveness of Hausaland but also in the fact that the emirates that succeeded the old Hausa kingdoms, although essentially political states, were bound to Sokoto primarily by religious allegiance. Allegiance was relative, however. Whereas in Zaria, Kano, or Bauchi there was peace in the land, and in Adamawa and Ilorin the Fulani were on the offensive, in other regions outbreaks were chronic. In Nupe and Guari and again in Gobir and Kebbi the idea of independence from Fulani rule was never abandoned and unrest continued; more generally the Fulani success evoked a revival of Hausa language and culture while traditional governmental administration survived largely undisturbed by an overlay of Fulani, Muslim procedure.

The main feature of the Sokoto jihad, therefore, came to be the political, cultural, and religious unity of Hausaland, although a secondary consequence was the renascence of the traditional commerce of the Sudan. From the capital city of Sokoto, built by Muhammad Bello, to peripheral communities like Raba in Nupe, there was evidence of the increasing commercial exchange that effective policing could provide. The English explorer, Hugh Clapperton, remarked in 1823 that Sokoto trade, though modest, included exports of local brass, pewter, and cloth, while among imports were spices, perfume, and beads from Tripoli and Ghadames, kola nuts from Asante, and Tuareg salt exchanged for local corn. Ten years later, Macgregor Laird, visiting Raba, spoke enthusiastically of the horses, donkeys, and raw silk brought from North Africa by Arab traders, while at mid-century Heinrich Barth made frequent note of this rising trade throughout Hausaland.

For Barth, the major emporium was Kano, by reason of her combination of household industry and commerce. Various cloths were woven in the baked-mud compounds and dyed in the municipal vats to be shipped off to consumers near and far—to the desert Tuareg for their veiling, to Timbuktu where Kano cloth was esteemed for its fineness, to Adamawa where its only competitor was nakedness, and to far-off Arguin Island on the Atlantic. Further, there were leather products, chiefly sandals and tanned hides much fancied in North Africa, as well as unprocessed goods including kola nuts, and, of course, slaves.

Slaves were a major element of the economy within the Fulani empire both as an item of exchange and a source of agricultural labor. The demand in the great markets such as Kano and Katsina led to the depopulation of territories on the periphery of the empire where raiding armies such as those of Raba were long in the habit of swooping down on helpless villages, and the infamous Ibrahim Nagwamatse, emir of Kontagora, ended his late nineteenth-century career of conquest and pillage with the taunting, "I shall die with a slave in my mouth." In Adamawa, Barth reported many private individuals with over one thousand slaves, while provincial governors controlled many times more, most engaged in cultivation. At Kano toward the end of the century, domestic slavery was common and slaves of various tribal origins were an important element in the economic life of the community as artisans, merchants, and cultivators as well as integral members of their masters' families. Others who came to Kano were less fortunate, for many were marched off along the killing desert tracks to the markets of Ghat and the Fezzan.

Seku Ahmadu in Masina

Usuman dan Fodio and his followers sought reform through a return to the principles that obtained in the days of the Prophet and the early Caliphates. In this sense the movement was conservative, attempting to reach back to earlier orthodoxy as a model for the present and future. The widespread conversions which took place among the Hausa and neighboring people therefore were to an established Islamic practice; for example, strict reference to the precepts of classic law, adherence to the Qadiriyya way long familiar in the Sudan, or a penchant for regarding the jihad as a latter-day parallel to the reforms of Songhai's Askia Muhammad Toure and his great scholarly adviser, al-Maghili. Circumstance eventually made the Sokoto empire much less than a thoroughgoing Islamic theocracy, nor was it nearly as centralized politically as the Muslim state that for a time held sway west of Hausaland, in Masina lying upstream from Timbuktu along the inland delta of the Niger.

Conditions in Masina in the early nineteenth century resembled those of Hausaland. There was a similar mixture of true believers and infidels—of Muslim Fulani and pagan pastoral Fulani, of Soninke, Songhai, and Kunta, long converted, poised against animist Bambara. The state of Masina was controlled by Fulani overlords, and the government was pagan in practice although the ruling *ardo* of Masina was in fact a Muslim. Further complications existed in that Masina, a Muslim state, was the vassal of pagan Segu, while the trading center of Jenne, harboring numerous Muslim factions, was essentially autonomous.

As in the case of Hausaland, such an uneasy equilibrium of antipathetical forces invited disruption and discord which came in 1818 in the form of a jihad led by Seku Ahmadu Lobbo, member of a minor clan of Fulani scholars. The seku, or chief, who was born about 1775, was educated in the traditional Muslim manner and according to the precepts of the Qadiriyya brotherhood, although his scholarly standing never approached the distinction of Usuman dan Fodio. Ahmadu visited Hausaland about 1805 in time to observe the early stages of the Sokoto jihad from which he drew considerable inspiration for his subsequent activities in Masina. Returning home, he established himself as a teacher and gathered a following, then ran afoul of the ardo of Masina when one of his students killed the ardo's son. In seeking to chastise Ahmadu, the ardo asked for the aid of the pagan Bambara king of Segu, and this event triggered the classic response of hijra to a new headquarters established at Hamdallahi, followed by jihad which defeated the Bambara, overthrew the ardo, and led to the creation of an Islamic state with Hamdallahi as its capital. A number of principalities were overrun, Jenne taken, and a measure of control gained in Timbuktu.

The Masina state of Seku Ahmadu ran along the Niger roughly from Jenne to Timbuktu, bordered by Kaarta and Segu to the southwest and the Mossi to the southeast. Much smaller than the Sokoto empire, it was more easily administered by the rigorous regime established by Ahmadu. A grand council of forty, of which Ahmadu was the leading member, dealt with all matters of government, including provincial administration, taxation, and military and diplomatic affairs. Noted more for their piety than their scholarship, Ahmadu and his ministers strongly opposed the use of spirits or tobacco, as well as dancing, prohibitions that ultimately proved vexing to their more worldly converts, particularly in the urban centers. With the death of Ahmadu in 1844, Timbuktu, for example, revolted and succeeded partially in easing the control of her internal affairs.

The disenchantment of the Timbuktu Muslims reflected the broad range of social and political complexities in the Masina area which had given rise to the movement of Seku Ahmadu in the first place. There were the differences between pagan and true believer, both within the Fulani community and between the Fulani and others. There were the rivalries among Fulani clans, and those between the Fulani and other people. There were the ambivalent relations between Fulani subjects and Bambara suzerains. Finally there were the conflicting views of Islam separating the puritan reformer and the cosmopolites of the trading centers.

This last dispute may have been decisive in the eventual fall of Masina. Initially Ahmadu seems to have aimed for an Islamic community that would offer rule of law for all, not merely for a dominant Fulani aristocracy. Large numbers of conversions were indeed obtained, particularly among the pastoral Fulani, but this support tended to change the nature of the jihad from broad egalitarian objectives to a movement propelled more by Fulani tribal unity.

It also embraced converts who did not share the puritanism of Ahmadu's more zealous followers. Ahmadu was able to hold his various factions together through astute leadership, but after his death schisms developed, among others, between the puritans and those newer adherents who chafed under what they regarded as excessive austerities. This proved to be a fatal rift that assisted the armies of al-Hajj Umar when he successfully invaded Masina in 1862. Thus when Masina fell, its demise was marked both by internal stresses and a holy war by Muslim against other professed true believers.

The Jihad of *Al-Hajj* Umar

Seku Ahmadu designated his son, Ahmadu II, as successor, and Ahmadu in turn was succeeded by his son, Ahmadu III, in 1852. It was during the reign of Ahmadu III that Masina ran afoul of the third great jihad of the western Sudan, that of al-Hajj Umar (b. c. 1794, d. 1864), the Tokolor warrior from Futa Toro.

The conquest of Masina was the culmination of developments long unfolding. Born into a scholarly family, Umar, like Usuman and Seku Ahmadu, was given a sound Muslim education, then in his early manhood he made an extended pilgrimage to Mecca, a journey of great consequence personally and to the subsequent history of Islam in the western Sudan. Pausing in Egypt, Umar met the scholars of the Azhar mosque in Cairo and doubtless observed the efforts of Muhammad Ali to strengthen the international position of his African Muslim state. In Arabia, the opportunity to visit the holy places would have played its part, while Umar must also have made note of the Wahabiyya activists in their reformist movement.

Of great significance while at Mecca, moreover, was Umar's designation as *khalifa*, or deputy, to al-Tijani, founder of the Tijaniyya sufist order. Umar had already become an enthusiastic supporter of Tijani doctrine which was disciplined and puritanical in spirit, strongly missionary in impulse, and thoroughly persuaded of the moral superiority of all Tijani adherents over the members of other brotherhoods. The way to God, argued the new message, need not be limited to an intellectual aristocracy as with the Qadiriyya. Spiritual salvation could be attained by anyone capable of the highest moral stability, a state of mind that was revealed by indifference to material pleasures such as tobacco, alcohol, or an excess of wives beyond the Quranic sanction. Such direct, unambiguous teaching penetrated deeply into the mind of Umar, and it was to play a central role in the subsequent organization and spread of his movement. As khalifa, Umar was authorized to reform the western Sudan, a sanction, when combined with Umar's intense commitment to Tijani doctrine, that made his movement the most imperialistic of the nineteenth century jihads.

Returning home from Arabia, Umar paused at Bornu long enough to marry into the ruling family, then stopped at the court of Muhammad Bello where he remained several years, taking one of Bello's daughters as wife. At Sokoto Umar gathered Tijani adherents, antagonizing the Qadiriyya leadership with his insistence on the primacy of Tijani doctrine and leadership. On Bello's death Umar was forced to move on, traveling to Masina where he stayed briefly, again stirring up local theological differences before passing on to Futa Jalon. There he paused for nine years, absorbed in the task of attracting and arming a following grounded in Tijani doctrine, a provocative activity that once again aroused uneasiness among local rulers. If Umar's doctrine was novel, so too was his armament, for, unlike other Muslim religious leaders, he equipped his *talaba*, or disciples, with firearms obtained on the West African coast. In 1848 he performed the hijra to Dinguiray, a military base from which he launched his jihad in 1852.

Early successes led to control of several Bambara and Mandinka states in the upper Niger and Senegal basins and brought Umar to Futa Toro where he already had much support among his Tokolor countrymen, but where he also encountered French commercial interests on the Senegal River. This was the first time one of the Sudanic jihads had confronted a European power, yet it seems probable that Umar's holy war was at this stage concerned only with extending his Tijani empire at the expense of Muslim and pagan African states rather than with an attack on the infidel Europeans. The French, however, were nervous and rebuffed Umar's suggested cooperation which would have given him a free hand to take control of the Futa while gaining him access to arms through the Senegalese entrepôt at Saint-Louis. Umar's reaction to French mistrust was first an attack on river traders, possibly in quest of the arms withheld, and then a siege of the river fort at Medina where he was repulsed in 1857 in a brilliant defense by the Saint-Louis mulatto commander, Paul Holle.

Umar had already begun operations against the Bambara of Kaarta and occupied their capital in 1854. He now turned his full attention eastward and defeated Segu in 1861, thus placing himself in direct confrontation to his former hosts and coreligionists, the Fulani rulers in Masina. Ahmadu III of Masina had already been greatly disturbed by the move against Segu and had persuaded her king to embrace Islam and then, unsuccessfully, had come to her support. Such an expedient conversion was no protection against the full flood of Umar's jihad which engulfed Masina in 1862, perhaps aided by local clerics, Tijaniyya converts disaffected by what they perceived as moral corruption and unsanctioned Islamic practice on the part of the ruling regime. Umar justified his move, which paralleled the Sokoto thrust at Bornu a half-century earlier, on the grounds that Ahmadu, like al-Kanemi, had allied with an infidel against a true believer and thereby had committed apostasy.

Thus Masina was absorbed by the Tokolor empire of al-Hajj Umar, but this height of success was also the point of undoing for the great conqueror, who lost his life in 1864 during an uprising at Masina. Umar's rule was carried on with great difficulty by his son, Ahmadu, who lacked his father's prestige and could control neither the partisan separatism of local people nor the independence of his own Tokolor governors. Nevertheless his political skill held the empire together at least in name until it was finally subdued by French arms many years later, the final blow coming in 1893.

The influence of Umar's conquests transcended the life of his political empire. Certainly he effected no permanent cohesion in the Sudan as the postmortem stresses within his realm amply demonstrated. Nonetheless, he did bring about widespread conversions to Islam, while the preeminence that the Tijaniyya brotherhood came to have throughout West Africa was largely traceable to his influence. Even in Hausaland the new movement has gradually come to supersede the Qadiriyya in a development that had its beginning in the visit al-Hajj Umar paid to Sokoto in the 1830s.

Al-Kanemi and His Successors in Bornu

The great jihads of the nineteenth century appeared to impose a vast Islamic unity throughout the western Sudan, but in fact relations between the major Muslim states were often seriously strained. The politics of empire did not always coincide with theological objectives, nor did worldly leadership necessarily agree with the aspirations of the more spiritually minded. Over the years Muslim Masina and Muslim Sokoto harbored small mutual esteem, while Masina found much political, if not spiritual, comfort in close relations with the pagan Bambara of Segu. For his part the religious reformer, al-Hajj Umar, showed no enthusiasm for fighting the infidel French but fell on his coreligionists of Masina with a gusto more appropriately reserved for the unbeliever. Similarly, the Fulani of Sokoto directed one of the major onslaughts of their jihad at the Muslims of Bornu, a gross perversion of the holy war, the defenders were quick to point out.

By the opening of the nineteenth century, Bornu had lost most of the strength inherited from the days of her great mai, Idris Aloma. Her most recent kings had proved effete, her administration overelaborate, and her armies ineffective. Former vassals such as Kano, Zaria, Daura, and Katsina no longer gave more than nominal allegiance, while Fulani dwelling within the borders of Bornu were becoming restive, stimulated by the revivalism of their cousins to the

Basutoland cattle range

WHO photo by D. Henrioud

People of Africa

Maasai herds and herders

Ethiopian farmland

Fishing canoes off Elmina Castle, Ghana

United Nations

west. When the jihad of Usuman dan Fodio was set in motion in 1804, the Hausa rulers of Kano and Daura appealed for assistance to their suzerain, the mai Ahmad (1793-1810); but the meager aid forthcoming was soon smashed along with the troops of Kano, and Kano fell to the Fulani. This success encouraged the Fulani of the western provinces of Bornu to rise in revolt, a movement so successful that it led to the establishment of a series of small emirates in western Bornu as well as the capture and sack of the capital city, Gazargamu, in 1808.

In this moment of extremity Mai Dunama, having succeeded Ahmad, called on the assistance of another of the many remarkable leaders that the Sudan produced during this age of religious revolution. Al-Kanemi, Muslim scholar and leader of the pastoral Kanembu people, had already been engaged in an informal war against the Fulani. Now, with official sanction, he moved his forces against the intruders, and succeeded in containing the jihad. Although the frontier emirates were permanently lost and Gazargamu eventually abandoned, al-Kanemi's exploits put an end thenceforward to serious Fulani designs on his country.

Al-Kanemi had therefore saved Bornu from what appeared to be certain extinction. Concurrent with his military action, however, this versatile leader had challenged the legitimacy of the Sokoto jihad, condemning it as an illegal exercise in imperialism. In the eyes of Usuman and Muhammad Bello, the government of Bornu had permitted pagan practice among its people, and worse, had given aid to pagan Hausa kings. Such an apparent approval of paganism was paganism itself, they argued, and consequently the fit object for a holy war. Al-Kanemi, with long residence and travel in North Africa and the Near East and with a sound reputation for scholarly theological commentary, contended that pagan practices performed in ignorance or weakness did not indicate paganism, that weakness was the unfortunate lot of all people, including the Fulani themselves. If all were to be condemned as unbelievers because of their sins, he insisted, there would be no true believers left to judge the infidels. "Tell us therefore why you are fighting us and enslaving our free people. . . . We have indeed heard of things in the character of the Shaikh [Usuman dan Fodio], and seen things in his writings which are contrary to what you have done. If this business does originate from him, then I say that there is no power nor might save through God. . . Indeed we thought well of him. But now . . . we love the Shaeikh and the truth when they agree. But if they disagree it is the truth which comes first."

Al-Kanemi's military successes catapulted this forceful leader into a prominent position at the mai's court, particularly after he was granted extensive lands by his grateful ruler. Other events soon followed, however, that cooled the mai's enthusiasm and led to a confrontation between the two men. Al-Kanemi's fiefs meant land for his Kanembu and other supporters and revenue from taxes, thereby yielding both wealth and the loyalty of a powerful following. In 1814 Kanemi established his own town at Kukawa while he strengthened his campaigning by enlisting aid of foreign governments. Such freedom of action, though taken in support of Bornu, bordered on an independence that could not be ignored by the Bornu ruler. In 1820 Dunama attempted to eliminate al-Kanemi by enlisting the aid of the neighboring state of Bagirmi. The effort misfired, Dunama died as his armies were defeated, and al-Kanemi placed Dunama's younger brother, Ibrahim, on the throne. Though he continued to recognize the ultimate authority of the mai, al-Kanemi had thus emerged as *de facto* ruler of Bornu.

In the ensuing years al-Kanemi continued his campaigning, but with varied success. Bagirmi was decisively defeated in 1824 and many areas regained that had been overrun during the initial period of the Sokoto jihad. The Bornu armies were badly mauled near Kano, however, and the western marches of Bornu were lost permanently.

At home al-Kanemi centralized the diffuse and complex administration of Bornu, relying largely on personal slaves as provincial administrators with his sons as army commanders. While Kukawa became in practice the nation's capital, al-Kanemi still recognized the mai's rule, taking only the modest title of Shehu. Devout Muslim, he relied on Islamic principle and law, but without the intensity that had marked the jihads of the west, and without naming himself Commander of the Faithful, religious leader of his people. Speculation over his continued tolerance of the old Saifawa dynasty have varied from al-Kanemi's sense of loyalty toward the ancient regime to a latent preference for the contemplative life of a scholar. Perhaps, too, his actions may have reflected an interest more in the practicalities than the symbols of power.

Al-Kanemi died in 1837 bequeathing the Bornu state to his son and successor Shehu Umar (1837-1881). It was, however, during Umar's long reign that the final disintegration of Bornu played itself out, for the vitality of al-Kanemi was evidently personal and could not be instilled into the ancient, failing kingdom. In 1846 Mai Ibrahim, chafing under the limitations of his subordinate position, precipitated civil war by plotting with the sultan of Wadai who invaded the kingdom and burned Kukawa. Umar, who had been absent campaigning in the vicinity of Zinder, was able to expel the Wadai army, but in the process of the war, Ibrahim was executed and his son Ali installed as a puppet by the Wadai army, was killed in battle. Thus in futility ended the thousand-year reign of the mighty Saifawa dynasty.

From that point forward Umar ruled directly although he eschewed the title of mai, resting content with the designation of Shehu. Somewhat indolent by nature, Umar gradually relaxed the centralizing efforts of his father, delegating authority to subordinates and allowing centrifugal forces to fracture the unity and efficiency of the state. Such a withdrawal from the daily responsibilities of rule, frequently characteristic of African monarchies, more than offset the long march toward centralization in Bornu's government. A king with only ceremonial functions and an aristocracy with privileges but no power led to administrative disorganization and regional particularism.

During Umar's last years the realm was in thorough disarray—the western provinces virtually independent, and Kanem to the east under the control of militant Wadai. After 1881 the decline continued under three of Umar's sons, ending once and for all in 1893 when independent Bornu fell before the armies of Rabih, a conqueror from the eastern Sudan.

Samori and Rabih

Viewed in their entirety, the great jihads may be regarded as an attempt by Muslim scholars—chiefly Fulani—to reestablish the primacy of Islam in the western Sudan as they felt it had once held sway in the days of the askia, Muhammad of Songhai. Thus they tried to restore the classic purity of the Islamic state, to purge the religious system of corrupt syncretistic and polytheistic forms, and to extend the domain of *dar al-Islam*, the abode of the true faith. Examined in still larger context, other factors may have played their part—the decline of Muslim prestige and authority throughout the world relative to the West, and the falling off of the trans-Saharan trade in the face of newer routes headed southward to the sea. Whatever their differences, therefore, the theological orientation of the jihad leaders binds them each to the others while separating them from other late nineteenth century Sudanic leaders whose motivation and activities seemingly derived from different sources. Of these latter, two stand out for particular attention—Samori Toure and Rabih Fadlullah.

Samori was born about 1830 in the Beyla region of what is today the southeastern corner of Guinea. His father, Lafiya Toure, was a farmer and cattleman who traced his descent to the Muslim trading community of the Dyula, but his mother came from local Mandinka stock of pagan, peasant background. The Toure clan had earlier migrated south from the vicinity of the Bure gold fields, in the process losing sight of their Dyula mercantile traditions and their Islamic faith. Samori, therefore, grew up as a typical farm boy in a pagan Mandinka village, yet he combined those elements that the times were to require—a clear if tenuous Dyula connection and a firm understanding of the indigenous farming mentality. To these he added creative imagination driven by an uncommon independence of character, qualities that were eventually to produce new combinations of political and religious power.

The high plateau country surrounding Beyla falls sharply away to the south toward the lowland rain forest, but facing north it leads up the valley of the Milo tributary to the great avenue of the Niger. Here Dyula traders had long been resident among the pagan cultivators, quietly promoting their mercantile prosperity, content to leave political matters to their animist neighbors. During the eighteenth and early nineteenth centuries, however, this easy social balance was upset by events that combined to stir the Dyula into a more active political role. First, there was the expanding Atlantic trade which gradually brought both prosperity to the Dyula and firearms to the interior; then, when the Fulani engineered their successful jihads in the Futa Jalon and elsewhere, these Mandinka coreligionists apparently determined that their own growing wealth and control of the gun trade called for a much more commanding position within the Milo region.

About the time of Samori's birth, there erupted a series of local jihads engineered with varying success by Dyula groups and establishing several Muslim states within which forced conversion to Islam soon roused resident pagan peoples to military opposition. Over the ensuing years, a chronic state of unrest gripped the Milo country as complex and shifting alliances of pagans and Muslims grappled with one another for control of territory and trade routes. It was these local conflicts that gave Samori his start, first as a simple line soldier, then as a quasi-independent military chieftain, and finally as the commander of an army of his own followers. By 1870 Samori had succeeded in recruiting a large, well-armed and loyal force which he then led through a decade of victorious campaigns that saw him become master of the Milo valley and commander of the most powerful force in the upper Niger country.

These initial successes had been due in large measure to Samori's exceptional personal qualities—an ability to arouse intense devotion among his troops, the talent for exploiting differences and divisions among his opponents, and a recognition of the need to maintain connections with both pagans and Muslims. Having earlier returned to the Islamic faith of his forebears, Samori secured further Dyula support with his determination to keep open the trade routes, while he calmed the fears of traditionalists by damping the missionary ardor of Muslims in his territories. Beyond this, he recruited his soldiery from a wide variety of Mandinka peoples, training them rigorously, making good use of firearms and to a lesser extent of cavalry, and in the process welding together a Mandinka army in which tribal attachments had been superseded by loyalty to Samori himself. Nevertheless, in 1884, he added what he felt was a necessary unifying capstone, declaring himself *almami*, or leader of the faithful, forcing Islamic instruction on the sons of leading pagan notables, and instituting a theocratic state in which conversion to Islam was to be required of all his subjects.

Whatever its appeal as a centripetal force, this decisive step in fact produced quite the opposite effect. Four years later, while Samori vainly attempted to reduce the Senufo fortress at Sikasso, his own peoples seized the opportunity for a general revolt, and were brought under control only with difficulty. From that point forward, Samori was obliged to abandon his rigid espousal of Islam, substituting in its stead personal loyalty and the organization of a thoroughgoing military regime as the foundations of national unity; yet already his power had passed its crest, and his final ten years in authority were occupied with an increasingly desperate defense of his state, primarily against the pressures of French colonial conquest.

During the early expansionist phase, Samori avoided any conflict with

Europeans, for his interests lay elsewhere, but his rising strength necessarily placed a barrier before European expansion into the savanna, and since Samori's appearance coincided with a growing European—particularly French—interest in the West African interior, a confrontation was sooner or later inevitable. Dyula concern for the trade in slaves, salt, and kola nuts had encouraged a southward-moving commerce that led to cordial relations between Samori and the English at Freetown who provided the firearms for his armies. The British government, moreover, was cool toward extending its authority inland whereas French visions of glory, in compensation for the humiliating loss to Prussia and Bismarck in 1871, called for an active advance from Senegal into the Sudan which might lay the basis for a vast empire stretching eventually from the Atlantic to the Red Sea.

By 1881 Samori had taken Kankan and established his capital at Bissandugu, his territory gradually blanketing the upper Niger basin in the regions of Bure and Wasulu. During the 1880s the French advance was intermittent and uncertain, and in any event was directed largely to the north against the Tokolor state of Ahmadu, the son of al-Hajj Umar. Samori was able to maintain his position through skirmishing and diplomacy—courting the British in order to offset the French, concluding friendship treaties with France herself, and seeking cooperation with Ahmadu as the best means of dealing with the intruder. It was in vain. The two could not bring themselves to work together, the British ultimately were not willing to oppose French pretensions in the interior, and France by 1891 had decided once and for all to push on with her imperial plans. Ahmadu was defeated by 1893, and Samori, though conducting a brilliant guerrilla action which enabled him to remove his state intact far to the east in the region of Kong, was finally run down and captured in 1898, dying two years later, an exile in Gabon.

Samori's initial motivation combined Dyula and Mandinka aspirations with a personal search for power, yet his ultimate fate was governed by other pressures he did not create and could not govern—a militant Muslim revivalism and the thrust of a determined French imperialism. Although he seems to have taken his religious obligations seriously, remaining a pious Muslim even after abandoning his policy of forceful conversion, Samori was in no way comparable to the great jihad leaders, Usuman dan Fodio, Seku Ahmadu, and al-Hajj Umar. First of all, his declaration of a Muslim state was tactical, not doctrinal, and was quickly abandoned when it no longer served his ends. Beyond this, in his extensive military activities he treated Muslim and pagan alike with fine impartiality, thereby earning the implacable enmity of Muslims in parts of the Sudan where his memory remains unpleasantly alive today. When he took the town of Kong in 1895, the Muslim scholars were slaughtered at the doors of the mosque and those who survived were later executed. If this was done in the name of military necessity, it also indicated an aloofness from religious scruples and commitments, along with a ruthless nature apparently indifferent to human life. Only a few years ago, a leading Muslim from Bamako remarked that Samori's sole endearing trait was his love for his mother.

Samori must be regarded, therefore, as a political, not as a religious figure—the architect of a resurrected Mali empire rather than a soldier of the Lord, Allah. Alternatively and in another light, he appears as an early nationalist leader trying to build and hold together a Mandinka state in the face of the growing pressure of French expansionism. His gifts were military and administrative. His system of government was practical and closely tied to military organization—each territory governed by a military commander of proven loyalty to the Almami, each conquered domain obliged to support the troops that maintained it in subjection.

Even more impressive were his actual military talents—in logistics no less than in tactics, in thoroughness of plan as well as determination in the field. His *sofa*, or professional soldiers, were supplemented by a conscripted army of citizens all drilled in the scorched-earth, hit-and-run tactics which were always the only possible means of success against the French artillery. His diplomacy kept the guns coming from Freetown, but he wisely supplemented this supply with workshops capable of turning out spare parts and effecting repairs. When the French set out to dispose of him in 1891 they anticipated a campaign of a few weeks in duration. Instead they were drawn into a wasting struggle in which Samori held off the attackers with his best troops while his auxiliaries conquered and organized a completely new state into which he was able to retreat with his government and armies intact, leaving only a thoroughly ruined countryside to be occupied by his French pursuers. Even his military intelligence was exceptional. Asked how he repeatedly discovered the French movements without giving away his own, he growled, "It is because I eat alone."

Nonetheless, a career of military conquest brought forth less admirable traits. Samori's political survival depended on guns and these, along with North African horses, were best obtained in exchange for slaves. A substantial portion of Samori's operations, therefore, consisted of fearful slave raids which devastated the countryside, bringing death and bondage to its population. Moreover, between 1891 and 1893, his grand retreat before the French from Bissandugu to the area of Kong was characterized by a systematic destruction of the land and its villages, culminating with the sack of Kong and the slaughter of its population in 1895. Understandably, such tactics have tarnished Samori's memory in parts of West Africa, although the age of African national independence has tended to excuse his actions as the necessary, if unfortunate, by-product of a desperate stand against foreign invasion.

The apotheosis of Samori as an early leader of African resistance to European penetration does not seem to have been granted to that other state maker in the nineteenth century Sudan who eventually fell before French arms. Possibly this is due to the paucity of information which survived the career of Rabih, information, moreover, supplied primarily by his conquerors and critics. Rabih first appeared in the Bahr al-Ghazal region of the southern Egyptian Sudan as a lieutenant of the powerful slave trader Zubair Pasha. When Zubair's son was defeated and killed in 1879 by the forces of General Gordon, seeking to stamp out the slave trade in the eastern Sudan, Rabih was suddenly a soldier without a patron. Rallying a few hundred survivors, he retreated westward, carrying on a precarious existence as a brigand but gradually building up an army that enabled him to advance from successful raids to permanent conquest. In 1893 he sacked the capital of Bagirmi, a few months later descending upon the failing Bornu kingdom. Destroying its capital of Kukawa, Rabih built a new seat of government but otherwise added little to the administration he had inherited. Master of the Chad basin, he tried unsuccessfully to extend his domain westward at the expense of Sokoto, and was obliged to content himself with consolidating the territory already conquered. His efforts were ultimately in vain. As in the case of Samori, Rabih ran afoul of European powers making determined probes deep into the Sudan. In 1900 Rabih was killed and his forces defeated by a French army at Kuseri, and although resistance continued briefly after his death, Rabih's kingdom was soon absorbed into the colonial holdings of France, Britain, and Germany.

A hard-bitten, self-made man, Rabih, like Samori, survived through his military prowess. How far his interests extended to the propagation of Islam is uncertain, however. His attitude toward the Mahdi of the eastern Sudan was ambivalent for he ignored the Mahdi's overtures while at the same time pursuing his conquests as a Mahdist army leader. There was, moreover, a Mahdist group in the western Sudan, and during the years of Rabih's ascendancy he maintained correct though hardly cordial relations with its leaders. It seems fair to conclude, therefore, that Rabih's motivation was more military than religious.

Suggestions for Further Reading

There has been a great deal of research during the past fifteen or twenty years covering the period of the jihads. While this work has added enormously to detail, intricacy of narrative, and, to an extent, approach, it has not greatly changed the broad outlines of the period. There is no reasonably brief, clearly-stated, study available; Bovill's *Golden Trade of the Moors* is dated and very sketchy in its treatment of the nineteenth century. The beginning students, therefore, may find heavy going in the fact-filled tracts, for example, by Murray Last, R. A. Adeleye and C. C. Stewart, or Louis Brenner and Ronald Cohen in J. F. A. Ajayi and M. Crowder, eds., *History of West Africa*, vol. II (Burnt Mill, Harlow: Longman, 1987). These, in turn, are based upon secondary works, monographs, and unpublished theses, of which a few may suffice here. See, among others, Last's *Sokoto Caliphate* (New York: Humanities Press, 1967), J. R. Willis, ed., *Studies in West African Islamic History*, vol. I (London: Frank Cass, 1979), or David Robinson, *The Holy War of Umar Tal* (Oxford:

Clarendon, 1985). For al-Kanemi and his successors, there is Louis Brenner, *The Shehus of Kukawa* (Oxford: Clarendon, 1973).

The accounts of travelers like Heinrich Barth, Hugh Clapperton, and others are basic sources for the period of the jihads and later, but more convenient is the excellent selection contained in Thomas Hodgkin, *Nigerian Perspectives* 2nd ed. (London: Oxford, 1975), which also includes excerpts from the writings of the leaders of the Sokoto jihad, including correspondence between Muhammad Bello and al-Kanemi.

The basic work on Samori is Yves Person's monumental three-volume biography, *Samori: Une Révolution Dyula*, 3 vols. (Dakar: IFAN, 1968, 70, 75). Briefer treatments in English by Person are available in Ajayi-Crowder, cited above, as well as in M. Crowder, ed., *West African Resistance* (London: Hutchinson, 1971) and R. Rotberg and Ali Mazrui, eds., *Protest and Power in Black Africa* (New York: Oxford University Press, 1970).

Information on Rabih is limited, but see W. K. R. Hallam, *The Life and Times of Rabih Fadl Allah* (Ilfracombe, England: A. H. Stockwell, 1977).

10

The Eastern Sudan— Egyptian Expansionism and the Mahdist Revolution

Invasion from the North

Muhammad Ali Pasha's motivation was always simple, his tactics complex. The building of a mighty Egyptian state as the vehicle of personal power was the lifetime objective of the great modernizer (1805-1848), but the means to this end were various. "You are aware," he wrote in 1823 to his forces invading the Sudan, "that the end of all our effort and this expense is to procure negroes." African slaves drilled into an efficient and loyal army would offset the losses suffered in his taxing campaigns against the Wahabiyya in Arabia and offer an inviting replacement for his insubordinate Albanian troops. There were other attractions, however. He hoped to gain access to the famed, if illusory, gold of the Sudan, deal a final blow to the Mamluk remnants who had survived the massacre he had engineered in 1811, and extend his hegemony south along the Nile as had the pharaohs of old, thereby placing his hand firmly on the profitable commerce of the Red Sea. For these reasons the Sudan was tempting to an ambitious ruler, and all the more so since its gradual decline into a number of petty moribund states promised success at little cost to any determined invader.

Necessarily, there were logistical problems involved in transporting a fighting force through hundreds of miles of difficult, little-known country, and had a serious and sustained military opposition been mounted, the intruders might easily have met disaster. A heterogeneous army of four thousand Turks and Albanians, Maghrib Arabs and Egyptian Bedouins, Barbary Coasters and black Africans was colorfully decked out in a great variety of costumes in which the bright-hued pantaloons, slippers, and short jackets of the Turks predominated, but which also exhibited Kurdish cavalry in steel breastplate and conical hat, Bedouins clothed in chain mail and helmet, and Arabs in their traditional flowing robes. A mercenary army, it was commanded by Muhammad Ali's third son, the twenty-five-year-old Ismail, who was assisted by an officer corps that included an American marine recently converted to Islam and the cause of Muhammad Ali. Uniformity and well-drilled precision were conspicuously absent in this motley assortment, but, fortunately for Ismail, its variety extended to its armament which included all-important artillery and a contingent of riflemen to sharpen its striking power.

The guns soon proved their utility. In the autumn of 1820 the army moved out from Aswan and swept past Dongola, lately deserted by its Mamluk contingent. Soon Ismail was confronted by the Shakiyya people whose warlike habits and splendid horsemanship were cancelled out by a medieval weaponry, and who were consequently slaughtered by the Turkish firepower in two engagements, their ears sent back to Cairo by the basketful for promised bounties. As it happened, the gallant but futile effort of the Shakiyya was the only opposition offered Ismail's troops by the demoralized and divided principalities along the Sudanese Nile. The army continued its march upstream, usually proceeding at night to the sound of kettledrums but often breaking ranks to wander off into the desert or to pause and plunder the local inhabitants. The next major objective was Shendi—a trading center not far beyond the ancient site of Meroe, a ragged, dusty, sun-scorched town where a splendid assortment of goods was on display but where slaves were the central item of commerce. Quickly securing the submission of the local ruler, Ismail pressed on, crossing the Nile into the Gezira and entering Sennar unopposed in June 1821. The unkempt appearance of town and inhabitants matched the ineffective bewilderment of Badi, the last of the Funj sultans whose pathetic final act of independence was the transfer of his faltering realm to the invaders.

In the summer of 1821 another column effected an easy conquest of Kordofan and the essential Sudan was now controlled by Egyptian power which would later add the wide spaces of Darfur in the west and the unknown and inaccessible reaches south of the Sudd, that vast papyrus swamp choking the Nile below her Bahr al-Ghazal tributary. The occupation had been simple— perhaps too simple—but from this point forward complications began to accumulate for invader and invaded alike. Sennar had been a shock, the famed capital a shabby village of grass huts housing a ragged population, docile yet sinister. Soon the summer rains poured down on the northerners, sapping their energy and eroding their morale, forcing them to sleep in the black mud and robbing them of even the will to bury the growing number of comrades dead with fever. In Cairo, Muhammad Ali was calling for gold and slaves but the response was disappointing for the gold supplies were exhausted and only half those slaves shipped on to Egypt survived the trip.

The Egyptian administration was not content merely with opportunities for slaving, however, and shortly proceeded to institute a comprehensive system of taxation, the severity of which amounted to confiscation, threatening the supply of slaves in the Sudan where specie was scarce and payment came in kind. The declining morale of the invaders was now matched by the disillusionment of the Sudanese whose initial reaction to the northerners had not been unfavorable. Numbers of Egyptian soldiers were ambushed and others murdered in their beds as they slept. Great migrations of people moved off to the wilderness, chiefly along the Ethiopian marches, placing the protection of distance between themselves and the Egyptian tax collectors. At Shendi, Ismail was assassinated in October 1822 when first he imposed an impossible assessment on the local ruler and then publicly insulted him. The incident set off a widespread revolt along the river from Shendi south, a revolt that might have succeeded even in the face of the northern firepower had the local people been able to suppress parochial differences and unite in adversity. With Ismail's death, the commander of the Kordofan army assumed responsibility for the occupation and soon his forces were burning, ravaging, slaughtering, and enslaving in a vicious outburst of retribution until the Sudan lay ruined and prostrate, its villages gutted and its land depopulated, denied even the sense of despair that had initially triggered rebellion. With the end of bloodletting came renewed taxation and further migrations, but in 1825 at last a more reasonable regime was instituted and the exhausted Sudan settled back to peace and the hope for some measure of rehabilitation.

The Ecology of Poverty

The troops of Ismail, pushing their boats through the Second Cataract of the Nile at Wadi Halfa, entered a land where civilization blossomed only under careful cultivation, where great kingdoms—Kush, Makouria, Alwa, Funj—had flourished in their time, but where severity of environment was endemic. The country was a vast, rocky plain, broken by occasional hills and crossed by dry ravines, a virtual desert almost as far south as the confluence of the White and Blue Nile, and thereafter a savanna scrubland suitable for the support of nomadic herders of camels, sheep, or cattle. Gradually the terrain below the confluence became more verdant, permitting cultivation of millet, groundnuts, and garden crops on terraced hillsides and well-tended orchards, but even here the basic industry was stock raising.

Through this difficult land flowed the great river, tracing a serpentine, green-edged ribbon across the sandy wastes, but in no sense a highway by reason of the half-dozen cataracts which obstructed travel over its thousand mile course between Aswan and the confluence. The Egyptians were able to move their craft up the river only with difficulty, and once they occupied Sennar and subdued the Funj, a far deeper penetration into central Africa was prevented by the Sudd which was not to be breached for another eighteen years. The land they traversed was hot and dry, the rainfall like the vegetation gradually increasing southward but arriving in a seasonal fall which punctuated, but did little to relieve, the blasting heat.

Muhammad Ali had invaded the Sudan in search of wealth, but little could be wrested from a land of worn-out gold mines and sparse population. Along the Nile floodplain, in the Gezira, and on the Kordofan steppe dwelt in the main subsistence farmers of many strains, the Arab being only the latest. Although their language and culture in most cases had become essentially Arab and their religion Islamic, their ethnic characteristics remained indigenous, the Arab blood absorbed in the dominant Sudanic type—Nubian in the north, with negroid people, such as the Funj, predominating in the central Sudan. Among the sedentary groups along the Nile, the Danaqla were Nubian speaking, yet the closely related Ja'aliyyin, occupying the river valley north of the confluence, were Arab speakers. Among the nomadic cattle keepers the evidence of Arab blood was somewhat more apparent. In the east, it is true, the Beja characteristically maintained their ethnic and cultural purity, adopting only the religion of the Arabs, but among the other pastoralists ranging both east and west of the Nile the Arab proportion was ethnically greater, a fact that, when added to the effects of a desert life, helped set off the nomads from the sedentary farmers.

Prominent among the pastoralists were the Baqqara, Arab camel herders turned cattle keepers, who ranged west of the river in Kordofan and Darfur, intermarrying with the farming population to form a virile nation of stock raisers, hunters, and slavers. These hard-driving, hard-riding individualists would in time indulge their love of booty and aversion to taxation by providing formidable support for the Mahdist revolution of the 1880s.

Superimposed on the agricultural economy of the Sudan was a pattern of trade following routes that moved north from Sennar to Egypt, and west-east to connect Darfur with Suakin on the Red Sea. The routes to the north by no means followed the course of the Nile with its long stretches of rapids and its great S-shaped loop which added hundreds of miles to the journey. Instead caravans struck out overland from Qarri to Kurti or alternatively followed the river through Shendi and Berber and then took the long trek through the Nubian desert directly to Aswan. Such travel, though common, was hazardous and uncomfortable—water was dangerously scarce, while the monotony of the daily round alternated between the scorching noonday heat and the intense cold of the desert night. The west-east track normally originated at Kubayh in Darfur and proceeded to El Obeid where the road turned north to Shendi, for the route directly to Sennar was threatened by the Shilluk people along the White Nile. From Shendi the caravans doubled back southeast to Quz Rajab from which point they moved northeast to Suakin on the coast.

These routes, converging on Shendi, established that river town as the prime market of the Sudan, and, indeed, its stalls contained a surprising variety of goods from three continents — spices from India, steel blades from German manufactories, leather from Kordofan, Egyptian soap, Venetian glass, Ethiopian gold, and Dongola horses, among many other items — the appeal of these products being fully matched by a port town's recreational diversions designed for the taste and appetite of those who had been weeks in the desert. Other entrepôts along the river, Berber, for example, were smaller versions of Shendi with its noisy clutter, its incessant argumentation and bargaining, its polyglot population of Muslim and pagan, African and Arab, its prostitutes, and its "bouza" grog shops.

The chief preoccupation of these market centers was commerce in slaves, both for the internal and external trade. For the most part the recruits came from afar, from Christian Ethiopia which provided women much prized for their beauty and loyalty, and from the pagan areas southwest of Darfur. Many bondsmen remained in the Sudan as servants, field hands, or retainers, but most went on to Egypt and Arabia. It is estimated that Sennar exported some fifteen hundred slaves each year to Egypt, while Darfur produced as much as six thousand annually, mostly girls destined for domestic service or harem residence. A goodly number of these naturally found their way to the Shendi market where a young male already marked with smallpox brought fifteen dollars but where girls were worth twenty-five. Treatment of slaves seemed to vary greatly. Although normally regarded only as livestock, they were reasonably well cared for, and their ultimate fate in Egypt and Arabia not infrequently involved manumission.

The fall of the Christian kingdoms to infiltrating Arabs from Egypt during the fourteenth and fifteenth centuries was accompanied by the introduction of Islam to the Sudan, but the uniformity it supposedly imposed was illusory, for intruding Islam was obliged to adapt itself to local customs even as traditional ways bent before the impact of the new faith. Thus, as the invading Arabs intermarried with the local people and merged their racial characteristics, so universal, flexible Islam adjusted to local practices and absorbed their animist elements into its own religious system.

In one respect, however, it was local conditions that imposed their uniformity on Islam. For the Sudanese peasant, living simply, religious practice tended more toward appeals to magic, while orthodox Islam with its system of abstract truths had little attraction. Consequently the Sudanese became highly receptive to the concept of sufism, in which mystical devotion to a Muslim saint, living or dead, enabled the follower of that saint to partake of his *baraka*, or God given supernatural power, and placed that follower in closer relationship to an otherwise remote and unapproachable deity. Islam in the eastern Sudan came to be identified with saint worship and the rise of religious brother-hoods, the external index of religious devotion showing itself not as the mosque, but rather the whitewashed, domed tomb of the saint. In the western Sudan,

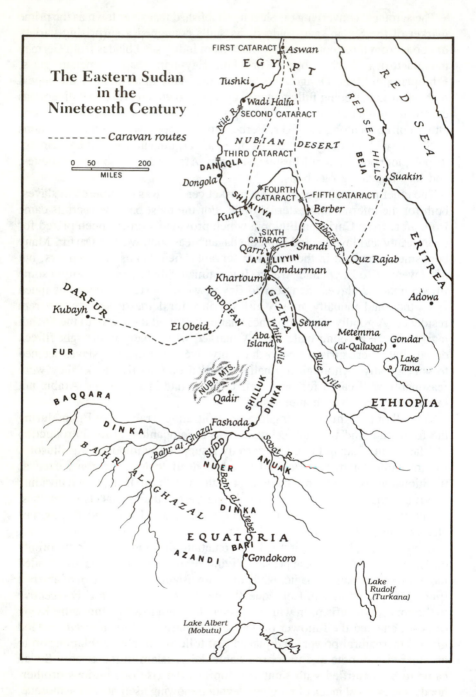

The Eastern Sudan
in the
Nineteenth Century

- - - - - - - Caravan routes

0   50   200
MILES

the Fulani clerics employed sufism primarily as a vehicle for puritan reform. In the east it was the emotional appeal of sufist mysticism that captured the heart of the peasant.

Egypt in the Sudan

The Sudan was but one of many enterprises in which Muhammad Ali was interested, and it was a minor one at that. Nevertheless, since his interest was essentially in the extraction of wealth, it was imperative that the initial occupation be followed as quickly as possible by a peaceful administration designed to restore some measure of prosperity to the land. Beginning in 1825 a series of able administrators bent their energies to that end. The first of these, Mahu Bey Urfali, ruled only one year, yet in that short time he set the tone of government which was followed by his successors, Ali Khurshid and Ahmad Abu Widan, who between them governed the Sudanese provinces until 1843.

Mahu's policy was based on reason, and reason dictated that a prostrated, frightened population be wooed by conciliation. To induce the people back from their refuge in the Abyssinian foothills, he promised a three-year tax holiday, imposed a tight rein on his army, sent food into the stricken Gezira, and took the shrewd if unexpected step of consulting Sudanese notables concerning his plans. Khurshid elaborated and enlarged on this beginning. On Mahu's recommendation he employed a local shaikh, Abd al-Qadir, as adviser, and al-Qadir was helpful in urging his people back to their fields, and later prevented a serious policy error when he persuaded the Egyptians to drop their plans for the forced military conscription of Sudanese freemen.

Khurshid's ultimate objective was a stable body of cultivators and pastoralists engaged in an expanding productivity which would serve as the basis for Egyptian taxation. That his administration was smiled upon in Cairo is attested to in the responsibilities and honors bestowed on him by Muhammad Ali. Beginning with Sennar province, he gradually was given control of Berber, Kordofan, and Dongola—all ruled from his capital at Khartoum. Throughout his domains a concerted effort was made to follow Muhammad Ali's bidding that the Sudan pay for itself, but since money was scarce, the payment of taxes was often difficult and the process of collection a grim business. There were taxes on land and taxes on livestock, taxes on water wheels, and customs duties on exports and imports. In Dongola, where Egyptian administration meant protection from Shakiyya raiders, collection was usually no great problem, but in the south Khurshid devoted much effort to attracting fugitives back to their lands and was obliged to exempt numerous chiefs from assessment in return for their cooperation in leading the exiles home. Tax gathering was usually accomplished through the use of Shakiyya irregulars supplemented occasionally by Egyptian cavalry, but in lean years even payments in kind were a great hardship; in 1835, the Sudanese pastoralists were obliged to part with their slaves in lieu of the usual levy in cattle.

The Egyptians were by no means content to tax the inefficient peasants as they had found them, but sought rather through a wide range of developmental schemes to improve productivity—to apply, in short, the Egyptian concept of modernization to this Egyptian colony. Agriculture, the basis of the economy, was fostered in a number of ways. Skilled workers were sent specifically to grow opium, indigo, and cotton, while more generally experienced Egyptian farmers and artisans were requisitioned from all Egyptian provinces on orders from Muhammad Ali himself. Irrigation was undertaken, Egyptian bullock-driven water wheels introduced, and improved pest control taught to the Sudanese. Many new crops were tried, and since their choice was often based on faulty information, most failed—for example, coffee, which was unsuited to the hot plains, silk, because the mulberry tree would not grow in the Sudan, and wool, when the Sudanese sheep could not be made to produce even a minimum quality for weaving. Some experiments were more successful, however. Indigo became a major crop; sugar cane, though unpopular with the Sudanese farmers, showed profit, while various types of fruit made good headway.

On the whole these were but minor additions to the two basic agricultural products of the Sudan, cattle and gum arabic, in which the northerners were interested. Draft animals for Egyptian farms and factories were cheap and abundant in the south, and demands were constantly coming from Cairo for new shipments that had to be kept within reasonable limits to forestall renewed emigration back to the wilderness. Since gum, which came from the widespread acacia and was used in the manufacture of paper and confectionery, presented no such problems, this Egyptian state monopoly proved most profitable over the years. The acacia was also widely used in boatbuilding, but its utility was not unlimited. When Muhammad Ali asked for samples suitable for rifle butts, it was found that nine hours and forty minutes were necessary to saw through one piece, the arsenal report concluding solemnly, "This shows that . . . this wood is indeed very hard."

Despite Egyptian exertions, the struggle for economic development in the Sudan came to very little. While military governors generally made poor production managers, Sudanese peasants clung tenaciously to their traditional techniques of cultivation, successfully withstanding the efforts of the Egyptian experts to convert them to the ways of scientific agriculture. Many schemes, moreover, were illusory; witness Muhammad Ali's lifelong search for gold supplies long ago exhausted, or the fruitless attempts to develop iron mining in Kordofan. Beyond this, as the pasha grew older, his energies flagged and his alertness was blunted with the result that a vacillating policy in Cairo soon enfeebled the administration in the Sudan. The death of Abu Widan in 1843 inaugurated a period during which no fewer than eleven administrators sat in Khartoum over twenty years. In 1848 Muhammad Ali died but this brought no relief for he was succeeded, first by Abbas I (1848-1854) under whose indifferent administration the Sudan atrophied, and then by Muhammad Said (1854-1863) whose capricious, lethargic nature perpetuated the drift that had set in during the last years of Muhammad Ali. Nevertheless, it was these unproductive years that witnessed an event of great importance in the history of the Sudan—the breaching of the Sudd and the penetration along the Bahr al-Ghazal and the upper Nile.

The Southern Sudan and the Slave Trade

The prime motive for Muhammad Ali's initial penetration of the Sudan was his desire for slaves to fill the ranks of the Egyptian army. He was soon disillusioned as to the utility of black troops outside their native land, but since the Egyptians and Turks fared ill in the south, these slave regiments, called *jihadiyya*, or regular soldiers, came in time to be the major support for the Egyptian administration in the Sudan. The harvesting of slaves, therefore, continued to be a major activity of the governors at Khartoum who organized armed raids annually into the Nuba hills in Kordofan, the mountains of western Ethiopia, or among the Dinka and Shilluk people living along the White Nile. Success was far from automatic, for local resistance was stubborn and resourceful; yet when Muhammad Ali dispatched an expedition in 1839 to explore the upper reaches of the White Nile, it was not a further search for slaves but curiosity over the river's source and the lure of gold that provided the initial impulse. The immediate consequence was the adventitious rise of an ivory trade, at first largely conducted by Europeans, and it was only later that large-scale slaving came to dominate the relations of upper and lower Sudan.

The Nile expedition, first of three led by a Turkish naval officer, Salim Qapudan, failed to discover the Bahr al-Ghazal channel to the west, but managed to find its way southward through the swampy maze of the Sudd, pushing upriver as far as the future site of Gondokoro. The initial reaction was disappointing, for Muhammad Ali's El Dorado still eluded him, but soon certain compensating factors became apparent. Great quantities of ivory were found to be available almost for the asking, while the local people, screened off until this moment from external influences, were an immediate attraction to European missionaries. Herein lay the seeds of future discord, hatred, and contempt. The intruders from the north, eager to exploit the area and possessing the technical superiority to do so, were at first totally ignorant of local custom and then learned to profit from its weaknesses. The indigenous people, fixed in their traditional ways and indifferent to the potentialities of change, fell victim to the invaders who used them and eventually enslaved them. The possibilities for progress were great, but human frailty led instead to human tragedy.

Through circumstance and habit, the local residents were peculiarly vulnerable, for their isolation had been complete and long-lived. To the east lay the Ethiopian highlands while the north and west were shut off by the Nuba hills and the swamps of the Bahr al-Ghazal watershed. On the south lay more mountainous country and the impenetrable equatorial forest. Hemmed in by these barriers a vast plain sprawled across the map, intersected by sluggish rivers, parched and bare during the dry season, flooded and covered with high grass during the rains, and capable of sustaining a scattered population only at a minimum level of subsistence.

Within this remote, monotonous land dwelt peoples with a splendid sense of isolation and a sublime self-confidence, but their isolation had shielded them from developments around them, particularly technological advances, and their self-confidence was that of individualism rather than of unity. Most were Nilotes—Luo speakers who had spread north from the Bahr al-Ghazal to form the farming and pastoral communities of the Shilluk and Anuak people along the White Nile and the Sobat rivers, Nuer and Dinka, tall, slim-hipped pastoralists spread widely through the Sudd and White Nile regions, or the more sedentary Bari located in the neighborhood of Gondokoro. Whatever their backgrounds many of these people joined in an aversion to organized government and lived instead in small, mutually antagonistic social units, the pastoralists indulging in a kind of organized feud in which cattle raiding played a basic role. In the western part of this area were Sudanic speaking groups who had migrated from the Lake Chad Chari River area, as well as peoples from the southwest, all of whom were sedentary farmers but none save the Azande any more friendly to strong leadership or united effort than their Nilote neighbors.

These were the people encountered as Salim led his first expedition up the Nile, and in its initial stages the confrontation was encouraging. The Shilluk, who knew the northerners, were not especially cordial and there were some early misunderstandings with the Nuer and Dinka, but on the whole the travelers were received by the wonder-struck inhabitants as nothing less than messengers from the gods. In the Bari country, the people were not only friendly but culturally more developed, and quickly produced quantities of cattle and ivory which they agreed to exchange for beads.

Gradually the bloom of cordiality faded in the face of growing familiarity. European traders soon appeared, drawn by the reports of ivory along the Bahr al-Jebel, or upper White Nile, but in time they were challenged increasingly by Arab merchants from the Sudan and Darfur. As the competition increased, the available supplies of ivory were exhausted, necessitating the organization of elephant hunts and the establishment of permanent colonies which relied on the local people for subsistence. Suspicion and hostility soon prevailed. The southerners could not accommodate the newcomers within their traditional systems of landholding and communal assistance—what the one regarded as a necessary sharing of the meager fruits of the land the other saw as dishonesty and avarice. By the 1860s the trade had come under the control of the Arabs who looked on the local people as savages, called them *abid,* or slave, and resorted increasingly to superior force to resolve disputes. The local people responded with growing truculence. Fearful and uncertain, unaccustomed to solidarity in the face of adversity, they were easily divided and exploited, their helplessness merely intensifying the scorn and impatience of those who had come to make profit from the land.

For a time the traders were held off by the southerners, pinned down to river posts, and prevented from penetrating the interior in a widening quest for fresh supplies of ivory. By the 1850s, however, the wars between tribal sections which had initially complicated the search for ivory were being turned to the traders' advantage. Rivalries were encouraged and alliances formed with different groups eager to enlist military assistance from the outsiders. Soon the trading post had become the sole point of stability in a sea of chaos, and its master the most powerful authority in his district.

The process was simple and effective. Raiding among the divided inhabitants, the armed bands employed by the traders captured supplies of cattle which were exchanged for ivory and the service of porters. In the process prisoners were taken and used in lieu of money to pay the wages of the armed retainers. Thus a commerce in slaves soon developed as a by-product of the ivory trade, for a single slave was worth three months' pay. For their part, the traders found it increasingly profitable to engage directly in slaving as they probed ever deeper into the virgin country away from the river.

In the Bahr al-Ghazal watershed, the trading camps developed into formidable strongholds, called *zeribas*, which were provisioned by the local people in return for a military support that soon reduced them to a state of vassalage. Here the slave trade was far more extensive than along the upper Nile, and the many slaves brought in by raiding parties were quickly bought up by numerous itinerant Danaqla and Ja'aliyyin traders, called *jallaba*, who swarmed down from Kordofan by the thousand, each to purchase a few slaves for eventual sale in North Africa. Superior armament usually spelled success for the raiders but occasionally they were badly defeated, particularly by the Dinka who had long experience in the thrust and parry of cattle raiding. In time one of the most powerful of the zeriba chiefs came to be al-Zubair Rahma Mansur who built a commercial empire based on the slave trade and ultimately became so powerful that the government in Cairo, despairing of controlling al Zubair, appointed him instead as governor of a Bahr al-Ghazal province it in fact did not control.

Backdrop to the Mahdi

In 1863 Ismail Pasha became viceroy of Egypt, an event that should have recalled the progressive days of Muhammad Ali, but instead led to the eventual loss both of Egypt's independence and her conquests in the Sudan. Ismail's troubles stemmed as much from personal shortcomings as from circumstance. He was intelligent, charming, energetic, and sympathetic to the process of modernization begun by his distinguished predecessor, but he was also impulsive and capricious in decision and totally bereft of judgment in financial matters. He introduced many public improvements but rarely saw them through to completion, while his efforts at national development eventually bankrupted the economy and opened the way to European intervention in support of his foreign creditors. Under Ismail, the Egyptian empire extended itself far into Africa, but ill-advised campaigns in Ethiopia in 1875-1876 destroyed the effectiveness of the army, rendering it incapable of providing the empire with adequate protection when the moment of crisis arrived.

It was during the years of Ismail's rule that the ground was prepared for the Mahdist revolution in the Sudan, and in this respect the Egyptian government's policy toward the slave trade was fundamental. Ismail's pro-Western orientation led him to favor abolition of the slave trade, but the inauguration of such a policy had profound ramifications in the Sudan. There, economic orthodoxy strongly supported by religious sanction had elevated slavery to the level of a natural law and established the slave trade as an honorable occupation. More specifically, two powerful groups were challenged—the Danaqla merchants who controlled the trade on the upper Nile, and the zeriba chiefs and their jallaba agents in the Bahr al-Ghazal.

Initial efforts at control were ineffectual, but in 1869 Ismail engaged the British explorer, Samuel Baker, to extend effective Egyptian rule along the Bahr al-Jebel, and four years later appointed Charles George Gordon to succeed Baker as the governor of the recently constituted upper Nile province of Equatoria, raising him to the position of governor-general of the Sudan in 1877. Baker was not a happy choice, for his heavy-handed methods not only antagonized Muslim slavers resentful over restrictions imposed by a European Christian, but succeeded even in alienating the southerners he was charged with protecting when he seized their cattle for food.

Gordon's administration of Equatoria was somewhat more accommodating, but as governor-general his first duty was to put an end to the slave trade in all areas, and by 1879, when Ismail was deposed, he had made substantial progress in that direction. In Equatoria he declared the ivory trade a government monopoly and forbade the formation of private armies, thus compelling many of the merchants to retire from business. In the Bahr al-Ghazal, where Zubair had already been eliminated, his son and successor, Sulaiman, and the other slavers were crushed after a hard campaign and their zeribas destroyed.

Such progress came at a price. The Bahr al-Ghazal lay devastated, its inhabitants scattered, and the jallaba driven into Kordofan and Darfur where they bided their time in sullen resentment over the loss of their goods and means of livelihood. Along the White Nile the commercial hegemony of the Danaqla was under increasing pressure from an apparently malign Egyptian administration directed by European unbelievers. Beyond this, the Egyptian government was in full decline, supported by an army that had lost its authority as a fighting force. By the time of Ismail's fall from power a potentially explosive situation had developed in the Sudan.

The Mahdist Revolution

On June 29, 1881, the Mahdi declared himself and shortly thereafter performed the hijra from the land of the infidels to his refuge at Qadir in the Nuba hills of southern Kordofan. Before that moment he had been Muhammad Ahmad, a Muslim ascetic, who was born a Danaqla in 1844 and who early showed preference for a life of religious study over the traditional boat-building trade of his family. Like so many Sudanese, Muhammad Ahmad's religious interests led not to the formalized Islam taught at al-Azhar in Cairo, but to the mysticism of a sufist brotherhood, and in 1861 he joined such an order, the Sammaniyya, when he was only seventeen years old. In the years that followed he gained a reputation for extreme piety and humility to the extent that when he went to live at Aba Island on the White Nile in 1870, he soon gained a large following among the local people attracted by his asceticism. His puritanical leanings were so pronounced that they caused Muhammad Ahmad eventually to break with his shaikh, Muhammad Sharif, and ally himself with another leader of the Sammaniyya order, a man presumably of less worldly nature but in any event of such an advanced age as to be susceptible to an early succession. When the old man died in 1880, Muhammad Ahmad became the acknowledged leader of his group—the possessor of a powerful baraka, or supernatural power, and an individual of proven piety whose growing appeal was especially strong among the people of Kordofan.

In a general sense, the Mahdist revolution in the eastern Sudan was a manifestation of the broad wave of spiritual unrest that swept the Muslim world during the late eighteenth and nineteenth centuries and resulted in such movements as the puritan, revivalist Wahabiyya in Arabia and the jihads of the West African Sudan. More particularly, it was a response of the people of the eastern Sudan, poverty striken and discontent, to gain some counterpoise to their misery and sense of frustration. Already fervent advocates of mystical sufism, they also subscribed to the doctrine of a Second Coming. Though such a belief varied throughout the Muslim world, in the Sudan, both west and east, it took the form of Mahdism whereby in the last hours of the world, a Mahdi or God-guided one would come to confirm the faith and proclaim justice. He would then fall before the Dajjal or Antichrist who in turn would be destroyed by Christ the Prophet as the world ended in the triumph of the true faith.

At the moment that Muhammad Ahmad became a leader of the Sammaniyya, there was a rising Mahdist expectation in the land, reflecting specific dissatisfaction with the lax morality and worldliness of Egyptian administrators as well as a more generalized sense of despair over the lot of humankind. It was not unnatural, therefore, that the new leader, with his reputation for extreme piety and his constant call for the renunciation of worldly vanity, was soon being regarded by some as the expected Mahdi. His own followers began saying that the Mahdi would come from among them, while one in particular, a new adherent from the Baqqara nomads of Darfur named Abdallahi ibn Muhammad, claimed to recognize Muhammad Ahmad as the Mahdi.

Doubtless these intimations influenced Muhammad Ahmad, but his own nature, rooted in emotional puritanism, required an inner conviction of divine calling, even as the movement he was to lead needed the genuine impulse of messianic expectations which could never have been transmitted by a counterfeit. In time such conviction came in a series of visions which Muhammad Ahmad was at pains to point out were revealed to him while he was in a state of wakeful good health. The secret was first communicated to his disciples; then after a trip to Kordofan to test popular opinion and settle on a place of refuge, the historic announcement was made, and Muhammad al Mahdi called on his adherents to rally to his person.

The remove to Qadir was consciously patterned in parallel to the flight of the Prophet from Mecca to Medina, and at Qadir the forces of the Mahdi steadily grew, partly in response to the appeal of his religious message, partly because of economic and political discontent, and partly because of the success of his arms against ineffectual Egyptian efforts to bring him to terms. Within a year he had won several important victories, gathered large quantities of war booty, and increased the number of his adherents from the few hundred who had assisted his departure from Aba to many thousand. Broadly these ansar, so called after the helpers of the Prophet Muhammad at Medina, fell into three categories. There was the growing body of disciples who came to the Mahdi out of religious conviction, persuaded of the need for reform leading to a new theocratic state. There were, moreover, the many Danaqla, Ja'aliyyin, and other disaffected traders and their mercenaries—particularly the jallaba sulking in Darfur and Kordofan—who saw in the Mahdi a means to regain their former economic and political ascendancy. Finally, there were the Baqqara pastoralists who had suffered at Egyptian hands, first in the person of Zubair who conquered their Darfur homeland in 1874 and then through the subsequent Egyptian administration which sought to impose onerous and unfamiliar taxation. In time another important element was added to his forces—black jihadiyya, professional soldiers captured in battle who served their new master as faithfully as they had the Egyptians. These troops greatly strengthened the Mahdi's forces through their use of firearms which were expressly denied the *ansar* as a violation of the Prophet's injunction concerning weaponry.

By the summer of 1882 the Mahdi had shifted from the defensive phase of hijra to the militant offensive of jihad, and there was much to commend this change. The government forces were plagued by bad leadership, difficult communications, and the confusion in Egypt caused by the Urabist army uprising of 1881-1882. Their line troops, moreover, had no heart for a fight in opposition to a holy war that compelled the support of all Muslims. The Mahdi, on the other hand, was campaigning on home ground amid friendly people caught up in the emotional surge of his cause. His guerrilla tactics were ideally suited to the capabilities of his own forces—ill-equipped but zealous levies from the local people who could move quickly, live off the land, harass marching columns, and bottle up the Egyptians in the towns to be cut off and starved out at leisure. In January 1883, El Obeid, the provincial capital of Kordofan, surrendered after a difficult siege, thus bringing a vast increase in wealth, power, and territory to the Mahdist cause.

The fall of El Obeid greatly raised the Mahdi's prestige but more impressive still was the annihilation in November 1883 of the expeditionary force sent south under the command of a British soldier, William Hicks, for the purpose of regaining Kordofan. This last vain effort by a failing Egyptian government to reassert its rule in the Sudan persuaded waverers that the northerners were finished. The following month the province of Darfur capitulated and in April 1884 Bahr al-Ghazal came over. Meanwhile the Beja had been persuaded to join the Mahdist cause bringing with them the Red Sea hill area, save only the port city of Suakin. By early 1884 it was clear that the Mahdi must prevail throughout the Sudan unless decisive action were taken, action that was beyond both the resources of the Egyptian regime and the determination of the British who had occupied Egypt during the summer of 1882 at the time of the Urabist revolt.

The final scenes of the Mahdist triumph, which took place at Khartoum early in 1885, involved the British more than the Egyptians—British governmental confusion, the force of British public opinion, and the activities of the energetic but unpredictable Gordon who had returned to the Sudan in February 1884 as governor-general. Gordon's instructions called for him only to explore means for evacuating the Egyptians in the Sudan, for the British were not willing to become involved in the interior and had committed troops solely for the protection of the Red Sea port of Suakin. Gordon, however, regarded his function as more executive than advisory and his erratic actions precipitated a crisis. First, he mistakenly announced a policy of evacuation, thus convincing waverers in the Sudan of Egyptian weakness. Then, after the Mahdi had rejected an offer of cooperation, Gordon proclaimed his intention to establish a strong government and defeat the Mahdi, presumably with the aid of troops Britain was not prepared to provide. Remaining stubbornly in Khartoum, the governor general was cut off as the sedentary people along the river north of Khartoum at last rose to join the Mahdi. In May, Berber was taken and the Mahdi's forces closed in on the doomed city. Pressed by public opinion at home, the British government finally organized a relief expedition which made its way south as the Mahdist army massed for attack.

The British reached the Khartoum area on January 28, 1885, but it was already too late. Two days earlier the defenses had been breached, the garrison overwhelmed, the city taken, and Gordon slain despite the Mahdi's orders that he be taken alive.

Epilogue — The *Khalifa* Abdallahi

With the fall of Khartoum the initial objective of the Mahdi had been achieved as most of the Muslim Sudan came under his control. At this point, however, facing the problems of consolidation and the further extension of his jihad, he died suddenly in June 1885, and a completely new phase of the Mahdist movement now unfolded. There was, first of all, a short power struggle which culminated in the accession of the Khalifa Abdallahi as the Mahdi's successor. Abdallahi was the same Baqqara adherent who had first recognized the Mahdi, and who had subsequently risen to prominence in the movement. His position as commander of the powerful Baqqara forces in the Mahdist army was decisive in bringing about his election, but it also indicated potential divisions among the Mahdist leadership which occupied the attention of the Khalifa immediately upon his assumption of power.

The chief division lay between the Baqqara nomads and the Danaqla and Ja'aliyyin river people, including the Mahdi's own kinsmen known as the *Ashraf*. Abdallahi met this problem with characteristic resourcefulness. He gradually circumscribed the power of the Ashraf by political and military means, finally eliminating them in the course of suppressing an abortive conspiracy in 1891. At the same time he attempted with varying success to tame his unruly Baqqara kinsfolk by forcing them to migrate to the region of his capital at Omdurman on the Nile where he could more successfully keep their refractory tendencies under control. By 1891 his authority over the land had become firmly established, but in the process the ideal of a Muslim theocracy governed according to the Muslim law of the Sharia had been converted into a conventional secular autocracy.

In defending his frontiers, the Khalifa embarked on the initial step in the Mahdi's grandiose objective of world Islamic domination. Here he was to meet ultimate defeat, although at first his affairs went reasonably well. A drawn-out war with Ethiopia between 1887 and 1889 ended in the defeat of Ethiopia and the death of her King Yohannes, while in 1887 an attempt to reestablish an independent sultanate in Darfur was crushed. Less fruitful was the effort to carry the jihad into Egypt, a move that ended disastrously at Tushki above Wadi Halfa in 1889. Indeed, this was a portentous defeat for it demonstrated a Western military superiority which, when later combined with growing Western interest in the African interior, was to culminate in the downfall of the Khalifa's Sudan as an independent African nation.

The final days of the Mahdist state were a reflection more of forces in Europe than in Africa, as demonstrated by the Anglo-Egyptian victory at Tushki. In the early 1890s the Belgians in Leopold's Congo began to probe the Congo-Nile watershed, and in 1895 the French decided to send an expedition into the Bahr al-Ghazal. The following year the British suddenly moved south from Egypt, presumably to protect the Italians in Eritrea from a Mahdist attack after their defeat at Adowa by the Ethiopians in March 1896. A series of engagements followed in which the defenders were successively driven back to Omdurman and there, just north of the city on September 1,1898, they suffered the final blow which put an end to the Mahdist regime in the Sudan. The Khalifa survived for another year before he and his shattered forces were finally destroyed, but by that time his conqueror, General H. H. Kitchener, had moved on to confront the French at Fashoda and another era had opened in the varied fortunes of the eastern Sudan.

Suggestions for Further Reading

The standard history covering the nineteenth-century Sudan is P. M. Holt and M. W. Daly, *A History of the Sudan*, 4th ed. (London: Longman, 1988). A briefer survey by Holt appears in the *Cambridge History of Africa*, vol. V (Cambridge: University Press, 1976). Vivid accounts are to be found in Alan Moorehead, *The White Nile* (London: Hamish Hamilton, 1960; New York: Harper, 1961), and *The Blue Nile* (London: Hamish Hamilton, 1962; New York: Harper, 1962).

The Egyptian occupation is examined in Richard Hill, *Egypt in the Sudan*, 1820-1881 (London: Oxford University Press, 1959); while the southern Sudan is dealt with in Richard Gray, *A History of the Southern Sudan*, 1839-1889 (London: Oxford University Press, 1961). See also Robert Collins, *The Southern Sudan*, 1883-1898 (New Haven: Yale University Press, 1962). Information on customs and traditions among some of the people of the southern Sudan is available in the writings of E. E. Evans-Pritchard and others, but most briefly in M. Fortes and E. E. Evans-Pritchard, eds., *African Political Systems* (London: Oxford University Press, 1940); Daryll Forde, ed., *African Worlds* (London: Oxford University Press, 1954); and Lucy Mair, *Primitive Government* (Baltimore: Penguin, 1962).

The standard work on the Mahdist state is P. M. Holt, *The Mahdist State in the Sudan*, 2nd ed. (Oxford; Clarendon, 1970); and this may be supplemented with J. S. Trimingham's *Islam in the Sudan* (London: Frank Cass, 1965; New York: Barnes & Noble, 1965). Sufism is also dealt with by Trimingham in *The Sufist Orders in Islam* (Oxford: Clarendon, 1971).

11

Population Explosions in Southern Africa

Mfecane—The Road from Zululand

Shaka Zulu is properly regarded as one of the great revolutionary figures in Africa's history. Like Philip of Macedon, he introduced changes in war making that spawned empires and altered the face of his world; yet he was as much the creature as the master of the events he precipitated.

The vast migration of the Bantu people, spilling over subequatorial Africa, appears to have crossed the Limpopo River in the early centuries of the Christian era. Recent archaeological explorations have identified probable Bantu artifacts in the eastern Transvaal and Natal coast, as long ago as the fourth century A.D. This is far earlier than previous estimates that placed the arrival of Bantu speakers in southeastern Africa as roughly contemporaneous with the founding of the Dutch colony at Cape Town.

It was the shape of the land that determined the nature and extent of the Bantu population movements. To the east between the coast and the Drakensberg Mountains lay a fertile valley attractive to a mixed farming people who could grow cereal crops to supplement their stock-raising activities. By the end of the seventeenth century, the Nguni-speaking Xhosa sections of the Bantu were ranged along the Fish River and were in contact with those other pastoralists, the trekboers, moving eastward from the Cape Colony. Farther to the west, the Sotho speakers had fanned out broadly across the plateau below the Limpopo, those to the east penetrating to the Orange River while farther west the Tswana, pressed against the inhospitable Kalahari Desert, were more limited in their southward movement. Finally, on the western side of southern Africa lay the Kalahari itself and the adjacent stretches of the Namib Desert, a last refuge of the Khoikhoi (''Hottentots'') and San

("Bushmen"), and a formidable barrier which held the Bantu advance well to the north.

If geography affected the rate of penetration of these colonists, it also helped to shape their daily lives, placing its mark on political institutions, social customs, and economic practice. The South African plateau was ideally suited to their pastoral-agricultural existence, but it was in its political manifestation that the adaptation to the land was best exemplified. A slow migration was most efficiently carried out by small, independent groups each organized around a royal clan, an arrangement that allowed a working balance between social cohesion and individual expression. Warfare was a small-scale affair involving either grazing rights and cattle, or defense against Khoikhoi and San raiding. There was no need for excessive political centralization. Along the eastern corridor families and settlements were scattered across the well-watered land. Inland on the dry veld, a greater concentration was called for around the few available water holes, but even here the authority of chiefs was limited by a popular assembly and a system of advisory councils, and everywhere chiefly power was forced to bow to the superior authority of public opinion.

Such an arrangement, centralized in conception but loosely administered in practice, readily led to political division as a solution for disputes arising from problems of royal succession and arbitrary rule or conflicts over land rights. Indeed, this had been the essential process of the Bantu dispersion— population growth bringing on social and political stresses which in turn were the basis for emigration and a new buildup of population. The system worked as long as there was free land for expansion, but there was bound to be trouble when the pressure of a rising birth rate could no longer be safely drawn off through migration and a fresh wave of colonization.

It was precisely this form of pressure that seems to have been developing, particularly among the Nguni speakers toward the end of the eighteenth century. On the coastal shelf, the fertile, disease-free country had apparently enjoyed excellent rainfall toward the close of the eighteenth century; then, as is so typical of African weather cycles, there was an abrupt change to serious drought. Thus good harvests and consequent population increase converted to famine in the now overcrowded corridor with resulting political convulsions. Good land became scarce and livelihood uncertain. The nature of warfare changed from a quasi-recreational pastime to a serious struggle for survival, necessitating the institution of a much more rigorously controlled politico-military system. Large-scale, strongly armed political configurations were called for and emerged. In the northern Drakensberg corridor of Zululand appeared three federations under strong leaders—the Ngwane under Sobhuza, the Ndwandwe of Zwide, and the Mthethwa led by Dingiswayo.

Political change necessarily led to social change, but most significant of all was a thoroughgoing revolution in military tactics which profoundly altered the shape of traditional society even as it sought to subserve changing political needs. First to go was the age-old custom of puberty rites involving circumcision, and consequent seclusion and vulnerability of fighting youth over protracted periods. Henceforth, proclaimed Dingiswayo—for it was the Mthethwa who perhaps first instituted the change—young men would be organized into military regiments based on age grades, and the achievement of their manhood would be accomplished on the field of battle, where it could be as effectively demonstrated as it was urgently needed. The new regimental organization soon became widely utilized, for it provided not only greater military efficiency but created a unitary, nationalized army which transcended parochial loyalties and converted the somewhat hypothetical powers of the chief into something more real.

Dingiswayo, however, lacked the ruthlessness and imaginative turn of mind necessary to carry these innovations to their logical conclusion, and it remained for his successor, Shaka, to respond to the demands of the changing times. Here was an outstanding military talent driven by consuming ambition and controlled by a pitiless, and apparently cruel nature. Born out of wedlock, the unwanted son of the chief of the Zulus, Shaka in maturity became physically powerful but psychically crippled by the need to compensate through acknowledged achievement as a man, for the years of ridicule and humiliation endured as a result of his clouded origins. His military prowess soon brought the favor of Dingiswayo who assisted Shaka, despite his disqualifications, to succeed his father as chief of the Zulus, then an insignificant people within the Mthethwa hegemony.

Once in control, Shaka moved swiftly and surely, putting into effect plans that had been long maturing. The traditional warfare of his day had been a casual business conducted by spear-throwing warriors who advanced in loose formation, hurling first invective and then their weapons, retiring when disarmed to fight another day. Little permanent damage was done by these war games which were designed not for slaughter but for cattle raiding. Shaka's innovations were shattering. In place of a handful of light spears, he provided his troops with a short, heavy, stabbing *assegai*, or spear, which was used as a sword at close quarters and discarded in battle only on pain of death. The Zulu regiments were thoroughly trained and disciplined to fight en masse by direction, never as individuals. They adopted and refined the "cow horn" formation, reminiscent of the Macedonian phalanx, which employed a massive center with swift, enveloping wings capable of attacking a flank and engulfing the enemy rear in a pincer movement. The close-formation advance behind a wall of giant cowhide shields was adequate protection against thrown weapons; then at close quarters, the heavy stabbing assegai came into murderous play, combining with the iron discipline and coordinated tactics to spread dismay and disaster among the enemy. Precision and discipline were provided by constant drilling, for Shaka placed his army on a permanent war footing, segregating his troops in training camps where they practiced and perfected their skills all the year round. The enforced celibacy which he imposed on his army may have been an effort at population control, but it also insured that individual zeal would be concentrated on military matters. Total warfare was the essence of Shaka's reforms, and none less well prepared could stand before his attack.

What followed changed the face of southern and central Africa. By the time Shaka became chief of the Zulu, the Ndwandwe had routed Sobhuza's forces which retired northward and eventually established themselves as the Swazi nation. Then, about 1818, the victorious Ndwandwe under Zwide met Dingiswayo's Mthethwa in a climactic battle during which the Mthethwa were routed and Dingiswayo killed. Whether by design or accident, Shaka and his Zulu took no part in the fighting, but whatever the circumstances, Shaka thenceforward stood unrestrained by obligation to any overlord, free to work for his own cause and to put his new ideas and military strength to the test. Thus began the *Mfecane*—the time of troubles.

Shaka added the remnants of the Mthethwa to his Zulu forces, then stood off the Ndwandwe hordes in the pivotal battle of Gqokoli Hill, his tactics and the discipline of his troops succeeding brilliantly against heavily superior numbers. Another engagement followed in which the Ndwandwe were routed and split, their power shattered, leaving Shaka master of Zululand. Zwide and a small contingent survived to renew the dispute with Shaka another day, but two other groups under Soshangane and Zwangendaba abandoned their lands to the victors, moving northward eventually to place their mark on the territories lying beyond the Limpopo.

Shaka's significance lies less in his career subsequent to this point than it does in the type of state he was able to develop as well as in the widening ramifications of the Mfecane (*Difaqane* in the Sotho tongue) throughout southern and central Africa. Initially, the Zulu nation had been tiny, but with the fall first of the Mthethwa and then the Ndwandwe, it grew rapidly by accretion, and as a result of subsequent campaigns, many additional groups and their territory were grafted on to the rapidly expanding Zulu state. The traditional pattern of Nguni society made this process easy, for each tribal unit was already organized along territorial lines with loyalties in terms of the chief, not the lineage, and groups had long contained people from many different unrelated clans. What Shaka did was greatly to accelerate this process through military conquest, insuring allegiance to the center by controlling and limiting the authority of territorial subchiefs, and ruling through his military *indunas*, the common-born leaders of his regiments.

Shaka's major political innovation, however, was the establishment of military barracks on the king's domain, which did much more than create an irresistible fighting machine—it brought together youth from all parts of the land and bound them together irrevocably in a common age grouping and a mutually shared mortal danger. All were dependent upon the king for their livelihood, all viewed him as the focal point of personal loyalty, all were imbued with a sense of Zulu nationalism which would stay with them for the rest of their days. Under Shaka, therefore, the Nguni state system with its centralization in embryo became a highly integrated political unity containing a thoroughgoing cultural assimilation. Herein lay the basis for a latter-day Zulu national cohesiveness and pride, a sense of unity that came to be imitated by other people in southern and central Africa.

Shaka's whole system was built on force, and this was both his strength and his weakness. The purpose of the state was the formation of a strong military establishment, and the purpose of this in turn was political aggrandizement. Year after year, the Zulu armies went forth to battle, and soon the territory between the Tugela River north toward Delagoa Bay was Zulu, while south of the river Natal lay devastated and Pondoland was under continuing pressure. In 1826 the remnants of the Ndwandwe were annihilated in a final battle, and several smaller groups were absorbed. By 1828, plans were maturing for a major push to the south against the people between Natal and the Cape Colony frontier. Not only would this put all of the Nguni under Zulu control but it would also bring contact with the Europeans and access to their trade goods and military knowledge. A decade of warfare had taken its toll, however. Even the most sanguine were tired of unrelieved campaigning and bloodletting; even the most savage spirits were shaken by Shaka's brutality. While the armies were far from home on campaign, an assassination plot was conceived and Shaka was cut down by his brother, Dingane, much to the relief of friend and foe alike. Shaka's career had lasted a brief ten years but in that short span a whole new nation and way of life had come into being; more than that, the ramifications of his conquests would carry on long after his death and far beyond the limited frontiers of Zululand.

Dingane became the new Zulu king and, despite the wave of reaction that raised him to power, he soon resumed the militarist policies of the great conqueror. Dingane's problems, however, were to originate in another quarter. A colony of British merchants and missionaries had for some years been gathering at Port Natal, which became a natural rallying point for Zulu dissidents as well as a potential colony of the Cape government. More serious still, the Boer cattle herders of the Great Trek, singling out Natal as an ultimate destination, had defeated the Zulus in 1838 and forced Dingane to evacuate all territory below the Tugela River. From that point forward the European influence slowly overwhelmed the Zulu state. The withdrawal north across the Tugela so undermined Dingane's prestige that he was unseated in 1840 by his brother, Mpande, who thenceforward carried on a conciliatory policy toward the Boers. Finally, during the 1870s, the Zulus unwittingly became an issue between the British and the Boers, which ultimately led to the defeat of Cetewayo, Mpande's successor, in 1879. Thus ended, for practical purposes, the independent Zulu nation.

Central Africa and the Great Ngoni Trek

Long before the final demise of the Zulu kingdom, the effects of the Mfecane were being experienced over a range of a thousand miles to the north, as far as the region of the great lakes of Malawi and Tanganyika. The violent defeat of the Ndwandwe by Shaka caused the movement of a number of people, including two sections of Zwide's defeated force, destined to play an important role in the subsequent history of central Africa. One of these groups under Soshangane paused near Delagoa Bay during the 1820s, then moved inland where it came into conflict with the other fugitives led by Zwangendaba. Ousting his rival who was sent reeling westward, Soshangane created the Gaza empire which imposed its rule from the Zambezi to the Limpopo and reduced the Portuguese trading settlements in Mozambique to tributary status. In time, however, the Gaza state came under increasing pressure from European imperial interests, and in 1895 it was finally incorporated into Portugal's African holdings.

The fate of the defeated followers of Zwangendaba was of more epic proportions—first, a long series of great victories and bitter defeats experienced in the process of a monumental migration which lasted a full generation and covered a march of a thousand miles and more; then, the establishment of major kingdoms comprising many diverse peoples, all in a world far removed from their original home in northern Zululand.

Such great achievements had modest beginnings. Zwangendaba's Jere people were but a minor group torn loose from their lands by the force of the Mfecane. Fleeing into southern Mozambique, they were badly mauled by Soshangane about 1831, passing into the Shona country of the Changamire empire where once again they suffered defeat, this time by another body of migrating Nguni speakers. Defeat was not unrelieved, however, for the Jere, or Ngoni, as they began to be called, brought Zulu fighting tactics with them which enabled them to subdue most local people encountered, many of whom were not only defeated but absorbed, thus expanding the size and strength of the Ngoni as their migration proceeded. In Mashonaland they devastated Changamire, then turned north to cross the Zambezi in November 1835, at which point a new phase in Ngoni history began.

North of the Zambezi, the Ngoni entered a region free of other southern marauders, inhabited partly by strong states related to the Lunda but also by decentralized villagers who were an easy prey for the invaders. Zwangendaba's hordes swept through the countryside, halting to engulf defenseless communities and ravage their lands, then moving on to new pastures to repeat the process. Although marked by protracted pauses of several years each, the line of march moved steadily northward, passing to the west of Lake Malawi until a point was reached east of the southern tip of Lake Tanganyika. Here Zwangendaba paused and built a center called Mapupo, for his people were weary, there were ominous divisions developing within the nation, and the

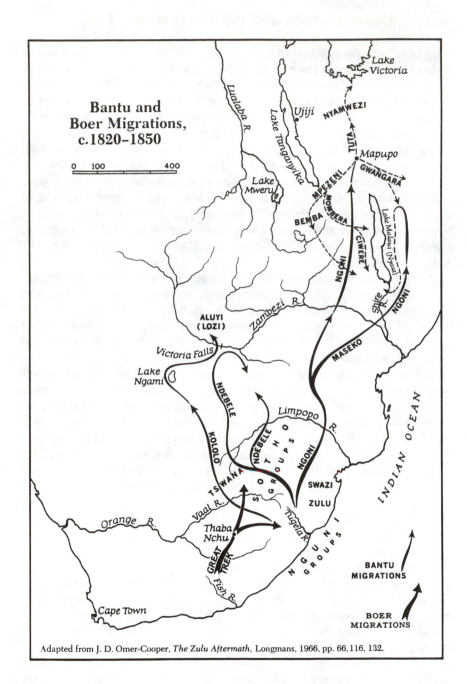

Bantu and Boer Migrations, c. 1820–1850

0   100   400

Adapted from J. D. Omer-Cooper, *The Zulu Aftermath*, Longmans, 1966, pp. 66, 116, 132.

old chief was ill and flagging in energy. About 1848 he died at Mapupo. It was twenty years since the great migration had begun far to the south in the defeat of the Ndwandwe.

Zwangendaba's own outstanding qualities of leadership aside, what had given the Ngoni cohesion and strength was the manner in which they dealt with those they conquered—that total political and cultural assimilation of one people by another which has frequently characterized African societies. Like the Lunda concept of positional succession or the extension of the original Asante royal clan to embrace former adversaries, the Ngoni system found a place for the vanquished which brought much-needed strength to the state and offered a new life to those who might otherwise have been faced with slavery and death. War captives were merely added to the homesteads of the original Jere families, becoming lowly but fully recognized relatives of their adopted masters. The young men were initiated into age-grade fighting regiments without prejudice and could rise to highest prominence solely on military ability. As more captives were taken, they too were absorbed, and so the nation grew through accretion and natural increase. Political unity was maintained by means of the original Ngoni clan pattern which developed in complexity to take account of the naturalized adherents who far outnumbered the first migrants from Zululand. The military efficiency and fighting tactics of Zululand and Jere social structure and cultural values survived, secure in the devotion accorded by all to the idea of Ngoni nationhood.

Nevertheless in time stresses developed. The death of Zwangendaba removed one major cohesive force while the growing size and complexity of the nation encouraged cleavages which were as natural as they were characteristic of the long-lived process of the Bantu dispersion. Eventually secessions took place which broke the Ngoni into five different groups, and in this form the final stage of the Ngoni migration was effected. Zwangendaba's death brought on a successional struggle which culminated in a complicated series of splits. First, a small group of dissidents fled northward along the eastern side of Lake Tanganyika. Known as the Tuta, they captured and absorbed many Nyamwezi, a people with whom they later cooperated, while contributing their share to the chronic unrest which so greatly assisted Arab slave procurement in the region of the Tabora-Ujiji route. Another section, called the Gwangara, escaped to the eastern side of Lake Malawi where they came to dominate what is now southeastern Tanzania, although ultimately dividing into two separate kingdoms. Meanwhile, the main body of Ngoni split in half, one group under Mpezeni moving westward into Bemba country and then eastward to the Fort Jameson area of modern Zambia; the other led by Mombera doubling back on Zwangendaba's route and settling in the highlands west of Lake Malawi. The fifth Ngoni state, Ciwere, broke off from Mombera and finally took possession of territory in the Dowa uplands in the southern part of present-day Malawi. A sixth group of migrants, generally classified as Ngoni and called Maseko after their leader, had journeyed northward independently of

Zwangendaba and, after many difficulties, finally established themselves in the Shire country south of Lake Malawi.

Thus the effects of the Mfecane came to central Africa in the form of wars and raids, but it was also responsible for the introduction of Ngoni culture and polity and the revolutionary idea in much of eastern and central Africa that people of different language and background could be welded into large-scale and lasting state systems. While the Ngoni kingdoms disappeared in the course of the European occupation of central Africa during the last part of the nineteenth century, the sense of common identity which they engendered has lingered on.

The Search for Security—Sebetwane and Mzilikazi

The upheavals in Zululand greatly intensified the social and political instability of the southern Bantu, tearing peoples from their lands, sending them scrambling for safety, both pursued and pursuer, both refugees and aggressors. Throughout the plateau west of the Drakensberg scarp ran the shock waves of the Mfecane, gathering intensity as they proceeded, dealing death and destruction, emptying habitable land, drawing together fugitives of diverse background into centers of desperate defense, and dispatching others in a flight from fear that begot violence and bloodshed.

It was quickly apparent that the effects of the Mfecane could not be contained within the narrow limits of the coastal shelf east of the Drakensberg Mountains. The early skirmishing between Ndwandwe and Mthethwa soon involved other people, for example, the Hlubi, costing them their cattle and their grazing grounds and forcing them over the scarp and up onto the plateau where the Sotho speakers predominated. At once the Hlubi fell on the Tlokwa, ousting them from their territory and sending them on an extended migration in search of survival and marked by warfare and pillage. Among those attacked in turn by the Tlokwa were a Sotho group, the Kololo, who lost their cattle in defeat and fled across the Vaal, starving but determined to recoup their losses at the expense of others.

There followed a long odyssey toward the northwest. Led by their young resourceful chief, Sebetwane, and employing Shakan military methods, the Kololo embarked on an extended trek fighting their way through the Tswana country, sometimes victorious, sometimes defeated, alternately losing their cattle and gaining new herds, enduring the rigors of the Kalahari, and finally after years of wandering arriving on the Zambezi above Victoria Falls. Here they encountered new hazards in the form of hostile people and an unfamiliar terrain, for this was the floodplain of the Zambezi, virtually submerged during part of the year and requiring mastery of radically different fighting techniques and methods of agriculture. Somehow the Kololo managed to adapt themselves to this new land and succeeded in subduing the local people in 1838, while beating off attacks of other marauding Nguni-speaking groups.

Once the Kololo had established themselves and eliminated outside threats, there remained the difficult problem of administering the more numerous indigenous Aluyi with their different culture and language. This was accomplished by fusion between the two groups through intermarriage and the elevation of local leaders to positions of prominence. The Aluyi soon accepted the name of Kololo and willingly adopted the language and traditions of the southerners. A strong, peaceful state emerged which greatly impressed David Livingstone when he first visited the Kololo kingdom in 1851, but in fact its strength proved more apparent than real. When Sebetwane died suddenly that same year, a problem of succession arose which could not be satisfactorily resolved. Fissures appeared between the Kololo and their local subjects, and in 1864 the former, already reduced by malaria, were overthrown and scattered. Kololo influence survived, however, for the Lozi, as they now called themselves, in effect continued to use the language of the intruders as well as elements of their customs. "We hear everyone around us speaking Sesuto," an observer remarked years later, adding, "The same customs, the same manner, the same dress, the same sociability and official code of politeness. . . . It really requires an effort of mind to believe oneself on the Zambezi."

Of the many threats which Sebetwane endured in his flight toward security, the most persistent was that of Mzilikazi and his Ndebele. This Nguni-speaking people spread terror and destruction in broad strokes across southern Africa during the years of their wandering, yet they too were fugitives, seeking refuge from attack, conquering in their rush to avoid being conquered. Their flight began, like many others, in Zululand where Mzilikazi committed the gross indiscretion as one of Shaka's military leaders of refusing to turn over to his overlord a number of cattle captured in a raid. This was bald rebellion, and Mzilikazi and his small group soon found themselves in headlong flight over the mountains to escape the avenging Zulu regiments.

This incident occurred about 1821, and for the next fifteen years the Ndebele became involved in a running struggle for survival which did not end until they had safely established themselves in Matabeleland. At first they paused in the northern Transvaal from where their hunting parties ranged widely in search of cattle and captives among the less martial Sotho and Tswana. In 1825, however, Mzilikazi was on the move southwestward in search of better range and greater security from Shaka's regiments. For almost ten years the Ndebele maintained themselves near the site of present-day Pretoria. It was a heavily settled area when they arrived but the systematic destruction of towns and seizure of livestock quickly depopulated the countryside. The local people were decimated, their men put to the sword and their women and children absorbed to add their strength to the Ndebele military state. Those who escaped lived wretchedly in marginal areas which they disputed with wild beasts, leaving the accessible land in the hands of the conquerors.

Still, security was elusive in this land of shifting fortune. Mzilikazi's growing nation lacked the stability that comes with longevity, and to his south were bands of Griqua and Khoikhoi whose mounted riflemen were more than a match for a massed assegai charge and whose hunger for cattle drew them to Mzilikazi's massive herds. Soon the Ndebele were under attack which they stood off with difficulty while their peril was compounded by a new Zulu punitive campaign ordered by Dingane. Once again the order was given and the Ndebele began moving westward into Tswana country.

In 1836 a new peril appeared in the form of the Boer trekkers. Attacked by the Ndebele, they struck back, routing the charging regiments with their rifle fire and eventually sacking Mzilikazi's towns and confiscating large numbers of cattle. This devastating rout precipitated a long march to the north across the Limpopo where, after more difficulties including a brush with the Kololo of Sebetwane, the exhausted Ndebele settled permanently in the country that had once been the domain of Changamire.

That the Ndebele survived as a unit and eventually emerged stronger than ever in Matabeleland reflected the toughness of the military-political state that evolved during their migration. Leaving Zululand with the classic Shakan battle techniques, Mzilikazi organized his people into military regiments which constituted individual settlements of soldiers with supporting civilian population, each commanded by a military leader and considered as part of the king's household. The older men served as reserves to a permanent standing army which was augmented from time to time by newly formed age regiments to which captive people were added. In this military hierarchy there was no room for traditional chiefs, and absolute power rested with Mzilikazi, the king, who owned most of the cattle, distributed marriageable girls among his warriors, and ruled through his regimental indunas. Upon the settlement in Matabeleland, the military towns grew into permanent geographic divisions and service in the age regiments became hereditary. The cohesiveness of the state was now enhanced by two additional factors. In the first place, the regional governors were the military leaders whose nonroyal origins precluded their organizing secession movements. Moreover, a class system slowly emerged which gave primary rank to the descendants of the original Ndebele, thus preserving Ndebele culture and language in the face of the massive infusions of conquered peoples. Nevertheless, when Mzilikazi died in 1868, these safeguards did not prevent a dispute over the succession which went to his son, Lobengula, only as the outcome of civil war.

Moshoeshoe and the Diplomacy of Self-Defense

Not all the victims of the Mfecane ran; not all sought to solve the problem of national security by adopting the violent tactics of Shaka. In Basutoland, security through the consolidation of diverse peoples was still the objective, but this was to be effected by diplomacy rather than by warfare. In the long run a policy of conciliation succeeded where violence failed—a new nation was conceived during the turbulent years following the rise of Shaka and that nation survives today, modest but independent.

The Basuto nation was the work of a most unusual and gifted statesman. During the early years of the nineteenth century, Moshoeshoe (Moshesh), the young prince of an obscure Sotho section, began to take account of the defensive possibilities of the flat-topped hills which were common to the mountainous region just west of the Drakensberg scarp opposite Natal. He saw that these heights could be defended against large numbers of attackers if properly provisioned and fortified. With a small group of young men he therefore established himself on an upland called Butha Buthe, and soon had the opportunity to test the validity of his strategy.

The repercussions of the Mfecane had thrown the Hlubi across the Drakensberg front and dislodged the powerful Tlokwa under their queen regent, Mma Ntatisi, and her son, Sikonyela. In their predatory migration, the Tlokwa attacked Butha Buthe on two occasions and were repulsed only with difficulty, carrying off Moshoeshoe's cattle and driving his people to the brink of starvation. It was clear that, although the principle of defense was sound, a better site than Butha Buthe was needed, one where not only an army but a whole people could stand off attack indefinitely. When such a place was finally located about 1824, Moshoeshoe led his people to the new site, called Thaba Bosiu, in a brilliantly executed march through bandit- and cannibal-infested territory. Now, at last, he had a firm base on which to build a viable state.

Although military defense was an essential element of Basuto policy, the success of the nation rested ultimately on the wisdom and diplomatic skill of Moshoeshoe himself, and Moshoeshoe's statesmanship in turn was based upon several major principles. In the first place, the psychology of military defense and the need for survival argued for the primacy of peaceful negotiation over warfare. Again and again, Moshoeshoe resorted to diplomacy in place of force and, more often than not, his patience was rewarded. The starving tribal remnants infesting the environs of Thaba Bosiu were won over from cannibalism and brigandage by the offer of food and shelter. The tough, vengeful Zulu were neutralized through a judicious use of tribute. In 1831, after repelling a fierce Ndebele assault on his stronghold, Moshoeshoe completely disarmed the attackers by offering them cattle in place of the usual insults.

This was no policy of weakness, but rather a shrewd strategy designed to exploit human vanity or to offer an adversary the opportunity for graceful withdrawal from an embarrassing position. If such means failed, Moshoeshoe had recourse to his second principle, that of dividing his opponents—for example, his successful elimination of the Tlokwa by inducing other groups to attack this aggressive people, and at a later time, his persistent efforts to woo the British as a counterbalance to the menace he saw in the Boer settlers.

Finally, Moshoeshoe possessed the imagination and flexibility to profit from the strength of his enemies, to use their techniques on behalf of his own cause. From the Griqua raiders he learned the use of firearms, guerrilla tactics, and the swiftness of horse-borne sallies, military skills that later stood him in good stead against the Boers in contradistinction to the suicidal assegai charges of the Ndebele. To meet European diplomacy Moshoeshoe encouraged missionaries to settle in his territories where they were able to render invaluable assistance in the complex dealings with Boer and Briton, but without being permitted to dominate and divert Basuto policy.

To some extent these were elements of a negative posture of defense, the positive side of which was the creation of a healthy, strong Basuto nation. Here again Moshoeshoe successfully brought into play his diplomatic talents. Persuasion, not force, held the loyalty of the many different people who came to live in the mountain refuge with its center at Thaba Bosiu. Small heterogeneous groups were permitted to retain their own leaders under the surveillance of members of Moshoeshoe's ruling family. Larger groups were essentially self-governing, required only to acknowledge the ultimate authority of Moshoeshoe. Cultural differences were gradually overcome by propinquity, and national bonds grew strong in a spirit of mutual need and respect. Above all was the example of Moshoeshoe himself, always the man of peace, always the diplomatist, always placing reason before choler. In the difficult days of the Boer expansion, Moshoeshoe was to be the salvation of the Basuto nation.

The Boer Trekkers

The land hunger that precipitated the Bantu Mfecane was also a major force behind the Great Trek of the Boer cattle herders, but there were other important factors working as well. First of all was the attitude toward race within the Cape Colony, which equated status with pigmentation. As the nineteenth century opened, the colony numbered approximately seventy-five thousand inhabitants, but only one in three was a free white, the others being slaves, freed bondsmen, Khoikhoi, or an emerging population of mixed blood, these latter the issue of interracial unions, many consummated legally or illegally in the interior. The sense of cultural and racial superiority that seemed to accompany European colonization in all continents was manifest in South Africa, reinforced both by the economic necessity of labor shortage leading to coercion and exploitation, and the policies of the East India Company that had legalized a stratified society under white domination. Though racial attitudes were somewhat more relaxed in the cosmopolitan ambience of Cape Town, on the eastern frontier geographic isolation and indifferent enforcement of law and order intensified a seeming need for discipline of servant by master in a narrow world that proclaimed the doctrine of human inequality. A second factor was the chronic distaste for authority which obsessed the trekboers' mentality. Already they had moved far to the east, vexed even by those uncertain and flaccid controls imposed by the Dutch East India Company. The administration of the British could only strengthen resentment and suspicion, especially since the new régime appeared to represent viewpoints that contradicted Boer principles regarding individual freedom and racial inferiority.

British rule, therefore, was a deeply disturbing factor, for it introduced concepts genuinely foreign to the South African society that had evolved over one hundred fifty years in relative isolation from European intellectual developments. For one thing there was the idea of administrative efficiency, particularly with respect to land registration, which attempted a systematic linkage of individuals to the land for purposes of taxation, orderly settlement, and more efficient farm management. To the Boer this smacked of tyranny, as did another British innovation, rule by law. The introduction of a professional judiciary independent equally of interested parties and executive pressure was a novelty which might have been better endured had the new magistrates been of higher competence. Unhappily, British zeal for reform did not extend to the desire to pay for it, with the result that officials were no more efficient and far less representative than they had been formerly. Worst of all, the British brought with them humanitarian impulses which preached such aberrations as emancipation for slaves, and equality before the law for all people. These notions shook a world long accustomed to a rigid caste system, and the paternalistic dispensing of ad hoc justice.

At first, the application of British rule seemed to favor the frontier farmer. To combat vagrancy, it was decreed in 1809 that Khoikhoi have a fixed address, thus virtually compelling them to take service and making extremely difficult the establishment of a free labor market. A few years later an ordinance permitted the apprenticing of Khoikhoi children to farms where they had grown up. The vagrancy code, however, also provided legal safeguards insuring equitable contracts, and in 1812 the so-called Black Circuit Court heard evidence in support of charges by Khoikhoi servants and passed sentence on white masters where accusations of mistreatment were proved.

Such steps were but a prelude to the far-reaching Fiftieth Ordinance of 1828 which sought nothing less than the complete overhaul of the codes governing the legal and civil status of the "coloured" population. Dr. John Philip, superintendent in South Africa for the London Missionary Society, had already attacked restrictions on Khoikhoi rights to freedom of labor and of movement. Whatever the influence of Philip and other missionaries, the government's Fiftieth Ordinance was instituted, banishing vagrancy and pass laws, at once guaranteeing freedom of work and the end of color discrimination by law. In 1834, with the abolition of slavery in the British Empire, former bondsmen automatically were brought under the provisions of the Fiftieth Ordinance, while concurrently an attempt by the legislative council in Cape Town to institute a new vagrancy law was disallowed in London.

Frequently reforms were tactlessly applied or gained little advantage to compensate for the ill will they engendered. The thoroughgoing and necessary revision of the administration of justice undertaken in 1828 was offset by a needless abolition of the old *heemraden* courts which were popular and familiar and could have been easily adapted to the new system. At the same time, the inauguration of a policy making English the sole official language in the country gained the resentment that was a first step toward eventual emergence of the Afrikaans language in South Africa. The abolition of slavery, moreover, was poorly implemented in the Cape Colony. Not only were farmers irritated by the prospect of former slaves possessing legal equality, but many were deprived of proper compensation through faulty administration and some forced into bankruptcy as a result.

British administration also interfered fatefully on the frontier, where Boer and Bantu contended with each other for possession of the same land. Rising population pressure meant chronic unrest which government policy was unable to soothe. First, the establishment of a fortified frontier in 1812 led to the outbreak of war and the substitution in 1819 of a neutral zone between the Great Fish and Keiskamma rivers. Unoccupied land such as this was no less than an invitation to violence which burst forth in 1834 after several years of drought had sorely tried black and white alike. In the fighting, the Xhosa were driven back and in 1835 Governor Benjamin D'Urban annexed the land between the Great Fish and Kei rivers, the neutral Fish-Keiskamma zone absorbed into the Colony, and the land from Keiskamma to the Kei designated as Queen Adelaide Province, to be henceforward available for further Boer colonization. The natural jubilation of the frontier settlers, however, was soon converted to outrage for, responding to missionary pressure, the government in London reversed D'Urban's policy and returned the annexed territory to African hands. The year was 1836, and the Great Trek, already underway, now began in earnest.

The Boer farmers had had enough of official policy. The philosophy of the Fiftieth Ordinance extended to the Bantu was anathema to these people; neither would their land hunger, long deprived, be satisfied by a pattern of permanent settlement with its entanglement of quitrents, land sales, survey charges, title deeds, and crown lands. A much more attractive alternative, more in keeping with their past history and spirit of independence, was a move on to new lands beyond the reach of the unsympathetic authorities and their hateful edicts. If the government chose to allow the Africans to remain in the coastal lands, they would move inland where their scouts reported vast expanses of unoccupied tracts. Here, where there was no Fiftieth Ordinance and servants knew their place, they could build a new life.

Altogether one out of every five Dutch-speaking South Africans joined the trek, drawn mostly from the less settled eastern regions. The parties went off in varying sized groups, sometimes only a handful of families, sometimes in larger companies. Their ox-drawn wagons contained all their belongings, moving along at the rate of about six miles a day which was the best that could be expected from grazing cattle, sheep, and goats. There was work for everyone. The men were busy with the livestock, repairs for the trek gear, hunting, and standing guard. The women cooked, mended, and cared for the children, while small boys were expected to help with the herds. It was desperately hard work in the face of a perilous present and an uncertain future. Variously searching for mountain passes, cutting tracks, dismantling wagons for the backbreaking passage across the mountains, enduring fevers, loss of livestock, dwindling supplies, and uncertain harvests, many were to perish and all would suffer.

Avoiding the heavily populated coastal strip, the trekkers moved inland, crossing the Orange River and skirting the mountain stronghold of Moshoeshoe's Basutoland. Here in Transorangia they paused, uncertain whether to strike north across the Vaal River or alternatively to turn east over the Drakensbergs into the valley of Natal. The land was empty and the Boer parties at first largely unopposed, but the reason was ominous for the silence was that of fear and devastation, not of peaceful solitude. The effects of the Mfecane were in full force—the high plains had been cleared by the rampaging Ndebele, Sikonyela's Tlokwa were harassing Moshoeshoe's fortress, Griqua parties were raiding across the Orange River, while the Zulu regiments of Dingane held the coastal belt in a grip of terror. As intruders, the Boers could have these new lands, but only if they were able to take them by force.

While the individual parties were congregating at Thaba Nchu in Transorangia, an engagement was fought to the north near the Vaal River which gave a taste of things to come. In October 1836, a party of trekkers beat off a series of furious attacks by Ndebele regiments, taking a heavy toll with their firepower but losing all their livestock in the engagement. Retiring to Thaba Nchu with difficulty, they there joined a growing debate as to the future direction and leadership of the trek. It was finally agreed to turn east to Natal under the experienced frontiersman, Piet Retief, but before the Drakensberg Mountains were reached, the group split, one wing led by Andries Potgieter turning north and crossing the Vaal. By this time there were already more than two thousand trekkers, all of an independent turn of mind, resistant to the idea of a coordinated, disciplined movement which their perilous circumstances demanded.

Thereafter success vied with disaster. Potgieter fell on the Ndebele in the autumn of 1837, defeating them so decisively that Mzilikazi decided to abandon his territories to the victors and take his people to the less fiercely contended regions beyond the Limpopo. Thus the Transvaal fell to the trekkers, but Retief's contingent suffered a far different fate beyond the mountains. Asking that his group be accommodated in Natal, Retief met a qualified acceptance from Dingane who required only that Retief regain some cattle taken by

Sikonyela, the Tlokwa chief. When this was achieved with relative ease and the trekkers had already begun to descend the scarp into Natal, Dingane became alarmed and put Retief and his party to death when they returned with the cattle in February 1838, then turned his troops on the Boer wagon trains, scattering them and almost succeeding in wiping them out. In the long run it was a vain effort, for assegai charges could not contend with rifle fire. With the assistance of reinforcements led by Andries Pretorious, the Boers counterattacked and in December 1838 routed the Zulus at Blood River, bringing about Dingane's eventual downfall and the accession to power of the tractable Mpande. The Zulu hold on Natal was broken.

The Shape of Things to Come— South Africa at Mid-Century

There was no precise end to the Great Trek. Settlers continued to cross the Orange River in their wagons, but already by 1840 the tone of the movement was beginning to change from a quest for new land to the consolidation of territory already acquired. The backbone of Bantu resistance had cracked with the defeats of Dingane and Mzilikazi, but military subjugation of the African nations would prove to be the least of the trekkers' problems. Both the Mfecane and the Great Trek were convulsive responses to population pressure and land hunger, and when the clamor and the dust of battle had subsided, it was found by Bantu and Boer alike that the people and the land were still there and the old problems persisted, albeit in vastly new dimension. The Great Trek, moreover, had been a flight from British authority—indeed, almost an anarchistic rejection of authority in any form—yet an ordered society and a stable government would be essential if the gains of the trekkers were to be consolidated. As always, dilemma was not to be resolved in flight.

In Natal, the Boers had no sooner won their haven from oppression than trouble began to pile upon trouble. The trekkers, handy with a rifle or a woodsman's ax, lacked either sympathy or experience for government. Insubordination and factionalism undermined authority and rendered futile any rational solution to economic problems rooted in the matter of land distribution. Farmers could not be prevented from moving over the frontier into Bantu country, cattle raids and hunting parties were unrestrained, many forays returned with Zulu orphan children under an apprenticeship that was tantamount to slavery, and attempts were made to clear Natal of her tens of thousands of Africans by driving them south into Pondoland. The land distribution policy, reflecting cherished Boer principles of freedom, dealt out six-thousand-acre farms with an open hand which took no account of valuation, occupancy, and tax assessment, let alone such refinements as land surveying.

Having fled from the jurisdiction of the Cape government, the settlers had

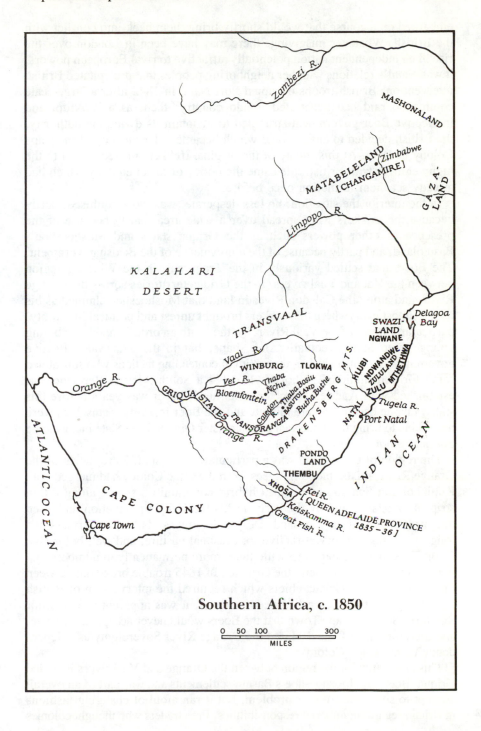

Southern Africa, c. 1850

MASHONALAND

MATABELELAND
[CHANGAMIRE]

Zimbabwe

GAZA-
LAND

Zambezi R.

Limpopo R.

KALAHARI
DESERT

TRANSVAAL

Vaal R.

Orange R.

WINBURG

Vet R.

Thaba
Nchu

Bloemfontein

Caledon R.

Thaba Bosiu

BASUTOLAND

Butha-Buthe

Orange R.

TRANSORANGIA

GRIQUA STATES

ATLANTIC
OCEAN

CAPE COLONY

Cape Town

CAPE COLONY

PONDO
LAND

THEMBU

XHOSA

Kei R.

[QUEEN ADELAIDE PROVINCE
1835–36]

Keiskamma R.

Great Fish R.

TLOKWA

SWAZI-
LAND
NGWANE

Delagoa
Bay

HLUBI

NDWANDWE

ZULULAND

ZULU MTHETHWA

Tugela R.

NATAL

Port Natal

INDIAN
OCEAN

DRAKENSBERG MTS.

0   50 100   300
MILES

embarked on a course that would shortly bring them back into conflict with the British. Whatever misgivings there may have been in London over the rise of an independent nation potentially attractive to rival European powers, it was Natal's relations with her neighboring peoples that precipitated British intervention. British troops occupied Port Natal in 1842 after a large-scale commando raid had penetrated Pondo country; then, as a bankrupt and ineffective Boer government struggled to maintain its dwindling authority, the British decided to annex Natal which became a dependency of the Cape Colony in 1845. At this, many of the original trekkers moved inland to the high veld, for with British rule came the policy of racial equality which had already set them in motion once before.

In the interior the situation, no less desperate, was more confused, partly because the trekkers were spread over a wide area, partly because of the presence of other powers such as the Griqua states and Moshoeshoe's Basutoland, and partly because of the ambivalence of the British government. The Boers had settled variously in the Transvaal, in the Winburg region between the Vet and Vaal rivers, in the Griqua territories across the Orange River, and along the Caledon River in land that Moshoeshoe claimed as his own. Almost everywhere the trekkers brought unrest and political instability, particularly north of the Vaal River. To the south an orderly and law-abiding Orange Free State eventually took shape, but in the Transvaal effective government remained elusive, the victim of contending factions who substituted force for constitutional authority. In 1844 a South African Republic was established with Andries Potgieter at its head, but it was years before this state in name became a state in fact, and the Boer trekkers themselves were never able to bring the Transvaal and her sister Orange Free State into a single political union.

The region of Griqualand was a particularly sore spot. Here, north of the Orange River, mixed-blood refugees from the Cape Colony had merged with Khoikhoi and San strains to form hybrid communities strung along a thin strip of arid land, and by the early 1820s the Griqua population had risen to approximately three thousand. Despite its low rainfall, Boer farmers had long found this territory attractive for seasonal pasture, and well before the Great Trek they had begun to settle there more permanently in numbers that would eventually overwhelm the Griquas. In 1845 trouble broke out between the settlers and the Griqua chiefs which required the intervention of British troops. By the time peace had been restored, it was apparent to Governor Sir Harry Smith at Cape Town that the Boers would never accept Griqua rule, and therefore in 1848 he declared the Orange River Sovereignty as a dependency of the Cape Colony.

This annexation of the region between the Orange and Vaal rivers included Griqua, Boer, and Moshoeshoe's Basuto settlements and was part of an overall attempt to solve the frontier problem, but it ran afoul of changing fashions in Britain regarding imperial responsibilities. Free traders who thought colonies expensive encumbrances combined with liberals subscribing to the doctrine of self-determination and together they raised questions about a deepening involvement in a worldwide colonial establishment. In addition, missionary influence was at low ebb after an expedition up the Niger in 1841 resulted in almost fifty European deaths from malaria. Reacting to these factors, Parliament began to favor withdrawal and retrenchment, and this mood hardened as far as South Africa was concerned when fresh hostilities broke out on the frontier in 1850. In 1852 the British concluded the Sand River Convention which recognized the independence of the Boers beyond the Vaal. Two years later the Bloemfontein Convention did the same for those settled between the Vaal and Orange rivers. The trekkers had at last succeeded in establishing the independent states they had set out to found.

British diplomacy and imperial strategy also had profound implications for the Basuto nation of Moshoeshoe where the pressure of settlers had been steadily building up around the edges of his mountain stronghold. As a result of a treaty with the British in 1846, Moshoeshoe set aside land along the Caledon River where the major Boer settlements had developed, but this arrangement was considered inadequate by those farmers located deeper in Basuto territory and they refused to give up their homesteads. Boer farms and Basuto villages were soon interspersed to a degree that made a fixed boundary difficult. When the Orange River Sovereignty was established, the question of boundary had been left unsettled, then was later defined by the British resident at Bloemfontein, H. D. Warden, to the intense dissatisfaction of the Basuto, many of whom now found themselves isolated across the frontier from their own people.

Moshoeshoe, who had long foreseen the danger of fixed boundaries, was unable to control his polyglot followers, and fighting broke out. Worse still, Moshoeshoe was confronted with a British power whose aid he had consistently courted as an antidote to Boer expansionism. In 1852, with characteristic deftness, he combined force and diplomacy to induce the withdrawal of a British expedition, but within two years the British had washed their hands of the problems of the interior, and Moshoeshoe was now alone facing the Boer republic of the Orange Free State. The wars that broke out in 1858 and 1866 ended disastrously for the Basuto with the loss of virtually all their fertile land. As his state tottered on the brink of total disintegration, however, Moshoeshoe once more sought British aid, and this time, in 1868 he secured protected status as a High Commission territory, thereby saving the Basuto nation from annihilation.

The salvation of Basutoland was gained at the price of independence, economic no less than political, for the territory that Moshoeshoe was able to salvage was a rocky height of limited resources and heavy population, and henceforth the Basuto people would be dependent upon their white neighbors for their livelihood. Herein lay the pattern that emerged from the Mfecane and the Great Trek. Two people, Bantu and Boer, sought land to accommodate rising numbers, hampered by an outdated, inefficient system of husbandry. The Boer, being technologically more advanced, was able to defeat the Bantu, pushing them by degrees off the land. The wars, those fought by the trekkers as well as the so-called "Kaffir" wars along the Cape Colony frontier, were always over possession of land, and the outcome of each encounter saw the Africans faced with further losses, ever less able to maintain their herds, sow their crops, or fuel their fires. In 1857, the Xhosa and Thembu gave dramatic and macabre emphasis to the process when, driven by superstition and frustration as their herds withered away in starvation and disease, they slaughtered their stock and scattered their grain in response to the vain prophecy that this would free them at last from the tribulations of warfare and land loss. The sequel of some thirty thousand dead of starvation and as many more driven into the colony in search of survival was symbolic of the breakup of the old way of life—a social and economic submission to match political subjugation.

The land had been the foundation on which traditional society rested. When one went, the other went. The African people, however, remained, obliged to embrace a new pattern of life, a pattern that was no longer theirs, but that of white society. Deprived of ownership, the Africans still remained on the land as squatters, tenant farmers, and laborers. They herded cattle and planted corn as before, but the cattle might be their master's, the corn pledged against future taxes, and their labor the property of others much as that of the serf in the medieval manors of Europe. Beyond this their growing taste for European consumer goods further mortgaged African resources to the new way of life.

The tragedy, however, was not so much in the disintegration of a traditional society that had its own shortcomings as it was in two other factors. The first was the subservient position of the Africans, locked in a social status wherein their meager share in the fruits of their labor was perforce established by others. Related to this was the system itself, as much behind the times as it was ahead of the Bantu society it had replaced. Obsolete agricultural techniques were applied to an infertile land, while capital accumulation, immigration, and foreign investment lagged in a land of wars, droughts, and insect plagues. Literacy was in small supply and economic planning primitive or nonexistent. Rugged individualism led not to political freedom, but to political fragmentation which in turn complicated the already difficult process of economic planning.

Even as modern science applied to problems of economic productivity was changing the face of nineteenth-century Europe and America, technology and industry remained largely unknown in this far corner of the world. The Cape Colony continued poor and the Boer republics many times poorer, eking out an existence on the sale of wool and hides which could not pay for much-needed improvements such as roads, railways, harbors, and local industry. The labor of the African, unskilled and inexpertly applied, consequently benefited no one, neither master nor servant. Each was bound up with the other, and both were caught in the toils of an ineffective, superannuated system.

The Mfecane and Great Trek had changed the face of South Africa, obliterating traditional society and throwing black and white into a complex of mutual interdependence. In the next stage of her history, South Africa would finally turn to the problem of economic reform—an industrial revolution based on the discovery of mineral resources which was to replace poverty with wealth and show the way to national unity. It would not solve the problem of racial harmony, however. It would succeed only in shifting the center of tension from the farm to the city.

Suggestions for Further Reading

The Mfecane and its consequences are set forth in detail in J. D. Omer Cooper, *The Zulu Aftermath* (London: Longmans, 1966; Evanston: Northwestern University Press, 1966). A briefer version by the same author is found in the *Cambridge History of Africa*, Vol. V, John E. Flint, ed. (Cambridge: University Press, 1976), but see also M. Wilson and L. Thompson, eds., *The Oxford History of South Africa*, Vol. I (Oxford: University Press, 1969), and Paul Maylam, *A History of the African People of South Africa* (New York: St. Martins, 1986).

The standard work on the Great Trek is E. A. Walker, *The Great Trek*, 4th ed. (London: A. & C. Black, 1960; New York: Barnes & Noble, 1960). The background of racial problems in South Africa is treated in W. M. Macmillan, *Bantu, Boer, and Briton*, rev. ed (Oxford: Clarendon, 1961) but see also T. R. H. Davenport, *South Africa: A Modern History*, 3rd ed. (Toronto: University Press, 1987) which draws from the latest research, well documented in the notes. The most recent and best overall perspective of what was taking place in nineteenth century South Africa is *A History of South Africa*, by Leonard Thompson (New Haven and London: Yale University Press, 1990).

12

West Africa and Europe's Humanitarian Revolution

The Enlightenment in West Africa

Africa and Europe—the relationship was long-lived, dating back to Roman times. It had been pervasive, touching African lands from the Mediterranean to the Cape, from West Africa to the Swahili coast. And it came to be profound.

The first contacts, however, were superficial. Rome never seems to have probed much beyond the desert edge in North Africa. The early Portuguese explorers and merchants, their thoughts on gold, Prester John, and a passage to India, touched mostly at coastal points, knowing little of the vast continental interior. Later others joined the Portuguese, all increasingly preoccupied with slaving to supply the plantations of the New World.

With slaving came a different character in Africa's relationship with Europe. First of all it altered the African ecology, removing millions from their native soil. The numbers are—probably always will be—in dispute, but even the more conservative estimates suggest 9.5 million during the eighteenth and nineteenth centuries, a substantial hemorrhage of humanity, even when spread from Cape Verde in Senegal to the southernmost tip of South Africa. Whatever the totals, however, such slaving brought changes to African societies although the nature of the changes still remains a subject of debate. Some say it was minimal, tangential to events within Africa, for example, the trade in captives resulting from the nineteenth century civil wars in Yorubaland. Others argue a possible benefit in that excess populations were dealt off from high density areas like Iboland as a conscious economic choice in exchange for weapons and other imports deemed necessary for national security. Still others insist that the result was a brutalization that depressed widespread areas and dehumanized the spirit of both the procurers and their victims. Whatever the conclusion, it was clear that the European trade in slaves and other commodities changed the character of many African communities. Old relationships based on clan and lineage were altered or replaced. New types of government emerged under unique forms of leadership, often self-made and warlike. Wealth and economic production became increasingly connected to indigenous slavery and an internal slave trade, particularly during the nineteenth century when the external trade fell before the onslaughts of the international abolitionist movement.

With the advent of abolitionism the European impact on Africa became more pervasive and much more profound. Forces were set in motion that in time would recast societies, first in West Africa and then elsewhere—a growing revolution, the most recent expression of which is found in the independence movements and the drive for modernization among the African peoples in the middle of the twentieth century.

By the close of the eighteenth century Europe had produced its Enlightenment, that set of principles that enunciated human perfectability, the primacy of rational thought, the effectiveness of scientific analysis, and the conviction that progress meant, among other things, the duty to bring the fruits of Europe's civilization to others deemed less fortunate. To be sure these fine ideals existed concurrently with the climax of an Atlantic slave traffic that produced such obscenities as the *Zong* incident, in which the captain of this slave ship was exonerated for jettisoning 132 sick slaves into the Atlantic because, as damaged payload, they were endangering sound cargo that was his responsibility to protect. Acting largely through its evangelic impulse, it was, nevertheless, the humanitarian component that ultimately prevailed. During the early years of the nineteenth century Europe's Enlightenment touched West Africa in two ways, both of far-reaching consequence.

First there was France's great Revolution of 1789 which transformed French society and eventually rearranged the map of Europe. From the crucible of revolution emerged the noble principles of liberty, equality, and fraternity— liberty to think, to speak, and to worship according to personal conscience, equality in the pursuit of happiness, and the mystical fraternity of all people seeking a better life. The Revolution also produced that outburst of patriotic feeling that argued national independence as the way to individual liberty, but that also insisted paradoxically that French culture was preeminent; therefore in practice French nationalism was the greatest nationalism, and colonial peoples should be encouraged to forget their own history and way of life that they might be assimilated into the higher civilization of France.

On the Senegal coast, the modest trading centers of Saint-Louis and Gorée, far from being abandoned to their own devices, were encouraged to share the fruits' of the revolutionary democracy unfolding in France. The slave trade was abolished and the slaves freed; all became citizens of the new French nation, and an invitation was tendered to send representatives to Paris. The Senegalese responded with appropriate revolutionary fervor and in 1793 subscribed an unsolicited sum to help toward the defense of the "motherland." During the reaction of the Napoleonic period, most of these liberal gains were wiped away, but already firmly fixed, both in France and in her small West African colony, was the idea that Senegal was French in fact and in spirit, and that liberty meant not independence from France but freedom to enjoy the fruits of French civilization, as much in Africa as in France herself.

Among other things, the Napoleonic era witnessed the reemergence of slavery and the slave trade within France's overseas possessions, but it was precisely in the final abolition of the slave trade in the nineteenth century that the European Enlightenment made its second major impression on West Africa, and in the process changed the future course of her history.

At first there were isolated voices raised in protest—clergymen and literary figures mostly, and as a group, the American Quakers. John Locke opened his first *Treatise on Civil Government* with an attack on slavery, and in 1748, Montesquieu remarked acidulously, "It is impossible for us to suppose these creatures to be men, because, allowing them to be men, a suspicion would follow that we ourselves are not Christians." Others were even more eloquent in action. In 1772 slavery was ruled illegal in England and Ireland, largely through the exertions of Granville Sharp, whose dogged industry and faith in English law led to the celebrated opinion of Lord Mansfield freeing the slave, James Somerset. The consequences were profound. First, there was the loss of property valued at hundreds of thousands of pounds, mostly the slaves of West Indian planters resident in Britain. Beyond this was the prospect that the end of slavery in the British Isles was but the first step toward its abolition throughout the empire. Next, there were the complications arising out of thousands of freed slaves cast loose in society without any means of support. Finally, there was the impact that Granville Sharp's success was to have on the subsequent fortunes of West Africa.

Colonization, Christianity, and Commerce

However tentatively, as the nineteenth century dawned, Europe's posture toward Africa was changing; the slaver was giving way to the humanitarian. Granville Sharp's personal crusade had achieved its desired result, but it had also set in motion its predicted consequences. In Britain a rising chorus of criticism against the slave system led finally to an organized movement launched during the 1780s to abolish the slave trade. For twenty years men like Sharp, Henry Thornton, James Stephen, and Thomas Clarkson hammered away at the evils of the slave trade, while in the crucial arena of Parliament the fight was carried by the eloquent and indefatigable William Wilberforce. More generally, support grew as the British economy shifted from a mercantilist preoccupation with the West Indian sugar plantation based upon slave labor toward a free trade emphasis on cheaper imports of food and raw materials to sustain a growing manufacturing establishment at home. In 1807 the slave trade was abolished, and the reformers were able to turn their attention to slavery in the empire which finally fell to their attack in 1834 with the passage of the Abolition Act during the previous year. Meanwhile, the Somerset case and the freeing of slaves by British forces during the American Revolution had led to the accumulation of a population of indigent blacks in London, destitute, homeless mendicants whose plight stirred the humanitarian spirit of Granville Sharp to action a second time.

Sharp's immediate solution was private philanthropy, but it was soon evident that a broader, more systematic, and permanent solution was needed. Never wanting in imagination, Sharp hit upon the idea of repatriation and, the objects of his concern being of African descent, it seemed reasonable that they be resettled in the land of their origin. It mattered not that few, if any, had ever seen Africa or that former slaves were unlikely to possess the skills and judgment necessary to make a success of a new settlement in a strange land. Private contributions were raised; the government agreed to underwrite part of the expense; and in the spring of 1787 a group of over four hundred set sail for Sierra Leone where they established a self-governing community, named by Sharp the Province of Freedom, on the site that later was to be known as Freetown.

Idealism and good will in London, however, were no compensation for settler inexperience, the hostility of the local inhabitants, and the ravages of fever. The colony foundered and was saved from extinction when it was reorganized in 1791 as the property of the Sierra Leone Company, a joint-stock enterprise of British philanthropists headed by Henry Thornton. Substituting a benevolent despotism in the person of Governor Zachary Macaulay for the failing democracy of the settlers, the company kept the colony alive, being greatly assisted in this respect by two much needed infusions of immigrants. In 1792 there arrived from Nova Scotia some twelve hundred former slaves freed by the British army during the American Revolution, who, suffering from the intolerance of Tory emigres, had not been successful in establishing themselves in Canada and who consequently seized the opportunity to gain homesteads in West Africa. Eight years later the Nova Scotians were followed by five hundred Maroons, runaway Jamaican slaves who had finally surrendered to the authorities in 1795, and after a brief, unhappy stay in Nova Scotia had agreed to repatriation in Sierra Leone. With this nucleus, the company hoped to develop a commercially profitable venture, but in fact it lost heavily and eventually was forced to turn over its undertaking to the British government. In 1808 the settlement of less than two thousand became a crown colony, a development of great significance for it coincided with the abolition of the slave trade and provided a convenient center for the rehabilitation of the tens of thousands of Africans who were soon being rescued by the British antislavery naval patrols operating in West African waters.

Herein lay the germ of a very different kind of European enterprise in West Africa. The abolitionists had hoped to establish missions among the indigenous inhabitants, and in 1799 the Church Missionary Society (CMS) was founded by Wilberforce and others with this purpose in view. These missions were to introduce Christianity, but also to encourage local agricultural production to take the place of slaving and thus develop a healthy, mutually beneficial commerce between Europe and West Africa. Slavery would shrivel and die, the abolitionists reasoned, while Western, Christian culture would gradually take hold, leading the Africans from what was regarded as a primitive barbarism to the higher civilization of the West.

In fact, circumstances played a variation on this theme. The internal slave trade and utilization of slave labor increased steadily over the decades while the missionaries found more fertile soil for Christian conversion not in tribal society, but among the recaptives who were pouring into Freetown harbor as a result of the exertions of the British antislavery squadron. Originating from West African points scattered between Senegal and the Congo, these refugees were settled in villages surrounding Freetown where, under missionary guidance, they became converts to Christianity and began to emulate the Nova Scotian settlers in their assimilation of Western culture. Although very few of the inhabitants native to Sierra Leone were affected, the rise in the Freetown area of a Christian community of liberated Africans, learning English and gradually becoming Europeanized, was a development of greatest consequence and cast a long shadow forward.

Sierra Leone was not the only West African experiment in the rehabilitation of former slaves. Some two hundred miles southwest of Freetown on the Grain Coast, another settlement struggled for survival. In 1822 a small group of American blacks arrived off Cape Mesurado, their voyage underwritten by the American Colonization Society which had come into existence some years earlier dedicated to the proposition that free blacks and manumitted slaves in the United States might gain a new start in life on African soil. There, it was argued, they would be safe from the discrimination and persecution that was their frequent lot in America, although the free American black looked on colonization more often than not as the enemy of abolition and racial equality, and was largely hostile toward the movement.

The early days of Liberia, so named for the freedom it signified, were a repetition of the difficulties encountered at Sierra Leone as disease, poor leadership, local hostility, limited numbers, and inexperience almost led to extinction. Once again, a single individual came forward to save the day. Yehudi Ashmun, a young white New Englander, assumed control when the authorized agent of the Colonization Society virtually deserted his charges. Like Zachary Macaulay at Freetown, Ashmun forced the reluctant colonists to work together, fought off attacks by the local tribal groups resentful of intrusion, and slowly brought an organized, permanent community into being.

By the time Ashmun departed in 1828, Liberia, though weak, was established.

After these early years, the similarity between the two philanthropic ventures ended. While Sierra Leone grew rapidly as a rehabilitation center, Liberia drifted aimlessly, weak, impecunious, and ignored. The problem of slavery in the United States was of a magnitude that could find little relief in the resettlement of a few thousand blacks; moreover, the political heat raised by the slavery issue made impossible any substantial assistance to the Liberian venture by the United States government. During the thirty years between the founding of the colony and the Civil War, only five million dollars was subscribed publicly and privately in America, and most of this sum went to defray the transportation expenses of the emigrants. Few American blacks were interested in colonization unless it was the price of manumission, and as late as 1850 the Liberian settlements numbered less than three thousand individuals. By that time, however, despite a faltering economy, political instability, and chronic troubles with the local people, Liberia had become an independent black African nation. As the colony of a private philanthropic society, it lacked sovereignty, and when its status was challenged under international law, there appeared to be no viable alternative to a grant of independence. In 1847 Liberia received its independence and thus began the history of an insecure, unwanted nation, small, weak, unstable, and frequently on the verge of collapse, yet somehow surviving to serve, among other things, as a symbol of the freedom to which others in Africa would in time aspire.

Senegal—The Jacobin Heritage

Both the British and the French were reluctant imperialists in the decades following the fall of Napoleon. Adam Smith's dry assertion that slave labor was more costly than free labor was matched by his conviction that colonies were a needless expense, and this view came to dominate the councils of economy-minded governments in England and France. Paris retained, but did little to develop, the few overseas possessions that survived Waterloo— Martinique and Guadaloupe in the Caribbean, Réunion Island in the Indian Ocean, and her trading posts in Senegal, these last returned at the conclusion of peace in 1815 after intermittent occupation by the British during a century of chronic warfare.

Senegal was the object for a time of a program designed to develop a wide range of agricultural products desired in France, but this mercantilist project fell victim to mismanagement, and its failure merely strengthened the views of those who regarded colonies as a drain without compensation on the national treasury. The local mulatto population was preoccupied with trade up the Senegal River, chiefly in gum used in France for sizing and dye-fast, but for this activity there was no great official enthusiasm since it implied costly military action against the tough, warlike Moors and Tokolor people who controlled the interior. Beyond this, there was a mild interest in coastal trade which brought French shipping to such places as Grand Bassam on the Ivory Coast, Whydah in Dahomey, and Gabon.

Reaction in Paris, however, did not necessarily suggest abandonment of the revolutionary impulse to extend Western civilization in its Gallic mutation to those parts of the world still in apparent need of its influence. To the governor charged with resuming French administration after the British occupation went unequivocal instructions. "The prime mover of the new colony," announced the ministry in Paris, "must be European culture driven by French energy, becoming through example, through persuasion, and through the appreciation of new achievements, the soul of the African."

Within the settled communities of Gorée, Saint-Louis, and the entrepôts along the Senegal, the French efforts at cultural assimilation were received with cordiality by both the *métis*, or mulattoes, and the small number of Africans who, like the mulattoes, were engaged in the river traffic. Typical of this group was Gabriel Pellegrin, a leading *métis* who had in his youth helped organize an insurrection unseating an unpopular governor to the cry of "Long live Robespierre," but who in middle age was a respected merchant, mayor of Saint-Louis, and trusted negotiator in commercial relations with the people of the interior. Another was the Abbé Boilat whose seminary training in France led to the priesthood and an attempt, albeit abortive, to establish secondary education on the French model in Saint-Louis. Still another was Paul Holle, a Saint-Louis mulatto who exchanged an early career as civil servant to become a celebrated Senegalese soldier and defender of the French post at Medina against al-Hajj Umar in 1857. Holle was a forthright protagonist for French civilization in Africa which he encouraged not only with arms but with words, urging the administration to subdue the interior by military force, to educate the people away from what he regarded as the retrogressive effects of Islam, and to step up economic development that the great potentialities of the country might be realized.

Such views were widely held by the small but important population of assimilated mulattoes and Africans, but for the most part the people of Senegal were as yet untouched by French culture. Most of those living in the cities were Wolof-speaking Muslims—household servants, artisans, and laborers, as well as a shifting number of Africans from up-country whose cultural habits and religious practices made them indifferent to Western ways. Despite the final abolition of slavery in 1848 and the extension of French citizenship, it was to be another half-century before the African people of the settled communities, let alone the interior, began to respond to the full cultural, economic, and political implications of the French presence in Senegal. Meanwhile, they remained subservient to the mulatto oligarchy which dominated Senegalese life during the second half of the nineteenth century.

The Bible and the Plough

By mid-century, a small but highly significant change was underway on the West African scene. Dotting the coast, a number of cities had sprung into existence, African in population but with growing European orientation, centers from which a Western way of life slowly began to extend itself outward, carried in the baggage of the African residents of these towns as they moved across the countryside as traders, missionaries, or government officials. Saint-Louis, Monrovia, Cape Coast, Accra, Lagos—government seats and market towns— they were developing that admixture of peoples and ideas which marks the authentic cosmopolitan center.

Freetown in Sierra Leone was the prototype. Over the years thousands upon thousands of rescued slaves had been put down in her harbor to be relocated in the satellite communities that surrounded the growing port. By 1850 Sierra Leone contained more than forty thousand of these liberated Africans, drawn from many points along the West African coast but dominated by large numbers of Yoruba, victims of the increased slaving occasioned by the civil wars which gripped Yorubaland intermittently after 1821. Uprooted and torn from their traditional way of life, the immigrants quickly accepted the standards they found at Freetown, sending their children off to study English and other subjects at mission directed schools, while striving to emulate their Nova Scotian and Maroon predecessors in absorbing elements of a Westernized, Christianized culture. Beginning life anew as laborers, apprentices, and farmers, they nevertheless turned naturally to trade as a means to self-betterment, and gradually there emerged a social and economic hierarchy reflecting middle-class standards of achievement.

At the bottom of the scale were the newest arrivals, unskilled laborers and cultivators struggling with an unfamiliar existence and suffering the stigma ever reserved for the newly arrived immigrant. Those who advanced beyond this stage became small traders and artisans, and higher still were the successful merchants with their European houses and furniture, their libraries, and their air of mid-Victorian domestic comfort. At the apex were the few large-scale merchants with extensive economic interests, community leaders notable for their public service as jurors, or in a few cases, as members of the colonial legislative council. Such were William Henry Pratt and John Ezzidio, Ibo and Nupe recaptives respectively, whose energy and imagination led to mercantile success and important trading contacts with England. Another was the self-made and industrious William Grant, who rose to become a leader in Freetown circles as merchant, legislative councillor, newspaper owner, and spokesman for the community of Creoles, as the Freetown Africans in time came to be known.

Although Creole culture dominated the city, Freetown nevertheless maintained a cosmopolitan quality. The Creoles, in their urge to become Westernized, adopted European dress, Christian worship, and Western education, at the same time developing their own language, Krio, which merged English and African tongues, while retaining a number of their traditional customs. Others were less assimilated, however. On the streets, stately Wolof women glided by in their mantillas, while half-naked Kru laborers jostled Fulani in their long white robes. The European community was small but important because of its association with government. British administrators generally lived in open-veranda houses, and the prevailing architectural standard was the one- or two-story clapboard building with shingled, steeply pitched roof, the simple hut inhabited only by those who could afford no better. Freetown still relied largely on the outside world for its amenities. There was little machinery and a chronic shortage of skilled workers. Church clocks were infrequently in working order, the government wharf possessed no crane for unloading, and even wagons and wheelbarrows were rarities. After 1852 the situation improved considerably as regular steamship service was instituted with England.

The Creoles of Sierra Leone were more than casual, passive agents for the spread of European civilization in West Africa, however, for they soon found themselves pressed into service as active participants in the continuing struggle of the abolitionists against the slave trade. Despite the naval squadrons, the trade had far from ceased while within West African principalities the utilization of slave labor continued to rise. At first, European enterprise took the form of a series of expeditions to investigate the interior, and particularly to determine the course of the Niger, as a means of opening up the country to legitimate trade from Europe. Such was the motivation that lay behind the major explorers of the early nineteenth century — Mungo Park, René Caillié, Denham and Clapperton, the Lander brothers, and Heinrich Barth — but while their exertions yielded much new information concerning the West African interior, they had little impact on the problem of abolition.

By the 1830s leadership of the antislavery movement had passed on to new hands; chief among these were Thomas Fowell Buxton, who had succeeded Wilberforce as the parliamentary spokesman for the abolitionists, and Henry Venn who became secretary of the CMS in 1841. Buxton and Venn felt that the slave trade would die only when it was replaced by something more profitable to West Africans; hence, said Buxton in his influential volume, *The African Slave Trade and Its Remedy*, it was necessary to explore the interior with an eye to the establishment of permanent missions which might conclude trade treaties with local chiefs while providing training in crafts and modern agricultural methods for their people. Manned at first by European technicians and missionaries — for Christian conversion was an essential part of Buxton's plan — the stations would eventually be operated by Africans trained especially for the purpose.

The object, said Venn, was the establishment of an independent West African middle-class society in faithful replica of Venn's own Victorian England. Ignorant chiefs governing primitive villagers subsisting on the edge of famine were always tempted to sell off surplus population, he continued, but West African communities of scientific farmers, merchants, and small-scale industrialists, reinvesting their surplus profits in an expanding economy, would combine an economic interest in the conservation and utilization of the labor force with Christian strictures against slavery, and thus the iniquitous trade would wither away in the face of a beneficent Western Christian civilization. It was one of the first arguments for the idea of technical assistance—economic aid and specialized training to the end of creating independent, productive, modernized communities of West Africans.

European merchants already operating in West Africa had little sympathy for this brand of economic and religious philanthropy, and indeed Buxton's plans received a severe setback in 1841 when a government expedition to establish an agricultural station on the Niger ended in disaster, a third of the European members perishing of fever. The idea persisted, however, and Venn turned a weakness to advantage by insisting that it was not the Europeans but the already Christianized, Westernized Africans, the liberated blacks of Sierra Leone, who were best qualified by training, background, and physical resistance to disease, to play the major role in West African regeneration. Let British business interests invest in a profitable venture of expanding trade, let British philanthropy underwrite the expenses of establishment and training, but let the mission stations be directed and staffed by Africans.

Sierre Leone, therefore, became a major center for the development of the apostles of modernization: formally trained missionaries to staff the proposed inland stations and institute what Buxton called "the Bible and the plough," along with less formal representatives of Westernized Africa, merchants and others among the liberated Africans who began to drift back to their homeland along the coast east of Badagry after 1839. In Freetown, Fourah Bay College was established by the CMS in 1827 for the training of mission teachers, and its first pupil, Samuel Ajayi Crowther, was also to become the foremost African exponent for the assimilation by West Africans of Henry Venn's Victorian bourgeois culture.

Crowther was indeed the classic product of British philanthropy. A Yoruba rescued by the antislavery squadron when still a boy and repatriated at Freetown in 1822, he showed a quick intelligence and sober application that commended itself to the missionaries in Sierra Leone and earned him educational opportunities which led to an early career as mission teacher. After a number of years of work in the Freetown area, he accompanied the Niger expedition of 1841, then went to England for seminary study, and after being ordained, was posted to the CMS mission at Abeokuta in 1845. When, with Crowther's active assistance, the CMS succeeded in establishing a number of permanent stations along the Niger, it became apparent that this mission network would require its own administration, and in 1864 the former slave boy, Samuel Ajayi Crowther, became bishop of a vast diocese comprising all of West Africa save the already established British settlements.

It seemed an ideal arrangement. Crowther worked with purpose and diligence building up his missions, gaining converts both to Christianity and to the ideas for economic development of his friend and sponsor, Henry Venn. Spiritual rehabilitation through Christ and temporal regeneration through improved agricultural methods and technical training was the path of progress which he saw and followed with a clear eye. When his stations prospered but fitfully, he redoubled his efforts. When his mission workers from Sierra Leone fell short of expectations, he sought out better recruits. When some suggested that Africa might better make her own way without Europe's paternal guidance, he condemned such a view as madness which denied the fruits of world progress to needy Africa. For Crowther, as well as for most of his generation of Westernized Africans, the material and spiritual development of Africa could only come in alliance with the progressive West. "Africa has neither knowledge nor skill . . . to bring out her vast resources for her own improvement, . . ." he informed his fellow workers on the Niger in 1869. "Therefore to claim Africa for the Africans alone, is to claim for her the right of a continued ignorance. . . . For it is certain, unless help [comes] from without, a nation can never rise above its present state."

Such views did not preclude the vision of ultimately independent, economically viable West African communities, but it remained for second-generation liberated Africans to give more specific definition to the idea of political independence. Most eloquent among these was James Africanus Beale Horton, who was born in Sierra Leone in 1835, the son of an Ibo recaptive. Horton showed early promise which aroused missionary interest and led to his education at Fourah Bay and eventual study at Edinburgh in the field of medicine. When he returned to West Africa in 1859, Horton came as a medical officer in the British army, serving for over twenty years in various stations from the Bights to the Gambia and thereby gaining an unusual familiarity with the peoples of West Africa.

Horton believed no less than Bishop Crowther in the importance of Western culture to the development of a modern West Africa, but he also took seriously statements emanating from England to the effect that the European presence in West Africa was temporary, limited both by European susceptibility to killing fevers and the conviction that the end of the slave trade would also mean the end of Europe's intrusion in African affairs. Surveying the many traditional societies with which he came in contact, Horton enunciated two axioms of West African life. First, he said, there was no physical or intellectual difference between the African and the European. If the West had in fact developed a more advanced culture, this was due to historical and environmental factors which could be offset by introducing West Africans to the best elements of Western civilization. Secondly, Horton continued, the process of social improvement must end in the establishment of free nations in West Africa. Through education, technical training, and economic development the people of West Africa would eventually achieve a political

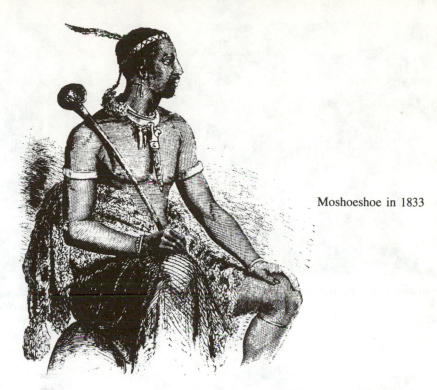

Moshoeshoe in 1833

Les Bassoutos, *by E. Casalis*

Shaka's indunas conducting parley

Illustrated London News, December 6, 1902

A slave market in the Eastern Sudan

The Pictorial Edition of the Life and Discoveries of David Livingston, by J. E. Ritchie

An audience of the Mai of Bornu, early nineteenth century

Costume Antico e Moderno, *by Ferrario, 1815*

Kano in 1850

Bishop Crowther

Africanus Horton

Author

Procession of Dahomey chiefs, their retainers and slaves

Graphic, 1876

King Kazembe, 1831

Omwata Kazembe, *by A. C. P. Gamitto*

Tippu Tip, c. 1885

Tippu Tip, *by H. Brode, 1907*

Zanzibar waterfront about 1875

Graphic, 187

Menelik II with young
Haile Selassie

and commercial stability, giving rise to a series of independent self-governing states, in the Gambia as well as Sierra Leone, among the Fante, the Yoruba, the Ibo, and other peoples. Horton's ideas, expressed in his extensive writings, were more than hot house theorizing, for they were produced in conjunction with the effort of the Fante community to create an independent government through the Fante Confederation constitution of 1871. They also appeared, however, at a time when the authorities in Britain were shifting from a policy favoring withdrawal from West Africa to one of permanent occupation. With this basic change, West African dreams of independence and modernizing states went a-glimmering.

West African Kingdoms in the Nineteenth Century

As the nineteenth century opened, the people of West Africa in their vast majority were quite unaware either of the changing European presence or the doings of the rising coastal communities such as Saint-Louis or Freetown. The traditional way of life was as yet substantially untouched by such external developments which only gradually intruded on the affairs of the inland societies, for example, the great forest kingdoms with their dynastic and other intramural preoccupations. Indeed, by the early nineteenth century the main external concern of West Africa's forest people was with the slave trade which in various ways they sought to direct to their own advantage.

Slaving had little immediate effect on the destinies of the Yoruba people whose unhappy history of chronic civil war during the nineteenth century reflected an internal chaos unanticipated after the eighteenth-century triumphs of the Oyo empire. The conquest of Dahomey, the securing of a trade route from the capital of Old Oyo to the coast, and the establishment of the culturally homogeneous and politically stable metropolitan provinces of Oyo seemed an unlikely prelude to disintegration; yet the death of the alafin Abiodun at the end of the eighteenth century was followed by deep political cleavages involving the royal succession and the authority of the king's advisers, the Oyo Mesi. The consequent weakening of the state permitted the Fulani in the flood of their jihad to overrun Oyo, occupy Ilorin, and compel the alafin to pay tribute.

These events had major repercussions throughout Yorubaland. A vast migration southward ensued which upset the ethnic and political balance of the Yoruba forest states and triggered a series of wars and local rivalries. The town of Owu, vassal and ally to Oyo, was destroyed and disappeared from history; others like Ibadan and Abeokuta were born from the pangs of conflict, while Oyo was forced to relocate herself a hundred miles to the south on the edge of the rain forest. Ilorin, an important center within the Oyo empire, defected under its governor, Afonja, who enlisted the help of Muslims and was then overthrown by his new allies as the Fulani jihad spread southward.

Even ancient Ife temporarily lost the protection of her privileged spiritual position and suffered attack. The southern remove of Oyo, which took place during the late 1830s, could not save the dwindling authority of the alafin who came increasingly under the influence of Ibadan which had grown rapidly as a refugee and war camp. Farther south, the Egba somehow evaded annihilation, and soon from their new city of Abeokuta they were competing with the Ijebu Yoruba as entrepreneurs in the arms and slave traffic which had risen sharply as a result of the civil wars. Political stability disappeared in a complex of shifting alliances, and every hand was turned against all others as the desire for profit from slaving added its measure to the confusion and the agony. Ibadan soon became strong enough to check the Fulani push southward but not strong enough to unite Yorubaland. Out of control, the wars dragged on.

The immediate beneficiary of Yoruba strife was Dahomey. The decline of Oyo meant the realization of a long-standing national purpose to be free from the foreign yoke, an achievement that King Gezo (1818-1858) secured when he ousted an Oyo garrison during the early years of the Yoruba civil wars. Gezo was interested in more than political independence, however. Dahomey's economy, geared to the slave trade, needed fresh supplies for foreign sale or domestic use and these he hoped to gain by taking advantage of Yoruba civil conflict. Such hope proved illusory. Some early victories over the Egbado neighbors of the Egba were more than offset when Dahomey came to face the rising power of Abeokuta and was forced to accept defeat after a series of bloody attacks ended in decimation of the Dahomean forces. The last of these came in 1864, a savage thrust at Abeokuta by Glele, son and successor to Gezo, which was so disastrous to Dahomey's strength that she never again attempted large scale military action and was compelled to simulate martial power by calculated acts of brutality against small communities and through baroque exhibitions of human sacrifice staged primarily for European audiences. In fact, the failure to overcome the Egba denied the Dahomean economy its needed expansion, but Dahomey was still a formidable power when she finally bowed in 1892 to the superior strength of a French army which occupied her capital city of Abomey and put an end to her independence.

On the Gold Coast, the major states of Fante and Asante found themselves similarly caught up in the complications of a growing European presence. By 1800 Asante was emerging from the civil and constitutional difficulties that had beset her in the second half of the eighteenth century and was prepared both to strengthen her commercial outlets on the coast and to reassert her control over conquered southern provinces such as Wassa, Denkyira, Assin, and Akwapim. Beginning in 1806, a series of southern invasions ensued which would have gone badly for the disunited Fante had not the British authorities in the coastal forts taken sides against Asante, eventually forcing the abandonment of the southern provinces in 1831 after the northerners had been defeated with British help on the field of Katamansu (Dodowa).

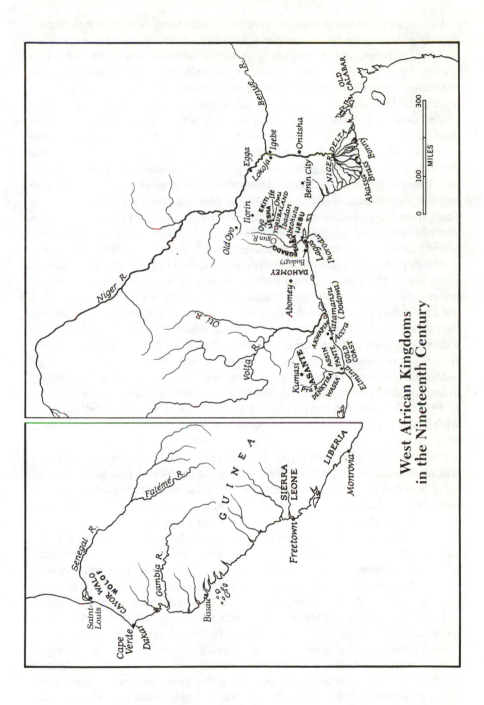

West African Kingdoms
in the Nineteenth Century

Vexing as these developments were to Asante, there was little satisfaction evidenced among the coastal people, for the British, Dutch, and Danes pursued different policies, and the British in particular seemed in African eyes to be guided by caprice as they alternated without apparent reason between indifference and interference regarding local affairs. In 1821, the British forts, which had been administered by an association of private merchants, were placed under the colonial authorities at Freetown. There followed a British disaster when the Asante overwhelmed the forces led by Sir Charles Macarthy in 1824, but just when this defeat was offset by the success at Katamansu, the forts once more were given over to private direction in an economy move which thoroughly perplexed and demoralized the coastal people. Next came an enlightened administration by George Maclean who served for a dozen years from 1830 as president of a council sponsored by the London merchants and whose tact and insight dissolved misunderstandings and went a long way toward establishing peace and increased trade between Asante and the coast.

Another seemingly inexplicable shift reintroduced in 1843 an official British presence in the forts and instituted a period of vacillating policy which undermined relations both with Asante and the coastal states. So disenchanted did the Fante become over the inconsistencies of British administration that they determined to form a political union capable of standing up to the Asante without reference to the government of the forts. In 1868, in the face of reviving Asante aggression, they formed the Fante Confederation as the basis for an independent state, but the Confederation soon collapsed when the British, in another unexpected change of direction, arrested its leaders as conspirators in 1871. This was but the prelude to a much firmer British colonial policy which was manifested three years later when the Gold Coast was annexed as a crown colony.

The introduction of alien forces that so complicated Fante-Asante relations was apparent in other parts of West Africa. In the Wolof and Serer country lying between the Senegal and Gambia rivers, Islamic and French influences laid a heavy hand on the structure of traditional society. The Wolof kingdom of Cayor which occupied the territory from Cape Verde to Saint-Louis contained a population of peasant farmers ruled by a slave-holding nobility and containing certain specialized castes of which the griot praise singers were particularly noteworthy. The abolition of the Atlantic slave trade had seriously eroded the income of ruling groups, now less able to dispose of war captives for guns and other European imports. At the same time growing French influence was converting the peasant loyalty to ground-nut culture while Islam increasingly replaced peasant loyalty to traditional religious practice.

Such imbalances led to new concentrations of power. At first there emerged a Muslim cleric, Ma Ba, who, with peasant support, established a small state north of the Gambia about 1861, but who a few years later was defeated and killed in action by the French when he tried to extend his influence into the Cayor. During this period the *damel*, or prince, of Cayor was Lat Dior, maintaining an intermittent rule through opportunistic alliances, now with Muslim clerics, now with the French, again with ill-disciplined *tyeddo*, royal slave soldiers, or with peasant farmer support. For more than twenty years Lat Dior held the stage amidst such shifting fortunes, but his eventual success was to be his downfall. When he attempted to gain control over ground-nut production, Lat Dior ran afoul of French mercantile and imperial pretensions. The French sought to convert the Cayor into a peaceful protectorate devoted to cash crop production, and to this end they spanned the region from Dakar to Saint-Louis, first by telegraph and then by railroad. For Lat Dior a forceful opposition was the only recourse. Fighting erupted, culimanting in 1886 in a climactic battle during which Lat Dior was killed and his army defeated. The Cayor was annexed and added to France's Senegal holdings.

The Vanishing Dream

The vision of a series of independent, prosperous African states, so vivid in the imagination of Fowell Buxton, Henry Venn, Samuel Crowther, and Africanus Horton, faded before the realities of individual ambition, human frailty, and economic motivation set in the rigors of the West African environment. European powers, economy minded and dedicated to the anticolonial principles of laissez-faire, nevertheless found themselves drawn inexorably into a deepening entanglement in West African affairs. African peoples, eager for the opportunities of increased trade but jealous of their sovereignty, experienced increasing difficulty in segregating political from economic involvement, and slowly lost the sovereignty that was the source of their economic strength. The idea of independence finally gave way to the fact of colonialism, and the dream of free and modern West African societies was forced to await its realization until the mid-twentieth century.

The heart of the matter lay in the legitimate commerce sought by Europe's merchants and encouraged by her missionaries, the latter eager to develop a substitute for the slave trade. In the Senegal Valley the traffic in gum was a modest but exclusive occupation of the mulatto and European traders of Saint-Louis and as such formed a fragile prop for local prosperity and an inconsequential element in the French national economy. The trade, moreover, suffered the further complication in the eyes of the French government of requiring substantial military assistance to neutralize the mercantilism of powerful indigenous states controlling both banks of the river. Nevertheless, there were offsetting arguments favoring greater involvement: the long-lived illusion of untold wealth in the interior and the nationalism of the French Revolution added to the ancient Bourbon dream of empire which began to revive during the 1850s with the rise of Louis Napoleon.

In 1854 a succession of ineffectual administrations came to an end with the appointment of Louis Faidherbe as governor of Senegal. Though sympathetic and informed regarding African civilization, Faidherbe nonetheless was a firm believer in the absolute superiority of French culture; neither did he shrink from the logic that commerce on the Senegal could not prosper without military support. Organizing the celebrated corps of African riflemen, the *Tirailleurs Sénégalais*, Faidherbe embarked on a series of campaigns which greatly expanded French influence beyond the coastal enclaves. The Trarza Moors were forcibly persuaded to respect the river traders, forts were built southward along the coast, and the Cayor and other territories were subjected to military and diplomatic pressures. Even the formidable al-Hajj Umar, hesitating over the direction of his jihad, was diverted from the Senegal Valley by the defense of Medina in 1857, and turned his attention inland toward the Niger.

Faidherbe's lengthy administration (1854-1861, 1863-1865) converted Senegal's modest mercantile pretensions to dreams of glory. He founded the port of Dakar, improved the facilities at Saint-Louis, joined the two towns by telegraph in 1859, and laid plans for extensive agricultural developments in the Cayor and adjacent areas. His vision of a link between the Senegal and Niger basins led to negotiations with al-Hajj Umar which, though they produced no immediate results, showed the way to subsequent French penetration of the interior late in the nineteenth century. Thus, in the French perspective, there emerged the image of a prosperous commercial and agricultural colony developing under the genial influence of French culture and the enlightened direction of French administrators. In the decades that followed Faidherbe, French influence spread inexorably. Chieftains like Lat Dior were subdued, albeit often with difficulty, French commercial interests centered in Bordeaux gradually ousted the mulattoes from control of economic affairs, while the thoroughly gallicized mulattoes gained compensation by maintaining political ascendancy over the rising African population in the expanding towns.

Increasing British involvement in the affairs of West Africa was similarly connected with the rise of those trading activities that replaced slaving. In the Niger Delta, palm oil had proved a ready substitute, and by mid-century there existed a lively exchange between the Liverpool merchants and the delta agents who had once been the principals of the slave trade. It was a rough and ready world, however; disputes were common, and in 1849 Britain agreed to the appointment of a consul, John Beecroft, to represent the English mercantile interests on the coast. A forceful individual, Beecroft was soon intervening in the affairs of local states like Bonny and Old Calabar, and his successors in the office of consul also found themselves drawn into intramural quarrels in their effort to protect the interests of the European supercargoes. Moreover, the temptation was always strong to increase outside pressure beyond the powers of mere persuasion, to introduce an element of force, and to argue for the establishment of some form of protectorate in the delta. The authorities in London would have none of this, however, and in 1865 the

House of Commons produced the report of its Select Committee on West Africa which recommended not further extension of British rule, but the preparation of Africans for self-government as a prelude to withdrawal from all territories except the repatriation center of Sierra Leone.

Such a view was out of step with events. In 1854 an expedition up the Niger under Dr. W. B. Baikie had demonstrated the efficacy of quinine as a malaria suppressant, and when regular steam navigation of the river was introduced three years later by Macgregor Laird, there developed the early prospect of direct commercial penetration of the interior and the eventual elimination of the African go-betweens of Bonny, Brass, Old Calabar, and other city-states in the Niger Delta. The opposition of these Oil Rivers communities was immediate, persistent, but unavailing, and even the widespread hostility of the inland people did not succeed for long in stemming the rising tide of Niger traffic. British official involvement followed the trade. A consul was placed up the Niger at Lokoja and warships were used for a time to escort the river steamers. The powers of the delta consulate were increased and its influence rose accordingly. The logic of circumstances pointed to the establishment of a protectorate which was finally proclaimed in 1885.

In Yorubaland a different set of events was leading to the same growing British involvement. Widespread slaving caused by the Yoruba wars brought direct intervention in the affairs of Lagos in 1851 when Consul Beecroft deposed the reigning king, Kosoko, replacing him with a more tractable member of the royal house. Intervention raised more problems than it solved, however, for the consuls subsequently based in Lagos soon found themselves increasingly entangled by the diplomatic complexities of the Yoruba wars as they sought to develop legitimate commerce with the interior as a substitute for the outlawed slave trade. Lagos was annexed by treaty in 1861, but the wars, which flared up again at the same time, brought a breakdown of inland commerce, worrying the new government at Lagos which was expected by the authorities in London to foster trade while maintaining a policy of noninterference in Yoruba affairs.

During the 1860s the administration at Lagos was under the direction of the vigorous Lieutenant Governor John H. Glover who viewed the Yoruba wars largely as a struggle on the part of the interior power of Ibadan to gain access to the coastal markets at Lagos despite the blockade of the trade routes by the Ijebu, and particularly by the Egba. Glover's tactics, therefore, called for pressure on Abeokuta to relax her restrictions while seeking alternate lines of communication between Lagos and Ibadan. This necessarily led to deteriorating relations with the Egba, which degenerated into open hostilities in 1865 when Glover's troops drove an Egba army from its siege of Ikorodu, and in 1867 precipitated the expulsion of the CMS mission from Abeokuta as a reaction to British interference. With the departure of Glover in 1872, tensions were eased somewhat, but intramural Yoruba disputes continued to be affected by the attitude of the Lagos government and merchant community, always intent upon seeking ways to increase trade with the interior.

In part, these difficulties grew from the contradictions of a policy that encouraged an increase of trade but refused to admit the political consequences; in part, they reflected the gap between the statesmanship formulated in London and the way in which officials in the field interpreted their instructions and met the exigencies of daily problems. Such complications were particularly pronounced on the Gold Coast after 1843 when direct administration of the forts was resumed. In 1844 a series of bonds were signed with coastal states introducing English justice in their territories and abolishing such customs as human sacrifice, but stopping short of any direct intrusion in the government of these communities. The signatory chiefs, however, felt they were gaining British protection along with British law, and were nonplused when in 1868 the Dutch and English, without warning, exchanged a number of their forts in a move that increased administrative efficiency by creating contiguous stretches of coast under British and Dutch control, but that seriously upset the local power balance, particularly in relation to Asante.

States like Denkyira or Assin, traditional enemies of Asante, suddenly found themselves tied to the pro-Asante Dutch and thereby susceptible to attack from the north. Elmina, Asante's long-standing coastal outlet, moreover, now came under Fante pressure to break with Asante, a situation that greatly disturbed the northerners who dispatched a raiding party to the coastal area around Elmina in 1869. Britain refused to be provoked into action and, as her prestige slumped, the Fante Confederation was formally launched to oppose Asante. At this juncture the Dutch withdrew leaving the British in sole possession of all the coastal forts, including Elmina. While London continued to avoid direct confrontation with Asante, her government on the Gold Coast wrecked the Fante Confederation and thus destroyed any concerted local opposition to invasion.

In 1873 the Asante armies crossed the Pra and moved against the coast to retake Elmina and at last London decided upon strong military action in support of the coastal position. It was a major turning point in British West African policy. Once the English government and people faced the fact of Britain's long-standing and deepening involvement in Gold Coast affairs, the victory in the Asante war of 1873-1874 was quickly followed by annexation of the coastal settlements as the Gold Coast Colony, and a new chapter opened in the history of British relations in West Africa.

If Africanus Horton's image of independent West African states disappeared in the wreckage of the Fante Confederation, the failure of the humanitarians to create a new civilization in West Africa was best exemplified in the fate of Bishop Crowther and his Niger missions. Partly the difficulty lay in a shortfall between theory and practice—the impossible task of creating in a few short years communities of Christian, bourgeois, Westernized yeomen and merchants capable of demonstrating the values of a completely new and strange way of life and persuading their neighbors to partake of its fruits.

Partly it reflected the force of circumstances which substituted imperialism for humanitarianism, converting the philanthropic ideals of the Buxtons and the Venns to the commercial designs of George Goldie Taubman, or the imperial dreams of Jules Ferry.

In building the Niger missions, Crowther faced an enormous task from the start. At once his appointment as bishop stimulated the jealousy of European missionaries and deprived him of effective control over the already established African churches in Yorubaland and Sierra Leone, a complication that blurred the conception of an indigenous church capable of propagating itself through missions founded by its own workers. In addition, there was the dependence of the Niger missions on traders, Europeans and Africans alike, for transportation and supplies, a dependence that strained relations between those interested in evangelization and those preoccupied with commercial gain. Nonetheless, the work went forward. Crowther had been instrumental in the establishment of stations at Onitsha and Igbebe (Lokoja) in 1857, and in time others followed—Akassa at the Niger mouth in 1861, Bonny and Brass in 1864 and 1868 respectively, and Egga beyond the confluence of the Niger and Benue in 1873.

Slowly, at first imperceptibly, a subtle change began to take form within the missionary movement. The rising interest in West African trade which led to the growing political involvement encouraged by people like Faidherbe, Glover, and Beecroft led also to a redefinition of European-African relations. The older notion of the equality of all people before God had formed the basis for Henry Venn's program of African regeneration with its principle of partnership between European and African. Now, during the 1870s and 1880s, this view was giving way to a doctrine of Caucasian superiority which, though rooted in the pseudoscientific pronouncements of Richard Burton and his school of thought, had educated European missionaries to a skepticism over the capacity of the African to digest the benefits of Victorian civilization.

Venn died in 1873 and his successors retained little of his faith in African capability. The chronic complaint by traders that mission stations were inefficiently operated by lazy, drunken, dissolute agents was given a hearing in London, presumably because the Niger missionaries were all Africans and thus not considered fully tested. In 1877 the CMS limited Bishop Crowther's authority by appointing a European lay worker to take charge of all temporal affairs connected with the Niger missions, and two years later financial control was vested in a committee of five Europeans and three Africans based in Lagos. Reports of mismanagement and irregularities on the Niger persisted, and in some cases were substantiated. In the changing context of the times these incidents prompted the conclusion at missionary headquarters in London that Crowther was an ineffective administrator, overindulgent with his erring charges, while his missions were sadly in need of European supervision. Bit by bit, the old bishop's position was circumscribed, his agents charged with various offenses which were followed with suspension, transfer, or dismissal.

By 1891, Crowther, a now-ailing octogenarian, had been in effect superseded by a group of European missionaries, and in December of that year he died. With him also died the idea of a new independent Africa through the vehicle of an indigenous, self-propagating Christian church. But by this time another age had dawned and the European scramble for Africa was in full flux.

Suggestions for Further Reading

Histories of West Africa have been written largely region by region, conforming to present-day independent nations. See, for example, the relevant chapters in J. F. A. Ajayi and Michael Crowder, eds., *History of West Africa*, Vol. II, 2nd ed. (Burnt Hill, Harlow, Essex: Longman, 1987), and a number of "national" histories. For Nigeria there is Elizabeth Isichei, *History of Nigeria* (London: Longman, 1983) and Michael Crowder, *The Story of Nigeria*, 4th ed. (London: Faber, 1978). The Gold Coast area is best served by David Kimble's *A Political History of Ghana, 1850-1928* (Oxford: Clarendon, 1963). For Sierre Leone there is Christopher Fyfe, *A History of Sierra Leone* (London: Oxford, 1962) concentrating primarily on the Freetown area. Liberia has no single satisfactory history nor is there any recent volume in English covering the regions that eventually became France's West African colonies.

Treatment of early nineteenth century influences in West Africa is contained in R.W. July, *The Origins of Modern African Thought* (New York: Praeger, 1967; London: Faber, 1968). For slave trade see Roger Anstey, *The Atlantic Slave Trade and British Abolition, 1760-1810* (London: Macmillan, 1975) and P. E. Lovejoy, *Transformations in Slavery* (Cambridge: University Press, 1983). The role of the missions is the subject of J. F. A. Ajayi, *Christian Missions in Nigeria, 1841-1891* (London: Longmans, 1965).

For West African kingdoms there is Ajayi and Crowder, cited above, as well as the older *West African Kingdoms in the Nineteenth Century*, D. Forde and P. M. Kaberry eds. (London: Oxford, 1967.) The classic Samuel Johnson, *The History of the Yorubas* (New York: Humanities Press, 1956) is still a major source of information on the Yoruba people.

The onset of the colonial period is the theme of Crowder, *West Africa under Colonial Rule* (Evanston: Northwestern University Press, 1968), but see also J. D. Hargreaves, *West Africa Partitioned*, 2 v. (London: Macmillan, 1974, 1985). Special studies include K. O. Dike, *Trade and Politics in the Niger Delta* (Oxford: Clarendon, 1956), J. E. Flint, *Sir George Goldie and the Making of Nigeria* (London: Oxford, 1960), Martin Klein, *Islam and Imperialism in Senegal* (Stanford: University Press, 1968), and Kimble, cited above.

13

Commerce and Statecraft in Eastern and Central Africa

The Rise of International Trade

When the Ngoni forded the Zambezi in 1835 and penetrated the savanna of central and eastern Africa, they brought revolutionary changes to a seemingly static pastoral scene. Their violent military tactics and novel political institutions meant annihilation for some, absorption into Ngoni life for others, and new social and political configurations for still others. Before their arrival, the countryside had been dotted with scattered villages sustained by a subsistence agriculture which provided a modest existence for a peasantry whose wants were simple and whose daily round had not greatly altered over the centuries. Although there were occasional fertile pockets, the rolling landscape was poor in soil and deficient in rainfall, and supported only a sparse population centered in tiny farming communities with little mutual economic and political contact, an isolation that greatly simplified the task of conquest for the invaders.

The Ngoni impact was shattering, but its long-range effect was no more profound and far less pervasive than that of its antecedent, which had begun to exert influence throughout East and Central Africa well before the intrusion from the south. This was the vast Bantu migration spilling over subequatorial Africa and early reaching the continental shores, both west and east. On the western side of Africa the Bantu were in touch with early Portuguese mariners; in the east there was some exchange with Arab and then with Portuguese traders involving ivory and gold in the Zambezi valley. For the rest of the vast interior, however, the outside world was unknown. From the forests of the Congo (Zaire) to the Limpopo valley, the savanna country stretched—isolated, remote, and introspective.

245

Small scattered communities and low population density reflected environmental insufficiency with its concomitant famine and disease. Some villages achieved a relative prosperity amidst the general poverty, thanks sometimes to location near salt, iron, or copper sources, sometimes because of control over scarce water or grazing grounds. Such advantages could be exploited by the energetic who accumulated wealth by trade or warfare, a wealth usually manifest in growing followings of clients and slaves, especially in women. Thus there was a tendency toward larger political units, but this was generally offset by a widespread system of matrilineal descent that deprived householders of control over the children produced by their wives and sisters.

In time, however, some larger states emerged. There were the Lozi, for instance, whose prosperity, both political and economic, rested in the fertility of their floodplain along the upper Zambezi. Emerging in the seventeenth century, the Lozi were a quasi-aquatic society; by contrast the contemporary Luba state, located near the Lomani tributary of the Congo River, occupied savanna grassland, its economy based in the control of iron and salt deposits. These assets served a commercial and political expansion led by a vigorous royal lineage that achieved its goal of a centralized kingdom through military force and astute use of genesis myths and royal ritual. The Luba state remained healthy well into the nineteenth century, by which time it had been joined by others which took shape, not through favorable indigenous conditions but from the growth of the international trade that pressed in on Africa with increasing intensity from the time when the Portuguese first circumnavigated the continent in the fifteenth and sixteenth centuries.

From bases in Angola and along the Mozambique coast, the Portuguese pushed their search for gold, slaves, and ivory, exchanging cloth, dishware, weapons, and varieties of beads in return. The possibilities for profit created powerful commercial centers along interior trade routes; in this manner the Lunda kingdom of *Mwata Yamvo* arose in the western savanna during the seventeenth century along with its counterpart in the east, the Lunda state of *Kazembe*. Though well inland, both were located along an east-west trade route that developed from the seventeenth century onward, linking the commercial activities of both the Atlantic and Indian Ocean trading areas.

The nations of Mwata Yamvo and Kazembe comprised a variety of local peoples, maintaining political cohesion through the devices of "positional succession" and "perpetual kinship." Positional succession joined local chieftaincies both to each other and to the crown, each new occupant divorcing himself from his own family ties to assume the wives, children, and lineage relationships that went with the office. In this way a perpetual kinship among offices and their occupants gave stability to a far-flung trading empire.

Like the Luba, the Lunda states remained powerful into the nineteenth century, their commercial and political strength constantly fed by the demands of the external trade in slaves and ivory. When the Atlantic slave trade dried up during the later nineteenth century, moreover, its decline had little initial

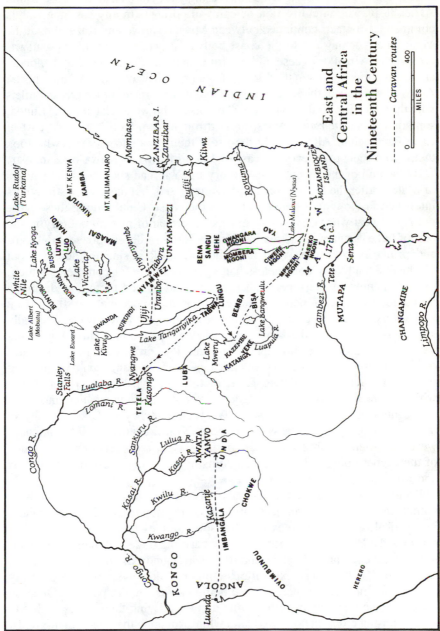

East and
Central Africa
in the
Nineteenth Century

‒ ‒ ‒ ‒ Caravan routes

impact upon internal slaving which increasingly provided chattels for use within Africa in plantation cultivation or caravan portage. In any case the Lunda commercial contacts continued between Mwata Yamvo and Kazembe, at the same time reaching out to the coast both west and east. In the west it was *pombeiros*, Afro-Portuguese traders from Angola, who moved Lunda goods, channeling much of them through Kasanje on their way to the Atlantic ports. Across the continent the Kazembe state sent its exports to Indian Ocean outlets with the aid of Bisa and Yao traders. The Bisa, who were related to the Lunda, sometimes sent their caravans straight through from their homeland east of Lake Bangweulu. Alternatively they sold their goods to the Yao who took them from their own territory east of Lake Malawi to Kilwa or Zanzibar.

By the end of the seventeenth century the Yao had succeeded the traders of Malawi after the Malawi state had disintegrated, but there were still others interested in the long distance traffic to the coast. Chief among these were the Nyamwezi who occupied an extensive stretch of plateau country to the east of Lake Tanganyika. Organized into a series of decentralized chiefdoms and primarily concerned with farming and stock raising in their dry but productive land, they nonetheless had evolved a taste for commerce which, by the opening of the nineteenth century, had gained them a widespread reputation as a trading people. These mercantile preoccupations arose from two factors. In the first place, the Nyamwezi country of Unyamwezi, poetically known as the Land of the Moon, was ideally situated to control a growing network of trade routes throughout the interior. From the principal center of Unyanyembe a major artery extended eastward to Zanzibar, five hundred miles distant. To the north was Lake Victoria and her bordering kingdoms, which by the late eighteenth century were receiving Indian calico and other goods, quite possibly via Unyamwezi. West and south beyond Lake Tanganyika lay the Katanga of Kazembe where traders, Nyamwezi presumably included, were exchanging manufactured goods for slaves, ivory, and copper, much of the copper going to the lake kingdoms in the form of ceremonial objects and articles of personal adornment.

Their strategic location aside, the Nyamwezi had developed a high competence as carriers, an occupation of prime importance in a land where in practical fact no other means of transportation existed. Pride in this skill reinforced a Nyamwezi monopoly of the carrying trade and manifested itself in the great caravans which wound their way, hundreds strong, to the coast each year. Though these expeditions contained donkeys, they were lightly loaded, the bulk of the merchandise being carried by the porters. Once on the coast, the men remained for some months busying themselves with odd jobs or raising crops on borrowed land while arranging the sale of their goods. Thoroughly professional as porters, they were less impressive traders, generally unfamiliar with the institution of credit and not especially mettlesome as bargainers. Possibly this was circumstantial, for coastal merchants could afford protracted negotiations, knowing that the Nyamwezi were obliged to return to their interior farms in time for the next growing season. In commercially sophisticated Zanzibar, this would have been a serious disability and an encouragement to the Swahili traders to venture inland, as indeed they subsequently did.

The Economic Imperialism of Sayyid Said

The outward commercial pressure of the Nyamwezi and other people of the deep continental interior was soon countered by a thrust from the outside inward, also primarily on behalf of trade. To begin, there were the Portuguese. Undismayed by the failure to gain control of the gold fields of Mutapa and Changamire, Portugal had subsequently looked northward where by the late eighteenth century her representatives had made commercial contact with the Lunda state of Mwata Yamvo via Angola, and Kazembe's kingdom by way of Tete on the Zambezi. In Lisbon the authorities contemplated establishing and controlling a transcontinental route which would connect Angola and Mozambique and bring forth great commercial and political dividends. With the occupation of South Africa by the British in 1795, this plan gained a new urgency and precipitated two expeditions in 1798 and 1806 with the purpose of surveying and securing a link across the continent.

The first reconnaissance, leaving Tete under the command of the explorer Francisco de Lacerda, reached the capital of Kazembe but was permitted to go no further, for there was fear that the Europeans might arrogate authority and usurp the westward traffic to the land of Mwata Yamvo. In 1802 two pombeiros were sent from Angola to cross to the east coast, and after many delays succeeded in reaching Tete and eventually in returning westward to their starting point. This journey brought no progress toward greater Portuguese influence in the interior; indeed, the earlier promise of trade between Tete and the Lunda states had failed to materialize, possibly because of competition from the Bisa and Nyamwezi. When in 1831 a third expedition was sent from Tete in quest of the Kazembe's patronage, it failed utterly, the king pointing out that he already had satisfactory commercial contacts with the Zanzibar coast through the Bisa.

It was, therefore, the energetic merchandising of the Nyamwezi, Bisa, and Yao that was in large measure responsible for the buildup of an external trade, and more particularly for the guidance of that commerce away from the Portuguese entrepôts to the Arab and Swahili centers such as Kilwa and Zanzibar. At the same time the international demand for slaves and ivory stimulated along the coast a great curiosity concerning the continental interior as a source for those commodities. Like the Portuguese, the Arab and Swahili merchants began to seek more immediate contacts with the inland people, and, unlike the Portuguese, they were largely successful in this effort. That this was so is closely related to the career of Sayyid Said, prince of Muscat from 1806 to 1856 and suzerain of the Arab settlements on the East African coast, for it was Said who played a leading role in organizing and directing the commercial penetration of the interior during the years of his long reign.

To a considerable extent Said's presence in East Africa was circumstantial. As ruler of the Omani empire, he was primarily interested in strengthening the traditional control of Muscat over shipping in the Indian Ocean—from the Middle East to India and from India to East Africa. During the early years of the nineteenth century Muscat prospered as the great naval powers of France and England, locked in combat, permitted the Indian Ocean commerce to fall to the Arabs. With the defeat of Napoleon, however, Britain reasserted her naval supremacy, encouraging traders from India and extending her influence along the Arabian coast. Stymied at home, Said turned his attention to East Africa where he gradually brought his dependencies under more direct control, while he grew increasingly impressed with the commercial possibilities of the interior trade.

In 1837, the occupation of Mombasa broke the last resistance of the Mazrui family, thus securing Said's authority on the East African coast and setting the stage for his permanent move from Muscat to Zanzibar three years later. Long before this, however, Said, with consummate tact and a sure economic instinct, had begun to lay the foundations for a commercial empire which linked the coastal markets with the peoples of the interior via the extended network of caravan trails already established by the Nyamwezi and other inland traders.

The key to Said's success was coordination and expansion of available resources rather than the introduction of innovations. The trails, for example, were already in existence and Swahili or Arab traders had begun to travel them in small numbers during the early nineteenth century. Under Said, however, the frequency and size of coastal caravans were greatly increased, communities of Arab merchants were strategically placed along the routes, and agreements were solicited with groups like the Nyamwezi guaranteeing protection and exemption from tolls. In this way Arab centers developed at Ujiji on Lake Tanganyika and Tabora adjacent to Unyanyembe where they served as staging areas for further penetration and commercial advantage such as the contacts made with the Baganda in 1844 and after.

Furthermore, Sayyid Said well understood the relationship between commerce and capital; hence he was at pains to encourage immigration of Indian bankers, the so-called *Banyans*, who were granted religious toleration and given control of the financial administration at Zanzibar, including the all-important customs. The Indian and Arab communities in East Africa were naturally antagonistic and were able to cooperate neither before nor after the time of Said, but during his reign he was able to combine their assets—the financial acumen of the Banyan, the toughness of the Arab soldier and trader— to the advantage of all. Finally, Said greatly solidified the economy of Zanzibar by encouraging the culture of cloves already begun before his arrival, a move that expanded annual exports manyfold while providing a local market for slaves from the interior needed to work the clove plantations. The resulting prosperity was demonstrated with dramatic clarity in export-import figures that increased enormously during the middle years of the century; by 1859, for example, Zanzibar stood as the world's foremost exporter of cloves, ivory, and gum-copal.

During Sayyid Said's day the Arab penetration of the interior was purely commercial and was meant to be no more. Caravans proceeding to the coast necessarily included armed guards, and the settlements such as Ujiji or Tabora could be defended if the occasion demanded, but basically these were peaceful, semipermanent settlements which rose and fell in numbers and activity with the volume of trade and which were characterized by comfortable houses, carefully cultivated gardens, flocks, and herds, well-stocked warehouses, and quantities of slaves for domestic service or eventual sale in the coastal markets. In time this purely commercial character changed to something more political, partly because the death of Sayyid Said in 1856 deprived the merchants of his clarity of purpose, partly because mercantile objectives tended to suggest political means, and partly because new forces from Europe began to influence the decisions of the sultan at Zanzibar.

The exact nature of the Arab presence in the interior varied greatly from place to place, however. The traders numbered only two or three thousand widely scattered individuals whose influence necessarily was conditioned largely by the reaction of the local people. In Unyamwezi the settlers at Tabora were able for a time to interfere successfully in parochial affairs, in 1859 unseating Manua Sera as chief of Unyanyembe when he sought to tax Arab caravans. Later they found themselves greatly restricted by the rising power of a neighboring chief, Mirambo, who between 1876 and 1880 took control of the roads northwest to Buganda and founded a market which offered a lively competition to the Arab emporium at Tabora. In Buganda the burgeoning Zanzibari trade was consummated in 1869 by formal diplomatic representation which exercised important influence in local politics, but in the highlands to the east the Arabs made little headway until late in the century because of the hostility of people like the Kamba, Kikuyu, Maasai, and Nandi. Far to the south they fared no better. East of Lake Malawi they came only as clients to trade with the Yao slavers, and a similar situation obtained north of the lake because of the strength of the Bena, Sangu, and Hehe people. To the west of Lake Tanganyika the Nyamwezi caravans kept the coastmen out of the Katanga, and it was not until the early 1880s, during the days of Tippu Tip, that the sultan at Zanzibar was able to assert authority south and west, an authority that on the eve of the European scramble for Africa turned out to be extremely short-lived.

In any event, it was already an empty authority, for the sultan, Sayyid Barghash, had long since lost effective control of his realm. During the reign of Sayyid Said, the British had exerted pressure at Zanzibar through a permanent resident, but Said's considerable diplomatic skill had minimized this influence, even succeeding in maintaining the slave trade without hindrance despite a treaty of 1845 designed to put an end to the traffic between Zanzibar and Muscat. Said's son, Majid (1856-1870) proved to be a weak ruler, however, whose indecision and procrastination led him to rely intermittently on the British for support with a consequent loss of his independence.

Majid's successor, Barghash (1870-1888), though much more assertive, soon found himself under similar obligation, so that the British consul, John Kirk, quickly became a major voice in the Zanzibari government. In 1873 a treaty was forced upon Barghash putting an end to the slave trade throughout his territories, and from this point Kirk urged Barghash to greater military and diplomatic penetration inland, partly to extend the force of the slave trade treaty and partly to counter growing interest in the interior by other European powers. This was the basis for the 1882 arrangement with Tippu Tip in which Tip was to administer his own extensive holdings in the eastern Congo under nominal Zanzibari authority while diverting all the ivory of the region eastward to Barghash's coastal markets. Despite Tippu's energy this move was soon rendered obsolete by the Berlin Conference of 1884, leaving Barghash bereft of both empire and illusions. "I must beg your forgiveness," he informed Tip when the latter returned to Zanzibar in 1886. "I no longer have any hope of keeping the interior. The Europeans . . . are after my possessions. . . . Happy are those who died before now, and know nothing of this."

Firearms and the Shifting Ecology of the Interior

The Arabs came to the interior, prodded by the external market for ivory and slaves. At first they offered in exchange those age-old commodities, cloth and beads, but by the middle of the nineteenth century the inland people were demanding and receiving firearms. Guns for ivory and guns for slaves was a certain formula for increased warfare and a declining political stability. Arms encouraged the natural aggressiveness of some, helped others in the killing efficiency of their ivory hunt, and tempted still others to indulge their predatory inclinations through slaving. As time passed, the system fed upon itself—more guns and an ever-rising demand for diminishing supplies of ivory led to increased raiding and slaving with consequent breakdown of village life and the rise of bands of rootless adventurers all too ready to add their measure of violence to the turbulent times. An oversupply of slaves developed as a result of the 1873 antislavery treaty, flooding the inland markets, cheapening life, and compounding human suffering. Perhaps the more fortunate were those who became the agricultural workers and concubines for traders like the Yao or Nyamwezi. Many others were pressed into service as porters for the ivory bound toward the coast and, judging from the accounts of travelers and missionaries, these were callously butchered or left by the wayside to expire of starvation or exhaustion when they were unable to carry their loads farther. Finally there were those who fell before the initial onslaught, cut down while fleeing blindly from the attack on their homes, their rotting corpses and bleached bones soon the only testimony to the futility of their fate.

Warfare, slaving, and political disintegration were by no means uniformly distributed in the interior, the highest incidence occurring around Lake Nyasa (Malawi) and in the Congo basin, territories characterized by isolated villages incapable of uniting in self-defense. In a massive demonstration of the laws of natural selection, only those survived who could adapt to the changing times. The Yao, for example, were a decentralized people living under petty, independent chiefs early in the nineteenth century. Finding themselves imperiled by gun-bearing neighbors, they quickly gained firearms themselves, then responding a second time to environmental provocation, became the chief procurers of slaves for the Kilwa market, extending their territorial influence and centralizing their political authority. Kindred Malawi people were unable, for their part, to make similar adjustments and paid the price as they marched in the columns of the slave caravans their Yao neighbors sent to the coast.

Others also fared variously, although it was not always guns that played the decisive part. The Bisa, who had stimulated the early trade with Kazembe, succumbed to their warlike Bemba neighbors once the latter obtained guns, and it was these guns along with a newly united chieftainship that enabled the Bemba to turn aside the Ngoni when they attacked in 1856. In the case of the Sangu, however, cohesion came from opposing the Ngoni and mastering their superior military tactics, and the same would appear to be true of the Hehe, who with the Sangu occupied the area north of Lake Nyasa (Malawi). Indeed, by learning well the military and political lessons of the Ngoni, the Hehe were able to keep Arab traders out of their country, thus denying themselves in their strength the very firearms that were so thoroughly transforming other groups. The effect of the Ngoni, like that of the Arab traders, was dual and contradictory—the weak were annihilated but the strong grew stronger in a setting of rising social disintegration and political anarchy.

Far to the north, beyond the limits of Ngoni penetration, the Arab traders encountered strong people, and their influence was limited accordingly. In the highlands between Mount Kilimanjaro and Mount Kenya were the Maasai, Kikuyu, and Kamba, in their several ways all resistant to outsiders. The Kamba had trading pretensions of their own and thus monopolized the coastal routes, the Kikuyu were essentially xenophobic, and the Maasai displayed their well-developed disposition toward warfare which led them to attack strangers with gusto. The traders were therefore obliged to approach the lake states in the Victoria region by way of Tabora. Here they encountered a number of strong, centralized kingdoms like Rwanda, which forbade entry to foreigners or severely limited their movements, or the powerful nations of Buganda and Bunyoro. These last, though well disposed toward the Arabs, were also quite capable of controlling and defining the external trade to suit their own pleasure.

When traditional societies broke down, their demise was often precipitated and their authority replaced by new polyglot kingdoms led by Swahili, Arab, or African opportunists taking advantage of the troubled times. Bringing together armies made up of fugitive slaves, deserting soldiers, refugees, detribalized brigands, and others torn loose from an orderly life by warfare and slaving, they moved about on massive elephant hunts, living off the land and terrorizing the local villages, or established more stable states on conquered lands. There were many examples. West of Lake Tanganyika along the upper Congo (Zaire) River, Arab and Swahili freebooters were particularly active as elephant hunters, raiding and pillaging on the strength of their superior firepower and eventually forming the basis for the more settled polity of Tippu Tip. To their south in the territory of Kazembe, the Nyamwezi state maker, Msiri, carved out and maintained his own realm which lasted for a generation until his death in 1891. Farther west, the Chokwe, an obscure group of highlanders, rose for a time to dominate the ivory trade in the Zambezi-Congo watershed south of the Lunda kingdom of Mwata Yamvo which they eventually destroyed.

The rise of Msiri was based on the classic combination of guns, ivory, and slaves to which was added the Katangan specialty of copper, but it must also be understood in terms of internal decay within the Kazembe kingdom. Msiri first visited the land of Kazembe as a member of a Nyamwezi caravan, then returned about 1856 to settle permanently with a colony of Nyamwezi known locally as Yeke. It was at this time that a long, wasting civil war erupted over the royal succession, and Msiri, by taking sides, was able to build up strength which led to his emergence as an independent power about 1865. His military strength was based on his Yeke warriors, well armed with guns which had been obtained through extensive trade connections and paid for with copper and ivory. Slowly the crumbling Kazembe kingdom was absorbed, and by 1885 most of the Luba kings to the north were paying Msiri tribute as well.

From the high point of his Luba campaigns Msiri's fortunes turned, essentially for the same reasons that had brought the Kazembe's downfall— excessive taxation and slaving practiced by a regime based solely on force. Msiri's rule was notoriously harsh. His palisades were festooned with skulls, not only of enemies, but also his subjects, for death was decreed often for trifling offenses. In 1886 a revolt broke out among the Sanga people but in the midst of this intramural difficulty, Msiri ran afoul of the forces of European imperialism bearing in upon Africa at this time. In 1891 he was shot by a member of an expedition sent by Leopold's Congo Independent State to occupy the valuable Katanga. From that point forward, civil order became Leopold's problem.

Msiri not only subjugated the Katanga but introduced many innovations into local society, not the least of which was smallpox vaccination. Nevertheless, in the long run it was the local culture that predominated, thoroughly

absorbing its Yeke conquerors who finally lost even the knowledge of their
native Nyamwezi tongue. To the west in the domain of Mwata Yamvo, a
somewhat different situation unfolded during these same years. Oppressive
royal taxation and a policy that arbitrarily designated villages to be sold into
slavery had turned the Lunda population against its rulers at the very moment
when the Chokwe to the southwest began to expand northward into the Kasai
country. Originally a small group of seminomadic hunters, the Chokwe had
collaborated with Ovimbundu traders from Angola in collecting and marketing
ivory, and with the aid of firearms had slowly expanded by a process of peaceful
infiltration into new lands, followed by a struggle with the local inhabitants
who were then absorbed into the widening Chokwe hegemony.

Internal dissension among the Lunda had reached the point during the early
1870s that periodically the Chokwe were invited by contending royal aspirants
to take sides, a development that greatly encouraged their northward migration
into Lunda country. By 1885 they had occupied most of the state of Mwata
Yamvo, sacked the capital, and sold its population into slavery. During the
ensuing decade they consolidated their position and began to move against
the Luba states. In 1898, the Lunda rallied and defeated the Chokwe in what
might have been the beginning of an important counterattack, but at this point
the military occupation by the Congo Independent State became effective,
and the Chokwe remained fixed over a vast area astride the Kwilu and Kasai
river basins and abutting on the western Katanga.

Mirambo, Tippu Tip, and the
Demise of Merchant Imperialism

At first blush, Mirambo, the Nyamwezi chief, and Tippu Tip, the Afro-Arab
ivory trader, might seem to be antithetical figures—the latter a coastal Arab
who made a career of extracting the wealth of Africa while forcing its people
to be his unwilling accessories, the former an indigenous ruler intent on rallying
his people against the encroachment of coastal invaders. Certainly Tippu was
an entrepreneur and an opportunist who practiced exploitation on the grand
scale, while Mirambo might be regarded as an early nationalist who brought
cohesion to his people in the face of foreign intrusion.

Viewed from another perspective, however, both men may be seen as similar
manifestations of the same process—the acquisition and consolidation of
commercial advantage through political power. Flourishing during the later
years of the nineteenth century, as the trade in ivory and slaves reached its
climax, both Mirambo and Tippu Tip instinctively built states which enabled
them to control that trade and protect it from competitors. The backbone of
commercial traffic in eastern and central Africa was the line running inland
from Zanzibar through Tabora and Ujiji, and across Lake Tanganyika into

the eastern Congo. Interestingly, it was on that line that the two leaders fashioned their commercial empires, even joining in a brief, belated alliance to preserve their control of this major route.

Mirambo was born of chiefly parentage between 1830 and 1840 at the time when Arab excursions into the interior were changing from occasional speculations to the more systematic penetration encouraged by Sayyid Said. Competition between the new arrivals and the established Nyamwezi gradually sharpened, and it was only a matter of time before a purely commercial rivalry descended to the use of force. While the Arabs at Tabora were resolving the question of toll charges by eliminating Manua Sera, the troublesome chief at Unyanyembe, the Nyamwezi were developing their own strength to the west where Mirambo had succeeded to his father's chieftaincy and was beginning to assert himself both as a mercantile and a military power.

The Arab challenge with its modern armament and streamlined merchandising called for and received an imaginative response from Mirambo who jolted traditional Nyamwezi political standards with the concept of a centralized state supported by vigorous military tactics, a concept that gradually enabled him to extend his sway far beyond his original modest patrimony. A series of petty strikes subdued and absorbed neighboring villages, their loyalty assured by the moderate rule of their new prince. Speed and surprise in attack, personal courage, and the promise of spoils brought more than victory, however, for it also attracted large numbers of *ruga-ruga* (Ngoni and other mercenaries along with detribalized adventurers, runaway slaves, and others uprooted by warfare), and these formidable warriors, armed with the guns which Mirambo was always at pains to obtain, soon developed into an army of unusual striking power.

Mirambo's objectives transcended booty for its own sake. He sought the establishment of a powerful Nyamwezi state which could stand off the intruding Arabs and control the growing interior trade to its own advantage. By 1871 he felt strong enough to give direct challenge to the Arab colony at Tabora, and there followed five years of warfare during which Mirambo was frequently reduced to extremity, managing to survive through tenacity of purpose while the superiority in arms of his foes was offset by their internal divisions. With the arrangement of peace in 1876, Mirambo was recognized as master of the region surrounding his capital at Urambo from which he quickly extended his control westward along the Ujiji route, and temporarily north toward Buganda. Though he never was able to challenge the Arabs successfully in the north, the Nyamwezi maintained their monopoly of the Katanga traffic and built Urambo into a market rivaling Tabora in importance.

During the years that Mirambo was consolidating and expanding his hegemony, his contemporary, Tippu Tip, was engaged in a similar exercise far to the west in the Congo area of the Lualaba and Lomani rivers. Born in Zanzibar about 1830, Tippu began trading as a young man for his father, a Tabora merchant, then struck out for himself during the 1860s in a series of wide-ranging ventures into Bemba and Lungu country at the southern end of Lake Tanganyika. Tippu Tip had early grasped the importance of armed retainers, and with these he was able to defeat Nsama, chief of the Tabwa people, adjacent to the Lungu, a coup that yielded Nsama's store of ivory and established Tip at once as a powerful and wealthy member of the immigrant trading class. Moving northward, the enterprising merchant prince combined trading and raiding, finally securing through a questionable claim of blood relationship a chieftaincy among the Tetela people in the Lomani area. By 1875 he had proceeded via Nyangwe on the Lualaba to Kasongo which became his headquarters. Here he reigned as a paramount chief among the Bantu people and as a governor chosen by the Arab traders, for none could challenge his force of arms.

Arabs had preceded Tippu Tip into the eastern Congo, and by the time of his arrival Nyangwe was recognized as a major entrepôt, filled with the harvest of raiding parties which roamed among the decentralized village communities hunting ivory and gathering slaves. Indiscriminate looting, however, by uncoordinated caravans was wasteful and untidy, and Tippu, who like Mirambo had a genius for political organization, soon had occupied a vast area in the Lomani and Lualaba basins, imposing taxes, building roads, staking out plantations, and regulating the hunting of elephants. He extended his authority downstream into the rain forest and in 1883 was already established at Stanley Falls. By 1890, although there were other important Arab traders in the area, Tippu Tip was preeminent; yet when he left the Congo in that same year on a trip to Zanzibar he was never to return, and a few short years later it was the Congo Independent State that controlled the lands over which he had once held sway.

Having established their commercial empires, neither Mirambo nor Tippu Tip was long able to hold and exploit the advantage they had gained, largely because of forces beyond their control. Mirambo had hoped for European support to secure the Nyamwezi state he was building, but this hope was seriously compromised in 1880 when he inadvertently killed two Europeans in the course of one of his campaigns and thus lost the confidence of John Kirk, the British consul at Zanzibar, who had been urging the sultan Barghash toward alliances in the interior. Even Mirambo's subsequent agreement in 1882 enabling Tippu Tip's caravan to pass safely through Nyamwezi territory failed to change opinions in Zanzibar. When Mirambo died in 1884, he still lacked European or Zanzibari backing for a strong and stable Nyamwezi kingdom, and with his death the people under his control soon reverted to their old parochial quarrels which continued until the area was occupied by the Germans in 1890.

In the case of Tippu Tip European conquest was also the ultimate consequence, ironically so because of Tippu's apparent awareness, even at the height of his power, that he could not long hold his domain. The Arab station at Stanley Falls was paralleled as early as 1883 with a European post founded there by H. M. Stanley on behalf of the International Association of the Congo, and the following year the Europeans attempted, albeit unsuccessfully, to prevent Tippu Tip from sending his caravans downstream beyond the falls. Tippu had already agreed in 1882 to cooperate politically and commercially with Barghash, but within a few years he had evidently resigned himself to the fact that the Europeans could not be ousted; hence, in 1887 he contracted to serve the Congo Independent State as its governor at Stanley Falls with the understanding that Arab trade, except for slaving, would be unimpeded in the territory below the falls. In this anomalous position he remained until 1890, distrusted both by the Arab traders and the Europeans. After his departure, even the fighting that broke out in 1892 between the Arabs and the Congo Independent State did not draw the aging political realist back to what he knew would be a futile defense of his domain. When Tippu Tip died in Zanzibar in 1905, his territories had already been incorporated into the Congo Independent State for over a decade.

Buganda and the International Trade

When the first Arab trader arrived at the royal court of Buganda in 1844, he found a powerful, unified state, its exceptional strength arising from a number of related factors. To start with, an abundant and well-distributed rainfall combined with a soil fertility unusual by tropical standards to provide a plentiful food supply with a minimum of labor. Indeed, cultivation of plantains, the main crop, was largely left in the hands of the women, thus freeing the Baganda men for political and military pursuits which placed the state at a distinct advantage over its neighbors. As national institutions evolved, they tended to place authority centrally in the hands of the kabaka who was able to employ his power toward the further unification and extension of his kingdom. The royal succession, for example, was afflicted with something less than the usual uncertainties, and once the king was firmly in control he became the unquestioned head of a military and administrative bureaucracy, each member of which held his position and wealth entirely at the kabaka's pleasure. Such a concentration of power in a relatively affluent, leisured society, offered unexampled opportunities for war making and economic imperialism. The result was that, by the early nineteenth century, Buganda had become not only an absolute monarchy, but also one that exercised extensive influence over the nominally independent adjacent peoples.

A despotism such as Buganda concentrated in the monarch's court not only power, but also the social and political nervous system of the country. Like the Versailles of Louis XIV, the kabaka's capital was filled with a domesticated aristocracy whose formula for survival was a shrewd mixture of obsequious flattery and palace intrigue. Here was dangerous ground, as was amply illustrated by the oft-noted anecdote of the English explorer J. H. Speke, who told of a Baganda shot arbitrarily on order of the Kabaka Mutesa to demonstrate the properties of a newly acquired carbine. At the same time the court was the locus of opportunity in a land where the standard of success was achievement rather than status, and where the rewards of the kabaka were as great as his punishments were severe. Here, then, came the ambitious and quick-witted to try their fortune, and here was developed in its highest form the inventive, receptive turn of mind made possible by leisure among a people already noted for their adventurous, acquisitive nature.

In this effervescent milieu, traders from the outside world were welcome as the means to greater glory and prosperity for king and subject, and none feared the strangers for they represented no danger to these virile people. On the contrary, they strengthened expansionist tendencies already underway, for they brought new products—particularly cotton cloth and, later, guns—which were in immediate demand and which could be obtained for slaves and ivory wrested from neighboring peoples by Buganda's long-established military superiority. Repeated predatory expeditions sent out by the kabakas Suna, who reigned until 1856, and Mutesa, who succeeded him for another twenty-eight years, yielded rich rewards in the form of produce and cattle as well as slaves and ivory. These goods were converted into an expanding national prosperity which was based solely on a redistribution of wealth by military force, Buganda's economy at this time experiencing no growth of its own.

In time the acquisition of firearms was to combine with Baganda intellectual curiosity to effect a profound social and political revolution in Buganda society, but in the days of Mutesa the guns he collected merely reinforced his military dominance over weak neighbors, as he established crack rifle companies recruited among young courtiers to supplement his peasant spearmen. Such added strength gave further assurance to Mutesa's diplomacy which was called upon during the 1870s to deal both with a renascence of power in Bunyoro and an imperialist thrust southward on the part of Egypt. In dealing with the Khedive Ismail's representatives, first Samuel Baker and then Charles Gordon, Mutesa consistently stressed an alliance against Bunyoro while the Egyptians spoke of an advance up the Nile which was initially thwarted by Mutesa's skillful combination of force and persuasion and eventually expired with the rise of the Mahdist state.

During the course of these events, the Buganda court was visited by the American journalist H. M. Stanley, deep in the midpassage of his continental explorations, and when Stanley spoke of Christian missionaries coming to Buganda, Mutesa strongly encouraged what he evidently took to be potential European support which could be used to help stand off the Egyptians. As the Egyptian threat faded, therefore, CMS missionaries arrived on the scene, but while they were to disappoint Mutesa as a means of military assistance, their long-run impact on Baganda society would prove considerable.

Suggestions for Further Reading

For Central Africa the best overall accounts are contained in David Birmingham and Phyllis M. Martin, eds., *History of Central Africa*, vol. I (London and New York: Longman, 1983). For East Africa see the older B. A. Ogot and J. Kieran, eds., *Zamani* (Nairobi: East African Publishing House, New York: Humanities Press, 1968) and Roland Oliver and Gervaise Matthew, eds., *History of East Africa*, vol. I (Oxford: Clarendon Press, 1963) which are preferable to the more recent *Cambridge History of Africa*, vol. V, edited by John Flint (Cambridge: University Press, 1976). The bibliographies in both the Cambridge and Oxford histories are excellent, though somewhat dated. There is a good history of Tanganyika, John Jiffe, *A Modern History of Tanganyika* (Cambridge: University Press, 1979) containing material on the nineteenth century.

Birmingham and Martin may be supplemented by the older Jan Vansina, *Kingdoms of the Savanna* (Madison: University of Wisconsin Press, 1966) and R. Gray and D. Birmingham, eds., *Pre-Colonial African Trade* (London: Oxford, 1970). For the East African coast, see C. S. Nicholls, *The Swahili Coast . . . 1798-1856* (London: George Allen and Unwin, 1971) and E.A. Alpers, *Ivory and Slaves in East Central Africa* (London: Heinemann, 1975).

There are a number of representative historical studies of indigenous African peoples — for example, B. A. Ogot, *History of the Southern Luo* (Nairobi: East African Publishing House, 1967), G. S. Were, *A History of the Abaluyia of Western Kenya* (Nairobi: East African Publishing House, 1967), Godfrey Muriuki, *A History of the Kikuyu, 1500-1900* (Nairobi: Oxford, 1974), S. Kiwanuka, *A History of Buganda* (London: Longman, 1971), and S. Feierman, *The Shambaa Kingdom: A History* (Madison: University of Wisconsin Press, 1974).

Much material can also be gained from the accounts of nineteenth-century travelers such as Richard F. Burton, J. L. Krapf, J. Thomson, and J. H. Speke; for example, see Burton's *Lake Regions of Central Africa*, vol.II (London: Sidgwik and Jackson, 1961).

For Tippu Tip see H. Brode, *Tippu Tib* (London: Arnold, 1907); Mirambo is examined in N. R. Bennett, *Mirambo of Tanzania* (New York: Oxford University Press, 1971).

PART THREE
Colonial Africa

14

The Partition of Africa

The Berlin Conference

On November 15, 1884 an international conference was convened in Berlin. Present was every nation of Europe, save Switzerland, and the United States of America, fourteen nations in all. The European locale and membership were notable in view of the expressed concern of the conference, which was the continent of Africa. It was proposed, first of all, to clarify the status of international trade on the Congo (Zaire) River and of navigation on the Niger. Secondly, an attempt was to be made to define conditions under which future territorial annexations in Africa might be recognized.

Also in attendance was the ill-understood International Association of the Congo. This self-styled philanthropic organization had been founded a few years earlier by King Leopold II of Belgium, ostensibly to end slaving and substitute legitimate commerce in the Congo basin, but in fact the vehicle for Leopold's imperial dreams in Africa. Lacking true sovereign status, it was already recognized by the United States as a *de facto* government — ironically the nearest thing to an African voice at the conference. No African state was represented.

That a conference concerned with Africa should be held in Europe, by Europeans, and exclusively on behalf of European interests, was a natural consequence of events which by the late nineteenth century had projected the Western powers far beyond the strength of the world's other peoples, propelled by the twin forces of nationalism and industrialization. Indeed, the concerns of the conference were essentially European concerns; the subject of Africa on the agenda was largely adventitious. Such a meeting might have dealt just as easily with free trade on the China coast or the rules of the game for acquiring islands in the Pacific. What was really at stake was the delicate balance of power among European nations, the projection of their rising mercantile interests throughout the world, and the nourishment of national pride which had recently begun to express itself through the acquisition of colonial territories in little-known, far-off places.

The history of the Berlin Conference amply bears out its European preoccupations. During the first half of the nineteenth century there had been no great interest among European nations in the Congo or Niger regions, but as ivory, rubber, and particularly palm oil took on increasing importance in Western commercial and industrial development, mercantile activity grew apace and combined with the work of explorers to stimulate at least an unofficial enthusiasm on the part of European governments. Portugal, whose early importance in the Congo area had declined with her dwindling national strength, now sought control of the mouth of the Congo and to this end secured a treaty with Great Britain in 1884 which conceded Portuguese primacy along the coast while guaranteeing freedom of navigation on the river itself. Thus were served both British economic interests and Portuguese political goals. In addition, Britain was able to check French expansion in the Congo region.

Events had already overtaken the Portuguese, however, and the treaty at once aroused opposition everywhere. For some years French interest in Africa had been growing, fed by a desire both for economic gain and national prestige. By 1884 she had her own substantial claim to Congo territories as the result of a treaty which the explorer de Brazza had secured, giving France the north side of Stanley Pool at the head of the navigable Congo. At the same time, Leopold II was establishing the basis for his personal interests in the Congo area. Even as de Brazza was pursuing his explorations, Henry M. Stanley was engaged in similar activities for Leopold's International Association of the Congo; thus whatever the rival claims of Leopold and the French, both were of the same mind in opposing Portuguese pretension in the area.

Into this situation of growing complexity was introduced the further complication of Prince Bismarck, chief minister of Imperial Germany which in the few short years since the Franco-Prussian War of 1870-1871 had established herself as the major power of Europe. Bismarck was essentially concerned with securing German preeminence in Europe, and consequently was at first indifferent to colonies as emblems of national prestige. He was, however, under increasing pressure from German commercial interests who wished to see the flag and the gunboat follow their widening trade, and in any case the artful chancellor was well aware that gains in Europe sometimes were best obtained through exertions in other latitudes. In this connection, he had gradually become uneasy as signs mounted that other European powers were edging toward territorial acquisitions in Asia and Africa. What if German trade should be denied access to these areas? How would German prestige weather a situation that found France and others controlling colonial empires while Imperial Germany had none?

Beyond these considerations, Bismarck's foreign policy was based on soothing French national pride, rubbed raw by the disaster of Sedan, the German occupation of Paris, and the loss of Alsace-Lorraine. He thereby encouraged the French in colonial adventures which might compensate for humiliation in Europe, and sought to draw closer to France by controlled quarreling with her chief colonial rival, Great Britain. This could be done by laying claim in Africa and the Pacific to territories, the main value of which lay in the annoyance their occupation would cause Britain, while acquisition had the additional asset of placating the expansionist and commercially minded groups within Germany. In 1884 Bismarck suddenly announced protectorates in South-West Africa, Cameroun, and Togo, as well as a portion of New Guinea in the South Pacific. At the same time the foundations for German East Africa were being laid even as the Berlin Conference met, a conclave called jointly by France and Germany at Portugal's suggestion in an effort to solve the Congo impasse which had resulted from the breakdown of the Anglo-Portuguese treaty.

If Bismarck's objectives in calling the conference were centered primarily in Europe, they involved as well the formulation of a set of rules defining the orderly extension of European influence in Africa. During their three months of deliberations, the participating nations appeared to achieve much in this respect. First, they accepted not only freedom of trade and navigation in the Congo basin, but freedom of navigation along the Niger as well. Second, their final agreement, the Berlin Act, provided that any power henceforward annexing territory or instituting a protectorate would at once notify all signatories while guaranteeing effective occupation of the regions in question through the establishment of political stability.

These paper accomplishments, however, meant little in practice. Freedom of navigation was left to national, rather than international, control, while the concept of effective occupation proved unenforceable in any particular instance. Of greater moment were the agreements reached outside the regular sessions whereby the Congo region was partitioned. The German claim to Cameroun was recognized, the limits of Portuguese hegemony clarified, French rights along the north bank of the Congo River conceded, and most astonishing of all, the sovereignty of Leopold II over the Congo Independent State legalized by treaty.

In sum, the Berlin Conference neither precipitated nor regularized the so-called scramble for Africa; it merely punctuated the fact of Africa's partition. European encroachment had already been under way for a considerable time before the congress convened and the rapid occupation that followed was scarcely a direct result of its deliberations. Rather, it was the logical consequence of a larger historical evolution.

Partition—The Causes

The partition of Africa is best understood as the culmination of those expansionist forces that shattered Europe's relative isolation at the dawn of the Renaissance, prompting her intrusion into other parts of the globe in a series of ever-widening waves. In Africa this was marked, first of all, by the search for trade which brought on the West African slave traffic; then, by the early nineteenth-century antislavery, humanitarian movement which attempted to atone for earlier sins through a program of rehabilitation, casting African societies in Europe's image.

Implicit in the humanitarian crusade was the conviction that Europe's presence in Africa was temporary and disinterested, that the development of prosperous African societies meant closer commercial attachment, but political divorce, between Africa and Europe. If Portugal held stubbornly to her possessions on the Guinea coast, in Angola and Mozambique, France showed at best sporadic inclination to expand her West African holdings, while the official and public attitude in Britain, exemplified by the conclusions of the 1865 Select Committee of the House of Commons, was distinctly anti-imperial. Nevertheless, concurrent with the spirit of isolation were factors leading toward a steadily deepening entanglement.

The mere presence of European powers encouraged involvement. Sierra Leone, for example, had become a colony in order that slaves freed by the British naval squadron might be effectively rehabilitated, and the success of this venture was reflected in the thriving community of Freetown. But Freetown did not exist in a vacuum. She had growing mercantile relations with the inland people as well as territorial interests along the coast which necessarily drew her government into an active prosecution, here of boundary claims on the Liberian border, there of suspected slave trading in Portuguese Guinea, now of indigenous chiefs for alleged treaty violations, or again in reprisal for destruction of property or the death of British subjects caught in the chronic tribal skirmishing. Similarly, the French posts in Senegal and down the coast, however tentatively held, invited defense against apparent threats from Muslim revivalists of the interior, while the French continually entertained dark suspicions regarding British designs in their area. Far to the southeast, Britain had occupied Lagos in 1861 as a means of combating the slave trade and furthering commerce, a move that soon forced her to participate, unhappily but increasingly, in the complexities of Yoruba politics.

One source of growing involvement was the relative autonomy of colonial administrators whose freedom of action was directly proportionate to their degree of remove from home governments. Parliamentary questions or ministerial instructions could be ignored or subverted by energetic or strong-willed executives, while changing circumstances might necessitate actions not encompassed by initial instructions. "Insupportable pro-consuls," grumbled Lord Salisbury, the British foreign secretary during the height of the partition, but who could deny the influence on colonial policy of the energetic Governor Faidherbe and his disciple, Brière de l'Isle, advocate of "*le go-ahead des Americains*," of that intrepid trailblazer, de Brazza, whose popular appeals over the head of the government brought France into the Congo, or of the

German adventurer-explorer, Carl Peters, whose unsolicited exertions gave Germany an empire in East Africa?

The example of the Gold Coast is illustrative. There, British policy had clearly vacillated over the years, but there was no mistaking the differences in style and effectiveness of a series of colonial officials. In 1824 the ill-prepared expansionism of Sir Charles Macarthy led to death and defeat at the hands of the Asante and eventual abandonment of the coastal forts by the British government. Contrariwise, during the 1830s George Maclean's tactful diplomacy greatly revived British prestige and influence in the area, stimulating the local authorities to look to Britain for assistance and guidance which his successors were not always able to provide. Later, the liberal-minded governor Sir Arthur Kennedy lent encouragement to the spirit of self-reliance among chiefs which culminated in the Fante Confederation movement, but unhappily the movement expired at the hands of others. First, the acting administrator, C. S. Salmon, arrested its leaders, convinced as he was that the confederation was a conspiracy against British authority; then, as the confederation showed signs of revival, it was smothered by the ineffectual sympathy of Kennedy's successor, J. Pope Hennessy, who approved its objectives but could not bring himself to recommend its acceptance in London.

The personal factor aside, expanding economic interests drew Europe inexorably into a deepening concern with African affairs. As the slave trade died, new demands for new products were generated by the growing industrial establishment of Europe. Palm oil came into prominence as a lubricant for machinery; there was a fast-rising consumption of cotton in the mill towns of England; ivory was found to have a wide range of ornamental and practical uses; gum was needed in the manufacture of paper and confectionery and as a dye fixative and fabric sizing; while a host of other products—groundnuts, tobacco, indigo, sugar, coffee, tea, tropical fruits—along with the generally vain hope of mineral wealth, stimulated European commercial enterprise. For their part, African societies developed an abiding desire for the manufactures of Europe—fabrics and utensils, but also alcoholic spirits and firearms, as well as the ever-popular beads.

Mercantile activity more than implied political and military pressures which were exerted both inward and outward, for Africa was as quick, if not as adept, as Europe in prosecuting its commercial interests. A major factor in the difficulties encountered by the British on the Gold Coast during much of the nineteenth century was the unceasing urgency of the Asante thrust toward the coast in search of the European trade. It was the British decision to meet this pressure with force in the interests of political stability which led to the Asante War of 1873-1874 and the establishment of the British Gold Coast Colony. On the Senegal River, the Brakna and Trarza Moors had controlled the gum trade over the years through the force of their arms, a situation that was regularly deplored by the traders of Saint-Louis, but never resolved until Faidherbe subdued the Trarzas in 1858. Faidherbe's relations with al-Hajj

Umar were also influenced by economic considerations as indeed were most of his programs for colonial development in Senegal. Later the imperial ambitions of French soldiers would trigger major moves inland across the western Sudan.

Circumstances were much the same in other areas. Like Senegal, Sierra Leone existed on trade, and trade meant an aggressive policy toward the people of the interior, advocated by the Freetown merchants and prosecuted by vigorous governors like S. J. Hill who in 1861, despite misgivings in the Colonial Office, annexed territories in the hinterland in order that commerce might prosper. On the Niger, trade was even more completely a major factor touching all activity—the Christian missions, the social and political organization of the delta states, the establishment of British consuls, and finally the breaching of the delta and the mercantile-cum-political activities of George Goldie Taubman. When Bismarck made his sudden territorial moves in Africa in 1884 and 1885, the wonder is that he was able to base them on political considerations within Europe, ignoring in the main the growing clamor of the merchants of Hamburg and Bremen.

Yet Bismarck's motivation was characteristically sound. The African commerce, for all its rising importance, was but a minor matter compared with the great political and strategic factors generated by Europe herself. Africa, for example, supplied only two percent of Britain's foreign commerce prior to the First World War. Similarly Germany's West African trade for 1882 represented only 3/10 of one percent of her total imports, but by that date Germany had already become the most powerful nation in continental Europe, and Bismarck's main concern was to maintain and strengthen this position. The other colonial powers were no less preoccupied with European affairs. France looked for the day of revenge when the Germans would be humbled and Alsace-Lorraine regained. Britain, though aloof from Continental involvements, was nonetheless intent upon preserving her world mercantile and industrial supremacy, a major requirement of which was the maintenance of open sea lanes for her shipping.

None of these matters had any direct connection with Africa although they were to play a decisive role in her final partition. Bismarck's decision to annex Alsace-Lorraine after the Franco-Prussian War was based primarily on considerations of military strategy, but this advantage was gained at the expense of a deep-seated bitterness in France. In time the French reaction took two antithetical forms. The first was a straightforward desire to regain the lost provinces and with them France's shattered national pride. This "doctrine of effacement" concentrated on Europe, equated colonialist arguments with national treason, and dreamed of the day of revenge. The other position was equally patriotic but saw a world changing before the force of industrialism, and argued that France's future greatness depended upon her ability to change with the times. Here was a doctrine of compensation which freed France from her myopic preoccupation with the "blue line of the Vosges" beyond the new Franco-German frontier, which spoke of markets and raw materials for France's growing industrial machine, and which offered imperial vistas to refresh the flagging spirits of all true French patriots.

The principal architect and theoretician of this new colonialism was Jules Ferry who, as premier in 1880-1881 and again in 1883-1885, brought large areas under French control in Indochina, Madagascar, and Africa. In Africa he engineered protectorates in Somalia and Tunisia, and supported explorations in the Niger and Congo basins. One such expedition, although not directly attributable to Ferry's encouragement, was that led by the young naval officer, Pierre Savorgnan de Brazza, who in 1880 secured a French protectorate over vast but ill-defined territories on the north bank of the Congo, and thus greatly stimulated in response the acquisitive instincts of both the Portuguese and Leopold II. At the same time, French activity on the West African coast alarmed Britain into a defensive posture regarding her commercial interests which led directly to her securing a protectorate in the Niger Delta area.

Such colonial adventures ideally suited Bismarck's objective of neutralizing the power of France in Europe and setting the French and British at odds as colonial competitors. The joint French and German invitation to the Berlin Conference was but another element in this complex diplomacy. Not only did it suggest closer Franco-German cooperation, but it brought Bismarck squarely into the African scene where he might exercise a measure of control over the shape of Europe's impending occupation of Africa, partly to guarantee an appropriate share for Germany, partly that no difficulties might emerge in Africa to complicate Germany's European position.

The chief beneficiary of the conference, however, was not the German chancellor but Leopold II of Belgium who has been aptly described as a "royal speculator . . . masquerading as a philanthropic society." This ambitious monarch, frustrated by the limitations imposed by his small kingdom, sought and eventually found expression for his imperial aspirations in the creation of the Congo Independent State with himself as its sovereign. He achieved this improbable objective in a series of artful maneuvers, first through the establishment in 1876 of the International Association for the Exploration and Civilization of Central Africa (International African Association), a private organization formed under Leopold's presidency with ostensibly scientific and humanitarian objectives, and then via the International Association of the Congo, controlled by Leopold and presumably interested in the commercial development of the Congo basin.

By the eve of the Berlin Conference, Leopold's Congo Association had laid claim to a large area through the treaty-making exertions of its agent H. M. Stanley, and the Belgian monarch was already hinting at the idea of a strong indigenous state in the Congo directed by Leopold himself. Such a concept was attractive to Britain and Germany as a check to French ambitions in the area, and all sides were cordial toward a scheme that blocked Portugal. France was finally brought into concurrence when she was assured the right to assume Leopold's obligations in the event he were unable to maintain the costs of administration. As the conference proceeded, a series of bilateral agreements were concluded recognizing the sovereignty of Leopold's International Association of the Congo which thereby became a signatory in good standing when the Berlin Act was confirmed by the powers in February 1885. Five months later the association became the Congo Independent State.

In addition to Bismarck, Leopold, and France was a further factor, acting powerfully as a catalyst to partition. In 1798, when Napoleon invaded Egypt, Britain's reaction had been quick and unequivocal in the protection of her lifeline to India and the Far East. Now, three-quarters of a century later, the stakes were that much higher in an era of rising industrial competition, and Egypt was even more the key to the East now that a canal at Suez had at last become a reality. The reign of the khedive, Ismail, which began in 1863 with high promise of fulfilling Muhammad Ali's program of modernization, soon foundered in mismanagement and extravagance. The canal was completed in 1869, a fact that greatly intensified Europe's interest in Egyptian financial and political stability. Hence by 1879, when Ismail had brought the country to bankruptcy despite recourse to foreign loans, he was forced from power by his European creditors who took financial control of the country as advisers to Ismail's successor, Tawfiq. The economy measures they introduced struck hard at the Egyptian army, already a center of nationalist opposition to foreign interference. Disaffection among Egyptian officers led to the military revolt in 1881 led by Colonel Urabi Pasha, an uprising that was put down only when Britain invaded and occupied Egypt in 1882.

The occupation was to have been a joint French-British venture but France was prevented from participating because of a cabinet crisis, and Britain consequently found herself *de facto* ruler of Egypt, a role she accepted reluctantly as necessary to the protection of her communications to India and beyond. Such a situation, however, stimulated European rivalries already in motion as a result of economic competition, the rise of Imperial Germany, and the emergence of a spirited sense of nationalism. French confrontation with Britain, thwarted in Egypt, was thus intensified in West Africa while she vied with Portugal and Leopold's International Association of the Congo. Bismarck, in effect, exchanged his support of British intervention in Egypt for acquiescence in his African protectorates, while Britain and Leopold both responded to French pressures by developing their claims in West Africa and the Congo respectively. By 1885 the partition of Africa had indeed accelerated into a scramble.

Partition—The Process

The partition of Africa, then, was the result of a number of factors, primarily European in origin, which gradually accumulated momentum until by the time of the Berlin congress their combined force had reached explosive proportions. To the early mercantilism, which brought the French occupation of the Senegal coast and the British posts on the Gambia River and the Gold Coast, were added the antislavery haven of Sierra Leone and the port of Lagos, annexed in 1861 also as a blow against the slave trade. In 1874 Britain gave up its efforts to withdraw from the Gold Coast, reversed its policy, and assumed the responsibility of governing the newly created Gold Coast Colony. For her part, France extended her authority far along the course of the Senegal during the administration of Faidherbe while the expansionism of Napoleon III pressed the conquest and occupation of Algeria, begun under the reigns of Charles X and Louis Philippe. Portugal maintained her holdings on the Guinea coast, along with Angola and Mozambique, and dreamed of empires her weakness would not allow.

For a time there was a pause in the formal extension of British and French authority in West Africa while privately inspired and semiofficial forces built up pressure for eventual occupation. French commercial enterprise, echoing Faidherbe, proposed railroad schemes for opening up the Niger watershed, connecting it alternatively with Algeria or the Senegal River system. Such proposals, which anticipated a deep penetration of the West African savanna, were followed by exploratory, quasimilitary probes from Senegal which, however, were largely checked by the Tokolor state of Ahmadu to the east and the Mandinka power of Samori on Ahmadu's southern flank. Undaunted, French traders began to appear along the lower Niger where they at once came into conflict with the United African Company (later named the Royal Niger Company), formed in 1879 by the merchant prince, George Goldie Taubman, from several independent British mercantile establishments long active up the Niger beyond the preserve of the African trading states in the delta. The consolidation by Goldie, the surname he preferred, had been frankly monopolistic and was followed by a commercial war which by the end of 1884 had succeeded in forcing out or absorbing the French.

Goldie's ultimate solution was political, however. He sought a charter, finally granted in 1886, giving him not only a commercial monopoly but political authority over the Niger territory in question. His treaties with local potentates in effect set up a sphere of influence which his company administered by what later came to be known as indirect rule and which eventually was absorbed into the Niger Districts Protectorate. Proclaimed by Britain in 1885, this protectorate included the coast between the Lagos colony and German Cameroun, extending inland as far as Lokoja and eastward two hundred miles along the Benue to Ibi. Thus was formed the basis for the modern state of Nigeria. Already this action had been preceded by the German protectorates in Togo and Cameroun in 1884, while the French, undeterred by their problems on the lower Niger, moved in 1883 to secure their Slave Coast trade by occupying Porto Novo and Cotonou, and therewith divorced Lagos from the Gold Coast by the intrusion of what eventually became the colony of Dahomey.

The Berlin Conference was also preceded by the reluctant British intrusion into Egypt in 1882, a temporary occupation that nevertheless dragged on in varying form until after the Second World War. In other parts of Africa, however, the conference marked a new and accelerated stage in the partition. De Brazza consolidated French claims to the territory between Gabon and the north bank of the Congo by the classic practice of treaty making, in this case with local chiefs in the Sangha and Ubangi river basins, thus providing a point of departure for subsequent explorations northward toward Lake Chad.

On the other side of the river, Leopold proceeded energetically to implement his successful claim at Berlin for control over the huge Congo basin. First, there was the business of exploration, already underway before the sovereignty of the Congo Independent State was achieved in 1885, but thereafter greatly intensified with the help of steam-powered river craft which were able to reach all parts of the huge Congo watershed. Interior river communications, however, were of little consequence as long as access to the sea was blocked by the rapids below Stanley Pool, and Leopold therefore very early began surveying a railroad link to the coast. Construction started in 1890 and the line was completed eight years later at a great cost in life, not only among the local people who were employed largely as porters between Leopoldville and the coast, but also among the West Africans, chiefly Krumen, brought in to help with the construction.

Leopold's problems were not entirely limited to extending effective communications over vast distances, for his hegemony was sharply contested in two major areas—the east and the Katanga. In the east were the Arab traders, well established along the Lualaba River since the 1860s and headed by the redoubtable Tippu Tip. Their slaving activities extended far to the west and north of the Lualaba beyond Stanley Falls, and Leopold, weak in resources and manpower, was unable to establish *de facto* authority farther than Bangala near the top of the Congo bend. In 1887 his agent, Stanley, managed to persuade Tippu Tip to become governor of the eastern region, an alliance of convenience based on Leopold's weakness and Tippu Tip's realization of the long-range power of the Europeans compared with Sultan Barghash's failing authority at Zanzibar. Tippu Tip could not control all the Arabs, however, and after he departed for Zanzibar in 1890 relations quickly deteriorated.

Not only were the Arabs suspicious of the European connection, but Leopold soon found himself embarrassed by his alliance with a notorious slave dealer when in 1888 Cardinal Lavigerie, founder of the White Fathers missionary movement, began a crusade to end the Arab slave trade. Converting a weakness into a strength, Leopold now came forward as the champion of African freedom and called an antislavery congress in Brussels in 1889 from which he extracted the right to charge import duties as a means of support for a campaign to end the Arab slaving once and for all. His mercantile and political objectives thus attractively concealed in humanitarian dress, Leopold abandoned further efforts to cooperate with the Arabs. In 1892 hostilities broke out and were largely ended three years later with the Europeans victorious under the leadership of Francis Dhanis, later made a baron by the grateful Leopold.

While the eastern provinces were being subdued, Leopold was similarly engaged in extending his rule to the Katanga. There Msiri had long held sway, but by 1890 he was under pressure from Cecil Rhodes and the British South Africa Company seeking control of the Katangan copper, an external complication added to the revolt of the Sanga people which had plagued Msiri since 1886. Msiri would have none of Rhodes's protection, nor was he any more receptive to Leopold's emissaries when they arrived in 1891 with similar overtures. Pressure by the Belgian king became so intense, however, that violence broke out and the uncooperative Msiri was killed. His death at once gave Leopold effective occupation of the Katanga although in the process he inherited the Sanga revolt which was not put down for another decade.

The Berlin Conference also marked, but did not greatly affect, a movement toward occupation in East Africa which was more particularly the result both of European international diplomacy and the activities of official and unofficial agents on the ground. The unsponsored harvest of treaties gathered by Carl Peters on the mainland back of Zanzibar in 1884 suited Bismarck's momentary purpose of embarrassing Britain, and a German protectorate was proclaimed just as the conference concluded its deliberations in March 1885. This development led to a British-German agreement in 1886 dividing the vast area between the Tana and Rovuma rivers along the line of the present Kenya-Tanzania frontier, Zanzibar, although not represented, being granted possession of the coastal islands and a shoreline strip ten miles deep. Zanzibari independence disappeared in 1890 when Britain gained the right to "protect" the island, at the same time being conceded primacy in the Great Lakes area which was to become the territory of Uganda. In return for this she ceded Germany the strategic North Sea island of Heligoland, and consented to outright German control over the Zanzibar coastal strip in Tanganyika, a foothold that was quickly extended inland to the region of Lake Kivu and Lake Tanganyika. Once again European diplomatic considerations had proved paramount in the partition of Africa.

As the decade of the eighties drew to a close, the quickening pace of partition came to southern Africa. Cape Colony and Natal had long been British possessions, but when Bismarck appropriated South-West Africa in 1884, Britain blocked possible German linkage with the Transvaal the following year by establishing a protectorate over Bechuanaland. Such a move also was to serve the imperial design of the Salisbury ministry, just come to power and dedicated to control of the Nile highway that would eventually expand into the idea of a Cape to Cairo axis. During the early 1880s gold was discovered in the Transvaal, attracting, among others, Cecil Rhodes, already possessing a fortune in Kimberley diamonds, but Rhodes's enormous appetite for commercial and political conquest was scarcely satisfied thereby, and he pressed northward through his British South Africa Company toward the

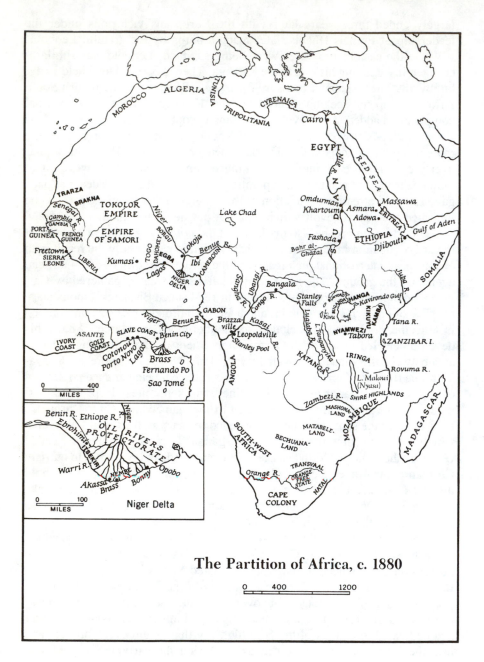

The Partition of Africa, c. 1880

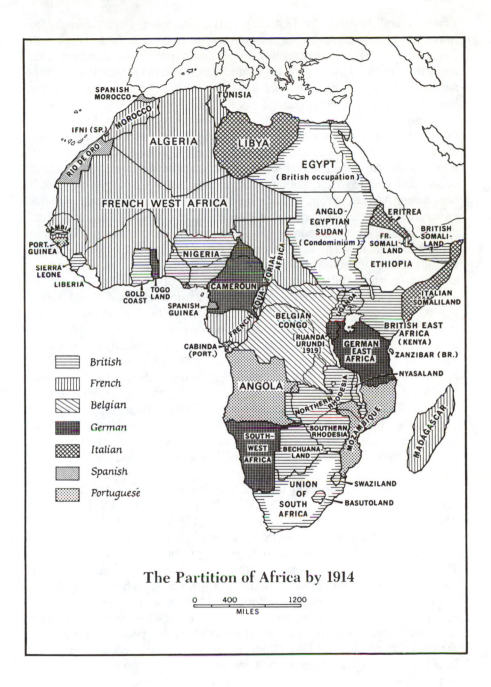

SPANISH
MOROCCO
TUNISIA
IFNI (SP.)
MOROCCO
RIO DE ORO
ALGERIA
LIBYA
EGYPT
(British occupation)
FRENCH WEST AFRICA
GAMBIA
PORT.
GUINEA
SIERRA
LEONE
LIBERIA
NIGERIA
GOLD
COAST
TOGO
LAND
SPANISH
GUINEA
CAMEROUN
FRENCH EQUATORIAL AFRICA
ANGLO-
EGYPTIAN
SUDAN
(Condominium)
ERITREA
FR.
SOMALI-
LAND
BRITISH
SOMALI-
LAND
ETHIOPIA
ITALIAN
SOMALILAND
UGANDA
BELGIAN
CONGO
(RUANDA
URUNDI
1919)
CABINDA
(PORT.)
BRITISH EAST
AFRICA
(KENYA)
ZANZIBAR (BR.)
GERMAN
EAST
AFRICA
NYASALAND
ANGOLA
NORTHERN
RHODESIA
RHODESIA
SOUTHERN
RHODESIA
MOZAMBIQUE
MADAGASCAR
SOUTH-
WEST
AFRICA
BECHUANA-
LAND
SWAZILAND
UNION
OF
SOUTH
AFRICA
BASUTOLAND

British
French
Belgian
German
Italian
Spanish
Portuguese

The Partition of Africa by 1914

0　　400　　　1200
MILES

Zambezi and beyond. In 1890 his settlers founded Fort Salisbury in Mashonaland while company agents pushed on to contest the Katanga with Leopold. In 1891 protectorates were proclaimed in the trans-Zambezi area, as well as in the Shire highlands around Lake Malawi where British missionaries had been gathering since the 1870s, inspired by the work and the example of David Livingstone.

British economic and political imperialism was now in full flower; Portuguese designs on Central Africa were rudely turned aside, while expansionists like Rhodes and Harry Johnston extended British primacy by treaty with the indigenous people. In Matabeleland and Mashonaland occupation resulted from military conquest in 1893 and suppression of a subsequent African revolt, leading in 1898 to the creation of a colony with an elected white settler minority in its legislative council. In South Africa, the determination of Britain to dominate the Transvaal and its growing economic strength led to the defeat of the Boers in the war of 1899-1902 and the ultimate unification of South Africa under British imperial direction although internal affairs were held firmly under Boer (Afrikaner) control.

French expansionism found its most fruitful expression in the great savanna belt of the western and central Sudan. Checked by the United States when in 1879 she proposed a protectorate over Liberia, France nevertheless emerged as master of vast stretches of West Africa and architect of an east-west axis which for a time challenged Britain's grand design from the Cape to Cairo. Pursued with enthusiasm by French officers in the Sudan, her strategy was to link the valleys of the Senegal and Niger rivers, to connect these in turn with her North African centers in Algeria and Tunisia, then to push eastward to the Lake Chad region where French interests were aiming northward from de Brazza's Congo, and finally to press on to Djibouti on the Red Sea in a maneuver that would sever Britain's north-south line and loosen her hold on Egypt.

Britain, with no comparable territorial aspirations in West Africa, did not generally interfere with the French military operations which subdued Ahmadu's Tokolor empire between 1890 and 1893, established French rule in Guinea and the Ivory Coast by 1893, occupied Dahomey in a hard campaign in 1892, and finally put an end to Samori's prolonged resistance in 1898. The French advance to the east was forced to swing northward around the Fulani emirates when Captain Frederick Lugard, acting on behalf of Goldie's Royal Niger Company, occupied Borgu in 1894, a scant two weeks before the arrival of French forces. Another serious reversal occurred four years later far to the east when France's grand imperial strategy collapsed at Fashoda. A thrust into the Bahr al-Ghazal was approved by the French government in 1896, and two years later a small column under Captain J. B. Marchand arrived at Fashoda on the upper Nile after a fourteen-month march from Brazzaville. By this time, however, the British were well embarked on the process of taking the Mahdist Sudan, and in September 1898 the Khalifa was defeated by General Kitchener at Omdurman, thus ending effective resistance from the Mahdist state. Kitchener immediately marched south to Fashoda where he threatened Marchand's much smaller contingent. After several uneasy weeks during which the two forces represented potential large scale war, the French backed down, and with Marchand's departure so faded the threat to Britain's hold on Egypt and her control of the Nile.

In northern Africa, one other European power asserted herself. The process of Italian unification, achieved for practical purposes in 1861, now suggested the further embellishment of a colonial empire, and soon Italy was joining in the partition of Africa. Massawa on the Red Sea was taken in 1885, and then in 1889 the whole Eritrean coast and Asmaran highlands were occupied at the expense of Ethiopia. At the same time Somalia from Cape Guardafui to the Juba River became an Italian protectorate while the French established themselves at Djibouti and the British took that section of the Somali coast facing the Gulf of Aden. Italian pretensions were much greater than these modest acquisitions, but they also exceeded her strength, and she failed to occupy Ethiopia, checked by Menelik's stunning victory at Adowa in 1896. Later, however, in 1911-1912, she gained further African territories in Tripolitania and Cyrenaica. The last piece of independent Africa to fall was Morocco, divided between France and Spain in 1912.

On the eve of the First World War, the partition of Africa was complete. Only two territories, Liberia and Ethiopia, had escaped European colonization, and Liberia, at least from the viewpoint of the indigenous people of the area, might well have been regarded as a special version of the Western occupation of Africa.

Partition—The African Response

Throughout the process of partition, particularly during its climactic stages, the African people were little able to check the tidal wave of foreign control that swept over them. Unable to resist partition, they were by no means passive bystanders—impotent perhaps, but not passive and not unresponsive. There were, of course, many chiefs of small, isolated communities who ill understood the significance of their mark on treaties that compromised their authority and potentially limited their freedom of action. Others, however, were quite well aware of their sovereignty and approached the Europeans, even as they were being approached in turn, as agents in the solution of economic problems or possible allies whose friendship might assist in the realization of a diplomatic victory at the expense of some belligerent neighbor. Africa therefore was not a dull, uncomprehending, inert mass, apathetic in the face of the force that bore in upon her; neither were African leaders necessarily high-minded, patriotic leaders defending honor and territory. They were human beings caught up in dynamics they could not control. Their eventual loss of land and liberty was due essentially to a want of technical sophistication, not to a lack of will or vigor to respond.

Examples abound. In Buganda, the kabaka, Mutesa, ruled with a firm hand, sure of his authority over a virile, imperialistically minded power. When, during the early 1870s, Egypt began to probe southward in search of trade and empire, both Bunyoro and Buganda saw the intruder not as an object of fear, but as a means for gaining advantage in their intramural struggle. When the possibility of European support against both Bunyoro and Egypt later presented itself, Mutesa, like any resourceful statesman, reached out for help where he could find it, confident that in his strength he could use the Europeans to his own advantage.

Similarly, Mirambo in his struggle to establish a trading empire among the Nyamwezi, consistently regarded Europeans as his vehicle to success. Europeans had guns and understood mechanics, they possessed wide knowledge and influence; hence they could help him to gain power within his sphere, to control the passage of caravans, and with them, their wealth. His preference for Britain was a direct reflection of her influence in Zanzibar, even as his hopes for an enduring and powerful inland nation rested on the possibility of an alliance with the British state. Much the same considerations prompted the Hanga (Wanga) chief, Mumia, to encourage coastal traders and seek a British alliance during the 1880s as a means of offsetting a loss in local authority. So successful was Mumia's policy that his village north of Kavirondo Gulf grew in wealth and importance and later became the administrative center for Kavirondo while Mumia's influence increased proportionately.

These essays in international diplomacy by Mirambo and Mumia were made in the interests of political power linked to economic advantage. A profitable commerce was the aspiration of many an African people, and when that commerce involved Europe, as it frequently did, the European trade was assiduously wooed. When European merchants first appeared in West African waters in search of gold and then to barter for slaves, the goods they offered in exchange were exotic by local standards, but soon became necessities, not of life, but in the satisfaction of prestige and the desire for luxury. Spirits and tobacco developed into steady favorites; a taste spread for European and Indian textiles, for mirrors and ornamental jewelry, while firearms were quickly found to be indispensable to successful statecraft. When the slave trade was abolished, other products were substituted, and desolate indeed was the countryside which could provide no goods of interest to the Europeans. Far from opposing the arrival of traders, the local people frequently fought one another to gain access to the European commerce; as long as trade was the object, the European was more than welcome.

Commerce, therefore, was one of the forces leading to partition which found the Africans as quick as the Europeans to press for advantage, and nowhere were they more resourceful than in the mangrove swamps of the Niger Delta coast. There, as elsewhere, European traders were encouraged, but only to exchange their goods with the delta agents who in turn monopolized the trade with the interior. When the Europeans attempted to penetrate up-country and make direct contact with the inland markets, trouble resulted.

In the tidewater creeks, those familiar with the area were able to move swiftly and silently in their small craft, and when the occasion called for force, they could bring to bear large numbers of fully manned war canoes complete with cannon and riflemen. The prize was trade monopoly; in this respect the objectives and the tactics of George Goldie and the Royal Niger Company were identical with those of such delta merchant princes as Jaja, king of Opobo, and Nana, the Itsekiri governor of the Benin River.

Both were hard-bitten realists, and Jaja in particular had risen from unpromising slave beginnings to become, first, head of one of the main trading houses of Bonny, and then, when the prospect of dominating Bonny faded, the founder of the new state of Opobo which soon emerged as the most important power in the Niger Delta. Such pretensions with their corollary of mercantile dominance came under increasing pressure from British traders, particularly when the Berlin Conference proclaimed freedom of commerce on the Niger and a British protectorate was established throughout the delta. Jaja had already secured a treaty sustaining his monopoly which he proceeded to implement by direct trade with England, threatening to destroy any up-country producers who might try to deal with British merchants, and carrying on a vigorous diplomatic offensive to force Whitehall to honor the terms of his treaty. Since the British merchants in the area had formed a trading cartel, the issue was not free trade versus monopoly, but whether the monopoly would be African or British, and there was the further question of which government, British or African, in fact ruled the creeks. Reduced to these essentials, the dispute was clearly foreclosed against Jaja who, faced with the prospect of overwhelmingly superior force, surrendered in 1887 to the British consul, Harry Johnston, and was eventually deported.

The fall of Nana was also a history of mercantile competition played out in terms of political authority. In the far northwestern edge of the Niger Delta below Benin City, the Itsekiri traders had long been active, first in the slave traffic and later in the export of palm oil. In the 1850s on the urging of the British consul they had established the office of chief or governor of the Benin River as a check to unrest in the area. After a series of occupants, the post went in 1879 to Olomu, the most prominent Itsekiri trader of his day. His son, Nana, succeeded in 1883 on his father's death, using both his inherited wealth and his official position during the ensuing years, to build up an impressive trade monopoly covering not only the creek region but the palm oil hinterland along the Benin, Ethiope, and Warri rivers.

Such a monopoly irritated many people. First, it was vexatious to the growing number of British traders coming into the area. Next, it was cited by the African oil producers as the chief cause for their falling prices during the 1880s. Further, there were disaffected elements among the Itsekiri who resented

Nana's power. Finally, his strength was regarded by the British protectorate administration as a challenge by a local chief who was also strongly suspected of engaging in an illegal slave trade. In 1891 the Itsekiri country was placed under the new Oil Rivers Protectorate, now constituting the southern portion of the Niger districts, and shortly thereafter the mercantile and political opposition to Nana accelerated rapidly. In 1894 the acting consul general reported to his government a virtual stoppage of trade due to unrest created by Nana's men. Nana was ordered to withdraw his war canoes and when the answer was unsatisfactory, a blockade was placed on his headquarters at Ebrohimi in the mangrove lowlands near the Benin River. The town was shelled and several attacks were mounted but these were driven off by well-armed and entrenched defenders. Finally, after adequate reinforcements had been called up, the town was taken in September 1894, but by that time most of the population had melted into the forest. Nana escaped, later to give himself up in Lagos, and like Jaja he was subsequently tried and banished.

In some instances the commercial-political opposition to European pressure ended more happily for the defenders; for example, with the Egba, who survived Governor Glover's energetic interference, maintaining their independence until 1914. Usually, however, the results were disastrous, as in the case of the Brassmen, who attacked the Royal Niger Company post at Akassa in 1895 in a desperate protest against the loss of their inland markets to the company's monopoly, then were overwhelmed, despite determined resistance in their home delta country of Nembe, and their town of Brass destroyed.

Occasionally what began as a matter of commerce took on a different color with the passage of time. Asante, defeated in 1874, soon endeavored to regain her old authority while European states during the 1880s stepped up their mutual competition in the extension of protectorate areas. The Gold Coast government, prodded by local African merchants on the coast, sought to impose its rule on Asante while Prempeh, the asantehene, moved to evade entanglement, his position progressively weakened by the defection of former allies asking for protection by Britain. In 1896 the British occupied Kumasi and deposed Prempeh, establishing a protectorate the following year. This action was deeply resented locally, and, when in 1900 the Gold Coast governor committed an unpardonable blasphemy by demanding to sit on the golden stool, that ancient symbol of the Asante state and spirit, the people united in a rising which was put down only after months of hard campaigning. In 1901 Asante was annexed directly to the British crown.

The struggle of the Asante people to preserve the spirit and fact of national integrity was paralleled in other African societies. If Moshoeshoe sought protectorate status as the means of national survival and Tippu Tip opted to join the forces he realized he could not beat, others fought stubbornly to stave off annihilation, their motivation often as diverse as their objective was identical. In the Katanga, Msiri paid with his life for refusing to give up the commercial advantage which Tippu Tip knew could not be held. In West Africa, the driving force behind the Senegalese Muslim leader, Mamadu Lamine, was partly religious zeal and partly pride in his Sarakole origins, while Ahmadu, son and successor to the great jihad leader, al-Hajj Umar, seems until too late to have been preoccupied with the rigid defense of a Tokolor state that had seen its best days. With Samori it was the preservation of his Mandinka empire with a series of imaginative political and military maneuvers, as brilliantly conceived as they were ultimately futile.

East Africa also witnessed uncompromising resistance along with accommodation. If Mirambo had sought an alliance with Britain, his compatriot Siki was of another mind, and thwarted German occupation from his center at Tabora for several years until his defeat and death in 1893. Similarly, the Hehe chief, Mkwawa, held out against the Germans in the Iringa region of Tanganyika for the better part of a decade until he was overwhelmed in 1898. To the north, opposition was likewise variable—witness the Nandi in western Kenya who were not to be finally subdued until 1905, the Kikuyu who were sometimes cooperative, sometimes antagonistic, or the Kamba who generally were receptive to European penetration. Far in the south, resistance, though unavailing, was bitter and shaped an equally bitter course for the history of an unhappy land—the determined defense of the xenophobic Boer and the futile struggle of the ill-starred Lobengula against the relentless force of British penetration.

Modernization and Independence in Ethiopia

Political disintegration had settled over the Ethiopian highlands during the long royal residence begun at Gondar by Fasiladas in the mid-seventeenth century, and as such seemed to be preparing the ground for the accelerated process of partition that was to consume Africa during the nineteenth century. Intrigue and regicide were commonplace while monarchs degenerated into ineffectual puppets, corrupt and impotent within the remote splendor of their palaces. Only the Ethiopian Church managed a show of national cohesion, if not authority, while political power was captured by the nobility, the great princes of Tigre, Shoa, Amhara, and Gojjam ruling, for practical purposes, as independent sovereigns. Of these, Shoa, though peripherally located to the south and long beset by Galla pressure, had a particular destiny, for its royal house was to bring forth the rulers who would lead the country back to national unity and in the process protect it from annihilation by foreign powers.

Tewodros, the first of the reformer-kings was not a Shoan, however, nor was he even of the main royal houses. The son of a minor chief in western Ethiopia, he was born about 1818 and given the name Kassa, coming to manhood in a period of growing chaos during which civil war descended into anarchy and brigandage was a plausible road to power. Living a life of chronic uncertainty in the unrelieved turmoil of the day, Kassa did indeed operate for a time as the chief of a band of highwaymen, a successful vocation that led eventually to political recognition and marriage with the daughter of the *ras*, or prince, of Gondar in 1847. Within a few years he had gained control of both Gondar and Gojjam, and when this was followed by victory over the ras of Tigre in 1855, Kassa was able to have himself crowned *negusa nagast*, king of kings, with the throne name of Tewodros or Theodore. The king of Shoa having died shortly thereafter and his young son, Menelik, fallen into the emperor's hands, Tewodros was established as the undisputed head of an Ethiopian nation once more united.

Tewodros had unified the country by force, but, like Muhammad Ali, he now sought to build a modern state, making unity permanent through administrative reform and the nation powerful by means of an up-to-date army. He attempted to place civil control over the lands and the wealth of the Ethiopian Church, the state undertaking to pay the salaries of the clergy. He moved to break the power of the provincial nobility by instituting districts under his own appointed governors. He transferred his capital from the inaccessible center of Gondar, and instituted the first system of roads for better communication and military transport.

It was to military reforms that he gave chief attention, however, for he was aware of the shortcomings of the traditional means of warfare in Ethiopia in a context of growing imperial interest by European nations in the affairs of Africa. "I know the tactics of European governments," he announced. "First they send out missionaries, then consuls to support the missionaries, then battalions to support the consuls." As it happened, the missionaries became Tewodros's own military vanguard when they were obliged by the emperor to concentrate on casting cannon and shot rather than converting souls, finally producing a great mortar capable of firing a thousand-pound shell, as well as several other artillery pieces of lesser caliber.

Such novelties as bronze cannon were much needed by the emperor who was beset not only by foreign enemies actual or potential, but by rising opposition at home on the part of both nobility and clergy, unwilling to give up their long-standing authority to a central government, or to part with their vast accumulation of landed wealth. Deprived thus of an adequate financial base for his reforms, Tewodros ultimately failed in his attempted modernization of Ethiopia, although the immediate cause of his downfall came from another quarter — a dispute with Britain over a request for technical assistance which involved misunderstanding and pride, tactlessness and arbitrary behavior.

In 1862 Tewodros asked that artisans be sent to help him in his plans for military development. When this appeal was ignored, he took it to be an unfriendly act and responded by detaining the British consul and mishandling several other Europeans. Tewodros's conduct was characterized by a lack of restraint which increasingly marred his later years, but his behavior may also have been caused by a determination to gain the help of craftsworkers capable of manufacturing arms. In any event, relations gradually deteriorated between the two countries, and a military expedition was finally dispatched in 1867 under Sir Robert Napier to rescue the consul and his companions. By this time much of Ethiopia was in open revolt and the invaders had little difficulty reaching the fortress of Magdala where Tewodros stood at bay. His small force was easily defeated in April 1868 by the larger, better-equipped British expedition, and even his great mortar exploded on firing, thus punctuating the futility of Tewodros's position. On defeat he committed suicide, and there ended this first attempt at Ethiopian modernization and unification.

For a time it appeared as though Ethiopia would revert to its earlier pattern of internal chaos, but in 1871 the ras of Tigre succeeded in outdoing his rivals, and early in 1872 he was crowned Yohannes IV, king of kings. Throughout his reign, the new emperor was to have little time for internal reform and, unlike Tewodros, sought national unity by granting considerable local authority to regional princes in exchange for their loyalty to crown and nation. This loyalty left him free to deal with the mounting foreign threat to Ethiopia. Initially, there were the Egyptians who were subdued during 1875-1876 in their attempt to expand inland from the old Turkish coastal foothold at Massawa. More serious, however, were growing European interests in territories bordering Ethiopia. Particularly active in this respect was Italy, which first converted her Red Sea foothold of Assab into a colony in 1882, and then occupied Massawa in 1885 with British acquiescence, combining this expansionist policy with a diplomatic offensive designed to split Menelik, now king of Shoa, from his nominal overlord, Yohannes. Such machinations received a temporary setback when the Italians were defeated at Dogali in 1887, but Yohannes was now obliged to face yet another foreign enemy in the Mahdist armies of the Khalifa which attacked and burned Gondar in 1887. Two years later at Metemma (al-Qallabat), an Ethiopian victory was turned to defeat when Yohannes was mortally wounded, and his troops, suddenly demoralized, abandoned the field to the badly mauled Sudanese. Once again the threat of disintegration faced Ethiopia.

Although the death of Yohannes was a blow to national security and unity in these parlous times, Ethiopia continued to enjoy prosperity in its succession of kings. Menelik II, who now proclaimed himself negusa nagast without serious dissent, had already served a royal apprenticeship since 1865 in Shoa, and for some years had been absorbing valuable experience in two activities vital to the survival of the Ethiopian state, the achievement and extension of national cohesion and the frustration of European aspirations in his country.

Menelik II's long career was characterized by good fortune leavened by an enlightened opportunism. Grandson of the celebrated Shoan king, Sahle Selassie (1813-1847), he became Tewodros's prisoner in 1855 but profited from his confinement, observing at first hand the business of statecraft; then taking advantage of Tewodros's failing hold on the government, he escaped from the fortress of Magdala in 1865. Back in Shoa, he assumed the crown of what was virtually an independent principality, and with the death of Tewodros claimed the title of king of kings. This placed him in direct confrontation with Yohannes, but potential civil war was avoided through negotiation in 1878 whereby Yohannes assumed the crown and Menelik the succession, while the latter maintained all but the name of independence in the southern kingdom of Shoa.

Yohannes was thus free to turn his attention to foreign threats while Menelik busied himself in reasserting hegemony over what he regarded as Ethiopia's traditional tributaries to the south and west. "I shall endeavour," he was to inform the European powers some years later, "to re-establish the ancient frontiers of Ethiopia," and these he indicated to be Khartoum in the north and Lake Victoria to the west with all the Galla territories included. The process began with his accession to the Shoan throne. The Galla were cultivated by diplomacy or conquered by military action and an attack made on the Muslim state of Harar which still prevailed in the southeast. Menelik first subdued the Wello Galla located north of Shoa who had long isolated the Shoans from the rest of Ethiopia; then by both force and persuasion he formed the Shoan Galla Confederation around the area of what was later to become the capital city of Addis Ababa, finally pressing outward into Gurage and Kaffa to the southwest, Arussi, Sidamo, Bali, and Borana in the south; Wallaga in the west, and Ogaden to the east.

These areas were taken between 1875 and the end of the century—both before and after Menelik's accession to the Ethiopian throne—and were joined by the emirate of Harar which was subdued in 1887. Unlike previous conquerors, however, Menelik was interested in occupation, not ransom, and consequently introduced a permanent administration, either in the form of local rulers loyal to him or his own military garrisons where necessary. Hence his provincial government took on some of the quality of the European colonial regimes, at least in the eyes of those whose lands had been invaded, and in fact several of his campaigns were made expressly to forestall European colonial ambitions. "If powers at a distance come forward to partition Africa between them," he stated his philosophy to Europe, "I do not intend to be an indifferent spectator."

Whatever may have been Menelik's own imperial aims, he certainly was fully aware of the serious nature of the European threat, and his whole career as Shoan king and Ethiopian emperor was devoted to thwarting the expansion of western colonialism to his homeland. This objective he pursued as Tewodros had by securing modern arms, a process at which he was far more successful than his ill-starred predecessor. Through purchase and diplomacy he steadily accumulated firearms, particularly from Italy, whose fruitless attempts to seduce Menelik into a betrayal of Yohannes cost her dearly when the guns sent to the Shoan later were used to repel the Italian invasion at Adowa.

By the time that Menelik succeeded Yohannes in 1889, the Italians were actively fanning out from their Massawa beachhead onto the Eritrean plateau and the French were entrenched in Djibouti. Vigorous countermeasures were therefore needed to check this latest manifestation of European expansionism. One of Menelik's first diplomatic acts was to sign the Treaty of Wichali (Ucciali) which conceded the Italian holdings in Eritrea but recognized Menelik's own imperial status in Ethiopia and guaranteed his access to the sea through Italian territory. The treaty, nevertheless, soon became a source of dispute, for the Italians claimed that it bound Menelik to consult Italy in the conduct of his foreign relations, thereby converting Ethiopia into an Italian protectorate, whereas the Amharic version of the text made such consultation optional, not obligatory.

Menelik denounced the treaty in 1893 and, convinced of Italian designs on Ethiopia, prepared for the expected invasion with steady imports of weaponry for his growing army. When the Italian attack began in 1895, the situation was far removed from what had faced Napier almost thirty years earlier. In the first place, the Ethiopians were now better united behind their emperor and in opposition to the invaders whose appropriation of land for Italian colonists had particularly angered the local population in Tigre. Moreover, Menelik fielded an army of a hundred thousand well-armed troops, more than five times the Italian force, which was further embarrassed by unfamiliarity with the terrain, resulting in fatal tactical miscalculations against the soundly conceived Ethiopian battle plan. The Battle of Adowa, fought in March 1896, therefore, brought crushing defeat to the invaders, a unique reversal to the partition of Africa, which put the quietus for a long generation on European designs in the Abyssinian highlands.

Menelik's subsequent diplomacy, perhaps mistakenly, did not attempt to dislodge the Italians from Eritrea. It did, however, achieve the immediate, unqualified recognition in Europe of Ethiopian strength and independence, while encouraging European interest in Ethiopia's economic possibilities. This was an important development for it enabled Menelik to enlist European assistance toward one of the major objectives of his reign, the modernization of Ethiopia. Always cautious of entanglements that might compromise his independence, the emperor began to entertain arrangements that would develop and open up his country.

Modernization was carried out along familiar lines. Bridges and roads were built and a railway projected in 1894 connecting Djibouti with Menelik's new capital of Addis Ababa, founded about 1886. To this was added a postal service, as well as telegraph and telephone systems, all operating by the early years of the twentieth century. State administration was made more efficient, education modernized, and up-to-date banking facilities introduced along with the beginning of hospital and public health installations. These innovations, which were just a beginning and scarcely affected the daily existence of most Ethiopians, were invariably achieved with the help of Western technicians, a reflection of continuing European political interest in the area. Menelik, therefore, was at pains to arrange firm boundaries for his empire, and between 1897 and 1908 international frontiers were settled by treaty with all his neighbors.

To these formal developments, Menelik added a number of arrangements with private and public concessionaires designed to promote commercial, agricultural, or industrial development. Many of these grants were to prove illusory for the canny emperor was capable of awarding conflicting rights or claims to nonexistent resources, pocketing the concession fees for the state, particularly in support of the excellent Ethiopian army.

Menelik's careful program, jointly standing off European efforts at economic and political domination while building up his internal resources, was sound policy. When in 1906 his health and vigor began to fail, Britain, France, and Italy, quickly reacting to a sign of weakness, concluded a treaty proclaiming their right to intervene in Ethiopian affairs "to protect their nationals" in the event of internal unrest. As the emperor grew progressively weaker, the possibility of a struggle for succession arose, and with it mounted the prospect of foreign interference. When Menelik died in 1913 on the eve of the First World War, however, the European powers were fortunately preoccupied at home, and Ethiopia survived intervention for another twenty years.

Suggestions for Further Reading

For the newcomer to Africa's history, the best introduction to the era of partition is the essay chapter by G. N. Sanderson, "The European Partition of Africa . . ." in Vol. VI of the *Cambridge History of Africa* edited by Sanderson and Roland Oliver (Cambridge: University Press, 1985). This piece may be supplemented by J. D. Hargreaves, "The European Partition of West Africa," J. F. A. Ajayi and Michael Crowder, eds., *History of West Africa*, Vol. II (Burnt Mill, Essex, England: Longman, 1987).

The complex subject of the partition of Africa has been treated in a large body of works, a few examples of which are cited. For the Berlin Conference, see W. R. Lewis, "The Berlin Congo Conference," P. Gifford and W. R. Lewis, eds., *France and Britain in Africa* (New Haven: Yale University Press, 1971). British imperial policy is set forth in Ronald Robinson and John Gallagher, *Africa and the Victorians* (London and New York: Macmillan, 1961), a controversial work that has caused much subsequent discussion—for instance, see W. R. Louis, ed., *Imperialism* (New York: Frank Watts, 1976). For West Africa see J. D. Hargreaves, *West Africa Partitioned*, 2 v. (London: Macmillan, 1974, 1985). Biographies of major actors in the partion process include John Flint, *Sir George Goldie and the Making of Nigeria* (London: Oxford University Press, 1960); Roland Oliver, *Sir Harry Johnston and the Scramble for Africa* (London: Chatto and Windus, 1959); Margery Perham, *Lugard*, 2 v. (London: Collins, 1956, 1960; New York: Oxford University Press, Vol. I, 1956), and Robert I. Rotberg, *The Founder: Cecil Rhodes and the Pursuit of Power* (Oxford University Press, 1988).

The story of the African response to partition is scattered through many works, including several already listed. For Jaja, see K. O. Dike, *Trade and Politics in the Niger Delta, 1830-1885* (Oxford: Clarendon, 1956); and G. I. Jones, *The Trading States of the Oil Rivers* (London: Oxford University Press, 1963); as well as Roland Oliver, *Harry Johnston*, cited previously. Nana is dealt with in P. C. Lloyd, '' The Itsekiri in the Nineteenth Century,'' *The Journal of African History*, Vol. IV, No. 2 (1963); and in the full-scale biography of the delta leader Obaro Ikime, *Merchant Prince of the Niger Delta* (London: Heinemann, 1968); the Brassmen in John Flint, cited before, and in E. J. Alagoa, *The Small Brave City-State* (Ibadan: Ibadan University Press, 1964). See also Obaro Ikime, *Niger Delta Rivalry* (London: Longmans; New York: Humanities, 1969). There is much material on African response to the partition of East Africa in *History of East Africa*, already cited, but see also G. W. Were, *A History of the Abaluyia* (Nairobi: East African Publishing House, 1967.) Professor Norman Bennett has published a full-length biography of Mirambo, *Mirambo of Tanzania* (New York: Oxford University Press, 1971); and the military resistance to European penetration by various West African societies is recounted in M. Crowder, ed., *West African Resistance* (London: Hutchinson; New York: Africana, 1971). For Asante see Ivor Wilks, *Asante in the Nineteenth Century* (Cambridge: University Press, 1975).

Further discussion of Ethiopia may be pursued in Richard Greenfield, *Ethiopia* (London: Pall Mall, 1965; New York, Praeger, 1965); and E. Ullendorf, *The Ethiopians*, 2nd ed. (London: Oxford University Press, 1965). See also Alan Moorehead's entertainingly written *The Blue Nile* (London: Hamish Hamilton; New York: Harper, 1962). For Tewodros, see Sven Rubenson, *King of Kings: Tewodros of Ethiopia* (Addis Ababa: Haile Selassie I University and Oxford: 1966). Menelik is covered in Harold G. Marcus, *The Life and Times of Menelik II* (Oxford: Clarendon, 1975).

15

Early Nationalist Stirrings in West Africa

Adaptation and Survival

As the nineteenth century unfolded and European influence steadily reached out, probing ever deeper into the world of West Africa, the African reaction to Europe grew correspondingly, both in its extent and its force. It came from two distinct sources of the African population. On the one hand, there were the traditional societies, attempting to contain an alien presence within the definition of their time-tested way of life. On the other, there were those West Africans educated in Europe, who had already accepted in whole or in part the standards of Western civilization and who therefore sought to utilize their newly acquired skills both to strengthen their Africa and to protect it from annihilation at the hands of a foreign culture.

Traditional Africa was by no means inert or unproductive, but her rate and direction of change were scarcely relevant to the forces that bore in upon her, and her response, however determined, was thus foredoomed. Direct confrontation, diplomatic or military, was futile in the face of European technological superiority. In West Africa the end was invariably defeat and submission, whether it was decided by the sword in Niger Delta creeks and western savanna, or by negotiation in a chiefly compound.

Foredoomed in its immediate defense of the indigenous African state, the traditional response was even more grievously deficient in its understanding of the ultimate shape of African society. In the thrust of events, the classic village life was to become slowly more obsolete; the future of African societies would require an appreciation of such modernizing forces as national unity,

288

technological development, and international involvement, concepts largely beyond the comprehension of traditional leaders, but well understood by those Africans whose education and experience had exposed them to the ways of colonial powers. Survival in a modern world, therefore, suggested accommodation, cooperation rather than conflict in an effort to understand and to control this new, alien civilization destined to introduce much of its substance into the old world of Africa.

Accommodation with Europe promised much, but it also bristled with difficulties. Not only did it require a thoroughgoing knowledge of the two worlds of Africa and the West, it also called for a nice judgment of how far European civilization could be used to benefit African society without destroying it. Not only did it point the way to African independence from Europe through the very ideas and institutions used by the West to dominate Africa; by the same token it posed the problem of keeping that domination from becoming permanent. Not only did it hold the promise of modernization and political freedom, it also contained the threat of cultural extinction. Those who practiced accommodation, therefore, were obliged to live at an advanced level of sophistication, to be able to move with easy assurance in the two worlds of Africa and Europe but never to forget their identity, to poise themselves between acceptance and rejection of the West without losing their sense of balance and proportion, to seek a secure marriage between those European institutions best suited to African growth and the most substantial elements of traditional African life—in short, to assimilate, not to be assimilated, as Leopold Senghor was to put it.

It is not surprising that such demands brought varying responses. At one extreme were those Africans fully persuaded as to the superiority of European civilization, who saw African progress in terms of the degree to which Western culture could be absorbed and Western influence made dominant in Africa. At the other extreme were those who saw Europe as decadent and her civilization, if not her technical powers, of dubious advantage. The first group was exemplified by such assimilated Africans as Abbé Boilat and Paul Holle of Senegal, or, in a later generation, the Nigerian, Kitoyi Ajasa. Examples from the second group included the generation of cultural nationalists who professed the faith of negritude in the years following the Second World War. Between these two lay a wide range of opinion which was to a considerable extent a reflection in West Africa of the differing approaches of Britain and France to the administration of their colonies.

Since the Revolution of 1789, France had based her colonial policy on the idea of assimilation which argued the superiority of French language and culture and the necessity that each colonial absorbs with dispatch all things French. Where French influence was directly felt—among the urban mulattoes of Senegal for example—this policy was successful to a surprising extent. French-educated Africans tended to equate progress in Africa with mastery of European standards, to vest their status within the world community on French not

African qualities, to regard African identity as irrelevant to the reality of French cultural superiority.

British colonial practice, on the contrary, stressed, if anything, the differences between Africa and Europe, but at the same time unconsciously inculcated a wide range of Anglo-Saxon predilections extending from constitutional law to black silk umbrellas, and from Anglican theology to afternoon tea. The result was a greater independence of European standards and more diversity of response to colonial rule, combined with a degree of devotion to European culture as total as anything to be found within the French territories. Nevertheless, two main streams of thought were discernible among educated Africans in the British areas. The first held close to the French doctrine of assimilation, arguing that where European institutions were superior to those of traditional Africa, they should be introduced as quickly and thoroughly as possible, the better to get on with the business of social and cultural betterment. The other was much more self-consciously nationalistic, insisting that African civilization must develop along its own lines or perish, but often employing ideas and skills acquired in Europe to formulate its views and to attack the colonial policy and government it came to oppose.

Politics and Commerce in Senegal

The administration of Governor Faidherbe was pivotal in the development of French colonialism in West Africa. Before his time, the French presence, for all its longevity, had been tentative, and French commitment to her posts in Senegal remained equivocal. By the end of his tenure of office, the colony had been transformed not so much physically as in its sense of mission. Instead of a precarious coastal foothold, Senegal had become a permanent base from which would one day be launched the conquest of an empire. Moreover, in the years following Faidherbe, there was growing assurance from the slow but steady development of the economy, while the second half of the nineteenth century saw the colony at last secure a definite participation in French political life, so long promised and so long withheld.

Faidherbe had laid the foundations for economic expansion both through his "pacification" policy for the interior country and his program of public works designed to facilitate agriculture and commerce. To be sure, the gum trade of the early nineteenth century was little affected and exports rose with disappointing modesty from 2,500 tons in 1854 to 4,000 during the 1880s. This lackluster record was more than offset, however, by the emergence of groundnuts as a major product. In 1853 only 3,000 tons were exported, but this figure rose dramatically in the years that followed—8,700 tons in 1870, 34,000 in 1881, 45,000 in 1885, and 65,000 in 1894. Such statistics were accompanied by corresponding increases in the value of exports, a development that was nevertheless somewhat dampened by the fact that Senegal continued to be saddled with a single-crop economy, groundnuts now having replaced gum as her major product. Although diversification was attempted fitfully with such crops as indigo, rubber, and cotton, little resulted; the groundnut yield of 1883, representing more than 70 percent of the value of exports, typified the problem.

With expanding commerce came the rise of the city, slowly at first and then with increasing velocity in the decades preceding the First World War. Saint-Louis was already an established center; by the end of Faidherbe's administration it had a population of approximately fifteen thousand, mostly Africans, with Europeans and mulattoes numbering but a few hundred each, the African community containing substantial numbers from the inland territories. Since Saint-Louis was situated on a small island in the Senegal River, the African neighborhoods had gradually spilled over to the suburbs of N'Dar Tout and Guet N'Dar on the Barbary peninsula which separated Saint-Louis from the Atlantic Ocean and which served as well as a terminus for the caravans from the interior. Here on the edge of the city were the compounds crowded with their traditional round straw huts, and the colorful, noisy markets where the products of Africa and Europe changed hands to the accompaniment of shouted abuse and finally of mutual congratulations. In the middle of town, where the Europeans and mulattoes were dominant, the mood was vastly different: quiet streets lined with whitewashed buildings shimmered in the tropical heat, a scene that, according to the novelist Pierre Loti, invariably evoked a feeling of melancholy and lassitude.

Saint-Louis was not only the chief port by reason of its location at the head of the Senegal River; it served also as the seat of government for the colony. Nevertheless its preeminent position was challenged increasingly by other municipalities as the century drew to a close. While the island of Gorée gradually declined into picturesque decay, the nearby centers of Dakar and Rufisque were emerging in response to the new commercialism. Dakar, founded by the French administration in 1857, grew slowly at first. As late as 1881 it languished with fewer than 2,000 inhabitants, but once the railroad to Saint-Louis had opened in 1885, growth was rapid. By 1895 the population had risen to 8,000, in 1904 to 18,500 and on the eve of the First World War Dakar had become the first city of French West Africa, the capital and chief port for France's vast West African territories.

For its part, Rufisque experienced a growth only comparatively less spectacular. Arising spontaneously and without official assistance a dozen miles down the coast from Dakar, Rufisque was the result of the groundnut trade. With less than 1,200 population in 1878, it rose to 4,000 in 1883 and 8,000 by 1891, almost doubling its size again by 1914. As early as 1885 this lively port controlled 40 percent of Senegal's groundnut exports, and in 1914 still challenged Dakar's more diversified commerce with mounting control of the groundnut trade. In the face of this economic expansion, Saint-Louis gradually faded, joining Gorée as a relic of days gone by.

The rise of Senegal's cities reflected political as well as economic growth, for it was in these communes that the French system of representative government was transplanted and developed during the second half of the nineteenth century. In both France and Senegal a brief experiment with democracy followed Europe's liberal revolutions of 1848; then after the autocratic reaction experienced during the regime of Napoleon III, parliamentary government was once again established as the French Third Republic was launched in 1870. In Senegal this was reflected in a series of related moves. To begin with, the colony was granted the right of choosing through universal male suffrage a representative to the Chamber of Deputies in Paris. This privilege was made permanent in 1879, the same year that Senegal formed her first territorial general council, also elected through universal suffrage and exercising substantially the same legislative responsibility for local administrative and financial matters as did the general councils of France's own metropolitan departments. In 1872, moreover, both Gorée and Saint-Louis were incorporated as full-fledged municipalities with their own democratically chosen municipal councils, Dakar at first sharing this authority with Gorée. In 1880 the growing port of Rufisque was also elevated to this status of *commune de plein exercice*, and seven years later Dakar and Gorée were separated, thus forming the so-called Four Communes of Senegal. Since universal suffrage was defined through usage to include all male individuals who could show a five-year residence in the communes, the vast majority of African males were thus able to join the mulattoes and Europeans as electors for deputy, for the general council, and for the municipal councils.

It did not follow, however, that the African vote meant African political power, since there were many complex facets to Senegalese politics during the decades leading up to the beginning of the First World War. First, there was France herself, whose rising interest was reflected both in the growing political and economic activities of the merchant houses of Bordeaux and in the colonial government concerned with the administration of an expanding empire. Bordeaux saw to it that her commercial stake in Senegal was protected by Bordelais agents on the ground, some European and some mulatto. For its part, the government introduced as much authoritarianism as the local traffic would bear, for it could not permit local parliamentary exercises in the general and municipal councils to interfere with its surveillance of the gradually expanding interior areas coming under its control.

These forces from France were offset by the mulattoes who, though they normally gave Bordeaux weak economic competition, were generally able to control local elections and offices, including the position of deputy to Paris. That they were successful in the face of an overwhelming African electoral majority was a measure of their control of the African vote by reason of their wealth, position, and education through which they dominated former slaves and present servants. Election frauds were common during these years and

African support was regularly bought to keep mulattoes in parliamentary control. Indeed, if they had been able to maintain a united front among themselves, the mulattoes would have been a great embarrassment to Bordeaux and the colonial administration; instead intramural cleavages based on family feuds and economic competition kept them divided, thus simplifying the task of the French in maintaining their own political and economic influence.

One reason why political power was slow to develop among the Africans dwelling within the communes was their laggard rate of assimilation into a French way of life. While the mulattoes had long since become completely converted to French culture, the Africans remained largely unabsorbed — speaking only Arabic or African languages, and on the whole illiterate in any tongue, Muslim in religious persuasion, and quite unfamiliar with the constitutional bases of government as imported from France. In 1857 Governor Faidherbe had guaranteed their special status as Muslims with an order that permitted the use of Islamic law in the settlement of civil disputes connected with such matters as inheritance and marriage. This decree, while protecting the personal status of the Africans, also tended to set them apart from the Europeanized population, an isolation that not only contributed to political exploitation but to other types of discrimination as well. Toward the close of the century, as French settlers arrived in Senegal in increasing numbers, it was alleged that these immigrants were being given preference in employment both by the government and in the commercial establishments of Saint-Louis, Dakar, and Rufisque.

Whatever the merits of these charges, there was no blinking the move, which gathered momentum both in France and her colonies during the early years of the twentieth century, to abandon the concept of assimilation in favor of "association," a doctrine that admitted the integrity of indigenous culture but only at a level inferior to French civilization. The consequence for people living under the policy of association was arbitrary rule, administrative justice, and forced labor imposed by a quasi-military colonial authority, and this was in fact the type of government that emerged in those areas of West Africa gained through France's late nineteenth-century conquests. In the Four Communes, however, the so-called African *originaires*, having long enjoyed political and civil rights guaranteed by the French constitution, considered themselves to be French citizens in good standing, and they therefore greatly resented official steps to limit their privileges by reducing them to the status of French subjects.

In Paris, nonetheless, it was argued that the special status as Muslims enjoyed by the originaires necessarily made them ineligible for French citizenship and its attendant obligations and privileges. In a complex series of administrative orders and court decisions made between 1907 and 1914, the Africans of the Four Communes were systematically deprived of their French citizenship along with most of their civil and political rights, a development that was checked only by the outbreak of war in Europe and the rise of that master politician and defender of African rights, Blaise Diagne. Even before the advent of Diagne, however, the Africans had rallied in defense against their oppressors, organizing a mildly nationalist political party, the Young Senegalese, which was able to elect a few candidates to the local general and municipal councils but which had no pronounced effect in checking the new colonial policy. Interestingly, in view of Senegal's long-standing loyalty to France, the Young Senegalese demanded not home rule or African independence, but a guarantee of their rights as Frenchmen, for the originaires had now come to regard themselves as full-fledged sons of the great Revolution of 1789, as French as any citizen dwelling in France herself. Thus by 1914 the African population of the Four Communes, at any rate, viewed assimilation into French civilization as a major political, if not cultural, objective.

Sierra Leone and African Nationalist Self-Consciousness

If African self-awareness in the French areas was emerging as an offshoot of French nationalism, a different set of circumstances in English-speaking West Africa was bringing forth a correspondingly different African response. The Sierra Leone rehabilitation center for former slaves continued to radiate influence wherever its people went, and most of these found their way eastward to parts of what later became Nigeria—in Yorubaland and the regions bordering the Niger River. What they brought in their intellectual baggage was partly a reflection of personal conviction and partly a measure of the Sierra Leone community they had left behind.

Already by mid-century the Creoles of Freetown were shifting from the relatively uncritical acceptance of European civilization which had characterized the generation of Bishop Crowther to something more demanding, both of Europe and of their own African antecedents. If Crowther's son-in-law, the Reverend George Nicol, considered a Cambridge education as the ideal preparation for his son as a clergyman-to-be in Africa, Nicol's contemporary, the merchant William Grant, would be satisfied with nothing less than the establishment of West Africa's own university designed to focus attention on African history and culture and thus avoid the emotional and intellectual confusion that so often accompanied education by a foreign set of standards. Again, James Quaker, trained for the ministry in London and for many years head of the CMS grammar school in Freetown, could scarcely envision the development of an independent Christian church in West Africa except through continued and intimate association with British philanthropy. By contrast, the British-trained West Indian barrister and long-time Freetown resident, William Rainy, devoted himself during the same years to a career of exposing the extravagances and inequities of British rule in Sierra Leone, and found steady applause among the Creoles for his exertions.

Such eclecticism was readily exportable. Bishop Crowther's great missionary work on the Niger on behalf of the "Bible and the plough" was carried out while another Sierra Leone emigre employed his own grasp of European institutions precisely to ward off prospective European influence. In Abeokuta, the Egba resistance to the belligerence of the Lagos administrator, J. H. Glover, found its most vigorous expression in the hands of George W. Johnson, sometime tailor and amateur musician, late of Sierra Leone. Colorfully known as Reversible Johnson, a name that did justice to his political prowess, he succeeded for a time in gaining a measure of support from the people of Abeokuta for his modernized Egba foreign office, the Egba United Board of Management, through which he mounted a successful diplomatic defense against the expansionism of the Lagos government.

Such action was scarcely appreciated by Crowther, the churchman, for it resulted among other things in the expulsion of the Church Missionary Society's European missionaries from Abeokuta in 1867. "Half-educated, unprincipled young men," Crowther described Johnson and his helpers, blaming them for the troubles of his co-workers, but the difficulty may have been in part caused by the Egba themselves, individualists to the core and nonpartisan in their resistance to all alien efforts to save their souls. During the 1870s they forced the departure of another missionary, James Johnson, a Yoruba from Sierra Leone, dispatched to Abeokuta to reestablish the CMS mission. Johnson was known as Holy Johnson among his contemporaries because of the puritanical nature of his Christianity, and it was his excessive zeal in propagating the faith in Egbaland that aroused the ire of the local people and led to his withdrawal.

This incident, which occurred early in Reverend Johnson's long career, was scarcely an accurate gauge of the man. Devoted Christian he was and his ecclesiastic abilities led ultimately to his appointment as assistant bishop in charge of a West African diocese. Moreover, during the last decades of the nineteenth century when African frustrations over the intrusions of colonial rule were sublimated in the form of independent church movements, Johnson remained staunchly loyal to his Anglican ties. Nevertheless he was one of the outstanding nationalists of his age, stressing the values of Africa's own culture, better suited to African needs than alien imports from Europe. Christianity was universal, insisted Johnson; it was no more European than it was African, but Western education, language, thought, and such external trappings as dress were parochial qualities to be imitated only at Africa's peril. Let the African cleave, therefore, to his ancient social practices, his time-tested ethical and moral codes. Johnson, the Christian cleric, had long been indulgent toward such indigenous customs as tribal markings, traditional marriage ceremonies, and local dress, while the use of African baptismal names was celebrated as part of his churchly ritual. Even domestic slavery he thought might be left to the "quiet ameliorative influence of the missionary's teaching," and late in his career he countenanced polygamy under certain circumstances as not incompatible with the teachings of Christ.

Preoccupation with Africa's welfare came in many guises. During this period, for example, the most distinguished Creole name in Freetown was without doubt Samuel Lewis. Widely known up and down the coast as learned barrister, member of the Sierra Leone legislative council, and Freetown mayor, Lewis exercised great influence in establishing standards of behavior and belief within his own community and beyond. His personal code was unquestionably Western—Christian faith, hard work, and public service with a modicum of personal profit to provide life's necessities, the very Victorian virtues that had been urged by Fowell Buxton and Henry Venn as the basis for social and economic reform in West Africa. As legal practitioner, he worked diligently for his clients who, he felt, also worked hard and deserved painstaking service in return. As appointed member of the legislative council which Lewis joined in 1882, nineteen years after its establishment, he saw himself as the servant of his community and constructive critic of official colonial policy. When he was knighted in 1893 he regarded this less as a personal honor than as a measure of West African progress, and took the occasion to urge greater public service on his contemporaries.

There was no gainsaying the extent of Lewis's own public service. During twenty-one years of faithful attendance in the legislative council until his death in 1903, Lewis was the guardian of popular rights—here forcing the withdrawal of an ill-advised law censoring the press, there criticizing executive usurpation of legislative functions, regularly calling for wide public representation on the council, and always filling the role of responsible spokesman for his people. As mayor of Freetown, he assumed the task of teacher, carefully instructing his fellow citizens in the obligations and privileges of self-government. As a public-spirited citizen, he conducted many experiments in the cultivation of new crops and urged agricultural improvement as a means to economic development. As a Sierra Leonean he regularly criticized a weak-willed colonial policy for failing to extend its influence into the interior, thus mortgaging, in his view, the economic and political future of his country. Withal, he called for sobriety, diligence, and responsibility from his people, for he saw no hope of ultimate self-government until they had in fact learned to govern themselves.

To many, Sir Samuel Lewis seemed too rigidly guided by an unreflective acceptance of European standards early instilled, perhaps, by a thoroughly British education. Nevertheless, a closer examination reveals something more—a careful mind at work, searching for the advancement of the African people, and backed by the courage to choose the unpopular over the expedient. Lewis was roughly handled at times, both by his own Creole community and by the colonial administration, each of which tended to regard him as an occasional apostate, neither group really understanding his unfailing devotion to inner principle. Thus his desire to give legal service to his people was ever tempered by an unwillingness to sacrifice justice to cheap favoritism. Similarly, his principle of loyalty to constitutional authority did not preclude opposition to arbitrary rule. What appears in the works and working principles of Samuel

Lewis, therefore, is a capsule version of West Africa's urgent problem of the nineteenth and twentieth centuries—how to build a modern society based on the best of both the African and European worlds.

Edward Blyden Creates a Philosophy
of African Nationalism

Although, like Samuel Lewis, many West Africans wrestled with the difficult question of modernization and Westernization, few grasped the problem in its entirety or were aware of its massive complications, and only one seemed to see the necessity for creating a complete philosophy of African nationalism which permitted the full use of European ideas and institutions without damage to racial dignity or loss of a sense of African integrity. That one exception was Edward W. Blyden whose brilliance dominated the West African scene during the half-century leading up to the First World War, and whose ideas not only aimed at the psychic security of Africa in the face of European intrusion, but also anticipated the need far in the future for cultural and economic independence when African nations came to achieve political freedom in the mid-twentieth century.

Blyden was a West Indian by origin, born in the Danish island of St. Thomas in 1832. Though his antecedents were solidly West African—probably Ibo—he might never have come to the west coast had it not been for the accident of an educational opportunity lost in the United States through racial prejudice, and a consequent trip to Liberia, where he settled in 1851, to gain the training denied. In Liberia, Blyden, whose scholastic aptitude had early been noted, quickly mastered Greek and Latin at school along with Hebrew as an extracurricular pursuit, his abilities earning him the editorship of the *Liberia Herald*, which he held for a year in the mid-fifties. Soon, however, he was teaching full-time at his own school, becoming its principal in 1858, the same year he was ordained a minister of the Presbytery of West Africa. In 1862 Blyden took a chair as professor of Greek and Latin at the newly formed Liberia College, having journeyed to the Americas during the previous year in search of settlers for Liberia, the beginning of a long-lived career of public service and activity.

The recruitment trip was no accident, for Blyden was already formulating ideas regarding the role of Africa and Africans in the upward thrust of civilization; only in Africa, he argued, could the black race realize its own native genius, and this idea was to become one of the chief, albeit most controversial, aspects of his philosophy of Africanness. "I believe nationality to be an ordinance of nature," he declared at the time, "and no people can rise to an influential position among the nations without a distinct and efficient nationality. Cosmopolitanism has never effected anything."

Such a concept flowed from a more generalized philosophic stance. It was true that the races of the world differed physically and emotionally, shaped by long exposure to the forces of environment, agreed Blyden, accepting current European anthropological doctrine. They could not be ordered into a hierarchy of ability and achievement, however, as the whites invariably arranged them, placing themselves at the head of the list; they were merely different. Indeed, continued Blyden, each race had its own peculiar assets, excelling in certain pursuits and less successful in others. Races were therefore not competitive or comparative so much as complementary, and in their totality they made up God's divinity. "Each race sees from its own standpoint a different side of the Almighty," said Blyden. "The whole of mankind is a vast representation of the Deity."

If the races were coequal but different, it followed that each had its own special contribution to make to the sum of human civilization. White Europeans had their virtues and faults—didactic and strong-willed, accomplished in the sciences and preoccupied with material betterment. This could lead to salutary ends; for example, in Africa it meant an end to the slave trade and intertribal wars, economic improvement, and the introduction of modern medicine. But, Blyden went on, these advantages came at a price. The European was also domineering and materialistic, selfish and essentially irreligious. Humanity, not the Deity, became the sole object of human endeavor; the white race enslaved and bent others to its will, while religion was made to subserve material and temporal purposes.

Here was no person for blacks to imitate, warned Blyden, particularly since they possessed uncommon characteristics of their own. First, there was the concept of community in African life. "What is mine goes; what is ours abides," Blyden quoted a Vai proverb to emphasize the harmony in unity of African society. Property was communal, and the fruits of the earth belonged equally to all. No competition separated people into antagonistic groups, no individuals gathered wealth at the expense of others, all were cared for—the aged, sick, and helpless along with the healthy—in the genial protective atmosphere of the family.

Secondly, there was the African consonance with nature, the ability, said Blyden quoting the Book of Job, "to speak to the earth and let it teach him." Thus did the black race observe nature's rhythm of creation and recuperation as the model for a healthy polygamy, thus did the Africans follow the example of the industrious termite in constructing their own cooperative society, thus did they dwell outdoors, unburdened by clothing, using the whole book of nature for their school.

Finally, said Blyden, to communion with nature was added communion with God. Unlike Europe, African society made little distinction between the temporal and spiritual worlds; all existence was a continuum comprising the ancestors, the living, and the yet unborn. Religious thought and practice was no sabbath ritual but the essence of everyday life, reflecting a religious sense among the African people of highest refinement. That this had always been so, he insisted, was witnessed by the shelter that Africa had given the Jews and then the infant Jesus, as well as the cordial reception subsequently accorded the great religions of Christianity and Islam.

These special African qualities, Blyden continued, not only established the blacks as coequal and complementary to God's other people; it also gave a clue as to Africa's position in the advancement of civilization, a matter of the greatest importance to Blyden who insisted that racial achievement must be measured ultimately by its contribution to the sum total of human accomplishment. Clearly, said Blyden, past performance by the black race suggested not mastery but service. "Africa's lot resembles Him also who made Himself of no reputation, but took upon Himself the form of a servant. . . . He who would be chief must become the servant of all, then we see the position which Africa and the Africans must ultimately occupy."

Service to humanity, harmony with nature, and communion with God, then, suggested to Blyden the unique and essential offering that Africa would make in a materialist, soulless world—"the mighty principle of Love." "Africa may yet prove to be the spiritual conservatory of the world," he rejoiced.

> When the civilized nations, in consequence of their wonderful material development, shall have had their spiritual perceptions darkened and their spiritual susceptibilities blunted through the agency of a captivating and absorbing materialism, it may be, that they may have to resort to Africa to recover some of the simple elements of faith.

Thus, from his basic proposition describing the races as equivalent facets of a unitary godhead, each with its original and necessary contribution toward humanity, Blyden had secured African self-esteem in the face of Europe, but there were still some corollaries to be drawn from this scheme. First, there was the proposition that racial individuality called for social and biological segregation, and Blyden cited the American black and the Sierra Leone Creole as flagrant examples of effete and confused people resulting from miscegenation. Nothing less than physical isolation and biological purity would therefore suffice, a point of view that evoked much controversy among Blyden's contemporaries even as it was to do in the days of Marcus Garvey and later.

Such radical notions, though they followed the logic of Blyden's argument, also had the practical advantage in his eyes of forcing Africans to stand by their own cultural, intellectual, political, and economic institutions. Blyden insisted, for example, that education must necessarily be tailored to African needs—no foreign educational philosophy, no study of European heroes, no examination of alien biology or geography could meet Africa's requirements— and it was he who greatly influenced William Grant through his own detailed plans for a West African university. In the same way, Blyden urged the importance of African history to signal past accomplishment and thereby reestablish the dignity of the black race. Finally, Blyden, the Christian minister, was one of the strongest critics of European missionary practice in Africa. Citing the universality of Christ's message, he urged his people to organize their own churches—just as Christian but far less European—another declaration of racial independence.

Many of Blyden's pronouncements were highly theoretical, and he was frequently guilty of idealized history, anthropology, or biology. Nonetheless his ideas were developed in no vacuum, for he lived in daily acquaintance with the great issues of his day, as Europe subjected Africa to military conquest and political control; hence his philosophy had an immediacy for his contemporaries, helping to shape their actions and build their sense of racial identity in response to the European intrusion. His personal following was always small, for the educated Africans of his day were few; but his and their importance was disproportionate to their number and was ever growing. Consequently, he was able to exert a widening influence which ultimately transcended his own times, for Blyden's basic demand was the restoration of human dignity, a plea that has had continuing relevance in Africa, and indeed throughout the world.

Liberia and the Tribulations of Independence

Throughout his writings Edward Blyden stressed the importance of Liberia as a haven for the rehabilitation of former slaves from America. Stimulated in part by his doctrines of racial segregation, but also by his image of an independent nation of blacks, Blyden employed the most glowing terms in a recurring rhapsody over Liberia and her prospects. "It is the only spot in Africa where the civilized Negro—the American Negro without alien supervision or guidance is holding aloft the torch of civilization," he stated. This theme sometimes was supplemented by more poetic flights: "I am kindled into ecstasy as I contemplate the future of that infant nation. . . . The hills . . . covered with flocks, and the valleys with corn; the increase of the earth . . . fat and plenteous. . . . . Language fails. . . . Imagination itself is baffled . . . and pauses with reverent awe before the coming possibilities."

This romantic expression of hope was scarcely supported by the fact of Liberia's faltering start as a self-governing nation. Independence had come initially in 1847 largely because a colony for repatriated American slaves was an embarrassment to the United States government, caught in the toils of its domestic slavery issue. When the colonists began to agitate for greater freedom from control by the American Colonization Society and Britain called into question the sovereignty both of Liberia and its parent organization, the slavery issue prevented any action by the American government, and Liberian independence followed.

Unhappily, the new state was ill-equipped to deal with problems which beset it from the start, many of them carry-overs from the colonial period. In the first place, immigration, chiefly from America, had always been low, producing a mere fifteen thousand colonists during the forty-year period from the founding of the colony to the time of the American Civil War, and gaining only a few thousand more thereafter as emancipated blacks chose almost exclusively to remain in the United States.

Moreover, these arrivals from America had divided into factions based partly on mercantile-agrarian rivalries, but even more on social grounds with ancestry as the measure of acceptance. This unfortunate but understandable cleavage gave rise to a two-party system based largely on skin color, and at first it was the Republicans led by the octoroon Joseph J. Roberts who gained control of the government. Roberts, a prominent merchant, served as governor during the last days of the Colonization Society and then became Liberia's first president during several successive terms. In 1870 the opposition True Whig party was successful when Edward J. Roye, a full-blooded black, became president. Victory nonetheless was brief. Roye first of all negotiated a disastrous foreign loan and then attempted to remain in office unconstitutionally, thus leading to a successful attempt by the Republicans to oust him and his supporters. Within a few years, however, the Whigs had returned to power and by 1884 were in such complete control that Liberia ceased to be a two-party state from that point forward. Gradually, the color issue died away, and by the end of the nineteenth century the mulatto faction among the settlers had quite lost its identity. Unfortunately, other related controversies had long since emerged to plague the struggling Liberian state.

From the earliest days there had been a basic cleavage between the settlers and the indigenous people of Liberia. The former with their Westernized background looked on the local inhabitants as uncivilized, much in need of spiritual and physical rehabilitation. This attitude, not unlike that of the European authorities assuming control in other parts of West Africa, looked to the development of a Liberian state under the leadership of a settler oligarchy with gradual participation by the indigenous population as its membership became absorbed into the Western culture of the immigrants. In fact, very little assimilation was encouraged or effected over the years, and relations between the Americo-Liberians and the local people remained at the level of unrelieved hostility punctuated by frequent outbreaks of violence. The settlers tended to adopt an attitude of superiority, based on culture rather than color, and they steadily extended their control inland by treaty, land purchase, and protectorate, maintaining that control in many instances by force.

The administration of the hinterland was neither clearly defined nor efficiently managed, and the process by which political and civil rights were extended to the local people was complex and difficult to follow. A Department of the Interior was created in 1868, and five years later limited parliamentary representation was accorded the various tribal groupings. Not until the early years of the twentieth century did the people in the interior gain status as Liberian citizens, and it was to be almost another half-century, during the

administration of President William Tubman, before any concerted effort was
made to bring the local African population into national life through genuine
social and political reform.

Chronic financial difficulties were another burden that complicated Liberian
national life, all the more so since they invited intervention by Liberia's British
and French neighbors. Outright absorption through the establishment of a
protectorate was probably prevented by the United States, which expressed
a "peculiar interest" in Liberia's independence while making no attempt to
impose its own colonial controls. When Liberian state finances reached an
advanced level of chaos, as they did periodically, there was generally sufficient
interest within the American government to arrange new financial terms without
the necessity of European intervention. Nevertheless, although total absorption
was avoided, Liberia lost several boundary disputes east and west to the French
in the Ivory Coast and the British in Sierra Leone, respectively. In 1882,
for example, territory in the Gallinas district west of the Mano River was
annexed to Sierra Leone after a protracted dispute. Ten years later, France
absorbed into the Ivory Coast a large area claimed by Liberia, and further
cessions along the Guinea and Ivory Coast borders were extracted in 1910.

The Demise of the Forest Kingdoms

European expansionist activity at Liberia's expense was sometimes attempted
through encouragement of tribal resistance, but the more usual European
relationship with the traditional societies during the last decades of the
nineteenth century was one of conquest, then occupation and absorption into
expanding colonial territories. None was immune as European nations
intensified their acquisitiveness in mutual competition. If smaller principalities
like Nembe and the Itsekiri were overwhelmed, so too were such almighty
but fading empires as Dahomey and Benin. The former, its illusion of military
invincibility shattered on the walls of Abeokuta, gained some compensation
during the 1880s in sacking the Yoruba kingdom of Ketu. Such victories were
vain, however, in the face of a Dahomean economy no longer sustained by
the slave traffic and unable to achieve economic security through legitimate
commerce. French control of the coast introduced new complications
concerning trading outlets and customs receipts which seemingly could only
be resolved by military action. Behanzin, succeeding to the throne at Abomey
in 1889, provoked the French by calculated slave raiding and an attack on
a French gunboat, then despite stubborn resistance was defeated and finally
exiled in 1894, his kingdom converted into French colonial territory.

Benin, like Dahomey, with a reputation for human sacrifice, was brought
under British protection in 1892 by a treaty that specifically abolished both
slavery and sacrifice, while providing for trade relations. When the oba,

Ovenramwen, appeared slow to comply, the acting consul general proceeded inland in 1897 to investigate and was massacred with most of his party. The intruders had arrived with unfortunate timing at the moment of a great Bini festival marked by wholesale human sacrifice, and closed to all strangers on pain of the displeasure of the gods. A punitive expedition followed in 1897; Benin was captured and the oba exiled, and this once-great kingdom became just another part of Britain's Niger Coast Protectorate.

Such basic misunderstandings were not uncommon in the clash of unequal forces that punctuated the final colonial occupation of West Africa. In 1896 the British proclaimed a protectorate over the Sierra Leone hinterland beyond Freetown, an area defined by international treaty with France and Liberia but occupied without consulting the local chiefs. Administration of the protectorate was to be in the hands of the chiefs under the surveillance of a British district commissioner with governmental cost defrayed through a per capita levy, the so-called hut tax, of five shillings on each house. The tax was unfamiliar and unpopular, the protectorate government unwanted, and in 1898 mounting tension and mistrust erupted in war, the resistance led by Bai Bureh, a chief from Kasse on the Small Scarcies River. As Bai Bureh's forces were slowly reduced by a West Indian regiment, the revolt spread to other parts of the hinterland and a great many Creoles and Europeans were killed in the spasm of resentment that welled up among the local people. The uprising, however, collapsed as quickly as it had arisen, and with Bai Bureh's capture and exile, all formal opposition ended. The hut tax remained and the protectorate continued to be administered indirectly through the numerous chiefs who had taken no part in the war.

The outburst which briefly shook Sierra Leone in 1898 was a minor reflex compared with the great and complex fratricidal struggle that had divided and devastated Yorubaland since the disintegration of the Oyo empire began toward the end of the eighteenth century. The first phase of the nineteenth-century Yoruba civil wars covered the period from 1820 to 1837 and was characterized by several factors—the destruction of Owu, the defection of Afonja, the alafin's governor in Ilorin, and the subsequent Fulani capture of that northern stronghold, the destruction of the ancient capital of Old Oyo, and the remove of its people to the forest edge at the new Oyo, and the rise of independent Ibadan and Abeokuta. The second period, from 1837 to 1878, saw a complex struggle among the successors to Oyo which gradually polarized around Ibadan and Abeokuta. Despite her many opponents, Ibadan grew progressively stronger while Abeokuta was hard pressed to hold her own, faced as she was during this period by determined political and military attacks from Dahomey, as well as by the pressure of the British in Lagos who sought to reach the interior through Egba territory.

In their last stage, from 1878 to 1893, the Yoruba wars achieved new climaxes of complexity and animosity. By the 1870s, Ibadan had emerged as the most powerful of the Yoruba states, a fact that lent urgency to the formation of a coalition among her opponents. To the south, the Egba and Ijebu sought to limit Ibadan's power by blockade, forcing the Ibadans to gain their military supplies chiefly through Benin. To the east the Ijesha and Ekiti Yoruba were ready to join the alliance which also gained the support of Ilorin. Despite this formidable array, lbadan more than held her own in a series of engagements, but neither side could gain the upper hand and the conflict dragged on.

With the Fulani no longer a decisive factor and Dahomey in decline, the combatants turned in upon themselves, preoccupied with their parochial quarrels; yet this was to be the period when a major external force would finally bring peace to the tortured land. Constant warfare, particularly in the interests of shutting off supplies to Ibadan, necessarily meant a serious dislocation of trade, a condition that greatly disturbed the merchants and government at Lagos. As early as 1882 the British intruded themselves as peacemakers, the urgency of their mission underscored by the rising threat that the wars posed to the survival of Lagos as a major entrepot. By 1890 the cosmopolitan port with its polyglot population and its normally colorful, lively markets lay mournful and deserted, its shops empty and its trading canoes idle. There was a growing desire, therefore, among the commercially minded Africans of the city that the authorities accelerate their quest for peace, by whatever means were required.

A negotiated peace concluded in 1886 almost succeeded in stopping the war, but the moment had not yet arrived and fighting broke out anew. Both the Egba and Ijebu tightened their blockade, the Ijebu adding a calculated insult to the government at Lagos, an incident that finally resolved the British to resort to force An expedition under Governor Carter quickly subdued the Ijebu in 1892 and the following year the governor was able to establish a *de facto* protectorate over the various states of Yorubaland. At last peace had arrived. Samuel Johnson, the Yoruba historian who had played an important role in the diplomatic offensive for peace, caught the sense of relief of an exhausted people. "To the vast majority of the common people," he reported, "it was like the opening of a prison door: and no one who witnessed the patient, long-suffering, and toiling mass of humanity . . . could refrain from heaving a sigh of gratification on the magnitude of the beneficial results."

Abortive Alliance—The Westernized Africans and the Traditional Authorities

In the face of the alien European intrusion, both traditional authorities and educated Africans sought effective means of response, whether in accommodation or opposition, and it was quickly evident that in the process some form of united effort by both old and new Africa would be attempted. In this respect it was the educated Africans who took the lead, representing themselves to the chiefs as Africa's most eloquent spokesmen before European governments, and to the colonial administrations as an ideal liaison between the alien worlds of Africa and Europe. This attitude was generally resisted by the traditional powers who were disinclined to share their dwindling authority with parvenu commoners, and by the colonial administrations, suspicious of educated elite as potential sources of disaffection. Rather, colonial administrators sought some sort of partnership in government with the long-established African leadership.

The French areas of West Africa scarcely knew the problem before the period of the First World War. In a few coastal points like the Four Communes of Senegal, the principle of assimilation, though under rising attack, still prevailed. In the hinterland a difficult conquest in the face of stubborn opposition led to a quasi-military regime imposed with rigid authority by French administrators.

The British approach was more flexible and pragmatic, but tended to keep cooperation with legitimate African rulers through which the colonial administration could operate. The classic prototype was the Protectorate of Northern Nigeria, proclaimed in 1900 and placed under the governorship of Sir Frederick Lugard. Northern Nigeria coincided roughly with the Fulani empire, no longer in its virile expansive stage by the end of the nineteenth century, but still a well-knit and effectively administered state, its provinces clearly responsive to the authority of its ruler, the sultan of Sokoto. Lugard's first task, therefore, was effective occupation which was achieved through a series of military actions ending in 1903 in the dethronement and subsequent defeat and death of Sultan Attahiru I of Sokoto.

Faced with the problem of governing a huge territory with a massive fifteen million population, Lugard ruled through authorities already in place in an administration already foreshadowed by Goldie and others that came to be known as indirect rule. With the capitulation of the Fulani emirates, the established African administrations were retained intact, British resident commissioners added at the apex, and a number of basic legal changes instituted such as the abolition of slavery, at least in principle, and the introduction of British law to supplement the Muslim codes. Thus Lugard was able to impose his policies over a vast region without the necessity of an expensive network of administrators, while the emirs, in return for cooperation, were permitted to retain much of their traditional authority.

The concept of working with and through traditional authorities was tried in other British-held areas, its success varying to the extent that there were local administrations through which colonial policy could be applied. In eastern Nigeria where no chiefly system existed, indirect rule was necessarily an almost total failure. In western Nigeria where the chief was no autocrat, his sanction carefully defined by a complex system of customary law, district officers often weakened the fiat of a traditional ruler by inadvertence or carelessness. Ignorant of local usage, they might overlook the importance of royal ceremony or chastise a chief publicly before his people, thereby complicating the imposition of their own colonial authority.

On the Gold Coast a well-defined hierarchy of traditional leaders had long been a fact. In the regions south of Asante the British early attempted to impose their rule through the chiefly agency, and here the educated community made its most concerted effort to join with the chiefs in opposition to the colonial regime. There was already some precedent for this. The Fante Confederation had been an initial effort to marry the special attributes of the educated African to the chiefly power, while in his time Africanus Horton had devoted much attention as a member of the elite to the question of national independence in West Africa through the combined efforts of the educated and traditional leadership.

With the establishment of a Gold Coast colony and protectorate in 1874, the British sought to clarify the role of the chief in their government. Recognizing the organizational and fiscal economy of an administration that made use of the indigenous rulers, they introduced regulations that attempted to link the chief to the colonial power and redefine his jurisdiction. Greater definition necessarily meant limitation and supervision by a higher authority, however, while, at the same time, the more the chiefs were supported by the colonial government, the less their people came to look upon them as consequential units in that government. A series of ordinances made local rulers responsible for new but undignified and untraditional duties, removed the dispensing of justice from their hands, and gave the British governor the power to dismiss the native authorities who in the past had been responsible only to their own people. Other enactments by the officially controlled legislative council provided for municipal reforms which violated age-old township organization and completely upset customary law regarding land ownership, that fundamental foundation of traditional African society.

Under these circumstances, a small but influential group of educated Africans from the coastal areas stepped forward to protect the authority of the traditional rulers, to push their own claims to increased participation in local affairs, and indeed to challenge the very right of the British to govern in the Gold Coast. Some were successful merchants like James H. Brew, John Sarbah, and J. W. Sey, but particularly T. Hutton Mills, John Mensah Sarbah, and J. E. Casely Hayford, whose understanding of the British constitution was matched by long study of Fante customary law, a combination ideally suited to a judicial challenge of the British presence in the Gold Coast.

Of particular prominence was John Mensah Sarbah, a Fante from Cape Coast of scholarly disposition and conservative habits, who utilized his training in English law to call into question both the legitimacy and the practicality of alien rule. The first Gold Coast African to be called to the English bar, Mensah Sarbah in a series of learned constitutional treatises pointed out that the British had resorted to force, not to law, in establishing themselves on the Gold Coast. They had pressed without justification the advantage that the bonds of 1844 had given to English jurisprudence in the administration of local justice. They had assumed quite unreasonably that in signing protection treaties African rulers willingly parted with their sovereignty. This, insisted Mensah Sarbah, was an arbitrary and unlawful imposition of colonial rule.

Moreover, the argument continued, having secured their position, the intruders instituted laws and procedures totally alien to local custom, thus enormously complicating not only their own administration, but also the lives of the people they had come to govern. "Gold Coast territory was not an uninhabited district . . . . or [one] obtained by conquest or cession," Mensah Sarbah explained. "Whether the inhabitants were taken to be half or wholly savages, they had their aboriginal tribal government . . . invested with the rights of sovereignty and exercising its powers."

Nevertheless, Mensah Sarbah was forced to recognize the reality, if not the legality, of alien rule; better, then, to seek means for more effective African participation in government than to waste time in idle lamentation. To this end he urged expanding responsibilities for the educated African both as a leader bringing his people into a new, changing world and as an individual "racy of the soil," in Mensah Sarbah's words, who would know how to preserve the best qualities of Africa's ancient communal virtues. Suiting the action to the word, he devoted his brief years—he died in 1910 when only in his mid-forties—to both the defense of traditional institutions and the demand for a larger degree of self-government.

As a private citizen and public petitioner, and later as a member of the legislative council, Mensah Sarbah consistently urged greater attention to the African and his institutions in the formulation of official policy. He argued for a wider utilization of community leaders as members of the legislative council, the better to represent the needs and desires of the people. He criticized British-imposed municipal government, based as it was on English, rather than African, experience. He pointed out the difficulty of enforcing taxation foreign to local usage. He spent long and frustrating years urging broader chiefly responsibility and independence in the administration of justice, one of the major strengths of traditional society. Undergirding all these practical everyday suggestions lay his painstaking studies in customary law produced in several massive volumes, of which *Fanti National Constitution*, appearing in 1906, represented his most mature philosophy of government.

Like so many West Africans of his day, Mensah Sarbah was particularly exercised over government policy concerning land ownership. In 1897 he helped to organize the Aborigines' Rights Protection Society as a focal point of popular protest, and led a determined fight before the legislative council in opposition to proposed legislation offensive to local customs of land usage. The administration had been concerned with the protection of African land from alienation by European concessionaires seeking timber, subsurface, and other rights, and therefore introduced bills in 1894 and 1897 applying, in effect, British standards for determining ownership and inheritance of land in its Gold Coast colony.

There was at once sharp opposition within the African community, showing itself in public demonstrations, in a deputation sent to London in 1898 by the Aborigines' Rights Protection Society, and in learned briefs prepared by both J. E. Casely Hayford and John Mensah Sarbah. Mensah Sarbah used his material to support representations before the legislative council, the burden of his argument resting in the familiar claim that all land in Africa was always under ownership, that no lands were unoccupied no matter how long they appeared abandoned or remained out of cultivation. Hence, concluded Mensah Sarbah, there could be no legal expropriation of any territories to be classified as crown land. In this instance African customary law carried the day, and the legislation finally enacted was carefully defined to protect African land titles while still maintaining close preventive surveillance against alienation.

The defense of customary African rulers and traditional institutions mounted by John Mensah Sarbah and his educated contemporaries was based only partly on conviction, for there was also the growing desire to reach out for power in a changing society. Hence, in time the chiefly authority came to be as much a point of competition as of cooperation, the new and old elite locking in conflict over the leadership of their people in a fast-changing world. This struggle, which continued in parallel with the opposition to colonial government, did not reach its fullest dimension in the Gold Coast until the years after the First World War. By that time colonial rule had hardened everywhere in its most restrictive form, and West Africans of every definition needed all the mutual aid they could muster to keep in view the fading dream of national self-determination, a dream that had been one of the noble ideals of the war that hoped to make the world safe for democracy.

Suggestions for Further Reading

This chapter relies substantially on R. W. July, *The Origins of Modern African Thought* (New York: Praeger, 1967; London: Faber & Faber, 1968); other studies are helpful, for example, Michael Crowder, *West Africa under Colonial Rule* (London: Hutchinson, 1968; Evanston: Northwestern University Press, 1968). For Senegal, see Michael Crowder, *Senegal: A Study in French Assimilation Policy*, rev. ed. (London: Methuen, 1967; New York: Barnes & Noble, 1967) and G. W. Johnson, *The Emergence of Black Politics in Senegal* (Stanford: University Press, 1971). Sierra Leone is covered in detail in C. Fyfe, *A History of Sierra Leone* (London: Oxford University Press, 1962); and in J. D. Hargreaves, *A Life of Sir Samuel Lewis* (London: Oxford University Press, 1958). H. R. Lynch, *Edward Wilmot Blyden* (London: Oxford University Press, 1967), deals with the important West African nationalist; and J. H. Kopytoff, *A Preface to Modern Nigeria* (Madison: University of Wisconsin Press, 1965), studies the role of the emigres returning home to Yorubaland from Sierra Leone. About the only material on Liberia is found in R. L. Buell, *The Native Problem in Africa*, 2 vols. (London: Frank Cass, 1965; Hamden, Conn.: Shoe String Press, 1965); and in *Liberia: A Century of Survival*, 1847-1947 (Philadelphia: University of Pennsylvania Press, 1947), by the same author. For the Gold Coast, see David Kimble, *A Political History of the Gold Coast*, 1850-1928 (Oxford: Clarendon, 1963).

The best volume on the Yoruba wars is Samuel Johnson, *The History of the Yorubas* (Lagos: C.M.S. Bookshops, 1921); but this should be supplemented by J. F. A. Ajayi and R. Smith, *Yoruba Warfare in the Nineteenth Century* (Cambridge: Cambridge University Press, 1964); S. O. Biobaku, *The Egba and Their Neighbours*, 1842-1872 (Oxford: Clarendon, 1957); and S. A. Akintoye, *Revolution and Power Politics in Yorubaland* (London: Longmans; New York: Humanities, 1971). Both Michael Crowder, *The Story of Nigeria*, 4th ed. (London: Faber, 1978) and Elizabeth Isichei, *History of Nigeria* (London: Longman, 1983) may also be consulted.

This chapter stresses growing contacts between Africans and Europeans on the eve of the colonial era. For greater emphasis on internal African affairs, see the relevant chapters in J. F. A. Ajayi and Michael Crowder, eds., *History of West Africa*, Vol. II (Burnt Mill, Essex, England: Longman, 1987).

16

The Foundations of Progress and Poverty in Southern Africa

The Birth of a New Society

The hard outline of South African society in the middle years of the twentieth century took its first firm shape during the half-century preceding the unification of 1910. It began with the concluding stages of the great migrations of Boer and Bantu which thoroughly interspersed African and European communities across the vast southern veld. It continued as European farmers appropriated new lands to their own use, denying them to the Bantu cattle herders who were thus obliged to become tenant farmers and rural laborers as the price of survival. It was given a dramatic thrust toward eventual prosperity as a modern industrial nation with the discovery of mineral resources in diamonds and gold. Despite parochial jealousies and a shifting British colonial policy, it moved uncertainly in the direction of the political unification that economic advance dictated.

Finally, unified and with national prosperity in sight, South Africa committed itself to a policy of social and economic discrimination based upon color. Asian, Coloured, and most especially the indigenous Africans, were relegated to an inferior position, the latter fixed in the status of rural and urban pauper, denied the exercise of political and civil rights, and proclaimed unworthy of the fruits of their own labor. Thus did the long-lived Boer philosophy of human inequality achieve its logical conclusion in a way of life that was eventually to bring forth the apartheid state of the Republic of South Africa.

Britain and Complexities of Colonial Stewardship

The ambiguity of Britain's colonial policy in South Africa emerged from the fact that she alone possessed the authority to deal with the complexities of government on the ground, yet her actions were often dictated by domestic pressures irrelevant to the situation in South Africa. By projecting the Boer farmers far into the interior, the Great Trek gave an entirely new amplitude to the old problem of relations between white settlers and their Khoikhoi or slave laborers. Henceforward, there was to be a Boer-Bantu confrontation which dwarfed previous racial problems; moreover, by removing themselves from the jurisdiction of the Cape Colony, the trekkers had given geographic and political dimension to a social and cultural cleavage within the white population, long in development. The forces of racial antipathy and division had now been given new impetus. Only a strong, wise, and consistent policy might have succeeded in checking faction and replacing it with harmony and unity. Unfortunately, the British government was bound to pay greater attention to its constituents at home than to the necessities of the South African situation; worse still, British imperial and humanitarian impulses were a complex of contradictions which inexorably intruded their own ambivalence into the policies applied to South Africa.

One overriding consideration guiding Britain's statesmanship in South Africa was the strategic position of that land athwart the route to the Orient where British interests of long standing resided in India, the Antipodes, and the Far East. Beyond this was the concern of humanitarians for the indigenous African in need of conversion and regeneration, as well as the merchant's preoccupation with expanding commerce. Such matters were forced to contend, however, with the abiding absorption in London with economy in government and noninvolvement in colonial entanglements. Hence supremacy had to be maintained and tribal rights protected without the financial commitment necessary to do the job. The Colonial Office was obliged to keep the peace without troops and to rule without power, while administrators on the ground found their assessments set aside by the exigencies of broader global strategies, and their policies reversed by local election results at home.

After the Great Trek, the balance of tensions set up by these conflicting forces emerged initially in an effort to exercise indirect control over the trekkers, by trying to extend the jurisdiction of Cape courts to the interior beyond the colony's frontier, and by isolating the Boer farmers from coastal outlets and possible understandings with other European powers. Thus the annexation of Natal in 1845 served the double purpose of checking potential intervention from abroad while putting a stop to Boer commando raids into Zulu and Pondo country.

In 1848, a similar search for order prompted the Cape Colony governor, Harry Smith, to annex and proclaim the territory between the Orange and Vaal rivers as the Orange River Sovereignty in a move to avoid Boer outbreaks in the Griqua states. This action meant deepening British involvement in the border dispute between the Boers and Moshoeshoe along the Caledon River. Nevertheless, rising free-trade, anticolonial sentiment at home led to a reversal of policy in 1852 and 1854 as the independence of the trekkers beyond the Orange River and in the Transvaal was recognized through the Sand River and Bloemfontein conventions. This withdrawal effectively freed the Boers to deal with Moshoeshoe and led eventually to the wars between the Orange Free State and the Basuto which cost Moshoeshoe most of his best land and reduced his people to desperation. To avoid the total breakup of the Basuto state and large-scale migrations of landless wanderers into Natal, Cape Colony, and elsewhere, policy was once more reversed and Basutoland was annexed by Governor Wodehouse in 1868.

Colonial administrators saw readily enough the need for coordinated policy which would unify weak European communities, poor in resources and labor, and in their separateness incapable of solving the complexities of African relations. In 1858, High Commissioner and Cape Colony Governor Sir George Grey stated the case convincingly in his call for federation. The very weakness and isolation of the European communities, he said, encouraged an unrest among the African people which could not be contained by isolated, feeble governments. Whatever their differences, the European settler states could hope to survive only through fusion which would bring more than uniformity and wisdom to ''native policy''; it would also offer political stability and economic strength to all. Fifteen years later, Lord Carnarvon, the secretary of state for the colonies, was arguing much the same thing. ''The most immediately urgent reason for general union,'' he said, ''is the formidable character of the native question, and the importance of a uniform, wise, and strong policy in dealing with it.'' Preoccupation in Westminster with economy in government had blocked Grey's proposal in its time, and now, in the mid-1870s, Carnarvon's urgings would go unheeded in the face of other factors that had arisen to complicate questions of union in South Africa.

The Revolution of Diamonds and Gold

In 1867 diamonds were found in the alluvial soil of the Orange River near the Vaal confluence, and two years later the discovery of the eighty-three-carat ''Star of South Africa'' lent drama to the inauguration of the world's greatest diamond industry and the beginning of South Africa's economic revolution. It also added a new dimension to the problem of political unity.

The diamond finds necessarily precipitated a stampede of claims over semiarid lands previously utilized as marginal pasture. Long in dispute between the Griqua chief, Waterboer, and certain sections of the southern Tswana, the region had also been infiltrated by Boer trekkers trickling across the Orange River. Now, however, the diamond rush also brought tens of thousands of fortune hunters from the world over and led to the creation of a short-lived Diggers' Republic in 1870. To these growing complexities were added claims to sovereignty pressed by both the Orange Free State and the Boer South African Republic in the Transvaal, while the Cape Colony somewhat reluctantly urged British annexation. The British government as usual viewed involvement with mixed feelings, but finally in 1871 sanctioned annexation to the Cape of the territory that was called Griqualand West, realizing that if the diamond fields went to the Orange Free State, there could be little likelihood of subsequent confederation under the leadership of the Cape Colony.

The Cape Colony occupied a prominent position in imperial policy at the moment. Nineteenth-century political liberalism argued for colonial self-government, a condition that had already been achieved in Canada, New Zealand, and parts of Australia, and the Cape was expected to follow shortly. In 1853 Cape Colony had received a constitution granting representative, though not responsible, government; then in 1872 responsible government was instituted with British control exercised only in external affairs. Britain now began to look once again toward union, stimulated by examples throughout the world—the American Civil War, Imperial Germany, Italian unification, and her own creation, the Dominion of Canada—as well as an awakening uneasiness over the rise of Germany as a world power.

There were also internal factors clamoring for unity, factors closely linked to the rise of the diamond industry. The dusty, untidy boom town of Kimberley became a magnet equally to people and to capital, both of which had long shunned South Africa. Imports in Cape Colony and Natal more than doubled between 1871 and 1875, interest rates on foreign investments declined sharply in response to a heavy capital influx, port facilities were improved by governments suddenly affluent through rising customs receipts, while railroad and telegraph lines reached out from the coast to tap the swelling resources of the interior. Within a few years the value of diamond exports had far exceeded the products of local agriculture. Financial unification seemed well on the way with the development of a regional banking system throughout Cape Colony; surely, circumstance had joined logic to demand political unification as well.

Lord Carnarvon, urged by Disraeli, moved to achieve confederation, and there was some prospect that the liberal-minded President Brand of the Orange Free State, President Burgers of the South African Republic in the Transvaal, and J. C. Molteno, first Prime Minister of Cape Colony, might prove cooperative. A differing ''native policy'' among the constituents appeared to be the most difficult, though not insuperable, obstacle, but in fact trouble, when it appeared, came in another guise. Both the Transvaal and Orange Free State were sulking for having been deprived of what they considered to be their valid claims to the diamond fields of Griqualand West. More crucial still, Cape Colony, newly raised to virtual independence and jealous of her status, her economy booming as never before, was in no mood to share her gains with others less fortunate. Molteno emerged as a tenacious though not very farsighted politician whose vision of the future did not extend far beyond the immediacies of parochial Cape politics. Fearful of his position as first minister, and sensitive to possible interference from a former master, he declined to attend Carnarvon's federation conference in 1876, and the scheme collapsed.

In a fateful sequel, unification failed even more ominously in the north. There on the barren plains across the Vaal, the trekkers had squeezed out an uncertain existence, hampered not only by the infertility of their country but also by rural isolation and a conservative resistance to modernity. An open-handed land policy yielded inadequate revenue for the government and discouraged efficient cultivation, at the same time building expansionist pressures that would eventually bring conflict with neighboring Africans. In 1876 the xenophobic Transvaal settlers attempted to sever their connections to the south, with its nascent industrialism and its custom duties, by seeking a rail outlet through Portuguese territory to Delagoa Bay, but this venture came to nothing. The same year war broke out with the Pedi over land claims, and resulted in both military setback and the financial and administrative collapse of the Transvaal. In April 1877 Britain annexed the demoralized country, to the relief even of some in the South African Republic itself.

Carnarvon took over the Transvaal to end the warfare but also to advance his confederation plans. In fact, events marched steadily toward disunity. Molteno had lost none of his earlier suspicions, and the Orange Free State was unenthusiastic despite a £90,000 award in compensation for her claims to Griqualand West. When in 1878 Carnarvon was replaced in a cabinet reshuffle, Sir Bartle Frere, the South African high commissioner, became the chief protagonist for Britain's federation policy, but his exertions only succeeded in nudging that elusive objective even farther out of reach. Intent on gaining Transvaal friendship through the acquisition of territory in Zululand, Frere helped precipitate a war with the Zulu which led to the annihilation of a British column at Isandhlwana in 1879. The defeat, though later reversed at Ulundi, soured British public opinion over Disraeli's South African policy and added disrespect to Boer dislike of things British. Already Transvaal leaders, headed by Paul Kruger, had charged Britain with arbitrary rule and the frustration of Boer rights of self-determination; now, their demands for independence grew more insistent.

Basically, the difficulty lay in the same incompatibility that had plagued Boer-British relations throughout the century. British imperial policy demanded support of each colony's administration through local taxation but effective public finance and administrative orderliness were not a conspicuous part of the Transvaaler character while British administrative efficiency in practice often fell short of its own ideal. Resentment over these matters soon escalated into violence. When the Gladstone government, replacing Disraeli in 1880, withheld independence, frustration burst forth in a successful revolt which was followed by a grant of independence in all but foreign relations through the Pretoria and London conventions of 1881 and 1884. Another battle had been lost by the forces of unity, but with the discovery of gold in the Transvaal in 1884 the confederation struggle resumed once more.

At Kimberley, after the first wild rush had subsided, the task of sorting out thousands of claims began, to the end that the mines might be efficiently worked with modern equipment. During this process a few men of energy and foresight emerged to excel in the business of consolidation, particularly Cecil Rhodes, arriving in Kimberley when the initial waves of prospectors were already ebbing in the face of barren claims and rising costs. Rhodes pursued his goal of amalgamation, buying up digger rights and eventually forming one of four major concerns that came to control the Kimberley diamond production. Unsatisfied, Rhodes pressed on, finally swallowing his three rivals in massive purchases involving millions of pounds of sterling. By 1890 he had extended his ownership to all of South Africa's diamond mining.

Rhodes sought monopoly for efficiency and profit, but his ambitions extended far beyond Kimberley—to lands beyond the Limpopo and the Zambezi where he envisioned greater profits still, financial, to be sure, but also imperial— the vision of British empire in Africa. Such a quest would lead him eventually to contest the Katanga copper with Belgium's Leopold II, and, along with Harry Johnston, to argue a Cape to Cairo route under British paramountcy. First, however, his attention was to be diverted by the Transvaal and the great gold-bearing veins of the Witwatersrand, where modern industrialism was clashing with Boer pastoralism.

The existence of gold deposits in the Transvaal had been known for some years, but only by the mid-1880s were they demonstrated to be economically viable, and then only under circumstances that were bound to create profound economic and cultural changes among the Boer farmers still searching for sanctuary from the pursuit of British-imposed modernization. Suddenly they were descended upon by hordes of *uitlanders*, or foreigners, an Afrikaans term with pejorative overtones. Ten times the numbers that had invaded Kimberley fifteen years earlier, they arrived from far-off places—from Australia and New Zealand, America and the ports of Europe, as well as from the Cape and other points nearer at home. They sprawled across the veld, and at the site of the main reef a city sprang up with speed and without plan, noisy, dirty, busy, preoccupied with the business of gold, and indifferent if not impatient with the simple beliefs and customs of the Boer farmers.

From their capital at Pretoria, forty miles removed from Johannesburg, the Boers watched with mixed feelings, for wealth began to pour into the land along with the confusion and foreign ways. From the first, Johannesburg was destined to be no boom town, to rise up suddenly and die away as quickly, for the gold, though present in enormous quantities, could be obtained only by use of the most expensive, up-to-date equipment. Individual prospectors could not flourish here, only large-scale industrial complexes backed by vast capital resources from Europe, employing great gangs of labor, and penetrating deep into the earth by means of modern machinery and sophisticated scientific techniques. Tiny gold particles fixed in an ancient metamorphic rock were expensive to extract, and profits, though ultimately great, were small in margin and available only through a vast economic enterprise keyed to the subtleties of an international money market.

However distasteful this foreign intrusion may have been to the Boer farmer, it offered him at last an unparalleled opportunity for escape once and for all from the British to the south. At the same time it sharply increased the danger of imperial British interference. On the one hand, a bankrupt government was suddenly converted to affluence, and in the dozen years between 1883 and 1895 its revenues increased twenty-five-fold. Nonetheless, the financial windfall came from tax levies on a wealthy, growing population, intense and dynamic, intolerant of Bible-reading farmers whose land it threatened to dominate. Again, the mines brought dramatic increases to the value of land and the price of foodstuffs, while the new industry introduced improvements in transportation and communication which had so long shunned the remote veld across the Vaal. These gains, however, threatened closer links with the south and with the British from whom the Boers had fled a half-century earlier, and whose controls they had only recently shuffled off.

Shrewd, if isolated, the Transvaalers saw well enough that their newfound wealth was a means to political viability and independence, and, under the leadership of their president, Paul Kruger, they moved to exploit their greatly improved position. Kruger revived plans for a railroad to Delagoa Bay which would free him from dependence on southern outlets. He solicited advice and assistance from European powers, particularly Germany, thereby challenging British hegemony in South Africa. He sought room for expansion across the Limpopo, and in 1887 concluded the Grobler Treaty with the Ndebele king, Lobengula, which secured special privileges for Boers traveling and trading in Matabeleland. Thus, in strength, the Transvaal turned its back on union, but the very conditions that produced her strength were also to defeat her policy. In the end, it was the discovery of gold on the Witwatersrand that made certain the unification of South Africa.

The Road to Union

British statesmen aside, there had been few serious moves toward consolidation in South Africa during the nineteenth century. Following the Great Trek, an effort by Andries Pretorius to bring Natal, Winburg, and the Transvaal Boers together had come to naught, and in 1860 his son, Marthinus, had attempted to join the South African Republic and the Orange Free State, resorting to the remarkable but nonetheless unsuccessful maneuver of securing election as president in both states. Such efforts were, to say the least, premature, since the South African Republic could scarcely maintain its own unity, while the Free State, contiguous with Cape Colony and containing many English settlers, had never shared the extreme sensitivity to British institutions of the trekkers to the north.

In the years that followed, the miscarriage of both the Grey and Carnarvon schemes complicated any subsequent attempts at unification. The aftermath of Lord Carnarvon's failure was the annexation and release of the Transvaal, the net result of which was a nascent Boer nationalism based on race, manifesting itself in a pronounced leaning toward Germany, with all the paraphernalia of foreign loans and advisers, of visiting war vessels and tariffs, all in all a complication to internal South African unity. Unhappily, there were few offsetting factors at work among the Transvaal's neighbors. It is true, in Cape Colony, Jan Hofmeyr, through his Afrikander Bond, led the Cape Boers steadily away from racism to a doctrine of Boer-British cooperation, urging his people to greater participation in the public life of the Cape. Moreover, in the Orange Free State, President Brand, whose loyalties extended equally north and south, would not join Kruger in a proposed military and mercantile union which would have effectively isolated the two Afrikaner republics from their British-oriented neighbors.

Otherwise, Cape Colony and Natal seemed no more enlightened than the northerners. In 1885, Kruger, having failed momentarily to arrange for a rail line from Johannesburg to Delagoa Bay, asked for a customs union with the Cape which would have involved extending the Cape Town-Kimberley line to the Transvaal gold fields. Brand, sensing possibilities, urged a more general customs arrangement, but Cape Town was evasive, and Natal no less so. When the Cape belatedly suggested a conference in 1888, the moment had passed. Kruger had glimpsed the prospects that his gold deposits laid before him, and was already turning to the device of economic nationalism and a second, and this time successful, attempt to gain a rail outlet to Delagoa Bay. The others finally had their conference, without the Transvaal, which completed its line in 1894, but even then the Cape and Natal failed to reach agreement over uniform import duties. All that was salvaged was a customs union between the Cape and the Free State which gave the Cape railroads access to Free State territory.

Nevertheless the forces of unification were also in motion. The German protectorate over South-West Africa, proclaimed in 1884, stimulated the British to block a linkup with the Transvaal by annexing a portion of Bechuanaland to the Cape in 1885 and proclaiming a protectorate over the rest. This action not only eliminated German influence in the central plateau but checked Transvaal expansionism along its western frontier while maintaining control over the so-called Missionaries' Road which proceeded from the Cape Colony northward through Mafeking, skirting the western edge of the Transvaal on its way to Matabeleland and Mashonaland beyond the Limpopo. Such a move had been strongly urged by Cecil Rhodes, now a millionaire many times over with a fortune in diamonds and gold, and fully engaged in his drive to promote British influence across Africa on behalf of wealth and empire.

To pursue his ends, in 1888 Rhodes intensified his participation in Cape politics, becoming the colony's prime minister two years later, and in 1889 he succeeded in obtaining a royal charter for his British South Africa Company, the agency of his thrust to the north. In 1890 a column under company direction arrived at the site of Salisbury to lay claim to Mashonaland and to open yet another chapter of British imperial history. The immediate objective, however, was further to contain the landlocked Transvaal in a tightening vise of British-controlled territories, thereby fastening her irrevocably to the British imperial interest. Rhodes had done his work well, and Kruger's persistent efforts to free his country from Britain's domination resulted only in deepening his involvement. In 1895 he succeeded in negotiating a protectorate over Swaziland which brought with it the long-sought territorial access to the sea, but simultaneously Kruger made such cordial overtures to the Germans as to frighten Britain with the specter of a renewed German influence in the Transvaal. The Swaziland protectorate was forthwith revoked, Kruger lost his coastal outlet, and the Transvaal in effect was reduced to the position of a suzerain state, ringed on all sides by foreign territory and dominated by Britain.

Rhodes now stepped up his pace, spurred by the growing competition among European nations in the partition of Africa and the knowledge that his own failing health left him little time. His objectives involved annexation of unclaimed territory in the interior through his chartered company, and the establishment of a customs union in South Africa which, he felt, the Transvaal would eventually be obliged to join. From this would follow South African political federation, the extension of British hegemony to the north, and finally a British steel spine down the eastern side of Africa, the Cape to Cairo railroad.

By 1895, therefore, unification seemed to be on the way despite the Transvaal, but Rhodes, ever in a hurry, was prepared to force a showdown. The Uitlanders, probably already outnumbering the Boers, had been denied political rights and treated as aliens by their hosts who feared that a grant of political equality to the newcomers would cost them control over their own land. Although Uitlander discontent was more apparent than real, the mining corporate leadership had come to regard the Transvaal government as an impediment to industrial progress. Rhodes now helped organize a conspiracy to overthrow the Transvaal government by means of an internal uprising to be supplemented by a raiding party of five hundred Rhodesian police and volunteers under Dr. L.S. Jameson who would come in on appeal by the Uitlanders. The secretary of state for colonies, Joseph Chamberlain, was privy to the plot, which, however, totally misfired when the ill-prepared and divided Uitlanders lost heart and Jameson foolishly attacked despite instructions that he abandon the invasion.

The raid began on the last day of 1895, but without effective support within the Transvaal, Jameson and his men were speedily subdued. What did not end so quickly were the repercussions of this ill-starred adventure which, on the contrary, proceeded in ever-increasing intensity until they burst forth in the Boer War four years later. The raid necessarily cast the Boers in the role of patriots defending their land, while Rhodes lost much prestige along with the support of Hofmeyr and the moderate Cape Boers, and was forced to retire from politics.

The British government was deeply involved. Control of South African gold meant domination of worldwide money markets at a time of great international commercial and industrial growth, not to mention the continued strategic importance of southern Africa to Britain's far-flung empire. Such naked imperialism backfired, however, strengthening the position of the Boer republic. In sympathy, the Orange Free State finally concluded a military alliance with the Transvaal, whose leaders, for their part, were driven further toward a German entente while maintaining and adding to the restrictions on the Uitlanders.

Steadily the chasm of misunderstanding widened as the area of accommodation narrowed. In 1897 Sir Alfred Milner was appointed governor and high commissioner of Cape Colony, and the following year Kruger was reelected president of the Transvaal. From this point forward there ceased to be a basis for reconciliation. The Transvaal would not voluntarily give up its relations with European powers while Britain could not permit these alliances to threaten her predominance in South Africa. In the end, union was achieved, but only at the expense of war, which broke out in October 1899.

The Transvaal and Orange Free State lost the Boer War after three years of bitter conflict. In the end the commando and guerrilla tactics of the Afrikaners could not match the British numbers and a scorched earth policy which weighed heavily on both military and civilian populations. A peace treaty was finally signed, in May, 1902, calling for large-scale rehabilitation of the country, and eventual responsible government in the two former republics, at first to be administered as crown colonies by Lord Milner, now colonial governor as well as high commissioner. Basically Milner's policy was designed to secure South Africa's territories under a British hegemony—political rehabilitation by means of a thoroughgoing anglicization of the predominantly Afrikaner population of the South African territories and economic regeneration based on the gold production of the Witwatersrand. These objectives achieved, representative government might then be introduced in the Afrikaner territories leading to internal self-government within the British Empire.

Economic progress was at first halting, largely because of a shortage of labor on the Rand. The African miners, having been scattered during the war, were reluctant to work at the low wages offered, but they soon returned, possibly stimulated by the competition of contract Chinese labor utilized between 1904 and 1910.

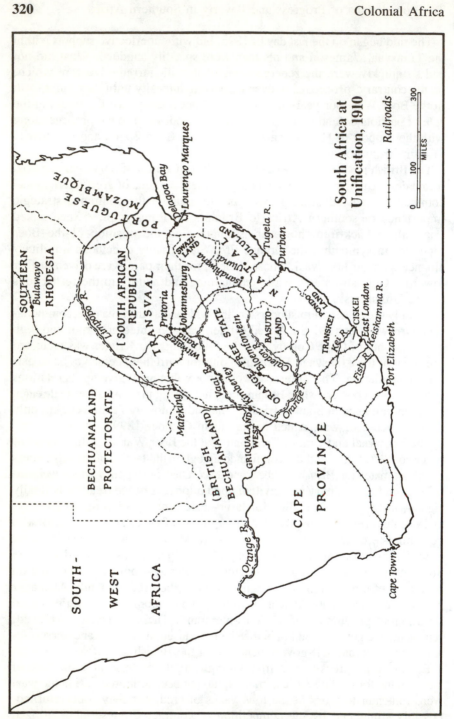

South Africa at
Unification, 1910

⊢⊢⊢⊢ Railroads

MILES
0   100   300

Milner's political moves were revolutionary, given the South African situation with its population majority of Dutch antecedents, its long history of Boer discontent with British rule, and a bitter war just concluded in which two Boer republics had been defeated and occupied. Under these conditions Milner instituted a program of cultural assimilation involving the use of English as the official language and principal medium of instruction, the encouragement of English settlers, and an end to the acutely provincial Afrikaner school curriculum, all looking forward to an eventual federation under the British crown. In fact, this policy was not ruthlessly pursued after Milner's departure in 1905, while Boer reaction to the hardships of the late war and the perceived indignities of British cultural domination led to the renascence of a particularly powerful brand of Afrikaner nationalism.

The most immediate nationalist manifestation was the formation of political parties—*Het Volk*, "the People," in the Transvaal led by the Boer military figures Louis Botha and Jan Smuts; the *Oranje Unie*, or Orange Union, of J. B. M. Hertzog, Abraham Fischer, and C. R. de Wet in the former Free State; and Jan Hofmeyr's revived Cape Colony Afrikander Bond under the name of the South African Party. The tides of nationalism and anti-imperialism were soon running so strongly that both the Transvaal and the Free State received new constitutions providing for self-government in 1906 and 1907 respectively, and by 1908 all these new Afrikaner parties were in complete control of their respective governments.

At last with the arrival to power of Boer (Afrikaner) governments, the time for union was drawing near. Britain looked on unification as strengthening her international position, especially in relation to Germany; by contrast, some Afrikaners saw it as the road to national independence, while moderate Afrikaners like Smuts and Botha thought in terms of a healthy merging of English and Dutch stocks to build a strong nation within the British Empire. In 1908 a convention met, finally producing a constitution which went into effect in May 1910, eight years after the signing of the peace treaty. It provided for a unitary government under the British crown, the former colonies transferring their sovereignty to the central authority. It also provided for a legislature wherein only Europeans could sit, and for which, the Cape Province excepted, only Europeans could vote. Hence union came only for the European; it was not meant to include the 80 percent of the South African population that was not white.

The Other Union

The Union of South Africa had at last been achieved, emerging from the tensions of international politics and the necessities of economic development. The Boer War added forceful persuasion to the logic of modernization, and Afrikaner nationalism awoke in time to crown the process with its own unity.

What seemed to be missing was that fundamental preoccupation of all South Africa, that other union that bound two races together in a common destiny: the relation between the African and the European.

Quite the contrary, it too was present. Spoken or unspoken, it had long since become part of each individual nervous system; consciously or unconsciously, it affected decisions, influenced attitudes, and determined the policies of state. When union was finally mooted, it might yet have failed had there been no agreement on so-called "native policy." The Cape delegates were determined to sustain their long-standing tradition of a common voting roll without racial qualifications, while those of the Transvaal and Free State were equally unbending that no African might have the franchise. Union was salvaged only through compromise permitting local control of suffrage; in the end, the racial issue was the ultimate, irreducible obstacle which had to be circumvented to achieve political unity. With unification, moreover, came the principle that South African society was to be based upon racial privilege and exploitation, a principle that has shaped South Africa's affairs to the present, just as it had in turn been shaped by pressures over the long years stretching back to the first confrontation of Boer and Bantu on the Fish River.

The Great Trek had signaled the great change, that is, the beginning of the end for African independence, the first steps in the disintegration of traditional African society. The competition of rising populations, black and white, for decreasing supplies of arable land manifested itself in two forms. First and more dramatic was the series of wars begun in the eighteenth century and concluded only in the early years of the twentieth whereby the Africans resisted the engrossing of their land and the imposition of foreign control over their activities. Sometimes successful for a time but more often disastrous, African resistance usually ended with the European occupation of African territory and the compression of the indigenous people into more congested areas on ever-poorer land.

Such a progression was particularly well marked on the eastern frontier of the Cape Colony. The old Xhosa area beyond the Fish River had been annexed by Governor Harry Smith in 1847, the former neutral zone contained between the Fish and Keiskamma being added directly to Cape Colony, and the territory between the Keiskamma and Kei rivers organized as the colony of British Kaffraria. Beyond lay the Transkei, a large area extending north to Natal, which would eventually become the main reserve for Africans under the latter-day policy of apartheid. Here developed a vast refugee camp for uprooted people, Mfengu (Fingo), Mpondo, and Griqua, as well as broken remnants of Thembu and Xhosa retreating from the devastation of their self-inflicted genocide of 1857 in British Kaffraria. Such a multiplicity of insecure groups led to sporadic outbursts, which in 1877 involved forces of the Cape government in an unwanted and expensive war. The sequel was not European colonization, but the extension by Cape Town of colonial controls which gradually introduced both Europeanization and a double standard, both in the Transkei and in Cape Colony proper. By the 1890s there were stiff vagrancy laws on the books, no African could purchase alcohol, and the indigenous people were being encouraged to secure their land on the basis of survey and individual title. At the same time, the franchise was open to all, although literacy and property qualifications meant that most Africans, along with some Cape Coloureds and Europeans, were unable to vote.

Basutoland already having been taken over in 1868, the final annexation of Pondoland to the Cape in 1894 closed the gap between the Cape and Natal, and left only Zulu country and Swaziland unaccounted for south of Portuguese Mozambique. Swaziland lingered on until annexation by Britain in the mid-90s, but in the Zulu territory, where the Shakan Mfecane had instilled proud martial traditions, there were the makings of trouble with a renascent Zulu nation. The Zulu warriors chafed over their encirclement by colonial territories which limited their raiding and traditional "washing of spears." Moreover, Cetewayo, the Zulu king, was in dispute with the Transvaal over frontier land claims. When an arbitration commission found for him in 1878, the high commissioner, Sir Bartle Frere, insisted that the Zulu land cession be accompanied by the breakup of the Zulu military machine and the installation of a British resident in Zululand. Such terms led straight to the disaster at Isandhlwana early in 1879, a setback that was not recouped until six months later at Ulundi, when Cetewayo was defeated and exiled. For a time Zululand survived under the rule of thirteen chiefs established by the British, its final years marked by petty civil war and Boer incursions. In 1897 it was finally annexed to Natal.

During much these same years there was unrest and dissatisfaction among the Africans living in Natal. Not long after her annexation by Britain, the colony had established a series of reserves where Africans dwelt under traditional law administered by their own chiefs, but under the surveillance of European magistrates directed by Theophilus Shepstone, the Diplomatic Agent to the Natives. This policy of indirect rule, so different from that of the Cape, introduced a number of vexatious regulations and levies which were poorly administered and inadequately financed. In 1873 the situation led to a minor breach of the peace which resulted in the eventual banishment of a Hlubi chief, Langalibalele, the severe punishment reflecting a sense of European insecurity in the face of the thousands upon thousands of Africans residing in European-administered territories under circumstances that satisfied neither white nor black.

As always the essential problem was land. The Natal reserves seemed commodious, but their terrain was poor and was continually being chipped away to create white farms. The Europeans complained that the African locations drained off labor needed to cultivate their own fields, but the Africans were in fact moving away from the reserves due to crowding, poor soil, and odious regulations. Despite the extensive acreage set aside for their use, more than half the Africans were squatters on private or crown lands.

Analogous circumstances obtained in the other territories. For practical purposes Africans were denied land title in the Orange Free State and the Transvaal, although some freeholds did materialize under liberal interpretation of the law. As for the Cape, while freehold was countenanced, it was sometimes designed more to harvest African labor for European use than to protect African property in the land. The Glen Grey Act of 1894, for example, sponsored by Rhodes, established freeholds in the Cape reserves in such a way as to insure a surplus landless population that could be attracted to white farms or to the industrial centers.

Here, then, dwelt the second, less spectacular but more profound, competition for land. The Boer farmer thought in terms of a minimum tract of six thousand acres for each family, and with an expanding population and absentee ownership, enormous acreages were quickly preempted. The original trekkers, moreover, had arrived in Natal, Transorangia, and the Transvaal at a time when the shock waves of the Mfecane had temporarily scattered the African peoples so that there was an illusion of empty land which soon faded with the return of more peaceful times. Beyond this, European and African concepts of land ownership and utilization differed profoundly; what was alienation in the eyes of the one might to the other involve no more than a temporary right to pasturage. By the end of the century growing demands of white farmers and the appearance of large land companies had brought legislation throughout South Africa that engrossed tribal lands, forcing the Africans to dwell on reservations or relegating them to the role of squatters or tenants on land they might have formerly occupied, now permitted to remain by their new European landlord in return for labor or rent.

There were Africans who prospered despite this unpromising regimen. A class of peasant producers emerged, some purchasing their own tracts, many others working terrain of absentee owners, using their personal equipment to produce profitable cash crops. Their very success, however, intensified the pressures of white-controlled governments on the black population. White farmers feared the economic competition of black production, while in both town and country the need for cheap controllable labor remained undiminished. To stamp out the independent African farmer legislation was eventually drafted — the Natives' Land Act of 1913 — limiting privately owned holdings by Africans to 13 percent of the land, roughly coincident with the reserves. Like the Resident Natives Ordinance in Kenya and the Land Apportionment Act of Southern Rhodesia, the 1913 Native's Land Act thus insured for South Africa a supply of African labor for European use, forcing the bulk of the African population into a landless labor force for either white-controlled farming or industry.

With the coming of diamond and gold mining, the pattern of an agricultural, rural proletariat was extended to these new urban industries where once again the Africans were compelled to work for the benefit of others under conditions of growing social, political, and economic limitations. They came, prodded by various factors. The primary imperatives were the tax laws, designed to raise revenue for administrative expenses but also to drive the African into the labor market. During the 1890s the rinderpest epidemic was another major stimulus, but there were attractions in the mines as well. There was the appeal of European manufactured goods that soon became necessary luxuries, the allure of city life, the desire for personal freedom and money in pocket often denied on the farm with its monotony and its poverty. Among other things money offered the prospect that an early acquisition of bridewealth would soon lead to marriage and family. What the African workers also encountered, however, was a depressed wage scale that exploited their lack of skill and want of unity, and in fact based the industrial prosperity of South Africa as much on their unrewarded labor as on the presence of precious ores in the earth.

From the first, therefore, the double standard on the farm between European owner and African tenant was repeated in the industrial town. White labor came to mean skilled labor at high wages, whereas black labor was always unskilled and low paid. In the mines white workers often were in fact skilled, their talents much needed in engineering the extraction of low-grade ore. Nevertheless, the principle held that, regardless of skill, white labor must command a high price based on skin color, that the color bar when applied to industry decreed a continuing gap between African and European, with no prospect that the African could close that gap and gain access through excellence to the privileged class.

The mining companies would have preferred low wages for both white and black, arguing that narrow profit margins in deep-level mining made necessary stringent economies in labor costs. White labor organized in opposition, however, insisting on high wages and job preference segregated by color, adding an economic argument to their racial prejudice, much like the Free Soilers of pre-Civil War America. Such an arrangement made for great inefficiency, and was questionable economics as well. A large unskilled labor force was an ineffectual tool despite its cheapness, its depressed condition and easy availability a deterrent to increased competence, its low earning power an impediment to national prosperity. Yet, worse still was the utilization of a high-wage white labor supply, at first predominantly skilled but in the years after the First World War including more and more unskilled workers who, because of their color, had to be paid at a rate considered appropriate for so-called civilized labor. In 1936, for example, the earnings of 47,000 Europeans in the mining industries amounted to £16,700,000, £4,000,000 more than the combined income of 395,000 unskilled Africans. In economic terms this had several consequences. First, in times past, it had led to labor shortages caused by lack of African incentive, and the importation of contract laborers like the indentured Indian sugar workers in Natal after 1860 and the Chinese brought into the Transvaal at the conclusion of the Boer War. Next, it encouraged industrial inefficiency through the use of cheap labor. Finally, the depressed African wage scale choked off a large potential purchasing power.

More than this, however, the double standard in labor meant an economic system wherein a large unskilled work force existed at submarginal levels in order that a small privileged segment of the population might achieve a standard of living comparable with that of the world's most advanced countries, despite the relative poverty of the South African economy. Hence, it was no wonder that the pattern of discrimination and segregation, which had emerged in the preindustrial years, should be perpetuated and strengthened when the center of economic life shifted from the farm to the city and South Africa's industry promised something more than the subsistence agriculture practiced so long by the trekboer farmer.

Such a drift of events might have been checked on several occasions by British intervention, the final opportunity coming at the conclusion of the Boer War. But Lord Milner's conviction that inferior blacks should be ruled by more advanced whites conceded the logic of the Afrikaner position regarding a franchise restricted to whites and foreclosed the possibility of genuine reform. Thus was the war won and the peace lost for the African population. Moreover, when the concept of federation gave way to a centralized government under unification, Cape liberalism was bound to be swamped sooner or later in facing contention from other quarters that the foundation and future of South African society rested in racial privilege.

Beyond the immediate circumstances, Britain's inadequacy was defined by the limitations of her own domestic and imperial necessities. As for the Africans themselves, their powers of resistance and range of action were even more acutely limited. Direct confrontation by tribal military force was futility conclusively demonstrated by the crushing of a Zulu uprising under Bambatha in 1906. Africans therefore turned increasingly toward other means to compensate their growing sense of frustration.

First of all, there was the rise of an independent church movement which drew the sting from racial discrimination and permitted self-government in the world of religion where none was permitted in secular affairs. The earliest manifestations of these Ethiopian churches occurred during the 1870s and 1880s with such nationalist religious groups as Nehemiah Tile's Thembu church. More significant, perhaps, was the later development of intertribal churches among mine laborers in the Transvaal organized by M. M. Mokone, James M. Dwane, and others. All these movements had the same motivation, however—to compensate for the restrictions of white rule by providing African organizations directed and controlled by Africans.

A second path led in the direction of more overt political action, but its first manifestations were mild and largely ineffective; witness the activities of John Tengo Jabavu, an enfranchised Cape Xhosa who sought unsuccessfully to extend political rights through an alliance with white liberals. Jabavu and others, like Walter Rubusana, were deeply disappointed by the discrimination against Africans contained in the Union constitution, taking their case in futile protest before the British people at the time of Parliamentary ratification in

1909. The shortcomings of Jabavu's program, with its misplaced reliance on black-white partnership, led to somewhat more vigorous measures in 1912 in the formation of the South African Native Congress which was later renamed the African National Congress. This organization, the work of Dr. Pixley Seme, Sol T. Plaatje, and others, sought full African citizenship through the franchise and the end of restrictions on landholding and personal movement— moderate objectives which were nonetheless anathema to a philosophy of white supremacy that would relentlessly steer the country in the direction of apartheid. During the years that followed, this educated African leadership, so moderate in its objectives and methods, might well have echoed the cry of anguish that had emanated some time earlier from the unhappy Africans of Natal, "If we Natives could only have feathers we would put on our wings and fly to another country."

Beyond the Limpopo—

The Union of South Africa united only the white South Africans. The black population remained outside, either physically in the territories of Bechuanaland, Basutoland, and Swaziland which came under British protection, or in the form of the Union's segregated African community—wanted only for its exploited labor, and denied all rights and privileges that a long residence in the land seemed to warrant. Beyond the Limpopo, however, another white community hesitated, and then declined to join, uncertain of its position and unready to lose its identity within the vast state taking shape to the south.

There was a certain historical logic to a unification that would have extended South Africa's hegemony to the Zambezi and perhaps eventually beyond. Both African and European had moved north not many years earlier, occupying the vast territory that had once been the land of Mwene Mutapa, placing upon it the stamp of conquest that had become familiar during the days of the Mfecane and the Great Trek. In June 1890, a column of "pioneers," dispatched by Cecil Rhodes and accompanied by Rhodes's agent, Dr. L. S. Jameson, crossed the Limpopo and marched to the site of Salisbury, thereby basing themselves in Mashonaland. A half-century earlier, the Kololo people of Sebetwane had finally reached safety in the waterlogged Aluyi (Lozi) country up the Zambezi above Victoria Falls. During much the same years, Mzilikazi and his Ndebele had abandoned their troubled land in the Transvaal in a final successful flight to security beyond the Limpopo, far from the reach of both the vengeful Zulu hordes and the guns and horses of the Boer trekkers. Now, it seemed, circumstances had again overtaken them; flight had gained not sanctuary, but only respite from the menace of the white people who once again confronted the Ndebele and challenged their rule.

The settler column that planted the British flag at Fort Salisbury in September 1890 was the instrument of Cecil Rhodes's particularly virile form of European imperialism. The first step had been the establishment of the Bechuanaland protectorate blocking the Germans in South-West Africa and securing the Missionaries' Road north to Matabeleland, the domain of the Ndebele, or Matabele, people, led by their paramount chief, Lobengula. Having seen Imperial Germany checked, Rhodes next hastened to contain the move of the Transvaal across the Limpopo, set in motion through the Grobler Treaty of 1887. At his urging, the British South African high commissioner, Sir Hercules Robinson, negotiated the Moffat Treaty in February 1888, which bound Lobengula to consult the high commissioner before undertaking any dealings with other powers involving territorial cession. The Moffat Treaty thus canceled out the implications of a Transvaal protectorate contained in the Grobler agreement which, in any case, Lobengula had apparently regarded as no more than an expression of mutual friendship.

While the Transvaal government bitterly, but vainly, protested this check to its expansionist enterprise, Rhodes now moved to monopolize the economic exploitation of Matabeleland. Nine months after the Moffat Treaty, in October 1888, Lobengula was induced to sign the Rudd Concession under which he assigned to Rhodes exclusive mineral rights throughout his domain in exchange for one thousand breech-loading rifles and a monthly stipend of £100. Both Lobengula and Rhodes regarded Ndebele suzerainty as effective within Mashonaland to the northeast as well as in Matabeleland proper.

The Rudd Concession not only provided Rhodes with important economic privileges in Ndebele country; it also enabled him to apply for a royal charter forming a company that could exploit the advantages gained through the Moffat and Rudd agreements. In 1889, the charter was granted, creating the British South Africa Company with powers to engage in various economic pursuits, to maintain its own police force, and to arrange political relations by treaty with African powers. Territorial definition did not exclude the possibility of expansion northward across the Zambezi. Thus Rhodes had gained the authority to occupy Central Africa, a step that he initiated when his "pioneers" crossed the Limpopo and, guarded by a company police force of five hundred, headed into Mashonaland.

Lobengula was under no illusions as to the threat that these developments posed for his kingdom which was one of the major African powers south of the Zambezi. By the 1880s, the Ndebele nation had grown by accretion of conquered people to a population of one hundred thousand, capable of fielding an army upwards of twenty thousand disciplined spearmen. Here was a strong, centralized state which had avoided much of the divisiveness that had plagued the Ngoni, which had absorbed many neighboring Shona people and reduced still others to vassalage, and which showed a marked antipathy toward Europeans and a resistance to their way of life.

Nevertheless, the Ndebele position reflected basic weaknesses of which their king was only too well aware. The classic military tactics and traditional armament of the Shakan period were passing out of date as firearms became increasingly available. Ndebele society, however, had grown rigid, impeding any genuine military reform, while guns were expensive and difficult to keep in good operational condition. The Ndebele economy rested on cattle for food, for reward, and for prestige, but raiding was becoming more and more hazardous against well-armed neighbors, and prospective victims grew scarce as European control closed in from the south. Finally, many Ndebele, particularly among the young warriors, seem to have underestimated the magnitude of the European threat. Their hostility toward the white people led them on occasion to counsel annihilation of all whites in Matabeleland, a suicidal policy, as Lobengula fully realized, chiding his impetuous warriors with the remark, "You want to drive me into the lion's mouth." Such belligerence greatly complicated the king's diplomacy which was essentially designed to discourage the white advance without involvement in the direct military confrontation he knew would be fatal to his cause and people.

From Lobengula's point of view, then, he had conceded little in signing the Moffat Treaty unless he planned to give away his country, which was certainly not the case. Moreover, to Lobengula the Rudd Concession had the advantage of limiting foreign penetration to what the king mistakenly took to be one small group of ten miners under his royal authority, a grant for which he received in return a substantial supply of modern arms and a handsome monthly royalty. When Lobengula discovered his error, he moved to repudiate the concession as contrary to his understanding, but events were already moving beyond his control. Caught between the militants in his own camp and the pressure exerted by Rhodes, Lobengula in the autumn of 1889 granted the company limited prospecting rights which were promptly used as the excuse for the pioneer column that established itself on the site of Salisbury (Harare) in the autumn of 1890.

Such an action clearly exceeded Lobengula's authorization but it was only the opening move in a gambit that would lead to full-scale occupation and control. The settlers, some two hundred including South Africans, British, Canadians, and Americans, were awarded extensive mining and land claims in Shona country that was ostensibly, though in most cases not actually, subject to Lobengula's rule. The real objective, however, was Matabeleland which Rhodes thought would eventually develop into a second Witwatersrand, and would sooner or later have to be taken and developed.

In 1893 Jameson used a border incident to make war on the Ndebele, the result of which was Lobengula's defeat and subsequent death, reportedly from smallpox. Matabeleland was occupied and Ndebele cattle confiscated, mining and land companies were established and African labor recruited by company police action and through taxation. In 1896 the Ndebele rose up against these iniquities followed shortly by the Shona whose land had been similarly appropriated although, unlike the Ndebele, they had ceded no territories through conquest. After fierce resistance the Ndebele and Shona were finally induced to lay down their arms; however, control over their territory and their destiny had now passed from the Africans to the Europeans.

Such miseries were compounded by natural disasters in the form of plague and drought, capped by the devastating rinderpest epidemic of 1896. What was also apparent was the imposition of a new way of life, a permanent encumbering of African land and labor by the European intruder in a pattern not unlike that concurrently unfolding in South Africa. Although the roseate prospects of the Matabeleland reefs soon gave way to more modest appraisals, mining remained an important industry, gradually joined by staple agriculture, particularly in maize, tobacco, and livestock. Production relied on good land and cheap labor, the former obtained by confiscation, and the establishment of "native reserves," the latter by taxing and coercing the Africans as well as restricting their access to the agricultural economy.

Recruitment of labor for low wages was not easily achieved, especially in face of competition from the South African mines. Typical devices were pass laws and labor contracts that impeded free individual movement and restrained the growth of a labor market based upon supply and demand, as well as so-called hut taxes, the payment of which forced the African into the labor market. Such restrictions were carefully designed to create migrant labor rather than a landless work force; in this fashion a worker could be billeted at their workplace at minimum cost, the expenses of their family being met, not by their employer but by the productivity of their own farm normally located in the reserves. Inevitably this system led to submarginal working conditions, malnutrition, debilitating disease, and high mortality.

The reserves were initiated in Matabeleland in 1895 and augmented periodically until the end of company rule after the First World War. By that time some 23 percent of the land had been set aside for African use, 32 percent earmarked for European ownership, with the company holding the remaining 45 percent which was eventually designated as Crown Land, open to purchase by anyone but in practical economic terms limited to Europeans. Without taking account of the population ratio of one European for every twenty Africans (approximately fifty thousand against one million by 1930), there were the additional circumstances that European land was well served by railroads, was of generally good quality, and was to a considerable extent unused.

There were chasms of ambiguity if not deceit separating the theory and practice of so-called native administration in Southern Rhodesia. Reserves were established officially to protect Africans from land encumbrance, yet the practical effect was to produce labor for European farms and mines. More generally, unlike the situation in South Africa, assimilation was to be the stated policy in Southern Rhodesia, although it was to be the assimilation of the African into a Europeanized society. As soon as they had learned through education and experience to deal with a Western, modern way of life, it was argued, the Africans would take their place as equals in the new society, and there were electoral laws to prove the point, for from the first the only restrictions on the franchise were based on property and literacy.

Yet even here, as in other phases of Southern Rhodesian life, elements of discrimination were apparent. Property qualifications effectively excluded Africans from political activity, and were periodically raised to maintain that distinction; juries were necessarily white because they were drawn from the voting rolls, and a double standard came to obtain in the judgment of criminal cases; the constant and growing need for labor made for an insistent, though officially resisted, European demand that Africans be forced to work; while land apportionment continued to favor white occupation. When the occasional African began to make economic and social progress, his advance was feared and blocked, first by custom and finally by official policy. In 1930 the Land Apportionment Act was passed whereby all Africans not under contract as laborers were relegated to the reserves. Thus did early principle of racial cooperation degenerate into racial segregation, capped in Southern Rhodesia by this final sanction of law.

Such legislation had been enacted by the European-dominated, self-governing colony of Southern Rhodesia which came into existence in 1923. During the earlier period of company rule, economic development was restricted to mining and land companies and the growing body of white settlers. Development took place in various forms—railways which connected Southern Rhodesia to the south and brought an outlet as well through Portuguese Mozambique; gold mining which, modest in output, was yet the basis for the economy with an annual production worth £3,580,000 by 1914; agriculture which slowly provided exportable quantities of beef cattle, tobacco, citrus fruits, and some grains; and a gradually expanding population, the settlers rising from 13,000 in 1898 to 24,000 in 1911, and to 36,000 by 1923, the fast-growing African population being estimated in 1911 at 750,000 and over a million twenty years later.

Political advance, limited for practical purposes to whites, began in 1898 with the establishment of a legislative council providing for a popularly elected minority which became a majority in 1907 and was increased in 1913. By the time of the First World War, the settlers were demanding self-government, and in 1915 the Colonial Office agreed in principle. Over the years, the direction of the company had grown irritating, and when a satisfactory formula was developed for its withdrawal, a draft constitution was prepared calling for responsible government, and in 1922 this was accepted by the electors who at the same time rejected the proposal that they be absorbed into the Union of South Africa. The next year Southern Rhodesia was annexed to the British crown as a self-governing colony.

—And Across the Zambezi

The expansionist drive of Cecil Rhodes which produced the Moffat Treaty and Rudd Concession for Matabeleland had, by 1889, already crossed the

Zambezi into Barotseland. There the Lozi king, Lewanika, actively sought a helping hand from Europe, for he was haunted by the possibility that he might be dethroned by his own people, as had occurred once before, or destroyed by the Ndebele, who were threatening a military invasion. Emulating the Tswana chief, Khama, Lewanika approached the administrator of Bechuanaland requesting British protection. This overture was referred to Rhodes who had just obtained the charter of his British South Africa Company, and Rhodes immediately dispatched a representative, F. E. Lochner, to Barotseland. In 1890 this emissary concluded an agreement with Lewanika and his chiefs, the Lochner Concession, by which the company obtained mineral and commercial rights throughout Barotseland and adjacent suzerainties, in return for which Lewanika was to receive a subsidy of £2,000 a year.

This arrangement was conceived in misunderstanding. Lochner had implied that he represented the British government directly, whereas the protection for which Lewanika had contracted was provided only by the South Africa Company. Rhodes was interested in political control and commercial profit, but it soon became evident that there was no gold to be had in Barotse country, and interest in the area flagged. The company defaulted on its annual payments to Lewanika and did not send him an official resident until 1897, by which time he had long since repudiated the concession.

The arrival of the British resident, Major R. T. Coryndon, introduced a more active period of colonial administration, one that brought an end to Barotse sovereignty and a steady diminution of Lewanika's freedom of action. First of all, in 1898 and 1900, Coryndon renegotiated the old concession, adding the important provision that disputes involving whites would be judged by the British South Africa Company which also might make farming grants to Europeans in the suzerain territories outside Barotseland proper. A few years later a hut tax was imposed, to be collected by Lewanika but only as an agent of the administration, and to be shared by him in a formula imposed by Coryndon. In 1904, Lewanika was obliged to surrender jurisdiction over civil and criminal justice for Africans outside the Barotse reserve, at the same time also losing control over certain types of cases within his own domain. Finally, two further agreements, reached in 1906 and 1909, forced the king to concede all authority over the disposition of lands outside Barotse country proper. Thus, by the time of his death in 1916, Lewanika had been reduced to the level of a local chieftain, wielding limited powers in his own territory, and even there, his sovereignty resting, at least in British eyes, with the English queen, not with the Barotse king.

Nevertheless, when company rule was supplanted by a directly administered British protectorate for Northern Rhodesia in 1924, Barotseland identity had not been lost, and there were good reasons for this. In the first place, the Lozi vigorously challenged the legality of their various concessions, thereby at least forestalling further erosion of their authority. Secondly, the company was careful to preserve some semblance of a Barotse state for it did not wish to jeopardize the legality of the mineral rights obtained from Lewanika in the original Lochner Concession. Moreover, it was during the 1920s that Sir Frederick Lugard's doctrine of indirect rule was at the height of its influence in shaping British colonial policy. Finally, in Rhodesia, there was the conviction that encouragement of traditional authorities might neutralize any movement toward larger, potentially dangerous, intertribal racial cohesion.

Far to the east of Barotseland, events took a somewhat different turn, although imperial expansion was still at the heart of the matter. In the Lake Malawi (Nyasa) area, for example, a series of European interests converged. There were the Scottish missionaries who arrived in the 1870s and who were soon calling for a British consul as protection against quickening Portuguese designs in the region. There were the Portuguese, long interested in extending their influence inland from their coastal possessions and connecting with a land bridge their holdings in Angola and Mozambique. Finally, there were Leopold of Belgium, the Germans in East Africa, and the omnivorous Rhodes, all expressing a lively preoccupation with central Africa. In the Nyasa country, however, it was the British who finally established themselves, proclaiming a Nyasaland protectorate in 1891.

As usual Rhodes had a hand in these developments although the principal agent was Harry Johnston, appointed British consul to Mozambique in 1889. To forestall the Portuguese, Johnston and his deputy, Alfred Sharpe, secured a number of protection treaties over a broad area west of Lake Malawi and south of the Lake Tanganyika-Lake Mweru region. These pacts, along with additional treaties obtained concurrently by a representative of Rhodes's South Africa Company, assured British supremacy north of the Zambezi between Lewanika's domains and Lake Malawi, but Portugal did not accept defeat until forced to acquiesce in the face of a British ultimatum in 1890. The following year, a treaty delineated the present Mozambique frontier, excluding Portugal from the Shire highlands south of Lake Malawi where many of the Scottish missions were located. Prior to this, in 1890, an Anglo-German agreement had fixed the boundary with German East Africa, while, in 1894, the line of the Congo Independent State was established as it is today.

The Portuguese threat removed, there followed the problem of colonial administration. The South Africa Company agreed at first to finance the peace-keeping functions in Nyasaland of the African Lakes Company which had been organized originally as a commercial aid to the Scottish missions. Later this responsibility was given to Johnston, appointed commissioner in Nyasaland, and in 1891 a boundary was drawn west of Lake Malawi, roughly parallel with the axis of the lake. Thus, in deference to the missionary distrust of Rhodes, Nyasaland was placed under separate administration as a British protectorate, although Rhodes's company continued to finance its police-keeping functions. In 1895, however, Nyasaland was taken over completely by the British government, the company maintaining responsibility for the interior territory, now called Rhodesia. In 1899, a further division was made between Lewanika's domains, officially named North-Western Rhodesia, and the vast plateau of North-Eastern Rhodesia lying west of Nyasaland and south of Lake Tanganyika. A final adjustment followed a few years later, placing what was to become the copper belt within the North-Western zone.

The conflicting claims of colonial powers were not the only sources of contention within Nyasaland and North-Eastern Rhodesia. Harry Johnston, whose duties as commissioner included policing in both territories, used his South Africa Company subsidy to support a small army, primarily of Sikh soldiers, a force soon brought into play against local peoples unwilling to accept European domination. In the Yao country south and southeast of Lake Malawi, for example, a number of chieftains confounded Johnston's troops between 1891 and 1893, and were not finally subdued until 1895 with the defeat of Makanjira, the most successful of the Yao warrior chiefs. In the Shire country, there was a brief rising among the southern (Maseko) Ngoni in 1896, but resistance was light and easily suppressed. More difficult was the situation in North-Eastern Rhodesia, near the Nyasaland boundary. There the Ngoni of Mpezeni had been tricked into a fraudulent concession which opened up their country to white prospectors, brought deteriorating relations with the authorities, and ended in an outbreak in 1898 which was smashed by military action, the Ngoni herds being confiscated in penalty.

Others were more easily reconciled. The Tonga welcomed missionary assistance that brought an end to their long-standing victimization by the northern (Mombera) Ngoni. Again, the Bemba, with a reputation for war making and an active alliance with Arab slavers from the coast, might have been expected to offer Johnston formidable opposition. Instead, they submitted to British control, perhaps because of the decline of the Arab caravan trade, perhaps, in realization of growing European power.

The Arab slavers, intruders in their own right, were difficult to eliminate for they were well armed and tenacious adversaries. This was especially true of Mlozi, a Zanzibari trader, who established an armed village at the northern end of Lake Malawi during the 1880s, from which he dispatched slave caravans to the coast. Over the years, he withstood a number of efforts to dislodge him, but in 1895 Johnston besieged him with an overwhelming force, and he was defeated and executed.

Resistance to European domination also emerged from another, entirely different, quarter. As in South Africa and elsewhere, African dissatisfaction with the limitations of white rule found release in religious expression through the independent church movement. In Nyasaland, a series of African revivalist churches appeared at the beginning of the twentieth century, stimulated by fundamentalist missionary activity and critical of many of the features of colonialism. Taxation and forced labor on European plantations were sources of discontent which combined with pressure for land, and all became factors

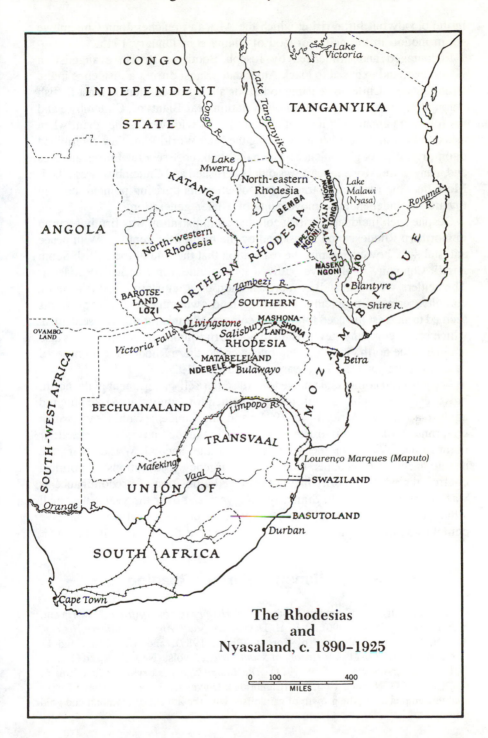

The Rhodesias
and
Nyasaland, c. 1890–1925

in the bloody but futile rising which the African preacher John Chilembwe set in motion in the neighborhood of Blantyre in January 1915.

Encouraged and influenced by Joseph Booth, a British evangelist in Nyasaland, and exposed to black American protest during a residence in the United States, Chilembwe came to harbor a deep resentment against British colonial practice. In his small mission station near Blantyre, Chilembwe and his followers apparently lost patience bit by bit with white rule; then, when asked to fight in the British army during the First World War, they determined upon protest through violence. Their outbreak cost several European lives and many more African, but it was quickly crushed and Chilembwe was killed. More than the reaction of traditional societies his uprising pointed the way toward the independence movements of a later generation.

Despite such incidents, British colonial administration was firmly secured in Northern Rhodesia and Nyasaland by the turn of the century. With peace and stability, however, came the realization that the rule of the British South Africa Company might have outlived its usefulness in Northern Rhodesia. The settlers were demanding representation on a legislative council, and a complex series of problems concerning land ownership and mineral rights seemed to suggest the need for a direct colonial administration. The settlement which ended company stewardship in Southern Rhodesia, therefore, was also applied to the north, and a protectorate over Northern Rhodesia, administered as a single unit since 1911, was established in 1924.

There was no comparable move toward settler self-government in the north, however. The number of Europeans remained low, only thirty-five hundred against a million Africans in 1921, and the concept within the British government of colonial trusteeship put a brake on moves toward settler domination. When, in the years prior to the Second World War, the development of the copper industry lent urgency to questions of political control, the white minority had not achieved a position of predominance as was the case in the south. Similarly, in Nyasaland over the years, the small white population gained no important political privileges which might have complicated the African independence movement that eventually emerged.

Suggestions for Further Reading

For South Africa see Leonard Thompson, *A History of South Africa* (New Haven: Yale University Press, 1990); T. R. H. Davenport, *South Africa: A Modern History*, 3rd ed. (Toronto: University of Toronto Press, 1987); and M. Wilson and L. Thompson, eds., *The Oxford History of South Africa*, 2 vols, (New York and Oxford: Oxford University Press, 1969, 1971). *The Cambridge History of Africa*, Vol. 6, R. Oliver and G. N. Sanderson, eds. (Cambridge: University Press, 1985) has effective chapters emphasizing the growth of capitalism with the advent of diamond and gold mining.

For the Union of South Africa, L. M. Thompson, *The Unification of South Africa, 1902-1970* (Oxford: Clarendon, 1960), is definitive. Some information on early African nationalism in South Africa is available in Thomas Hodgkin, *Nationalism in Colonial Africa* (New York: New York University Press, 1957; London: F. Muller, 1956); B. G. M. Sundkler, *Bantu Prophets in South Africa*, 2nd ed. (London: Oxford University Press, 1961); and Peter Walshe, *The Rise of African Nationalism in South Africa* (London: Hurst, 1970; Berkeley: University of California Press, 1971). The story of the Zulu nation is set forth in D. R. Morris, *The Washing of the Spears* (New York: Simon & Schuster, 1965); while the fortunes of other African societies may be followed in J. D. Omer-Cooper, *The Zulu Aftermath* (London: Longmans; Evanston: Northwestern University Press, 1966). The most recent study of Cecil Rhodes is R. I. Rotberg's *The Founder: Cecil Rhodes and The Pursuit of Power* (New York: Oxford University Press, 1988).

For the Central Africa of the Rhodesias and Nyasaland see *The Cambridge History of Africa*, Vol. 6 already cited as well as relevant chapters in David Birmingham and P. M. Martin, eds., *History of Central Africa*, Vol. II (New York: Longman, 1983), the latter stressing capitalist exploitation of African land and labor from a Marxist point of view. Other histories include the lively Philip Mason, *The Birth of a Dilemma* (London: Oxford University Press, 1958); T. O. Ranger, ed., *Aspects of Central African History* (Evanston: Northwestern University Press, 1968); and *The Zambesian Past* edited by E. Stokes and R. Brown (Manchester: Manchester University Press, 1966; New York: Humanities, 1966). For John Chilembwe, see G. Shepperson and T. Price, *Independent African* (Edinburgh: The University Press, 1958; Chicago: Aldine, 1958).

17

Colonialism and Nation Making in East Africa

The Logic of European Imperialism

The partition of Africa was set in motion by forces largely outside Africa's experience. National rivalries within Europe, a rising international commercial competition, the exigencies of geopolitical strategy, the aspirations and conceits of Western leaders, even the exertions of European proconsuls, adventurers, and clergy in Africa, all placed their imprint on the African land—here staking German claims, there intruding French interests, urging the rights of Britain, the sovereignty of Portugal, or the pretensions of Leopold of Belgium. For a time, the fate of the Nile highway passed from African into European hands, the Islamic way in the western Sudan was forced to accommodate Gallic and Anglo-Saxon Christian controls, while the vast Congo watershed faced the alien demands of a Belgian royal administrator.

If European occupation of Africa was largely unrelated to African circumstances, occupation nonetheless implied control, and control in turn demanded some form of government—an administration that would deal with alien peoples in ways that not only satisfied imperial strategies, but also sought to reconcile African and European views of the respective roles of ruler and ruled. Here there was little uniformity of governmental pattern. Colonial theory and practice varied enormously from power to power, but no more so than the African societies on which colonialism was imposed. The range of these societies extended from simple hunter-gatherers to sophisticates thoroughly at home with European culture, from those who regarded the West as the key to progress in Africa to others who looked upon the colonial presence as meaningless and irrelevant to their way of life.

Nevertheless, some uniformities were discernible. First of all, there was the attitude of the European government seeking maximum control with minimum expense, tending to support the status quo, smiling on entrenched African oligarchies, and indifferent to costly and politically dangerous social reform. Secondly, as external power was extended across the African map, the diversity of indigenous societies was forced into unique conformities, artificial and arbitrary in their initial conceptions, to be sure, but the beginnings of the African nation-states which were to achieve national independence in the mid-twentieth century. Thus was modern Africa conceived, shaped in the uneasy union of two alien civilizations.

British Paternalism in Uganda

During the final decades of the nineteenth century, a number of factors combined to bring about extensive changes in Buganda, the nation that was to provide the foundation for the British protectorate of Uganda. First, there was the sense of skepticism, opportunism, and innovation which had long marked the national character of Buganda, particularly among the nobility of the kabaka's court. Next was an expanding international commerce introduced by coastal Arabs who brought in their baggage not only Western firearms but also the Islamic faith. Beyond this was a more direct and immediate European influence represented by Protestant and Catholic clergy — missionaries who arrived respectively in 1877 and 1879, their object Christian conversion, but their effect Baganda parochialism and religious civil war. Finally, there were the imperial rivalries of Europe which led to the partition of Africa and the establishment in the Great Lakes region of a British protectorate over Uganda, agreed to by Germany and Britain in 1890 and formally instituted by Whitehall four years later.

The intellectual curiosity afoot in Baganda society and the concurrent weakness of Buganda's traditional religion made for easy conversion to new faiths, particularly among the lively, ambitious youth at court. Parties of adherents, Muslim, Catholic, and Protestant, quickly emerged among the young courtiers, already in a powerful position as special riflemen in Mutesa's armed forces. When the kabaka died and was succeeded in 1884 by his vicious and vacillating son, Mwanga, a potentially unstable situation disintegrated into open civil war, brought on by Mwanga's treacherous and maladroit statesmanship and encouraged by the ill-advised sectarianism of the missionaries.

In 1890 further complications developed when Captain Frederick Lugard, later to serve as colonial governor in Nigeria, arrived in Buganda representing the Imperial British East Africa Company which in turn embodied British interests in the area. There followed an involved series of military engagements and diplomatic thrusts which established British suzerainty while greatly reducing Mwanga's authority in relation to the Christian chiefs, especially those led by Apolo Kagwa, the *katikiro*, or first royal minister. When the British East Africa Company was dissolved and a British protectorate proclaimed over Buganda in 1894, Kagwa and his party acquiesced after some hesitation, riding with the British against the forces of Mwanga who was finally captured and exiled in 1899.

Throughout these developments, the kabaka had steadily lost authority to the religious factions among his followers, so that by the time of Mwanga's overthrow, Buganda was in fact a limited monarchy governed by an aristocratic oligarchy. At the same time the chiefs were admittedly dependent upon the British; hence, when Mwanga's departure removed the last opponent of the status quo, a long period of relative political stability ensued. Suddenly, the dynamism of Baganda society was replaced by an inertness which reflected both the general contentment of the Baganda nobility and the disinclination of a new colonial administration toward change.

The mutual objectives of both the Baganda chief and the British administrator were embodied in the Buganda Agreement of 1900. In the first place, the Baganda undertook to collect and pay taxes to the colonial administration, thus acknowledging the sovereignty of the British crown. In return for this, the traditional ruling hierarchy was retained complete with kabaka, *lukiko*, or legislature, katikiro, and other chiefly offices, all with full government functions but always subject to the ultimate authority of Britain. Finally, Special Commissioner Harry Johnston, who negotiated the agreement with the Baganda chiefs, instituted a revolutionary system of land tenure whereby all land was divided, half for the crown and half for some four thousand chiefs, the chiefly portion henceforward to be maintained on the basis of individual private ownership. If the peasants did not resist this development, it indicated that they gradually were able to transform their farm tenancy into quasi-freehold tenure. The chiefly aristocracy naturally regarded the Agreement with the deepest satisfaction.

During the half-century up to the conclusion of the Second World War, therefore, Buganda was administered by a cluster of British officials headed by the governor and superimposed upon an African chiefly hierarchy. The indigenous authorities were present in the person of the kabaka and his regional administrative chiefs called *bakungu*, in the lukiko, and the katikiro. To this the British added a series of minor district chiefs while broadening the functions of the lukiko chiefly council to include judicial and parliamentary responsibilities. The colonial administration laid down general policy but the details of government were left in the hands of the Baganda chiefs, and indeed the Baganda regarded the Agreement of 1900 as something like a treaty between sovereign states and managed over the years to maintain a show of autonomy although conceding ultimate authority to their British protectors. What emerged, therefore, was a system akin to what later was called indirect rule during Lugard's days in Nigeria, a system, however, not without friction, sometimes between Baganda and British, sometimes reflecting political stress among the Baganda themselves. Nonetheless by and large, the chiefs remained secure in their dual role as rulers and as hereditary landed gentry. Thus when Buganda took her first steps toward modernization, they were made through the agency of traditional institutions, not through a new way of life, through acknowledged leaders like Apolo Kagwa, not through an educated elite divorced from the chiefs.

The Buganda government by hereditary ruler and appointed chief was extended without substantial alteration to the other territories which were successively occupied by force of arms against strenuous but futile resistance to form the Uganda Protectorate. In such traditional kingdoms as Bunyoro, Toro, and Ankole, the new system fitted reasonably well, following the Buganda example. Among the smaller principalities of Busoga and the even less politically cohesive Gisu, Teso, Lango, Acholi, and others, adaptation to a strange political configuration came less easily, but in all cases the Buganda model was finally established, often with the assistance of Baganda agents who acted in some cases as surrogate rulers, in others as advisers to the locally appointed chiefs. By the time of the First World War, a complete Baganda-style colonial administration had been substantially achieved in Uganda, a series of mutually exclusive African governments responsible only to the British protectorate authority at the apex. Few larger attachments thus emerged to compete with local loyalties, the Baganda proving particularly jealous of their sense of identity and prerogatives. Such parochialism was to prove a serious impediment to national cohesion during the trials of nation making that were to come with independence.

Furthest advanced politically, Buganda also took the lead in the modest economic development that occurred during the years of British rule. Colonial policy, formulated as usual in terms of economy and local self-sufficiency, encouraged the emergence of a tax-paying peasantry, while prohibitive transportation costs, an unpromising world market, and a discouraging official attitude eliminated the possibility of European settlers and a plantation economy. Prodded by an administration in search of viable exports, the African farmer, though long accustomed to providing only for his own immediate needs, began to experiment with cash crop production. Led by Baganda peasants whose land purchases over the years gradually expanded the original four thousand freeholds of the 1900 agreement to over fifty thousand, Uganda agriculture began to grow cotton commercially which quickly proved to be an outstanding success. From a mere £1,000 in 1905-1906, cotton exports jumped in value to £369,000 in 1914-1915, stimulating total exports to a virtual sixfold increase over the same period.

Nevertheless, this early promise was not sustained. Other crops offered less prospect than cotton, and the few cash crops that were developed involved a relatively small number of producers. Transportation costs continued to

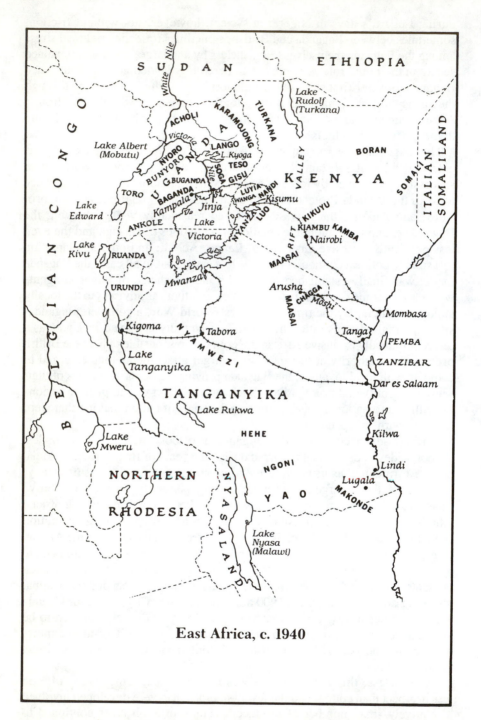

East Africa, c. 1940

impose severe limitations despite the increased activities of traders. Chiefs and landlords levied prohibitive requisitions on their tenants, while essentially the economy remained that of a subsistence peasant society. Not until the years after the Second World War would expanding revenue and a colonial policy devoted to development and welfare bring about basic changes in the traditional pattern of leisurely rural poverty.

Kenya—Racialism in a Colonial Society

As a colonial possession, Kenya offered few initial attractions, even to British imperialists of the Victorian Age. The main prize lay far inland where the Great Lakes held the strategic headwaters of the Nile, and the sophisticated Baganda offered the prospect of a fruitful partnership in colonial management.

The British East Africa Protectorate which was proclaimed in 1895 was regarded largely as a vast wilderness, inhabited by wild beasts and primitive peoples, which had to be traversed to reach the more consequential interior. The coastal strip above and below Mombasa was nominally under Zanzibar's suzerainty and coveted by her sultan, but it was also claimed by the Mazrui who, during 1895-1896, raised a brief but vexing rebellion that had to be put down by force. Inland for hundreds of miles were stretches of plains and hills, woodland and scrub, which Maasai, Kamba, Kikuyu, and others contested with the great game herds and with each other. The Maasai, in particular, seemed to have a penchant for civil strife, and all nations appeared to the British to lack even the rudiments of political organization. At the close of the nineteenth century, African energies were further eroded by famine and dulled by disease—precious cattle melting away before the dreaded rinderpest, crops devoured by locusts, and populations decimated by smallpox. This was country to be traversed, not occupied.

Yet to traverse was to occupy. Buganda and her neighbors had to be reached first by road and then by railway, and to keep these lines open and protected required "pacification," either by diplomatic agreement, as with the Maasai, or by force, as imposed upon the Nandi who were subdued in a series of difficult campaigns between 1895 and 1905. A number of fortified posts were gradually established which were linked together in 1901 when the railroad from Mombasa reached Lake Victoria, thus providing a framework for the extension of British authority throughout the vast expanse of the East Africa Protectorate. Portentously, the railway also led directly to the increase in population of European and Asian settlers destined to play major roles in the future Kenya Colony.

The Asians came up the rail line as traders, an extension of the ancient Indian mercantile connection with East Africa. The Europeans, for their part, were actively solicited by the government with the objective of developing the country through which the railroad ran, thus offsetting the costs of administration and public works. They came in various sorts — impecunious adventurers seeking a new stake in life, land-poor gentry from Britain, retired soldiers on pension, and Boers dissatisfied with conditions in South Africa — and they settled themselves on lands that careful and skillful British diplomacy had persuaded the Maasai to vacate, the so-called White Highlands stretching north and west from Nairobi along the line of the Rift Valley. Most lacked sufficient capital, and in any case, the initial tracts granted were too small for profitable farming. There were not many who could afford to wait the long years until coffee or sisal plantations began to yield profit, and few could engage in the extensive wheat and livestock production which characterized the handful of large holders like Lord Delamere.

There were additional complications. Even where European truck farming could be managed, it was undersold by African producers; beyond this, Europeans were not expected to engage in competition with native Africans nor to perform manual labor. Custom dictated, therefore, that farmers employ black workers, even if few could afford to pay wages attractive enough to entice the peasant from his familiar way of life. Similarly, custom forbade escape into small-scale commerce or a craft labor which were the province of the Asians and therefore considered socially demeaning.

The white settlers began arriving in numbers as the twentieth century opened, and in the years that followed, slowly and with difficulty, they began to make profit from their farming. Trial and error eliminated cotton, flax, and rubber culture, pointed up the viability of coffee and sisal, and discovered the value of maize. Because periodic depressions and the vagaries of world commodity markets presented their problems, gradually the small entrepreneurs were eliminated and land consolidated into larger, more economical units. In 1923 the authorities inaugurated a protective tariff which effectively subsidized cattle, dairy, and wheat producers, providing them with a local market, the expense of subsidy being passed on to the rest of the community in the form of higher prices.

Over the years, the settlers pressed the administration unceasingly for privileges they felt were theirs by right of position and talent, their demands developing a particular urgency regarding the question of labor. While London vacillated, various devices were introduced through the Protectorate government, as in South and Central Africa, the net effect of which was to lead or drive the African into the labor market.

In 1901 and on subsequent occasions head taxes were imposed, mainly to create a class of taxable, wage-earning African workers. It was not long, however, before this indirect compulsion had been supplemented by an informal system of labor conscription, both for public and private use. In time the Kikuyu, on the edge of the White Highlands, began volunteering their labor in return for grazing and cropping rights on European lands, but government action continued to tighten the bonds of coercion. In 1915 the Natives Registration Ordinance undertook to control labor movement in the interests of recruitment, and subsequent official interpretation of the law became tantamount to direct compulsion. Three years later the Resident Natives Ordinance decreed that only essentially full-time agricultural laborers might remain on European held land, thus ruling out any possibility of an African tenant or peasant proprietor class.

Finally, economic pressures were also exerted. Beginning in the 1920s, for example, African coffee culture was virtually forbidden, the chief reason being settler fear that agricultural prosperity among the Africans would force up the price of labor to prohibitive levels. The implications of these measures reached far beyond their immediate economic objectives. They helped set a pattern of two societies, segregated economically and socially, the one resting on the privilege of race and status supported by official fiat, the other locked in a position of inferiority and made to subserve the interests of the first.

The widespread view within the British government, which had originally encouraged white settlement and had envisioned a sturdy Anglo-Saxon yeomanry breathing life into a rich but unexploited land, was thus obliged to give way to the realities of racial discrimination. As in South Africa, a society arose dominated by a white minority that maintained its privileged position through manipulation of the machinery of government. By and large settler exploitation of the African was resisted by the home government sensitive to humanitarian pressures in Britain, but administrators in Kenya were more susceptible to settler demands, yielding to persistence or their own prejudices. Over the years favorable economic decrees were complemented by other official acts on behalf of the settlers, for example, in 1906 the introduction of a constitution and legislative council with unofficial settler representation, in 1907 the establishment of the protectorate capital at the former railway staging area and settler stronghold of Nairobi, and in 1908 the institution of an informal policy prohibiting the White Highlands area to Asian settlement.

This last reflected a European settler attitude toward the Indian community as inflexible as that facing the African. Although there were chronic divisions among the settlers, they always presented a united front on racial issues and were implacable in their hostility toward the Asians, especially during the years following the First World War. They themselves received elected representation in the legislative council in 1920 as the East Africa Protectorate became the Kenya Colony, but in the face of similar demands on behalf of the Indians, the European view was simply that Asians might be represented by the official membership on the council, or, alternatively, by a specially appointed European. During the early twenties, the Indians pressed their demands while the settlers sought to dominate official policy. In 1923 a compromise British Government White Paper was issued which satisfied neither side. The Indians gained five council seats but were denied inclusion on a common voting roll; furthermore they could not obtain relaxation of the policy restricting non-European landholding in the White Highlands. For their part, the settlers lost the monopoly of the franchise they had previously held, at the same time being rebuffed in their bid to have Kenya declared a self-governing colony on the Southern Rhodesian model.

These disappointing developments defined the highest point of settler influence which was further checked when the White Paper went out of its way to declare Britain's primary responsibility for Kenya's 2.5 million Africans, not to be forgotten in the face of the articulate and self-serving exertions of ten thousand Europeans and twenty-three thousand Asians. In 1924, the appointment of a European missionary gave the Africans a special representative on both the legislative and executive councils, and five years later African precedence was once again officially pronounced in a report which urged a common voting role, equal franchise, and no racial discrimination.

That same year, 1929, the Labourites returned to power in Britain and soon made known their position on colonial matters in East Africa—rigorous protection of African land rights, an increase of African representation on the legislative council, and eventual responsible government only when all sections of the population were assured adequate representation. In 1931 a special committee of the two houses of Parliament in effect killed any lingering hope for local self-government under settler control, and a few years later European special privilege was further undermined by an income tax designed to redress what was officially regarded as an inequitable tax burden borne by the African population. If the outbreak of the Second World War in 1939 put a temporary end to politics, war's end and ensuing African political pressures also brought the realization that Kenya with its tiny European population would never follow the Rhodesian example, never fulfill that long-nourished settler aspiration, "white man's country."

Kenya—Alien Rule and African Response

If an early objective of British colonial administrators was the introduction of a white-settler community, their philosophy of government was necessarily committed, consciously or unconsciously, to the idea of settler dominance with both African and Asian playing subordinate roles. Such a view could scarcely have raised humanitarian scruples in the minds of the first Protectorate officials as they compared their European skills and institutions with the apparently backward societies surrounding their early outposts. Unlike the people of the Great Lakes area, the Kenyan Africans appeared in the eyes of colonial administrators to possess little political sophistication and, indeed, most national groups (Mumia's small state of Wanga [Hanga] excepted) were organized primarily on kinship relations. This was as true of the Nilotic Luo and Bantu Luyia dwelling east and north of Lake Victoria as it was of the pastoral Nilotes, Maasai and Nandi herders of the Rift Valley region. It applied equally to seminomadic Boran and Somali cattle keepers roaming the arid stretches toward the Ethiopian and Somali frontiers, to those Nilotic Turkana west of the waters of Lake Rudolf, or to the Kikuyu and Kamba farmers of the central Kenya plateau.

So-called statelessness did not greatly confound the authorities, however. Within the first decade, military expeditions had brought large areas under control, and the threat of force extended the British fiat much farther still. Once peace had been secured, a profound ecological revolution ensued as embattled communities spread out of their fortress villages, hill dwellers were converted into plains dwellers, and the voice of arbitration replaced strength of arms as a means of settling disputes. Moreover, the early rustication of the Maasai in special reserves soon opened to cultivation by other African peoples, land previously regarded as too dangerous for occupation.

Conquest and occupation nevertheless proved simpler than ongoing administration. Imposition of law and order, collection of taxes, introduction of public improvements, and recruitment of labor all required a hierarchy of officials in societies where none had existed traditionally and where appointed bureaucrats were politically meaningless and personally irritating. Only the sanction of British authority backed by the presence of district officers gradually gave a degree of legitimacy to the administration-selected chiefs who continued to be an alien, albeit increasingly efficient, institution.

In one respect in particular, the matter of land policy, the Africans of Kenya never became reconciled to British rule. Their suspicions ever roused in defense of deep-seated attachment to the life-giving soil, they reacted as much to the potentiality as to the actuality of land alienation; fear of loss was at the bottom of much of their persistent sense of insecurity and injustice. Many groups were only lightly affected (those in the Kavirondo or Nyanza area, for example) but others had much more substantial grievances. The Maasai became thoroughly disillusioned with their relegation to inadequate reserves, an experience that explains much of their apparent indifference to modernization and their retreat into xenophobic tribalism. In particular, the Kikuyu, closely attached to the land and with serious population pressures, suffered from both real and imagined alienation.

The Kikuyu system of landholding was based upon the *githaka*, an assemblage of land, not necessarily contiguous, owned by a subclan or small lineage called *mbari*. Traditionally each mbari member was entitled to a portion of his clan's githaka, thus providing him with both economic support and secure personal position within his section of the Kikuyu nation. Since the whole of Kikuyu society was built upon the mbari system, loss of githaka was more than an economic disaster; it involved the very identity of individual or group, therefore ultimately the coherence and cohesion of the Kikuyu people. As it happened, Kikuyu territories lay adjacent to the White Highlands; consequently, many misunderstandings concerning ownership and occupancy arose over the years. To the European settler, loss of one piece of land could be compensated for by another or by cash payment, if indeed he felt its ownership could be demonstrated at all. To the Kikuyu, however, githaka provided social and psychological security along with economic support; land alienation, therefore, came to be an abiding source of Kikuyu discontent right down to the days of the Mau Mau upheaval.

Beginning about 1930, Kikuyu resentment over loss of githaka was further heightened when the long-lived custom of tenancy on white settler lands was curtailed in the interest of more efficient scientific husbandry. This action added the pressure of new numbers to ancestral Kikuyu territory, already filling up through population increase, and focused dissatisfaction on yet another aspect of government land policy, the system of tribal reserves, which had long troubled Africans.

The Maasai at an early date had been placed on reserves while Nandi and Kikuyu reserves were established before 1909, but most nations obtained no such guarantee. Moreover, the Crown Lands Ordinance of 1915 defined all land occupied and utilized by Africans as crown land, and empowered the governor to sell portions of reserves if he felt they were no longer needed. Such legislation contributed no little to the widespread insecurity which, however, was somewhat alleviated in 1926 when reserves were proclaimed for all people throughout the country, and in 1934 when the Carter Land Commission recommended important extensions to lands already held in reserve.

Unfortunately, the strengthening of the reserves also stiffened lines of racial segregation, while ignoring the growing problems of urbanization manifest in centers like Mombasa and Nairobi. During the 1930s these towns began to attract numbers of uprooted, unskilled Africans, poised uneasily between their traditional mode of life and a novel but insecure existence. Here then was a paradox of policy. Just as the separateness of white and black was being further defined by official decree, the two worlds of Africa and Europe were in fact being thrown together in a new and complex relationship.

Kenya—The Onset of African Political and Social Aspirations

During the half-century concluding with the Second World War, colonial occupation brought extensive change to Kenya—a changing economy and a changing society—not all of which was welcome and little of which occurred without some measure of response from the African people. Slowly a wage-earning money economy took hold, forced by the taxation and labor policies of the government and urged by a growing taste for European consumer goods. Accompanying this was a new individualism, fostered in part by missionary training, competing with traditional authority, and developing new sources of personal wealth and extratribal power along with a growing attraction toward middle-class, Westernized social standards. To long-standing resentment over land were therefore added further misgivings concerning latter-day official policy seemingly designed to obstruct African advance toward economic sufficiency, toward educational opportunity, and toward a share in the standard of living introduced by the European.

As ever, social resentment found political expression. The earliest manifestations of political unrest took place within the traditional societies where young men, emancipated through education and escaping to the town or the European farm, began to take exception as early as 1912 to outmoded customary authorities or to chiefs owing their power to the European administration. The issues were various but one recurrent theme, at least among the Kikuyu, was the perennial question of land alienation. Between 1903 and 1906, during the initial wave of settlement in the White Highlands, large tracts had been appropriated, particularly in the Kiambu district to the north of Nairobi, for which compensation was trifling or completely lacking, and where Africans were forced to become squatters on land they continued to regard as their own.

During the 1920s a number of protest organizations emerged, most of them founded by politically self-conscious Kikuyu. Although these groups enunciated specific grievances concerning such matters as land alienation, taxes, or labor policy, there was implicit in their protest a deeper sense of outrage over the basic implication of all official measures, namely that the African was a second-class human suitable only for exploitation. The first of these organizations to appear was the most moderate, however—the Kikuyu Association founded about 1920 by Kiambu farmers intent upon blocking any further alienation of their lands, but willing to work toward reform within the existing colonial structure.

Such sweet reasonableness was not for everyone. In Nairobi young clerks and domestics of various tribal origins came together in 1921 to form the East African Association under the Kikuyu leadership of such individuals as Jesse Kariuki and Harry Thuku. Thuku, literate and member of an influential Kikuyu family, held a clerkship in the Treasury, using his prestigious position to move into the front rank of those intent on challenging European authority. In 1921 he also founded the Young Kikuyu Association, apparently a temporary outgrowth of the East African Association, and the following year another Kikuyu, James Beauttah, was instrumental in the appearance of the Young Kavirondo Association in Nyanza, its membership made up of youthful educated Luo and Luyia. These organizations were uniform in rejecting the premise of white rule, basing themselves on the principle of political change. They attacked labor policy, the head tax, and land alienation, and were particularly opposed to the despised *kipande*, an identification card required of all Africans.

Thuku's militant program began to gain a following outside Nairobi, thereby insuring official concern and an early end for his movement. In 1922 he was arrested, this step leading directly to a protest rally that ended tragically when police fire killed over twenty members of the greatly excited crowd. On that note of violence the East African Association quickly collapsed, but in Nyanza, the Kavirondo Association experienced a somewhat different fate. Its initial political character was altered by missionaries who by 1923 had diverted its energies into welfare work, while political activities in the Kavirondo area tended increasingly over the years to degenerate into an unproductive intertribal rivalry irrelevant to any effective opposition against the inequities of colonial rule.

These were but temporary setbacks, at least in Kikuyuland. With Thuku in prison, leadership fell on others including Beauttah and Joseph Kangethe who helped found the Kikuyu Central Association (KCA) in 1924 which listed among its several demands the release of Thuku, still the spiritual head of the protest movement. Gradually the KCA gathered adherents, particularly among the younger generation, and within a few years of its appearance it was admittedly speaking authoritatively for the Kikuyu people as a whole.

Among its early recruits was Jomo Kenyatta who became general secretary of the association in 1928, as well as editor of its monthly journal, but Kenyatta was soon dispatched to London to present the grievances of his group directly to the British government. As Kenyatta later testified, these grievances centered on questions of education, of legislative council representation, and particularly of land ownership. "If you woke up one morning," said Kenyatta, "and found that somebody had come to your house, and had declared that house belonged to him, you would naturally be surprised, and you would like to know by what arrangement. Many Africans at that time," he continued, "found that, on land which had been in the possession of their ancestors from time immemorial, they were now working as squatters or as labourers."

Kenyatta remained almost continually in Europe until 1946, acting as KCA representative in Britain and for a time pursuing postgraduate study at the London School of Economics. Thus, he avoided the crisis of leadership which threatened to destroy the KCA movement in the 1930s. The schism developed with Harry Thuku's release in 1931, his by then moderate views appearing to disqualify him for KCA membership, at least in the eyes of Jesse Kariuki, the association's vice-president, and other activists. Thuku left to found the progovernment Kikuyu Provincial Association in 1935 but the KCA survived the split and by 1940 was the most powerful and widely influential organization in Kikuyuland as well as the most radical. With the commencement of the Second World War it was proscribed and its leaders arrested, their release not coming until the closing years of the war.

In 1929, shortly before the outbreak of dissension within the KCA, Kikuyu society, slowly evolving before the pressure of Western ideas and institutions, was caught up in a crisis over the traditional custom of female circumcision. Attacked by the missionaries, the practice was held as an essential of Kikuyu culture, and the missionary censure was therefore widely interpreted as an effort to undermine that culture and gain further alienation of Kikuyu land.

Freetown, Sierra Leone, 1856

Saint-Louis in 1865

Cape Coast c. 1890

Edward W. Blyden

Samuel Lewis

Rev. James Johnson

John Mensah Sarbah

Mutesa I and his court

Brown Brothers

Nana Ofori Atta

UPI/Bettmann

Henry Carr

J. E. Casely Hayford

Lamine Guèye

COLONIE DU SENEGAL

ELECTIONS LEGISLATIVES DU 1er MAI 1932

PARTI RÉPUBLICAIN SOCIALISTE

Blaise DIAGNE, Député sortant, Candidat

PROFESSION DE FOI

ELECTEURS du SENEGAL

Pour la cinquième fois, je viens demander au collège électoral le renouvellement de mon mandat à la Chambre des Députés. Depuis dix-huit ans que vous m'avez fait confiance, j'ai, non seulement défendu avec succès vos intérêts généraux et particuliers, mais encore étendu et élargi mon mandat au profit de toute la Fédération de l'Afrique Occidentale Française. La communauté d'intérêts qui lie toutes les Colonies du Groupe oblige d'ailleurs votre mandataire à une conception d'autorité qui prend sa source dans le principe même de la Représentation Nationale. Au surplus et par là même, Député du Sénégal, et parce que tel, je l'ai été totalement pour tout

vaux pour fins d'utilité publique, et non le travail des indigènes au profit des particuliers, qui reste toujours libre parce que soumis à la seule loi des parties intéressées.

Sous-Secrétaire d'Etat dans dans les deux Ministères LAVAL pendant plus de treize mois, je me suis appliqué à défendre et à servir les intérêts généraux de nos colonies en général, et en particulier le Sénégal.

La grande Exposition Internationale Coloniale de Vincennes, vit ce spectacle grandiose d'une plus grande France symbolisant par un Ministre des Colonies européen et un Sous-Secrétaire d'Etat noir fraternisant dans une collaboration d'intime

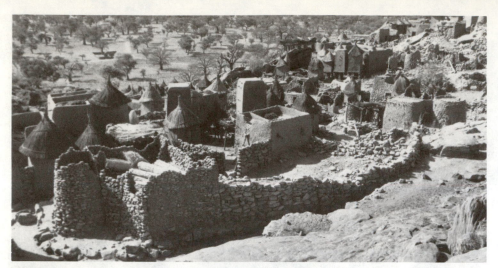

Dogon Village

Marketplace, Western Sudan

The great majority of people rallied in support of tradition and were led in this respect by the Kikuyu Central Association. The net result of the controversy was a temporary breaking away from the churches, but a permanent estrangement also arose between the missions and the schools, many of which thereafter came under the sponsorship of independent Kikuyu associations. Thus Kikuyu grievances against colonial rule found focus and release in the circumcision issue and the rise of African-controlled schools. The movement also served the postwar rise of Jomo Kenyatta who used the Kenya Teacher Training College, founded in 1939 in support of the independent schools, as a channel for the spread of his political influence.

By the outbreak of the Second World War, therefore, at least among the Kikuyu of Kenya, were to be found indications of the shape of things to come. Already evident were the lines of defense on behalf of tradition and the patterns of resistance against alien rule. What was also present, if less noticed, were the intertribal tensions which would eventually complicate the process of nation making.

The Tanganyikan Colony and Mandate

Having gained a colonial empire in Africa as the by-product of Bismarck's powerful diplomacy, Germany undertook to administer her African holdings primarily as suppliers of raw materials for the German economy. In Togo and Cameroun the objects were ivory and palm products, and then cultivated crops such as coffee, cocoa, cotton, and rubber. Similarly, German East Africa was soon engaged in agricultural development—coffee, copra, and groundnuts, to which cotton and sisal were subsequently added.

To extract these products and govern their newly won territories, the Germans were at first guided by a policy of expediency which relied heavily on arbitrary, coercive methods of labor recruitment, but the completeness of colonial control was nonetheless compromised by a paucity of administrators and limited funds. Lack of personnel led to a system of indirect rule through local chiefs with whom treaties were signed wherever possible. In areas of former Arab influence, their officials, or *akidas*, were retained, each exercising a degree of authority over several villages, often in concert with local chiefs or *jumbes*. If African governments appeared inconvenient, however, they were quickly reordered to different specifications, and always the ultimate authority was the German district officer. These officials were sometimes guilty of ruthless enforcement of the hut tax imposed first in 1897, a line of conduct that added fresh unrest to the chronic outbreaks of violence that had greeted German rule from its inception.

In 1888 the initial colonial government, the German East African Company, was challenged by an outbreak among coastal Arabs fearing the end of their traffic in slaves, and when direct administration by the Imperial German government was instituted in 1890, there was other opposition to command attention. The Hehe maintained a determined resistance for a half-dozen years after their initial annihilation in 1891 of a "punitive" expedition; in the Kilwa area Hasan bin Omari led a revolt during 1894-1895, while military action was required in 1893 to subdue the Chagga as well as the Nyamwezi chief Siki. The Makonde of Lugala, followers of the Yao leader Machemba, held off the Germans until 1899, and the Ngoni living back of Lindi had to be visited by a military force in 1897.

In 1901 more flexible government policy was introduced. For example, an attempt was made to collect taxes by nonviolent means; nonetheless, while this shift seemed at first to bring results, there was a fresh outbreak in the south in 1905 which quickly developed into a major rebellion. The initial manifestations of unrest in the Kilwa district seemed related to forced labor and the harsh methods employed by akidas in carrying out their duties. More particularly, there was objection to a government experimental program in cotton culture which the African farmer regarded as inequitable, uneconomic, and damaging to subsistence food production. When the movement received religious sanction in the form of a special water, or *maji*, given each fighter, supposedly rendering him immune to gunfire, there developed a unity among diverse people, a fanaticism in battle, and a sense of commitment which quickly spread the Maji Maji Rebellion far beyond its original nucleus. Such circumstances joined with German unpreparedness to sustain the conflict during a two-year period before it was finally extinguished in 1907, and then only through scorched-earth tactics which supplemented military action in subduing the insurgent forces with heavy casualties. It was estimated that at least seventy thousand Africans perished, many of disease and malnutrition.

By the end of the Maji Maji uprising, therefore, German administration in East Africa had been forced to conduct fully twenty years of warfare to achieve peace through African submission to colonial rule. There was a more positive side to the occupation, however. Despite limited resources, a number of public improvements were soon introduced—harbor development, bridge and road construction, and the establishment of institutions for scientific research. Some attempts were made to assist African agricultural production, while missionaries brought the beginnings of elementary educational instruction.

In 1907, a more liberal regime softened the harsher aspect of the earlier administration and concentrated on reform and economic expansion. Missionary schools were encouraged, public health services and further agricultural research inaugurated, while the arbitrary corporal punishment of Africans practiced in former times gave way to formalized judicial procedures. The development of settler plantations devoted to rubber, sisal, coffee, and cotton was assisted through special government institutes, pricing schemes, and improved communications. By 1914, a railroad line had been completed from the coast to Kigoma on Lake Tanganyika and another to the coffee districts located around Moshi. The settler community, steadily growing in importance, gained much from these improvements, but so too did African farmers, for they came in time to dominate the production of coffee, copra, and groundnuts. Hence, by the eve of the First World War, German administration had overcome many of its former limitations and converted an unsettled land, plagued by slaving and chronic warfare, to a peaceful colony with an expanding economy.

If latter-day German administration was enlightened as well as paternalistic, paternalism also characterized the period of international trusteeship that emerged from the Peace of Versailles under the mandate of the League of Nations. Most of the former German East African colony was placed under British responsibility and renamed Tanganyika while the tiny but heavily populated Hima-Tutsi kingdoms of Rwanda and Burundi became the Belgian mandate of Ruanda-Urundi. In Tanganyika, the new administration was at once characterized by a sense of commitment to protect colonial charges against exploitation while preparing them for eventual self-government. Laudable as was this attitude, it nevertheless tended to engender cautious, conservative trusteeship, and indeed during the immediate postwar period little was done in the Tanganyika mandate to fashion a new world in place of the dislocated society and ravaged land resulting from four years of hard military campaigning by German and Allied forces.

With the arrival of Sir Donald Cameron as governor in 1925, a more coherent and active administration emerged. The governor's personal temperament, his experience as chief secretary to the government in Nigeria, and his conviction that effective administration could only exist when based on indigenous institutions all contributed to his establishment of a system of indirect rule. The Native Authority Ordinance of 1926 undertook to govern through local authorities, investing them initially with responsibility for maintenance of order and collection of taxes, later adding judicial functions, while encouraging local financing and direction of community development projects.

Cameron's philosophy argued that the League's mandate was a trust leading to ultimate self-rule; therefore, training of Africans in self-government was absolutely essential. Traditional authorities were the logical agents, he insisted, as was customary law the chosen vehicle, although precedent and accepted practice were always subject to adaptation on behalf of modern requirements. In his day, Cameron's policy was criticized by settlers in Tanganyika as suppressive of quick modernization under European leadership, and later it was argued that his selection of native authorities had been precipitous and maladroit, leading in fact to a confusion within traditional modes of government and their disintegration in the face of British procedures directed by British administrators. Although there may have been an element of justice in these charges, there were also a number of accomplishments to mark Cameron's stewardship.

In addition to invaluable experience in local government, the people of Tanganyika gained an expanded system of education adapted to their needs, aid toward agricultural development, particularly in teaching and research, and improved public health services especially designed to deal with endemic trypanosomiasis. Finally, there was progress in alleviating the distresses of forced labor which so sorely troubled African societies across the continent during the interwar period. A labor department was established in 1926 which encouraged better working conditions and provided medical care for workers, while at the same time wage payments in cash were guaranteed by law. Compulsory labor continued for public works but remuneration was usual, while the number of workers gradually declined in the face of growing voluntary employment. Nevertheless, although the government exerted no overt pressure on individuals to work either on public projects or private plantations, professed official neutrality was criticized in 1929 by the Permanent Mandates Commission of the League of Nations as tantamount to actual compulsion.

The departure of Cameron in 1931 marked no significant change in government policy. Even the worldwide depression of the 1930s and the crises of the Second World War lightly touched the sprawling mandate as yet so little affected by the stresses of Western civilization. There were of course changes. Education and public health moved forward very modestly, the economy slowly shifted from subsistence to cash crop production, porterage declined in the face of improved roads and motor transport, and a gradual rise in living standard was reflected in better domestic housing and the beginnings of public sanitation. Nevertheless consequential economic changes were obliged to await the dynamics of the postwar years.

In much the same way, the pattern of traditional village life slowly evolved, giving ground before such pressures as British administration, population movements, and the emergence of mixed urban centers. Regional loyalties and intertribal political configurations were still developments for the future, however. As yet few individuals conceived of themselves as members of a Tanganyikan nation.

Multiple Colonialism in Zanzibar

Colonization and colonial rule by alien groups had long been a fact of life in Zanzibar. For centuries, Arab merchants had maintained small communities up and down the East African coast, spreading Islamic culture along with their trade goods, and the Shirazi Persians in particular had through permanent immigration introduced a Middle Eastern and Muslim quality which came to be characteristic of the African population of Zanzibar and other island and coastal settlements. The resultant Swahili civilization maintained sufficient mercantile relations with inland Africans to interest traders, chiefly Arab and

Indian, and eventually in the sixteenth century to attract the attention of Portuguese conquerors in process of asserting their commercial domination of the Indian Ocean. The ousting of the Portuguese by resurgent Omani Arabs at the end of the seventeenth century reestablished Arab primacy along the coast, but this authority remained nominal until Sayyid Said succeeded to the Omani throne at Muscat in 1806 and then transferred his seat of government to Zanzibar in 1840.

Thus Zanzibar became the center of an Arab state on the East African coast, preoccupied at first with trade, particularly in slaves, and then during the second half of the nineteenth century shifting to the cultivation of cloves as the British antislavery crusade spread into the Indian Ocean. This development had profound implications for the Africans of Zanzibar and to a lesser extent for the people of neighboring Pemba. First, it introduced an immigrant Arab aristocracy increasingly involved in plantation management. Next, it meant a thoroughgoing political and economic domination by the Arabs over the African population, their best lands alienated, their labor exacted by corvée, and their communities isolated from the ruling Arab class.

Beyond these groups there were plantation slaves and a small number of Asian clerks and shopkeepers. The latter were financially important but politically inactive, while the slaves gradually became converted into tenant farmers as servitude faded before the insistence of British abolitionism at the end of the nineteenth century. British officialdom, the smallest group of all, was at the same time of greatest consequence. Beginning with resident-advisers in the days of Sayyid Said, their representatives gradually increased their influence to the point of dominance during the consulship of James Kirk in the 1870s and 1880s; then in 1890, Britain imposed a protectorate which in practice became unadulterated colonial control.

As elsewhere, British colonial practice supported the status quo which in this case meant government through the agency of the Arab oligarchy. When at first the sultan's administrative machinery was completely overhauled in the interest of efficiency, Arabs were used to staff the new bureaucracy; then, in the 1920s a legislative council was introduced on which Arabs, despite their small numbers, had representation equal to that of the Africans and Asians combined. This was a particularly striking reflection of the unresponsiveness of official policy to changing times for it occurred during the interwar period which saw the rise of an African peasantry, steadily acquiring land from the failing Arab plantation aristocrats.

In the years following the Second World War, the general liberalization of colonial control in the British areas led in 1956 to popular election of half the unofficial legislative council members, a development which surprisingly was at first urged by the Arab minority rather than by the Africans who outnumbered all others by three to one. Arab leadership apparently hoped thus to maintain governmental control at the time of independence which was drawing near, and indeed in 1961 when responsible, ministerial government was instituted, the Arabs managed to form a coalition with sympathetic Africans. In time, however, political authority for the Arabs was to follow in the path of their economic decline.

British Rule and Nationalist Stirrings in the Nile Valley

From ancient times, Egypt and the Sudan had been bound up in each other's affairs; now at the turn of the century as the Khalifa's armies fell before Kitchener's firepower, the Nile Valley was once again unified, this time within the embrace of British imperial power. Having occupied Egypt in 1882 at the time of the Urabist revolt, a move designed initially to protect European investments in Egypt, Britain remained as *de facto* ruler, her position reflecting both the quickening of the imperial pulse and concern for the safety of the Suez link with the East. When the Sudan fell to British arms in 1898, and France had been faced down at Fashoda in her effort to break the British hold on the Nile, the vast Mahdist state also came under Britain's control, to be administered through the device of the Anglo-Egyptian agreement known as the Condominium.

The Condominium was the creation of Lord Cromer, British consul general in Cairo from 1883 to 1907, who governed Egypt indirectly through the local regime headed by the khedive. Nominally the khedive was both vassal of the Ottoman sultan and ruler of his own Sudanese dependency. To preserve these legal niceties, the Condominium proclaimed a dual sovereignty in the Sudan, Britain joining Egypt as coruler by right of conquest. Thus Cromer was able to impose effective control in both territories without the necessity of undisguised annexation. For the moment, at least, British control was unclouded by those qualifications which later came to embarrass her hegemony in the Nile Valley.

In Egypt and the Sudan, as in other areas, British imperial rule followed the familiar pattern of securing the status quo, content to insure protection of the Suez Canal and unwilling to embark on major social reforms which, it was felt in Whitehall, might bring unrest along with rising expectations. In Egypt extensive economic development was therefore undertaken only within the framework of the existing social order. Agriculture, particularly cotton production, was greatly stimulated by improved hydraulic engineering in the Nile floodplain, harbors were modernized and railroads built, and the economy thereby firmly directed away from subsistence farming to cash crop cultivation. Ownership of land, however, was permitted to accumulate in the hands of a local aristocracy which also monopolized the benefits of the modest, Western-oriented educational system, and exercised such limited parliamentary powers as were permitted by the British authorities.

In the Sudan, a combined British and Egyptian civil service conducted all official business, Sudanese at first having no share in the administration. As with Egypt, long-staple cotton production was encouraged, chiefly through an irrigation scheme begun in the Gezira before the First World War, while steam-driven river transport, railroads, and improved port facilities added their measure of modernization. These advances were financed, partly by Britain, but chiefly through interest-free Egyptian loans contributed at British insistence. Unlike cotton development in Egypt, the Gezira project was designed to encourage peasant farming, and indeed by the time it was nationalized in 1950, the scheme had grown into a large and successful agricultural cooperative involving the government, private concession companies, and tenant cultivators.

Despite its caution Britain's colonial policy of paternalism and limited reform provided the classic formula for nationalist discontent, a reaction that broke with particular violence in Egypt in the years following the First World War. Before the war some nationalist agitation had been apparent in the frustrations of European-educated civil servants who, in spite of their Westernized background, saw the wisdom of appealing to Egypt's Muslim peasantry, ever resentful over the inequities of taxation and land distribution. Nevertheless, it was the 1914-1918 conflict in Europe that crystallized local dissatisfaction — vexation over wartime sacrifices unrewarded, and bitterness in the knowledge that the great principle of national self-determination enunciated at Versailles was to be applied exclusively to European soil. The resultant rise of the Wafd party under Saad Zaghlul, and the rebellion that followed when Zaghlul and his aides were exiled to Malta, emphasized the seriousness of the Egyptian movement and led to a qualified grant of independence in 1922. Britain reserved for herself several important powers including security of imperial communications, responsibility for Egyptian national defense, protection of foreign nationals, and British preponderance in the Sudan.

In time the Wafd showed itself to be essentially conservative, representing affluent landed and financial interests; yet at this stage it was loath to accept any limitations imposed on Egyptian sovereignty, nor did it welcome recognition of Britain's paramountcy in the Sudan. In 1924, however, there expired any lingering Egyptian illusions concerning her share in the Condominium as her troops and officials were forced to withdraw from all Sudanese stations in retaliation for the assassination in Cairo of Sir Lee Stack, governor-general of the Sudan. The Condominium remained in name, but Egypt's interests in the south were thenceforward more appropriately to be reflected in the recurrent and vain Wafd assertion of Egypt's legal and historical position in the Sudan, rather than in any actual exercise of sovereignty.

British conservatism, responsible for the virtual end of Egyptian authority in the south, was also directed against a small but growing nationalist movement within the Sudan itself. As elsewhere in her African colonies, Britain was devoted during these interwar years to rule through traditional authorities who were treated with as much confidence and affection by administrators in the field as the educated Africans were mistrusted and shunned. Thus isolated in frustration, Westernized elite, already trained in such schools as Khartoum's Gordon Memorial College to extol European liberal and democratic values, came together in political opposition to the seeming hypocrisies of established authority. The first Sudanese to express a specific nationalism was Ali Abd al-Latif, a young Dinka whose political organization founded in 1921 brought him a jail term during which he developed the conviction that success could henceforth come only by making common cause with Egyptian nationalists. The result was a second party, the White Flag League, founded by Abd al Latif in 1924 and dedicated not to Sudanese freedom, but to unity with independent Egypt.

Ali Abd al-Latif's movement once again collapsed in the face of official displeasure, and the expulsion of the Egyptians in 1924 completed the isolation of his early nationalist followers. Moreover, the government pressed forward with its policy of indirect rule through the chiefly authorities, and educated Sudanese were actively discouraged from participation in government, even as minor members of the civil service. Nevertheless, circumstances were already developing which in time would not only produce a Sudanese nationalism, but one marked indelibly by the quality of Sudanese character and the necessities of Sudanese history.

This parochial manifestation was bound up with the particularities of Islam in the Sudan. In the days before the Mahdi, one of the most powerful sects was the Khatmiyya headed by the Mirghani family, its particular strength lying in the north and east. Long associated with Egyptian rule and resistant to the Mahdist impulse, the Khatmiyya and their Mirghani leaders were over-shadowed during the years of the Mahdist state, reemerging with the Condominium which gained their hearty cooperation as a return to the golden days of Egyptian influence in the south. For its part, Britain looked on the Mirghani as allies and influential leaders, in appreciation of which the head of the order, Sayyid Ali al-Mirghani, was knighted in 1916. During the interwar period, however, the Mahdists made a strong comeback as the British found another useful political friend in Abd al-Rahman, the posthumous son of the Mahdi. When political activity developed in the Sudan during the years of the Second World War, it quickly polarized around these two figures and their families.

In 1938, the Graduates' General Congress was founded by Sudanese government workers, now long established in the lower and medium ranks of the civil service. By 1942 the congress was demanding self-determination for the Sudan at the end of hostilities, and when rebuffed, it split into two factions, the activist Ashiqqa founded by Ismail al-Azhari and a more moderate Umma party. The Ashiqqa, seeking Egyptian aid, also found themselves drawn to the Khatmiyya with its traditional orientation toward the north. The Umma responded by supporting Sudanese independence without Egypt, allying itself with the Sudan's leading nationalist symbol, Abd al-Rahman al-Mahdi. Thus each group gained mass strength among the politically inexperienced but devout Sudanese people. At the conclusion of the war, as Britain faced the multiple problems of relations with Egypt and the future of the Sudan, this basic political split within the Sudan conditioned her deliberations even as it was to shape Sudanese politics and relations with Egypt during the years leading to independence and beyond.

Suggestions for Further Reading

Most of the recent research on East Africa dates from the 1960s and 1970s; hence the best overall survey of the subject is the *Oxford History of East Africa*, 3 v. (Oxford: Clarendon, 1963, 1965, 1976), especially Vol. II, edited by Vincent Harlow and E. M. Chilver. See also B. A. Ogot and J. A. Kieran, eds., *Zamani: A Survey of East African History* (Nairobi: East African Publishing House and Longmans, 1968; New York: Humanities, 1968), and the *Cambridge History of Africa*, Vol. VI, edited by Roland Oliver and G. N. Sanderson (Cambridge: University Press, 1985) and Vol. VII, edited by A. D. Roberts (Cambridge: University Press, 1986).

For Uganda, there are a number of helpful studies including D. A. Low and R. C. Pratt, *Buganda and British Overrule, 1900-1955* (London: Oxford University Press, 1960); and D. A. Low, *Buganda in Modern History* (Berkeley: University of California Press, 1971). Several more specialized works shed light on particular aspects of Uganda history; for example, R. Oliver, *Sir Harry Johnston and the Scramble for Africa* (London: Chatto and Windus, 1957); M. Perham, *Lugard: The Years of Adventure* (London: Collins, 1956; New York: Oxford University Press, 1956). For a study of Buganda based on written and oral materials, see S. Kiwanuka, *A History of Buganda* (London: Longmans, 1971).

Kenya is surveyed by many works, but see C. G. Rosberg and J. Nottingham, *The Myth of Mau Mau* (New York: Praeger; London: Pall Mall, 1966). Histories based on oral tradition should be mentioned: B. A. Ogot, *History of the Southern Luo* (Nairobi: East African Publishing House, 1967); G. S. Were, *A History of the Abaluyia of Western Kenya* (Nairobi: East African Publishing House, 1967); G. Muriuki, *A History of the Kikuyu, 1500-1900* (Nairobi: Oxford, 1974); and R. L. Tignor, *The Colonial Transformation of Kenya: The Kamba, Kikuyu and Maasai from 1900-1939* (Princeton: University Press, 1976). *Facing Mount Kenya* by Jomo Kenyatta (New York: Vintage, 1962) is a classic exposition of the Kikuyu point of view and may be supplemented by Kenyatta's *Suffering Without Bitterness* (Nairobi: East African Publishing House, 1968). The settler viewpoint is set forth in the works of Elspeth Huxley, particularly her *White Man's Country: Lord Delamere and the Making of Kenya*, 2 Vols. (London: Macmillan, 1935; New York: Praeger, 1968). For the Asian community, see J. S. Mangat, *A History of the Asians in East Africa* (Oxford: Clarendon, 1969); and R. G. Gregory, India and East Africa (Oxford: Clarendon, 1971).

For Tanganyika, see J. Iliffe, *A Modern History of Tanganyika* (Cambridge: University Press, 1979); and the relevant chapters in P. Gifford and W. R. Louis, eds., *Britain and Germany in Africa* (New Haven: Yale University Press, 1967). For the Maji Maji revolt see J. Iliffe, "The Organization of the Maji Maji Rebellion," *The Journal of African History*, Vol. VIII, No. 3 (1967). Zanzibari history leading to the political upheaval of 1964 is reviewed in M. F. Lofchie, *Zanzibar: Background to Revolution* (Princeton: Princeton University Press, 1965).

For Egypt and the Sudan, see John Marlowe, *Anglo-Egyptian Relations, 1800-1953* (London: Cresset Press, 1954); P.J. Vatikiotis, *The History of Egypt*, 3rd ed. (Baltimore: Johns Hopkins Press, 1986); R. L. Tignor, *Modernization and British Colonial Rule in Egypt, 1882-1914* (Princeton: Princeton University Press, 1967); P. M. Holt and M.W. Daly, *A History of the Sudan*, 4th ed. (London and New York: Longman, 1988); and the chapters by Daly and G. M. Sanderson in *The Cambridge History of Africa*, Vol. VII (Cambridge: University Press, 1986).

18

Between Two World Wars— Nationalist Frustrations in West Africa

West Africa and the First World War

Recent research has demonstrated that the impact of the First World War on Africa was both extensive and profound. The immediate pressures of war led colonial powers greatly to intensify their demands for labor and supplies, often threatening or upsetting delicate ecological balances and economic systems. Eventually, Germany's colonies were parceled out among the victors, plans were laid for the recouping of Europe's materiel and personnel losses at Africa's expense, while colonial administrations were tightened into much greater efficiency. All this cast a deep shadow across African hopes for a liberalization of colonial controls let alone for an ultimate independence.

In West Africa the most devastating initial impact came in the form of troop requisitions. Both France and Britain were determined to carry the war to Germany on African ground and African soldiers were designated as the appropriate instrument. France sought African troops for action in Europe as well, particularly in light of her mounting losses on the Western Front. Recruitment methods were harsh and arbitrary, little more than forced labor levees bordering on slave raids that left villages bereft of their young men. Such recruitment caused desertion and malingering and frequently escalated into widespread open rebellion. The British demands were relatively modest with only about 26,000 men-at-arms eventually called to do service in West and East Africa. France's mobilization goals were far more ambitious and equally unrealistic. Officials in Paris projected one million potential soldiers despite the disclaimers of West African administrators like Governor-General J. Van Vollenhoven, and indeed some 180,000 were eventually recruited, one-third provided through the exertions of Blaise Diagne, the Senegalese delegate to the Chamber of Deputies in Paris.

Such losses weighed sorely on villages scattered across a thinly populated countryside, and were compounded by requisitions for foodstuffs that had to be provided by communities already robbed of much of their labor force. These burdens, when added to unpopular taxation, the imposition in many areas of nontraditional rulers, and an unwanted alien regime, fed the fires of rebellion that were only quenched with difficulty by skeleton administrations badly understaffed through war's attrition. Unrest in the British territories was more muted, if only because there the afflictions of colonial rule were somewhat less severe.

In both British and French West Africa the small number of western-educated Africans looked to a new order at war's end, a relaxing of colonial restraints in return for African contributions to the war effort. As reward for his recruitment effort, Blaise Diagne had received explicit promises of an extension of French citizenship to returning war veterans. British West Africans also hoped for reforms that would involve them more directly in colonial administration, delimit paternalism, and introduce more of the benefits of modernization. It was this mood that characterized the pan-African congresses organized by the black American leader W. E. B. Du Bois, that lent urgency to the program of J. E. Casely Hayford's National Congress of British West Africa, and that prompted nationalist leaders in their demands for extension of political rights, improvement of educational and public health facilities, or equality of economic opportunity between whites and blacks. Unfortunately, factors operating within the colonial powers of Europe were to render such aspirations vain. At the conclusion of hostilities, England, and particularly France, moved to strengthen and to systematize, not to weaken, their machinery of colonial government in West Africa.

The Theory and Practice of Colonial Administration

Both England and France had developed systems of colonial administration during the nineteenth century that differed markedly each from the other in their theoretical definition but that were not always so easily distinguishable in practice. French administrators had long followed techniques of colonial government based on the doctrine of assimilation, that view which held that French civilization should be shared by all people living under French rule, that those who dwelt in territories overseas were just as entitled to the exercise of full political and civil rights as were citizens of France itself. In practice this doctrine was applied only to limited portions of France's overseas holdings during the nineteenth century. In Senegal, the coastal communities were treated substantially like provincial districts of France, but in the hinterland French authority gradually extended itself primarily through force of arms, and led to a form of local government largely military in direction and nature.

Toward the end of the century, as French arms subdued larger and larger areas in Africa, colonial theorists in France became increasingly dissatisfied with the principle of assimilation. They argued that it was impossible to expect millions of people of totally different background and level of civilization to absorb what they saw as the subtle qualities of French culture and to operate the democratic machinery by which the French governed themselves. They therefore proposed the alternative doctrine of association which encouraged colonial people to retain their traditional culture but which placed them in a clearly subservient position to their European masters. By the end of the war in 1918, association had become the dominant note in French colonial policy, and in West Africa a highly centralized, authoritarian regime emerged. At the apex stood the colonial ministry in Paris wherein originated all policy for the colonies. In the overseas territories were the colonial administrations, a hierarchy of officials from metropolitan France headed by a governor and charged with carrying into effect the designs of the ministry. At the bottom of the scale were the provincial, district, and village chiefs whose job it was to enforce the edicts of the administration — taxation, labor requisitions, and the maintenance of law and order. These chiefs were appointed by the colonial government which sometimes ratified the position of a traditional ruler or alternatively chose a chief arbitrarily where no appropriate indigenous authority existed. The standard of chieftaincy in the French African colonies was efficiency, not legitimacy; hence, French direct rule tended not only to be autocratic but erosive of native custom as well.

Administration in the British colonies was less responsive to any exact theory of colonization, but as with the French territories, lines of authority were tightening in the British possessions at the conclusion of the First World War. During the nineteenth century, England had administered her West African holdings in a variety of ways that reflected a characteristic pragmatism. By and large, however, colonial possessions were ruled arbitrarily by appointed governors assisted by their administrative staffs, and in the process no consistent or systematic attention was paid to the preservation or utilization of traditional customs and institutions. This lack of uniformity was checked, however, by Sir Frederick Lugard, who took charge of the Protectorate of Northern Nigeria in 1900, instituting the system of indirect rule which came to be the standard of Britain's administration in her West African colonies during the period following the First World War.

In theory, indirect rule was the antithesis of the French administration. It emphasized the maximum use of traditional law and governmental machinery, encouraging the people to continue in their indigenous patterns of government, substituting only the ultimate appeal to the British crown for whatever had been the sovereign authority in the land. From the point of view of national self-determination for West Africa, however, indirect rule offered little more guarantee than did the direct administration of the French. For one thing, although indirect rule sounded superficially like virtual local autonomy, it was in fact a system whose ultimate authority clearly lay beyond the grasp of the Africans themselves. Some things were left in place, for example, slave labor that both French and British administrators saw as essential to local economic efficiency. There were, however, innovations such as direct taxation, justice by administrative officers, and compulsory labor often introduced arbitrarily to unwilling or uncomprehending African populations. Chiefs were normally chosen by their people, but their authority was known by all to reside in the British power which paid them salaries and advised them in their governmental duties through colonial administrators assigned for that purpose. Indirect rule, moreover, worked best in those areas like northern Nigeria where traditional governments most resembled European prototypes—large-scale states with a clearly defined, centralized authority administering a system of direct taxation. In other regions like eastern Nigeria, with its decentralized societies and absence of chiefs, indirect rule was virtually impossible to initiate and an amended form of direct administration had to be substituted.

A second major shortcoming of indirect rule arose from the anomalous position in which it placed the growing body of educated Africans. By its nature, indirect rule emphasized the legitimacy of traditional authorities, but it was precisely the traditional chiefs who were least able to adapt themselves to the changing social and political conditions that followed the introduction of colonial rule. The small body of Africans trained in the West was best qualified to interpret the two worlds of Europe and Africa, each to the other; yet colonial administrators on the whole resisted the opportunity to make use of this African resource. Partly, this was a defense of the traditional authority, but more often it emerged from a distaste for Africans capable of detecting and criticizing shortcomings in colonial administration. Educated Africans were said to lack the respect of their own people, but in fact it was the support of the colonial governments that was more often missing.

In one final respect both French and British colonial administration was antagonistic to West African nationalist aspirations after the First World War. France, emerging from the war economically prostrated, quickly rallied to the proposal put forward by the colonial minister, Albert Sarraut, for a massive development and utilization of French colonies designed to help rehabilitate the national economy. This latter-day mercantilism demanded a total political control, especially when it involved large-scale utilization of forced labor in the construction of major public works projects. While an analogous exploitation of the English colonies did not develop, a policy of laissez-faire in British West African trade was followed which meant in practice that economic power tended to fall into the hands of European firms. That the colonial government favored these large overseas corporations in its regulations may only have reflected administrative convenience, but the result nonetheless was a depressing effect on local West African economic enterprise.

Nationalist Politics in West Africa
Between the Two World Wars

Colonial rule in West Africa in the years following the First World War permitted little effective political activity on the part of those Africans seeking broader economic and constitutional advantages. It was therefore a difficult era for African nationalists, an age in which the politics of accommodation with colonial governments often seemed to promise the greater reward. On the Gold Coast, for example, political, social, and economic reform resulted more from the exertions of a paternalistic colonial administration than from African political pressures, whereas in Senegal local political leadership was content to develop a privileged position for a small section of the population by coming to terms with the French colonial administration. In Nigeria the nationalists were largely frustrated with only token headway to show after years of aggressive agitation. At the same time some of their countrymen more sympathetic to British rule were favored with honors and positions of responsibility in government.

It was in Senegal that the greatest shortfall developed between hopes for reform toward democratic self-determination and the reaction of postwar French colonial policy. In the spring of 1914, just before the outbreak of hostilities in Europe, a remarkable event had appeared to signal the beginning of a major trend in political liberalism for French West Africa. For some years, the French had been moving to restrict the political and civil rights of the originaires (those Africans living in the four communes of Dakar, Saint-Louis, Gorée, and Rufisque), and by 1914 the French citizenship of these Senegalese had been revoked and inroads made on their voting privileges and their right to protection in French courts. The people of the Four Communes, accustomed to being treated as French citizens, had fought back for their rights and organized a small political party, the Young Senegalese, which made some modest gains in local elections. Political power in the communes, however, had always rested with the mulatto and French mercantile groups, and the Africans were not expected to be able to develop a political force of any consequence.

Fortunately for the African cause, there arrived in Senegal early in 1914 an obscure African customs official named Blaise Diagne, who had been born in Gorée many years earlier but who had lived away from his native country almost continuously throughout his adult life. Diagne returned at this time to contest the seat as representative from Senegal in the French Chamber of

Deputies, a post that theretofore had always been filled either by a French or mulatto candidate. In an exciting election in which Diagne's own energetic and resourceful campaigning played an important part, he was elected deputy, thus becoming the first African ever to fill that post.

Diagne's campaign had gone to the heart of the matter, accusing the Europeans and mulattoes of both economic and political discrimination against Africans, and pledging himself if elected to regaining the lost citizenship of his people. "The majority of the voters are black," he assured his rapt African audiences. "It is their interests which must be represented." True, his father had only been a cook, but he, Blaise Diagne, was proud to come from such humble surroundings. "Your candidate is the candidate of the people," he went on. "I am not ashamed to be a black man."

The election won, Diagne continued the assault. Hammering steadily in the public press on the subject of economic exploitation, social prejudice, and political discrimination against the Africans of the Four Communes, Diagne set a memorable example as an aggressive African capable of standing up to the European. At times he seemed obsessed by his campaign to gain respect for blacks, for example, when he almost precipitated a riot in Dakar after taking violent offense when he discovered that a European resident had given his dog the name of Blaise. Later, during the last year of the war, he insisted on the strictest regard for protocol while traveling in West Africa during his recruitment campaign, in order that the dignity of the first African deputy might not be compromised. Most important of all, taking advantage of France's need for troops from her colonies to fill the trenches in France, Diagne in 1916 secured a complete and unequivocal grant of French citizenship for the people of the Four Communes. "The natives of the incorporated communities of Senegal and their descendants," the law stated simply, "are and remain French citizens."

These were exciting days, not only for the citizens of the Four Communes, but for all the people of French West Africa. For the first time in the lives of many of Diagne's contemporaries, the age-old feeling of inferiority had been replaced with a sense of dignity and self-respect. What was more, Diagne did not appear ready to call a halt to his reform movement after he had regained the constitutional rights of the people of the Four Communes. Already idolized by a large following throughout the French territories of West Africa, he seemed on the verge of a fight to extend political and civil rights beyond the limited bounds of the Four Communes. In 1918 Diagne recruited over sixty thousand West Africans for the French army, and he was on public record as favoring the enlargement of the franchise to include those West Africans who had fought for the mother country in her needy hour. Moreover, he appeared capable of carrying out such a reform. A clever political tactician, he had quickly consolidated his position at the expense of the old conservative oligarchy in the Four Communes, and in 1919 was reelected deputy. As the war ended, he was conspicuous in his support of a move by the colonial ministry to grant the privilege of municipal incorporation to a number of communities beyond the Four Communes, and at the same time he called for the extension to West Africa of labor legislation already in force in metropolitan France guaranteeing improved working conditions, greater leisure time, and the use of arbitration in industrial disputes.

In the years that followed, Diagne's proposals somehow never progressed beyond the talking stage. The plan for the extension of incorporated municipalities was dropped during the reaction of French postwar colonial policy, and in 1920 the old colonial General Council was replaced with Diagne's blessing by a Colonial Council ostensibly more democratic but actually designed to give the administration a tighter control over colonial affairs. Throughout French West Africa, forced labor for public and private use was thrust on an indigenous population unable to defend its position in the face of the *indigénat*, the system of administrative justice that dealt arbitrarily with minor offenses and screened the African from the protection of French courts.

This was the situation that developed during the 1920s for the approximately fourteen million inhabitants of French West Africa. Classed as French subjects under the policy of association, these people had virtually no political or civil rights, and were represented only in the colonial council by chiefs whose own offices rested squarely on the sanction of the colonial administration. In the Four Communes, some fifty thousand citizens protected by Diagne's law represented an island of privilege, and it soon became apparent that Diagne and his party had become uninterested in the needs of any outside this small group. In 1923 Diagne reportedly reached an agreement with the merchants of Bordeaux who had long held a major interest in the West African trade. Under this arrangement, the deputy received the support of Bordeaux for his political activities. in return for which he agreed not to interfere with Bordeaux's economic prerogatives in Senegal. Thereafter, though Diagne gave occasional lip service to a more liberal colonial policy—greater representation for West African territories in the French parliament, for example—most of his eloquence was utilized in eulogizing the French colonial system. In 1930 when France needed a defender of her colonial labor program at the conference on forced labor held by the International Labor Organization in Geneva, it is significant that she turned at once to Blaise Diagne.

The changing attitude of the Diagne party in the postwar years brought a natural disillusion to many of its early followers who felt that their cause had been deserted by a political opportunist ready to exchange independence for the honors and perquisites of public office. In 1928, and again in 1932, Diagne's longtime lieutenant, Galandou Diouf, ran against his former chief, but the Diagne machine was too strong, the deputy was returned in both instances, and Diouf did not finally gain the parliamentary seat until 1934 after Diagne's death. On the face of it, the charge against Diagne of opportunistic capitulation to pressures from France appeared only too well substantiated, but in a deeper sense the problem was more complex. Diagne was a product of French assimilation and like most Africans educated by France, he had become thoroughly committed to a belief in the superiority of French civilization and the ultimate necessity for African absorption into the French way of life. For him, association was an interim state which would be followed in time by true assimilation. Ultimately, he was certain, there could never be any distinction between metropolitan and overseas France. "I belong to those," he once told a cheering Chamber of Deputies, "who believe that France's traditional posture . . . can only find its resolution in unity . . . of the spirit between France and the peoples or races scattered across her overseas territories." To Diagne there was much to be said for the policy of teaching young Africans about "our ancestors the Gauls."

One reason that Diagne's political opponents enjoyed so little success during his lifetime was that they were in essential agreement with his politics and philosophy, and consequently represented no basic change from his program. When Galandou Diouf had opposed Diagne, Diouf was accused of Communist affiliation, Diagne of being an imperialist agent. Once Diouf succeeded to the position of deputy he became the established symbol of colonial rule and another opposition arose with the taint of radicalism.

Diouf's most successful opposition came from Lamine Guèye who during the twenties had been variously the ally and the foe of Diagne and of Diouf in the shifting pattern of local politics. When Diouf became deputy, Guèye moved into opposition, seemingly justifying the charge of radicalism leveled at him by aligning his local following with the French Popular Front from 1936 onward. This was no true reflection of leftist sentiments, however, for Guèye's party, like those of Diagne and Diouf, consisted of privileged African citizens, not of workers or peasants. To be sure, Guèye's Popular Front connections did prompt him to demand an extension of French citizenship beyond the Four Communes, a view that Diagne himself had once held. More significantly, however, Guèye was at one with Diagne, Diouf, and other political leaders in the view that the future for Africa, lay in political if not cultural assimilation with France. To a great extent the reactionary development of French colonial policy between the two world wars was the result of policies determined in Paris. In some measure, however, its success was also caused by the deference to the basic principles of French colonialism accorded by the West African political leaders of the day.

In the British West African territories, the system of indirect rule was applied in differing degrees to suit local circumstances and the convictions of individual colonial governors. The result was a variety of administrations less rigorous and exploitative than those of the French, but essentially paternalistic in philosophy and resistant to local African movements for a greater share in the economic and political activities of the colonies.

In tiny Gambia, for example, the legislative council, first constituted in 1843 to advise the governor, contained only two Africans, both nominated by the administration from the port of Bathurst. It was not until 1932 that the people of the Protectorate hinterland were given any representation when provision was made to add a British Protectorate Commissioner to the council.

In Sierra Leone, a legislative council had existed since the mid-nineteenth century, and Freetown had been a largely self-governing municipality since 1893 when the distinguished African barrister, Sir Samuel Lewis, had persuaded the government to create an elected municipal council with taxing authority, Lewis serving as the first mayor of Freetown. The experiment was no great success, however. As mayor, Lewis had labored diligently to instill in his Creole neighbors both a sense of administrative responsibility and a willingness to submit to tax assessment for rating purposes, but to no avail. Few valued the franchise as something worth being taxed for, and in 1926, after a generation of inept and occasionally corrupt administration, the experiment in municipal self-government was discontinued by the authorities.

Representative government in the Colony and Protectorate fared better, and in 1924 the legislative council was enlarged to give greater African representation. Provision was made for eleven official and ten unofficial members, three of the latter elected by voters within the colony possessing appropriate property and literacy qualifications. Of the remaining seven, all nominated by the governor, two were always Africans from the Colony, two representatives of the commercial interests, and three were paramount chiefs drawn from the three provinces of the Protectorate.

It was in Nigeria, where Lugard's system of indirect rule had originated, that the greatest opposition to British colonial practice developed, an opposition that was a combination of resistance by traditional authorities and an effort of western-educated Africans to introduce principles of democratic, representative government which they claimed were in the best traditions both of indigenous society and of their colonial masters. The opposition of traditional authorities was to a considerable extent a carry-over from the days of nineteenth-century independence when local rulers like Nana, the Itsekiri leader, or the emir of Kontagora, had unsuccessfully held out against the imposition of British protectorates. In 1918 the Egba people of Abeokuta had rioted and in 1929 there was an outbreak of violence among the market women in the Aba district of eastern Nigeria, both disturbances essentially protests against unfamiliar administrative practices imposed from above as part of the ostensibly indirect system of British rule.

The most persistent and effective reaction to the colonial administration came, however, from the educated classes located largely in Lagos. Their disaffection was complex and to a degree contradictory. In the first place, they were offended by the attitude of British officials, missionaries, and traders who introduced Western social and cultural standards, and then ridiculed African attempts to emulate the European. Further, they wished to introduce political reforms based on British democratic traditions and resented any efforts to impose arbitrary colonial rule. Finally, although they disliked indirect rule by indigenous authorities, they were troubled by the deteriorating effect that colonial government was having on traditional institutions.

During the years of the First World War, these Lagos nationalists had carried on an unrelieved campaign of opposition to the administration of Sir Frederick Lugard. Lugard's system of judiciary by administrative officers was for them no more than an inefficient tyranny, his policy of indirect rule a deception behind which British district commissioners might operate without hindrance, and the amalgamation of northern and southern Nigeria effected in 1914 but a device for the extension of military rule to the south where constitutional government had once reigned. When Lugard left Nigeria in 1918, the sense of relief among the nationalists was unrestrained, their attitude summed up by Thomas H. Jackson, editor of the *Lagos Weekly Record* and one of their leading spokesmen. "For six long years," Jackson complained, "we have lived under the cramped condition of military dictatorship when the law from being a means of protection had become an instrument of crime and oppression. . . . The last administration has made the very name of the white man stink in the nostrils of the native."

Such strong feelings reflected years of frustration, a frustration illustrated by the chronic dispute between the people of Lagos and the government over the king, or *eleko*, of Lagos. Lagos had been annexed in 1861 under a treaty with Docemo, the then-reigning eleko, wherein Docemo was given an annual stipend, but no provision was made for his heirs despite the fact that the sovereignty of the house of Docemo had been relinquished in perpetuity while the royal line continued to function as the traditional authority of the people of the city. The grievances of the Lagos nationalists came to be focused in this eleko issue and were pressed upon the administration by Herbert Macaulay, a civil engineer whose talents as a public speaker and polemic writer had made him the leading figure among the nationalists by the end of the First World War.

Macaulay and his followers had vainly urged Lugard to provide an adequate stipend to sustain the eleko, but instead the government had finally deposed the king and installed another candidate, accusing the eleko of having joined the Macaulay party to embarrass the authorities. This was in 1920, and from that point forward the eleko issue became an obsession to Macaulay and a major source of embarrassment for the administration. The Macaulay party circulated a petition for the reinstatement of the original incumbent, and, backed by public opinion in Lagos, continued to regard the "destoolment" (dethronement) as unconstitutional. Both Macaulay and Jackson carried on an incessant editorial campaign over the years against the colonial government, Macaulay's denunciations in 1928 gaining him conviction for criminal libel and a short prison term. Finally in 1933, under a more benevolent administration of Governor Sir Donald Cameron, recently arrived from Tanganyika, the eleko controversy was settled when the government agreed to the restoration of the popular claimant. It was a small victory in the sense that the position of eleko had long since become largely ceremonial. Viewed from another perspective, however, it demonstrated the character of a determined and resourceful African leadership, as well as the virility of traditional customs facing the pressures of external change.

In part the eleko controversy reflected deep differences, not only between Nigerians and British, but between different groups within Lagos itself. Macaulay represented one extreme, a West African version of twisting the British lion's tail. Many western-educated Africans, however, were out of sympathy with what they defined as undignified conduct. For them, British rule represented a major step forward and upward, and they regarded progress in West Africa in terms of how quickly Nigerians could absorb and utilize the best aspects of Western civilization. Theirs was a view not dissimilar from the assimilation theories put forward by French colonialists and embraced by Senegalese leaders like Blaise Diagne and Lamine Guèye. In Lagos this assimilationist position was typified by such respected members of the community as the eminent barrister C. A. Sapara Williams, Dr. John Randle, the physician and political figure, Sir Kitoyi Ajasa, who founded the *Nigerian Pioneer* in 1914 to defend the policies of his friend Lugard and the educator and public servant Henry Carr.

Henry Carr had also been in the thick of the eleko fight, but on the opposite side from Macaulay, for Lugard had made Carr Resident of the Colony in 1918 and in this office he was obliged to defend the government's position. Not that Carr was reluctant to do so, for he was thoroughly unsympathetic with the views of the Macaulay party. To conservatives like Carr, the position of eleko was an anachronism which, having lost its original function, could only serve the antisocial purposes of attracting dissident groups within the community, providing them the opportunity to plot mischief within the eleko's compound. Encouraging such a weakened institution could only invite trouble, Carr insisted. It was better that the sons of the house of Docemo be given a sound Western education so that they might qualify to serve their people anew, not as faltering relics of a dead past but as well-integrated African members of a new Afro-European civilization. Such assimilationist ideas may have appealed to the authorities, but they were unequivocally rejected by most of the people of Lagos who preferred the more exciting approach of Macaulay and his followers.

One event that stimulated the Macaulayites and lent them a measure of success for a time was the constitutional change in 1922 that provided for the popular election of one member from Calabar and three from Lagos to a new and larger legislative council. This reform precipitated a flurry of political activity led by Macaulay and Jackson who founded the Nigerian National Democratic Party and placed three candidates before the Lagos electorate in 1923. Macaulay was ineligible for office, having been imprisoned over a misuse of trust funds ten years earlier, but his popularity proved transferable and his handpicked candidates won the quinquennial elections for Lagos without any difficulty between the years 1923 and 1938.

As it happened, winning three seats on a council of forty-six of which twenty-seven were government officials offered more electioneering excitement than actual political power as Macaulay and his Democratic Party soon discovered. In the first flush of enthusiasm, the Lagos members pledged themselves to cooperation and constructive criticism of official policy, but gradually their optimism was replaced with disillusionment. It became clear that the official majority on the legislative council was not to be influenced by unofficial opinion, and the elected representatives soon found themselves venting their frustration through exhaustive but fruitless questions in the council regarding governmental policy. Public interest in the elections gradually declined, and the work of the unofficial members became a sterile exercise in voicing their dissatisfaction with legislation that was forced upon them by the council's overwhelming official majority. This official majority, reported Dr. C. C. Adeniyi Jones, Macaulay's party colleague and longtime council member, "has practically reduced the unofficial members, especially the elected members, to the role of mere recording instruments of official sweet will."

In 1938 the Macaulay monopoly over the legislative council elections was broken by the Nigerian Youth Movement which signaled the beginning of a newer, more militant brand of nationalist politics. At the same time there returned to Nigeria Nnamdi Azikiwe, who soon added his journalistic dynamism to the new nationalism. Thus, on the eve of the Second World War, Nigerians were looking forward to nationalist politics well beyond the parochialism of the Herbert Macaulay era. But this was a development that was not to have consequence until the postwar period.

On the Gold Coast a similar set of circumstances was creating a somewhat analogous group of frustrations. Historically, the Gold Coast had been the first home of a West African independence movement, reflected by the Fante Confederation and the writings of Africanus Horton. Through the closing years of the nineteenth century and up to the beginning of the First World War, the Gold Coast westernized elite had been especially active in pointing out their traditional constitutional and historical rights to a colonial administration then tightening its grip on the reins of government.

Influenced partly by Lugard's theory of indirect rule and partly by past experience, the Gold Coast governors of the war years and immediately thereafter followed the general British pattern in West Africa and sought to strengthen the chiefly authorities. In 1916 the legislative council was substantially enlarged, the most notable additions being three western-educated representatives of the coastal cities and three paramount chiefs to speak for the provinces, all to be nominated by the governor. In 1925 another constitution brought further changes. The urban representatives remained fixed at three and would henceforth be elected by manhood suffrage based on a property qualification. However, the number of chiefs was doubled, the six representatives to be elected by newly formed provincial councils made up of the leading traditional authorities.

Two years later, a Native Administration Ordinance gave the provincial councils specified administrative and judicial functions in a further effort to secure the power of the chiefs. British official policy at the time was based on the conviction that West African societies were evolving toward modern western-style civilization only very slowly, and that until a greater degree of Westernization had been achieved, it was necessary to maintain the authority and integrity of the native authorities in order to prevent social disintegration.

Such a view was totally unpalatable to the western-educated classes in the Gold Coast, who had long fought to preserve traditional practice and authority but who felt increasingly that they were entitled to share in such local government as there was, first, because they represented a segment of the population of growing importance and, second, because they saw themselves as the most effective link between the old world of traditional Africa and the new world of Europe. By the close of the First World War most of the old leaders had disappeared from view, men like John Mensah Sarbah, James H. Brew, or T. Hutton Mills, but one of their most important spokesmen was more active and influential than ever. In J. E. Casely Hayford, the Cape Coast barrister and journalist, the Gold Coast African had a champion of long experience both in defending the virility of traditional institutions, and in arguing the qualifications for leadership of the educated classes.

If Casely Hayford's prewar exertions had concentrated on explaining the importance of traditional government to British administrators often too prone to discount the importance of native institutions, his postwar activities within the Gold Coast were devoted to checking the excessive growth of the chiefly authority encouraged by the British doctrine of indirect rule. At the root of the controversy lay a struggle for power between the leaders of the old Africa and those of the new. The chiefs felt their authority slipping away from them in the face of a Western intrusion which challenged them both in the form of a European administration and a Westernized African elite. The educated Africans, willing to protect the traditional authorities against the erosion of British government, were no longer content to submit to the dictates of unlettered chiefs. When the colonial administration attempted to strengthen the chiefs, therefore, a split developed within the Gold Coast between the chiefs and the elite.

The chiefly position was ably argued by Nana Ofori Atta, paramount chief of Akim Abuakwa and one of the representatives of the native authority appointed to the legislative council under the changes of 1916. Ofori Atta questioned the right of westernized Africans to speak for the people. The chiefs, he insisted, were the rightful leaders in the land, and as long as they remained on their stools they were the appropriate medium through which local government should be conducted. Casely Hayford took a contrary view. According to tradition, he pointed out, chiefs were not the voice of their people;

indeed, they were specifically denied this function which could either be expressed informally by any member of the community or officially by a specially chosen spokesman or linguist.

Beyond this, continued Casely Hayford, it was the educated African who was becoming a natural leader in a modern, changing world, for it was he who understood the Westerner and it was he whose literacy made him best qualified to deal with the alien presence in the land. "The educated class represents substantially the intelligentsia and advanced thought of British West Africa," he stated before the legislative council. "It also represents the bulk of the inhabitants of the various indigenous communities and with them claims, as sons of the soil, the inherent right to make representations as to extinguishing disabilities, and to submit recommendations for . . . necessary reforms."

Such logic failed to impress the administration which continued to support the role of the traditional authorities, much to the distress of the westernized groups. The constitutional and administrative changes of 1925 and 1927 were received with extreme distaste by the elite who at first boycotted the new constitution and refused to cooperate in the choice of a legislative council. The progressive coastal cities were being discriminated against, they argued, and the chiefs encouraged beyond their capacity and their right to govern. It was nothing but an attempt to divide and rule. "That is no franchise at all," Casely Hayford cried out in protest. "It is a mockery. It is a sham, a humbug." Yet it was also a reality which the educated community eventually was forced to recognize.

Casely Hayford finally made his peace and stood successfully for election to the legislative council in 1927, pointing out the possibilities that lay before the educated African if he chose to exert his influence as an adviser to the chiefs. Others like J. B. Danquah, a younger brother of Ofori Atta and future head of the United Gold Coast Convention, agreed, observing that the real power in the Gold Coast was, after all, the British government which had to be endured in the form it chose to assume. A basic instability had been established, however, for the administration was attempting to rule indirectly through a traditional authority attempting to sustain itself in the face of changing conditions and new forms of African leadership. The results of these uncertainties were to become manifest in the changing politics of the period following the Second World War.

The National Congress of British West Africa

During the period between the two world wars, Casely Hayford was to a large extent preoccupied with a movement that went beyond the limited question of national politics within the Gold Coast. For many years he had come to regard international cooperation among Africans as the most effective means to the achievement of greater self-determination by the peoples of West Africa;

hence, when democratic ideas at the end of the First World War stimulated nationalist aspirations in Africa, Casely Hayford saw his opportunity to translate his long-standing plans into actuality. Unity in thought, in aspiration, and in objective could best be served through unity in action, through a united West Africa. True patriotic love of country was love of humanity, he said. "I venture to commend . . . the coming together of entire West Africa as one man to think together, and to act together in matters of common need."

Following this conviction, Casely Hayford led a group of educated Africans in organizing a conference of West African leaders drawn from the Gambia, Sierra Leone, Nigeria, and the Gold Coast to be held in Accra in 1920. The conference was based on three major premises—that the western-educated African had become the natural leader of his people, that Wilsonian self-determination was a proper basis for political, economic, and social reform in British West Africa, and that community of interest would henceforth lead West Africans to work in close concert in achieving their mutual objectives.

These objectives took many specific forms as they emerged through the resolutions of the conference. Constitutional reform was demanded in terms of municipal self-government, the end of courts presided over by British administrative officers, popular election of half the membership of the legislative councils, and the creation of special houses of assembly, containing popularly elected majorities, which would be responsible for colonial taxation and budget policy. Equality of opportunity between European and African was stressed in civil service, medical service, and judicial appointments. Similarly, there was urged the end of economic discrimination against Africans in favor of European business interests, especially in connection with indigenous land ownership and the right to sell or lease land without interference by the government. Further, it was argued that more efficient self-government might be fostered through a strengthened African press and particularly through more extensive, improved education capped by a West African university. Finally, the idea of national self-determination was given a special African relevance in the demand that no disposition of the former German colonies be made without reference to the wishes of the people of the territories involved.

As the conference concluded its work, it formed a permanent National Congress of British West Africa and subsequent meetings were held at Freetown in 1923, in Bathurst in 1925-1926, and at Lagos in 1929-1930. Much the same demands were put forward at these later conferences, an indication of the lack of practical success of the congress's demands. Casely Hayford argued that the congress had been responsible for the legislative council reforms of the 1920s and for the founding of Achimota College in the Gold Coast, but beyond these questionable claims there was little concrete progress to show.

The fact was, the National Congress had been founded well ahead of its time. Not only did it get a cool reception from colonial administrations suspicious of a movement which challenged their authority and questioned their competence, but it never was able to capture the united backing of all indigenous groups within West Africa itself. In the Gold Coast, many chiefs were unsympathetic to a movement made up of westernized Africans, whereas political divisions within the educated community of Nigeria robbed the congress of effective support in that country. Moreover, the congress never made clear its determination to speak for all the people. Its rallying cry that "taxation goes with effective representation" had a deceptively authentic ring, but what it seemed to mean in practice was that the rate-paying, educated Africans wanted effective political control of the machinery of government they felt they were supporting through their taxes, and there was little indication of their genuine interest in true popular government. Be that as it may, political reform in British West Africa was not to be found in an interterritorial congress movement during the period between the two world wars. When Casely Hayford died in 1930, the National Congress lost its chief supporter, and it too soon expired.

The Pan-African Movement

The National Congress of British West Africa had sought to secure greater economic, political, and social privileges for the people of the British West African territories. Nevertheless, it was also part of a larger movement for unity among members of the black race the world over, and it attempted as an organization made up of native Africans to give world leadership to this pan-African movement. Actually the congress did little in a practical way to assume such leadership, although Casely Hayford, particularly through his journal, the *Gold Coast Leader*, gave enthusiastic applause to evidence of black solidarity in various parts of the world, and laid claims for Africa as natural leader of worldwide pan-Africanism. His argument was simply one of antecedents. Black people originated in Africa, and it was to Africa that they might appropriately turn for refreshment and inspiration. Under African leadership, Casely Hayford argued, the black race could harness the discoveries of science, throw off the yoke of oppression, and eventually employ an elevated sense of right and wrong to assume moral leadership in a sick and materialist world.

As it happened, the guiding hand for a nascent pan-African movement came in another form from another source. First, there was the abiding interest in Africa maintained by New World blacks throughout the nineteenth and into the twentieth century. For those burdened with slavery and the subsequent inequities of segregation and discrimination, Africa was a continuing source of inspiration for racial accomplishment and solidarity as well as a destination for emigration schemes put forward occasionally within the black community of America. Next, the idea of racial solidarity transcending continental limitations was given specific manifestation in the first pan-African conference convened in London in 1900 by the West Indian barrister Henry Sylvester Williams. This meeting, called to protest colonial rule in Africa, was attended by blacks largely from the West Indies and the United States, but it gave concrete definition to the idea of black unity, for the first time expressed through the technique of a pan-African congress.

Finally, pan-Africanism reached full dimension in 1919 when the black American leader W. E. B. Du Bois organized a pan-African congress in Paris coincident with the Versailles peace conference. Du Bois's objective was simple and clear—to seize the opportunity presented by the assembled delegates from the powers of Europe in order to demonstrate the solidarity of the black race, and to lay claim to the importance of Africa in the postwar world. Resolutions were passed calling on the great powers to establish codes of law, to be enforced by the League of Nations, which would protect the racial, economic, and political interests of Africans.

These were utopian hopes quite out of touch with the realities of postwar colonial policy in Africa. Indeed, Du Bois was fortunate to be able to gain permission from the French government to hold his conference at all, since martial law was still in force in France. He succeeded only because of Blaise Diagne's intercession with the French premier, Georges Clemenceau; yet, despite this modest beginning, Du Bois was pleased with the results. The conference had asked specifically that the German colonies be turned over to an international body rather than to various colonial powers, and in this suggestion Du Bois saw the germ of what came to be the mandates commission of the League of Nations.

Two years later in 1921, Du Bois brought together another, more ambitiously conceived, pan-African conference which met in London, Brussels, and Paris with larger representation, particularly from Africa itself. This time, however, Europe was much less receptive. When a resolution criticizing the Belgian colonial regime was passed, there was sharp reaction in Brussels and an innocuous substitute was proposed and declared passed despite what Du Bois described as a clear majority in favor of the original version. This parliamentary maneuver was the work of Blaise Diagne who was acting as presiding officer at the time and who had now become a critic of Du Bois's pan-African movement. The second congress had taken as its theme the idea of racial equality as a basis for eventual self-government in Africa. Diagne declared himself opposed to any implied criticism of France's colonial policy, and succeeded in adding to the final resolutions of the conference a statement citing what Diagne regarded as the liberalism of France in dealing with her colonies.

Diagne claimed that Du Bois had become a dangerous and misguided man whose internationalist, bolshevist tendencies were obscuring the benefits that European powers had brought to their colonial peoples. Diagne had supported the first conference because he thought he saw an opportunity for Africans in the French colonies to educate their American brothers by comparing France's liberalism with the repressive measures used in the United States against American blacks. The continued radicalism of the Du Bois contingent had made this difficult, said Diagne, although he felt that he had succeeded in some measure in forcing Du Bois to abandon his extremely critical stand on colonialism. For the assimilated Diagne, the only true cooperation in Africa was that between whites and blacks. "To isolate the black race," he wrote, "and to let it work out its own evolution is ridiculous . . . The evolution of our race . . . requires the cooperation of everybody."

This rebuff to the pan-African aspirations of American blacks was later underscored by the exchange that Diagne carried on with Marcus Garvey who had attempted to enlist Diagne's support for Garvey's own pan-African movement with its strong criticism of European colonialism and its expressed purpose of creating a black empire in Africa. Once again Diagne cited the persecution of the American black in contrast to the African under French rule. Improvement in the conditions of blacks living in America, said Diagne, could never come by preaching revolution, but only through emulation of the example in the French colonial territories of peaceful, progressive government. "We Frenchmen of Africa wish to remain French," he concluded, "for France has given us every liberty and accepted us without reservation along with her European children. None of us aspires to see French Africa delivered exclusively to the Africans as is demanded, though without any authority, by the American Negroes," at the head of whom Garvey had arbitrarily placed himself.

As with other efforts to effect social, economic, and political reform for blacks during the interwar period, pan-Africanism eventually fell on hard times. Garvey's back-to-Africa movement collapsed in 1925 when he was convicted of fraud and finally deported by the United States to his native Jamaica. Meanwhile, the pan-African conferences of W. E. B. Du Bois continued to meet intermittently, without great achievement. A third convened in London and Lisbon in 1923 and another in New York in 1927, but neither of these had much success in terms of black solidarity or social progress for the black race. The London-Lisbon meeting was marred by the split among blacks occasioned by the Garvey movement and by the continued opposition of the colonial powers. The New York congress, which was sponsored by American black women's organizations, dealt largely with questions of social welfare in Africa but had little direct African representation. In 1929 a fifth congress had to be canceled because of the economic crisis in the United States. It was not until the end of the Second World War that this fifth congress was finally held, by which time the course of world events had put an entirely new complexion on the pan-African movement and the nationalist aspirations of Africa's people.

Liberia and African Nationalism

The pan-African movement during the years after the First World War became involved with the affairs of the Republic of Liberia, pursuing her uncertain existence as the only independent black nation in West Africa. At his first pan-African congress, W. E. B. Du Bois had suggested an internationalized Africa formed of the former German colonies, to which could subsequently be added sections of Portuguese Africa and the Belgian Congo. Marcus Garvey had also talked of an independent African empire, and then had negotiated specifically with the Liberian government for a grant of land to accommodate his African colonization movement. Liberia was initially cordial to the idea which called for the repatriation of between twenty and thirty thousand black families from the Americas, each representing a worth of $1,500, the whole operation to be financed by Garvey's Universal Negro Improvement Association to the extent of $2 million. The suspicion soon arose within the Liberian government, however, that Garvey might be conspiring to unseat the True Whigs who had long been the reigning party within the country; what was more, the Liberians seemingly were warned by neighboring colonial powers that there could be no toleration of an organization within Liberia that admittedly was working to overthrow European authority in Africa. In 1924, therefore, the Liberian pledge was rescinded in a move that was shortly followed by the general collapse of the Garvey movement.

Marcus Garvey was among the least of Liberia's troubles, however. After three-quarters of a century of independence, the country was still beset by the same problems that had long complicated healthy national growth—an inefficient, arbitrary, and often corrupt government, chronic insolvency resulting from an impoverished economy linked with administrative laxness, an uncertain national sovereignty threatened by European colonial expansionism, and a repressive "native policy" that maintained insecure but tyrannical control over the tribal areas. Politically, the country had continued under the domination of the descendants of the original black settlers from America who, by the conclusion of the First World War, numbered about twelve thousand against an indigenous population of perhaps as much as one million. Among the settlers, the True Whig Party formed an oligarchy, which not only denied the indigenous peoples any meaningful political representation or self-expression, but also presented the Americo-Liberians with a bureaucratic regime perpetuated through such devices as election irregularities, political patronage, censorship, and arbitrary presidential rule.

Much of Liberia's trouble was financial. Inadequate and badly administered revenue policies had led to foreign loans in 1871, 1906, and 1912, negotiated on unfavorable terms which increased the country's debt burden and invited the possibility of intervention by creditor nations. In 1920 an American loan was tentatively arranged, but no final agreement was forthcoming, failure resulting in large measure from a lack of enthusiasm both in Liberia and in the United States. Nevertheless, the initial interest of the American government at least forestalled intervention by European powers, while the final breakdown in negotiations in 1922 forced Liberia into certain financial reforms at home. New tariffs and domestic taxes were imposed and methods of collection given a thorough overhaul. By 1925, revenue was almost three times that of 1918, and there was even a small budgetary surplus.

The basic problem of economic development remained, however, along with the need to liquidate expensive foreign loans. During the 1920s these pressures combined with a search by American industry for sources of natural rubber, and all these factors led ultimately to the conclusion of the well-known Firestone agreements of 1926-1927. With encouragement from the United States government, the American industrialist Harvey S. Firestone negotiated a series of concessions which enabled the Firestone interests to obtain ninety-nine-year leasing rights to tracts totaling one million acres for development as rubber plantations. In return, Firestone paid rental fees and certain customs duties and agreed to construct harbor facilities at Monrovia. The total investment was protected by a controversial $5 million loan which funded previous Liberian foreign indebtedness, but at advanced interest rates, and in effect introduced American control over the collection of revenue in Liberia. Thus Liberia traded a loss of authority concerning national affairs for increased income from taxes and rentals, a measure of protection against potential intervention by neighboring colonial powers, and a general economic upturn based upon the introduction of American capital and organizational efficiency.

In fact, the Firestone connection did much to pioneer economic development, although initial miscalculations by Firestone over the availability of an adequate supply of workers raised the delicate question of compulsory labor such as was commonly practiced under the concession systems in the French and Belgian Congo and elsewhere. As it happened, in 1929 Liberia was accused by the United States of condoning a regimen of forced labor tantamount to slavery, and the following year an International Commission of Inquiry appointed by the League of Nations was invited to investigate. Although Firestone was shown to employ only voluntary labor, a number of prominent Liberian officials were charged in the commission's report with conducting a system of compulsory labor "hardly distinguishable" from true slavery. The findings forced the resignation of highly placed government officers, including President Charles King, brought legislation designed to correct the abuses in question, and almost led to the imposition of a foreign protectorate under League of Nations auspices.

Aside from the reforms, which outlawed slavery, pawning, and the export of contract labor, international intervention was forestalled largely by Liberian determination to direct its own affairs. At the same time, administration of the hinterland continued substantially unchanged in its long-standing authoritarianism designed to maintain the ascendancy of the Americo-Liberians. Settler domination was assisted by the ignorance and isolation of the indigenous population hampered by a poor transportation and communications network and a rate of illiteracy exceeding 90 percent. Nonetheless, other more direct means remained in effect.

Beginning in the first years of the twentieth century, a system of government through local rulers had been instituted which not only reduced the costs of administration but kept the interior divided and isolated along tribal lines. In addition there were hut taxes, labor requisitions for public works, and control of residence and population movements all imposed through recourse to military force. When necessary, moreover, there was no hesitation to reshape traditional institutions to suit official convenience, and to all these repressive measures was added an informal exploitation in the form of such tactics as unauthorized taxes, crop seizures, and illegal forced labor. All in all, the generally harsh and arbitrary policy induced a response of "sullen restless fury" punctuated by bloody outbreaks of violence.

With the inauguration of William V. S. Tubman as president in 1944, a fundamentally new approach was introduced in the form of Tubman's Unification Policy. The underlying philosophy of this approach was directed toward giving the traditional societies a sense of genuine participation in national life in place of their former exploitation. Extended suffrage and parliamentary representation, introduction of programs for health, education, and public works into the hinterland, guarantees against alienation of tribal lands, improvement of the professional quality of the interior administration, and a campaign to promote appreciation of traditional culture all combined to attenuate the old animosities. Thus, as the tide of African nationalism flooded in the years following the Second World War, Americo-Liberians were able to take the lead as patriots within their own country, avoiding the forces which, for example, relegated the Creoles in Sierra Leone to a subsidiary role in national politics. For, despite the many changes which introduced vast social, economic, and political improvements for the indigenous people of Liberia, it was the settler minority that remained firmly in control of the sources of power and wealth as the era of African independence dawned.

Suggestions for Further Reading

For the First World War see the chapter by Michael Crowder and Jide Osuntokun in *History of West Africa*, Vol. II, 2nd ed. (Burnt Mill, Harlow Essex: Longman, 1987) edited by J. F. A. Ajayi and M. Crowder, as well as the issue of the *Journal of African History*, Vol. XIX, No. 1, 1978, all of its articles devoted to this subject.

Both British and French colonial policy is discussed in detail in R. L. Buell, *The Native Problem in Africa*, 2 vols. (London: Frank Cass, 1965; Hamden, CT: Shoe String Press, 1965). Also to be consulted is *Africa Under Colonial Domination, 1880-1935*, A. A. Boahen, ed., Vol. VII of the *UNESCO General History of Africa*. For the ideas on colonial administration of Lord Lugard see Margery Perham, *Lugard:*

The Years of Authority (London: Collins, 1960); and Lugard's own *Duel Mandate in British Tropical Africa*, 5th ed. (London: Frank Cass; Hamden, CT: Shoe String Press, 1965). French policy is set forth in R. Delavignette, *Freedom and Authority in French West Africa* (London: Oxford University Press, 1950; Frank Cass, 1968); and Michael Crowder, *Senegal: A Study in French Assimilation Policy*, rev. ed. (London: Methuen, 1967; New York: Barnes & Noble, 1967). For more recent detailed studies of colonial rule, see J. A. Atanda, *The New Oyo Empire: Indirect Rule and Change in Western Nigeria, 1894-1934* (London: Longman; New York: Humanities Press, 1973); and A. I. Asiwaju, *Western Yorubeland Under European Rule, 1889-1945* (London: Longman; New York: Humanities Press, 1976).

National politics, covering both British and French West African territories, are discussed particularly in terms of the ideas of nationalist leadership in R. W. July, *The Origins of Modern African Thought* (London: Faber & Faber, 1968; New York: Praeger, 1967). See also J. A. Langley, ed., *Ideologies of Liberation in Black Africa, 1956-1970* (London: Rex Collings, 1979). Pre-World War II French West African politics are studied in part in G. W. Johnson, *The Emergence of Black Politics in Senegal* (Stanford: Stanford University Press, 1971). Harry A. Gailey, *A History of the Gambia* (London: Routledge and Kegan Paul, 1964; New York: Praeger, 1965) deals with that British colony. For the Gold Coast see David Kimble, *A Political History of Ghana*, (Oxford: Clarendon, 1963; New York: Oxford University Press, 1963). Nigeria is covered by M. Crowder, *The Story of Nigeria*, 4th ed. (London: Faber, 1978) and Elizabeth Isichei, *History of Nigeria* (London: Longman, 1983); and J. Coleman, *Nigeria: Background to Nationalism* (Berkeley: University of California Press, 1958). Some of the flavor of West African nationalist thought may be obtained from the writings of nationalist leaders; for example, J. E. Casely Hayford, *Ethiopia Unbound* (London: Frank Cass, 1969); Herbert Macaulay, *Justitia Fiat* (London, 1921); and Henry Carr, *Special Report on the Schools of Southern Nigeria* (Old Calabar: Government Press, 1900), and in Langley cited already.

July, Coleman, Buell, and particularly Kimble discuss the National Congress of British West Africa, which is also the subject of a chapter by M. Kilson in R. I. Rotberg and Ali Mazrui, eds., *Protest and Power in Black Africa* (New York: Oxford University Press, 1970). See also Magnus J. Sampson, ed., *West African Leadership* (Ilfracombe, England: A. H. Stockwell, 1949).

The role of Blaise Diagne at the pan-African congresses after the First World War is discussed in July, but see also George Padmore, *Pan Africanism or Communism* (London: Dobson, 1956); as well as Imanuel Geiss, *The Pan-African Movement* (London: Methuen, 1974), and V. B. Thompson, *Africa and Unity: The Evolution of Pan-Africanism* (New York: Humanities Press, 1969). For Diagne and the election of 1914, see G. W. Johnson, "The Ascendancy of Blaise Diagne and the Beginning of African Politics in Senegal," *Africa*, vol. 36, No. 3 (July, 1966).

On Liberia, see Buell's *Liberia: A Century of Survival, 1847-1947* (New York: Kraus Reprint, 1969) as well as the chapter on Liberia by J. G. Liebenow in G. Carter, eds., *African One-Party States* (Ithaca: Cornell University Press, 1962). See also Liebenow's *Liberia: The Evolution of Privilege* (Ithaca and London: Cornell University Press, 1969) and the chapter by M. B. Abasiattai in *History of West Africa*, Vol. II, cited already.

19

In the Heart of Darkness

The Unity of Adversity

Despite its vastness there was a certain unity to the great central block of Africa that came to comprise colonial empires for France, Belgium, and Portugal. From the Sahara to the Zambezi, from Angola to Mozambique, it was primarily Bantu country, and it was poor—poor in people, in resources, and in standards of living. Thin soils, a capricious climate, and endemic disease had kept populations low, scattered, and on the move. Depressing the quality of life, such afflictions had discouraged political stability as well, and bred geographic isolation. Yet over time a traffic had developed in desired commodities like iron, copper, and salt, and trade routes emerged that gradually formed commercial unities over widening areas.

The arrival of outsiders from Europe and the east African coast accelerated and eventually dominated these growing mercantile networks. In eastern Africa it was Swahili and Portuguese in search, first of gold, then of ivory and slaves. In the west the Portuguese quickly instituted a commerce in human chattels to feed the growing demands of New World plantations. By mid-nineteenth century, on the eve of the colonial era, this vast central African territory had fallen increasingly under foreign influence, its production moving outward into the markets of the world.

Nevertheless when European powers rushed to establish their colonial empires late in the nineteenth century, there was a marked disinterest in the Bantu heartland. France and Britain were preoccupied elsewhere, principally in West Africa. The Germans at first were content with a few coastal enclaves, while southern Africa below the Zambezi was already a special case unto itself. With the international slave trade headed toward extinction, these poverty-stricken latitudes hardly seemed worth the effort of colonization. Portugal, it is true, was vigorous in asserting its prior claims in Angola and Mozambique, but her hegemony ultimately rested on the acquiescence of apparently disinterested powers. For its part, France took over what became French Equatorial Africa, but there was no great enthusiasm in this move. Most astonishingly of all, the great watershed of the Congo and its tributaries was allowed to slip away, almost as an afterthought, to become nothing less than the personal fief of Leopold II, king of the Belgians.

The Belgian Congo

Conceived in the fertile imagination of the Belgian monarch, the Congo Independent State was brought into the world of nations in 1885 through his skillful machinations at the Berlin Conference. It was a unique phenomenon, the total creation of a remarkable man, the fulfillment of his imperial ambitions, and the outlet for his royal energies. "There are no small nations . . . only small minds," he pronounced, and not being one himself, proceeded to give shape and substance to the vast realm he had brought into being.

This was no mean task, even for an empire builder. Vague treaty rights had to be confirmed through effective occupation which meant, among other things, subduing the tenacious Arab slavers in the Lualaba country to the east and checking the energetic expansionism into the Katanga of that other African imperialist, Cecil Rhodes. Not content with mere consolidation, Leopold II sought, through the Anglo-Congolese agreement of 1894, to occupy the Bahr al-Ghazal, but this move was thwarted by the French, intent upon keeping the way open for their east-west axis. Such undertakings were enormously expensive, and their cost had to be added to already mounting outlays for routine exploration, occupation, and administration. During the five years following 1885, Leopold was obliged to pay out twenty million francs of personal assets in support of his African adventure, a ruinous reversal even for a royal speculator.

This state of affairs could not long be endured by a man who regarded the Congo as his private property and who expected substantial returns on such valuable real estate. Beginning in 1887, Leopold granted extensive landholdings to a Belgian firm organized by Colonel Albert Thys who undertook to construct a rail line past the Congo River rapids, from Stanley Pool to the sea at Matadi, a link with the outside world essential to the exploitation of the Independent State's resources. The railroad was completed in 1898, by which time Leopold had hit upon other sources of financial assistance. At the Brussels Conference for the Abolition of the Slave Trade in 1889-1890, he succeeded in obtaining international agreement to a 10 percent import duty, ostensibly levied as a means of combating the Arab slave trade. At the same time, in 1889,

Leopold II willed his African empire to Belgium, a calculated action that immediately yielded a ten-year, interest-free loan of twenty-five million francs.

This was a good beginning, but the Congo had much more to offer, and Leopold moved systematically toward a fuller exploitation of his domains. The initial policy adopted in 1885 had conceded commercial freedom to European traders as stipulated in the Berlin agreement, while providing that the state would claim title only to vacant lands, that is, lands not actually occupied by Africans. Such laissez-faire principles had brought little benefit to the Independent State, and soon were set aside in favor of a more remunerative regime. First, Leopold tightened up land policy by defining African land ownership in 1891 to comprise only areas under active cultivation, a most serious restriction considering indigenous agricultural practice which usually involved a periodic movement from exhausted lands to unoccupied, fresher tracts. Next, he earmarked all land now defined as vacant to be the *domaine privé*, the domain of the state, the natural products thereof, chiefly wild rubber and ivory, being the exclusive property of his government. In practice, this restricted zone came in time to comprise approximately half the total area of the Independent State, virtually all the territory north of the Congo (Zaire) River as far as Stanleyville, parts of the Kasai, and the vast Katanga which was divided between the state and the Katanga Company chartered in 1891. Other private concessionaires were licensed to assist with the harvesting of produce from these state lands, to which Leopold added a large tract of royal terrain, an enormous personal preserve staked out in the Lake Leopold region in 1896.

The commercial monopoly of Congo assets now safely in hand, for the Independent State was a stockholder in most of the private companies involved, Leopold now moved to the business of extracting the wealth of the land. First, there were the mineral resources of the Katanga, to be developed and controlled through a series of public and private bodies of which the *Union Minière de Haut-Katanga*, chartered in 1905, was to become most widely known. Next were the important resources of ivory, and particularly of rubber, their harvest resting heavily on the availability of indigenous labor. In 1892 a tax was imposed, payable in kind, expressly to encourage the gathering of rubber, and in 1903 Africans were required to work forty hours a month for the state or the private concessionaires, again with the harvesting of wild rubber particularly in view. Beyond these exactions were a variety of obligations involving construction labor, food requisitions, and military service.

One feature of this system of forced labor was the looseness of its administration which permitted wide discretion concerning methods of enforcement by local agents; another was the policy of production premiums paid to company employees and state officials, an open invitation to the abuses soon to become the hallmark of the Congo regime and the object of widespread international censure. Indeed, a constant, compulsive demand for rubber combined with few scruples about methods led straight to a system of unrivaled barbarism. The labor regimen meant virtual servitude for workers isolated far from home in strange and difficult surroundings; worse still, when villages failed to produce their assigned quota of rubber, chiefs and women were held captive against collection which was also urged by a liberal use of the *chicotte*, a hippo-hide lash of severely punishing qualities.

The variety of the atrocities and the vindictiveness of their perpetrators strain the limits of credibility. Armed African soldiers or company guards raided villages, looting supplies while taking hostages against deliveries of rubber. Others assigned the task of guarding villages established themselves as local despots, making free with women and food supplies, killing and maiming those who resisted their tyrannies. Mutilation became a common practice, employed as punishment or even as a form of census, and stories were numerous of soldiers returning from expeditions to be congratulated on their collections of amputated right hands or garlands of ears festooned on a string. These obscenities added macabre punctuation to the rape, pillage, and murder that ravaged wide areas, and greatly reduced the population, in the process also effectively limiting the harvesting of rubber.

Such atrocities, reported in a swelling chorus of protest by missionaries and other observers, led first to investigation and then to conversion of the Congo State into a Belgian colony. Much of the criticism originated in Britain where humanitarian scruples were combined with objections over Leopold's commercial monopolies violating the free-trade guarantees of the Berlin Act of 1885. Both the Aborigines' Protection Society in London and the Congo Reform Association of E. D. Morel played their parts, but particularly damaging was the report filed in 1904 by Roger Casement, British consul to the Congo. Casement's eyewitness account of brutal malfeasance was soon substantiated in the conclusions of Leopold's own investigating committee, and with international criticism mounting, the Belgian king finally capitulated. In November 1908, his home government annexed the Congo Independent State which thenceforward became the Belgian Congo.

There had been humanitarian misgivings in Belgium itself over Leopold's Congo administration, but annexation was greeted with no great enthusiasm in the tiny country where a pragmatic view of the world could envision only trouble and expense in connection with this vast new acquisition. In fact, however, the main financial liability continued to fall on the Congo African, not on the citizen of Belgium. Under royal management, the king's private domain in the Lake Leopold area had yielded an estimated 71,000,000 francs between 1896 and 1905, much of this fortune expended for personal and public purposes in Europe. In transferring Congolese sovereignty to Belgium, Leopold also passed on assets valued at 110,000,000 francs along with assorted debts and liabilities amounting to 246,500,000 francs.

Whatever income the Belgian state received from its newly acquired holdings of concession company securities and real property, it regarded the carrying charges on fully 200,000,000 francs of its Congo obligations as chargeable against the Congo itself. Thus the Congo, having contributed so generously to Leopold's personal wealth, was now obliged to service a heavy debt, much of which had been incurred by Leopold to finance lavish public works in Belgium. Moreover, for the time being, the shift from personal to colonial rule left unaffected the special position of the concessionaires which continued to control land in the Congo many times the size of Belgium unencumbered by any rental obligation to the Congo government.

Eventually Belgium renegotiated most of the Congo concessions on terms more favorable to the state, but the basic concept of economic advance primarily through private capital was not to be altered by a nation that believed so firmly in the balanced budget and the inflexible equation of private profit with public good. Under Belgian administration, therefore, economy in government and development through sound business practice became one basis for colonial policy. Another was reform of the abuses that had characterized the days of the Independent State combined with a thoroughgoing paternalism toward the Congo people which, it was felt, would eventually bring civilization where darkness reigned—the concept of "white man's burden" in its pure form. Finally, there was that well-developed Belgian pragmatism which emphasized practical solutions to specific problems, which frowned on articulated, long range planning, and which denied colonial officers any recourse to guiding principles in moments of crisis.

What seemed in the abstract to be a well-ordered colonial administration devoted to human welfare emerged in practice, therefore, as an ill-designed authoritarianism based on misconception and fatally bound to the notion of human inequality. Examples abound. On the fundamental issue of land ownership and utilization, the colonial government made no essential changes from the policy of the Independent State. Occupation and ownership continued to be defined by European standards as large tracts were turned over to concessionaires and still larger sections reverted to state ownership. Moreover, Belgian concepts of economic advance in the Congo, formulated in terms of development by private European initiative, fully justified utilization of surface and mineral resources as a direct contribution to the improvement of African life, ignoring deep-seated anxiety among the people over alienation of their land.

Political administration and local government were constructed on similar miscalculations. Traditional custom and the chiefly authority were to be the basis for local rule, but in 1910 a decree was passed providing for the division of the country into chiefdoms which bore little relationship to the actualities of indigenous life and frequently placed authority in the hands of minor public figures or nonentities while the leading chiefs went unrecognized. In 1920 and periodically thereafter new administrative units were created lumping together peoples of diverse origins to be governed by nominated chiefs lacking traditional sanctions and responsible for executive and judicial duties without precedent in traditional society. Quite probably these changes were designed to make the chief more the member of a colonial civil service than the representative of a traditional society for which Belgian administrative officers had small respect in any case. Chiefs thus came to occupy an anomalous position—assigned leaders of their people, yet without status at home or substantive authority in the colonial regime; agents of the white rulers charged only with the administration of unpleasant tasks, such as road maintenance or law enforcement, meaningless in traditional society.

Labor policy was another fertile area for misunderstanding and mismanagement. The flagrant excesses of the Leopold era had been firmly suppressed, but recruitment continued unabated as concession companies engaged in vigorous competition for scarce workers. Inadequate administrative control resulted in malpractice such as organized hunts for labor and the custom of earlier times whereby women were made hostage until the men of a village agreed to sign on. A head tax instituted in 1914, and payable in cash, also encouraged villagers to leave their homes periodically, and in the Congo with its low population density (11.6 persons per square mile in 1923) there was always the danger of serious ecological dislocations if care were not exercised in restricting recruitment to allowable levels.

Programs regulating land, labor, and local government, however enlightened they might have appeared in the abstract, thus had little appeal for the African peasant. "What happiness have they brought us?" was the lament of one Congo chief. "They have given us a road we do not need, a road that brings more and more foreigners . . . causing trouble, making our women unclean, forcing us to a way of life that is not ours, planting crops we do not want, doing slave's work. . . . The white man . . . sends us missions to destroy our belief and to teach our children to recite fine-sounding words; but they are words we believe in anyway. . And we live according to our beliefs, which is more than the white man does."

Chiefly hostility toward the missions was natural in view of the missionary role in undermining the basic tenets of traditional Africa. The missionaries, both Catholic and Protestant, were quite genuinely horrified by what they regarded as the depraved quality of daily existence—polygamy, slavery, drunkenness, slothfulness, cruelty—and they attached small merit to African values that ignored individual initiative and cared not what tomorrow might bring. Before Christianity could be introduced, they argued, such barbaric customs and practices would have to be destroyed; yet in their zeal, the missionaries were sometimes guilty of a heavy hand and a myopic view that confused European social standards with absolute truth and saw little virtue in African ways. Nevertheless, those Africans who left their villages to live in the mission-sponsored communities found modern medicine in place of witchcraft, and well-constructed houses and sanitary living conditions to counter the unkempt squalor of some traditional villages. The end of polygamy meant a higher status for women, a settled existence offered the possibility of a more refined agriculture, while education opened a new world of literacy and technical skills. The whole aspect of these Christian assemblages impressed European visitors as one of comfort and prosperity.

To the missionary there were spiritual as well as material advantages. Christianity and literacy, it was felt, meant liberation from ancient fears and taboos, the tyranny of the sorcerer was to be replaced with a new sense of hope in achievement and rational thought. In this realm of intangibles, however, the advantages may not have appeared so clear-cut to the African neophyte. Traditional beliefs broken down were not so easily replaced with something new. If the old standards lost validity, new ones, half-learned and ill-understood, were not necessarily more relevant to the simple, bucolic world into which they were introduced. For many, the confrontation of two ways of life caused complications enough in everyday affairs but this was nothing to the trauma of conflicting beliefs involving ancestors, the spirit world, and the hereafter wherein a false choice threatened eternal darkness in isolation from all that was familiar and loved.

For the African who did succeed in transferring to the European world, there was the disquieting suspicion that the faith preached by the missionaries was not so much a means of liberation as an engine of subjugation. There were many Africans in the Catholic priestly hierarchy (six hundred on the eve of independence in 1959) and Protestant missions had a similar record of ordination; yet had not these priests been relegated to inferior positions, were not congregations segregated by color and churches dominated by white missionaries, and did not the Catholic missions use their state educational subsidies to indoctrinate the African into a permanent subservience? In short, was not Christianity designed to perpetuate racial inequality and colonial domination?

Such misgivings may well have been related to the rise of separatist churches and prophet movements which enabled the African to throw off European missionary control in preference to a self-directed religious expression. This development first manifested itself in the spring of 1921 in the Thysville district of the Lower Congo with the appearance of Simon Kimbangu, a carpenter and evangelical preacher, who quickly gained a large following drawn by his alleged powers as a healer. Although he urged neither heresy nor civil disobedience, Kimbangu soon ran afoul of the authorities who came to regard him as an insurrectionary and imprisoned him later in the year along with some of his disciples.

While Kimbangu remained continuously in detention until his death in 1951, his movement retained its vitality, breaking out periodically during the twenties and thirties with the recurrent rumor that, although he was presumed dead, the victim of the authorities, the prophet would rise again and lead his people. Such neo-Kimbanguist revivals were especially related in the popular mind with the arrival in the Congo of the Salvation Army in 1935, its members being regarded as the reincarnation of Kimbangu and his disciples, their white faces the color of the departed spirits and the letter S on their uniforms the symbol for Simon Kimbangu himself.

This particular variant of Kimbanguism was partly propelled by a minor Salvation Army adherent, Simon Mpadi, whose movement, concentrated during the late thirties in the French Congo, involved in outspoken form xenophobic and nationalist impulses which had always been implicit in the Kimbangu cult. Without doubt many purely religious factors explain the long-lived strength of Kimbanguism and other prophetic sects like the *kitawala*, or Watchtower, movement active in the Katanga during the interwar period. There was, for example, the insufficiency of emotional outlet in evangelical Christianity, or again, the inability of Christianity to deal satisfactorily with the problem of witchcraft or the role of ancestors.

Nevertheless, important extrareligious factors were present as well. Some of Kimbangu's early followers had predicted the end of the world in a cataclysm which would destroy the whites, and this initial anti-European element had remained. Kimbangu's anticipated resurrection and return was partly a protest against Western political and religious domination, while his stature as prophet raised him to a level with such figures as Christ, Muhammad, and Moses. European rule with its forced labor and its destruction of traditional society had weighed heavily, but overt resistance was useless and dangerous. Converted to religious expression, however, political protest was possible and proved to be a not altogether unsatisfactory means of dissent.

Belgian paternalism, so manifest in political and religious matters, was reflected in economic and social affairs as well. The great industrial concerns, *Union Minière, Forminière*, and others, solved their labor problems during the twenties and thirties with expensive but well-conceived welfare programs. Workers lived in attractive communities complete with public health services, schools, and recreation facilities. Workers received good pay, hours and working conditions were carefully regulated, while transportation from home, rations, and medical attention were extended to all members of a family. The rising number of experienced workers living healthy contented lives emphasized the apparent success of this system.

Yet paternalism had very serious limitations. The schools were excellent but scarcely extended beyond the elementary level. Public health facilities and housing were modern and efficient, but they were also strictly segregated. Economic opportunity was unrivaled up to a point, but management and the professions were closed to the African. An informed populace was thwarted by press censorship, and education found no fulfillment in the creation of an African leadership. When independence came in 1960, the Congo possessed scarcely two dozen university graduates.

The problem was based in the paradox of Belgian policy—the mixture of administrative efficiency with blindness toward human aspirations, the attempt to improve the economic lot of the Africans while suppressing their political impulses, the practice of racial discrimination by representatives of a Western civilization that in its finer moments at least preached human equality and perfectibility. The paradox did not go unnoticed in the Congo. "We are helots," remarked one African observer. "There is no real intercourse between Belgians and Africans. The crudest, stupidest, most recently arrived Belgian *colon* regards himself as my superior. . . . Officially there is no *racisme* in the Congo; but in practice we live in ghettos; in many shops we are served at separate counters; railway stations have separate entrances for *Européens* and *Indigènes*. Most of us in Leopoldville are too busy making money . . . to bother much about these things. But there is a *malaise*. Radical ideas reach us from across the Congo. . . . One day there will be an eruption. . . . We believe you mean to give us rights, but when?"

When the eruption finally came, the Belgian administration was no more ready than the Congo people. Belgian paternalism had stifled self-reliance and Belgian pragmatism could only precipitate the Congo into a sudden independence its people were ill qualified to sustain.

French Equatorial Africa

The enormous sprawling territory which France designated as Equatorial Africa in 1910 was a complete anomaly. Stretching eighteen hundred miles from the coastal palm forests of Gabon into the mid-Saharan highlands of Tibesti, it formed an area as great as Belgium's Congo but with little of the compactness, interior communication, and uniformity of its neighbor. In the north it contained desiccated wasteland, then stretches of such great savanna states as Wadai, Bagirmi, and Bornu—Muslim empires subsisting on slaving and the trans-desert trade, and including Arabs, Fulani, and Tuareg along with the local Kanuri, Wadai, and other peoples. Far to the south in the dense rain forests of the Ogowe, Congo, and Ubangi watersheds were numbers of small Bantu groups isolated in village communities and simple in their economies and sociology. With the exception of some hardwood stands in Gabon and wild rubber in the rain forest, the area seemed poor in resources, as indeed it was in population. In 1926, there were estimated to be but 3.1 million inhabitants in all French Equatorial Africa, a density of only 3.5 to the square mile.

French occupation of this immense territory arose from the exigencies of late nineteenth-century European power politics rather than from any intrinsic local attractions. Initial contacts went back to the decade beginning in 1839 during which years France established trading posts and antislavery naval stations on the Gabon coast, of particular note being Libreville, founded in 1849 as a repatriation center for a cargo of freed slaves. This Gallic counterpart to Britain's Freetown constituted France's major achievement in the area before the arrival of the explorer Savorgnan de Brazza in 1875. Brazza conducted a series of explorations in the interior, first along the Ogowe River and then in other areas, capping his investigations by the treaty of 1880 with the Bateke king Makoko, thus forming the basis for France's claims to the Gabon hinterland as far as the site of Brazzaville on the north side of Stanley Pool.

Brazza's activities, which included an infectious publicity campaign in Paris, stimulated a wave of expansionist enthusiasm in France and led to further explorations which, by the opening of the Berlin Conference in 1884, had firmly established French hegemony north of the Congo along the Ubangi River. France's imperial ambitions were now in full flood and further expeditions followed, culminating in the grand design to join central and north Africa at Lake Chad through which point an east-west axis would attempt to link Senegal with Ethiopia and Somalia. Such pretensions were only partially realized. During the 1890s both Britain and Germany forced their own colonial claims as far as Lake Chad, the former from northern Nigeria and the latter from its Cameroun protectorate. Moreover, in 1898 Captain Marchand was obliged to withdraw before Kitchener at Fashoda. Two years later, however, Major Lamy marched south from Algeria, linked up with Lieutenant Joalland's force coming east from Niger, and the two columns then joined Émile Gentil, already in Bagirmi country, where together they defeated the Sudanese conqueror Rabih at the battle of Kuseri in April 1900.

This imposing pattern of conquest, followed more modestly by occupation and interior consolidation, was forced to proceed slowly at first because of the difficult terrain, the scattered population, and resistance to the repressive tactics of the French forces which were at the same time so few in numbers. In 1905 four territories were organized, Gabon, Middle Congo, Ubangi-Chari, and Chad, all responsible to a governor-general at Brazzaville, and in 1910 a federation of French Equatorial Africa was formed. Poor communications, lack of personnel, and meager financing meant that administration was nominal, while public works, education, and health programs remained virtually nonexistent.

Colonial theorists in metropolitan France nevertheless had no doubts about the necessity for introduction of European civilization into what they regarded as a primitive land, nor was there great hesitation within official circles over the virtues of economic exploitation; hence by 1912 when peace had become more general, vast tracts were already long since in the hands of private concessionaires. Most of these lands had been granted in 1899 in the rain forest areas of Gabon, Middle Congo, and Ubangi-Chari with their extensive growth of wild rubber, the more arid stretches of savanna in Chad proving less attractive. Forty companies with a combined capitalization of 59,000,000 francs received a total of 665,000 square kilometers, more than the area of France, for which they paid a trifling rental and over whose products they exercised complete ownership.

As in the Belgian Congo, a head tax and forced labor were imposed locally to insure collection of rubber and ivory, while no realistic attempt was made to protect African land ownership and utilization, even in restricted areas. An insufficiency of government officials and indifference to the niceties of

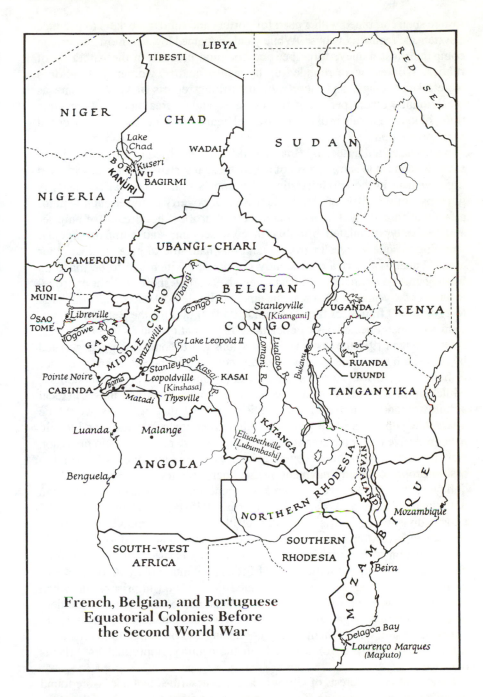

French, Belgian, and Portuguese
Equatorial Colonies Before
the Second World War

justice soon combined with a need for porters and rubber workers to produce a systematic regimen of abuse. While yields remained low and most concession companies lost money, force became common practice in the gathering of rubber. Workers were rounded up by armed guards, women and children were taken hostage, and there were disturbing reports of villagers shot as recalcitrants, others perishing from disease and ill-treatment. At the same time, bloody reprisals broke out, directed against Europeans by the incensed local population.

An investigation headed by Brazza in 1905 substantiated many of the alleged atrocities and led to some reform of the concession system, if not to any marked improvement in the administration of France's four equatorial colonies. A good part of the difficulty lay in the essential poverty of the French Congo, a fact that soon dashed hopes of commercial profit if not dreams of empire, and probably stimulated brutality in civil servants and company agents, straining to squeeze wealth from a land that had little to give. Unlike other areas, Equatorial Africa consistently ran deficits which had to be made up by the home government, while its sluggish economy showed slight improvement over the years. In 1924 revenue amounted to 18,650,000 francs compared to 21,000,000 francs for tiny Togo and 195,000,000 for the Belgian Congo, a situation that reflected basic deficiencies in population and natural resources.

Beginning in 1910 the system of concessions was to some extent renegotiated by the French government but without any conspicuous benefit either to France or her central African colonies. Vast areas remained under private monopoly, while during the 1920s evidence accumulated pointing to fresh abuses in local administration. It had been established in 1910 that Africans would be guaranteed a portion of all produce gathered on company lands, and would have exclusive use of the areas designated as "native reserves." No provision was made, however, for surveying the reserves, and no controls imposed to assure proper company payments for rubber gathered.

Beyond this, there appeared to be a recurrence of malpractices in connection with the requisition of African labor. During 1925-1926, for example, André Gide had visited Equatorial Africa in fulfillment of a childhood desire to see the Congo River, but this sentimental journey soon converted to a chronicle of indignation over atrocities witnessed, and his classic *Voyage au Congo* emerged as an eloquent indictment of French colonial policy. Gide spoke of enforced rubber requisitions which ended in fines and imprisonment when not properly fulfilled, of beatings and killings, and of the infamous incident of defaulting rubber gatherers made to carry heavy beams the day long in the broiling sun, one of them finally collapsing and perishing in his tracks — a tale of cumulative terror that had left the country empty and its villages deserted.

Conditions in the forests of Ubangi-Chari, as described by Gide, were found to obtain generally through French Equatorial Africa, the result of the same poorly supervised practices of private concessionaires unchecked by inadequate

numbers of civil servants working under a parsimonious colonial administration. Such circumstances were responsible for the loss of thousands of
lives during the construction of the railroad from Brazzaville to Pointe Noire
in the 1920s, and other tales of malfeasance and brutality continued periodically
to emerge from the Congo. Nevertheless, although occasional adverse criticism
helped put an end to particular abuses, up to the time of the Second World
War no fundamental change had been brought about in this unhappy state
of affairs.

Needless to say, African economic enterprise was not encouraged under
French rule, and only a few lumbermen and cocoa farmers from Gabon were
able to accumulate any appreciable capital before the era of independence.
At the same time a tradition of exploitation by concession companies and an
arbitrary if impecunious administration gave little encouragement either to
the doctrine of assimilation or the rise of a class of educated Africans. A few
small groups of elite had grown up in Libreville, Brazzaville, and Pointe Noire
over the years, educated in mission schools and attracted to a modest political
activity. In Libreville a branch of the French League for the Defense of the
Rights of Man was active between 1918 and 1930, protesting governmental
policy on such matters as land alienation and administrative justice. An allied
group, Young Gabon, was founded in 1920, opposing the rule of tribal elders
and demanding French citizenship. Generally these groupings tended to divide
along ethnic lines and their effectiveness was reduced accordingly.

Of more consequence were the mass movements of semireligious origin
which proved to be resistant equally to the direction of the colonial government
and of the traditional authorities. The Kimbangu cult spread across the Congo
River to gain a following among the Bakongo people living in Brazzaville,
and it was in that same city that violence erupted in 1930 in connection with
another popular leader, Andre Matswa. Matswa, a member of the Balali people,
had formed an Association of Natives of French Equatorial Africa in 1926
while living in Paris. Starting life primarily as a social organization, his group
soon developed political objectives, spreading at the same time to Brazzaville
where it began to attack racial discrimination and the *indigénat*, or administrative justice, as well as demanding French citizenship for Africans.

Returning to Brazzaville to take leadership of his movement, Matswa
attempted to organize a trade union, but was soon arrested and sentenced to
three years in prison. He subsequently escaped, but was eventually recaptured
and exiled to Chad where he died in prison in 1942 while serving a life sentence.
Matswa's trial in 1930 was the scene of rioting, reflecting not only popular
displeasure at the persecution of a local leader but a deeper discontent concerning political and social backwardness for which the colonial administration was held chiefly responsible. For years the Balali leadership, both educated
and traditional, cooperated in a passive resistance to the authorities which
was eventually crushed only by military action, and after the Second World

War an antigovernment messianic cult arose in Brazzaville in the name of André Matswa.

For its part, the French regime showed little interest in basic reform until forced to do so by the pressure of events outside Equatorial Africa. The trauma of France's military collapse before Hitler's armies in 1940 was followed by the slow rise of Free French resistance to the Vichy government in which Equatorial Africa played such a conspicuous role. Under her black governor-general from French Guiana, Félix Eboué, Brazzaville became the spiritual center of Free French activity; more than that, Eboué was able to inaugurate a fundamental change in colonial policy which looked to a completely new worldwide French union in the postwar period. Instituting improved medical and educational facilities, Eboué put an end to forced labor and moved toward the development of a peasant agriculture. Basing his system on a renascence of traditional sanctions, he encouraged authentic chiefs and strengthened indigenous institutions, offering the chiefs modern education to match their ancient status. Such changes were to be the foundation for a genuine partnership between European and African, and indeed, the Brazzaville Conference of 1944, over which Eboué exercised considerable influence, defined the future status of French African colonial peoples much along the liberalized lines he had suggested. Nevertheless a long history of neglect and oppression left the people of French Equatorial Africa ill-prepared to deal with the new world that awaited them in 1945.

Portuguese Angola and Mozambique

Portuguese occupation of Africa—predatory and corrupt—did not change in character over the years. There remained the same concentration on slaving which had typified the early relations with the kingdom of Kongo and the region of Angola; after 1700, moreover, growing poverty and stagnation in Portugal insured parallel decadence for her African colonies. During the seventeenth and eighteenth centuries, Angola in particular was ruled by administrators who were expected to profit from their position, and frequently did so. Legitimate commerce and capital investment were insignificant, education and health facilities nonexistent, and missionary work in full decline. Atrophy and tyranny marked this unhappy land.

In Angola, the interior was under ineffectual occupation by military governors whose single-minded policy was exploitation without revolt, a controlled warfare which brought in slaves while avoiding a general uprising. In the towns, such as Luanda and Benguela, there was a small population of Europeans, trader-officials, adventurers, and so-called *degradados* drawn from the ranks of criminals and political exiles. By 1845 Angola contained only eighteen hundred Europeans, most in Luanda. Benguela, for example, though important in trade, numbered only thirty-nine whites including one woman. These settlers were politically important because of their control of the town councils, much of their exertions being directed toward pushing the administration into armed slave raiding in the interior. Indeed, slaving dominated all activity and was the sole support of the economy. Toward the end of the eighteenth century, it was estimated to account for 88 percent of the colony's revenue, the rest coming from tithes and exports of ivory.

Mozambique presented a similar picture. By 1800 the coastal forts and trading posts had long since degenerated into centers of disease and decay, poverty-stricken slums matching the untidy dilapidation of Angola's ports. The towns contained Hindus and Goans along with Portuguese, most of them devoted to trade. Inland, during the seventeenth century, there had grown up a system of great feudal estates, or *prazos*, held by Goan or Portuguese landlords who governed their holdings without reference to the Portuguese authorities, granting such allegiance as they did to the inland rulers of the Mutapa kingdom. Thus, as in Angola, Portuguese control over the interior was nominal; yet it was the *prazeros* who probably held Mozambique for Portugal when they successfully resisted the war bands coming up from the south, set in motion by the Mfecane during the early nineteenth century.

By mid-eighteenth century, the economic life of Mozambique had swung squarely to the marketing of exploitable African labor. Earlier coastal trade had languished and gradually given way to slaving, particularly in response to Brazilian needs, while many a prazo operated gangs of workers who were in fact slaves, although they were not always called such. Despite the British antislavery patrols, various international accords, and Portuguese government decrees, slaving flourished along the Mozambique coast as late as the 1870s. Some cargoes headed for Cuba, others went to Zanzibar and Madagascar, while still others were sent to the French sugar plantations of Réunion in the Indian Ocean.

During these same years there had been an increasing flow of workers on their way from the Delagoa Bay area to seek employment on the farms of South Africa. In 1875 Mozambique and the British in Natal and Cape Colony reached agreement regulating this movement, the Portuguese gaining considerable income therefrom by substantially raising their passport charges. During the 1880s, however, the opening of the gold mines on the Witwatersrand in the Transvaal greatly increased the demand for labor in South Africa and recruiters began systematically to take workers from Mozambique. Soon half the mine workers were Mozambique Africans, and by 1910 some sixty thousand were laboring on the Rand.

Once again the Portuguese authorities insisted on regulating the supply, ostensibly on humanitarian grounds, but actually for the profit that could be gained. In 1901 an accord was reached that permitted controlled recruitment, and in 1909 a formal convention was signed to the same end. Service fees yielded substantial income which was supplemented by the provision of the 1909 convention that one-half of the total rail traffic from the Transvaal industrial area be channeled through Lourenco Marques on Delagoa Bay. Indirect gains were also impressive. Between sixty-five and one hundred thousand workers were contracted annually and each brought back accumulated savings which greatly stimulated the Mozambique economy. In 1903 the Portuguese estimated that two hundred thousand workers a year could mean an infusion of £3,000,000, and at that time it was reported that Africans were purchasing £600,000 worth of consumer goods a year, mostly in the southern districts where recruitment was heaviest.

Labor migration on this scale was much resented locally by public officials or private contractors relying on forced labor, for the workers clearly preferred the better conditions and assured wages of the Transvaal, and had to be coerced to work in Mozambique. In the Portuguese colonies, forced labor had long been considered an African birthright. When the government in Lisbon abolished the slave trade within Portuguese territory in 1836, there was such a violent reaction in Angola that for another decade no really effective action could be taken to implement this decision. Finally, in 1845 a prize court in Luanda put an end to the export of slaves, but only at the price of serious dislocations in an economy which was based largely on slaving.

During the 1850s, a series of decrees announced the gradual end of slavery in the Portuguese territories, but the provision of a transitional period of labor for each *liberto*, or freedman, was an invitation to abuse, and *liberto* soon became a euphemism for slave. In 1869 slavery was abolished immediately and without qualifications but again the law was evaded as masters made effective use of the uncertain status of the *liberto*. When the condition of *liberto* was finally terminated in 1876, workers were still obliged to contract their services, preferably with former masters, and vagrancy codes made continued forced labor an easy matter. Meanwhile, slave recruitment in the interior went on as before, now under the name of contract labor. The worst abuses and hypocrisy, however, were reserved for the labor market on the island of São Tomé, where, during the last decades of the nineteenth century, workers were shipped from Angola by the thousand each year to work the coffee and cocoa plantations. Many were listed as household servants, others as *libertos*, and some even came as freemen complete with passports, but all entered a world of virtual slavery.

Pressed from different quarters by British humanitarians and Angolan planters, the Portuguese had put an end to the worst abuses of São Tomé recruitment by 1915, and indeed the transitional years from the nineteenth to the twentieth century saw a concerted effort to institute a more comprehensive and coordinated colonial policy. First there was systematic subjugation of the interior, not completed until as late as 1930, then the imposition of an authoritarian regime under absolutist provincial administrators. During this process policies varied from a philosophy that frankly sanctioned white rulers exploiting black laborers, to that of a paternal humanitarianism designed to improve the African's lot materially and morally, and even to permit some few to achieve the status of *assimilados*, or thoroughly Westernized Portuguese citizens.

The changing fashion in colonial administration was largely responsive, not to circumstances in Africa, but to politics in Lisbon. In 1926 a military dictatorship was instituted and six years later the government of Antonio Salazar came to power. Over the years there had always been expectations in poverty-stricken Portugal that somehow her impecunious colonies would bring great wealth, but as always the colonies failed to throw off the weight of exploitation to which they were subjected. With Salazar, however, Portuguese mercantilism began to yield modest results—colonial production tailored to the home and world markets, Portuguese immigration and capital investment, and improved agriculture. The African worker continued to be the basis for colonial production, but some attempt was made to avoid the worst abuses of the contract labor system. There was, however, something more. Salazar talked of Portugal's need for colonies in order to maintain a position of world importance, and there were many official references to the noble and uplifting mission of civilization and to the solidarity and glory of an imperial Portugal.

For the African, this policy meant assimilation at glacial pace into a Portuguese way of life, an extended tutelage requiring what was regarded in Portugal as an enlightened if rigorous paternalism. Hence the principle of racial equality was subverted by the practice of cultural inequality, and reality unfolded in a repressive labor policy, continued economic backwardness, inadequate educational and medical facilities, and lack of technical development. A passbook system, the *caderneta*, enabled the authorities to keep all Africans under close surveillance while censorship, border patrols, controlled education, and ruthless police work prevented the development of cadres of local leadership. Hence, despite rural poverty and urban slums, there was little unrest in the years before the Second World War. A policy of calculated repression which discouraged literacy, withheld education, and isolated the African from the fast-changing world around him seemed ideally designed to maintain Portugal's colonial position indefinitely.

Nonetheless, a total quarantine could not be achieved. A number of Africans succeeded in gaining secondary-school training, while Angolan towns like Luanda and Malange contained industrial and clerical workers aware of the advantages of modernization. There had been modest political activity even before the Second World War, but more forceful mass organizations emerged during the 1950s. In 1956 the Popular Movement for the Liberation of Angola (MPLA) was formed in Luanda to represent urban dwellers and to voice their rising discontent. Two years earlier, another political grouping, the Union of the Peoples of Angola (UPA) had taken shape in Leopoldville where numbers of Bakongo migrants from Angola had gone in search of employment.

Whatever the initial objectives of these parties, they soon were caught up in the continental thrust of African independence. First there was the example of Ghana in 1957, then in the following year, self-government for the people of the French Community territories, including the Bakongo north of the Congo River. In 1960 the Republic of the Congo came into being, as Nigeria also gained its freedom, and it was clear that other nations were soon to follow. In Angola, by contrast, the administration mustered troop reinforcements, arrested many of the MPLA leaders, and sought to wipe out opposition by force. The Angolan Africans—their jobs and their land threatened by Portuguese immigration, their leaders imprisoned, their government at war with them—fought back, and the revolt of February 1961 began its long and torturous course.

Suggestions for Further Reading

Works covering French, Belgian, and Portuguese colonialism in Equatorial Africa are rare, but see R. L. Buell, *The Native Problem in Africa*, 2 Vols. (London: Frank Cass, 1965) for the French and Belgian territories, and the *Cambridge History of Africa*, Vol. 6, R. Oliver and G. N. Sanderson, eds. (Cambridge: University Press, 1985) and Vol. 7 edited by A. D. Roberts (Cambridge: University Press, 1986) for all three. Portuguese Africa is reviewed in Malyn Newitt, *Portugal in Africa, the Last Hundred Years* (London: C. Hurst, 1981) as well as the older *Portuguese Africa* by James Duffy (Cambridge, MA.: Harvard University Press, 1959), and *A Question of Slavery* by the same author (Oxford: Clarendon, 1967). See also P. J. Hammond, *Portugal and Africa, 1815-1910* (Stanford: University Press, 1967), John Marcum, *The Angolan Revolution* (Cambridge, MA: MIT Press, 1969), and the relevant chapters in *History of Central Africa*, Vol. 2, edited by David Birmingham and Phyllis M. Martin (London and New York: Longman, 1985), these last with heavy stress on economic factors.

For the Belgian Congo the two above-mentioned volumes of the *Cambridge History of Africa* are the place to begin, but see also the older *King Leopold's Congo* by Ruth Slade (London: Oxford University Press, 1962), Roger Anstey's *King Leopold's Legacy* (London: Oxford University Press, 1966), and L. H. Gann and Peter Duignan, *The Rulers of Belgian Africa, 1884-1914* (Princeton: University Press, 1979). S. J. S Cookey explores British relations with the Congo in his *Britain and the Congo Question, 1885-1913* (New York: Humanities Press, 1968), while Wyatt MacGaffey, *Modern Kongo Prophets: Religion in a Plural Society* (Bloomington: Indiana University Press, 1983) studies the Kimbanguist movement and its setting.

French Equatorial Africa is treated in *History of Central Africa*, Vol. 2, cited already and J. Suret-Canale, *French Colonialism in Tropical Africa, 1900-1945* (London: Hurst, 1971). Early political and messianic movements are discussed in Georges Balandier, *The Sociology of Black Africa* (New York: Praeger, 1970). For Eboué, see Brian Weinstein's volume, so entitled (New York: Oxford University Press, 1972). There are many accounts of Congo atrocities, but for the French areas see André Gide, *Travels in the Congo* (Berkeley: University of California Press, 1962), and the celebrated novel by Réné Maran, *Batouala* (Paris: Éditions Albin Michel, 1938).

20

The Two Societies of Southern Africa

Apartheid—Colonialism in South Africa

The years 1989-1990 marked a watershed in South African history. During that brief interval the Nationalist government embarked on an apparently irreversible course, no less than the establishment of a nonracial state, the dismantling of the notorious system of apartheid.

The term "apartheid" had first appeared much earlier, in 1948, during the election campaign that brought the Afrikaner National Party to power. An Afrikaans word translated somewhat awkwardly as "separatehood" or "separateness," apartheid had been largely unknown before that time, not to South Africa's population, let alone to the world at large. In substance, however, it was not nearly as new as it seemed.

Though the term "apartheid" was coined for the election, its underlying concept had been long in gestation among Afrikaner nationalist theoreticians. It argued that the races of the world embodied important cultural differences; thus racial groups were best kept physically separated from one another in order that each might develop its own genius uncorrupted by alien influences. The idea itself was certainly not new—witness the views on race of Edward Blyden and Marcus Garvey. In South Africa, however, it was no idle speculation. There, theory could be put into practice.

In 1950 Dr. Hendrik Verwoerd became Minister of Native Affairs in South Africa's newly-elected National Party government. As a leading Afrikaner intellectual and advocate of white supremacy, Verwoerd was a staunch supporter of apartheid and as minister he had a blueprint for action. What he envisioned was a series of self-contained communities, a central white state encircled by black satellites in training for possible self-government based

401

upon their own traditions. Black laborers, temporarily resident in the white state would be segregated in townships or "locations" where, as "foreigners," they had no political rights but where they were entitled to adequate housing and social amenities. Others would travel to work daily by means of a modern transportation system linking the satellite communities to the central industrial complexes. Cape Coloured and Asian (East Indian) populations were to be similarly segregated in what eventually might emerge as a commonwealth of nations in southern Africa, held together presumably by the political, social, and economic primacy of the Afrikaner state of South Africa. In the white areas, apartheid would mean "segregation," that is, separate amenities in public places—beaches, rest rooms, park benches, for example—the so-called "petty apartheid." Between South Africa and the Bantu states, or Bantustans, lay, in theory at least, a geographic gap that spelled "separation" or "grand apartheid" wherein citizens of each nation enjoyed the privileges and responsibilities of their citizenship at home but were to be regarded as resident aliens in each other's land.

Only just labeled and formalized in 1948, apartheid in its essentials had been part of South African life for a long time. Within a few years the first Dutch settlers at Cape Town had installed a restraining hedge and blockhouses to keep Khoikhoi out of their territory. Political and legal inequality was a well-established practice before the arrival of the British who, in their time, reintroduced pass laws, created "native reserves," and inaugurated hut taxes that controlled the land and labor of the indigenous population in ways that would have been thoroughly familiar to latter-day proponents of apartheid. Once union had been achieved in 1910, the government lost no time in adding legislation that intensified segregation in landholding, residence, work opportunity, and social freedom. With union, moreover, the African population was effectively disenfranchised, hence unable to raise any political opposition to these restrictions. Even the theory of racial segregation and separation had been earlier enunciated when Lord Milner, the South African High Commissioner after the Boer War, produced a report in 1905 that recommended strict geographic insulation of Africans who, Milner argued, should be taught habits of reliability in work but otherwise encouraged to retain traditional cultural and social institutions in their own territories.

Before Verwoerd's ministerial appointment the National Party government had already begun to explore the capabilities of the reserves as a basis for establishment of Bantustans, or "homelands" as they came to be called. A study was instituted, the results of which appeared in 1955 as the Tomlinson Report, and it was not encouraging. The deteriorating and overcrowded reserves could be rehabilitated, the report concluded, but at great expense and at best these lands would sustain only slightly more than half of the total black population that was expected by the close of the twentieth century. Tomlinson recommended large scale capital investment in the reserves to provide for soil rehabilitation, industrialization, new cash crops, and improved health, welfare, and educational facilities. Whatever their merits these proposals proved illusory when the Tomlinson population criteria were shown to be far below later projections, but in any case Verwoerd rejected much of the report on ideological grounds, resisting suggestions that would have encouraged industries, white capital investment, and private land ownership within the reserves.

Verwoerd's image of a future commonwealth of nations in southern Africa comprised an association of self-governing states but with the homelands economically dependent upon South Africa, a grouping to which he hoped the High Commission territories of Basutoland, Swaziland, and Bechuanaland, along with South-West Africa, might ultimately be added. In the homelands would dwell the "surplus" black population from the white agricultural and industrial areas, and Verwoerd moved to create his social and geographical "new vision" through fresh legislation that supplemented certain laws already on the books. Miscegenation in or out of wedlock had been outlawed in 1949 and 1950. In the latter year the Population Registration Act undertook to classify all persons in South Africa on a racial basis, thereby fixing the fate of each individual in relation to all subsequent and past racial legislation. The Group Areas Act also of 1950 provided for residential segregation by race; a series of Urban Areas Acts culminating in 1956 seriously limited the access of Africans to municipal localities; the job reservation laws and decrees determined which sort of employment was open to white and which to black; the Native Labour (Settlement of Disputes) Act of 1953 forbade strikes by Africans and discouraged their unionization; and the Reservation of Separate Amenities Act of the same year concerned itself with standards of public facilities, from hospital beds to drinking fountains, provided for the different races.

This was systematic, not random, discrimination designed to achieve total apartheid. Pass laws were extended to include women, squatters were moved off public and private land, and steps were taken to end long-standing black land ownership in white farming areas, the so-called "black spots." With the Bantu Authorities Act of 1951 and the Promotion of Bantu Self-Government Act passed eight years later, the logic of apartheid moved toward its goal of geographic separation. Together these laws sought to alter the constitutional status, and eventually to eliminate permanent physical residence, of Africans within the South African state, substituting the concept of Bantu nationhood in the "homelands." With the older African reserves as a territorial base, eight Bantustans were to be created, ultimately to become self-governing states to which Africans would in time return after their "temporary" residence in the white areas.

Armed with their two Bantustan acts, the South African authorities proceeded to organize governments within the reserves based upon traditional chiefly authority, the administration of Bantu governments at local, regional, and territorial levels closely supervised by a commissioner of the Department of

Bantu Administration and Development until the stage of self-government had been achieved. Over the years a total of ten homelands were established comprising slightly less than 14 percent of the South African land mass. In 1963 the Transkei became the first of these to reach self-governing status, its parliament a combination of elected and appointed members, its executive a chief minister and his cabinet, and its official language Xhosa.

The Transkei parliament was given control over its own budget and treasury as well as primary responsibility for local affairs. A European commissioner-general maintained liaison with the South African government which permitted no other form of African representation while it continued to manage all external matters along with surveillance of immigration, currency, and the Transkei constitution. As late as 1970 only the Transkei had come that far; by 1972, however, seven others had created governments with legislative assemblies. The following year the Ciskei, Bophuthatswana, Venda, and Gazankulu homelands joined the Transkei as self-governing territories—the last stage before total "independence." Thus the South African government seemed to have moved well along toward its stated objective—the establishment of a series of functioning Bantu states, self-directing to a degree but still largely subservient to the dictates of the parent South African Republic.

Despite expressions of independent thinking by the Transkei prime minister, Kaiser Matanzima, and particularly by Chief Gatsha Buthelezi of Kwazulu, continued subservience appeared probable in view of the formidable economic and political domination exercised by South Africa over its Bantustan clients. Until "independence" all political authority rested ultimately in Pretoria, and even after, the South African government controlled the disbursement of much-needed development funds; beyond this, the Afrikaner authorities further strengthened their dominance over South Africa's blacks by applying the concept of apartheid to education through the Bantu Education Act of 1953 and the Extension of University Education Act, passed in 1959.

These laws in effect segregated instruction at all levels, placing the control of education for Africans under the central government's Department of Native Affairs, shifting their curriculum away from the European syllabus toward traditional African materials with particular attention to Bantu languages, and establishing special universities for Africans, Coloureds, and Asians who, with some exceptions, were no longer permitted to attend the European institutions. Critics pointed to the emphasis on vernacular languages which effectively limited communication and cohesion among Africans of different tribal origin, and argued that the rigid personal and academic regulations imposed within Bantu universities would surely stifle African development according to any internationally acceptable principles of university education. But this was precisely the point. Divide and rule, and provide education, as Verwoerd had already observed, that trained its recipients for a servile position in society. Under the guise of autonomy the Africans were being fixed in an economic, political, and educational status that would insure their continued subservience to the ruling white society.

Thus the framework for apartheid was conceived, a classic form of indirect rule wherein an Afrikaner government dominated a series of neighboring Bantu regions, in theory the ideal separation of largely incompatible races, in practice firm control over an important reservoir of labor. For South Africa it was a new variation on an old story, and it contained elements that were at once bizarre, contradictory, and tragic. The contradictions were embedded in the imperatives of land, population, and urbanization. The urban-industrial centers—Johannesburg, Port Elizabeth, Durban, Cape Town and others— had been growing for decades, drawing into their vortex peoples of all races, as industry sucked up labor, both skilled and unskilled, and individuals sought a better living for themselves and their families. Between 1921 and 1960 the proportion of European city dwellers rose from 56 to 84 percent, of the Coloureds from 46 to 68 percent, of Asians from 31 to 83 percent, and of Africans from 12 to 32 percent. By 1980, as Verwoerd's successors strained to put his principles into practice, a third of 21 million Africans were estimated to be urban dwellers compared with approximately 500,000 seventy years earlier, drawn from an African population of but four million at that time. The number of urban Africans had therefore increased fourteen times, and the trend continued despite the apparent official determination to contain, even to reverse, this vast population movement.

The countryside was also beset with population problems along with an impoverished standard of living. Here a form of peonage kept the African rural laborer virtually outside the cash economy with a monthly income about equal to what a black industrial worker would make for two daily shifts. The result was a steady decline in the proportion of rural Africans, drawn to the cities or banished to the homelands, although in absolute terms there were more rural blacks than ever. The exodus might have been more pronounced except for the fact that a home on the countryside, mean though it might be, permitted a reasonably normal family life and healthy existence for some, conditions so conspicuous by their absence in the cities and particularly in the Bantu home territories. Other rural Africans, however, were homeless squatters—wives and children of migrant workers or refugees from the overcrowded reserves. The rural economy was thus overburdened by an unproductive population while suffering concurrently from a shortage of labor.

The African population continued to explode in all regions. The Tomlinson Commission had projected at most some 21,360,000 at century's end, a gross underestimate according to several subsequent counts that predicted 50 million or more. Even with the substantial economic and environmental homeland rehabilitation recommended by the commission and only incompletely implemented by the government, these territories—scattered, broken, scarred with erosion, and interspersed with white farms—could have supported adequate living standards for no more than a fraction of the numbers that were being thrust upon them. By the mid-1980s "independent" Transkei had about 60 percent of its ablebodied men working in South African factories, mines, and farms; those left behind were women, children, and the aged or infirm, producing only one-third of the food they consumed. For the Ciskei homeland that achieved "independence" in 1980 the situation was equally critical. More than half its food had to be imported while unemployment ranged between 25 and 50 percent, with per capita income less than $100 a year. The South African government supplied some 77 percent of the Ciskei budget, a level of support that underscored the bankrupt nature of the homeland people and policy. In 1984 it was estimated that there were 1.4 million destitute individuals residing in the homelands; nevertheless the government moved ahead with its plans. Attempts were made to persuade industries to decentralize and reestablish themselves near the homeland perimeters. These efforts largely aborted; hence a serious shortfall developed in job opportunities as the relocation campaign moved people from the cities and the countryside, eliminating numerous "black spots" in the process, depositing thousands upon thousands in the homelands.

By 1968 almost a half million Africans had been transplanted, but this was only a beginning. Between 1960 and 1982 some 3.5 million Africans were moved out of white areas and relocated, many in so-called "closer settlements" presumably because they permitted residents to commute daily to and from jobs in the white industrial centers. One such community saw its population density rise from 54 to 622 individuals per square kilometer, another from open fields to a sprawling slum of 120,000 souls. Thus was reflected the vast dimension of a relocation for which "forced removal" would be a much more accurate term. In the Transvaal over one million had been moved by 1982 with a half million more under imminent threat. Natal relocation involved some 745,000 up to 1982, almost as many again facing similar action.   By the process called "influx control" this segregation of "grand apartheid" was effected. A supply of black labor was made available, yet Africans were kept out of sight in the white areas, living their mean existence in homeland, settlement, or industrial compound.

The reverse side of this picture was the process of "resettlement," wherein residents in zones redefined as white areas were evicted from land they had occupied, sometimes for generations, their homes bulldozed as they were loaded aboard buses with their few portable belongings for a journey to their frequently far distant homeland, probably a place they had never before seen. Here they joined a swelling slum population in a rural ghetto of mud huts, shacks, and tents with inadequate sanitation and small plots suitable only for gardening, forcing family heads to remain away for protracted periods on contract or to endure the long daily commuter journey, the homeland economy resting upon small wages of these uncertain breadwinners.

It was an expensive program for the South African government but it seemed worth the price to a white population that knew blacks largely as domestic or industrial workers. Certainly white South African living standards have been among the best in the world today, characterized by comfortable homes, servants, free education, and frequently more than one automobile to a family. The country's 5 million whites own over 250,000 swimming pools while 800,000 servants cater to their wants, their personal wealth accounting for 60 percent of the national income compared with the 30 percent share of 30 million blacks.

Apartheid, however, involved subtleties and shades of meaning that are not apparent in bare statistics or government pronouncements. For many years labor shortages had brought informal relaxation of the system of job reservation and in 1979 it was abandoned altogether. Similarly, African unionization and the right to strike had been given limited sanction, while petty apartheid was allowed to lapse, at least officially, although local or individual prejudice still determined the status of a park bench, a beach, a restaurant, or a movie theater. The old pass laws were replaced by an identity card to be carried by all races, and a mixed population appeared in some white residential areas where blacks, coloured, or Asians were able to afford the rental. Most significantly, the resettlement program and influx control were suspended in the mid-80s, thereby eroding the segregated system of "grand apartheid," at the same time creating large pools of unemployed in the towns as a reverse flood of Africans engulfed the urban centers. As the decade drew to a close, therefore, there were indications of the revolutionary change that all at once seemed to point the South African nation irrevocably away from the bankrupt system of apartheid.

Apartheid and the Republic of South Africa

If apartheid was the logical extension of long-nourished Afrikaner views on society and race, its particular form and appearance was a direct result of South African white politics in the years following unification in 1910. The deeply felt patriotism of Paul Kruger—his view of the Boers as the chosen people fleeing the world's corruption to follow God's will in a new land—was easily transferable to others of like background, particularly after the trauma of defeat in the Boer War and Lord Milner's subsequent campaign to convert South Africa into an English-oriented component of the British Empire. British cultural assimilation not only failed in its objectives but greatly encouraged the rise of an emphatic Afrikaner nationalism, an anti-English sentiment which was to culminate a half-century later in the establishment of the South African republic, independent of any ties with Britain.

The move toward republicanism took time, for there were many, Boer and Briton alike, who were not immediately persuaded. The major figures in the years after union were moderates—Jan Smuts, Louis Botha, and J. B. M. Hertzog, Boer generals who were nevertheless advocates of a joint British-Afrikaner effort in building a South African state. Smuts and Botha argued the synthesis of two cultures as the basis for a strong and productive society. Hertzog agreed, but saw an initial need for raising the Afrikaner position culturally and economically (greatly extending the use of the Afrikaans language, for example) before the two streams could come together in total harmony. The difference was largely a matter of emphasis, but in the view of hard-core Afrikaner nationalists, Hertzog offered much more attraction, and it was to him that they initially attached their allegiance.

Nevertheless, Botha and Smuts formed the first governments, organized through their South African Party with Botha becoming prime minister in 1910 and Smuts succeeding when the former died in 1919. Their pro-English orientation, involving support for Britain during the First World War, greatly stimulated Afrikaner nationalism, however, which rallied behind the National Party formed by Hertzog in 1912. By 1924, the Nationalists were strong enough to unseat Smuts, his downfall coming significantly after he had broken a 1922 strike by white miners, called to protest the intended use of Africans in skilled positions on the Rand. This introduction into politics of the so-called ''native question'' further strengthened the Afrikaner position, and Smuts fell from power, accused not only of an antilabor bias, but of indifference to white superiority as well.

From this point forward, Afrikaner and National Party control over South African politics slowly tightened. Somewhat unwittingly and unwillingly, Hertzog was maneuvered into contesting the 1929 general election on the issue of race relations. Advocating segregation of the African population economically, socially, and politically, he particularly urged the removal of Africans from the common voter rolls in Cape Province, a privilege they had enjoyed from the time of unification in 1910. Although the time was not yet ripe for such a step, the emotion-charged racial issue enabled the Nationalists to win the contest and Hertzog to remain as premier.

During the depression years of the 1930s, Hertzog and Smuts effected a rapprochement, forming the United Party and directing a coalition government from 1933 onward, each man still holding to the two-stream conception of South African society. Such a view necessarily put them at odds with the *Broederbond*, a quasi-secret society of deeply nationalistic persuasion, founded after the First World War as an agency for the establishment of an Afrikaner-controlled nation. Politically the Broederbond movement was reflected in an intense dislike for the Smuts-Hertzog coalition and in the crystallization in 1933 of a right-wing movement among the Nationalists, the *gesuiwerdes*, or purified, who eventually went into opposition as the new National Party, under the leadership of a former Dutch Reform Church minister, Dr. D. F. Malan.

When Hertzog's bid for South African neutrality during the Second World War failed, his coalition with Smuts ended, and Hertzog soon retired from politics, for he could find little common cause with the extreme, anti-British views of the Nationalists. For their part, Malan and his colleagues refused to compromise the principles of Afrikaner nationalism, and saw their determination rewarded by victory in the election of 1948 that introduced the concept of apartheid. A rising industrialism had brought increasing numbers of Africans into the cities during the war while the worldwide liberalism of the immediate postwar years had encouraged African leaders to make political demands distasteful to white supremacy. The Malan victory was narrow, and indeed rested on coalition with a minor party, but once effected, it began a period of National Party domination backed by a steadily increasing support from all segments of the European population. Malan retired in 1954 and was succeeded by J. G. Strijdom who was replaced upon his death in 1958 by Dr. Verwoerd. Verwoerd's assassination in 1966 brought the minister of justice, John Vorster, to power as head of an all-powerful Afrikaner government.

Hertzog's views regarding racial segregation had finally forced a separate electoral roll for Cape Africans in 1936, and following the 1948 general election Verwoerd proceeded to convert the theory of apartheid into its practice. At the same time the Nationalists were determined to press forward to their major objective of an independent republic. Once again Dr. Verwoerd was the moving force, engineering a winning referendum in 1960 which was followed in 1961 both by the formal proclamation of the Republic of South Africa and by her withdrawal from the British Commonwealth.

Neither the Bantustan policy nor republicanism would have been easy to achieve without the tacit support of South Africa's English population. The vote for the republic in 1960 was indeed close, but the drift away from the United Party to the Nationalists after 1948 was unswerving and finally resulted in an overwhelming Nationalist majority. The causes appear to rest ultimately in the broad-based support among Europeans for white domination and segregation, if not for apartheid. After the proclamation of the Republic, moreover, a number of factors brought the white community into closer cohesion. First, Nationalist ascendancy muted the previously strident elements of Afrikaner nationalism, while increasing criticism abroad drove South Africans together in mutual defense. Next, the European community tended to regard the tribulations of the new nations of Africa as a clear indication of African incapacity for self-government. Finally, a growing spirit of militant nationalism among South Africa's own black population stiffened the attitudes of those who might previously have entertained some degree of sympathy toward the grievances of the African masses.

African Nationalism in South Africa

The many factors that so greatly stimulated nationalist development throughout the continent at the conclusion of the Second World War were perceived as clearly in South Africa as in other latitudes. There, too, were Africans who had fought the good fight defending the Four Freedoms and who looked forward at war's end to the rewards of loyalty. There, sensitivity to the coming possibilities was, if anything, greater than elsewhere. Were not the black people of South Africa more advanced than those in other parts of Africa? Were they not earlier introduced and more thoroughly assimilated into the urban world and the industrialized complex of modern society? Did they not far surpass the people of Africa's many territories in numbers of university graduates, degree of literacy, political and social sophistication, and economic development? Were not their grievances deeper, of longer standing, than those of any other people?

Such thoughts were much in the minds of the Africans in South Africa at the very moment that Afrikaner leadership was achieving its political victory of 1948 and thereby opening the way for its greatly accelerated regimen of racial discrimination. Here in fact was the disheartening climax to years of unrelieved defeat, and it marked the beginning of a new trend by Africans toward positive action rather than petition to gain the better life and the freedom they sought.

Black nationalism in South Africa had been conceived in adversity, in the disappointment of John Tengo Jabavu, Dr. Pixley Seme, and others over the unification constitution of 1910 which denied the African the right to sit in the Union parliament and limited his franchise to those resident in the Cape Province. From the first their response was insufficient, ineffective. The modest objective of Dr. Seme's African National Congress (ANC) which asked only for citizenship through constitutional means was no match for white opposition, which reacted not with concessions but with an increasing pressure of discrimination and segregation. As early as 1911, a Mines and Work Act reserved skilled jobs in the extractive industries for Europeans. Two years later, legislation was passed limiting the area of land available for African use to scarcely more than one-tenth of the whole South African land mass. At the same time, this Natives' Land Act directed the eviction of almost one million African squatters from white farms. The day after the bill was passed, as Sol Plaatje put it, "the African woke to find himself a pariah in the land of his birth."

Although the Afrikaner exponents of apartheid did not gain power until 1948, their work had largely been done for them by preceding governments. Directly after the First World War, for example, the Smuts ministry wielded an even hand in crushing labor unrest in Port Elizabeth, dispersing members of a millenarian religious sect in the eastern Cape Province, and chastising "Hottentots" in South-West Africa for tax default, all at a cost of hundreds dead and injured. In 1923, moreover, Smuts put through the Native Urban Areas Act permitting municipal authorities to control the number and location of Africans living in the cities.

For its part, the administration of General Hertzog, between 1924 and the outbreak of the Second World War, proceeded with a systematic delimitation of African civil and political rights. In 1926, the Mines and Work Amendment

Act extended and stiffened the definition of job segregation, while the Masters and Servants Act made it a criminal offense for Africans to break contracts. A year later the Native Administration Act gave the government the authority to appoint and depose chiefs, and threatened Africans with fines and imprisonment for causing "any feeling of hostility between Natives and Europeans." Other legislation circumscribed social and personal activity, virtually prohibiting the sale of alcohol to Africans, forbidding black-white extramarital intercourse, and further limiting urban residence for Africans.

The culmination of these restrictions came in 1936 with the Native Representation Act. This law relegated Africans in the Cape Province to a separate voting roll where they might elect three white men to represent them in parliament. Thus was the African vote segregated in the Cape, and brought a step closer to the total disenfranchisement which obtained elsewhere in the Union. The African community witnessed these reverses with growing anguish. "We have been denied all rights pertaining to human beings," cried an official of the African National Congress in 1929. "We are treated as aliens in the land of our fathers. . . . We are spoon-fed like children . . . denied all representation. . . . As a nation we are practically dead. . . . We are a race of servants . . . for the white man."

While the ANC continued to base its strategy in delegations and petitions, others sought more militant solutions. In 1918, the Industrial and Commercial Workers' Union (ICU) was founded by Clements Kadalie, an African migrant from Nyasaland of great energy and eloquence. At once Kadalie and the ICU organized a series of impressive strikes which captured the admiration of the African population and raised membership to a claimed figure of a hundred thousand. In the long run, however, administrative inexperience and implacable official opposition brought the union's undoing. Kadalie was embarrassed by the infiltration of white Communists whom he purged with difficulty, but whose departure deprived him of capable and experienced lieutenants. There followed an organizational deterioration which was hastened by defections, particularly that of the Zulu leader Allison Champion, who established a separate ICU in Natal. By 1930, the movement was finished; Champion was exiled from Natal, Kadalie was in obscurity, and only a handful of small unions, isolated and short-lived, signaled the passing of the once-powerful ICU.

The appearance of the Communists marked an important moment for it was the first of a series of efforts to organize and control black nationalism in South Africa, raising at once the question of whether leadership and objectives were to be exclusively African or whether they would be diverted to the service of international communism. For Kadalie the choice was clearly in favor of parochial objectives, the end of racial discrimination and the improvement of working conditions at home. Since that time, communism has maintained an uncertain influence, its revolutionary appeal clouded in the minds of African nationalist leaders by its association with white domination. At the same time, both before and after the outlawing of the South

African Communist Party in 1950, communism has offered obvious attractions in competition with Western constitutional forms which suffer the liability of example in the government of South Africa.

General Hertzog's introduction in 1936 of separate voting rolls in Cape Province gave rise to another African nationalist organization, the All-African Convention formed by Dr. D. D. T. Jabavu, the son of John Tengo Jabavu. The convention at once entered a vigorous if vain protest and refused to cooperate in the operation of the Natives' Representation Council, established concurrently with the change in voting procedures and given empty advisory functions connected with a broad range of African affairs throughout the Union. For a time, the African National Congress allowed its members to serve on the council, but over the years so little heed was paid to the council's deliberations that in 1946 its total membership resigned in protest, thereby signaling a virtual declaration of noncooperation against the South African government. With war's end, African demands had become much more insistent, even within the moderate African National Congress, but in 1948 the white position had also stiffened, and the result was not reform as in other parts of Africa, but rather the victory of Dr. Malan's National Party and the institution of apartheid.

Turning away from the traditional constitutional weapons of petition and representation, despairing of any ultimate prospect for political and economic emancipation, African leadership now began to shift toward direct action while avoiding recourse to outright violence. In 1946, a strike was called by the African Mine Workers Union which brought out seventy thousand workers and paralyzed the Witwatersrand mines for several days. Two years later, the ANC initiated two one-day work stoppages, and in 1952 the congress collaborated with the South African Indian Congress in a campaign of civil disobedience. Over a six-month period, eighty-five hundred African and Asian demonstrators were jailed, chiefly for deliberately breaking the color bar in public facilities. In 1957, there was a bus boycott in Johannesburg, while 1957 and 1958 were marked with further demonstrations, these by African women against their inclusion under the pass laws.

Such activities drew their inspiration from Gandhian principles of passive resistance, but frequently they led to violence in the course of police response. There was bloodshed in 1946 as the police drove to break the great mine strike. One of the 1950 sit-down strikes ended with rioting in Johannesburg during which eighteen Africans were killed and over thirty injured. The defiance campaign of 1952 was called off after a series of clashes with the police resulted in numbers of Africans shot dead or wounded. To rigorous police methods the government added other measures—proscription of the Communist Party in 1950, the inclusion of adolescents along with women under the pass-law regulations in 1956, a massive treason trial of ninety-one Africans, Asians, and European sympathizers begun late in 1956, and finally the outlawing of the African National Congress in 1960. These actions were usually effective in hampering African opposition. Even the treason trial, which ended in 1961 without a single conviction, succeeded in neutralizing the activities of most defendants.

As the lines of official repression hardened, African reaction grew correspondingly extreme. The traditional congress philosophy of racial equality achieved through nonviolence seemed bankrupt, its leadership, including Chief Albert Luthuli, vacillating and unrealistic, and its association with white liberals and Communists no longer acceptable. Luthuli had been elected congress president in 1952, but by 1958 he and other moderates were challenged by a group of young activists led by Robert Sobukwe, a lecturer at Witwatersrand University. Unsuccessful in capturing the congress, they formed the Pan-Africanist Congress in 1959 with a program of Africa-for-the-Africans, and a strategy of strikes and demonstrations designed to bring the downfall of the Nationalist government. The result was the anti-pass-law marches of March 1960 which culminated in the massacre at Sharpeville where sixty-nine people were shot down and many more wounded by a panicky police force.

By 1961, both congresses, acting underground, appeared ready to turn to sabotage as a weapon. With Sobukwe in prison, the Pan Africanists organized a movement called Poqo for purposes of sabotage, but its activities soon extended to political terrorism. In the ANC Chief Luthuli had reluctantly but gradually acquiesced in the weapon of sabotage, the function of the Spear of the Nation subsidiary of congress which came into being in 1962. In 1964, a number of younger congress leaders, including Walter Sisulu and Nelson Mandela, were brought to trial for sabotage. At this Rivonia trial Mandela freely admitted his participation, arguing that violence was the only recourse to the African, all other means of opposing white supremacy having been blocked by legislation. By the time of his sentence to life imprisonment, this seemed to be the feeling of a majority among the African population.

In the years immediately following Rivonia, however, apathy appeared to replace activism. With virtually all militant political leaders imprisoned, restricted, or forced into exile, there was little opportunity for overt agitation; moreover, a chronic shortage of labor forced up black wages while loosening the restrictions of job reservation laws. Even a modest prosperity brought into existence a small African middle class, and with South African living standards generally superior to those throughout the continent, there was a growing body of Africans with some investment in the status quo, unsatisfactory though that might be.

There was, moreover, the appeal, however limited, of local autonomy through the system of separate homelands. Against the unifying urge of African nationalism were poised local tribal loyalties, still a vital force for many and clearly encouraged by the Bantustan principle. The Transkei prime minister, Chief Kaiser Matanzima, maintained his position largely through the votes of government-nominated chiefs, but his policy of accepting the Bantustan philosophy while constantly demanding more rights within the framework of separate development was supported by a small but significant African following.

Matanzima has long been regarded as a genuine adherent of apartheid, in his judgment the best prospect for African advance. By contrast, the Zulu chief, Gatcha Buthelezi, emerged after 1970 as a tribal leader who accepted the Bantustan policy only as a necessary evil, trying to gain what advantage he could from the circumstances thrust upon his people. Pointing to the fragmented and overloaded character of the Zulu homeland, Buthelezi insisted that the South African government would be obliged to invest heavily in development; having committed themselves to separate homelands, he argued, the Afrikaners were bound to create viable and habitable Bantu territories or face the collapse of their apartheid philosophy. This position was difficult for Buthelezi. While working for his Zulu people within the constraints of the Bantustan principle, he exposed himself to attack by out-and-out nationalists who renounced all tribal commitments. At the same time Buthelezi's continuing insistence on a unified South African nation for the equal benefit of all races tended to be overlooked along with his steadfast refusal to move toward independence for his home Bantustan territory of Kwazulu.

South-West Africa and the High Commission Territories

At the time of South African unification, it was generally assumed that less developed neighboring territories such as Basutoland, Bechuanaland, Swaziland, and even the Rhodesias would ultimately be absorbed, and the South Africa Act of 1909 which set forth the details of union provided machinery for eventual incorporation. Britain was reluctant to see an immediate and unqualified transfer, however, and insisted on provisions that would protect the interests of the territorial inhabitants after transfer. The matter was not pressed at the moment, and did not rise again until 1935 by which time action without the consent of the African people themselves appeared increasingly remote. With the accession to power of the Nationalists in 1948, the question was again mooted, but by this late stage South African racial policies had thoroughly alienated world opinion, and the move toward incorporation was replaced by a growing demand within the territories for eventual independence.

The South African government's desire to absorb the High Commission territories was to a large extent bound up in the matter of apartheid and the administration of African reserves. Underdeveloped and impecunious, Basutoland, Bechuanaland, and Swaziland had long been heavily dependent upon South Africa, not only in economic terms but for many public services as well. Currency and banking, postal and telegraph facilities, and tariffs were all externally administered, while South Africa served as the chief market and principal source of goods coming into the territories. Significantly, a large proportion of the labor force from each territory found work in South Africa;

for Basutoland over 50 percent of its adult males at any one time were migrant workers in the Union.

Such close dependence involving much personal coming and going by individuals who suffered no economic or political color bar at home, was a source of embarrassment to the Afrikaner regime. Moreover, the Nationalists hoped through eventual absorption to reorganize the patchwork pattern of the Bantustans while adding vastly to their area of African reserves. In short, the South African government regarded the trust territories as "native reserves" in all but name, and sought to add them to the areas already held, thereby raising the proportion of the reserves from approximately 14 percent to near 45 percent of an enlarged South Africa.

In Basutoland, however, with its tradition of independence and its overwhelming African population, the British moved in 1959 to introduce a degree of internal autonomy which was designed as a first step toward total independence. Bechuanaland largely African in population, gained limited home rule in 1961 and subsequently forced further reforms which set her on the road to complete autonomy. Swaziland, with its considerable European influence and land ownership, encountered greater difficulty in drafting a satisfactory constitution, and suffered thereby a period of uncertainty, but in 1964 the Swazi paramount chief organized his own party and took power in a way that forecast eventual independence in the form of a constitutional monarchy. Thus South Africa, with absolute economic ascendancy over its indigent neighbors, was yet obliged to stand aside while they moved steadily toward political independence.

In South-West Africa, events took a decidedly different turn. This German protectorate had already been the scene of the infamous genocide campaigns of 1904-1907 which shattered the Herero and other peoples; now, at the conclusion of the First World War, it was mandated to the South African government and administered as an integral part of South African territory. Over the years the League of Nations Mandates Commission repeatedly criticized South African stewardship, pointing to exploitation of African labor, discrimination in favor of the white population, and an absence of much-needed educational and social development.

When in 1946 South Africa asked of the United Nations that South-West Africa be incorporated as part of the Union, her request was denied and the deficiencies of her previous administration cited as evidence of her unfitness. When the International Court of Justice handed down a nonbinding advisory opinion in 1950 that the United Nations had inherited League of Nations responsibility for South-West Africa, the Malan government countered by declaring that no United Nations responsibility existed for South-West Africa since the mandate had lapsed with the disappearance of the Permanent Mandates Commission of the League of Nations.

Subsequent efforts by the United Nations to assume her obligations were all thwarted. In October 1966 the General Assembly voted to end the South

African mandate but this action was repudiated by Pretoria as an illegal intrusion into South African domestic affairs. Two years later the United Nations renamed the territory Namibia and attempted to send a delegation to South-West Africa for the purpose of assuming control, but this move was blocked when South Africa refused to permit entry. In 1971 the International Court declared South African rule over Namibia to be illegitimate, a decision ignored in Pretoria where plans were already underway to divide the huge territory into a series of segregated reserves for Europeans and Africans alike.

Clearly South Africa was not ready to relinquish its hold on the territory and its 850,000 population in response to anything short of force. Essentially the circumstances paralleled those in the Republic itself. South-West Africa was rich in diamonds, copper, and other minerals, but labor was in short supply and had to be controlled to insure continued production in the mines. A system of separate homelands was not only consistent with the Bantustan program at home; it also facilitated recruitment of an essential work force. At the same time, a tightly controlled South-West Africa had strategic value as a buffer between South Africa and possible guerrilla movements entering from the north.

In 1968 the South African government announced plans for the eventual establishment of separate homelands for the black people of South-West Africa, at the same time inaugurating the first of the Bantustans in Ovamboland situated along the Angolan border. Labor unrest and a revolutionary movement subsequently taxed Afrikaner administration of the Ovambo region, but, as with South Africa proper, the Pretoria government moved steadily forward, apparently unswerving in pursuit of its stated objectives.

The Theory and Practice
of Partnership in Central Africa

For all its narrowness of vision, there was a certain perverse validity about the doctrine of apartheid. It offered the African little prospect but at least it told him squarely where he stood. To the north in the Rhodesias there was from the first much high-minded talk about responsibilities and privileges, civilizing missions and the promise of the future, but along with the oratory there developed a pattern of discrimination onerous in its uncertainty and vexing in its deception. After conquest and "pacification" in Southern Rhodesia, the official policy called for eventual assimilation of the African into European civilization, but circumstance imposed a *de facto* segregation based upon the differences between two cultures. When the Africans began to close the chasm, however, impediments were placed in their path as political rights were withheld so that social and economic advantages might be maintained.

Eventually discrimination was elevated to the status of a principle called "two pyramids" or parallel development.

In one essential this doctrine was philanthropic, enunciating the racial integrity of the Africans and the validity of their traditional institutions, and thereby providing a local argument both for the policy of indirect rule introduced by Sir Frederick Lugard elsewhere in Africa and the concept of trusteeship developed in the British Colonial Office. In another respect, parallel development stressed the antagonistic nature of the white and black races, confident in the superiority that the Europeans felt regarding their civilization and the need they saw for paternalistic rule to bring the Africans from the abyss of what was perceived as ignorance and barbarism. This second facet appeared prominently in an address delivered in 1938 by the Southern Rhodesian prime minister, Godfrey Huggins, whose words gave eloquent expression to the convictions of his European constituents. Western civilization, said Huggins, had brought peace, prosperity, and progress, offering Africans opportunities for advance which their own culture had long denied them. In this Africans should be given every encouragement, but their development should be separate and under no circumstances should it be permitted to interfere with progress in the white man's preserve. "To permit this would mean that the leaven of civilisation would be removed from the country, and the black man would inevitably revert to a barbarism worse than ever before. . . . The higher standard of civilisation cannot be allowed to succumb."

The "two pyramids" therefore became in fact a system of racial segregation imposed by the dominant European group. The establishment of Southern Rhodesia as a self-governing colony in 1923 provided the necessary constitutional authority, and legislation followed which insured that there would be no effective black challenge to white rule. First, there was the Land Apportionment Act, passed in 1930, which instituted a form of apartheid in landholding. To the African reserves of 21.6 million acres, this law added special areas totaling 7.5 million acres, open only to purchase by Africans. At the same time African squatters on 49.1 million acres of European lands were obliged to vacate, or remain as contract labor. The purpose was partly philanthropic—to protect land from competitive European bidding and insure its acquisition by African farmers. Nevertheless, the underlying philosophy was segregationist, and the practical effect was to create a landless African labor supply. Those who remained on European farms constituted a rural proletariat, while those who could not purchase and maintain a farm competitively on the generally poorer African lands gradually drifted to the cities for jobs in industry and life in a growing ghetto slum.

The second piece of discriminatory legislation was the Industrial Conciliation Act of 1934 which was later amended in 1945. This bill provided for Conciliation Boards to be composed of European employers and trade unionists, their function to set wage scales and working conditions in local industries. Specifically excluded were African unionists, however, for they were regarded as unready for skilled work. Although African unions, therefore, had no legal status, African laborers could in theory command the going wages established by the Conciliation Boards, for they were fixed regardless of race. Nevertheless, in practice it was the rare African chosen in preference to a European, and so in the towns a high European wage scale was set against the unprotected, unskilled labor of the African. In the countryside this legislation did not apply. The resultant wage differential between skilled European and unskilled African labor was of the order of fifteen to one.

For a time it appeared as though a form of settler domination would install itself in Northern Rhodesia as well, particularly when the discovery of large deposits of copper attracted European capital and settlers, and transformed a vast and poor land into an economic prize worth fighting for. The Rhodesian copper fields had long remained unexploited in the face of the richer, more accessible ores in nearby Katanga. During the 1920s, however, more sophisticated prospecting techniques began to reveal substantial deposits, but just at the moment when large-scale investment appeared worthwhile, the worldwide depression of the early thirties broke the market and momentarily killed interest. A slow recovery ensued, however, culminating in all-out production during the Second World War and establishing the Northern Rhodesian copper belt during the postwar years as the world's third-largest producer. By 1952 government revenue had increased eightyfold over the figure for 1924 while the value of exports climbed from $2 million to more than $230 million during the same period.

These spectacular financial progressions inevitably attracted settlers; thus the thirty-six hundred white inhabitants of 1924 had risen ten times by 1951 and reached a total of sixty-five thousand in 1956, this against an indigenous African population of something over two million. While such a proportion almost doubled the twenty-to-one black-white ratio in Southern Rhodesia, the prospect of economic gain joined hands with European consensus in racial superiority to bring pressure for preferential controls similar to those already exercised in Salisbury. When British South Africa Company rule was supplanted by a Protectorate government in 1924, a legislative council was formed with an unofficial minority of elected Europeans, but gradually the minority grew until in the years after the Second World War it had gained equality of numbers with the official members.

Nevertheless, there were complications in the Northern Rhodesian situation which had never been present in the self-governing colony to the south. A protectorate involved protection, in this case by the British Colonial Office on behalf of the African population, a fact enunciated most forcefully in 1930 by the secretary of state for the colonies, Lord Passfield (the noted Fabian, Sidney J. Webb). Thus a strong sense of colonial trusteeship combined with the fact of a smaller settler population to bring forth a doctrine, not of parallel development in racial isolation, but of cooperative partnership between white and black with the British government acting as a balance between the two.

The net result of this complex of forces was a steady move toward settler domination and a degree of economic color bar which, however, never quite achieved the complete political control that was the basis for racial discrimination in Southern Rhodesia.

In 1948 the settlers achieved parity on the legislative council and were represented on the executive council in a manner that was tantamount to responsible ministerial government. Nevertheless, in the same year Africans had been given appointed representation on both councils and in 1953 as the settlers gained a qualified legislative council majority, the African membership was again raised, representing a modest but clear-cut gain on white membership. Similarly, European trade unions on the copper belt monopolized the skilled jobs and commanded thereby during the postwar years elevated salaries fully twenty times the average of $25 a month which was paid the African miner. Such glaring discrimination, however, was never protected by law and was broken in 1955 by the major companies in a move that quickly brought Africans into a range of job categories hitherto controlled by white miners. At the same time the African Mineworkers' Union obtained substantial wage increases for the mass of unskilled labor. Color bar there was in Northern Rhodesia, but never was it absolute nor was it imposed through the legislation of a white-controlled government.

As a British protectorate, Nyasaland also enjoyed the sanctuary of trusteeship, but an even more powerful protection against white domination was her lackluster economic promise. A deficiency of mineral resources meant almost total reliance on agriculture, but even here production of coffee, cotton, tobacco, and groundnuts offered minimal attractions to European planters who numbered only a few hundred by the end of the Second World War. In 1946 approximately 5 percent of the total land area of the Protectorate was still in the hands of white settlers, mostly in the Shire highlands, but much of these holdings was subsequently purchased by the government, thereby replacing a status of tenancy with one of freehold for thousands of African families.

Such apparent advantages were not unmixed. Poor resources induced but few public improvements and if a small European population (only nine thousand out of almost three million in 1961) removed the problem of settler domination, it also meant that the country's modest economic potentialities were hardly worth contesting. With the constitutional reforms instituted in African territories after the Second World War, it was clear that European influence would decline in Nyasaland in the face of increasing African activity. It was equally clear that no degree of political autonomy could achieve prosperity in a poor land.

The Rise and Fall of Federation in Central Africa

Neither parallel development nor partnership appeared to offer much prospect for genuine multiracial cooperation in Central Africa. The "two pyramid" system of Godfrey Huggins was admittedly and irrevocably autocratic, while partnership as practiced in Northern Rhodesia evoked an image not of equal responsibility, but of the paternal relationship between senior partner and junior apprentice. Moreover, where the economic stake seemed worth the effort, the European community had imposed an effective color bar which checked African progress in favor of its own advantage. Any amalgamation of Central African territories based upon a concept of racial partnership thus seemed in the light of past experience to be in danger of a white domination and exploitation not unlike that already in effect in South Africa.

This was the opinion, at any rate, of the African community, particularly in the two northern protectorates, whenever the question of territorial merger arose. In Nyasaland and Northern Rhodesia, the Africans remained unmoved by arguments describing the economic advance and improved social services that would follow amalgamation. No more were they impressed with the guarantee that an interterritorial government would exercise no authority in the sensitive area of African affairs. For them the key was the potential withdrawal of crown protection and the likelihood of eventual independence for a white-dominated Central Africa which would place them at the mercy of a settler government such as had been the case with the Africans of Southern Rhodesia ever since 1923. This was no idle concern. Godfrey Huggins, the leading Southern Rhodesian advocate of fusion, had a notoriously low opinion of African capabilities which argued a long tutelage before racial partnership could mean racial equality. His chief supporter from Northern Rhodesia, the union leader Roy Welensky, admitted publicly that white domination would necessarily characterize federation, for, in his judgment, the African was clearly unqualified for full partnership.

Implacable African hostility delayed and altered the shape of federation, but it could not prevent it, for there were powerful forces within the settler community, and to a lesser extent within Britain, which urged some form of union. Many of the arguments were economic and administrative. Amalgamation would coordinate the resources of the three territories, it was said, bringing together Southern Rhodesia's industry and capital, Northern Rhodesia's copper, and Nyasaland's labor. Economic union would also mean administrative convenience in the sharing of public services and diminished expenses through common planning and joint utilization of personnel.

There were political and psychological factors as well. The Europeans of Southern Rhodesia had at one time considered throwing in their lot with South Africa, but for many the Afrikaner racial policies were too doctrinaire and unification northward now seemed preferable. For their part, the settlers in Northern Rhodesia felt themselves frustrated in their quest for self-government, and looked to a southern alliance as a possible means whereby British protection might be neutralized. Within Britain there were many who favored amalgamation on economic grounds, but the vision of a strong multiracial state in Central Africa also had appeal as a barrier against the possible expansion of South African racialism. Perhaps most of all was the long-lived and long-frustrated desire among the Rhodesian settlers for true independence and dominion status. Could not unification of the three territories be the first step in a process that would end when Central Africa achieved her place within the world community of nations?

British uneasiness over the intensity of African opposition ruled out any centralized union such as that of South Africa, but introduced the alternative possibility of federation, and so it was that a series of conferences led to the final shaping of a new state which made its appearance in October 1953 as the Federation of Rhodesia and Nyasaland (Central African Federation). Elections were held in each territory for a federal legislature of thirty-five, the two protectorates holding eighteen seats between them against seventeen for Southern Rhodesia. Each territory elected two Africans as well as one European who was specifically charged with looking after African interests; thus, overall, the whites had twenty-six and the Africans nine representatives. The election was marked by an emergent European opposition matching the African distaste for federation; in Southern Rhodesia a party formed to contest the election on the grounds that the new arrangement would undermine white supremacy. Nevertheless, the United Federal Party swept into power in all three territories and its leader, Godfrey Huggins, became the first federal prime minister while his lieutenant and eventual successor, Roy Welensky, was installed as minister of transport and development.

This initial success in no way meant the end of opposition which, on the contrary, continued to build up pressures in the ensuing years. The right wing among the settlers emerged as the Dominion Party, led by Winston Field, which set an antagonistic face against the concept of partnership. Too liberal on racial matters to suit the segregationists, the Federation leaders nevertheless impressed Africans as implacably hostile to genuine racial partnership. Moreover, Africans no longer were satisfied with partnership; increasingly they thought in terms of popular sovereignty—each individual equal in the voting booth. Under fire from both the European right and the African left, the Federation ultimately fell victim to what appeared at first as the less formidable of these factors, the force of African nationalism.

In Nyasaland and Northern Rhodesia, African resistance to European controls had been early marked by the Ethiopian church movement which brought forth the futile rising of John Chilembwe at Blantyre in 1915. Later it shifted toward an effort to gain representation and redress through constitutional means; then with industrialization came labor discontent, specifically directed at the discriminatory wage structure in the copper belt. By the time of federation, clearly defined nationalist movements in the northern territories had taken shape, the Nyasaland African Congress having been founded in 1944 while a Northern Rhodesia African Congress followed four years later. Within settler-dominated Southern Rhodesia, African nationalism crystallized later still, a militant congress movement emerging only in 1957.

The driving forces of nationalism were the usual ones—great social and economic changes leading both to self-awareness on a supratribal scale, and in the case of the people of Central Africa, to a resistance against the social and economic discrimination practiced by their white rulers. In nationalist eyes, the Federation was the capstone to the system of inequality which would place them in a position of permanent inferiority. At all costs it had to be destroyed.

In Southern Rhodesia there was some ambivalence in the African attitude toward federation. Many were opposed, but some saw cooperation with whites as the avenue to greater influence, while others argued that a federal connection bringing them closer to the great African populations in the northern territories would eventually facilitate liberal reform in the south. The reaction in Nyasaland, however, was immediate and intense, its hostility explained in part by the experience of many Nyasa laborers with racial patterns in Southern Rhodesia and in part by the absence of a strong settler community. In 1955 a constitutional change permitted the election of five Africans to the legislative council, and congress, led by the militant Henry Chipembere and M.W.K. Chiume, easily captured all five seats. Nonetheless, five votes out of twenty-three was a long way from political power, and the situation became more urgent in 1957 when Welensky, now federal prime minister, secured agreement in Britain for a review of the federation constitution to take place in 1960, the probable outcome to be Central African independence within the British Commonwealth.

Extraparliamentary tactics were clearly needed. Chipembere and congress urged Dr. Hastings Kamuzu Banda to return to his native land and assume the leadership of the nationalist movement. Banda's qualifications were maturity and an ease in dealing with Europeans gained from long years as a medical practitioner in England. What he also provided was an incendiary leadership which touched off the emotion-charged atmosphere in Nyasaland, leading to outbreaks of violence in 1959, and then to the declaration of a state of emergency, the banning of the Nyasaland African Congress, and the detention of Banda and a number of his congress lieutenants.

Explosions in Nyasaland were no isolated events during these fateful days; rather they were part of the upsurge toward independence in Africa which was quickly changing the map of the continent. In Kenya the Macmillan government provided for a new constitution early in 1960 which assured an African legislative majority, and shortly thereafter Dr. Banda was released from prison and invited to participate in a conference which introduced similar changes in Nyasaland. At the head of the newly formed Malawi Congress Party, Banda now gained full control of the territorial government as the result of general elections held in August 1961. With this victory, the stage was set for secession and the eventual dissolution of the Federation.

In Northern Rhodesia, African discontent was no less pronounced, but here the nationalist drive against federation faced much more formidable obstacles.

First there was a white settler community led by powerful European trade unions. Beyond this, there were important economic assets at stake. Welensky and the federalists could ill afford to let the copper belt follow Nyasaland; moreover, federation and ultimate independence rested on the continued union between north and south, and Southern Rhodesia—right-wing extremists aside—was as determined as the north not to allow a fatal split to occur.

In 1951 the Northern Rhodesia African Congress came under the leadership of a militant former schoolteacher, Harry Nkumbula, who renamed it the African National Congress and conducted a vigorous, albeit futile, fight against the inauguration of federation in 1953. Congress feared both the prospect of increased discrimination and the growing influence of Southern Rhodesia, and its apprehensions were heightened by such developments as the choice of Salisbury for federal capital and the shift of the Northern Rhodesian Kafue dam project to the interterritorial Kariba site on the Zambezi. When Welensky became premier in 1956 and stepped up his fight to loosen the controls of the Colonial Office, the situation appeared desperate to Northern Rhodesian Africans, long smarting under the indignities of social and economic color bar and aware of the far greater disabilities of the Africans in Southern Rhodesia.

Congress's main weapon against discrimination during this period was the boycott which was employed extensively but without great success and which usually resulted in violence and government reprisals. Both Nkumbula and the congress secretary-general, Kenneth Kaunda, were jailed briefly in 1955, a martyrdom that helped their cause but was more than offset by growing strains within the congress affecting its unity of purpose and action. Indeed, the two men were beginning to dispute leadership and tactics with each other, the popular Kaunda urging more vigorous political opposition, the less extreme Nkumbula losing rank-and-file support because of his apparent dictatorial manner.

Late in 1958 a formal split occurred when Kaunda and his militant colleague, Simon Kapwepwe, founded the Zambia African National Congress (ZANC), Kapwepwe inventing the name "Zambia" for the occasion. ZANC immediately made serious inroads into congress membership, but not enough to prevent Nkumbula's congress from conducting an effective electoral campaign early in 1959 under a new constitution which, however, most Africans, Nkumbula included, considered thoroughly unsatisfactory in its African representation. ZANC attempted to impose an election boycott by force, but this move was only partially successful as the new party was proscribed and its leaders placed in detention. Nevertheless, by 1960 they were all once more at liberty and a new party organized, the United National Independence Party (UNIP) with Kaunda as president.

Violence and unrest continued, largely stimulated by UNIP agitators, as gradually it became apparent that Northern Rhodesia, like Nyasaland, would sooner or later have its African-dominated government, an eventuality that could only mean secession and the end of the Federation. An African legislative majority in Northern Rhodesia was the recommendation of the Monckton Commission assembled by the British government in 1959 to advise on the future of federation, but such an unequivocal solution was as yet premature. Instead, the colonial secretary, Ian Macleod, put forward a complex constitution in the hope that neither Welensky's federalists nor the African nationalists would gain a clear majority, and federation would thereby be saved. Hence, as Banda and his Malawi Congress Party moved smoothly toward internal self-government, achieved early in 1963, and then proceeded with determination to total independence, elections were scheduled in Northern Rhodesia for October 1962 in an atmosphere of uncertainty. The results of the voting under the Northern Rhodesian constitution of 1962 gave a clear majority neither to Kaunda's UNIP nor to Welensky's United Federal Party, and placed the balance of power with the African National Congress and Harry Nkumbula. Nevertheless, an African government was formed when Nkumbula joined Kaunda in coalition, the white United Federalists acting as opposition.

Welensky and his federalists had now been compelled to yield control of both protectorates to the forces of African nationalism. In December 1962 they lost Southern Rhodesia as well, not to the Africans who were in firm check, but to the right-wing Rhodesian Front, a successor to the Dominion Party. In elections held that month, the Front defeated the United Federal Party when the latter proposed the end of color bar in public facilities. Hence all three territories had come under control of groups hostile to the concept and the fact of federation. There was no longer any basis for its survival, and at the end of 1963 the Federation of Rhodesia and Nyasaland ceased to exist.

Suggestions for Further Reading

For the system of apartheid see Leonard Thompson, *A History of South Africa* (New Haven and London: Yale University Press, 1990); T. R. H. Davenport, *South Africa: A Modern History*, 3rd ed. (Toronto and Buffalo: University of Toronto Press, 1987), and Thompson's *The Political Mythology of Apartheid* (New Haven and London: Yale University Press, 1985). These may be supplemented by works dealing with nationalism, African and Afrikaner, such as Tom Lodge, *Black Politics in South Africa Since 1945* (London and New York: Longman, 1983); Peter Walshe, *The Rise of African Nationalism in South Africa* (Berkeley: University of California Press, 1971); and the appropriate chapters in Monica Wilson and Leonard Thompson, eds., *The Oxford History of South Africa*, Vol. II (New York: Oxford University Press, 1971).

Some African perspective may be gained from literary sources, for example, E. Mphahlele, *Down Second Avenue* (London: Faber, 1959) and Alex La Guma, *A Walk in the Night and Other Stories* (London: Heinemann, 1967). A recent view of the effects of apartheid by an outside observer is Joseph Lelyveld's *Move Your Shadow* (New York: Times Books, 1985).

Brief accounts of affairs in Namibia (South-West Africa) and the High Commission Territories of Swaziland, Basutoland, and Bechuanaland are contained in Vol. 7 (Cambridge University Press, 1986), A. D. Roberts, ed. and Vol. 8 (Cambridge University Press, 1984), Michael Crowder, ed., both of the *Cambridge History of Africa*.

General histories dealing with Central Africa include Vol. 2 of D. Birmingham and P.M. Martin, eds., *History of Central Africa* (London and New York: Longman, 1986); A. J. Wills, *An Introduction to the History of Central Africa* (London: Oxford University Press, 1964); and A. D. Roberts, *History of Zambia* (London: Heinemann, 1976). For John Chilembwe, see G. Shepperson and T. Price, *Independent African* (Edinburgh: University Press, 1958). The growth of nationalism throughout Central Africa is traced in Robert Rotberg, *The Rise of Nationalism in Central Africa* (Cambridge: Harvard University Press, 1965).

Race relations in Central Africa is the subject of a trilogy produced under the auspices of the Institute of Race Relations in London: Philip Mason, *The Birth of a Dilemma* (London: Oxford University Press, 1958); and the same author's *Year of Decision* (London: Oxford University Press, 1960), which sandwich in time Richard Gray's *The Two Nations* (London: Oxford University Press, 1960).

The African view of events in Central Africa may be measured through a number of works by African leaders. See, for example, Kenneth Kaunda, *Zambia Shall Be Free* (London: Heinemann, 1962; New York, Praeger, 1963); Kaunda's speeches, edited by Colin Legum under the title *Zambia: Independence and Beyond* (London: Nelson, 1966; New York: International Publications Service, 1966); and a selection of his letters to Colin M. Morris, entitled *A Humanist in Africa* (London: Longmans, 1966). Also to be consulted are N. Sithole, *African Nationalism* (Cape Town: Oxford University Press, 1959; 2nd ed., London, 1968; New York, 1969); and Nathan Shamuyarira, *Crisis in Rhodesia* (Nairobi: East African Publishing House, 1967; London: André Deutsch, 1965; New York: Transatlantic Arts, 1965).

PART FOUR
Independent Africa

21

Toward Independence

The Foundations of Freedom

Colonialism contained the germ of its own destruction; indeed, the whole colonial system was a vast engine for the creation of a modern, self-governing Africa. By conquering, colonialism caused the desire to be free. By exploiting, it produced a growing resistance to tyranny. By introducing Africa to the modern world, it generated visions of a better life consummated in liberty. By demonstrating its own fallibility, it begot the hope that led to autonomy. By educating, it taught the skills of self-direction.

The educated African was the parent of the independent African. Missionaries, commencing their work in West Africa early in the nineteenth century, introduced literacy as a necessary avenue to Christianity, but with education came ideas and ideals that were to change forever the African world. European humanitarianism exemplified in the abolitionist movement and Western liberalism enunciated by France's democratic principles of 1789 made quick converts of educated West Africans like Paul Holle, Bishop Crowther, and Samuel Lewis. Nevertheless, admiration for Western civilization joined with the desire to share in its material improvement and its principles of self-government, while later observers like James Johnson, John Chilembwe, or Harry Thuku were not slow to note the shortfall that had developed between Christian ideals and the realities of colonial rule.

In South Africa, the religion of humility and poverty evidently meant to reserve those qualities only for blacks. In the Congo, brotherhood was somehow converted to parental domination, while in West Africa, despite European democracy, the fruits of European technology appeared to be limited largely to the colonial ruler. European education, introduced by Europeans, came to liberate, but remained to command. The Christian missionaries opened more and more schools but their products were permitted only to fill the lower ranks of governmental offices, of foreign trading establishments, of hospitals and schools, even of the Christian churches themselves.

Yet the effects of education could not be cut off at this subordinate level. New ideas not only stimulated new hopes, but also provided the means for their realization. With education came the professional and technical skills necessary for creating the modern society the educated African desired. An educated group gained cohesion through literacy, and found a common objective in its appetite for the advantages of Western technology. The educated African, through the medium of his or her education, emerged as the new leader of African societies, a leader whose whole being strained toward change.

As the network of education extended itself, it carried the doctrine of change farther abroad, and deeper into the new African mentality. To the evolving African, traditional society appeared no longer acceptable in what was seen as its poverty and sickness, its outmoded tribalism and antiquated values. Set against this unpromising picture was the West with its powerful technology, its wealth, its modern medicine, its dynamism, and its optimism. Those who glimpsed the vision of modernization wanted more—more economic development, more public improvements, more political expression, and above all, more education as their prime prerequisite to political, social, and economic emancipation.

These demands came gradually, proportionate to the introduction of Western education, but there were other factors also militating for change which would lead to eventual national independence. Missionaries had come to liberate slaves and save souls but they remained to initiate social and economic reforms to which European mercantile interests and colonial governments likewise lent force in their time. One such change was the gradual but portentous shift from an economy based on subsistence agriculture to one that dealt with cash crops in an international market. Such a shift held dangers as well as opportunities; in either case, however, there were ramifications well beyond the economic.

Not only did this changing economy introduce a common, compact currency, commercial agriculture, and prestigious, attractive manufactured imports; it also had profound implications for ancient concepts regarding land tenure, the individual and the family, social status, and rules of inheritance. New principles of land utilization, new standards for labor incentive reached out into villages, and as increasing numbers developed a stake in the new system, they were increasingly determined to have a say in its operation as well. By the conclusion of the Second World War, the degree of growing involvement was considerable. On the Gold Coast, for example, cocoa exports rose between 1901 and 1951 from 1,000 to 230,000 tons, the value of timber exports over the same period from £70,000 to £4,977,000. In Nigeria by 1948 more than two of every five adult males were active participants in the cash economy. Uganda cotton produced but 500 bales for the outside market in 1906, but by 1953-1954 the figure had risen to 398,000 bales yielding an income of £12,750,000.

The same forces driving the economic revolution brought other fundamental changes. Colonial governments, not noted for their open-handed approach to public improvements, nonetheless built roads, constructed harbors, dredged rivers, installed telegraphic communication, and even introduced expensive networks of railroads. In East Africa the railway from Mombasa to Kampala created the economy of the Kenyan White Highlands and established cotton production in Uganda. In Senegal, the line that was opened between Dakar and Saint-Louis in 1885 secured groundnut culture in the Cayor and converted Dakar from an insignificant administrative center into a great international port. Throughout West Africa railway and road systems were invariably directed toward the sea where they connected with a series of expanding entrepôts—Freetown, Dakar, Monrovia, Abidjan, Lagos, and others whose economic utility depended upon the breakwaters, channels, and other artificial devices introduced by European engineering.

These facilities did more than increase the economic activity which gave Africans a growing stake in their new society. They also helped create nations out of the colonial territories that had been stamped across the African map in the council chambers of Europe. Typically, transportation and communication systems were internal and extended only as far as colonial fronters, thus complicating international intercourse within Africa. Internally, however, they meant an easier movement of people and ideas, out of the isolation of village life, from countryside to city and back, from region to region, and among numbers of different ethnic and cultural backgrounds. If roads were a stimulant to commerce, they also helped spread the ideas that itinerant traders carried along with their goods, pollinating out-of-the-way communities with concepts that weakened their provincialism and broadened their experience. If rail lines were an aid to the administration of large areas by small cadres of European officers, they also moved Africans about in ever-increasing tempo, especially from the village to the town where the growing points of modernization were located.

The cities, crucial as a force driving toward independence, were essentially a new phenomenon, born out of the mercantile, cash crop economy. They wrenched Africans from the familiarity of their rural communities and thrust them into a strange world where they became dependent upon salaried jobs and where they were lost in the impersonality and competitiveness of urban life. At the same time, however, the city offered excitement and freedom from traditional restraints. There, aggressiveness and ability were rewarded, and new ideas and relationships became a common fact of life. Where these urban centers were carefully regulated as in the Belgian Congo, their inhabitants under close surveillance as with South Africa or the Portuguese territories, it was difficult for overt nationalist activity to take shape, but in other areas— British West Africa, for example—the development of an assertive leadership and a devoted mass following was much more easily brought into being.

The importance of cities was out of all proportion to their share of national population. The significance of the city rested in its strategic location at the center of power, of change, and of economic development. Even the tribal associations in the cities, arising out of a need to maintain connections with home, lineage, and the old way of life, played their part, for they were also important means for the dissemination of new ideas of urban origin back to the less sophisticated countryside.

Colonial rule was pointed toward self-destruction in yet another important way. Whether by direct administration through designated African agents or indirectly through established rulers, the regime steadily weakened the chiefly authority and the traditional sources of power. Appointed chiefs had no standing with their people and legitimate princes gradually lost respect and authority as they were obliged to perform unchiefly and unpopular duties, like tax collection, road maintenance, and public health enforcement, at the instance of their colonial masters. This situation lent circumstantial authority to the argument of the educated elite that they, and not the chiefs, were best qualified to lead their people in these changing times. Consequently, while colonial governments were systematically weakening themselves at the grass roots, they were elevating, despite their intentions, a new class of leaders who were a potential source of disaffection.

This need not have been the case, for the African elite with some exceptions were confirmed in their attachment to European institutions and values, and would have been pleased by nothing more than a genuine partnership with Europeans in administering colonial territories. Rejected by European administrators, however, they began to take advantage of their Western education to formulate concepts of African freedom and to organize vehicles for political action. This process had been first set in motion by nineteenth-century leaders like Africanus Horton and Edward Blyden, and continued through later critics like John Mensah Sarbah, James Johnson, or John Tengo Jabavu.

By the end of the First World War, educated Africans had become a thoroughly frustrated group, not only because they were forced to play what they considered to be an inadequate political role but also because they chafed as well under a discrimination that checked their professional and economic ambitions and rubbed raw their social sensibilities. It is probably no accident that Herbert Macaulay, one of the few West Africans trained as an engineer and thus foredoomed to a subordinate post in the government, turned to political agitation as an outlet for his energy and sense of self-respect. During the period between the two world wars, the African unofficial members of the legislative councils both in Nigeria and the Gold Coast maintained a continual barrage of complaints over discrimination against Africans in the appointment of magistrates, medical examiners, and other officials, over double-standard pay scales, and over economic policies that militated against Africans in business and in favor of their European competitors.

These complaints were accompanied both by an assertion of African cultural identity and a demand for political reform. Blyden had been an early advocate, though not practitioner, of the concept of an African personality, and he was followed in time by many others—the Nigerians, Majola Agbebi and James Johnson, the Gold Coast leaders, J. E. Casely Hayford and S. R. B. Attoh-Ahuma, and that later exponent of negritude, Leopold Senghor of Senegal, to name but a few. In the years after the Second World War and to a lesser extent before, African cultural identity found expression in literary and artistic output associated with such names as Ousmane Soce, Mongo Beti, or Chinua Achebe, as well as with that lively advocate of Africanness, *Présence Africaine*.

Political expression came in the form of properly constituted and legal parties such as Macaulay's Nigerian National Democratic Party or Casely Hayford's National Congress of British West Africa, of less acceptable political organizations like the Kikuyu-inspired East African Association or the African National Congress in South Africa, and of any number of journals with nationalist political sentiments. Where such developments were most thoroughly proscribed there were the nativist syncretistic movements, exemplified by Kimbanguism, to express nationalist discontent in sublimated form.

These organizations were part of a larger growth of so-called voluntary associations which arose throughout Africa in response to the developing needs of the new city dwellers. It was not merely a question of maintaining family or lineage links, although that was always important; these groups included as well trade unions, social clubs, sports associations, cultural fraternities, mutual aid societies, and religious movements, each with its special concerns. Whatever their origins, however, the voluntary associations came to have a political role as a training ground for leadership, as African-controlled information networks, as centripetal forces within a heterogeneous population, and finally as nuclei for organizing the mass supporters of overt political action. Some like the Kikuyu Central Association were initially political in objective. Others exerted influence by indirection—witness the connection between the Yoruba cultural society, Egbe Omo Oduduwa, and the Action Group of Chief Obafemi Awolowo or the subtle cohesion of ideas and objectives among the West African graduates of the Ecole William Ponty in Dakar.

Related to successful political organization was the public press with its ability to reach the growing numbers of literate individuals emerging from the expanding school systems. Newspapers had long been common in West African towns, but before the Second World War their appeal had been limited largely to the few educated elite. This pattern was destroyed forever in 1935 when Nnamdi Azikiwe, an Ibo representative of the new urban culture, became editor of the Accra *African Morning Post*. Two years later Azikiwe founded the *West African Pilot* in Lagos and a revolutionary brand of journalism had been launched.

Zik, as he was known to his contemporaries, was well endowed by temperament and training for the role he was destined to play in the rise of African nationalism. Born and reared outside the protective shell of traditional village life, he had gone to the United States during the mid-twenties for university study, receiving there not only his formal education but a liberal dose of survival techniques for a black man in a white-dominated world. When he returned to West Africa, he brought a practical firsthand experience with the race problem in America, its segregation, its lynchings, and its riots as well as the varying techniques of protest as practiced by such leaders as Marcus Garvey and W. E. B. Du Bois. Azikiwe had witnessed the spread of the back-to-Africa movement and the black flirtation with world communism, and he had watched the growth of a militant black press characterized by sensationalism and race consciousness.

Such experiences catalyzed personal energy and ambition to produce a different approach—demagogic and provocative—which replaced the urbane moderation of the established elite with the tactics of strident protest. Demands for measured constitutional reform were jettisoned, and in their stead were introduced appeals to racialism and positive action. Gone were the well-written but ponderous columns of Zik's predecessors, giving way to a fiery journalism that had great attraction for the growing numbers of urban dwellers with minimum education but expanding expectations. Azikiwe fixed upon specific grievances of farmers, clerks, unemployed, market women, and others, always associating their complaints in the popular mind with an anticolonial viewpoint. As imitators followed Azikiwe's lead, this lively penny press quickly extended its influence beyond local and ethnic limits, helped bring a new dynamism to nationalism in Africa, and in time served as a vehicle for the formation of actual political movements and parties.

The Changing World

The influence on Azikiwe of his foreign residence was repeated in many other instances, which in their aggregate were an important factor in shaping the African independence movement. As always, it was a question of education, direct or indirect, that exposed observers from Africa to the many expressions of humanity's constant quest to be free. The Gold Coast barrister, John Mensah Sarbah, had learned Victorian liberalism along with his Blackstone during a long residence in England, while Blaise Diagne's early assertiveness stemmed as much from close familiarity with French attitudes and institutions as from personal predilections. In Britain there were long-established philanthropic organizations like the Anti-Slavery and Aborigines' Protection Society ready to encourage the resident aliens from Africa, while after the Second World War the Labour Party gave direct governmental sanction to the idea of African reform. France, too, had her philanthropic societies, but political connections were more influential as evidenced by Diagne's association with the Republican Socialist Party and by the formation in 1936 of a Senegalese branch of the French Socialists under the leadership of Lamine Guèye.

These were but individual examples in retail. During the First World War, thousands of Africans served as soldiers in Europe and gained firsthand knowledge of the West, an experience that was greatly intensified during the conflict from 1939 to 1945. Between the wars, moreover, increasing numbers of students passed an extended residence in Britain and America, and, to a lesser extent, in France, Portugal, or Belgium, where they were able to observe the theory and practice of democracy along with colonialism and racialism. Between 1925 and 1945 the West African Students' Union, organized by the Yoruba, Ladipo Solanke, provided Nigerians in Britain with a sense of racial awareness and thus influenced a whole generation of future West African public figures. Of equal importance was a small group of Africans living in the United States during the late thirties and forties. Some of them had been encouraged to study in America by Azikiwe and came in time to share many of his experiences in a land where political democracy joined hands with anti-imperialism, and lack of class consciousness with individualism, all these qualities fused incongruously with a pattern of racial segregation and discrimination which spread across the land. Thus were such future leaders as Kwame Nkrumah, Ozuomba Mbadiwe of Nigeria, and the Sierra Leonean John Karifa-Smart enabled to develop a spirit of aggressiveness to accompany their sense of pride in race.

More than any other single factor it was the Second World War that signaled the shift in Africa from colonial control to ultimate independence. In the eyes of some a watershed between colonialism and freedom, for others an acceleration of a process already underway, the war pointed toward independence in a number of ways.

To begin with, there was the dawning recognition of the white man's fallibility. There were the personal experiences of black troopers fighting shoulder to shoulder with their white counterparts, conspicuously equal in matters of courage and skill. There were the humiliating defeats of European armies in the Pacific by members of a supposedly inferior race and the seemingly senseless butchery in Europe. There was the crucial contribution of African material and soldiery toward the insuring of Allied victory. Colonialism, it seemed, was not an inevitable condition made in heaven.

Secondly, there was the ambivalence of post-war colonialism. Just as they had after the First World War, European powers moved to reassert colonial controls and step up the production that had so greatly assisted the war effort. Such an action was necessary for national prestige and the rehabilitation of war-torn economies, it was said. But there was a difference this time. Colonizing powers now felt obligation as well as necessity toward their African wards for they were well aware of the important African contributions to the war effort. With development plans, therefore, went large investments in social, economic, and educational advance. With reassertion of political domination went concessions toward limited but greater participation in government. Generous in the eyes of their donors, these concessions were looked upon as niggardly in Africa where local leadership quickly responded with demands for far more radical reform. Such agitation had a serious impact on colonial administrations already under attack at home by critics of colonialism in a domestic atmosphere of growing public indifference to an imperialism no longer regarded as relevant, let alone imperative.

The Second World War, moreover, profoundly changed the international power balance, reducing once lordly colonial powers to the level of suppliants for American postwar aid needed to rebuild a shattered Europe, while the United States and the Soviet Union now took the stage as undisputed world leaders. Both had their reasons for disliking colonialism, and their influence was an important factor effecting change in imperial attitudes—for example, acquiescence to the idea of ultimate independence for the colonies under British control and the new concept of a French Union that spoke of citizens in overseas territories rather than subjects of France's colonies. To these changes was added the presence of a United Nations Organization which, among other functions, was expected to intrude a much greater surveillance over colonial affairs than had its predecessor, the League of Nations.

As the era of the ''cold war'' unfolded, the United States and the Soviet Union appealed increasingly for the support of the peoples of Asia, Africa, and Latin America, and in the process made no secret of their hostility toward colonialism. While Portugal remained fixed in her colonial possessiveness, and France withdrew but slowly from Indochina, the Dutch finally agreed to abandon Indonesia, and Britain arranged for independence in India, Pakistan, Ceylon, and Burma. The Atlantic Charter, pronounced by Roosevelt and Churchill during the years of conflict, had proclaimed the right of self-determination for all peoples, and when the British prime minister appeared later to repudiate his stand, this action merely stimulated further the rising aspirations to freedom in Africa.

At the conclusion of hostilities, the Labour government succeeded to power in Britain, and with Labour came a view of colonial stewardship that differed markedly from Churchill's concept of empire. Even as the French were reinterpreting colonial status in terms of partnership as enunciated at the Brazzaville Conference of 1944, the authorities in Whitehall were searching for new imperial definitions which would lead to eventual freedom for colonial people within a British commonwealth.

By war's end, however, these vague assurances were no longer satisfactory to African nationalists. The Fifth Pan-African Congress meeting in Manchester, England, in 1945 demanded immediate independence for Africa but that was only the beginning. Across Africa there was an awakening, a new awareness of the possibilities provided by political action. Parties were created and new dynamic leaders emerged with large popular followings, crying the cry of freedom. In some areas, like the Gold Coast, events moved quickly. In others, for example, the Belgian Congo and the Portuguese colonies, colonial administrations for a time contained growing nationalist pressures. In colonies with settler populations nationalist demands were met with forceful repression and the results were disastrous—witness Kenya's Mau Mau or the guerrilla warfare that eventually destroyed the white-controlled regime in Southern Rhodesia. In all cases, however, whether sooner or later, if by persuasion or by force, pressures within Africa led surely to the same ultimate result, the achievement of national independence.

Independence Movements in the Northeast

Ethiopia, the last African nation to lose her independence, was also the first to regain it. Menelik's failing health during his final years had introduced another period of political and dynastic uncertainty which was obliged to run its course through the brief, unsettled reign of the apostate to Islam, Emperor Lij Jasu (1913-1916), the accession to the throne of Menelik's daughter, Zauditu, under the regency of Ras Tafari, and finally the assumption of power in 1928 by Ras Tafari who was crowned Emperor Haile Selassie I in 1930 upon the death of Zauditu.

Haile Selassie's regency had been a period of slowly developing authority out of which he hoped to introduce reforms which would resume the modernization process begun by Menelik. Aside from progress in governmental administration and public works construction, a beginning was made toward the abolition of slavery and the replacement of feudal dues with controlled taxation. A ministry of education was formed in 1930, and the following year the emperor granted the country's first constitution, one, however, that provided only for an appointed parliament exercising limited advisory authority. Indeed, as emperor, Haile Selassie appeared to view his political role, not in terms of leadership toward democratic reform, but rather in the development of a loyal bureaucracy within the central government to offset the centrifugal force of the country's regional feudal barons.

These modest steps toward national strength were jolted to a standstill in 1935 by the rapid rise of a militant imperialism in Fascist Italy. Entrenched in Eritrea and Italian Somaliland, Mussolini precipitated a series of border incidents which were utilized as an excuse for invasion in October 1935. By that time, Haile Selassie had already been forsaken, for all practical purposes, by the impotent League of Nations which Ethiopia had joined in 1923, and by those Western statesmen unwilling to challenge Italian aggression at the price of possible war in Europe. Unlike the days of Adowa, the Italian armies came fully prepared to wage a modern, mechanized war, whereas the Ethiopian levies were neither well equipped nor coordinated to mass their strength at crucial points. In the end, antiquated tactics offset personal bravery, and the spirited defense of difficult mountainous terrain yielded to Italian firepower and the devastation of repeated unopposed aerial bombardment. By the spring of 1936 the Italians were approaching Addis Ababa, and when it was clear that the shattered Ethiopian forces were incapable of defending the city, Haile Selassie left the country to place his cause directly before the League of Nations. Within a few days of his departure, the Italians were in Addis Ababa, and Mussolini could announce to the world the annexation of Ethiopia.

Despite continued guerrilla resistance, Ethiopia had finally become an Italian possession, but in fact the triumph was short-lived. In 1941, in a campaign arising out of the Second World War, columns of British troops invaded Ethiopia from both Kenya and the Sudan, and, aided by guerrilla forces, were able within a few months to recapture the mountain kingdom. On May 5, 1941, five years to the day after Marshal Badoglio had entered Addis Ababa, Emperor Haile Selassie returned to his capital. Eritrea, taken at the same time, was administered by Britain under United Nations aegis until 1952, at which time it was federated as an autonomous unit with Ethiopia, the latter taking responsibility for external affairs. Such an arrangement appeared unlikely to endure in the face of economic interdependence, some mutual desire for union, and the ill-concealed pressures by the emperor's government to absorb the smaller territory. Despite growing misgivings within Eritrea over the absolutism of the Ethiopian regime, a series of steps brought the two units closer together until, in 1962, Haile Selassie annexed Eritrea as an integral part of the Ethiopian state.

The invasion of Ethiopia by Britain's military forces had been facilitated by her control of the neighboring Sudan, but in fact by the era of the Second World War colonialism was already reaching a dead end in that ancient land. The nationalist demands put forth by the leaders of the Graduates' General Congress, though peremptorily turned aside in 1942, arose at a time when the administration was already contemplating an extension of political responsibility. This was implemented in 1944 by the creation of a governmental advisory council of preponderantly Sudanese representatives, and by the end of the war, self-determination for the Sudan had been conceded in principle. What remained to be decided were details of timing and the matter of future relations with Egypt.

While the nationalists remained divided between the Umma party and the pro-Egyptian Ashiqqa of Ismail al-Azhari, the Egyptians continued to resist the idea of an independent Sudan until the military coup of 1952 brought the Nasser-Naguib group to power. The new military government, more flexible than its predecessor on the Sudan question, agreed in 1953 to immediate Sudanese self-government with self-determination to be settled within the following three years. This action, in effect ratifying what the British had already decided upon, set the stage for elections late in 1953 which resulted in a pronounced victory for Azhari and his Ashiqqa supporters, now reconstituted as the National Unionist Party.

The apparent preference of the Sudanese electorate for union with Egypt was in fact illusory, the strong support for Azhari reflecting rather a national dislike for the traditional Umma friendliness toward the British. The situation was misjudged by many outsiders including the Egyptians whose subsequent tactless diplomacy further alienated the Sudan, but Azhari correctly judged the popular tone and quickly converted himself from a unionist to the leader of the Sudanese independence movement. As prime minister, he moved without delay toward republican status which was formally declared on January 1, 1956. Autonomy brought little national unity, however. The old divisions remained between the Khatmiyya of Ali al-Mirghani and the ansar, or followers, of Abd al-Rahman al-Mahdi, while in the long run, Azhari's astute tactics in leading the country to independence deprived him of the rallying cry of union with Egypt which had hitherto kept his partisans united. The resultant deterioration of national politics into factionalism led to a fatal instability which was further aggravated by the growing problem of the southern Sudan.

This was another legacy of colonial policy. After the breakup of the Mahdist state, the British subjugation and subsequent occupation of the southern provinces had been conducted quite separately from the administration of the Muslim, Arabic-speaking north. Islamic influences were not countenanced by the British in the south; instead, indigenous institutions were encouraged, and Christian missionaries permitted to establish stations. As Sudanese independence approached, however, British officers in the southern provinces were rapidly replaced with northerners whose policy of forced assimilation into the Islamic-Arabic cultural orbit of the north led to reaction and rebellion in 1955, peace being restored only with difficulty. Having rejected union with Egypt, the Sudan now faced centrifugal forces within its own land which were intolerable to a growing spirit of nationalism. It was imperative that cohesion be effected between two regions vastly different in culture and background, the north often prejudiced and eager to force closer ties through Islamic education and religious proselytization, the south suspicious and resistant to the point of open hostility.

The south and other problems of early independence seemed to elude the solutions of increasingly opportunistic politicians. Western parliamentary government appeared ill-suited to a land where traditions were rooted in long-lived personal loyalties and deep religious commitments. When, in 1958, a bloodless coup was engineered which installed the army under General Ibrahim Abbud as the new agency of government, there was little protest from a people long accustomed to authoritarian rule.

The West African Catalyst

While Ethiopia and the Sudan may have been the first to regain their liberty, it was West Africa, and particularly the Gold Coast, that provided the essential impetus for the wave of independence which swept over the African continent in the years following the Second World War. At the outset this was unlooked for, since the Gold Coast impressed its rulers as a model colony, steadily growing in political maturity and economic strength; one that in good time would doubtless achieve self-government, but surely only through an orderly, measured advance. In anticipation of this eventuality, a new constitution in 1946 had provided for a legislative council with an elected majority, a concession that was hailed alike by the English and Gold Coasters as a fair indication of both past achievement and future promise.

In fact, appearances were deceptive, for the very state of progress on the Gold Coast was building explosive pressures which would not have been possible in a less developed land. First of all, there was a problem of rising commodity prices and scarcity of consumer goods caused by worldwide shortages at the end of the Second World War. Increasing numbers of urbanites with money to spend but few goods to buy suspected the government of using its position to assist European importers in manipulating the price structure for private profit, to public disadvantage. It was true that cocoa prices had risen with the rest, but at this point the outbreak of swollen shoot virus compelled the government to order the destruction of large tracts of diseased trees, consequently imposing great hardship on individual farmers. In many quarters the conclusion seemed inescapable—the government sought to ruin the farmer and take his land while encouraging the European merchants to make a killing out of the price spiral and market shortages.

In addition there were the numbers of soldiers returning home, their expectations unlikely to be met easily in a provincial West African society suffering economic dislocation. Beyond these immediate difficulties, however, was a basic shift in the community which upset long-standing social relations and encouraged a growing temper of opposition to authority within a large section of the population. The change was geared to an accelerating modernization which had more than doubled the numbers living in the major cities of the Gold Coast between 1931 and 1948, forced the commercialization of agriculture, and brought about the dramatic rise of a class of individuals only partly educated by a few years of indifferent primary school training. Semiliterate, unskilled, and often unemployable, dissatisfied with village life and unable to rise in the complex and unsettling world of the city, this new proletariat was resistant to the older chiefly authority and suspicious of a European-directed government. In January 1948 a successful boycott of European goods indicated the prevailing mood of unrest. A month later in Accra, a protest march by returing soldiers got out of hand and developed into rioting which quickly spread to other centers, resulting in considerable loss of life and property.

In this situation, the established, Westernized elite sought to assert their influence. A year earlier the United Gold Coast Convention (UGCC) had been formed by the merchant, A. G. Grant, the barrister and newspaper editor,

J. B. Danquah, and other western-educated Africans as a national movement dedicated to eventual self-government; now under Danquah's direction, the UGCC declared the colonial administration bankrupt and suggested that the convention be made the instrument of a new government. Such an action had little effect on the authorities who placed Danquah and some of his colleagues in custody, but more significantly it left the African population unmoved, awaiting the leadership that it instinctively felt could not be provided by the exclusive, educated elite.

The administration reacted in another way. The findings of the Watson Commission which investigated the riots and the Coussey Committee which explored the possibility of political reform in effect suggested nothing less than representative, responsible government as soon as practicable, but time was already running beyond this statesmanlike move, even as events overtook the ineffectual activities of the UGCC. In 1947, Danquah had appointed. Kwame Nkrumah as secretary of the convention in a move designed to spare its patrician officers the details of party organization while freeing them for larger political strategies. The move had misfired as Nkrumah quickly built a national organization based on the captivating slogan of "self-government now," then took his new following with him in 1949 when he founded his own Convention People's Party (CPP), an exciting, revolutionary, nationalist movement with direct appeal to the growing dissidents in the Gold Coast population.

Had Danquah and his associates been more searching, they would never have offered Nkrumah the position of UGCC secretary, for his career up to that point strongly suggested a revolutionary leader of uncommon ability, determined and capable of far exceeding their limited goals. Born in 1909 near Axim along the western Gold Coast, he had, like Azikiwe, graduated from local schooling to pursue his higher education in the United States where he learned the techniques of self-support to supplement formal study in economics, sociology, and education. His political education began as well during these years when he served as president of the African Students' Association of the United States and Canada, at the same time learning something of revolutionary tactics, particularly from the West Indian Marxist, C. L. R. James.

Already Nkrumah was thinking of the means by which colonialism might be destroyed, and when he left America for England in 1945, he was referred by James to George Padmore, another West Indian and former Comintern member who had defected from the Communist movement during the 1930s because he felt it to be insincere regarding national liberation in Asia and Africa. In London, Nkrumah and Padmore collaborated in organizing the Fifth Pan-African Congress at Manchester, with its ringing declaration for African independence which Nkrumah proposed to achieve through immediate organization of the African masses and the seizure of political power by means of strikes and boycotts. At the conclusion of the Manchester conference,

Nkrumah busied himself with plans to implement the congress's resolutions, and it was at this point that he answered the call to return to the Gold Coast and accept the post of UGCC secretary. Beyond his education, his growing political experience, and his determination to succeed through immediate action, Nkrumah possessed personal charm, eloquence, and a sure instinct for leadership. Here was the spark that would bring to life the potential within the Gold Coast for a mass nationalist movement.

Nkrumah's instinct told him to rebuff at first the constitutional reforms recommended by the Coussey report; instead, in 1950, he called a general strike and boycott, peaceful in intention but marked by violence, the result of which was imprisonment for him and his top aides and great excitement within the country for his cause. From his martyred position in jail he was now able to campaign successfully in the 1951 elections under the new constitution, and his CPP won a decisive victory at the expense of the UGCC. As the country's primary political figure, Nkrumah was released from prison and quickly shifted to a policy of cooperation with the authorities. Clearly the chief delegate in the new assembly, he was given the formal title of Prime Minister in 1952, and in 1954 he obtained a new constitution which did away with all special and nominated categories in the assembly and with any officially sponsored ministers in the cabinet, the governor, however, reserving authority for external affairs and defense. Nevertheless, internal self-government was still but a way station, and two years later Nkrumah was able to convince the British government that the country was ready for complete autonomy. On March 6, 1957, the Gold Coast became the independent state of Ghana.

In achieving his objectives, Nkrumah had been obliged to do battle with more than the colonial administration. The 1951 constitution had provided for a substantial number of assemblymen chosen by regional chiefly councils, an arrangement anathema to one seeking exclusive national authority. This impediment was removed by the 1954 constitution which provided for direct election of all assembly members, but at this stage another obstacle appeared in the shape of a new opposition made up of various regional, ethnic, and religious interests—Muslims, Ewe, Asante, to name the major components— which argued for a federal-type government in order to achieve a proper balance between national and local interests. The chief organs of the opposition, the Northern People's Party and the Asante based National Liberation Movement, banded together to contest the 1956 election, but the CPP led by Nkrumah and his lieutenants, K. A. Gbedemah, Kojo Botsio, Krobo Edusei, and Kofi Baako, once again demonstrated its primacy with a solid victory, and this achievement convinced the British government that Nkrumah had the national support it regarded as a necessary prerequisite to independence.

Apparently Nkrumah himself felt no such confidence, for once in power as head of a sovereign Ghana, he proceeded to demolish the opposition and establish a single-party dictatorship, the Republic of Ghana proclaimed in 1960, with himself as president and eventually as life president. Whether he was motivated by a sense of personal infallibility or by a fear that the newly independent nation, intent on accelerating its thrust toward modernization, could not afford the luxury of a locally oriented political opposition, the party nevertheless came to be equated with the nation while Nkrumah began to look beyond his position as national leader to the role of spokesman for all of Africa.

If Nkrumah's one-party state was a counter to the threat of regionalism, it was this same parochial tendency that complicated the search for an independence formula in Nigeria. Here, as in the Gold Coast, economic and social changes arising out of the exigencies of the Second World War had pushed Nigeria along the road to modernization. Strategic and economic considerations had greatly stimulated local production which received additional impetus from the passage of the Colonial Development and Welfare Acts in 1940 and 1945, born of a changing conviction in Britain regarding the responsibilities of colonial stewardship. Demand for raw materials, moreover, continued to expand during the postwar years, and as exports of cotton, groundnuts, palm oil, cocoa, and timber increased in a rising world price structure, the possibilities for internal development of the economy grew accordingly.

The result was a changing socioeconomic pattern characteristic of postwar Africa—the growth of industry, the expansion of cities, and the rise of organized labor; the steady extension of transportation facilities to meet insistent commercial needs; the frantic increase of the educational establishment in response both to popular demand and to shortage of skilled performers at all economic and technical levels; the involvement of ever-widening segments of the population into a cash economy; the development of a significant internal market to parallel an increased emphasis on exports and imports; the slow breakdown of a traditional way of life under attack by a new social dynamism.

Such changes were necessarily accompanied by emphatic nationalist impulses which were, however, complicated and diffused by Nigeria's historic heterogeneity. Despite the formation of the Nigerian federation in 1914, British administration between the two world wars had tended to emphasize regional diversity, especially the differences between north and south. The Muslim emirates, already isolated and xenophobic, were permitted to govern themselves largely according to long-standing feudal formulas, while the people of the east and west, although chafing under an ill-suited indirect rule, were nevertheless propelled forward into the contemporary world by their unwavering desire for the benefits of Western education. On the eve of the Second World War, the parochial politics of Herbert Macaulay were giving way to a broader nationalism exemplified both by the Nigerian Youth Movement of Ernest Ikoli, H. O. Davies, and others, and by the flamboyant exertions of Nnamdi Azikiwe.

For a time Azikiwe and the Youth Movement made common cause which, unfortunately, could survive neither the clash of personalities nor a sense of tribal identity, portentous in its implications—Zik with his solid Ibo support confronted by the large Yoruba block in the Youth Movement. In 1944 another attempt was made when Azikiwe formed the National Council of Nigeria and the Cameroons (NCNC) with himself as secretary and Herbert Macaulay as president. As the war ended, the NCNC set about building a national party dedicated to the achievement of internal self-government. As with the Gold Coast and the Sudan, Britain's postwar position regarding her colonies was not averse to a move toward self-determination, and the decade following 1945 was devoted not so much to a struggle for independence as to the search for constitutional stability in a land of centrifugal ethnic forces.

The first attempt was made by Governor Sir Arthur Richards whose constitution went into effect at the beginning of 1947. It was at once roundly criticized by nationalists, partly because it had been introduced without prior consultation within Nigeria and partly as a response to the undemocratic character of the new legislative council, its membership almost wholly chosen by indirection. The distinctive feature of the constitution, however, was its inclusion of the north in the central legislature and the establishment of three regional councils for north, west, and east. These bodies, though largely bereft of authority, were dominated by the chiefs and the British administration, and promised to become potential centers for a divisive spirit of regionalism.

This initial effort to balance unity and diversity was soon followed by discussions which led eventually to a second constitution under which general elections were held in 1951. This so-called Macpherson Constitution reflected the difficulties of formulating an effective government in a country of growing regional self-consciousness even as national developmental requirements called for increasing authority at the center. The constitution took effect at a time when cultural organizations like Egbe Omo Oduduwa the Pan-Ibo Federal Union, the Ibibio State Union, and the Jam'iyyar Mutanen Arewa, or Northern Peoples' Congress, were proclaiming the ethnic integrity of their memberships and finding themselves in the process more and more involved with political activities. The Pan-Ibo Federal Union had been one of the founding members of the NCNC, the Yoruba Egbe Omo Oduduwa sired its political wing, the Action Group, in 1951, while the Northern Peoples' Congress transformed itself into a political organ during the election campaign that same year.

The result of the new constitution, therefore, was a federation of three regional governments controlled by ethnic political parties all-powerful in their own areas and largely impotent elsewhere—the Action Group in the west, the National Council of Nigeria and the Cameroons (NCNC) in the east, and the Northern Peoples' Congress (NPC) in the north. The federal legislature and its council of ministers, chosen from the regional assemblies, could not operate as an effectively coherent entity with conflicting regional priorities complicating its deliberations. This was especially marked on the question of national self-government, the eastern and western regions pressing for early independence while the northern leaders wished to go more slowly, fearful that in an autonomous state their numerous but still largely illiterate population would be dominated by the more sophisticated, educated southerners.

In 1953 there were bloody riots in Kano reflecting local enmity toward the large numbers of literate southerners employed in the north as clerks in commercial establishments and government offices. When this outburst was followed by a motion in the northern parliament calling for the end of federation, the British government convened a new constitutional conference which met in an atmosphere of marked regional particularism, yet managed in its protracted deliberations to produce a new constitution which formed the basis for independence when it came in 1960.

This 1954 constitution seemingly placed the balance of power squarely in the three regions. The federal legislature was chosen according to electoral processes formulated by the regions; the central council of ministers was chosen on a regional basis; powers not delegated to the federation were reserved to the regions; each region was given a premier although none was designated for the federal government; and finally, although taxing powers were federal, distribution of revenue was made substantially proportionate to regional contribution. Lagos was designated a federal territory and the police remained federal, but other civil services, including the judiciary, were regionalized.

The strengthening of centripetal forces therefore remained a paramount necessity. For the moment, as the 1954 constitution came into effect, the major political figures were located in the regions—Dr. Azikiwe, the NCNC founder, as premier in Enugu, Chief Awolowo, head of the Action Group holding the same office in Ibadan, and Sir Ahmadu Bello, the Sardauna of Sokoto and leader of the NPC, the chief minister in Kaduna. Moreover, both the east and west looked to early self-government while the north still held back, thereby complicating the prospect of eventual national independence. At the same time, however, there were genuine efforts at unity. The NCNC and NPC succeeded in combining to form a coalition federal government with Awolowo leading the Action Group as a loyal parliamentary opposition, and in 1957 the constitution was revised in an atmosphere of determined and growing cooperation. A major change was the creation of a federal prime minister empowered to choose his own cabinet, and this position was soon occupied by the moderate deputy leader of the NPC, Abubakar Tafawa Balewa. At the same time, the west and east accepted local self-government while the north agreed to follow suit in 1959.

Thus the ground was prepared for the independence of Nigeria which was proclaimed on October 1, 1960. Nonetheless, the essential divisiveness of the country remained. The regional political parties, despite repeated efforts, continued unable to build national followings, while within the regions themselves, signs of further fragmentation appeared as smaller ethnic bodies demanded local autonomy in their turn, free from the controls of the already dominant larger national groups.

Independence—The French-African Variant

The conference of some twoscore French colonial administrators who met at Brazzaville in January and February 1944 marked an important turning point in French colonial policy. Recognizing Africa's contribution to the Free French cause, the provisional government of General Charles de Gaulle at once conceded a new kind of partnership, although equality between the French and the Africans was uncertainly defined by the delegates, now stressing the need for greater cultural assimilation, now arguing, with Félix Eboué, for the preservation of traditional values and institutions. Forced labor and the *indigénat* were to be abolished, modernization and French-style education greatly stepped up, and a broad-based franchise introduced along with a form of French citizenship allowing special cultural and religious status such as the *originaires* of the Four Communes of Senegal had long enjoyed. To a considerable extent the discussion centered on the question of administrative efficiency, with the federalists headed by Eboué arguing for decentralization on grounds of expediency. The conference finally urged the establishment of assemblies for various colonial territories, a decision that was of great moment in shaping the future independence of African peoples. Decentralization and democracy did not mean independence, however, as the delegates declared forever inadmissible the idea of self-government for France's colonies.

These recommendations comprised a major step forward even if all were not immediately brought into being. A liberal constitution was rejected by the French electorate in May 1946, and a second, which became the constitution of the Fourth Republic five months later, was much less open handed regarding colonial rights and status. The French Union which thereby came into being allowed no true confederation of states but classified former colonies as constituent territories of an indivisible republic. Greatest concessions were made in civil status and rights as the granting of French citizenship and its protection to all people of the Union meant a final end to forced labor and administrative justice. Nevertheless the franchise was for practical purposes limited to the 1.5 million overseas citizens who met specified property and literacy qualifications. Each territory received its own assembly, both West Africa and Equatorial Africa were given regional grand councils, and there was a special assembly of the French Union seated in Paris, but all these bodies enjoyed only advisory powers. Real authority remained with the French parliament, to which the African territories now elected a number of representatives, and indeed to a considerable measure the old prewar controls remained, for parliamentary ministers were empowered to govern the territories by decree in the absence of contradictory legislation. Thus France had made major concessions and old-fashioned colonialism was dead, but the overseas territories were still tightly controlled from Paris. French assimilation did not extend to the sharing of authority.

High centralization of authority was in the best Napoleonic tradition, but there were also practical considerations in the maintenance of close French colonial controls. The postwar years saw a vast rise in metropolitan overseas investment, French West Africa alone receiving up to $1 billion between 1947 and 1956 in French treasury grants and public low-interest loans for developmental purposes, as well as considerable direct support from the mother country for the local civil and military establishments. Along with investment went a substantial emigration of *petits blancs*, French petty bourgeois who became permanent residents—government workers, shopkeepers, clerks, and artisans whose livelihood had to be protected. Finally, French mercantile control of the overseas economies was tightened in an economic union that directed fully 70 percent of all exports to a protected metropolitan market, while receiving French goods on a similarly preferential basis.

That these benefits were reciprocal was affirmed by a developing African affluence. In the decade following 1947, for example, West African export of coffee and cocoa nearly tripled while groundnut shipments rose from 380,000 to 710,000 tons. To be sure these advances greatly benefited European planters as well, especially in the Ivory Coast where they had long been encouraged to settle and where their competition with African farmers led to the formation in 1946 of a political movement, the *Parti Démocratique de la* Côte d'Ivoire (PDCI), founded by a Baulé planter, Félix Houphouet-Boigny. By 1949 Houphouet and the colonial administration were locked in a struggle that involved police suppression and manipulated elections designed to break the impact of African-organized strikes and boycotts. After two bloody years, Houphouet, in a move reminiscent of the earlier accommodation of Blaise Diagne, made peace with the authorities and the French mercantile community, and within a few years capital investment and economic expansion had converted the Ivory Coast into one of the most productive territories in French West Africa.

This early postwar antipathy to colonialism was shared in other territories, although not on such explicit economic grounds. In 1946 Houphouet's party became a leading component of the grand interterritorial *Rassemblement Démocratique Africain* (RDA) which emerged from an historic meeting at Bamako called by several of the West and Equatorial African deputies to the French parliament as a reaction against the undemocratic constitution of the French Union. The result was a series of RDA sections organized within most of the French-African areas, including the United Nations trust territory of Cameroun, each section acting as a local political party but with a considerable interterritorial allegiance to the RDA caused by mutual commitment to the idea of African emancipation. Yet, despite the circumstances of its birth as well as its early association with the French Communist Party, the RDA maintained an essentially moderate position regarding the French Union. Less accommodating were the Senegalese Socialists, led first by Lamine Guèye and then by Leopold Senghor whose *Bloc Démocratique Sénégalais* (BDS) founded in 1948 as a farmer-intellectual alliance quite independent of the RDA, took the stand that some form of federation between Africa and France was preferable to the insufficient political assimilation provided by the French Union.

While in Equatorial Africa political inexperience and French overseas policy produced but faint echoes of events unfolding to the west, the more sophisticated West Africans now moved to test the strength of their affiliations with France, even as Paris was experiencing a fundamental change of heart regarding the nature of her overseas empire. Defeat in Vietnam in 1954, a reluctant grant of independence to the Tunisian and Moroccan protectorates in 1956, and the outbreak in 1954 of an increasingly ferocious civil war in Algeria all combined to shake the faith in French Union, as observers in Paris noted the growing power of national liberation movements all over the colonial world. Events in the Sudan and Ghana had their effect, the prospect of independence in the latter case leading to a new constitution granting internal autonomy to Ghana's neighbor, the French-administered United Nations territory of Togo.

This concession toward tiny Togo necessarily meant a fresh approach in all the French-African territories, and in 1956 there appeared a legislative *loi-cadre* which set forth the main outlines of a new policy for the overseas territories. The principle of assimilation was abandoned in favor of a revived concept of association in which a number of now semiautonomous territories with power over local affairs were placed in a federal relationship with France, the French government retaining control in external matters.

Local autonomy was granted, not as a step toward independence, but as its substitute; nevertheless the essential issue of the moment centered less on political liberty than on the fate of the two regions of French West Africa and French Equatorial Africa. These had been organized originally as administrative conveniences whereby the more productive areas could help defray the costs of government in the less developed territories. In time this situation became particularly vexatious to the more wealthy Gabon in Equatorial Africa and the Ivory Coast in West Africa, their accelerating development bringing with it a fast-growing burden in support of impecunious sister states. In 1954 the Ivory Coast was contributing over one-third of the total cost of administration in French West Africa and received back only half of that amount in local services. For its part, Senegal's record was distinctly better—a 30 percent return for a 39 percent output.

Under these circumstances it is not surprising that Houphouet, at this time serving as a French government minister, acted as a major influence in France's decision to establish a grouping based primarily on her direct relationship with each individual territory, the regional West African and Equatorial federations being considerably reduced in power and revenue. Against Houphouet was aligned Léopold Senghor whose espousal of negritude and African culture and whose genuine belief in equal partnership between France and Africa led him to criticize the *loi-cadre* as what he termed "balkanization" of French Africa. Senghor was not alone. Within the RDA were powerful

Kwame Nkrumah

United Nations

Nnamdi Azikiwe

UPI/Bettmann

East African independence leaders: from left to right,   *UPI/Bettmann*
Julius Nyerere, Milton Obote, and Jomo Kenyatta

President Félix
Houphouet-
Boigny of the
Ivory Coast

AP/Wide World Photos

Léopold Sédar Senghor

AP/Wide World Photos

Kenneth Kaunda,
President of Zambia

AP/Wide World Photos

J. J. Rawlings, Ghana Chief of State

Nobel Laureate
Wole Soyinka

elements led by Sékou Touré of Guinea and Modibo Keita of Soudan, who favored a strong federation as the prelude to independence for a massive and powerful West African state.

France now advanced an alternative, the celebrated offer of General de Gaulle, freshly come to power in the spring of 1958. He proposed that the African territories either ratify the constitution of the new Fifth Republic of France and thereby become autonomous states within a community whose external affairs would be controlled by France, or take immediate and absolute independence. With Ghana now free and others clearly on their way, the idea of independence was much in the African air, but only Guinea led by Sékou Touré voted against the constitution thereby gaining immediate and total separation from France in September 1958. The others accepted the constitution and the community, reluctant both to sever their long association with France and to put an abrupt end to the substantial developmental assistance that had poured into their territories ever since the conclusion of the Second World War.

The sudden, brusque divorce of Guinea did not settle the twin questions of federation and independence. In Equatorial Africa, Barthélémy Boganda of Ubangi-Chari, president of the regional Grand Council, carried on a campaign for continuation of the old federation; nevertheless both African groupings were terminated by the formation of the community, a move that merely intensified the search for unity. Senegal particularly dreaded isolation, not only on ideological grounds but because she was obliged to maintain and utilize the many federal installations at Dakar, for example, the port, the railroad to Bamako, and the university. In 1959, therefore, West African leaders formed the Mali Federation which initially included Senegal, Soudan, Upper Volta, and Dahomey, but which quickly reduced itself to the tandem of Senegal and Soudan when the others withdrew in the face of pressure from both Houphouet and the French.

The Mali Federation now moved toward total independence as France amended her constitution to permit complete autonomy within the community. In June 1960 the Federation became free, then, only two months later, split into the two independent nations of Mali and Senegal, unity proving impossible between such diverse groups as the dedicated, austere Marxists of the poverty-stricken interior and the wealthier sophisticates living in Dakar.

Meanwhile, in 1959, Houphouet had helped form the Entente, a loose grouping made up of Niger, Dahomey, Upper Volta, and the Ivory Coast, and designed as a counterweight to the Mali Federation. Houphouet-Boigny had consistently argued against independence, partly because he regarded it as expensive and dangerous to African development and partly because he valued the cultural advantages of the French connection. When France gave Mali its freedom within the community, however, his thesis was no longer defensible and the rush for independence began. Before the end of 1960 all of France's West African and Equatorial states had demanded and received their freedom. This included the United Nations trust territories as well. Part of Togo had already opted to join Ghana in 1957 and the remainder became an independent state in 1960, as did Cameroun. The following year a plebiscite in the British Cameroons resulted in the northern section remaining as part of Nigeria while the south voted to join the Federal Republic of Cameroun.

The Crisis of Independence in the Congo

Over the years Belgian paternalism effectively smothered any sense of Congolese nationhood, but it could not prevent Congo nationals from making note of the independence movements developing around them. Belgian efficiency wasted no energies training an elite for self-government which they were convinced would never come, but such a policy succeeded only in limiting the experience of those few leaders who did emerge. Belgian pragmatism rested secure in the knowledge of its realism and toughness, but in the crisis of independence it proved to be flaccid, purposeless, and unequal to the responsibilities that were thrust upon it.

The drive for independence came late in the Congo; having started tardily, however, it moved swiftly, borne along by African impetuosity and inexperience, matched with Belgian indecision. The independence of Ghana in 1957, General de Gaulle's dramatic *oui-ou-non* offer of independence or local autonomy within the French Community, the All-African Peoples' Conference held in Accra in December 1958, and the widened horizons of Congolese attending the Brussels international fair of that same year opened prospects undreamed of a few short years earlier. Inside the Congo, a modest and controlled political activity begun in 1956 suddenly broke loose, propelled by dawning ambition among the few educated elite, by economic and social grievances in the cities, and by an ominous tribalism springing up in diverse quarters of the country.

In 1957 limited reforms liberalizing representation in local government and introducing elections for the city councils of Leopoldville, Elisabethville, and Jadotville precipitated political organization: first, ABAKO (*Alliance des Ba-Kongo*), an ethnically rooted party which had originated in Leopoldville in 1950 as a Bakongo cultural society, then, CONAKAT (*Confédération des Associations Tribales du Katanga*), another tribally oriented confederation based in the Katanga, and in 1958, the *Mouvement National Congolais* (MNC) founded by a group of young educated Africans including Cyrille Adoula and Patrice Lumumba. ABAKO, led by Joseph Kasavubu, and CONAKAT, associated from the beginning with the name of Moise Tshombe, were necessarily regional in influence, but the MNC had gone beyond the limitations of parochialism and supported the concept of a national party dedicated to a united independent Congo. Local or national, however, all parties adopted a rapidly accelerating demand for democracy and early independence. ABAKO had called for an immediate grant of autonomy as early as 1956. The MNC grew steadily more radical throughout 1959, presumably a reflection of Lumumba's meeting with Nkrumah at the Accra conference. Each party found it expedient to step up its demands, fearful lest it be outdistanced by the others in the appeal for votes.

The response of the Belgian authorities was a rapid series of major concessions, culminating late in 1959 in the astonishing announcement that a conference would be held the following January, its predetermined outcome to be independence for the Congo in 1960. Such precipitous action reflected divisions within the government in Brussels, as well as fears that the Congo might fragment into a series of ethnic states if it were not allowed to go its way quickly. In January 1959 riots in Leopoldville had erupted, caused by resentment over unemployment and segregation, and profoundly unsettling to Belgian self-confidence. During the months that followed, the early party groupings, now joined by others including the PSA (*Parti Solidaire Africain*) led by Antoine Gizenga, showed increasing signs of regionalism along with their growing political extremism. Kasavubu and ABAKO were calling for virtual secession, the Katanga seemed to favor only a loose federalism, while rioting which occurred in Luluabourg and Stanleyville was based in ethnic animosities. Even the nationalist MNC felt the strains of divisiveness and broke into two with the departure of an independent Luba section favorable to federalism.

Belgian authorities had expected to retain control over external affairs even after independence, but the weakness of their stand drew forth even more extreme demands from the Congolese. At the Round Table Conference held in Belgium during January 1960, immediate independence was demanded and quickly granted along with the virtual assurance that the grant would be ratified by the Belgian parliament. Independence was set for June 30, 1960, with national elections to be held in May. Congolese leaders, momentarily united to face the Belgians at the conference, had found no opposition and, unopposed, had plunged on to gain even more than they had initially hoped for. It was a moment of missed opportunity. Lacking colonial resistance they also lost the necessity for a permanent unity which could have been the basis of a stable national government.

A constitution was drafted providing for a federal state of six provinces, the central government assuming such national responsibilities as military security, economic planning, federal currency, and higher education, while the provinces were given control in regional matters including local police and education at the lower levels. In the May election the strength of localism was all too apparent; although the MNC and its related smaller parties gained a solid plurality in the national lower house, Lumumba and his advocates of a unitary state were far outnumbered by the sum of other parties, all regional in appeal and federalist in orientation. When a government was finally formed with Lumumba as prime minister heading a broad-based coalition, this move was made possible only through the last-minute cooperation of Kasavubu who was named head of state.

The Republic of the Congo thus became a sovereign state under the most inauspicious circumstances. Indeed, on the day of national independence there was independence but as yet no nation. Fourteen million people drawn from over two hundred tribal groups had no sense of national identity, political leadership at the center was essentially dependent upon support in the regions, geographic diversity and enormous distances added their complications, while the sudden departure of a paternalist colonial regime removed restraints long endured and set free all of the centrifugal forces in this vast land. By the standards of Africa, the Congo was well developed in economic terms. There was a billion dollar annual production and one of the highest per capita incomes in the continent, but in its lack of political cohesion and its paucity of educated leadership it was certainly among the most poorly endowed of the new African nations.

The sequel to independence was virtual anarchy, succeeded by the four-year military occupation of a United Nations peace-keeping force, and then a slow, painful groping toward nationhood. Within a week of the celebration of independence, tribal disorders broke out, followed by a mutiny in the army which resulted in a number of European deaths and destruction of property. The ensuing panic and mass exodus of the predominantly Belgian European population deprived the country at its outset of much-needed trained personnel; then, less than two weeks after independence, Moise Tshombe announced the secession of the wealthy Katanga province which provided half the national revenue.

Lumumba and Kasavubu now appealed for intervention by a United Nations force which soon found itself caught up in a complex political and diplomatic tangle. There was the continuing influence of Belgian interests in the Katanga; the intrusion of international politics with unilateral Soviet encouragement and military supplies for Lumumba's government poised against strong American financial and logistical support for the U.N. action; the dismissal from office of Lumumba by Kasavubu in September 1960, and his assassination the following February while in the custody of Tshombe; the near breakup of the state which was checked only when Cyrille Adoula formed a government in August 1961; and the eventual occupation and reintegration of the Katanga in 1963 through United Nations action—all complicated by the continued incapacity of the Congolese army as an effective force for peace and security. On June 30, 1964, the United Nations mission and troops finally departed, but this was followed by another period of uncertainty during the 1964-1965 government of Moise Tshombe with its controversial white mercenary additions to the Congolese armed forces. Late in 1965 the Congo Republic was shaken by still another crisis when a bloodless coup installed General Joseph Mobutu at the head of a military government.

Although unsuspected at the time, the accession to power by General Mobutu represented a turning point for the troubled Congo state which henceforward began slowly to achieve the stability and cohesion so lacking during its early years—a practical working independence to match the nominal end of colonial control in 1960. Mobutu's start was not auspicious, however, for he was immediately beset by a series of political crises typical of the previous era; yet what gradually became apparent was his capacity for survival and a steady strengthening of the central machinery of state. First to be resolved was the problem of Moise Tshombe who, though forced into exile, nevertheless remained a source of potential national disunity. Fortunately for Mobutu, Tshombe died abroad in 1969; by this time, however, the government had faced a second embarrassment that threatened both Congo sovereignty and national self-respect. In 1967 white mercenary soldiers, former employees of both Tshombe and Mobutu, occupied parts of eastern Congo and threatened to shatter the ill-organized Congolese armed forces. With difficulty Mobutu prevailed as the insurgents were forced to retreat, eventually to be evacuated from neighboring Rwanda in 1968. Centrifugal problems persisted, however, in a series of stubborn internal rebellions, the most difficult and widespread of which, led by Pierre Mulele, was finally stamped out with Mulele's execution in 1968.

These threats to internal security, met and resolved, suggested a growing control over the army and the country. As Mobutu's strength increased, his administration concentrated on the encouragement of foreign investment in national economic development, and the end of regional divisiveness through emphasis on traditional Bantu values. A campaign for ''authenticity'' led in 1971 to the wholesale adoption of African names, for example, the traditional term of Zaire to denote the river Congo, the national currency, and most of all, the republic itself, while Mobutu dropped his Christian names to become henceforward Mobutu Sese Seko. These changes, said Mobutu, were to be more than nominal, however. Echoing African cultural nationalist impulses elsewhere, Mobutu saw himself moving to regain essential African values and national dignity.

As for Rwanda and neighboring Burundi, independence had come in 1962 after a lengthy Belgian administration of the Ruanda-Urundi mandate and trust territory. Here, as with the Congo, ethnic violence broke forth with the relaxation of colonial controls. In Rwanda the Tutsi, long-time aristocrats and traditional rulers, were massacred and driven out of the country by their subject Bahutu who pointedly established a republican government. In Burundi there was at the time no comparable outburst and a limited Tutsi monarchy was established.

East African *Uhuru*

As in other parts of the continent, the move toward independence in British East Africa was closely linked to the problem of ethnic exclusiveness. In

Uganda where the Baganda insisted on their own national integrity and in Kenya where the European community sought to maintain its dominant position, independence came slowly and painfully. In Tanganyika, far less developed in its economy and educational resources, little serious divisiveness emerged and it was there that the freedom cry, *uhuru*, was first converted into reality.

The British administration, not the African people, took the first steps toward Tanganyikan independence after the Second World War. Committed to a postwar liberalization of colonial controls and stimulated by its position as a United Nations trustee working toward eventual African self-government, Britain initiated several moves leading to greater local autonomy. In 1945 the legislative council was expanded to accommodate four African appointees along with the seven Europeans and three Asians. As investment in economic development and public works went forward, including heavy support for an ambitious but ill-fated scheme in mechanized groundnut production, there were further political advances. In 1951 an African was named to the executive council, and four years later the legislative council was again enlarged to include thirty unofficial nominees, ten representing each of the Asian, African, and European communities according to a principle of racial parity. Parity was the basis on which the governor, Sir Edward Twining, now moved to have the unofficial councillors brought to office through direct elections scheduled for 1958.

Such a liberalization of the political process, well ahead of the times in the late 1940s, was already out of date by the mid-fifties. In part, these constitutional reforms had been instituted to make more palatable the creation of the East African High Commission coordinating certain economic and administrative functions among the territories of Kenya, Uganda, and Tanganyika, but the fear of Kenya white domination made the move unpopular in Tanganyika. This opposition gradually took the shape of political parties, culminating in 1954 with the appearance of the Tanganyika African National Union (TANU) under the leadership of a young African schoolteacher, Julius K. Nyerere, recently returned from his studies in Britain. TANU and Nyerere at once opposed racial parity on principle and then further irritated the government by criticizing the prevailing system of indirect rule in the provinces, advocating an end to the old reliance on native authorities. Gathering overwhelming support throughout the country in competition with the interracial United Tanganyika Party, TANU circumvented the parity qualifications during the 1958 elections by nominating and sweeping into office its own candidates in all three racial groups, thereby controlling the unofficial membership of the legislative council from that point forward.

With such overwhelming African support in a country where no large tribal groups existed as potential centers of regional disaffection, Tanganyika was suddenly projected to the forefront of the independence movement in East Africa despite her deficiencies in economic resources and lack of a trained labor force. The principle of parity was dropped and the franchise broadened as Asian and European fears were assuaged by Nyerere's moderation, and in 1960 TANU again dominated the elections, now based on a single electoral roll. The following year came internal self-government which led to final independence in December 1961. By this time, TANU's political ascendancy had become so complete that as the Tanganyikan nation achieved its freedom, it did so in the form of a single-party state.

In nearby Zanzibar, one-party rule came via the route of revolution. On the eve of independence, it appeared that the Islamic solidarity of the population would enable the Arab oligarchy to maintain its established political control. A coalition of the Arab-dominated Zanzibar Nationalist Party (ZNP) and the African controlled but pro-Arab Zanzibar and Pemba People's Party (ZPPP) defeated the Afro-Shirazi Party (ASP) in the 1963 elections, winning a majority of seats despite the ASP poll of over 50 percent of the popular vote. Intent upon putting an end to the economic and political domination of the Arabs, and despairing of achieving this end by constitutional means, an opposition began to take shape within the African population, its sentiments strongly Marxist, and its object revolution.

On January 12, 1964, the government fell before a coup engineered by a small group of *ad hoc* insurrectionaries only one month after independence had been achieved. As a result of this upheaval, the opposition forces were able to seize power, led by the ASP president, Abeid Karume. At once, thousands of Arabs were arrested, much of their property confiscated or destroyed, the sultan banished, and the coalition parties proscribed. Beyond this, the new regime quickly instituted land reforms and other egalitarian moves designed to wipe out class privilege. In order to strengthen their political and economic program, the revolutionaries now looked abroad for aid through political alliance, and soon concluded an agreement with President Nyerere of Tanganyika which established the united republic of Tanzania in April 1964. Although the union provided for a marked degree of centralization under a Tanzanian national government, the Zanzibaris have since retained in practice a considerable independence of action in both their domestic and international affairs and probably were also responsible in part for Nyerere's own emergence as one of Africa's more eloquent advocates of state socialism.

The achievement of independence in Uganda was dominated throughout the period following the Second World War by the same Baganda isolationism that had conditioned British colonial rule during the protectorate period. Therefore, as Britain began to consider the possibility of colonial autonomy, she was obliged to deal with the fundamental difficulty of separatism in Uganda; the more her administrators argued the case for unitary government, the more they stimulated national exclusiveness in Buganda. The first serious disagreement came in the 1950s as the governor, Sir Andrew Cohen, attempting to point Uganda in the direction of centralization, succeeded in precipitating a Baganda secession movement led by the kabaka, Mutesa II. Mutesa's deportation and subsequent restoration marked a paper agreement in 1955 which found neither side essentially moved from its position, Buganda proclaiming its own solidarity and Britain determined to have a unitary state.

In 1960 the Baganda again threatened secession, and the following year, as Britain studied plans for a constitution on which Ugandan independence might be based, it was agreed that Buganda should have special status as a federated state within an otherwise unitary Uganda. This development naturally brought demands for equivalent federal status from the other kingdoms, and in 1962 this was conceded to Toro, Bunyoro, Ankole, and Busoga, the less cohesive Acholi, Lango, Gisu, Teso and other peoples being accorded a more direct form of administration. Buganda had gained her point and the constitution allowed the Baganda lukiko, or assembly, to choose representatives to the national legislature and guaranteed Buganda local autonomy within a Uganda federation. When independence came in October 1962, the kabaka was elected chief of state.

Indeed, the impasse was resolved, not so much by British acquiescence as by the refined political maneuvers of Milton Obote, a Lango leader with pronounced leanings toward a centralized welfare state and therefore a natural enemy to Baganda particularism. As the possibility of independence approached during the late fifties, political parties began to appear to contest upcoming elections, but no party was able to gain more than a regional following and none from outside Buganda could penetrate the exclusiveness of Baganda parochialism. This was true of the Democratic Party based on the Catholic Church as well as the Bantu-supported Uganda People's Union. The nearest thing to a national party was the Uganda National Congress based on a farmer's cooperative, but it too was unable to maintain a following in Buganda. In 1960 Obote merged the congress and union in the Uganda People's Congress (UPC), thereby gaining wide support except in Buganda; then in 1961 he concluded an alliance with the *Kabaka Yekka* (KY), an exclusively Baganda grouping emphasizing tribal solidarity, in the process risking his unionist support across the country. As it happened, the UPC had no difficulty in holding its adherents as the coalition won the 1962 elections, thus bringing the country to independence with Obote as prime minister.

It was a loveless marriage of convenience, however, a poor agent with which to solve Uganda's long-standing problem of separatism. Obote had gained nominal unity and national autonomy, perhaps hoping through coalition and the sobering responsibilities of independence to educate the Baganda away from their traditional aloofness. KY no doubt felt it could continue to serve its parochial interests, the government requiring its support to remain in power. Accommodation did not succeed. In 1966, in an atmosphere of growing crisis, Obote arrested several KY members in his cabinet, forced a unitary constitution through parliament which abolished the special position of Buganda, and drove the kabaka into exile by attacking his palace with troops of the predominantly

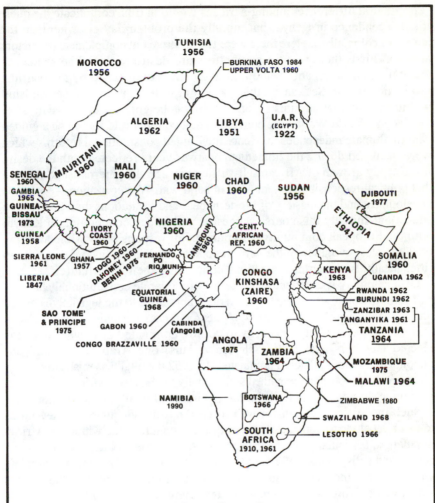

Independent Africa

non-Baganda army. Unity had been achieved, but its agent had been force, not consent.

Intramural differences among Africans would in time complicate the quest for independence in Kenya, but initially the problem lay elsewhere, in the legacy of colonialism. Here there were two discrete but complementary factors at work. First, there was the straightforward desire of the white settlers to maintain their dominant position, now greatly strengthened by the wartime production boom. Set against this was a long-standing sense of stewardship within the colonial administration which was heightened in the years after the Second World War by the conviction that colonial rule should be a guided path to ultimate independence. Hence the limited constitutional reforms which were instituted during the immediate postwar years reflected both the desire for a steady growth of African self-sufficiency and the paternalist conviction that political responsibility went hand in hand with Westernization—economic development and the mastery of Western ideas and institutions through Western education. Initially this course suggested multiracial cooperation in Kenya, with the European community assuming major responsibility while awaiting the long, slow evolution of the African population. Without a doubt such views fitted neatly with settler aspirations concerning their own future.

Official policy was reflected in a series of moderate constitutional changes. In 1944 provision was made for an African appointee to the legislative council and a second was added in 1947. A year later Kenya gained an unofficial majority in the council, a majority to be sure dominated by eleven European elected members against five elected Asians, one Arab elected and one appointed, and four Africans nominated. In 1952 the total was raised to twenty-eight but the proportions remained substantially unchanged, Africans, however, achieving an appointment to the twelve-man colonial executive council.

Such modest concessions proved to be far from adequate for they failed to meet, let alone to liquidate, basic grievances long forming within the African population, particularly among the Kikuyu. As ever the problem was economic, rooted in the dislocations of a rapidly developing society. The essential problem was simple; in the face of a spectacular rise in national prosperity, the African standard of living was in actual decline. Between 1938 and 1952 Kenyan exports increased in value seven times, based mainly on the production of white settler cash crops. Over these very years the African contribution to national production was minimal—6 percent in 1952, for example, compared with Uganda's 1951 figure of 63 percent; at the same time African real income from the market economy grew at the rate of only 1 percent per annum while the African population was rising at an annual rate of 3 percent.

In the fifteen years following 1938 the African labor force doubled and by 1951 accounted, through wages, for two-thirds of African earnings; yet per capita income was less than $10 a year, one-quarter of the figure for Uganda. Labor was low paid because it was inefficient, but a plentiful supply of cheap labor, ideally fitting the needs of European farmers, kept incomes low and thus frustrated African attempts at gaining new skills through training. For survival, laborers were compelled to supplement their wages by maintaining a stake in the subsistence agriculture of their village and reservation; hence, the tribal areas continued to provide quantities of cheap labor, but shared only the most minimal portion of the national prosperity. Well aware of this condition, Africans sought through political action to check their deteriorating economic position.

Led by the thin ranks of the educated, Africans in Nairobi and Mombasa began to form voluntary associations including an incipient labor movement, and out of this development emerged the Kenya African Union (KAU) in 1944. With the old Kikuyu Central Association outlawed and Jomo Kenyatta, recently returned home from England, assuming the KAU presidency in 1947, there seemed once again to be a vehicle for concerted African representations to government through a leadership of potentially supratribal appeal. As it happened the appeal was largely to the Kikuyu, located close to the government center at Nairobi and most directly affected by the land pressures from the White Highlands.

Between 1945 and 1953, the Kenya African Union petitioned the government repeatedly for political and economic reform, particularly a change in land policy and a more direct representation in the councils of government. Land would have to be redistributed, said the union, land which had been taken from Africans to begin with and now was desperately needed. Thus they might spread out from the overcrowded and overcropped reserves and put an end to the banishment of so many to starvation wages in the cities. At the same time, the argument continued, Africans were entitled to a higher proportion of the unofficial membership on the legislative council, a membership directly elected, not appointed by the colonial administration. Such appeals might have received a sympathetic hearing, especially from a Labour government in London, had not the settler oligarchy been quick and effective in guarding its own position. The result was that African representations were largely ignored, especially in the economic sphere. Specifically, there would be no land distribution, and no constitutional reform involving anything so radical as the single electoral roll demanded by the KAU. Failing to gain its objectives by peaceful petition, the African community slowly moved toward more violent means.

Disaffection grew gradually but inexorably as government policy continued to see progress only in terms of European leadership. Concurrently there arose among the Kikuyu the practice of oath taking, its purpose, as with many people the world over, to generate social cohesion and total commitment to a cause. By the end of 1950 the KAU leadership had recognized the emotional power of oathing and was using it as a conscious instrument of policy, hopeful of impressing their grievances on the government through mass unity. Now, however, the moderates in KAU began to lose control in the face of urban militants like the labor leaders Fred Kubai and Makhan Singh, whose radicalism combined with the discipline of oathing to radiate the concept of violence outward from the city to the rural Kikuyu areas. In the Fort Hall, Nyeri, and other districts north of Nairobi there were growing outbreaks in late 1951 and on into 1952 — minor civil disobedience, arson, destruction of property, and finally, murder. In October 1952 the progovernment Senior Chief Waruhiu was assassinated. Two weeks later a state of emergency was declared. Kikuyu complaints had at last gained official recognition through the resistance known as Mau Mau.

The "Emergency," with its wholesale bloodletting and its savage campaigning, was the ultimate spasm of a society pushed to extremity. It was consequently not the moderate nationalists of the KAU who were directly involved, as the administration believed, nor yet the ordinary peasant, but younger militants from Nairobi and the countryside whose flight to the forests of the Aberdares range and Mount Kenya was greatly accelerated by the declaration of emergency. The 1952-1953 trial and conviction of Kenyatta and his codefendants as instigators of Mau Mau was therefore futile, and the resistance had to be stamped out by a military action that had largely completed its mission by the end of 1955, although the "Emergency" was not officially terminated until early 1960. Unsuccessful militarily, the resistance succeeded, however, where other methods had failed in forcing recognition of African grievances and producing a genuine effort to deal with them.

In the all-important area of land reform, scattered holdings were consolidated into unitary farms, soil conservation was stepped up, and a program of cash crop development instituted, all underway well before the end of the "Emergency." All this might yet have been insufficient had it not been for political changes which were also instituted as early as 1954. Of these it was the introduction of the franchise for Africans in 1956 that overturned the administration program for controlled development of a multiracial state, and set Kenya on the path to African self-government. First, political groupings began to take shape and a Luo leadership emerged to complement the Kikuyu. Next, by refusing to cooperate in a ministry based on racial electoral rolls, the African parliamentarians wrecked the idea of racial parity and hastened the changes of 1960. A convention was called which produced a complex constitution, but the essential feature was a common-roll franchise. The one-man-one-vote ideal, so effectively dramatized by Tom Mboya's eloquence at the 1958 Accra All-African conference and elsewhere, had been achieved, and Kenya was on the way to becoming an autonomous African state.

An African-controlled government also marked the beginning of the end of land segregation in the White Highlands. Nevertheless, as the obstacle of settler domination receded and the vison of independence grew brighter, a new complication materialized in the form of a disturbing disunity within the African community. Two parties emerged. There was the Kenya African National Union (KANU) led by Kenyatta's old KAU colleague, James Gichuru, the young labor organizer Tom Mboya, and Oginga Odinga, who had built up a large following in the central Nyanza area. KANU drew its strength mainly from Kikuyu, Luo, and Kamba, but another party, the Kenya African Democratic Union (KADU), also appeared, headed by Ronald Ngala and Daniel arap Moi, and supported by a number of smaller ethnic groups fearful of Kikuyu and Luo domination. The election of 1961 was won by KANU which, however, refused to form a government while its leader by acclamation, Jomo Kenyatta, was still in detention. KADU then formed a government, but was embarrassed both by its minority position and by the release of Kenyatta in August 1961. Finally, in 1963, a new federal state was created as KANU and KADU settled their differences, and after further elections Kenyatta became Kenya's first prime minister. In December 1963 the country achieved independence, hopeful that, with the European question settled, a viable African nation was in the making.

Black and White Independence
in Central Africa

In Central Africa, the initial battle of African nationalists had been against federation, but the positive side of the antifederation struggle was national independence itself.

The combined strength of Nkumbula's African National Congress and Kaunda's UNIP easily insured an African legislative majority in the Northern Rhodesian general elections of October 1962. Nevertheless the two parties worked together poorly during their short-lived 1963 coalition, and the resultant sense of national uncertainty was clearly evident in chronic outbursts of violence which African leaders, including Kaunda, were hard pressed to contain. In part the lawlessness reflected urban unrest and unemployment on the copperbelt, but it also arose from an atmosphere of political frustration wherein an African majority had somehow lost its advantage and dissipated its energies in intramural conflict.

Such uncertainties were removed, however, when a new, uncomplicated constitution was introduced in 1963 which broadened the franchise to include over one million Africans and thereby insured victory for Kaunda's popular United National Independence Party. As expected, the elections held in January 1964 gave Kaunda and UNIP a solid legislative majority, although Nkumbula's Congress continued to show strength among the Ila-Tonga people in the southern districts and polled almost one-third of the 825,000 votes cast. With national leadership unambiguous at last, Kaunda moved steadily toward independence, using his new authority to regain the country's mineral rights from one of its major foreign concessionaires, the old British South Africa Company, while steps were taken at the same time to soothe the pride of the traditional royal house in Barotseland and thus forestall any separatist tendencies in the northwest. On October 24,1964, independence was proclaimed in the new state of Zambia.

Once the antifederation spasms in Nyasaland had ended and Dr. H. K. Banda gained his overwhelming victory at the head of the Malawi Congress Party in August 1961, the small highland territory moved smoothly toward independence. During 1962, Banda conducted the nation's affairs as unofficial head of government, he and his fellow ministers introducing numerous reforms with the cooperation of the governor, Sir Glyn Jones. In February 1963 Banda became prime minister in name as well as in fact, and Nyasaland proceeded to the stage of internal self-government. A little over a year later, on July 6, 1964, complete independence came to the new country known as the Commonwealth of Malawi.

In Southern Rhodesia the achievement of independence had a far different history. Here the force of African nationalism developed late and here it was fully tested and contained by a strong group of white settlers long resident in the territory and long accustomed to directing national affairs without the assistance of those they considered their inferiors. The controlling factors went back half a century and more, to the defeat of Lobengula and the subjugation of Ndebele and Shona, to the gradual emergence of a modern nation based on white management and black labor, and to the establishment of *de facto* segregation and discrimination by color which seemingly relegated over nine-tenths of the population to a permanently subordinate position.

Even under ideal circumstances it would have been well-nigh impossible to soften attitudes and relationships long since hardened into prejudice, to reverse the trend of decades and build a society based on genuine partnership. As it was, circumstances were much more conducive to the emergence of extremism, both European and African, an extremism which led to the crisis of UDI (Unilateral Declaration of Independence) in November 1965.

A number of factors were involved. First, there was the late but forced growth of African nationalism in Southern Rhodesia. The Southern Rhodesia African National Congress was not founded until 1957, when the one-time trade union leader Joshua Nkomo breathed new life into an older, moribund congress movement. Spurred in its aspirations and demands by the example of nationalists in neighboring Nyasaland and Northern Rhodesia as well as by the flooding tide of independence throughout Africa, the congress soon became the target of an uneasy government which banned it in 1959 in order, it was said, to forestall the type of violence that was taking place at the time in Nyasaland. The nationalists immediately reappeared in new forms culminating in the Zimbabwe African People's Union (ZAPU), formed early in 1962 with Nkomo as president. In whatever form, however, the thrust of African nationalism was directed against the system of white supremacy. What it sought was majority rule, a political condition clearly unacceptable to the settler community.

Poised against the African was the European, but the white settlers were by no means united in their position. At one extreme was the Dominion Party led by Winston Field and dedicated to a European-dominated, independent Rhodesia. At the other were the liberals, exemplified by Garfield Todd, the Southern Rhodesian prime minister during the early federation years, who favored the end of color bar and the institution of a multiracial society. Between these poles were the majority who supported Welensky's United Federal Party in its program of partnership, a policy that argued for the very gradual sharing of power with Africans over a long, evolving period of apprenticeship.

In 1958 Todd was replaced as Southern Rhodesian premier by Sir Edgar Whitehead of the United Federal Party, and it was Whitehead who in 1959 proscribed the congress movement and placed many of its members in detention. Somewhat paradoxically, he defended his action as a blow for multiracialism which, he said, could not survive fanaticism by either black or white, and concurrently Whitehead moved to do away with legal and customary color bar which he felt was an impediment to the healthy growth of a modern society. Under his guidance, the Land Apportionment Act was amended to allow for a degree of African residence in urban areas, and a campaign was instituted to do away with the social aspects of racial discrimination. In 1961, moreover, the Southern Rhodesian constitution was amended in such a way as to give modest legislative representation to Africans, but the prospect that they might eventually gain majority control was uncertain, estimates ranging from a dozen years to Ian Smith's not-in-my-lifetime declaration made in 1964.

Such tentative steps toward partnership were satisfactory neither to African nationalist nor to European conservative. Nkomo at first accepted with reluctance, then rejected, the constitution, yielding to the mounting criticism of Africans both inside and outside Southern Rhodesia. It was nothing but a device to perpetuate settler control, he insisted, and called for a boycott of the general election of December 1962, thus ruling out any possibility of racial partnership.

The white community, in its own eyes having made great concessions only to have them spurned by ungrateful Africans, was further upset by what it regarded as British duplicity and weakness in bowing to black pressure in Northern Rhodesia. There, Whitehall had granted a constitution in 1962 which, the whites felt, would establish an African state to the north and spell the end of the Federation of Rhodesia and Nyasaland. Having placed their faith in federation as a means to independence, the Southern Rhodesian settlers now turned in disgust from the ineffective moderation of the federalists and voted the newly formed Rhodesian Front into power. An outgrowth of the old Dominion party, the front in victory therefore could be expected to institute a right-wing segregationist regime, in every way anathema to African objectives.

Nevertheless the African nationalists regarded the Rhodesian Front victory as clearing the air of the ambiguities of federation, and prepared to do battle with their new opponents. While the front lifted former restrictions and released numbers of detainees, Nkomo intensified his opposition, insisting that Southern Rhodesia was African territory and that the ZAPU objective was nothing less than the end of minority rule. Even so, this was not enough for the more militant nationalists led by the Reverend Ndabaningi Sithole who formed the more belligerent Zimbabwe African National Union (ZANU) in 1963, thereby splitting and seriously weakening the nationalist effort. The two groups vied with each other in pressing their demands and wasted much effort on an intramural struggle that played straight into the hands of the authorities.

The Rhodesian Front's initial amnesty may have deceived the nationalists into misjudging the essential inflexibility of the front leaders on the issue of white supremacy, but they were soon disabused as the government put through legislation designed to contain any manifestations of African belligerence. Stiff laws were introduced against criminal acts of a political origin, nationalist leaders were kept under close scrutiny, and eventually both Nkomo and Sithole were placed in detention with numbers of the followers. While violence continued to break forth periodically, a good deal of it continued to stem from the rivalry between nationalist groups, and in any event the government was able to control concerted action by identifying and restricting new leadership as it emerged. By the end of 1964 the nationalist movement appeared well under control.

Having contained the Africans, the Rhodesian Front, led by Ian Smith after April, 1964, turned to the major issue of Rhodesian independence, an issue that was soon narrowed to the question of whether independence would be granted or seized. Successive British governments had uniformly insisted that the independence movement would have to show clear evidence of African backing as well as a guarantee of steady advance toward majority rule. Smith tried to prove African support through the testimony of chiefs, a tactic unacceptable in London. As for majority rule, he clearly had the settlers with him in setting his face against such heresy. In 1964 the Rhodesia Party was formed under the leadership of Roy Welensky, dedicated to moderation and constitutionalism and opposed to any extralegal unilateral move toward independence. That October Welensky and his party were soundly beaten in two by-elections, and Smith's hand immeasurably strengthened thereby. Another year of intensive negotiation followed, but there appeared to be no basis for compromising the essential quarrel over whether power would ultimately rest with the majority, which would mean African rule, or with the settler minority and their position of racial supremacy. On November 11, 1965, the Unilateral Declaration of Independence was broadcast by Smith, and the last of the Central African territories found its independence.

The Haves and the Have-Nots

For the African population of Rhodesia, UDI meant anything but independence, and there were others placed about the continent who saw themselves in similar condition. In South Africa, whatever their views about the Bantustans, few Africans deluded themselves with the thought that they possessed independence, or even true self-government. In the Portuguese territories of Mozambique, Angola, and Guinea, a classic colonial regime still prevailed, scarcely altered since the heyday of the slave trade, while in 1965 Spain still held minor and little-publicized African territories in varying stages of colonial status. In a different category, far to the east on the Somali "horn," the Djibouti enclave, now known as the Territory of the Afars and Issas, remained under French protection, having so voted in March 1967 in preference to absorption into neighboring Somalia.

For the rest, independence came early and late. With United Nations assistance, Libya had secured her freedom in 1951, while to the west Algerians fought their way to liberty in 1962 after seven years of bitter warfare with France. If the Afar and Issa people of the former French Somaliland preferred their protected status, those in the Italian and British Somaliland protectorates opted for independence which arrived in 1960 as the two territories merged to become the Republic of Somalia.

In West Africa, the smaller British colonies followed the path trod by Ghana and Nigeria. Sierra Leone achieved independence in 1961 and the tiny enclave of the Gambia in 1965. In both territories, smallness of size posed the problem of economic viability, a question that arose again in connection with the High Commission territories embedded in the South African land mass. Nevertheless, Moshoeshoe's Basuto nation became the kingdom of Lesotho in 1966 with his direct descendant and namesake Moshoeshoe, as constitutional monarch and Chief Lebua Jonathan as prime minister. In the same year the vast but impecunious Bechuana protectorate gained its freedom as the Republic of Botswana led by its president, Seretse Khama. Two years later, Swaziland followed her sister territories to independence.

Independence for Spain's modest colonial holdings brought difficulties along with freedom. In 1968 the island of Fernando Po located in the Bight of Biafra was joined with the mainland enclave of Rio Muni (formerly Spanish Guinea) to become the state of Equatorial Guinea, but the new nation's prospects were clouded by a meager economy and political instability. In 1975 an agreement with Morocco brought withdrawal from Spanish Sahara, a phosphate-rich territory which was then divided between neighboring Morocco and Mauritania. This move was deeply resented by Algeria, which had backed the Saharan independence movement known as POLISARIO (Popular Front for the Liberation of Saguia Hamra and Rio de Oro), and had hoped thereby to extend her own influence in the area. The subsequent guerrilla activities undertaken by POLISARIO seriously strained Algerian-Moroccan relations and placed the region's mining production in some jeopardy.

Finally, despite long-standing mutual antipathy and the territorial ambitions of nearby Ethiopia and Somalia, the 250,000 Afar and Issa herdsmen decided in a referendum to end their status as France's last African colony. In June 1977 the tiny rock and sand enclave surrounding its deep-water port and railhead became the Republic of Djibouti.

Suggestions for Further Reading

The literature on nationalism and independence in Africa is indeed extensive, and only a small portion of it is listed here.

General works include the *Cambridge History of Africa*, Vol. 8 (Cambridge: University Press, 1984) edited by Michael Crowder; Lord Hailey's *African Survey*, Revised 1956 (London: Oxford University Press, 1957); the two collections edited by Prosser Gifford and W. R. Louis: *The Transfer of Power in Africa: Decolonization 1940-1960* (New Haven, CT: Yale University Press, 1982), and *Decolonization and African Independence 1960-1980* (New Haven, CT: Yale University Press, 1988), and Thomas Hodgkin's classic *Nationalism in Colonial Africa*, (New York: New York University Press, 1957; London: F. Mueller, 1956). See also Hodgkin's *African Political Parties* (Harmondsworth, Middlesex: Penguin, 1961); and G. A. Almond and J. S. Coleman, eds., *The Politics of Developing Areas* (Princeton, NJ: Princeton University Press, 1960). A number of group studies dealing with a variety of African nations before and after independence include two edited by Gwendolen Carter, *African One-Party States* (Ithaca: Cornell University Press, 1962) and *National Unity and Regionalism in Eight African States* (Ithaca: Cornell University Press, 1966); as well as J. S. Coleman and C. G. Rosberg, eds., *Political Parties and National Integration in Tropical Africa* (Berkeley: University of California Press, 1964).

For northeastern Africa see Richard Greenfield, *Ethiopia* (New York: Praeger, 1965); and P. M. Holt and M. W. Daly, *A Modern History of the Sudan*, 4th ed. (London and New York: Longman, 1988). See also I. M. Lewis, *A Modern History of Somalia* 2nd ed. rev. (London: Longman, 1980) and P. J. Vatikiotis, *The History of Egypt*, 3rd ed. (Baltimore: Johns Hopkins Press, 1986).

Histories of British West African nations already mentioned in other chapters deal with independence individually but special attention should be given to J. S. Coleman, *Nigeria: Background to Nationalism* (Berkeley: University of California, 1958); D. Austin, *Politics in Ghana, 1946-1960* (London: Oxford University Press, 1964); R. L. Sklar, *Nigerian Political Parties* (Princeton, NJ: Princeton University Press, 1963); and P. T. Bauer, *West African Trade* (London: Routledge and Kegan Paul, 1963). The writings of nationalist leaders include George Padmore's two works, *Pan-Africanism or Communism* (London: Dennis Dobson, 1956), and *The Gold Coast Revolution* (London: Dennis Dobson, 1953); Kwame Nkrumah's autobiography, *Ghana* (Edinburgh: Thomas Nelson, 1959); Sir Ahmadu Bello's *My Life* (Cambridge: Cambridge University Press, 1962); and *Awo: The Autobiography of Chief Obafemi Awolowo* (Cambridge: Cambridge University Press, 1960).

The French-African territories are served by the two volumes of V. Thompson and R. Adloff, *French West Africa* (London: Allen and Unwin, 1958; Stanford: Stanford

University Press, 1958), and *The Emerging States of French Equatorial Africa* (London: Oxford University Press; Stanford: Stanford University Press, 1960); R. S. Morgenthau, *Political Parties in French-speaking West Africa* (London: Oxford University Press, 1964); Michael Crowder, *Senegal: A Study of French Assimilation Policy*, rev. ed. (London: Methuen, 1967).

For the Congo (Zaire) see Roger Anstey, *King Leopold's Legacy* (London: Oxford University Press, 1966); and Crawford Young, *Politics in the Congo* (Princeton, NJ: Princeton University Press, 1965).

There is considerable literature on the independence background in East Africa. One may begin with the *Oxford History of East Africa*, Vol. III edited by D. A. Low and Alison Smith (Oxford: Clarendon, 1976). For Uganda, see D. A. Low, *Buganda in Modern History* (Berkeley: University of California, 1971). Zanzibar is dealt with in M. F. Lofchie, *Zanzibar: Background to Revolution* (Princeton, NJ: Princeton University Press, 1965), and Kenya is served by G. Bennett, *Kenya: A Political History* (London: Oxford University Press, 1963), and C. G. Rosberg and J. Nottingham, *The Myth of Mau Mau* (New York: Praeger, 1966). For Tanzania see John Iliffe, *A Modern History of Tanzania* (Cambridge: University Press, 1979). A number of works present the views of African nationalists, for example, Jomo Kenyatta, *Suffering without Bitterness* (Nairobi: East African Publishing House, 1968); Oginga Odinga, *Not Yet Uhuru* (London: Heinemann, 1967; New York: Hill & Wang, 1967); Tom Mboya, *Freedom and After* (London: André Deutsch, 1963; Boston: Little, Brown, 1963); and Julius Nyerere, *Freedom and Unity* (Dar es Salaam: Oxford University Press, 1967).

Nationalism and independence in Central Africa has been treated in a variety of works, for example, David Birmingham and P. M. Martin, eds., *History of Central Africa*, II (London and New York: Longman, 1986). R. I. Rotberg, *The Rise of Nationalism in Central Africa* (Cambridge, MA: Harvard University Press, 1965); D. C. Mulford, *Zambia: The Politics of Independence, 1957-1964* (London: Oxford University Press, 1967); and James Barber, *Rhodesia: The Road to Rebellion* (London: Oxford University Press, 1967). An African view of events may be seen through Kenneth Kaunda, *Zambia Shall Be Free* (London: Heinemann, 1962; New York: Praeger, 1963); and Nathan Shamuyarira, *Crisis in Rhodesia* (Nairobi: East African Publishing House, 1967; New York: Transatlantic Arts, 1965; London: André Deutsch, 1965).

For studies of Africa and the Second World War there is Vol. 26, No. 4 (1985) of the *Journal of African History* as well as Vol. 8 of the *Cambridge History of Africa* cited already.

22

Independence Economics

The Meaning of Freedom

Independence was both end and beginning. A successful climax to long years of nationalist struggle, it also brought the realization that new-born liberty meant new responsibilities and an obligation to high purpose. Along with the pageant and the oratory, the parades and the dancing in the streets, the foreign dignitaries and the champagne toasts, there was always the sobering image of much work to be done. At Accra, in midnight solemnity, as the red, green, and gold colors of Ghana replaced the Union Jack, Kwame Nkrumah exulted, "The battle has ended! . . . Ghana . . . is free forever." Free, he was quick to add, but with a mission. "There is a new African in the world," he continued, " and that new African is ready to fight his own battle. . . . It is the only way in which we can show the world that we are masters of our own destiny." In its turn Tanganyika marked independence with a beacon light on Mount Kilimanjaro. "It will shine beyond our borders," Julius Nyerere remarked, "giving hope where there was despair, love where there was hate and dignity where before there was only humiliation."

This was more than mere rhetoric. Caught up in the flush of African enthusiasm, the rest of the world paused, half persuaded, half skeptical. In its time, European colonialism had created new territories of a scale and complexity reminiscent of ancient empires in other eras long gone. Could Africans now muster the discipline and sophistication necessary for self-government? Western imperialism had opened a wider world to African experience. Would African statesmen be equal to the opportunity for a constructive role in international affairs? Increasingly over a century and a half, the West had dominated ever broader aspects of African life. Were the Africans prepared to support their

468

political freedom with the cultural and intellectual independence that would establish a genuinely African identity in world civilization?

More than that, independence itself had not yet been fully achieved. There remained the vexing problem of the European-dominated south, the arbitrary rule over African majorities by white oligarchies in Rhodesia and South Africa, as well as continuing colonial control in the Portuguese territories. Even in the proud flush of enthusiasm that marked the independence celebrations in Lagos and Accra, in Dakar and Brazzaville, in Dar es Salaam and Lusaka, there was a nagging sense of unfinished business. "Our independence is meaningless," Nkrumah warned as Ghana was born, "unless it is linked up with the total liberation of the African continent."

Alternatives of Economic Development

Political independence brought with it yet another overriding question. Colonialism had exploited, but it had also developed. Schools and literacy, railroads, highways and harbor facilities, scientific agriculture and the beginnings of industry, economic growth and rising standards of living had all marked the era of colonial control. If these advances had been introduced chiefly for the profit of others, national freedom demanded that they now be turned to African advantage. Nnamdi Azikiwe had already perceived the imperative years earlier—political freedom was not enough, he said; economic independence would have to follow. Now, early in 1965, as his compatriots pondered the consequences of their sovereignty, President Kaunda of Zambia put the question once again. "Political independence only serves as a key to the door of economic and social progress. . . . We must . . . open the door . . . for all the people. . . . The question now is—how do we do this?"

It was a big question and there were many answers. Two main strands of thought predominated, however. Most outspoken were those who felt that true economic independence could be attained only by forceful action, that political freedom was essentially a sham screening continued colonial control over national economic assets. Kwame Nkrumah was an eloquent advocate of this viewpoint, and there were others—Sékou Touré of Guinea, Modibo Keita, the president of Mali, as well as the radical leadership in Algeria. Their point of departure was Marxist, their rallying cry "neocolonialism," and their argument that the colonial system had survived independence and was thriving through a variety of devices—economic alliances engineered between former dependencies and imperialist nations, support of puppet regimes frequently come to power through corruption, deliberate sabotage of efforts at genuine inter-African unity, economic infiltration through loans and capital investment, even direct monetary control over emergent states whose finances remained in the hands of one-time colonial powers.

For these activists, the answer to neocolonialism was "African socialism," a rigorous state control of the economy, the nation's wealth reserved for the nation's citizens. Through state planning and regulation, they said, the government could mobilize surplus production for investment, and foreign aid would be carefully scrutinized, to be accepted only where clearly consonant with the goals of national development. Economic growth, therefore, was to be largely self-contained — industry providing surplus capital for the development of the countryside which in turn produced foodstuffs to support the burgeoning cities. There would be experiments in collective farming, their anticipated effectiveness to be matched by a system of labor mobilization reminiscent of the communal work pattern of the traditional African village. In Ghana workers' brigades made their appearance, while the poetic "human investment" encouraged in Guinea and Mali sought to offset the need for foreign infusions of capital through voluntary labor on a vast array of public projects. It was *travail obligatoire*, as Sékou Touré explained, the difference between the hated forced labor of colonialism and the obligation to work for their state that all free citizens gladly recognized.

If this were Marxism, it spoke in an African idiom. Touré, for example, argued that no class war existed, for there were no classes; the struggle was external, waged against the continuing influence of colonialism. The ultimate goal was not international communism but pan-African unity; meanwhile, growth would be determined and measured in terms of national development. Nkrumah concurred wholeheartedly with the objective of pan-Africanism, but detected a pernicious class structure lingering in African society, its foundation those ancient customs related to family relations and landholding that he claimed rewarded indolence, retarded productivity, discouraged savings, and discriminated against the creative urge.

In Tanzania Julius Nyerere formulated what was in fact a variation on the Marxist approach to African development, an East African version of African socialism. Like Sékou Touré and others, Nyerere stressed the socialist way that preached equal access for all to the fruits of land and labor, and he also rejected the European brand of socialism as combative and dedicated to a class warfare foreign to Africa. Nyerere envisioned a new society based upon the tenets of an older, traditional, precolonial Africa wherein all had worked and shared in the harvest, where no special privilege existed, where no one starved either for food or self-respect. This was a utopian view of the past; nevertheless Nyerere hoped to fashion a new society in its image, and he set forth his ideas in numerous writings, most specifically in the celebrated Arusha Declaration of 1967. Stripped to essentials, the declaration called for national self-reliance, group cooperation that involved state direction of industry and commerce, Western technology where appropriate but minimal foreign assistance with its attendant controls, and an ethic of selfless service that banished personal acquisitiveness and emphasized communal sharing. Agriculture, the basis of Tanzania's economy, would receive priority, its effectiveness embodied in the *ujamaa* village community which brought scattered farmers together to form a close-knit family-like solidarity.

The second major approach to the strategy of development largely contradicted the assumptions and conclusions of the first. Pragmatic, capitalist, and materialist, it encouraged foreign assistance and entertained few suspicions of the West; indeed, a major tenet was the need for continued aid along the lines that former European powers had established during the last stages of their colonial occupation. Most of the new states of Africa found this an attractive alternative to the austere, doctrinaire proposals of the African Marxists, but perhaps its most enthusiastic support came from Kenya, under the leadership of Jomo Kenyatta, and from the Ivory Coast of President Félix Houphouet-Boigny.

Despite his alleged association with Mau Mau, Kenyatta was no revolutionary. His instincts were conservative and his social ethic the Victorian credo of hard work; family solidarity and the virtues of a hierarchical society were the basic lessons he had set forth in 1938 in his classic study of the Kikuyu nation, *Facing Mount Kenya*. Under colonialism it was not freeholds in the White Highlands that Kenyatta and his people had found objectionable; it was the exclusion of the African. When political independence was followed by transfer schemes that settled Africans—mainly Kikuyu—on the Rift Valley lands once exclusively occupied by European farmers, there was slight inclination to follow the socialist ideas of men like Nkrumah and Touré. National economic development, said Kenyatta, would come from a mixed economy of industry and agriculture. At first, African initiative would concentrate on agricultural production by individual farmers, their property held not in traditional communal tenure but as privately owned tracts of land. Industry for the moment would remain in the hands of European management, sustained by large infusions of private capital from abroad, nationalization occurring only in those areas where lack of interest compelled the government to assume an active role. To be sure, government was paternal, but support of official policy offered many advantages to Kenya citizens in public service jobs or licensing and loans for small businesses.

Like Kenyatta, Houphouet had also emerged among his people as a nationalist leader protesting the inequities of colonial rule; like the Kikuyu elder, he too experienced no embarrassment in establishing close and fruitful connections with former rulers after independence. In fact, Houphouet had openly questioned the wisdom of Ghana's independence in 1957, remarking that no nation could afford to live in isolation in the modern world, particularly those developing states requiring vast amounts of capital for heavy and continuing expansion. At the time, he had expressed a preference for Ivory Coast membership in the French Union, but when events swept his country into a declaration of political independence, he was careful to maintain the cordial relations already achieved with France.

In terms of development, the results were spectacular. French assistance and investment helped propel an annual growth rate approaching 8 percent during the decade following independence in 1960. Over that period the gross domestic product increased by 250 percent as the Ivory Coast became a major exporter of cocoa, coffee, and hardwoods; nevertheless, industrial production increased from 6 to 14 percent of the gross domestic product, while reliance on agriculture, despite the spectacular success of exports, was reduced from almost half to less than one-third the total national output. Reflecting this steady growth of local productivity, surpluses were plowed into development and the proportion of foreign assistance was thereby steadily reduced.

Critics were quick to point out, however, that the economic advances in the Ivory Coast were illusory, and were, in fact, a classic example of national growth without national development. To begin with, the rising exports of cash crops could not be expected to continue indefinitely in the face of finite international demand, while the national resource of hardwoods would soon be exhausted through overzealous cutting. At the same time, it was argued, local food production was being neglected, thereby necessitating expensive imports, a condition that also characterized the development of Ivory Coast industry. Preoccupation with light manufacturing for import substitution was of little long-range use, the critics said; what the country needed was heavy industry in mining and processing of metals and chemicals, but the scale in cost and productivity of these base industries lay beyond the resources of a small West African nation. Faced with falling exports and the necessity for continued import of foodstuffs and heavy goods, the Ivory Coast economy would sooner or later stagnate.

Worse still, the argument continued, the national economy remained securely in the hands of foreign capital, operating in concert with a local African oligarchy. As with Kenya, industry was European-financed and -managed, while land had gone largely into the hands of a small group of well-to-do African planters. In the cities, the African elite was concentrated almost exclusively in government service, while commercial activity remained overwhelmingly French. A large and impecunious African proletariat in the city and on the farm lacked the savings that might have helped propel a healthy national development, while those who possessed the resources to invest in growth—African planters and European merchants—failed to do so, the Africans because they felt no obligation and the Europeans because their savings were sent back to France. The conclusion was inflexibly pessimistic—the Ivory Coast was a country with a European bourgeoisie and an African proletariat, a supplier of raw materials and financial profit to French capitalism.

By the mid-1970s, such gloomy predictions seemed as yet unfulfilled. Maintaining close ties with France and liberal policies governing foreign investment, Houphouet continued to guide his country from success to success. During eighteen years of independence, the gross domestic product had increased tenfold, the annual growth rate was holding at 7 percent, while the Ivory Coast budget had grown from 26 to 480 billion francs. By 1978, industrial production accounted for 18 percent of the G.D.P., yet growth was firmly based in agriculture, reflecting a diversification that placed the Ivory Coast among leading exporters of timber, cocoa, coffee, palm oil, and tropical fruit.

One final generalization may be added. Whether motivated by Marxist or capitalist principles, all newly independent African nations introduced various degrees of state planning, but at the same time all held close to the structure of inherited colonial economies. Thus they remained exporters of raw materials needed in the industrialized West and importers of manufactured goods, machinery, and entrepreneurial or technological skills. With the rapidly expanding world market that characterized recovery from the Second World War, African primary agriculture and mineral products prospered with both growing demand and rising prices, at least until the eve of independence. Between 1947 and 1957, for example, West African cotton production tripled, East African coffee production rose over one and one-half times, while the continental output of copper, iron, zinc, or bauzite, made substantial advances of 50 percent or more. All this gave a roseate hue to prospective independence, but it also raised potential dangers, for African economies were therefore tightly linked to the activities of the industrialized world, leaving Africa less able to determine its future fortunes whatever the theoretical assertions of African socialism.

The Problems of Modernization

Agriculture

An economic neocolonialism aside, there were problems intrinsic to modernization, but in general newly independent nations faced their future with high hopes and enthusiasm to match.

Perhaps the most difficult impediment facing African developers was the African environment. Although this environment is often and correctly described in terms of the caprices of the weather acting on a land of indifferent fertility, it is probably the very geniality of Africa's climate that has constituted a major hinderance to progress and growth. Tropical temperatures, lacking a period of winter frost, encourage proliferation of species and heavy population expansion, but the resultant multiplicity of animal and plant life has meant an intense competition for survival and a consequent limit on the numbers and geographic concentration of any particular species. Each organism encourages in its existence a natural enemy which flourishes by feeding on its victim but which eventually declines in numbers as the population of its prey is destroyed. In Africa, therefore, survival of species ultimately has rested upon small numbers spread over wide areas, and this limitation has applied equally to all. Thus, when Africans graduated from hunting and gathering to the stage of cultivation, they were compelled to practice a shifting agriculture and to be content with subsistence production in the face of voracious pests which limited their harvests while they themselves continued to endure the lethal and enervating attacks of tropical diseases.

During the era of colonial control, the development of modern medicine and scientific agriculture introduced for the first time the possibility of overturning this dismal balance of nature and converting crop production into a major engine for a rising standard of living. Since, throughout the world, economic growth has usually sprung from a base in agriculture, and since at independence nine out of ten Africans were farm dwellers, modernization in Africa was linked in the eyes of many to a revolution in crop production. Not only was this a shorter route than industry could provide toward increasing total exports and building budget surpluses, it also leveled the most direct attack on the problem of unemployment while stimulating other sectors of the economy—service industries, transport, and, ultimately, manufacturing.

Realization of the prior claims of agricultural development had not escaped economic planners in the newly independent African governments, but achievement was beset with complications. Beyond the ecological balance of a tropical environment with its downward-leveling pressures, Africa suffers widely from a thin and infertile soil cover which is alternately washed away by excessive rains and burned out by an equatorial sun. Further, though generally lacking the conservatism of the peasant with deep attachment to a particular parcel of land, the African farmer has been nonetheless hampered by limitations of technique and outlook. Over the centuries the pressures of environment had forced farmers to adopt a migratory, subsistence cultivation, a system that exploited land instead of improving it, producing for survival and security, and this subsistence agriculture still dominated wide areas across the continent. Since production was linked in the main to local consumption, the more modern concepts of a market economy, of cash crops, the accumulation of surpluses, and production specialization grew but slowly. Furthermore, traditional patterns of land tenure have militated against the idea of private ownership, thereby inhibiting any tendencies by individual farmers to introduce physical improvements or to invest capital and labor in anticipation of a greater productivity.

Environment and custom, therefore, combined to frustrate the development of scientific cultivation and commercialized production in a money economy, but there were factors working for change. The growth of urban markets, the introduction of a system of cash exchange, expanding educational opportunity, the rise of part-time farming linked to migratory labor, and the development of export crops beginning during the colonial period, all pointed African farming in the direction of market production, and, once in power, African governments added the thrust of their own economic planning.

Official activity attacked the problem on many fronts. The identification and encouragement of cash crops was an early activity both of colonial regimes and independent governments—cocoa, groundnuts, and palm products in West

Africa, coffee and tea in East Africa, cotton in the Anglo-Sudan, and rubber in the Congo as well as in independent Liberia. In Kenya the government's land resettlement program begun in 1954 was greatly accelerated after African political ascendancy was assured in 1960, and large blocks in the White Highlands subsequently came under African control. Similarly, freehold tenure and settled farms began to appear in a number of other countries, either countenanced or actively encouraged. A form of private land holding, for example, had already been in effect among the Baganda since 1900; in Ghana and southern Nigeria a combination of land scarcity and cash-crop agriculture led to a gradual spread of individual ownership; and freehold tenure as practiced in the Ivory Coast after independence was the basis for much of that country's subsequent acceleration of plantation agriculture.

There were many other government activities. State-directed pest control, better transportation, irrigation and erosion projects, the production of fertilizers, government agricultural credit and crop storage facilities, as well as improved genetic strains resulting from publicly supported research were all widely employed to increase productivity, while the demonstration farm and extension service remain standard devices for educating individual farmers and for identifying and attacking their problems.

Some undertakings came in the form of vast projects like the Gezira cotton-growing scheme which evolved successfully in the Sudan over the early years of the twentieth century. Governments, both before and after independence, tended to favor such large-scale ventures for their greater visibility and potential efficiency in production and marketing. Not only was this a major consideration in support of the ujamaa villages of Tanzania, it also played a similar role in other countries, in Ghana's Volta resettlement cooperatives or the farming communities begun about the time of independence in the eastern and western regions of Nigeria.

Despite the exception of the Gezira scheme, however, large-scale agricultural ventures did not prove successful, and some have been spectacular and expensive failures. The British government lost $80 million in a disastrous attempt to grow groundnuts in Tanganyika between 1948 and 1950. Across the continent, a program begun in 1932 for the irrigated production of rice and cotton in Mali achieved only limited output after an investment of $180 million and forty years of effort. The reasons for these failures were various—deficient planning and unskilled technicians, inadequate roads, water, and other services, labor shortages, farmer conservatism, and political complications.

Whatever the form or size of any particular project—a fertilizer plant in Senegal, a palm tree nursery in Nigeria, an irrigation demonstration farm for Ghana, or a self-help housing scheme in Kenya—the ultimate objective was always the same. Agricultural production had to be dramatically increased, greatly improved in quality, and concentrated on essential crops. Food supplies to meet the needs of the home market would eliminate costly imports, while agricultural exports steadily developed as an essential prerequisite to economic growth.

Mining

Fundamental though it may be, economic growth through agricultural development was painfully slow and difficult. Production barely matched population increase, there was a discouraging lag in the application of modern methods and technology, while droughts and other natural disasters took their toll, forcing the import of food with consequent inflation. The new states of Africa therefore turned where possible to other sources of wealth, in particular to the continent's vast mineral resources which, in some cases—copper, petroleum, or industrial diamonds, for example—had already become important contributors to world supplies, while other minerals such as iron ore and uranium gave promise of future development.

Given sufficient capital the exploitation of subsurface assets offered many attractive prospects. It was diamonds and then gold that financed modernization in South Africa, while copper mining in Zambia had placed that country's production—averaging over 700,000 tons a year during the 1960s—behind only the United States and the Soviet Union and about on a par with Chile. Neighboring Zaire with probable reserves of 600-800 million tons of especially rich ores accounted for about 6 percent of the world's annual output of copper, but the country also possessed a variety of other minerals such as cobalt and industrial diamonds.

Other territories showed similar possibilities. Gabon, already relatively affluent because of its timber, saw post-independence crude oil production soar to 5 million tons by 1970, while her hundred-year reserves of high-grade manganese were yielding close to 2 million tons per annum. To this must be added valuable deposits of uranium averaging a 1500-ton annual yield as well as the huge Mekambo iron ore fields with their 60 percent or better iron content.

Similarly, if less spectacularly, the Mount Nimba fields lying in Liberia and Guinea held 250 million tons of 66 percent ore which by 1970 had made Liberia the third-largest exporter of iron in the world. Iron also began to rescue Mauritania from a desert poverty, while deposits of iron and uranium may yet do as well for impecunious Niger. Bauxite, which is the industrial arm of Ghana's Volta River power project, is present in Guinea in extensive, high-quality reserves; Sierra Leone has long been a diamond and iron ore producer, while rich stores of phosphates have been identified and developed in Togo and Senegal.

The export of minerals not only earned foreign exchange and invited investment; it also required sophisticated harbor, transportation, and power facilities which were of value to agricultural and industrial producers who might not otherwise have been able to afford their construction. During the colonial era the need for such expensive facilities was often an impediment to development, but subsequent improved techniques of mineral extraction and dwindling world supplies worked in favor of Africa in this respect. To return to the example of Gabon, French aid and French-inspired European Common Market grants doubled between 1960 and 1962, while a $360 million development plan for 1966-1970 anticipated a 60 percent contribution by private capital, chiefly foreign investment in mining, forestry, and manufacturing, with foreign loans supporting another 60 percent of the plan's public sector allocations. Liberia experienced similar largesse—$30 million in loans and grants from West Germany in 1961 and 1962, American A.I.D. support totaling over $88 million up to mid-1964, along with Export-Import Bank loans of $92.8 million into 1965, to say nothing of substantial foreign loans to the mining companies working the Liberian ores.

There have been other serious challenges to African hopes for development, however—competition between nations inside and outside Africa or from new products, the wastage caused by political unrest, or the fact that some nations simply lack the natural resources for development or find their supplies running out. For example, in Ghana some gold mines were earmarked for shutdown because of the declining supplies, while such countries as Mali, Chad, Malawi, or Tanzania have shown little evidence of any important mineral resources. Faint hopes sometimes arise, however, as in the case of petroleum and uranium reserves that have been identified in the parched wastes of Somalia.

Perhaps most frustrating of all were the situations where development was blocked not by lack of resources but by human frailty. In Nigeria the civil war of the 1960s seriously reduced oil production, depressed economic growth, and discouraged foreign investment; by contrast, after the collapse of the Biafran secession movement early in 1970, the economy recovered in spectacular fashion. Oil production tripled during the first postwar year, foreign capital renewed its former interest with enthusiasm, and national economic vitality manifested itself in a growth rate approximating 10 percent. Similarly, economic advance badly compromised by the unrest which followed independence in the Congo (Zaire), accelerated once again with the establishment of political stability. Other states, notably Zambia and Egypt, long paid a heavy price in economic dislocation as a result of international political disputes—Zambia's chronic quarrel with white-dominated Rhodesia and Egypt's problems arising from the Arab-Israeli wars.

Industry

While the base line for modernization in Africa rested in agriculture and initial economic stimulus wherever possible seemed best provided by mining, it was the development of industry that first attracted African planners, for industrialization was widely regarded at independence as the key to a breakthrough from poverty to affluence.

Belief in industrialization as a panacea grew from the general understanding across Africa that the world's industrialized countries were rich countries, a fact that was easily distorted to mean that the wealthy nations were wealthy because they were industrialized. Economists were quick to point out that no such causal relationship existed, but they did identify another economic consideration—the progressive deterioration in the trading position of primary producing countries in relation to the advanced industrial nations. Put simply, the argument went thus. The capacity of societies to absorb foodstuffs or other raw materials is limited, but no such limitation applies to consumption of manufactured goods. Therefore, as national incomes rise, a greater proportion goes toward purchase of industrial goods, a condition that militates against those states exporting foodstuffs and other primary products while importing the bulk of their manufactured commodities. Under these circumstances, economists advised developing nations to restrict industrial imports and encourage a domestic manufacturing establishment; the alternative was a steadily worsening balance-of-payments relationship with the industrial world.

As professional assessment thereby converged on popular aspiration, the discussion shifted to the choice of industrial effort. What type of industry was best adapted to national development? Should it be one that stimulated local primary production in agriculture or mining? Were the possibilities more promising in domestic or foreign markets? How could industrial job opportunities best be expanded? What balance should be struck between capital and consumer goods? Where lay the competitive advantages for challenging imports in the domestic market? Where should industries be located? How large should their plants be? There was a seemingly endless succession of difficult questions.

Difficult questions brought difficult answers. Rapid industrial growth was the goal, but indirection seemed the quickest route. Successful industry required a strong internal market; most domestic consumers were farmers; hence, developing nations were thrust back once more on agriculture. At the same time, social justice and political discretion suggested broad improvement in purchasing power, even though economic realities sometimes seemed to argue for diverting a substantial portion of national income to a restricted class of citizens affluent enough to purchase manufactured goods.

As for foreign markets and capital goods production, these presented many problems involving sufficient underwriting, skilled labor, transport, power, and experienced management, yet such ingredients applied also to domestic markets, and were notoriously hard to come by. Efficient management tended to originate with immigrants or foreign residents like the Asians of East Africa, the very groups that governments were often under pressure to drive out, precisely because of their efficiency. Finance capital was available largely in the industrialized world, and it came primarily to seek investment opportunities. Agricultural development usually had little attraction for outsiders, while investment in minerals, though frequently massive, was narrowly specialized with but slight impact on the broader national economy.

Labor supply raised other complications. Independent governments hoped that a manufacturing establishment would help absorb large populations of workers, a vain illusion since even the most optimistic industrial growth rates were unequal to the substantial numbers generated by simple population increase. To cite one example, by 1970 the entire Zambian economy had generated approximately 350,000 paying jobs, yet each year fully 50,000 seventh graders left school intent on gaining employment.

In the face of such figures, it was ironic that skilled labor was in chronic shortage, itself a factor hampering industrial development. Part of the problem rested in the steady turnover of migrant workers, part-time farmers habitually moving between town and their family land in the provinces. While this phenomenon seemed to ease somewhat during the early independence years, it was more than offset by the vast pools of the unskilled that accumulated in the cities, pushing up the unemployment totals and depressing the very national purchasing power so necessary for a buoyant domestic market.

The particular choice of industries was keyed to such factors as markets, available raw materials, and transportation costs. One approach, already begun in colonial times, favored the processing of primary commodities for export. Substantial reductions in bulk or weight could be translated into freight savings on long international hauls; hence, for example, Zambian copper was exported as ingots, while Liberia began to ship its iron ore in the form of processed pellets of uniform size and excellent quality. Agricultural products were susceptible to similar refinements. A number of countries locally converted their groundnuts to oil, cotton was typically ginned to separate seed from fiber, coffee beans were hulled, sugar refined, and tea processed.

There were limitations, however. Competitive processing industries in consumer countries normally enjoyed high tariff protection; thus, Ghana and other cocoa producers were compelled to limit exports to cocoa beans in lieu of the finished chocolate products they might have preferred. More generally, it was an unhappy economic fact that greater savings could be had when final processing was located in the industrially advanced countries with their technical sophistication and experienced management. African sugar refineries, therefore, produced mainly for African markets. Zambian copper could not advance beyond the stage of electrolytic bars to the production of copper sheets and wire. Cotton was exported, not as cloth but in its raw state, and cotton seed was rarely converted to the form of oil and cake.

The process of industrialization also took advantage of shipping economies by importing parts manufactured elsewhere for final assembly at home. In this way savings in freight could be augmented by using cheap local labor, provided, of course, that the savings in low wages were not offset by inefficient productivity. This tactic produced numerous enterprises such as oil refineries, car and truck assembly lines, or manufactories of radios and other electrical equipment. Some critics questioned the wisdom of refineries since they are capital intensive; that is, they contain a high proportion of investment in plant as against labor. With high fixed costs, economy is gained only through high production, a questionable eventuality in countries with limited local markets. Internal market size also posed questions for motor vehicle assemblies, although in that case the industry is much more labor intensive, and can absorb the output of other manufacturing efforts such as textiles for upholstery or glass for windows and mirrors.

Beyond the priorities of raw material processing and the assembling of imported parts, there was the basic thrust toward import substitution to secure more favorable trade balances and much needed foreign exchange. In this case the concentration was on consumer industries such as textiles, footwear, foods, and household articles. A new textile mill in Togo, a distillery in Uganda, a brickyard in Ethiopia, or a soap factory in the Ivory Coast were matched by shoe manufacturing in Tanzania, paper mills in the Sudan, and cement works in Nigeria. In some cases, these industries served both local and export markets. Kenya, for example, was able to ship much of its processed meat and dairy products abroad, and fully 90 percent of its canned fruit and vegetables in 1963 were marketed outside East Africa.

Most production, however, was linked firmly to domestic consumption, and in some cases served to stimulate other local efforts as well. Furniture and paper manufacturing contributed to wood processing, while the distilling of spirits made good use of refined sugar byproducts. Again, the manufacture of kitchen utensils or corrugated iron roofing stimulated an iron and steel industry which in turn drew heavily on supplies of electrical power. To take one specific case, Ghana developed an industrial complex situated at the artificial deep-water port of Tema. Here, in addition to modern docking facilities, were located a variety of establishments including an aluminum smelter, oil refinery, electric steel furnace, vehicle assembly plant, and a number of light industries, all drawing power from the hydroelectric plant at Akosombo on the Volta River.

Poor planning or political motivation caused failures in particular instances, but there were more fundamental difficulties. Most industrial development occurred in light manufacturing as engineering and heavy industries lagged, thereby stunting essential industrial growth. Excessive reliance on foreign technology and skills created industries designed to the advantage of outsiders and gave minimal support to the basic agricultural and mining sectors so important in attacking rural poverty and urban unemployment. Finally, growth and planning were national rather than regional in scale and relied too much on foreign investment. Thus there was little incentive promoting national savings for reinvestment while local business ventures lagged and profits went overseas to the advantage of foreign capital.

Milling industry in Abidjan

United Nations

Downtown Nairobi

United Nations

Agricultural modernization   *United Nations*

Copper refinery, Zaire   *United Nations*

Arts Faculty Quadrangle, University of Ibadan

Muslim worship in Mali

United Nations

Poorland farming in Cameroun — United Nations

Drought—Burkina Faso — United Nations

The Vagaries of Economic Growth

The problems of development were complex enough in prospect but as African societies proceeded beyond the initial stages of an independence so eagerly sought, the realization slowly dawned that prospective complications were as nothing to the tangled realities of growth and development. Agricultural states soon found themselves paradoxically obliged to import the produce their own farms did not yield, income from mineral exports rose and fell unpredictably with the caprices of international markets, growing inflation wiped out savings and confounded economic stability, budget deficits jumped along with external debts, rapid population increase, especially in the cities, brought urgent demands for jobs and food that new economies could not provide, world depression cut demand for exports while dramatic increases in energy costs, chiefly petroleum, during the 1970s added intense strains to small, weak economies.

Piled upon these woes were the natural disasters of periodic drought, and the human weaknesses of inexperience, inefficiency, and corruption intensified by an erosion of national morale and a growing "every-man-for-himself" psychology. By the beginning of the 1980s the heady prospects of twenty years earlier had given way to a pessimism sometimes bordering on despair. The Ghana of Nkrumah that had shown the way to freedom was an admitted economic shambles. Zaire, rich in copper, oil, and diamonds, was in a chronic state of financial collapse. Even the affluent faltered. Nigeria, despite its petroleum, saw its economy sag with falling oil prices in the early 1980s. The Ivory Coast, the envy of all during the 1960s and 1970s, entered upon an era of falling commodity prices and heavy external debt with sobering prospects and problems to match.

Economic statistics were impressive indicators of epidemic difficulties. During the 1960s the economic growth rate of black Africa as a whole had registered a modest 3.7 percent rise per annum, a figure comparable with the performance of developing countries in other parts of the world. During the 1970s, however, the figure had dropped to 1.7 percent a year, and many of Africa's low income states actually registered negative growth rates. Overall between 1965 and 1989 sub-Saharan Africa had registered a disappointing annual growth rate of 0.3 percent. Starting from a very low base in the late 1960s, industrial production in Africa showed increases of 3 percent during the ensuing decade, but low productivity and marginal profits were matched by growing unemployment and poor utilization of plant capacity, while this modest industrial growth was more than offset by a crisis in agricultural production. By 1980 the per capita output of foodstuffs had fallen by more than 20 percent below the 1960 level. At the same time production of export crops, that had increased 2 percent per annum during the sixties, declined by the same amount between 1970 and 1980. These alarming developments were all the more disturbing in view of a continentwide population growth of 2 percent a year, a rate that rose to 3.2 percent during the 1980s.

There were severe political and financial consequences for hard pressed governments. Urban populations, jobless and unproductive, had nevertheless to be fed, yet as farm productivity declined, food had to be imported in ever increasing quantities despite the shrinking value of exports needed to pay for such imports. Balance of payment deficits mushroomed and were met by heavy international borrowing that increased black Africa's external debt fivefold between 1970 and 1979. Internally, the quality of life declined as governments found it increasingly difficult to maintain services; consequent political unrest led to rioting, abrupt and violent changes in government, and a steady decline in morale, personal and national.

What had gone wrong?

The reasons were many — a web of political, economic, social, psychological, and environmental factors, cause and effect intertwined, local influences vying with pressures from international financial and commodity markets, economic decisions often made for political reasons, political consequences frequently the result of faulty or ill-informed economic judgment or the vicissitudes of a tropical climate.

As always the African environment played an influential role. Between 1968 and 1974 severe shortage of rain gripped the Sahel, those lands bordering the Sahara from Senegal across the bulge of Africa to Ethiopia and Somalia. Always a region of marginal rainfall, supporting grains that require little moisture along with such livestock as goats, camels, and drought-resistant cattle, the Sahel is particularly susceptible to drought because of the seasonal rhythm of the rains; when they fail in one year there is a twelve month wait for relief in the next. Submarginal rainfall over several years culminated in 1973-1974 to bring widespread disaster to the estimated 25 million inhabitants of this broad belt. Resultant hunger and malnutrition invited diphtheria, measles, cholera, and tuberculosis that claimed tens of thousands of victims. Herds were wiped out, an estimated 25 percent overall, a disastrous loss for predominantly pastoral people like the Fulani and Tuareg. Refugees poured into overcrowded relief camps where the United Nations and other international agencies struggled vainly to distribute supplies of food and medicine in the face of inadequate storage, handling, and transportation facilities — the irony, for example, of frail roads washed away by rains too feeble to produce a necessary supply of food.

In 1982-1983 and 1984-1985, renewed droughts struck the Sahel, affecting nations from Mauritania and Mali in the west to Sudan and Ethiopia in eastern Africa; at the same time a similar dry spell settled over southern Africa, devastating harvests in Zambia, Mozambique, and Zimbabwe, to say nothing of South Africa and the adjacent nations of Botswana, Lesotho, and Swaziland. The extent of human suffering quite aside, such natural disasters sorely pressed the fragile economies of developing nations. Not only was there little foreign exchange to purchase food imports, even relief donated from abroad threatened internal economic balance. Unfamiliar foods like wheat began to alter local dietary preferences while free or subsidized distribution discouraged indigenous farmers through falling prices. Whole ecologies changed, converting numbers of self-sufficient pastoralists like the Somali or the Tuareg into permanent unproductive refugees eking out a marginal existence in the squalor of urban slums.

Paradoxically, despite the heavy loss of life to famine and disease, populations in Africa continued to expand, indeed accelerate, thereby providing new governments with the delicate ecological and political problem of feeding ever ballooning numbers of largely unproductive citizens. The figures were sobering, if not frightening. According to growth rate projections, Africa's 353 million as of 1980 would almost double to 679 million by the year 2000. In forty years Nigeria's 1980 population of 85,000,000 would have more than quadrupled, Kenya risen from 16 million to 81 million, and Zaire from 28 million to 95 million. Not surprisingly a growing number of African governments began to sponsor family planning programs, but the problems presented by raw population growth were further complicated by movements of people, both local and regional, particularly from the countryside to the cities.

In 1965 African cities contained approximately 14 percent of the total population; by 1989 this figure had risen to 28 percent and it is estimated that urban population will continue to rise by at least 6 percent annually, bloating the cities, most of which did not exist a century ago. The young people pile into the towns, drawn by the bright lights and the illusion of opportunity, repelled by the monotony and rigidity of rural life. But the cities cannot support them. Living in hovels of castoff lumber and corrugated iron, lacking water, electricity, and plumbing, to say nothing of refuse collection and paved streets, unemployed and frequently unemployable but educated in skills that draw them further away from the land, they join a growing, disenchanted urban constituency that forces unsound economic decisions for political reasons.

The policies of many African governments during the early independence years tended to accelerate the trend from countryside to city that had already begun during colonial times. Colonial governments, chiefly in southern Africa, had forced farmers off the land into industry through taxation, thereby damaging traditional rural economies. After independence African leaders reinforced this trend, stressing industrialization and urban development as the road to affluence, at the same time supporting large scale, capital intensive agricultural projects which frequently were far less productive than the efforts of small scale farmers. This trend is now being reversed and the small farmer encouraged, but potential gains are offset by price declines and inefficiency in marketing and research along with the pressure of ever-expanding populations.

Falling prices reflect world market conditions, but they are also the result of government policy that has favored politically sensitive urban areas at the expense of the agricultural community. The prices governments pay for food have been kept artificially low to mollify the volatile cities; those left on the land, therefore, had no incentive to produce beyond their own needs, agricultural production declined and governments were obliged to import foodstuffs, paying for them with scarce foreign exchange that has been diverted from rural development. Add to this the gross overevaluation of many African currencies, a factor which further limited farm income and encouraged food imports relative to local production. The case of Nigeria is illustrative. At one time self-sufficient in food production, Nigeria became a heavy importer of produce needed to feed multiplying urban populations. During the 1960s agriculture contributed 56 percent of the gross domestic product; by 1985 it had dropped to scarcely more than 20 percent. The problem affected everyone, however. The World Bank has estimated that, during the 1970s, agricultural production across the continent increased at only half the rate of population growth.

To these melancholy developments must be added the weight of inefficiency and corruption, a disintegration of the public ebullience that had so characterized the early days of independence, and the chronic inability of African nations to work together in concerted effort toward solving their problems. To be sure, pan-African unity has received much support over the years, but despite compelling political and economic imperatives, such support has frequently been a matter more of principle than practice, with centrifugal pressures consistently offsetting the forces of unity.

The economic arguments for a united Africa have centered on the frail condition of infant states, which are poor in resources and depressed in purchasing power. Development efforts would have to transcend limited national markets and modest productivity, it was felt, uniting within regional, inter-African economic groupings that permitted maximum utilization of financial and natural resources. Thus, markets of scale would be created that attracted foreign investment, utilizing that investment for development strategies unhampered by parochial limitations.

Here was sound reasoning and the best of intentions, but accomplishment lagged well behind motivation. There were many practical impediments to be overcome—differing currencies, conflicting tariff schedules or customs regulations, railroad gauges that varied country to country. Home markets were weak, united or not, and each African nation tended to produce the same goods as its neighbor, more competitive than complementary. Political leaders were loath to share sovereignty and power while ideologies and local interests frequently placed firm barriers in the way of cooperation. Foreign investment, following its own interests, sought opportunity in mineral-rich or more industrialized states, thereby tending to widen the gap between the impecunious and their more fortunate neighbors.

What resulted was an impressive array of conferences and treaties of cooperation that launched organizations, however, often more apparent on paper than in practical fact. The former French territories were most active and effective in developing cooperative groupings, reflecting both the old regional federations of West and Equatorial Africa as well as their continued association with metropolitan France in such matters as trade preferences, technical assistance, currency control, and cultural affairs. There was, among others, Houphouet's Council of the Entente States, founded at the time of independence; the West African Customs Union of the early 1960s that was replaced in 1970 by the West African Economic Community (CEAO); the 1968 Organization of Senegal River States (OERS); and the central banks of West and Equatorial Africa issuing common African francs as part of the French franc zone.

Less cooperative were others, notably the former British colonies. In East Africa, for example, the common services union established by the colonial regimes in Kenya, Tanganyika, and Uganda was converted in 1967 into the East African Community (EAC), a step toward a hoped-for common market that was expected to expand eventually to include neighbors such as Ethiopia, Somalia, Rwanda, and Zambia. During the 1970s, however, the Community foundered on the shoals of competitive economies, incompatible political ideologies, and the disastrous interlude of the Idi Amin years in Uganda. Concurrently some sixteen West African states attempted to form their own common market through the Economic Community of West African States (ECOWAS), created in May 1975.

There is no denying that ECOWAS began as a serious attempt at economic cooperation, emphasizing the ultimate objective of unhampered commercial and population movement throughout West Africa. Fifteen years of activity have not been reassuring, however. An initial problem arose when several member states expelled foreign nationals during the early 1980s, a gesture of economic nationalism that reflected bad times and unemployment but offered doubtful prospect for cooperation in times of stress. Liberalization of trade regulations, begun in 1980, moved forward fitfully, hampered by lack of funds promised but not provided, and a preoccupation with parochial economic and political demands. Heads of state continued to attend annual meetings, but, as press reports indicated at the conclusion of the 1988 session, the atmosphere has tended much more toward showcase than substance.

Foreign observers of Africa's economic problems tend to stress circumstances within Africa itself whereas African leaders cite the impact of world conditions and particularly the matter of dependence which they regard as another unfortunate inheritance from colonial times. Certainly external factors have played an important role. Between 1973 and 1982 the dramatic tenfold rise in oil prices introduced by the Organization of Petroleum Exporting Countries (OPEC) forced the nations of Africa to a 600 percent increase in the proportion of their export earnings spent on energy. Moreover, the worldwide economic dislocation and inflation that resulted from the OPEC action was soon joined by a collapse in the prices for raw materials which were the main prop of most African economies. During the last six months of 1974, the overall market dropped 49 percent, the flaccid demand for African exports continuing through the 1970s into the next decade. In 1981, for example, cocoa prices declined by 10 percent, sisal by 17 percent, copper by over 20 percent, and timber by 25 percent. Thus at the very time energy costs were soaring, Africa's ability to pay was seriously reduced, forcing heavy international borrowing at record interest rates and a mounting external debt with servicing charges that threatened bankruptcy and economic collapse.

To these woes were added high inflation-driven prices for manufactured imports, a growing protectionism throughout the world, and reduced foreign aid budgets among most nations of the industrialized world. Many African political leaders have found these external conditions particularly irksome. They argue that their economies were originally shaped to accommodate colonial masters and since independence they have been compelled by circumstances to continue serving the affluent West at African expense. Mineral and agricultural exports for the metropolitan centers of Europe have increased unfavorable trade balances, augmented external debt, forced the import of food, and thereby made "independent" Africa more dependent than ever.

Whatever the weight of the argument, there is evidence that both internal and external factors have played their parts in Africa's worsening economic situation. In Ghana, for example, fifteen years of alternating civilian and military rule had reduced the economy to disarray by the end of 1981. A good deal of the responsibility belonged to the military governments of the 1970s, their fiscal and economic mismanagement leading to an excess of expenditures beyond the nation's productive capacity, thereby inviting budget deficits, inflation, unemployment, and shortages. As corruption in government joined economic incompetence the economy virtually stopped functioning, its ultimate collapse marked by breakdown of machinery, lack of spare parts, disintegration of transport and communication, and a deepening sense of public despair.

During these economic agonies Ghana's international debt approximated $1 billion, a substantial proportion in repayment arrears. Nevertheless such a figure would have raised a few concerns in Zaire where the external debt for 1980-1981 reached $4 billion, where budget deficits, corruption, inflation, and currency devaluation were chronic, and where total export earnings, chiefly in copper and cobalt, amounted to only two-thirds of the 1982 debt obligation.

Zaire's problems were due partly to the economy's heavy dependence on primary commodity exports, partly to maladroit leadership. In Tanzania President Nyerere's hopes for affluence based upon self help seemed to founder as much on internal inefficiency and corruption as on the cost of petroleum imports or falling world commodity prices. Some observers saw Nyerere too rigidly committed to a socialism that his country could not sustain. The state-controlled companies that directed much of the economy had failed to operate effectively as had the ujamaa agricultural communities. Food production for market fell sharply as more and more farmers retreated into a subsistence economy or sold their produce on the black market. Another essentially agricultural country found itself compelled to import food to avert a crisis in the cities.

In the Ivory Coast political stability and prudent economic management seemed to offset reliance on raw material exports as high growth rates continued to be the envy of less affluent neighbors. Beginning in 1979 and continuing through the 1980s, however, prices of coffee and cocoa fell sharply. It was felt at first that the loss could be offset by more efficient production and the sale of newly discovered petroleum resources, but subsequent economic projections were less encouraging, citing overproduction and a too-intimate client relationship with France. Balance of payment deficits beginning in 1979 were traced not to falling export prices but to the cost of salaries, profits, and interest payment on debts—all going to France to pay for heavy capital investments and the maintenance of French nationals working in the Ivory Coast. President Houphouet-Boigny was not persuaded. In 1988 he accused "international speculators" of impoverishing Africans by artificially driving down cocoa prices, and he threatened to withhold the Ivory Coast production, almost a third of the world crop, unless a fair price could be obtained on the world market.

Not surprisingly, differing views of the crisis in development in Africa have produced differing solutions. The World Bank, stressing internal factors, has urged local action centered on small scale agriculture, to be encouraged through price incentives and devaluation of inflated currencies, while private initiative was developed to insure the return of local efficiency. The Organization of African Unity (OAU) took quite a different approach in its Lagos Plan for Action which stressed regional cooperation in industrialization and food production in such a way as to make entire sections of the continent less reliant upon and vulnerable to the vagaries of the world economy. During the 1980s, however, this debate was superseded by a new concern that African nations shared with others, particularly the countries of Latin America. This was the growing crisis of foreign indebtedness.

The Debt Repayment Crisis

Foreign indebtedness had marked African economies almost from the initial days of independence. At first it seemed a legitimate, indeed, a welcome, device for lifting African societies into the orbit of prosperity. Loans would help build infrastructure, develop industry, and expand agriculture, loans easily serviced through resurgent economies and eventually retired by prosperous nations. During the 1960s and into the 1970s, as African nations wrestled with development, they borrowed heavily to obtain foreign exchange that would finance industrialization and make available desired imports. Fragile economies, however, made halting progress in the face of population increase, falling commodity prices, inexperienced management, inflation, and the other ills that beset them. When the OPEC nations forced up fuel prices during the 1970s, this created a crisis, a need for much heavier borrowing to pay for energy imports essential to ongoing development.

Private commercial banks in the West, already affluent with a flood of deposited OPEC profits, were only too glad to oblige. Borrowing intensified dramatically in Africa, and also coincidentally in Latin America. When struggling nations found difficulty in meeting interest payments, more loans were offered and debts rescheduled over longer periods. The International Monetary Fund (IMF) and the World Bank (International Bank for Reconstruction and Development), both dominated by the creditor nations in the West, lent additional funds that were tied to seemingly sound advice on efficient economic management, austerity measures that would alleviate growing debts while simultaneously stabilizing erratic national economies.

Conditions had degenerated too far, however. By the early 1980s there was a crisis in both Latin America and Africa marked by debt so enormous that annual interest payments and debt retirement had begun to exceed the actual volume of new loans. In Latin America accumulated debt had ballooned to $350 billion, a tenfold increase in the decade ending in 1983. African obligations had also exploded, the sub-Saharan states nearing $135 billion by the end of 1988, eighteen times the 1970 figure and equalling the sub-Sahara region's total gross domestic product. Though a much lower total than the Latin American obligations, the African debt was in fact a critical burden for nations with far less robust economies. The national figures were frightening—Zaire and Zambia, each over $5 billion; Zimbabwe, $2.5 billion; Ghana, $2 billion. Even the affluent Ivory Coast had accumulated a $10 billion indebtedness that was one and one-half times the gross national product. Finally there was Nigeria, her $21 billion 1984 debt mounting to $33 billion by 1991 and threatening default. Debt service payments alone for thirty-eight sub-Saharan countries exceeded $11 billion annually.

By 1988 a financial emergency had become apparent, to the creditors as well as to the debtors. In a number of cases private banks had begun to write off what were regarded increasingly as uncollectible debts. In Africa, countries were falling in arrears and balking at the austerity clauses attached to IMF and World Bank loans. In 1987, for example, Zambia abandoned the stringent measures imposed by the IMF, citing the impossible political costs. Debtor nations argued that they could not afford the consequences of food riots, commodity scarcity, and black markets caused by currency devaluation, reduced government spending and the freeing of prices long held artificially low through official subsidies. By 1989 governments and banking interests in the West were exploring devices for discounting substantial portions of Third World debt in order that debtor nations might retain sufficient capital for investment and local consumption to propel their economic growth. In the long run such a move was seen increasingly, if grudgingly, in the West as the best form of self-interest, assisting the recovery of much-needed Third World customers for the industrial and other products of the developed nations.

In 1989 the World Bank was able to express a note of cautious optimism. The gross national product of sub-Sahara Africa, the Bank reported, was expanding faster than population growth for the first time since 1970. Between 1984 and 1988 agricultural production had risen to 4 percent annually, up from 1.25 percent over the 1970-1984 period, all this despite the usual problems of population, climate, and civil strife.

This reversal was no accident. The reasons lay in a sea change across the world map as nations began to introduce new measures in approaching their ongoing problems of growth and development.

The New Pragmatism

At the time of African independence in the 1950s and 1960s, conventional wisdom prescribed a benevolent authoritarianism as the best vehicle for economic development. Stable governments led by single parties, it was argued, would stay the course through the erratic shifts of short term populist demands, holding to unpopular but necessary reforms that would eventually achieve much desired national prosperity. Throughout Africa there quickly arose a complexity of state regulations—licensing requirements, price controls, export-import restrictions, and other restraints that aimed at reducing imports and encouraging domestic industrial output, while holding at bay perceived "neo-colonialist" efforts to gain economic control of newly independent national economies.

During the 1980s it became increasingly apparent that these devices were not working, that government interference in economic affairs often proved disastrous for development. As the decade drew to a close the dramatic growth of East Asian countries and the collapse of socialism throughout eastern Europe brought home the realization that state socialism was inefficient, if not outright destructive of development efforts; more particularly, that economies seemingly worked best when governments limited their activities to the encouragement of free competitive markets. Such a course resulted in greater efficiency of production, a sharper competitive edge in world competition, and a fuller participation in the benefits of an expanding world market.

Typically, economic problems found political expression. Across Africa widening popular discontent began to force authoritarian governments to introduce democratic reforms, one objective of which was economic regeneration. Single party regimes started to give ground, from vague assurances as in Ivory Coast, Cameroun, or Togo, to more concrete moves toward constitutional change characterized by developments in Gabon, Congo, Nigeria, and Benin. It remained to be seen what these political moves would achieve in terms of economic rehabilitation, casting off the old bonds of state control in favor of a free market, liberating private enterprise, or encouraging foreign investment. In this respect the experience of Ghana might prove instructive. When the Rawlings government lifted market restraints—for example, the end to a 50 percent confiscatory tax on cocoa production—exports soared and Ghana embarked on a 5 percent annual growth rate beginning in 1983. The World Bank has argued that similar actions would produce similar growth in other developing countries. As the 1990s opened, it was still too early to know whether this judgment would reflect hope or reality.

Suggestions for Further Reading

For historical background there are A. G. Hopkins, *An Economic History of West Africa* (New York: Columbia University Press, 1973); Ralph Austen, *African Economic History* (London: Heinemann, 1987); and C. C. Wrigley "Aspects of Economic History," *Cambridge History of Africa*, A. D. Roberts, ed. (Cambridge University Press, 1986). For economic development in the early years of African independence, consult Andrew M. Kamarck, *The Economics of African Development*, rev. ed. (New York: Praeger, 1967). William A. Hance's *Geography of Modern Africa*, 2nd ed. (New York: Columbia University Press, 1975) contains a wealth of useful information. For multinational cooperation in Africa, see John P. Renninger, *Multinational Cooperation for Development in West Africa* (New York: Pergamon Press, 1979). See also A. Adedeji's chapter in the *Cambridge History of Africa*, Vol. 8, Michael Crowder, ed. (Cambridge: Cambridge University Press, 1984).

For differing approaches to development see Samir Amin, "Underdevelopment and Dependence in Black Africa," *Journal of Modern African Studies*, Vol. 10, No. 4 (1972); Colin Leys, *Underdevelopment in Kenya* (London: Heinemann, 1975); and Cranford Pratt, *The Critical Phase in Tanzania, 1945-1968* (Cambridge: Cambridge University Press, 1976). These may be supplemented by the writings of African leaders such as Julius Nyerere, *Ujamaa, Essays on Socialism* (Dar es Salaam: Oxford University Press, 1968) and other collections; Kwame Nkrumah *I Speak of Freedom* (New York: Praeger, 1961) among others; and Kenneth Kaunda, *Independence and Beyond* (New York: International Publications Services, 1966).

Government reports and the publications of international agencies are most helpful for both analysis and statistical information, for example, reports of the United Nations, the World Bank, and the International Monetary Fund.

Much information and analysis is available in journals and press reports. *West Africa* offers a steady supply of economic news for its region, while other periodicals such as *East Africa Journal, Africa Report*, or *African Affairs* perform similar services. The field staff reports of the American University Field Service should also be consulted. More particularly, there are the professional journals dealing with African economies, including *The Journal of Modern African Studies, The Journal of Development Studies, The International Labour Review*, and *The American Economic Review*. Finally there is the wealth of information accumulated in the yearly issues of *Africa Contemporary Record* (New York: Africana Publishing Co., 1969-   ) and *African South of the Sahara* (London: Europa Publications.)

23

States and Nations

The Indispensable Unity

During the colonial era, the African map was a patchwork of territorial possessions; no more. Internal administrative organization or the fixing of international boundaries was purely a matter of convenience for ruling powers that felt scant compulsion to think in terms of some indefinite future when freedom might come for a colonial people. It was, therefore, of little consequence that Ewe dwelt equally in Togo and the Gold Coast, that Uganda gathered a clutch of Nilotic pastoralists into an improbable unit with the massive Bunyoro and Buganda kingdoms, that Upper Volta would appear and disappear intermittently with France's periodic reorganization of her West African possessions, or that Muslim emirates from the sprawling savanna plains would be combined with southern forest dwellers to form the region known as Nigeria.

With the arrival of independence, however, a lack of national cohesion raised new and vexing problems. People held together by a colonial administration had no loyalties to states that were not nations. Centrifugal forces gathered strength, fed by economic frustration, ethnic animosity, religious contention, or personal ambition; yet, the creation of vital modern economies demanded national cohesion, and development was stymied without the firm foundation of political stability. It was ominous, though not surprising, when dance groups from the Congo could train together over weeks for the Brussels fair of 1958 and show no trace of interest in one another's art, when Kikuyu and Maasai might live only a score of geographic miles apart while separated by an infinity of cultural light years, or when some Yoruba were moved to describe their national University of Ibadan as "that nest of Ibos."

An infectious sense of unity had marked the independence struggle, and all had combined momentarily in support of the common goal. Nevertheless, those who looked beyond the immediate success saw disturbing signs—political parties in Nigeria or the Congo that were essentially tribal; regional, ethnic, and religious fissures that quickly appeared to challenge Nkrumah's leadership in Ghana; the lamentable collapse of the Mali Federation within a few short weeks of its founding; or the continuing search for a separate independence by peoples like the Baganda and Bakongo.

Decline of the Parties

In leaving Africa, former European colonial powers were at pains to ensure that the new states would function as multiparty democracies, following roughly the example of western Europe. Particularly in the British areas there had been a policy change from indirect rule through so-called native authorities to a two-party system now regarded as essential to political stability and economic growth. Perhaps it was felt that what was British was best and most appropriate; perhaps that a parliamentary democracy might in future prove more sympathetic toward a one-time colonial master.

Such presumptions were not to be. Even before independence, African leadership turned progressively away from multiple parties and the give-and-take of legislative debate, favoring a more authoritarian design and persuaded that there were good reasons for its adoption. To begin with, those who had fought the good fight for independence were propelled by a sense of mission. The party—their party—had banished colonialism and opened windows to a new world of freedom. Still, they saw the job only half done. Were they not in victory the ones with the battle-tested experience to fashion a new nation and a better society? Who but they were their people's leaders, touched by fate for a great purpose? Surely, there was little reason for an opposition of similar background and education, its objectives perhaps only the arrogation of power for its own sake.

National unity was essential, the argument continued. There could be no compromise with regional, ethnic, or religious divisiveness disguised as loyal opposition. Better no parties at all, as all united in a common cause, but if a nation free of parties was utopian, then at least one unifying grouping was a reasonable alternative. In the course of their struggle against colonialism, moreover, nationalist leaders had absorbed in full measure the Marxist-Leninist perspective of history, a view which instilled an image of the state and its welfare prospering through the doctrines and activities of a single-party structure.

Such natural inclinations were undergirded by circumstance. Populations in nations yet imperfectly formed leaned heavily on a party organization that was easily recognized and identified with national progress. The new governments, furthermore, had inherited from the colonial past a tradition of centralized authoritarian control. Habits thus formed led more readily to the perpetuation of bureaucratic government, a tendency that was further strengthened by the association in popular thought of the ruling party as a true vehicle of the African revolution.

Given their sense of mission, political leaders themselves did much to hasten the movement toward a single-party government. Opposition forces were harassed or absorbed; trade unions, youth groups, and other extrapolitical organizations were attached variously to the ruling national party; and a judicious use of patronage was employed to build up a broader following. In developing nations where much economic activity and public works construction came from direct government action, there were myriad opportunities for persuasion. Jobs, career advancement, fellowships, housing and social amenities were offered or withheld through official action. Furthermore, when gentle persuasion failed, there was always recourse to restrictive or punitive tactics such as press censorship, sedition legislation, deportation, and detention. Finally, the dominant group possessed the parliamentary authority to strengthen its legal position, often capping the process by outlawing the opposition while endowing the single party with the ultimate legitimacy of constitutional sanction.

It was Nkrumah's Ghana, showing the way to national independence, that was among the first to move toward arbitrary rule. Nkrumah had managed to head off federalism and achieve his country's freedom in March 1957 under a unitary form of government; shortly thereafter there began a series of moves that soon destroyed and scattered organized political opposition. Colonialism typically held back subject nations, Nkrumah had explained in the 1956 preface to his *Autobiography*. Independence, he continued, demanded a total national mobilization for development, a socialist economic system to bypass the complexities of capitalism, and, when necessary, "emergency measures of a totalitarian kind" to ensure the survival of social justice and a democratic constitution.

Less than six months after independence day, the "emergency measures" made their first appearance; within three years Ghana had a totally new constitution featuring an all-powerful executive, the opposition was a spent force, its leader in exile and others in prison, and Nkrumah had been elected president of Ghana by nine of each ten who voted. The Convention People's Party (CPP) had taken control; indeed, as Nkrumah stated it, "the CPP is Ghana and Ghana is the CPP," Henceforth it would be the function of government to subserve the interests of the party.

In some respects it was a sour victory. Nkrumah was able to point to considerable economic progress, but no overall development policy emerged, and there was growing criticism of inefficiency, graft, and corruption in government. As early as the middle of 1957 the administration found itself confronted with labor unrest, ethnic divisiveness, and quarreling within the CPP. Subsequent deportations, including members of the foreign press, brought sharp criticism from abroad, as did the notorious Preventive Detention Act of 1958 under which individuals could be detained without trial for conduct suspected of being a threat to national security.

Increasingly the government felt compelled to make use of the Preventive

Detention Act, at first against the opposition, although eventually in an attack on leading CPP politicians themselves. Meanwhile, the web of party control was steadily widened. Workers were obliged to join the party trade union; negotiations over agriculture were made the responsibility of the party-related farmer council; youth, women, ex-servicemen, students, and others were similarly organized and attached to the party. Slogans, parades, and pageantry contributed ceremonial affirmation and were matched by the imposing party headquarters structures erected conspicuously in downtown Accra. Nkrumah became *Osagyfo*, the War Victor — some translated the term as Redeemer; his statue was raised in front of the parliament building, and his likeness appeared on the new national stamps and currency. There was little expression of surprise when, in 1962, Nkrumah was named life president of Ghana.

By 1960, then, Nkrumah, his party, and his government had reached a position virtually without challenge; yet, already, disruptive factors were taking shape that in a few years time would devastate his policies, destroy his effectiveness, and finally bring about his complete downfall. The most serious difficulties Nkrumah faced were economic in nature, although their effect was greatly intensified by maladroit leadership and unsophisticated development planning.

Determined to force the pace of modernization, Nkrumah and his ministers began to commit the government to massive expenditures in industry and mechanized agriculture, their purpose to create jobs, increase the scale of production, and bring the economy more directly under state authority. These changes were largely unaccompanied by appropriate economic controls and planning. Consequently, when world cocoa prices dropped sharply during the early 1960s, Ghana faced a severe balance of payments crisis, her declining income unable to match rapidly rising expenses. To meet this problem the government resorted to heavy external borrowing, but the terms were often inappropriate for long-term development projects, which, in any case, were themselves often poorly conceived, badly managed, and intrinsically unprofitable.

Unwilling to curtail its plans for expansion, the government sought additional income, drawing heavily on its reserves and imposing special taxes, import duties, and compulsory savings, along with so-called voluntary contributions. Heavy expenditures and restricted imports brought both sharp price rises and shortages; these in turn affected productivity and employment, leading to labor unrest and, more ominously, to a growing popular disenchantment with the regime. Despite marked advances in such services as public health, village development, and education, it was clear that the standard of living was in decline; what was worse, those associated with the party and its many auxiliaries were seemingly unaffected by the economic malaise and continued to live their accustomed lives of affluence. Had the nation struggled free of the special privileges associated with colonialism only to fall victim to a new tyranny?

For Nkrumah, troubles came in multiples. Despite his repeated exertions, Ghana gradually lost leadership within the pan-African movement as large numbers of newly independent countries began to contest his objectives and strategies for Africa's position in world affairs. At home, economic difficulties were forced to share the stage with a new problem—dissention within the CPP itself. The destruction of political opposition was an initial factor, for it removed the old need for unity and encouraged the factiousness of personal ambition. Beyond this, Nkrumah's search for an ideology to fuel his new socialist society caused him to turn from his older CPP colleagues, who were successively dismissed as both bourgeois and corrupt. While more power thereby came directly into Nkrumah's hands, he was handicapped during a period of mounting crisis by a new group of inexperienced, sometimes incompetent, lieutenants, by the decline of the CPP as an effective instrument of government, and by his own lack of systematic attention to political and economic problems within Ghana itself.

At the close of 1965 the $500 million of reserves registered at the time of independence had converted to an estimated external debt of $600 million, the national growth rate had virtually disappeared, unemployment was severe and rising, and prices, led by foodstuffs, were up 65 percent over 1963. Such statistics were the stuff of popular unrest, a fact that was punctuated by a series of bombings and unsuccessful attempts on Nkrumah's life. Nkrumah's sense of purpose regarding Ghana and Africa remained unshaken, but he became increasingly isolated both from people and party, and his last months in power were marked by a personal rule that could not control the rush of circumstances.

In the face of a deepening national crisis, it was the army and police of Ghana that abruptly ended Nkrumah's rule in February 1966. While the president was absent on a visit to China, police rounded up ministers and CPP officials as the army seized the government house by force. A military regime took control and a new era opened in Ghana's history.

Among those states that were former French colonies, there was a similar tendency toward single-party rule. The starting point had been regional unity— both that provided by the two great federations that France had instituted in West and Equatorial Africa, and by the political union of the interterritorial *Rassemblement Démocratique Africain* (RDA). Although the pan-African design of regionalism quickly faded with the *loi-cadre* of 1956, the component sections of RDA were able in most instances to develop their strength within the individual territories and to serve as the vanguard for nationalist movements in those emerging nations.

In Guinea, for example, Sékou Touré made use of trade unionism in bringing the *Parti Démocratique de Guinée* (PDG) to a dominant position during the 1950s. Precipitating his country's independence, Touré described colonialism as a continuing threat, vulnerable only to the forces of national and international cohesion. Here, the party would play a vital role, said Touré. Ethnic and religious loyalties rarely conformed to national boundaries, and nationalism itself was still too vague a concept for a people newly independent. It fell, therefore, to the party to provide the idea of community, and in Guinea, all were encouraged to join. Opposition groups were suppressed, differences of opinion were worked out within the unity of the party, and the party in its unity became the nation and, in effect, the people of Guinea.

Touré's political ideas were heavily sauced with a Marxist doctrine also to be found in the pronouncements of Modibo Keita and his colleagues of the *Union Soudanaise* (US) of Mali. Such leanings doubtless helped influence the rise of a single party in that state as it did in the Senegal of Léopold Senghor. In neighboring Ivory Coast, however, philosophy was tempered by the pragmatism of Houphouet-Boigny, although the end result, in 1946, was the formation of a single party, the *Parti Démocratique de Côte d'Ivoire* (PDCI) every bit as ascendant as any in Africa.

Taking advantage of the growing accommodation that characterized French policy during the 1950s, Houphouet and his PDCI colleagues shifted from the anti-colonial struggle to join the French administration in sharing political power and the perquisites of office. Under the circumstances it was relatively easy for PDCI to absorb the opposition, and, once independence had been achieved, to alter the form of government, giving Houphouet, as president, a dominant position in relation to the legislature and the courts. Though universal suffrage was maintained in Ivory Coast, elections soon lost their competitive character. Critics or opponents were contained through persuasion and reward, and, if necessary, through coercion. While superficially a political democracy appeared to function, in fact the state was operated by an oligarchy, and the government, including its laws and constitution, shaped to the needs of its rulers.

Such a pattern appeared widely throughout French-speaking Africa—in Upper Volta, Gabon, or Chad, for example, if not in unstable Dahomey with its coalition governments. Nevertheless, despite the apparent strength of the single-party regimes there was always the threat of faction and the possibility of overthrow for their reigning authority. President Senghor imprisoned his premier, Mamadou Dia, when the latter appeared to usurp power late in 1962, and in Ivory Coast, Houphouet experienced similar crises in 1963 and 1964. Moving swiftly and efficiently, the Ivory Coast administration smashed two plots based upon a combination of ethnic tensions, ideological differences, and the upward pressure of younger leadership.

Sékou Touré's passionate cry of neo-colonialism reflected deep and abiding French economic interests in many of her former colonies, and France was ready to come to the aid of friendly regimes when in trouble. In Ivory Coast, French arms may have helped sustain the government during its troubles, and French military bases were said to lend the stability of their presence to Senegal. Certainly, French arms were active against revolts in Chad and Gabon; in the case of the latter, it was French paratroopers who in 1964 restored President Léon Mba to power after he had been ousted during a short-lived coup. At the time Mba was moving toward a single-party state while consistently promoting ties with the France he regarded as a second fatherland. When he died in 1967, he was succeeded by his vice president, B.A. Bongo, who proclaimed his own one-party government and maintained his predecessor's friendly and encouraging attitude toward French capital investment.

As with Gabon and Ivory Coast, close French ties to Senegal reflected cultural affinity and economic interest. Thoroughly at home with French culture, President Senghor deeply admired General de Gaulle, and, with many other Africans, applauded the grant of independence when it came to France's territories in 1960. At the same time, admiration was nourished by much needed economic assistance in support of a single-crop economy based in groundnuts which unaided would have been hard pressed to maintain Senegal's national establishment with its large civil service, its university, and its great harbor installations. After the retirement of President de Gaulle in 1969, there was for a time some uncertainty over the continuation of various forms of French aid, not only in Senegal, but in other favored states as well. France wished to maintain her old influence, while the francophone states sought greater independence of action. Nevertheless, close relations remained much as before.

Whatever the philosophical or political persuasiveness of single-party rule, the centrifugal pull of regional, religious, or ethnic loyalties within African states continued to argue the need for unity. Chronic political instability in Dahomey, for example, was in no small measure traceable to regional rivalries. Again, Chad's religious and ethnic differences ultimately forced that needy country into a civil war it could ill afford. It was tribal animosity that marred the arrival of independence in both Congo-Brazzaville and Congo-Kinshasa (Zaire); the same was true for Rwanda and Burundi, Uganda and Kenya, among numerous others.

In time, one-party governments came to be the hallmark of African states. In some cases—the Tanganyikan African National Union (TANU), Nkrumah's CPP, the *Mouvement Populaire de la Révolution* (MPR) in Zaire, or the PDG of Guinea—they were officially proclaimed monopolies. In others like the United National Independence Party (UNIP) of Zambia and Kenyatta's KANU, they developed into *de facto* one-party regimes, attempting in their omnibus character to neutralize parochial exclusiveness. For example, President Kaunda of Zambia briefly threatened to resign his office in 1968 in a moment of exasperation over tribalist tendencies among political leaders, while at the time of independence the nation experienced a stubborn defiance of governmental authority arising from a dispute with the Lumpa church of Alice Lenshina Mulenga. Concentrated in the Bemba country to the northeast, the fifty thousand Lumpas reacted violently during 1964 against pressures to bring them into the reigning UNIP organization, fighting neighboring peoples incited to attack them, resisting government troops with heavy loss of life, a large contingent finally retreating into the nearby Congo (Zaire).

In Zaire, where zionist churches had long flourished, prophetic sects posed a periodic threat to civil order, abandoning village life, refusing to pay taxes, and sometimes resorting to brigandage and kidnapping as in the case of the Kitawalistes in Equateur province to the northwest. Otherwise tribal loyalties still threatened slowly growing political stability. The insurrection of white mercenaries in 1967 gained the immediate support of Katangese gendarmes bent on achieving the secession that had eluded Moise Tshombe after independence, and touched off local unrest when the mutineers marched through Kivu and Orientale provinces. Between independence in 1960 and the advent of General Mobutu's government five years later, Zaire had known far more anarchy than order, an order that gradually began to assert itself, as Mobutu's regime slowly consolidated its authority.

Political stability was halting and it came at price, for government authority under Mobutu was based upon arbitrary rule and a pervasive corruption through which the administration gained loyalty and neutralized opposition. Considerable energy and resources were invested in popularizing the symbols of Mobutu's MPR, the nation's only legal party as of 1970, as well as fostering the image of the president himself as party leader, head of state and rallying point for national unity. Essentially, however, Mobutu ruled by combining tough action with a corruption that destroyed or seduced potential foes and fragmented opposition, an adroit process that fostered survival by permitting no focal point of dissent to emerge.

Nevertheless it remained an intrinsically unstable system and in 1978 and 1979 it received a serious challenge when a force of Katanga exiles in Angola invaded Shaba (formerly Katanga) Province. The action resulted in hundreds of fatalities and a scare for the copper and cobalt markets, as well as for Mobutu's ineffectual army. The revolt eventually collapsed, put down by French and Moroccan troops brought into Shaba at Mobutu's request.

In Kenya, the personality of a national leader also served as counterpoise to actual or potential ethnic divisiveness. President Kenyatta, however, was not content to let the matter rest on his individual prestige as he moved to neutralize the opposition. For a time he harassed but tolerated the Kenya People's Union (KPU) led by Oginga Odinga. However, Luo unrest following the assassination of Tom Mboya in July 1969 eventually led to the proscribing of KPU and Odinga's house arrest. Later the two leaders were reconciled as Odinga rejoined his old Kenya African National Union colleagues, but Kenya continued under the control of its strong president essentially as a one-party state.

Government dominated by one party was an old story in Liberia where the True Whigs had long maintained a monopoly of political power. From its earliest days, the country had been dominated by its American colonists who gradually extended their authority over the indigenous population, ruling arbitrarily and culminating their exploitation of land and people during the period between the two world wars when the ugly charge of slaving reached as far as the president's office. With the accession of William V. S. Tubman as chief of state in 1944 there followed an improvement in relations, and local leaders were encouraged to join with the settler aristocracy in government. After 1964 representation of one million indigenous Liberians in the legislature was made equal to that of the thirty thousand Americo-Liberians, a degree of parity that took little account, however, of the economic ascendancy of the settlers or the absolute political power wielded in the presidential office.

With the death in 1971 of President Tubman, national leadership was assumed constitutionally and peacefully by the vice-president, William R. Tolbert. Although the settler oligarchy remained firmly in control both of the True Whigs and the government, the Tolbert administration made an effort to introduce greater efficiency in government and freedom of political expression along with more effective industrial growth and improved agricultural production. Nevertheless corruption and inefficiency remained endemic, economic planning lacked any genuine concern for an improved standard of living, while government continued to be essentially the action of presidential fiat.

The Soldiers

Already frustrated by problems of national cohesion and domestic stability, the people of Africa were obliged to endure as well an epidemic of military upheavals substituting army dictatorship for civil rule. Far from being an isolated instance, the coup in Ghana illustrated a trend of no less than continental proportion. Between 1952, the year that Colonel Nasser staged the revolt that overthrew the government of King Farouk, and 1968, which closed out with a bloodless coup in Mali, there were over seventy incidents, either staged or planned with military collusion, and twenty of these led to the institution of new army-led governments. Dahomey endured six successful coups through 1972, and General Mobutu twice took charge of the government in Zaire where lack of public order and indiscipline in the armed forces had been chronic.

It was an army revolt in June 1965 that deposed Ahmed Ben Bella and installed Colonel Houari Boumedienne in his stead as chief of state in Algeria, while military revolts swept away civilian rule in Burundi, Upper Volta, and the Central African Republic in 1966. President Sylvanus Olympio was assassinated in 1963 during a successful coup in Togo, while the unseating of President Nkrumah occurred scarcely a month after a major upheaval in Nigeria had overthrown the federal and regional administrations in January 1966. Sierra Leone experienced two successful military coups, the first which did away with civilian rule in March 1967, and the second which reestablished it in April 1968. Late in that same year, the long-lived government of Modibo Keita came to an abrupt but peaceful end when the president's army deposed him in favor of a military administration.

In 1969 it was the turn of both Libya and Somalia. In Libya the monarchy was toppled by a group of young army officers under the leadership of Colonel Muammar al-Qaddafi and dedicated to a more forcefully independent role toward the West. The Somali experience was similar—a left-oriented group of army officers taking control from what they termed a corrupt and ineffective governing class. The year, 1972, was marked by a second army coup in Ghana, led by Colonel Acheampong. During 1973, a bloodless coup upset the Bahutu government of Rwanda; the following year Upper Volta returned to the full military rule it had tentatively abandoned in 1971, while army officers seized power from the civilian authorities in both Niger and Ethiopia. The year 1975 saw two more army actions—the assassination of President Tombalbaye of Chad, and the abrupt change in Nigerian military leadership from General Gowon to Brigadier Mohammed. It was also the year the military regime in Dahomey changed not its government but its name to the People's Republic of Benin. In 1978 General Acheampong resigned, presumably in response to pressure from his fellow officers, and the Mauritanian president, Mokhtar Ould Daddah, was unseated by his army in a bloodless coup. Less than one year after taking office, Acheampong's successor, General S. W. K. Akuffo, fell to still another coup, engineered by junior airforce officers, most particularly Flight Lieutenant J. J. Rawlings. Even the seemingly stable were not immune. The Liberian military, headed by an army sergeant, Samuel K. Doe, unseated President Tolbert's government and two years later Kenyatta's successor in Kenya, President Daniel arap Moi, was hard pressed to fight off a military takeover. By that time, some two score states were under control of full or quasi-military administrations.

This impressive record of political instability reflected the complexities of societies under stress and change. Aside from the tenacious hold of "tribalism" with its ethnic diversity and its clan loyalties, there was the disappointment of people who soon discovered that political independence did not automatically assure an improved standard of living. When dissatisfaction reached epidemic proportions, the atmosphere became charged with the intensity of crisis. When disillusionment reached the soldiers, it touched individuals capable of translating anxiety into action.

There was more than social malaise, however. The instability of new societies created tensions within the military itself, parochial tensions involving such matters as competition for promotions or personal jealousies, inter-corps rivalries, and ethnic animosities. What was more, national armies in Africa were not necessarily detached, disciplined apolitical bodies, capable of standing aloof from the forces that surrounded them, stepping forward reluctantly and only when the political or economic imperatives allowed no alternatives. Most were marked by inconsistent patterns of recruitment, superficial training, and limited professional experience. Africanization applied too quickly brought a few junior officers to high position prematurely, then blocked advancement for those who followed. Often shot through with corruption, as well as their own cleavages, armies erupted into action for their own reasons, unseating weak, inefficient civil governments incapable of effective resistance and bereft of popular support.

In 1963, for example, President Olympio of Togo was gunned down by veterans of the French colonial forces when he refused them employment in the Togo army. The following year, simultaneous army mutinies in the East African countries of Kenya, Uganda, and Tanzania were suppressed with British help, the cause no more elevated than a dispute over pay and job advancement. Again, the well-known mutiny of the Congo *Force Publique* at the moment of independence in July 1960, was traced to resentment in the ranks over what was regarded by the troops as an excessively slow program of Africanization. Even the military coup that toppled Nkrumah in Ghana was apparently precipitated by the fear of interference by civil authorities in what the army felt to be its professional autonomy. During the last years of Nkrumah's regime, a deep uneasiness spread throughout the officer corps over promotions and retirements looked upon as political, over cutbacks in amenities and services, over attempts at CPP indoctrination, and over Nkrumah's special praetorian corps responsible to the president alone.

The military leaders who seized power in Ghana formed a National Liberation Council headed by Lieutenant-General J. A. Ankrah and through this agency they proceeded to govern the country by decree. There was a general sense of relief throughout the population over the fall of Nkrumah, yet, at first, the Council saw its role as temporary, its responsibility to reverse the ruinous course of the previous government while reestablishing civilian rule as quickly as possible. To this end, a series of economic measures halted the trend toward state ownership, retrenched public expenditures, and moved to liquidate the massive foreign debt through renegotiation. At the same time the CPP and its affiliates were dissolved and a substantial number of civilians recruited to assist the Council in its activities. In 1969 a new constitution prepared the way for a return to civil government; that same year elections returned Nkrumah's old antagonist, Kofi Busia, as prime minister heading a parliamentary government.

Unhappily, the Busia ministry was unable to make effective headway in economic matters while antagonizing important segments of the population, notably civil servants, trade unionists, and finally and fatefully, the army's officer corps. Failing in his efforts to reduce and reschedule Ghana's foreign debt, Busia introduced austerity at home in the face of steady inflation and rising unemployment, and restrained government expenditure while permitting apparent extravagances by individual ministers. As his problems mounted, Busia also introduced economies in defense spending, officer salaries, and fringe benefits. Thus threatened, the army responded in January 1972, deposing the authorities and reinstituting a military government, the National Redemption Council, under the leadership of Colonel I. A. Acheampong.

Echoing the actions of General Ankrah, Acheampong immediately restored all cuts in military expenditures and emoluments, at the same time, inaugurating a regimen of mismanagement marked by continued inflation and commodity shortages and complicated by the oil crisis of 1973 and its subsequent world depression. Less capable even than its predecessor in effecting fundamental economic reform, the military government steadily lost popularity, under both Acheampong and his successor, General Akuffo, the opposition marked by strikes and industrial sabotage.

The Rawlings coup of June 1979 was achieved, therefore, in an atmosphere of public frustration that lent support to the change, especially since Rawlings expressed his intention to clear out corruption in government as a prelude to the return of civilian rule as had originally been announced by the Akuffo government. In September, a constitutional government headed by Dr. Hilla Limann took office, confronting at once what Limann described as a "economic shambles" marked by stagnant agricultural and industrial production, a weakened infrastructure of plant and equipment, and a sagging public morale that encouraged corruption and contributed to a declining productivity. As with his predecessors, Limann was unable to make the necessary and unpopular economic decisions or to check the growing corruption in and out of government. On New Years Eve, 1981, Rawlings and his fellow officers once more stepped in, deposing Limann, suspending the constitution, and instituting yet another era of military rule for Ghana.

Alternating civilian and military rule also characterized the fortunes of Ghana's Upper Volta neighbor. After 1974 civilian government was gradually restored, but in 1980 the army seized power and over the ensuing decade other coups followed, a total of five from the time of independence. In 1983 the government was overthrown by a young charismatic army captain, Thomas Sankara, then in 1987 Sankara was in turn replaced and subsequently assassinated, his former friend and colleague, Captain Blaise Compaoré, taking control. Sankara had come to power declaring a crusade against neocolonialism, but his most enduring action while governing a poor and drought-stricken people may have been the 1984 proclamation renaming the country Burkina Faso, "Land of the Upright Men."

Happily, some nations were able to avoid the trauma of military intervention. Civilian governments have long remained in control in Zambia and Malawi, while in 1982 both Tanzania and Kenya managed to overcome army-inspired efforts to replace the civil authorities. In Gambia a 1981 attempted coup was put down with the help of Senegalese troops, while both Cameroun and Senegal survived presidential successions without any major upheaval. At the beginning of 1981 Senegal's President Senghor stepped down in favor of a hand-picked successor, Abdou Diouf, who was reelected in 1982 in his own right. Late in 1982 Ahmadou Ahidjo abruptly resigned as head of state after twenty-two years as President of the Republic of Cameroun, naming as successor his prime minister, Paul Biya. Eventually the two men fell out, but Biya has maintained control, successfully suppressing a 1984 coup attempt designed, it was said, to return Ahidjo to power.

Orderly transition was not for others, notably Uganda and the Central African Republic. In the latter country, the single-party government of David Dacko was unseated by his cousin and army commander, Colonel Jean-Bedel Bokassa, on New Years's eve, 1965. Budgetary problems, arbitrary government, and corruption were the ostensible reasons, but Bokassa's anxieties in fact were stimulated by reductions in military appropriations and his fear of losing control in a power struggle that had developed between the army and police. The flamboyant regime that Bokassa instituted, however, became increasingly embarrassing to a French government that was its chief economic support. In 1979 French paratroopers swept Bokassa out of office and into exile, replacing him with Dacko, but the latter soon succumbed to still another military government in 1981.

For Uganda events had been long unfolding, events culminating on that January day in 1971 when General Idi Amin moved his armor into Kampala and ended civilian rule for his country. The steps that Milton Obote took against Buganda and the kabaka in 1966 were accompanied by proclamation of a military state under a constitution that created an executive presidency and abolished the old kingdoms of Buganda, Bunyoro, Toro, and Ankole. Having thus for the moment rid himself of effective political opposition, Obote announced his Common Man's Charter in 1969, a call for state socialism to be implemented by development of collectives, government-operated industries, and nationalization of commercial and financial institutions.

Obote's economic reform soon brought problems in the form of capital outflow, commodity shortages, and inflation, as Asian traders and foreign corporations sought to avoid losses to nationalization. The president's main concerns were political, however, involving continued regional and cultural divisions as well as control over the Ugandan army that was both his protection and a source of potential opposition. The mutiny of 1964 had brought immediate pay rises and rapid promotion through Africanization; more fatefully, it gave the army a taste of its own power in the face of a civil government. Armed forces recruitment was conducted largely among northern Nilotes and led to internal factionalism that involved the president through his Lango cohorts and eventually precipitated a feud between Obote and his army commander, General Amin. Resenting Lango influence and anticipating his own arrest and removal from command, Amin seized power at a convenient moment during Obote's absence from the country. It was not just another army coup for it led to one of the bloodiest and most destructive intervals of misrule to mark Africa's difficult independence years.

Civil War

The political instability and economic uncertainties that encouraged military intervention were nourished in country after country by ethnic, regional, and religious divisions that paralyzed authority and compromised the process of nation making. In the majority of cases — Cameroun, Ghana, Senegal, Sierra Leone, Ivory Coast, or Zambia are good examples — centripetal forces prevailed and national unity was preserved, whether under civil or military rule. Others not so fortunate saw these divisive stresses overwhelm the center and plunge their countries into the perplexities and agonies of civil strife.

In the Sudan and in the former Belgian Congo, for example, the malady of internal warfare came early and remained long. Elsewhere, in Chad, Burundi, or Rwanda, events followed much the same disheartening course. The military government that toppled Emperor Haile Selassie of Ethiopia in 1974 inherited his powers along with a bitter struggle to retain the separatist territory of Eritrea. As for Angola, that country finally reached statehood in 1975 after four centuries of Portuguese colonialism, only to emerge a divided land at war with itself. Most spectacular of all was the fate of some 60 million Nigerians. As they embarked upon independence in 1960 with high hopes and great expectations, their country was widely applauded for its stability and promise. Less than six years later, the Nigerian government had perished, victim of a brutal military coup, and the Nigerian nation appeared to be breaking up before the force of the civil war that followed.

The scenario was near-classic. Initially, on January 15, 1966, a rebellion of young army officers overthrew the constitutional government, replacing it with military rule, a form of administration that controlled the country into 1979. In time, complex events led to the secession of the Ibo-dominated eastern region and the establishment of the Republic of Biafra in May 1967. A long, grinding civil war ensued which ended early in 1970 with the total defeat of Biafra and the reaffirmation of Nigerian unity, under the leadership of General Yakubu Gowon. The circumstances of rebellion and national collapse, however, were embedded in history and in the character of Nigeria's people.

First, there was the existence of many powerful ethnic groups artificially bound together into one nation essentially as a convenience of colonial administration. Introverted in their cultural pride, and intolerant in their mutual isolation, they were notably unsympathetic, if not uncomprehending, toward each other's efforts at self-improvement. Next, there was the shape of the British colonial government, at first concerned primarily with the economy and efficiency of its own organization, a conception that suggested regional cohesion and rates of modernization keyed to local rather than to national circumstances. When the era of the Second World War first brought serious thoughts of national independence for Africans, the regional orientations of Nigeria's colonial administrators were given constitutional sanction, the resultant decentralization encouraging the forces of ethnic separateness which in turn supported it.

Over the years, Ibo aggressiveness in many areas of national endeavor had collided with a growing resentment, especially in the north where a conservative, traditionalist Hausa-Fulani society feared for its ability to control its own destiny in a fast-changing world. When independence brought those standard problems of growth rates and debt servicing, of inflation and unemployment, of inexperience and immorality in government, the stresses on an incoherent national society proved too great. Anti-Ibo pogroms in northern towns resulted in a massive bloodbath in which thousands of Ibos perished, their homes and property destroyed. Those who returned to the east came back to a shocked population wherein virtually all sense of Nigerian national loyalty had been destroyed. The logical consequence was secession which, when contested, led to civil war.

The sequel to Biafra was mixed. The military regime headed by General Gowon clearly saved the nation in its hour of extremity; at the same time Gowon made another signal contribution to national cohesion when in 1967 he replaced the old federal regions with twelve states, thereby at once strengthening the center and creating areas that conformed more comfortably with ethnic groupings. Post-war problems proved more intractable for military rulers, however, and eventually brought about Gowon's own downfall in July 1975.

Indeed, it was Nigeria's strengths that were her chief weakness. A large wartime army, resisting demobilization, became a financial drain and threat to political stability. Oil revenues invited rapid economic development but taxed the nation's capacity in management and facilities to move rapidly forward in financing basic industries and a revitalized agriculture. Inflation accompanied heavy expenditures on capital goods, but there was also inefficiency and corruption in government, characterizing an administration inexperienced in the intricacies of national development. Public confidence waned in the face of official paralysis and the postponement of a promised return to civilian rule.

Gowan was removed from office while attending an OAU conference in Kampala, and the new military government headed by Brigadier Murtala Muhammed at once advanced briskly on a number of fronts—attempting to clean up official corruption, dealing with the minority issue by adding seven more states for a total of nineteen, and, most particularly, arranging for a new constitution and return to civil government by 1979. Murtala's assassination by disgruntled army officers failed to check these developments, and his successor, General Obasanjo, was able to pass on control of the state to a new civilian administration in October 1979. After more than thirteen years of military rule, Nigeria had returned to a government of law and of democratically elected representatives.

It was a government of something old and something new. The old was the reappearance of Nigerian politics in all their idiomatic artistry, the enthusiasm, energy, and excitement of the early independence years. The new was a different form of government, patterned not on the parliamentary system bequeathed by Britain but on an American model that stressed separate state and national governments, an executive president and explicit representation of regions and constituencies in Senate and House, separation of powers and constitutional guarantees of fundamental political and civil rights. Especially Nigerian was the emphasis on safeguards for ethnic minorities, particularly in the structure of political parties; there could be no return to the "tribalism" that had marred the First Republic and led to civil war.

The transfer of authority was made smoothly and the military leaders relinquished power as they had promised. The new government, however, faced immediate problems, some inherited from Nigeria's past, others emerging from current circumstances. To begin with, constitutional precautions against ethnic exclusiveness failed to prevent an electoral polarization along regional lines, a chilling reminder for some Nigerians of earlier divisiveness. Only one of the five parties contesting the elections, the National Party of Nigeria (NPN), was able to demonstrate a truly national base, although even NPN required a special last-minute interpretation of the new constitution to insure the election of Shehu Shagari, the party's candidate for president. There were other difficulties that were the natural consequence of a new system of government. As in the early years of the United States under its new constitution, relations had to be tested—House versus Senate, state versus the federal government, executive versus legislature, the role of parties, the limitations of the civil service, the functions of the Supreme Court.

More vexing for Shagari's administration were economic problems, also old and new. The Nigerian economy had become far too dependent upon its resources in petroleum, 90 percent of its foreign exchange, for example, derived from oil revenues. There was need, therefore, to press forward with industrialization and to revitalize sagging agricultural production while fuel reserves lasted. Mounting revenues during the 1970s had followed OPEC price rises in 1973-1974 and 1979-1981, but the economies of the oil consuming industrialized world began to falter in the late 1970s, a worldwide oil glut developed by 1981, and Nigeria found itself with large expenditures and commitments matched by ever fading petroleum revenues. Faced with high public expectations for advances in living standards, with heavy expenditures committed to agriculture, industry, and the move of Nigeria's capital to the centrally located site of Abuja, with continued inflation and an accelerating corruption, the government also saw its oil revenues abruptly fall by half, a crippling economic blow that greatly complicated political life.

It was no surprise, therefore, that Shagari's reelection in 1983 was followed early the next year by the country's sixth military coup, installing General Muhammed Buhari at the head of a new regime. Inexperienced soldiers no more than corrupt politicians were capable of resolving Nigeria's economic and political complexities, however. Shrinking oil revenues, a population exploding upward beyond 100 million, chronic religious strife, the pinch of devaluation and austerity, and a characteristically outspoken press insured continuing popular agitation. In 1985 fellow officers removed Buhari in a bloodless coup, installing General Ibrahim Babangida in his place. Babangida's administration proved relatively restrained and, although politics were banned, he promised a return to civil rule by 1992.

Parochial loyalties and economic ills led to military coups and civil war in Africa's largest state, the Democratic Republic of the Sudan. There, in a country with a long history of religious and regional differences, a series of civil and military regimes attempted to overcome factionalism with varying success. In 1964, the military government of General Abbud bowed to growing popular demands for renewed civilian rule, not as a gesture toward constitutionalism but as an admission of continued impotence before seemingly intractable problems, centered on national unity and economic development. The return of the politicians brought little relief, however, for their parties were no more able than the generals to resolve long-standing differences impeding economic and social progress. In 1967 the old Mahdist Umma Party lost its effectiveness by splitting into liberal and conservative wings, while the National Unionist Party (NUP) of Ismail al-Azhari amalgamated with the pro-Egyptian People's Democratic Party which had departed the NUP in 1956 after al-Azhari turned away from his original support for union with Egypt.

These shifts and schisms, based partly on the old Mahdiyya-Khatmiyya division, partly on a family quarrel among the Mahdist ansar followers, and partly on the recurrent issue of relations with Egypt, impeded national development, but nonetheless remained secondary to the unresolved problem of relations between the north and the southern provinces of Bahr al-Ghazal, Upper Nile, and Equatoria. There, the Nilotic people long argued neglect both during colonial times and since independence while claiming that the northerners in control of the government in Khartoum were attempting to thrust their Islamic way of life on the Christian and pagan south. In 1961 long-lived discontent broke out in the form of a guerrilla revolt marked by bitter fighting which drove almost two hundred thousand refugees out of the country, mostly into Uganda. Some southerners tried to secure concessions by working within the government, but this policy further complicated and intensified the revolt which also became the source of border problems and strained relations with Uganda. By early 1969 final agreement on a constitution had yet to be reached because of uncertainties as to whether the Sudan should be a centralized state as favored by the north or a federation preferred by the southerners.

In the spring of 1969, the army took power once again, impatient with the continued sectarian disputes among political parties, disturbed by the inertia of a stagnant economy and the steady drain of an expensive military commitment in the south. Led by General Gaafar al-Nimeiry, the ruling

Revolutionary Council survived a series of counter-coups but made little progress with the old difficulties of economic development and political unity.

General al-Nimeiry's government achieved a signal triumph in 1972, however, when it succeeded in bringing a stop to the bloody civil war in the south. After much negotiation, an agreement was reached granting internal self-government to the southern provinces under a federation wherein Khartoum would retain control over foreign affairs, currency, and defense. One year later, in May 1973, a constitution was adopted embodying these provisions. At last peaceful and seemingly united, the Sudan was nonetheless unable to exploit its new-found stability.

The reasons were apparent, partly in the country's long-lived religious and ethnic divisions, partly in the problems of yet another poor African state struggling to modernize and develop its economy. During the 1970s and into the 1980s, the Sudanese government failed to sustain economic growth although the presence of oil fields in the south offered some hope for the future. Beset by inflation, mounting foreign debts, corruption, and widespread public disaffection, Nimeiry became increasingly dictatorial. In 1982-1983 he moved to dilute the autonomy of the equatorial provinces, and purge the army officer corps of southerners. Faced east and west by hostile Ethiopian and Libyan neighbors and increasingly unpopular at home, Nimeiry was unseated in 1985 and replaced by an elected government of shifting coalitions headed by Sadiq al-Mahdi. Mahdi owed his prominent position largely to tradition, for he is the great-grandson of Muhammad Ahmad, the Mahdi, who had routed Anglo-Egyptian forces a century earlier to establish the Mahdist state. Such a lineage had little currency in the southern provinces, however, where the long-lived civil revolt was resumed in 1983 under the leadership of John Gareng, a defected army officer, who formed the Sudan People's Liberation Movement and its military wing, the Sudan People's Liberation Army to resist what he termed an attempt to reimpose Islamic law and culture on the southerners. By mid-1989, as still another military coup unseated the al-Mahdi civilian regime, the Sudan seemed still to be adrift in a sea of civil war, economic stagnation, and political instability, thereby intensifying the suffering of a population that had endured during the 1980's afflictions of drought, plague, and famine sometimes reaching almost biblical intensity.

Years of drought, famine, and plague were also the lot of Sudan's Ethiopian neighbor where political unrest and civil conflict had been almost continual since the absorption of Eritrea in 1962. Guerrilla warfare that broke out shortly after Eritrean annexation gradually escalated into a full-scale revolt, and by early 1978 most of the territory had been wrestled from Ethiopian control. The Eritreans, aided, it was alleged in Ethiopia, by the Sudan and other Arab states, gained their initial successes against the government of Haile Selassie; then, as the emperor was deposed by his army in 1974, they continued their revolt against the military regime that followed.

The Ethiopian army action began early in 1974 with demands for higher pay that soon expanded to include political reforms. Gradually the army substituted its authority for civil rule, finally removing and detaining the emperor who died in custody the following year. The new regime introduced social reform, especially in land redistribution, but contributed little to improve the country's political stability. Indeed, Ethiopia's historic regional divisiveness was compounded by an internal struggle for power within the *Dergue*, or provisional military council, and the Dergue soon found itself pitted also against radical groupings, particularly the Ethiopian People's Revolutionary Party. For a time, a confusion of ambushes, shootouts, arrests, assassinations, and executions elevated internal unrest to the level of virtual civil war, but in 1978 the Dergue leader, Colonel Mengistu Haile Mariam, seemed to have gained control over the army and therefore over the machinery of state.

Ethiopia's internal uncertainties precipitated yet another crisis, partly intramural but mostly external. In 1977, Somalis from the Ogaden region began a guerrilla action, strongly aided by forces of the neighboring Somali Republic, and together they succeeded in overrunning the Ogaden area that the emperor, Menelik, had annexed to Ethiopia toward the end of the nineteenth century. In his extremity, Mengistu now turned to the Soviet Union, and, with the aid of Soviet arms and Cuban troops, launched a counterattack that forced the Somalis to withdraw their forces in March 1978.

With the Somali threat momentarily dormant, Mengistu was able to deal more directly with domestic discord—the stubborn rebellion in Eritrea and a movement for secession in Tigre province, active since 1975. In neither case was he successful; after a decade of military confrontation both the Eritreans and the Tigreans appeared stronger than ever. Urged to conclude a political settlement by his Soviet sponsors, Mengistu was obliged to beat off an attempted coup in 1989 engineered by officers of his war-weary army. It was but a temporary respite. As his regime collapsed before Tigrean and Eritrean pressure, Mengistu fled the country in the spring of 1991, his army beaten, the Eritreans in *de facto* control of their territory, and a provisional government led by Tigreans directing the nation's affairs from the capital of Addis Ababa.

The virus of civil war struck at small and large with equal impartiality. Ethiopia and the Sudan were large states and so too was Chad where a civil struggle broke forth in 1965. Rwanda and Burundi, by contrast, have been among Africa's smallest nations to endure the ordeals of ethnic animosity. Rwanda's tribal crisis came first, even before independence, and was solved only with heavy loss of life and the removal of many thousands of refugees to nearby countries. The essential conflict lay between the Tutsi pastoralists who had ruled the mountain highland ever since their arrival in the fifteenth century, and the servile, but far more numerous, Bahutu farmers. During the period of colonial control, there were introduced egalitarian ideas which threw into question Bahutu serfdom, and led to eventual Bahutu political ascendancy achieved by the time of national independence in 1962. Between

1960 and 1964 up to two hundred thousand former Tutsi overlords left the country, some returning in 1963 as a rebel army which, however, was unsuccessful, in its effort to unseat the regime. The price of revolt was a large-scale massacre of Tutsi in 1964 followed by periodic outbursts of violence and further migrations of refugees. While the military coup in 1973 deposed the civil leadership, the upheaval appeared to be caused essentially by intramural differences among the Bahutu. Nevertheless, the implacable hostility between Bahutu and Tutsi remains undiminished, its potential for bloodshed well illustrated by the murderous conflict which has continued to embitter relations between these same two peoples in neighboring Burundi.

Migrations notwithstanding, the Tutsi have maintained a 10 to 15 percent proportion of Rwanda's 5 million people, a share which approximates the population balance in Burundi where 650,000 Tutsi have been locked in a power struggle with six times that many Bahutu. At independence the Burundi Tutsi managed to retain political control, first in the form of a monarchy, then, in 1966, as a republic which was established through an army coup engineered by Captain Michael Micombero. These intramural changes left the Bahutu unsatisfied and they responded with two unsuccessful risings in 1965 and 1969, followed by a much more violent rebellion in April 1972. Despite its dimension, the revolt was crushed, to be succeeded by several weeks of reprisals in which Bahutu leadership was systematically exterminated. As many as 100,000 Bahutu were reported killed in an ethnic conflict which flared again in mid-1973.

Efforts at intertribal reconciliation have had mixed results. In 1988 after Pierre Buyoya of Burundi had moved many Hutus into his Tutsi dominant government, there were further clashes as Hutus apparently felt reforms to be too slow. Estimates of fatalities ranged upward to 20,000, victims of tribal animosities that continue to plague the African continent.

The vast African state of Chad blankets the natural boundary between desert and savanna which has witnessed conflict between southern farmers and northern pastoralists as old as African history itself. During the apogee of the great savanna kingdoms, the southerners were able to impose their rule on the nomads; when independence from colonial rule came, the Christian or pagan farming population of the south once more prevailed, providing Chad with much of its administration which, the northern Muslims maintained, ruled largely in the interests of the southerners.

In 1968 Chad's president, Ngarta Tombalbaye, a southerner, enlisted the aid of French troops in an effort to contain a widening revolt in the north, a vain action as northern insurgency steadily intensified. By 1979 civil war had descended into anarchy—Tombalbaye had been assassinated during the 1975 army uprising, successor regimes had collapsed, and orderly government had given way to a land dominated by diverse guerrilla bands.

Up to 1975 the conflict in Chad had been essentially a north-south, Muslim-Christian confrontation, but southern intramural factionalism combined with northern military strength to put the country largely in the hands of the northerners, not, however, a united north but a series of military forces largely devoid of program or ideology and dominated by loyalty to individual warlords. Of these, two emerged as predominant—the Northern Army Forces (FAN) of Hissen Habré and Goukouni Woddeye's Popular Army Forces (FAP). In December 1980 Goukouni established a *de facto* government, occupying the capital of Ndjamena with the crucial assistance of a Libyan army sent by Colonel Qaddafi, seemingly bent upon extending his influence into Chad. By 1982, however, Habré had gained control of Ndjamena and begun an offensive against Libyan forces, scoring decisive victories in 1987 that rid the country for a time of the northern influence.

With the arrival of the 1990s there was cautious hope that Africa's seemingly endemic strife might be on the wane. To begin with, the end of Cold War contention between the United States and the Soviet Union had removed one major source of violence—the military support of surrogate forces in Africa. Furthermore, the intolerable cost of lives and property resulting from interminable civil war was beginning to outweigh any perceived advantages in continued military action. The result was an uneasy balance between peace ventures and chronic violence that showed some tendency toward negotiation over warfare.

It was a mixed bag of examples. The defeat and departure of Mengistu had finally halted the conflict in Ethiopia. In Somalia the government of Siad Barre was unseated early in 1991 by insurgent groups but with uncertain prospects for future peace and stability. The recurring warfare between north and south in the Sudan appeared to have halted momentarily, perhaps as much from exhaustion as from conviction. In Chad the Habré regime was ousted in 1990 in a brief campaign by a little-known faction apparently supported by Colonel Qaddafi and Libya. In Liberia the year 1990 was occupied by a growing civil conflict that ultimately toppled President Samuel Doe and his unpopular government but left a vacuum of uncertainty as to which of several insurgent groups might succeed to power.

Somewhat more promising were the truces involving Angola and Morocco. Prodded by American and Soviet diplomacy, the Angolan government and UNITA ended their sixteen-year civil war in a May 1991 agreement designed to prepare the way for free elections to be held in 1992. Concurrently, after fifteen years of strife, Morocco and the POLISARIO Front guerrillas moved to accept a cease-fire at United Nations urging, the outcome to be a referendum to determine the future status of their disputed territory in the Western Sahara, the former region of Spanish Sahara.

Throughout the wartorn regions of Africa, the need for an end to death and destruction was evident enough. What was not so clear was whether common sense and the instinct for survival would prevail in the long run over national self-interest, ethnic rivalries, and religious intolerance.

Suggestions for Further Reading

For assessments of Africa's independence years up until about 1980, see Vol. 8 of the *Cambridge History of Africa*, Michael Crowder, ed. (Cambridge: Cambridge University Press, 1984), and Prosser Gifford and W. R. Louis, eds., *Decolonization and African Independence* (New Haven: Yale University Press, 1988). There are good studies of individual countries, for example, Dennis Austin's fine *Politics in Ghana* (London: Oxford University Press, 1964), Crawford Young, *Politics in the Congo* (Princeton: Princeton University Press, 1965), or Richard L. Sklar, *Nigerian Political Parties* (Princeton: Princeton University Press, 1963).

Numerous writings by African leaders themselves will provide the reader with an image of events as seen by the principal participants. See, for example, Kwame Nkrumah's autobiography, *Ghana* (New York: Thomas Nelson, 1957), or his *I Speak of Freedom* (New York: Praeger, 1961); Julius Nyerere's *Freedom and Unity* (Dar es Salaam: Oxford University Press, 1966), and *Freedom and Socialism* (Dar es Salaam: Oxford, 1968); Kenneth Kaunda, *Zambia, Independence and Beyond* (New York: International Publications Service, 1966), and *A Humanist in Africa* (London:Longmans, 1966); Tom Mboya, *Freedom and After* (Boston: Little Brown, 1963); Oginga Odinga, *Not Yet Uhuru* (New York: Hill and Wang, 1967); Jomo Kenyatta, *Suffering Without Bitterness* (Nairobi: East African Publishing House, 1968); or L. S. Senghor, *On African Socialism* (New York: Praeger, 1964), among others.

Periodicals like *West Africa, Africa Report*, or the *Journal of Modern African Studies* have offered numerous pieces dealing with the military in Africa, but there are also a number of book-length works to be consulted. See, for example, Claude E. Welch, ed. *Soldier and State in Africa* (Evanston: Northwestern University Press, 1970); or Samuel Decalo, *Coups and Army Rule in Africa* (New Haven: Yale University Press, 1976) for differing views of the subject. A useful summary of military coups is offered in Kenneth W. Grundy's pamphlet, *Conflicting Images of the Military in Africa* (Nairobi: East African Publishing House, 1968). A convenient collection of essays is to be found in Robert I. Rotberg and Ali A. Mazrui, eds., *Protest and Power in Black Africa* (New York: Oxford University Press, 1970). For those interested in the Nigerian coups, see B. J. Dudley, *Instability and Political Order* (Ibadan: Ibadan University Press, 1973); Robin Luckham, *The Nigerian Military* (Cambridge: Cambridge University Press, 1971); and for the civil war in Nigeria, A. H. M. Kirk-Greene, *Crisis and Conflict in Nigeria*, 2 vols. (London: Oxford University Press, 1971).

Information on a wide range of African affairs is available in encyclopedic fashion in *Africa Contemporary Record* (New York: Africana Publishing Co., 1969-   ).

24

Disintegrating Citadels in the South

Portugal Bows Out

It was with equanimity that, in 1960, the Portuguese dictator, Dr. Antonio Salazar, examined the winds of change then sweeping their way toward freedom in Africa. Even as his Angolan subjects stood poised on the brink of revolt, he spoke repeatedly of Portugal's historic civilizing mission. "We have been in Africa for 400 years. . . . We are present there with a policy." And, again, "[Emancipators] come too late, for the job has already been done. Portuguese unity does not allow for transfers, cession or abandonment."

For a long time it appeared that Salazar was right. Tiny, impecunious Portugal seemed to have done it again. Centuries earlier she had led the way outward to break Europe's long isolation, thrusting her influence deeply west and east, carving herself an empire on three continents. Now, almost half a millennium later, she still maintained her possessions overseas—Macao on the China coast and the province of Goa in western India; most incredibly of all, the vast African territories of Angola, Mozambique, and Guinea, firmly Portuguese, it appeared, at the very moment other powers were quitting the turbulent seas of African independence.

At its onset the revolt in Angola went badly for the insurgents. During the early months of 1961, spontaneous uprisings occurred in several locations. All were put down with brutal thoroughness; in six months an estimated 20,000 Africans lost their lives, and by year's end resistance seemed largely to have ceased. It developed, moreover, that the revolutionaries were far from united. In the northern districts, the Union of the Peoples of Angola (UPA) led by Holden Roberto held sway, a movement based in the Bakongo people and essentially antagonistic to the Popular Movement for the Liberation of Angola

513

(MPLA) centered in Luanda and supported by the Kimbundu speakers of central Angola.

Despite its inauspicious start, the revolt did not expire. Roberto's UPA was able to maintain occasional guerrilla activity in the north while the MPLA, rallied by its Marxist leader, Dr. Agostinho Neto, managed to shift its campaigning to the grasslands of eastern Angola, operating from bases in Zambia. In 1963, moreover, Portugal faced a fresh uprising as the nationalists of Portuguese Guinea, long discontent, graduated from political protest to armed struggle. The following year it was the turn of Mozambique where FRELIMO (the Front for the Liberation of Mozambique) began military operations in the northern districts near the Tanzanian border; then, in 1966, the National Union for the Total Independence of Angola (UNITA) broke away from UPA and under the leadership of Jonas Savimbi organized a guerrilla movement in the Ovimbundu country of south-central Angola.

The operations were modest but persistent. Ambushes or hit-and-run mortar attacks goaded rather than hurt, but they forced Portugal to a steadily growing military undertaking that by the late 1960s consumed almost half the national budget. A small nation of limited resources was obliged to put over 170,000 men in the field in its three African territories, a substantial commitment pinned down by a far smaller opposition. Still, casualties were light, the economic promise, especially in Angola, was great, and the regime remained unshaken in its devotion to Portugal's self-proclaimed imperial destiny. When Salazar died in 1970, his policies continued unchanged, the direction of his leadership reaffirmed. Conservative politicians, army officers, and business executives appeared to be in complete control.

Nevertheless, it was the Portuguese army, protector of the metropolitan regime and defender of Portugal's colonies, that introduced revolution at home and independence abroad. As Amilcar Cabral, head of the insurrectionist party in Guinea had predicted, grinding colonial wars would steadily bleed the metropolitan government of men and resources and bring ultimate freedom overseas. Ironically, discontent built up first in the very forces sent to stifle the guerrillas in Africa. Condemned to unrelieved bush campaigning, leading sullen conscripts, and influenced by the political sophistication often displayed by captured Africans, young Portuguese officers came eventually to resent the inefficiency and corruption of their leaders in Lisbon. Neglected and exploited, they began to think in terms of social revolution; radicalized toward an ideology not dissimilar from that of the African liberation movements they faced, they finally turned on their own government, toppling the regime in April 1974, swinging their country sharply to the left, and abruptly forcing the abandonment of the long-lived dream of a greater Lusitanian empire. In September 1974, Portuguese Guinea was granted formal independence as Guinea-Bissau. The next year, the Cape Verde archipelago, São Tomé and Principe islands, Mozambique, and Angola, all followed.

For Guinea-Bissau the grant of freedom was no more than ratification of an accomplished fact. By 1972, a United Nations observation team reported that approximately two-thirds of the country was already in the hands of Cabral's liberation movement with Portuguese garrisons limited increasingly to the port of Bissau and other towns. That same year a national assembly was formed after a general election throughout the unoccupied areas, and in October 1973, Guinea-Bissau declared its independence. This action came only a few months after the assassination of Cabral by a disgruntled follower with the help of Portuguese connivance, a fate that had also befallen Eduardo Mondlane, the FRELIMO leader in 1969.

In Mozambique, Mondlane's FRELIMO nevertheless continued its campaigning—forcing the colonial government to commit large numbers of troops in response to hit-and-run raids, rocket attacks on convoys, or mining of paths and roads. Though these tactics yielded little territorial control, they produced their desired result in the endless, expensive war that eventually brought disillusionment and revolution in Lisbon. Mondlane's death, although probably caused by dissention within FRELIMO, resulted in no important schism as the liberation movement came under the control of Samora Machel, leader of FRELIMO's more radically Marxist wing. When independence came in the summer of 1975, it was Machel who was sworn in as first president of an independent Mozambique.

In Angola, the path to independence was a good deal more circuitous. Although the new revolutionary government in Portugal was ready to evacuate the territory at mutual convenience, there was a serious problem of orderly succession. Initially, the Portuguese encouraged coalition among the three national movements of UPA, MPLA, and UNITA, suggesting a joint Angolan-Portuguese transitional regime to be established in Luanda. Twice a coalition was formed and twice it collapsed. When, in November 1975, the Portuguese finally withdrew as agreed, they did so from a badly divided country where civil war had replaced the older anticolonialist struggle.

Such circumstances were a guarantee for instability and an invitation to external intervention. At independence, the MPLA held only Luanda city and a narrow corridor running eastward toward Zaire, Holden Roberto and UPA were dominant in the Bakongo north, and Savimbi's UNITA ranged across the Ovimbundu plains to the south. Of the three, the Liberation Movement (MPLA) of Agostinho Neto appeared weakest, but on the eve of the Portuguese departure, the MPLA seized the port of Luanda as prelude to a rapid military buildup through the introduction of Cuban soldiers, Soviet technicians, and Communist-bloc arms. Despite subsequent infusions of American supplies and direct intervention by South African troops, the Cuban-Soviet presence quickly proved decisive. By February 1976, the UPA and UNITA opposition had been routed, the oil-producing enclave of Cabinda secured, and Neto's MPLA recognized as the legitimate government of Angola by the Organization of African Unity and a growing number of nations both in and out of Africa.

For Angola the end of Portuguese rule was only the beginning of new tribulations. Refusing to accept MPLA legitimacy, Savimbi and UNITA instituted a guerrilla action that quickly escalated into civil war. With the help of clandestine and often overt material and troop support by South Africa, and supplemented by American aid particularly after 1986, Savimbi was able to force a stalemate war on the Angolan government, despite heavy Soviet aid and the continued presence of some 50,000 Cuban troops.

In 1988, however, a settlement seemed to be in the making. Brokered by the United States with apparent Soviet acquiescence, a pact was signed between South Africa, Angola, and Cuba calling for a phased evacuation of Cuban troops. The withdrawal was tied to independence for Namibia based upon UN-supervised free elections, part of a larger regional settlement urged by a number of African nations. In June 1989 President J.E. dos Santos, who had succeeded Neto on the latter's death in 1979, signed an accord with the UNITA insurgents providing for a cease-fire to their twelve-year civil war. By the end of 1990, however, little progress had been made toward a settlement. Mutual suspicion between Savimbi's UNITA and the MPLA government remained the chief obstacle, each side fearful that the other might ultimately prevail, each determined to maintain its own position of power.

Civil war was also the fate of independent Mozambique. In 1976 an anti-government organization, the Mozambiquan National Resistance (RENAMO) instituted guerrilla warfare against the government that has caused widespread loss of life and property and greatly complicated plans for economic development. Formed originally by the white Rhodesian state during the 1970s and subsequently given covert support by South Africa, RENAMO, like UNITA, has underscored the basic instability of many newly independent states. In 1989 talks were proposed by the Mozambican government, the purpose to bring an end to the hostilities so costly to a land already mired in poverty. As in Angola, however, progress was slow as the conflict continued unresolved into 1991.

From Rhodesia to Zimbabwe

The collapse of Portugal's African empire changed the whole balance of power in the south; indeed, it threw open no less a question than the future survival for white governments in southern Africa. Nowhere was this shift of fortune more apparent than in Rhodesia.

At the time, Ian Smith's Unilateral Declaration of Independence of November 1965 (UDI) had seemed audacious in concept and uncertain in consequence, yet its immediate disabilities were few. The British government declared the UDI action illegal and economic pressure was applied by the United Nations in 1966 and 1968 in the form of trade and travel embargoes. A ban was placed on the sale of oil to Rhodesia and a number of her products, notably tobacco and chrome, were prohibited to United Nations member states. Briefly,

Rhodesian exports sagged, but her minerals and other goods continued in worldwide demand, and her trade quickly revived, albeit in clandestine form. Oil imports flowed freely from South Africa; even the faint prospect of military chastisement vanished when Britain declined to back her diplomacy with force.

Force was applied in sporadic and largely ineffective form from another quarter, however, as guerrillas based in Zambia and the FRELIMO-controlled areas of Mozambique instituted occasional forays along the northern and eastern Rhodesian borders. These forces were recruited from membership in exile of the Zimbabwe African People's Union (ZAPU) and the Zimbabwe African National Union (ZANU), their respective leaders, Joshua Nkomo and Reverend Ndabaningi Sithole, still in detention in Rhodesia, their mutual rivalry momentarily submerged in the Front for the Liberation of Zimbabwe, a joint guerrilla effort formed in 1971.

Apparently the combination of sanctions and guerrillas was sufficiently vexing for Smith's Rhodesian Front government to bring forth a renewed effort at settlement with the British, and a tentative agreement was reached in November 1971, that would have ended UDI and brought the eventual achievement of African majority rule. The plan called for the end of sanctions and the introduction of constitutional changes charting a slow advance toward political power for Africans. It also required approval by Rhodesian people as a whole, and on this qualification the proposal ultimately collapsed. While white Rhodesians voted overwhelming acquiescence, black reaction was negative. In part, the black view reflected the exertions of a new political figure, Bishop Abel Muzorewa, who founded the African National Council in 1971 expressly to oppose the settlement. The prospect of any quick transfer of power was anathema to the European electorate and essential to the Africans; hence, on the eve of the Portuguese collapse Rhodesia remained much as she had at the time of UDI—enduring international sanctions and censure, refusing any rapid accommodation of black political power, and combating increasingly insistent guerrilla activity through harsh controls over the population in the affected border areas.

The Portuguese army revolt of 1974 forever altered the status quo. With the independence of Mozambique and Angola, Rhodesia found herself at once surrounded by unfriendly African nations, her 250,000 whites confronted by a domestic black population of 6.8 million, her only outlet to the sea through South Africa where the government of Prime Minister John Vorster was pressing for action that would secure some form of peaceful coexistence in place of an inevitable racial conflict. Reluctantly in 1974, Ian Smith released all political prisoners, repealed the ban on ZANU and ZAPU, and began to think of what he had proclaimed unthinkable "in my lifetime"—black power in Rhodesia.

Indeed, the circumstances left little alternative. Rhodesia's white population, already losing 10,000 annually through emigration, could not indefinitely sustain itself in a guerrilla war wherein Rhodesian government forces won most battles but took casualties leading to an ultimate loss of the war. Economically, the country had also come to suffer heavy damage, caused by the continued sanctions on Rhodesian trade by an increasingly hostile world community. Sanctions could be circumvented with ingenuity, but the process was costly, an estimated 10 percent of the country's gross domestic product. To this burden was added the global slump of the late 1970s, as well as the constant financial drain of the shooting war.

By 1975 ZANU, or its guerrilla component, had come under the leadership of Robert Mugabe, a Shona and former schoolteacher, and a professed Marxist, who had been jailed for subversive activities in the 1960s but who was released in the 1974 amnesty, only to devote his time to surreptitious recruitment of guerrillas billeted and trained in Mozambique. Unlike Bishop Muzorewa, Mugabe became convinced that nothing but armed insurrection would bring down the Smith government; his forces, which soon rose to an army of 18,000, rapidly intensified the war with strikes from Mozambique that carried ever deeper into Rhodesia while inflicting heavy losses in life, property, and morale.

ZANU's founder and nominal head, Ndabaningi Sithole, remained in Rhodesia as, for a time, did the ZAPU leader, Joshua Nkomo. Nkomo was persuaded to try for reform from within, but by 1976, like Mugabe, he had left the country to direct guerrilla action, his ZAPU forces striking from bases in Zambia.

Together Nkomo and Mugabe joined in the Patriotic Front, an alliance of the former's largely Ndebele guerrillas and Mugabe's Shona contingents. To an extent it was a marriage of convenience between two potential rivals for national political power, each drawing support from different sections of Rhodesia's African population, Nkomo with a record of many years devoted to the nationalist cause, but Mugabe directing guerrillas who were to bear the brunt of the fighting that eventually forced capitulation of the white government.

In 1978 Smith announced a new constitution based upon the sharing of power between white and black, but there was much skepticism at home and abroad since the arrangement reserved substantial political and economic privileges for Rhodesian whites—for example, a guarantee of parliamentary seats, cabinet posts, and property rights along with administrative control of the army and police. Elections held in April 1979 produced a government with Muzorewa as prime minister, and Smith as a member of the new cabinet. The bishop hailed his accession to power as a genuine shift toward the concept of majority rule and racial cooperation, but it was soon apparent that he could not direct his own government in the face of Smith's constitutional and administrative restraints. Denounced by the Patriotic Front and unable to gain diplomatic recognition from any foreign quarter, Muzorewa's ministry failed as well in its attempt to end the economic sanctions against what was now officially called Rhodesia-Zimbabwe, or to secure an end to the fighting. It had become increasingly apparent that there could be no political solution without the participation of the Patriotic Front. It was also clear that such participation would spell the end of white rule in Rhodesia.

Ian Smith had at last run out of options. Determined guerrilla action had demonstrated the incapacity of an African country governed by a small European minority, even of a compromise administration that offered at least the illusion of power sharing.

Despite the 1965 Unilateral Declaration of Independence, Rhodesia was still technically a British colony. In September 1979, the British government called a conference designed to settle the fourteen-year dispute over the future of Rhodesia, an invitation that was accepted by the war-weary Muzorewa government as well as by the Patriotic Front, prodded by neighboring countries like Mozambique and Zambia that had suffered much physical damage and financial drain from their support for the guerrillas. There followed almost four months of delicate but wearing negotiation which culminated in December 1979 with acceptance of a cease-fire and new constitution based upon majority rule. Rhodesia reverted temporarily to its status as a colony, Britain established a transitional government that supervised the cease-fire and the ensuing political campaigning, and in February 1980, Rhodesians, black and white, went to the polls, giving an absolute majority to the party of Robert Mugabe. Two months later Zimbabwe became an independent nation with Mugabe as its first prime minister.

The election was a satisfying conclusion to the long and bitter history of Rhodesia's racial strife, substituting a political for a military solution and banishing at last special privilege based upon ethnic prejudice. Nevertheless there were initial fears over the possible direction of the new government. His power established, Mugabe thus moved quickly to placate the white population and to reassure potential foreign investors. Zimbabwe was well endowed with a diversified economy and a skilled labor force, but much of its assets, particularly its productive agriculture, were European owned and operated and its future development remained dependent upon favorable foreign loans. There was concern both inside and outside over Mugabe's Marxism and African hunger for quick rewards to a successful revolutionary struggle. Mugabe's initial efforts aimed therefore at restraining his own followers in order that their eventual prosperity might be ensured.

There were other disturbing signs, however, that quickly emerged from another quarter. These had already been perceived in the pattern of voting, not for the whites who were clearly overwhelmed, but between groups within the black population. Muzorewa's negligible support reflected the damage of his association with Ian Smith, but the vote between Mugabe and Nkomo was ominous in portent. The former had the solid backing of the Shona people, some 80 percent of the population, while Nkomo appealed only to the 18 percent Ndebele proportion, neither candidate showing significant strength outside his own region. The result was a bitter disappointment for the ZAPU leader after the long years of struggle to realize an independent African nation.

Nkomo immediately agreed to join the Mugabe cabinet, but resentment smoldered, doubtless on both sides, recalling earlier years when Shona and Ndebele fought each other in the time of Lobengula.

Within two years of his election, Mugabe had dismissed Nkomo from the cabinet, citing acts of lawlessness on the part of former ZAPU guerrillas, allegedly with Nkomo's acquiescence. Mugabe charged Nkomo followers with potential disloyalty to his government; for Nkomo the prime minister was guilty of utilizing force to establish total political power, as government army units occupied Matebeleland, often employing rough tactics in the search for those who were officially designated as dissidents. From the government point of view the victims were lawless former guerrillas waging renewed tribal war. To the Ndebele they were innocent victims of atrocities by an arbitrary dictatorship. In 1983, Nkomo fled the country temporarily citing a threat to his personal safety.

Fortunately the mistrust was not allowed to escalate. In 1987 Mugabe and Nkomo agreed to merge their two parties as a symbol of a united nation. Although this action seemed to assure Mugabe's ascendancy, for the time being at any rate divisive tribalism had been set aside and Zimbabwe was free to turn to problems of economic and social betterment, at least a nominally united nation.

Namibia—The Last African Colony

If Portugal had been the key to white power in southern Africa, the South African Republic was the force that dominated the affairs and the fate of Namibia.

Namibia, the name adopted by the United Nations in 1968 to identify the territory of South-West Africa, was another of Africa's anomalies—a diversity of mutually exclusive or antagonistic peoples, brown, black, and white, thinly inhabiting a vast stretch of quasi-desert twice the size of California; a region of surface poverty that masked mineral riches in diamonds, copper, lead, and zinc; a geographic entity of boundaries drafted originally in far-off Europe, including an incongruous 300-mile panhandle created only to satisfy the geopolitical concerns of a one-time German chancellor.

In its people Namibia has been more various than in its land —the greater part an arid plateau suitable mainly for grazing. Indigenous were the San (Bushman) hunters, but by 1000 A.D. Bantu-speaking, iron-using farmers had arrived to establish themselves in the better watered, partly wooded pastures of the northern districts. Chief among these were the Ovambo but these people were supplemented eventually by warlike Herero pastoralists who filtered through the Ovambo and settled in the drier steppes farther south. By the seventeenth and eighteenth centuries varieties of Khoikhoi cattle herders were coming up from the Cape region, driven north by Boer expansion but bringing with them horses, guns, and substantial proportions of white blood.

European colonialism caused European settlement too, first in the form of German farmers, missionaries, and officials at the end of the nineteenth century, then Afrikaners from South Africa, particularly after the Second World War. Today, the overall Namibian population of some 1.3 million is approximately 78 percent black African, 12 percent European, and about 10 percent Khoikhoi or mixed. The Ovambo are far and away the most numerous numbering approximately 600,000 (46 percent of the total population). Of several other Bantu-speaking groups, the modest Herero numbering under 100,000 still show the effects of the disastrous German pogrom of the early 1900s. Afrikaners form the majority of 120,000 whites, although there is a substantial community of Germans along with some English-speaking Europeans. The Khoikhoi are similarly divided, most notably between the Nama and the Rehoboth Basters, the latter a hybrid population of European and Khoikhoi, as are more recently arrived Cape Coloureds. Racial variety does not make for overpopulation, however; the average density of the country is only about two people to a square mile.

Both before and after the Second World War, South Africa dominated her South-West African territory, politically and economically. It was South African investment that developed the pastoral industry, and converted fishing into a major source of export earnings; by 1970 Namibia sold half her exports and bought fully four-fifths of her imports from her powerful neighbor. Railway, road, and harbor construction, moreover, were the result of South African initiative and were integrated into South Africa's own system of transportation. Similarly, South Africa managed police, defense, and customs for many years, and by the late 1960s was administering mining, health, education, and labor relations as well. The local legislature at the territorial capital of Windhock possessed little authority, much of its function already encumbered by the South African parliament to which South-West Africa had been given direct representation in 1949.

For South Africa, then, it was elementary logic to fashion a homelands program in South-West Africa similar to her own domestic policy of separate development. Such a program, it was felt, would not only assist in reinforcing the apartheid orthodoxy but would also facilitate control of the territory's many ethnic divisions, and prepare South-West Africa for a possible absorption into the South African Republic proper. The organization of Ovamboland in 1968 as the first homeland was thus part of a plan to establish six or more so-called native nations for Herero, Nama, Damara, Baster, and others, their total area an estimated 40 percent of the territory as against approximately 44 percent to be set aside for the exclusive use of the European population.

Denying any United Nations jurisdiction over Namibia, South Africa was jolted from any possible complacency by the fall of the Portuguese African empire in 1975. Faced with new and changing conditions, the South African Republic evolved a policy that was both more supple and more subtle, employing force along with subterfuge while concealing any predictable objectives for the ultimate disposition of the Namibian territory.

In 1975 South Africa began its new policy with the formation of a multiethnic political coalition, an ostensible first step toward a federated state designed to become independent by the end of the decade. This so-called Democratic Turnhalle Alliance emerged stillborn, however, for it lacked Ovambo participation, particularly by the South-West African People's Organization (SWAPO), a militant nationalist grouping formed in 1960 of largely Ovambo membership. During the 1960s under the leadership of Sam Nujoma, SWAPO had inaugurated a guerrilla liberation action, operating from bases in Angola. In 1976 the United Nations General Assembly recognized SWAPO as the sole representative of Namibia and endorsed its struggle for freedom. Two years later the U.N. Security Council approved Resolution 435, proposing free elections for all the peoples of Namibia to be supervised by the United Nations, a proposition to which South Africa gave grudging agreement in principle while making no specific moves toward its implementation.

The more belligerent side of South African policy consisted of military action, chiefly in southern Angola where it combined support for UNITA insurgents with strikes against SWAPO bases and those Cuban forces assisting the Angolan government of President dos Santos. By 1982 South Africa had begun to insist that any implementation of U.N. Resolution 435 would require concurrent evacuation of Cuban troops from Angola, a linkage originally suggested by the United States government, intent upon offsetting Soviet influence in southern Africa. There followed several years of inconclusive military skirmishing and unsuccessful attempts by South African to establish an interim Namibian government without SWAPO participation.

In 1988, however, a solution was forthcoming. The regional settlement that had brought an uneasy truce to Angola yielded much more successful results for Namibia. In 1989 the United Nations supervised elections for representatives to a national assembly, their initial purpose to write a constitution leading to an independent Namibia. The election was contested by a number of political groups, including SWAPO which gained only a moderate majority of assembly seats, thus assuring that SWAPO would not dominate the assembly. The resultant constitution called for a democratically chosen government complete with a bill of rights, press and speech freedom, and an independent judiciary. Independence came without incident in 1990 under a government headed by Sam Nujoma as president.

The Afrikaner Laager

The collapse of Portugal put an end to South Africa's hope for a protective shield of friendly white communities to the north, a comfortable buffer to complement Pretoria's black African diplomacy which dominated the satellite

Robert Mugabe,
President of Zimbabwe

AP/Wide World Photos

Sam Nujoma,
President of Namibia

United Nations

The gravestone reads:

BANTU STEPHEN BIKO,
HONORARY PRESIDENT
BLACK PEOPLE'S CONVENTION.
BORN 18 – 12 – 1946.
DIED 12 – 9 – 1977.
ONE AZANIA ONE NATION.

Apartheid's victim

United Nations

Squatter shanties, Cape Town   *United Nations*

Nelson Mandela   *United Nations*

states of Botswana, Lesotho, and Swaziland while cultivating such independent nations as Malawi, Ivory Coast, or Senegal. In its external policy the Vorster government was ready to endure neutral, if not friendly, African neighbors, their economic and political stability to a considerable extent reliant upon South African sufferance. It was this strategy that caused Vorster to urge Ian Smith to accept the inevitability of a black majority government in Rhodesia, to encourage the Turnhalle coalition in Namibia, and to give support to the UNITA movement of Jonas Savimbi.

In Mozambique South Africa pursued a similar carrot and stick strategy. While maintaining its support of the RENAMO rebels, South Africa also provided technicians and continued to remit a substantial portion of the wages paid Mozambican miners at the outdated and deflated official price of gold. The gold payments provided Machel's government with a substantial profit and South Africa with a grateful, and more particularly, a dependent neighbor.

Whatever its particular effectiveness, South African foreign policy was designed to gain time—time to establish an overwhelming national strength in resistance to external hostility, time to encourage economic growth and domestic prosperity that would blunt the point of internal African opposition to apartheid. It was hoped economic growth would end in self-sufficiency, but where it began was with a dependence upon world supplies of investment capital and technology, of weaponry and industrial energy. In this respect South Africa held many important assets. Not only did she serve as the source of the free world's gold supply, she also possessed substantial reserves of other minerals much in demand, including coal, iron ore, uranium, industrial diamonds, copper, and chrome. Nevertheless, gold revenues were dependent upon international money markets over which South Africa had no control, and development required investments of a scale beyond the nation's domestic financial capacities. South Africa would have to rely on vast infusions of foreign capital for such facilities as power, water, and transport, capital from sources increasingly critical of South Africa's racial policies.

Even more disturbing than the massive needs in foreign capital, trade, and technology, however, was the nagging awareness that, despite its considerable industrial sophistication, South Africa was neither wealthy nor developed, that its apparent affluence was illusory and based upon exploited black labor, that its industry was not competitive in world markets, that its international dependency might prove permanent should the domestic economy remain too small, unable itself to capitalize proposed plans for domestic growth.

If national economic advance stood in danger, the causes appeared to lie squarely with the Afrikaner government and it supporting white population. Successful development rested ultimately on a large and healthy domestic market, and an attractive international posture, both of which appeared to be fading from sight. Whatever the allure of South Africa's minerals and the appeal of her investment possibilities, world opinion was bound to depress the availability of international loans, to encourage demands for economic sanctions, and to dampen the interest of large transnational corporations.

Afrikaner policy nevertheless remained unmoved, designed to protect and preserve white privilege. There was considerable debate among Afrikaners along conservative-liberal lines, among those intent upon maintaining the status quo and those who argued for flexibility in racial relations. Neither side disputed the principal axiom of white power; the question was how to maintain ultimate control while accommodating the thrust of African nationalism. Since the conservatives controlled the National Party and the government, theirs remained the prevailing policy, based on the concept of racial segregation through separate homelands.

The government moved forward inexorably to implement its program. In October 1976, the Transkei was led to independence by its prime minister, Chief Kaiser Matanzima, and a year later Transkei was followed by the Bophuthatswana Bantustan, a territory comprising a half dozen scattered tracts located near the Botswana border. By the end of 1980, two others had achieved independence — Venda, a tiny enclave of mainly Shona-related people in northern Transvaal, and the Xhosa state of Ciskei located near the town of New London. Others appeared less determined, particularly Kwazulu, where its elected leader, Chief Gatsha Buthelezi, attacked the homelands program as divisive and refused to apply for independence. In the urban centers of South Africa, black opinion was largely hostile, regarding the homelands as irrelevant to their condition and unresponsive to their needs. In the countryside the rural population dominated by local chiefs seemed favorably disposed, and it seemed possible that all homelands, with the Zulu exception, might eventually take the road to independence.

There was no mistaking government pressures for sovereign homelands. Over the years more than half the Transkei budget was supplied by Pretoria, and South Africa also supported substantial programs for buildings, roads, and schools. An analogous situation applied to the other "national states" which, in addition to direct budgetary support, derived substantial capital infusions from South Africa for public construction or industrial estates. Political and civil rights also came with local independence, but homeland citizenship, written into the enabling legislation, also explicitly denied South African citizenship to all Xhosa, Tswana, and Venda, whether or not they happened to reside in the newly created states. Indeed the South African government went further, announcing that rights to start businesses and to sign long-term leaseholds in South African black townships like Soweto were permissible only for those who possessed homeland citizenship.

In 1978 John Vorster was succeeded as premier by his minister for defense, P. W. Botha. Botha was as determined as his predecessor to maintain the system of apartheid, but continuity now called for flexibility and a subtlety of execution in place of the more rigid orthodoxy of the Verwoerd and Vorster years. As Botha took office apartheid was already under strain, both through its own contradictions and from the hostility of an increasingly unsympathetic world community. How could white supremacy be sustained in the face of vast changes, both national and international?

Within South Africa the economy had become sluggish and inflation was on the rise. The homelands were proving expensive and inefficient, sapping the prosperity of the nation and failing to provide the labor controls promised. At the same time the African population, rising in numbers, was gaining political strength and purchasing power, its unions illegal but flourishing, its labor vital to industrial expansion. Moreover, the Afrikaner population had become restive, those on the right fearing for their institutionalized privileges, on the left searching for fresh solutions to growing problems. The need for new policies had become evident.

Botha tackled these matters in several ways, his essential tactic to divide apartheid's opponents and to repair its tarnished image. One major move was political, a constitutional reform shrewdly designed to grant nominal governmental representation to Asian and Coloured populations, the object to ally them with white power while weaning them away from African political aspirations. In 1984 a new constitution went into effect calling for a parliament with three chambers, for whites, for Coloureds, and for Asians, and a powerful executive president elected by a white-dominated college not responsible to the legislatures. Expressly excluded were the Africans, for, according to Afrikaner logic, they were in the process of becoming citizens of their own national states, the homelands, and it was there that they were expected to express their black political interests.

For the African there were economic and social concessions. The system of petty apartheid was dismantled, thus largely abandoning racial segregation in public facilities. More important, most job reservations were discontinued and black unions legitimized along with the principle of collective bargaining. To a large extent this merely recognized the reality of growing black economic power, based on union membership that had risen to over one million by the mid-1980s. Union demands for better wages had been singularly successful, for example, the differential between black and white workers in gold mining dropping from over 20-1 in 1971 to 5.5-1 by 1982. Finally the pass laws were in large measure abandoned along with the system that relegated blacks to homeland ghettos. These were major changes but they had no effect upon political matters which remained firmly in the hands of the white population.

There were concurrent moves in international affairs, once again to neutralize the foes of apartheid and brighten the image of the South African state. Throughout southern Africa a combination of military and economic persuasion kept overt opposition in check. Military support for rebel groups in Mozambique and Angola, South African troops in Namibia and occasional commando raids into neighboring territories reminded bordering states of their weakness, while economic pressures compelled discretion in dealing with the South African colossus. South Africa's railways dominated regional transport, its industry provided jobs vital to national economies, while Swaziland,

Lesotho, and Botswana were locked into a customs union that offered economic stability as a price for fiscal control. From Zambian copper exports to mining jobs for Mozambicans the so-called front line states were forced to acknowledge need for South Africa's cooperation, aware that it could be unilaterally removed at any moment.

In its relations toward a wider world, South Africa possessed less leverage and its exertions were consequently less successful. For its own reasons the United States continued to give support to Angolan insurgents and Great Britain refrained from adopting economic measures against the apartheid government, but increasingly world opinion rejected the argument that South African comprised a community of cooperating independent states black and white. Beginning with Transkei no nation gave official recognition to "independent homelands," while a growing antiapartheid movement gathered momentum, especially within the United States, exerting pressure that withheld investment and withdrew corporate presence from a South African economy already under stress.

Botha's new flexibility appeared not to be working. While international resistance grew, internal problems multiplied. The three-headed parliament was largely ignored by Asians and Coloureds. Africans increasingly confronted apartheid with violence, strikes, and boycotts. Bloody demonstrations became a daily diet on television broadcasts throughout the world, featuring a police state under siege. In 1985 these broadcasts were forbidden, but as violence continued to escalate, the government declared a state of emergency the following year. The system of apartheid had entered a new era.

"Freedom in Our Lifetime"

Over the years South Africa had maintained its dominance, mainly by force much less through persuasion. Both inside and outside the Republic blacks steadily lost their illusions that the South African authorities were serious about genuine reform through mutual citizenship or power sharing. Consequently the earlier strategies of the African National Congress based upon nonviolence and constitutional procedure were abandoned step by step, leaving violence as the only remaining agent of reform. Such a view was implicit in the campaigns of sabotage and terrorism sponsored by the militant wings of the African National Congress and the Pan-Africanist Congress during the 1960s, and it was stated explicitly by Nelson Mandela during his Rivonia trial testimony in 1964.

Whatever its theoretical attraction, violence was not a recourse that could be sustained over protracted periods. What emerged in South Africa in the years following the enunciation of apartheid in 1948 was a pattern of alternating quiet and violence, some outbursts planned, others seemingly spontaneous, and all escalating on a growing curve of frustration and fury. The first manifestation of this cycle showed itself in the wave of strikes, boycotts, and civil disobedience that marked the years immediately following the Second World War, a transitional watershed between the orderly protests of the prewar years and the disorder that followed. These initial disturbances were eventually contained through massive arrests and judicial proceedings, the ensuing interval of calm only to be shattered in 1960 by the pass law demonstrations organized by Robert Sobukwe that led to the massacre at Sharpeville and the emergence of the militant movements of Poqo and Spear of the Nation.

Once again the authorities were able to clamp down the lid of police containment, once again respite was temporary, broken with sudden violence in June 1976. At the African township of Soweto on the outskirts of Johannesburg, rioting erupted without warning, the spark a relatively minor irritation—a regulation requiring the Afrikaans language as a medium of instruction in the schools. The consequences were major—a series of racial conflagrations that exploded intermittently over a six-month period at various points across the country, including the Johannesburg townships, Pretoria, Durban, Cape Town, and a number of the African universities, outbursts that reflected a spontaneous spasm of rage over conditions long endured.

If there were leaders, they belonged to a newer, younger generation, their identity eluding the perplexed security administration that had been so certain of its ability to detect trouble before it emerged. Alternatively, the spontaneity of the uprisings may have been stimulated by the Black Consciousness movement that had coalesced in the late 1960s with its stress on the values of an African identity, its palpable manifestation in the South African Students Organization (SASO) founded in 1968 and the Black Peoples Convention that was formed four years later.

The South African Students Organization, led by its president, Steve Biko, specifically rejected cooperation with whites, who, it was felt, had dominated African nationalism in the past and who, in any case, by their nature could not understand the experience and aspirations of black people. SASO emphasized the achievements of traditional African heroes like Shaka and Moshoeshoe in preference to the moderate, cooperative, but unsuccessful efforts of more recent leaders like those who had directed the affairs of the African National Congress over the years. For its part, the ANC driven into exile with the Pan-Africanist Congress, escalated its militancy, training young guerrillas in Mozambique for the coming armed intervention, and, like SASO, stressing African consciousness as well as cooperation with Coloureds and Asians, in a union of racially oppressed peoples.

This more radicalized trend, propelled in large measure by urban youth, left the moderate position primarily to Chief Buthelezi. His was difficult ground. A leading Zulu spokesman, he urged economic development for the homelands, yet he attacked the Bantustan system and refused independence for Kwazulu. Speaking to whites as well as to blacks, but as a major African leader, he called for a united South Africa governed by majority rule on behalf of the people of all races. His position scarcely endeared him to the authorities, but he was also rejected by those Africans dedicated to armed revolution, and others caught up in the mutual antipathy between Xhosa and Zulu.

Still confident in the effectiveness of its police, the government gave no ground. Both the ANC and PAC were infiltrated by informers, their efforts to slip terrorists into the country stymied by quick action of security forces. Leaders of various nationalist groups were detained or harried into ineffectualness. Nelson Mandela still languished in his Robben Island prison. Sobukwe, jailed in 1960, released, then "banned" in 1969, remained under house arrest in Kimberley until his death in 1978. Biko was banned in 1973 and constantly harassed by police until detained in August 1977. A month later he died of injuries sustained in police custody. Overall the toll of the Soweto uprisings was fearsome—approximately 600 dead, some 6000 arrested, many to be detained or later tried, convicted, and jailed.

In September 1984 chronic unrest abruptly escalated as a protest at Sharpeville against rent increases erupted in violence, claiming twenty-nine lives. Slowly the violence spread, engulfing the districts around Johannesburg and Port Elizabeth, then extending to other centers such as Cape Town and Durban. Mobs of rock throwing blacks invaded and set fire to buildings, chiefly dwellings, increasingly turning their rage on fellow blacks such as policemen or township officials regarded as government stooges. Black against black was also marked by tribal animosity—clashes between urban radicals of often Xhosa origins and cohorts of Inkatha, the political arm of Chief Buthelezi's Zulu movement. Funeral for victims shot by police became occasions for political expression, an expression of mass discontent that seemed as universal as it was spontaneous and undirected, for no central leadership emerged, not from the ANC, not from the unions, not from any particular organization.

Month after month the disturbances continued and intensified, paralleled by paralyzing labor unrest, for example, over one thousand strikes in 1987 by unions of growing power and political radicalism. In 1985 the government declared a state of emergency around Johannesburg and the eastern Cape Province, and began a process of banning, both institutions and individuals (usually house arrest with visitors and public expression forbidden), to supplement the thousands of arrests that had become a routine occurrence.

Government action included persuasion as well as force. Relocation and influx control had been suspended in 1985, and pass laws abolished the following year. Certain leading African blacks were treated with discretion, for example, Bishop Desmond Tutu, head of the South African Anglican church, 1984 Nobel Peace Prize recipient, and frequent critic of the government. Even Nelson Mandela, still imprisoned, received increasingly delicate treatment, and there were hints of his release—a dangerous move, for Mandela, widely regarded throughout the world as the primary leader of the black cause, was still nominally committed to violence as the only recourse to his people.

The government moved with circumspection, however, trying to hold a middle ground between black demands and the growing alarm of right wing white segregationists outraged at what they regarded as cowardly abandonment of the apartheid principle. Business leaders were said to urge the end of apartheid as economically untenable, as foreign pressures mounted. Particularly distressing was the "disinvestment" campaign, originating in the United States with its strong and active civil rights movement.

Buffeted by such diverse forces, the basic government posture remained firm as police action continued without letup. In 1988 there was renewed banning of many organizations including the Congress of South African Trade Unions and the United Democratic Front, a multiracial antiapartheid group formed in 1983 as a rallying point for political action. The cost of militant opposition came high. In 1989 more than 4,000 deaths, mostly black, had been reported. The irony was that many casualties resulted, not from clashes with the authorities but between blacks, once again led by the chronic violence between Inkatha and Xhosa supporters of the United Democratic Front.

In 1989 there came a sudden and fundamental change in the course of events. President Botha abruptly retired, to be replaced as National Party chief and Republic president by F. W. de Klerk, a political figure said to be ready to talk with black leadership about providing the African population with some form of satisfactory political voice. All at once the unthinkable had become a distinct possibility—the dismantling of apartheid leading at last to that longstanding African objective, "Freedom in Our Lifetime."

A Turning Point

Once in authority President de Klerk moved quickly, implementing his promise to replace the system of apartheid with a government in which all races might share. Political prisoners were freed, most particularly the African National Congress (ANC) leaders, Nelson Mandela and Walter Sisulu. The Congress and other antiapartheid groups were restored to legal status. The 1986 state of emergency was lifted, except in Natal where ethnic strife still raged. Responding to de Klerk's pledge, the South African parliament in 1991 scrapped major foundations of the apartheid system. Repealed were the Natives Land Act of 1913 that had dictated racial segregation of land, the Group Areas Act defining neighborhoods segregated by race, and the Population Registration Act, that cornerstone of apartheid, by which all South Africans were classified at birth by race. Radically altered was the Internal Security Act of 1976, eliminating or severely limiting sections that had permitted indefinite "preventive detention" for purposes of interrogation, provided for house arrest, authorized the banning of individuals and organizations, and prohibited political publications by government critics.

In a largely successful effort to ease international economic pressures, sanctions in particular, de Klerk journeyed to the United States, Europe, and a number of African countries to reassure the world of the seriousness of his intentions. Seeking to assuage the fears of the white South African electorate, he promised an eventual constitution that would protect white interests while extending political rights to blacks. Despite these concessions, however, the government remained firmly in control, the police active, and, according to ANC accusations, holding more than 1,000 political prisoners in custody.

The de Klerk administration was obliged to tread softly, to yield to black aspirations without losing the backing of its white supporters. Black leadership was under similar constraints, for among Africans there were numerous divisions to be reconciled. Aside from the deep cleavage between Buthelezi's Inkatha movement and the ANC, there were other black groups to be taken into account, for example, the Pan-Africanist Congress (PAC) and the African trade unions as well as factions within the ANC. Mandela agreed to abandon the ANC policy of armed struggle, but he and other senior Congress leaders had difficulty controlling the ANC rank and file who elevated him to the ANC presidency in 1991 but demanded an aggressive policy maintaining pressure on the South African government. One major point of contention involved the nature of the government while a new constitution was in the making. The ANC demanded there be an interim government representing all races, while de Klerk insisted that his government would remain in power until the new constitution was adopted.

By mid-1991 many changes had taken place and apartheid was finished, but more changes were in the offing and it was difficult to predict their shape and direction. There were conflicting factors at work, some signaling change, others resisting any move to a new order. As might be expected, the thrust of change came mainly from Africans. Increasingly they were a force in the land, in their ever-growing proportion of the population, in economic power through rising income and greater control of skilled as well as unskilled labor, in the political strength of effective public agitation. Other influences came from abroad—sanctions and disinvestment that bruised a South African economy already weakened by its own sluggish behavior.

There were also pressures from within the white population, more particularly among Afrikaners, many of whom had abandoned their farm life with its rural conservatism to share in the country's industrial and commercial affairs, joining the South African business community in the realization that apartheid was economically inefficient, an anachronism in the modern world. This was an attitude increasingly shared among Afrikaner intellectuals, a fundamental shift signaled by the Afrikaner Broederbond which in 1990 discarded its traditional support of apartheid, backing de Klerk in his call for a multiracial constitution, arguing that benefit for one race could only come through benefit of all. There was more than philosophy in the new Broederbond position. The apartheid system was proving itself expensive and unworkable, consuming some 15 percent of the national budget and providing few returns on investment. The homelands were a good example of failed policy—sustained at the cost of $2 billion a year, they were corrupt and inefficient, lacking international recognition, incapable of supporting their own populations or of containing the population flow to the cities.

Nevertheless apartheid was not without its supporters. De Klerk had come to power following an election victory, but the National Party majority had been seriously eroded and it was said that de Klerk lacked support of the security and police forces, even of members in his own cabinet. A strong conservative backlash was signaled by the rise of the Conservative Party led by Andries Treurnicht, but serious divisions among the African population were also likely to complicate change to a new order, as violence and bloodshed marked continuing clashes by black against black.

Finally there were the imperatives of history. South Africa had lived its entire 340-year existence as a racist society. Apartheid arrived in 1948 but racial prejudice was as old as the original Cape Town colony. A sharing of political power would mean the end of centuries of white domination and economic privilege. Would a white-controlled society voluntarily concede its advantages and join hands with its black population in creating a newer, more just society? Alternatively, would it make some final move to protect and preserve its long-lived way of life? For their part, would black Africans be content to live peaceably with former white masters? Or would they choose to dominate others, perhaps using their new-found political power to gain for themselves the prosperity so long denied?

Suggestions for Further Reading

For Portuguese Africa, see Ronald H. Chilcote, *Portuguese Africa* (Englewood Cliffs, NJ: Prentice Hall, 1967). The origins of the nationalist movement in Angola are fully covered in John Marcum, *The Angolan Revolution* (Cambridge, MA: MIT Press, 1969); the revolution in Guinea-Bissau is covered in Basil Davidson, *The Liberation of Guiné* (Harmondsworth, Middlesex, and Baltimore: Penguin, 1969) which may be read in conjunction with Amilear Cabral, *Revolution in Guinea* (New York and London: Monthly Review Press, 1969). Eduardo Mondlane's *The Struggle for Mozambique* (Harmondsworth, Middlesex, and Baltimore: Penguin, 1969) may be consulted for Mozambique.

For Rhodesia to Zimbabwe there is David Martin and Phyllis Johnson, *The Struggle for Zimbabwe* (London and Boston: Faber and Faber, 1981), and Patrick O'Meara, *Rhodesia: Racial Conflict or Coexistence* (Ithaca and London: Cornell University Press, 1975). A brief survey of affairs in Namibia is Peter Duignan and L. H. Gann, *Southwest Africa-Namibia* (New York: American African Affairs Association, 1978) to be supplemented by material in the *Cambridge History of Africa*, Vol. 8 (Cambridge: University Press, 1984) edited by Michael Crowder.

Pertinent literature is a good deal richer for South Africa. See, for example, Leonard Thompson, *A History of South Africa* (New Haven and London: Yale University Press,

1990); T. R. H. Davenport, *South Africa: A Modern History*, 4th ed. (Toronto and Buffalo: University of Toronto Press, 1991; and John de St. Jorre, *A House Divided* (New York: Carnegie Endowment for International Peace, 1977). For the economic effects of apartheid there is Merle Lipton, *Capitalism and Apartheid* (Totowa, NJ, 1985). Afrikaner racial concepts are examined in Leonard Thompson, *The Political Mythology of Apartheid* (New Haven and London: Yale University Press, 1985).

25

African Cultural Independence—Ideals and Complexities

Negritude

Independence took many forms, and Africans had long understood that political freedom was but part, albeit important, of a greater whole. Europe had exercised colonial rule scarcely three-quarters of a century, yet in that time she reached out fatefully, intruding her influence on African life in diverse and subtle ways. National sovereignty, when it came, had arrived for most with relative ease. Could Europe's economic ascendancy be conquered quite so simply? More uncertain still, could Africans regain control over their own way of life; indeed, would they be able to assert their independence as black men and women in a white-dominated world?

It was an old question. many times asked; thus stated, independence became deeply psychological, rooted in long-lived racial attitudes. Africanus Horton had voiced it in the face of Europe's first imperialist ventures; later, in the years between the two world wars, poets of the Caribbean and the Harlem Renaissance had composed rhapsodies to blackness and the holy heritage of Africa, seeking to combat prejudice and achieve emotional security in racial pride. The movement was quickly picked up and transported to Paris, and there it was nourished, chiefly by expatriate blacks from the French West Indies. On the eve of the Second World War it emerged as the concept known as *negritude*, a term supplied by the Antilles poet, Aimé Césaire, that in time came for many to embody the essence of pan-Negro cultural affirmation.

In the post-war years negritude lent its weight to Africa's independence drive, in the process precipitating a debate among Africans as to its essential meaning and substance; more generally, negritude came to embody the search for true racial emancipation, in Africa, a final freeing of those real or imaginary bonds that had compelled colonial subjects to defer to Europe. It was no accident that the movement gained its greatest impetus in the French colonies, where French assimilation had extolled the virtues of French language and culture, but where the reaction, when it came, was most direct. Perhaps, too, it was not surprising that negritude drew support from cultural and intellectual activities in Paris, most particularly from the philosophy of existentialism and its chief advocate, Jean-Paul Sartre.

The existentialists saw reality in terms of individual perception, each life cycle determined by the freedom of individual choice. Such a view equating all people had much to offer the world's oppressed, including blacks come from Africa and the Americas seeking to validate their culture. Disillusioned by world war and the emptiness of Western industrial society, Paris made much of these newcomers. As early as 1921 there was critical acclaim for the West Indian René Maran and his prize-winning novel, *Batouala*, while six years later André Gide's *Voyage au Congo* echoed Maran's attack on colonialism. Black American jazz vied in vogue with the black music-hall *vedette*, Josephine Baker, and the attraction of Picasso and others to African sculpture reflected a growing public interest manifest in the large audiences at the Colonial Exposition opened in 1931. By the end of the Second World War, Sartre's preoccupation with negritude had crystallized in his celebrated essay, "Black Orpheus," appearing in 1948 as an introduction to Léopold Senghor's anthology of poetry by black and Malagasy writers.

Sartre began with the problem of individual identity — was each man free to be himself, he asked, or was he the captive of another's perception? Historically Europeans had looked down on Africans, enslaving and exploiting them, relegating them to an inferior status based on color. Eventually, the blacks came to accept the condition of their color, Sartre observed, but with negritude, racial humiliation was converted to racial pride. Like Orpheus seeking Eurydice in the underworld, the black poet descended into his own being, wrestled the serpents of European culture, and finally, triumphant, regained his Africa, his negritude.

It was but a short-lived triumph, continued Sartre. As Orpheus had lost Eurydice, the black poet embraced his negritude only to see it vanish in the act. Negritude was a necessary stage, said Sartre, an anti-racist racism, but the paradox of racism arising from its opposition was resolved through black self-abnegation leading to the ultimate synthesis of human brotherhood. "Strange road," concluded Sartre. "Offended, humiliated, the blacks probe to the most profound depths to find again their most secret pride, and when they have finally discovered it . . . by supreme generosity they abandon it." Renunciation, this act of love, was not vain. The particularism of negritude expires along with racism, but as it does, it is born again in the future universalism.

Sartre's dialectics leading to a European-African synthesis had strong appeal for Léopold Senghor, the Senegalese poet soon to become a leading African nationalist statesman. An early advocate of African cultural emancipation, Senghor also exhibited the deep mark of his European education. Like the writers of the Harlem Renaissance, Senghor was much attracted to Western achievements. For him, Western rationalism, materialism, and technology inspired awe as well as misgivings. French language and culture was a ready vehicle through which to assure the advance of Africa's peoples. Negritude must not deny, said Senghor, it must oppose; but opposition was qualified, a stage in the process of worldwide cultural synthesis.

During the nineteenth century, the West African nationalist, Edward Blyden, had suggested the complementary character of the world's races. Now, in the twentieth, Senghor revived this concept in his "Civilization of the Universal." Negritude, firmly placed in Africa, reaches out to Europe, he asserted. With its intuition it enriches Western logic. Its music softens the jangled clatter of industrial society. The power of its masks nourishes a whole generation of artists, while its supernatural insights support the philosophers and poets of surrealism. Above all, with its humanity Africa assuages the agonies of the industrialized world—"the sense of life, the joy of life, that which is daughter of rhythm, of earth forces."

Despite Senghor's intellectual leadership within the negritude movement, most of its practitioners shied away from his admiration of European civilization. Certainly it had no charms for Frantz Fanon, the Martiniquan psychiatrist whose sympathies for the Algerian independence revolution led him to expound the virtues of violence as the only response to Europe's colonialism. Freedom bestowed on former colonies gained nothing, Fanon insisted. True liberty came only with violent struggle, a cathartic that purged the shame of inferiority and left the individual with a secure self-image of human dignity.

The main thrust of negritude, however, was neither Senghor's synthesis nor Fanon's violence. More typically, it accented a straightforward African or black cultural renascence to match the movement toward political independence that was sweeping the continent. Most of its exponents were French-speaking Africans—Alioune Diop, editor and founder of the influential journal, *Présence Africaine*; the Guinean, Keita Fodeba, both politician and director of the national dance troupe, *Ballets Africains*; historians Abdoulaye Ly and Cheikh Anta Diop of Senegal and Joseph KiZerbo from Upper Volta; the Ivoirian writer, Bernard Dadié, to name only a few of the many. Sometimes its message was gentle, as with Camera Laye's celebrated novel of 1954, *The Dark Child*, projecting with tender nostalgia the exile's longing for his beautiful homeland in Guinea. Sometimes the accents were harsh and the sentiments unyielding, as expressed in the indictment of the white man by the Senegalese poet, David Diop:

> Is this really you this back which is bent
> And breaks under the load of insult
> This back trembling with red weals
> Which says yes to the whip

Where British colonialism had prevailed, negritude was regarded with mistrust by Africans more concerned with national independence than vague and romantic appeals to a cultural mystique. Kwame Nkrumah's concept of the "African personality" was no more than independent Africans working out their own destiny in their own way; in any case, a different system of colonial rule had brought forth its own form of African reaction. British administration had emphasized indirect rule through the chiefly authorities and had expressly excluded the educated Africans as unqualified to govern, being neither Western nor indigenous. Those Africans who had studied in Europe had different ideas, however—concepts like self-determination, democracy, or responsible government by law, gained from a study of British history and political institutions.

The idea of independence in the British colonies was therefore enunciated chiefly in political terms; in the realm of cultural affairs there was indifference, and, if not that, uncertainty and contradiction. On the one hand, there was a strong suspicion of anything thought to be primitive in African life, to be banished as retrogressive and out of joint with the thrust of modernization. In South Africa, the Bantustan system was more than enough to stigmatize traditional culture in African eyes, but elsewhere there were similar reactions to the old arts and religion. In Nigeria, for example, the folk tales of Amos Tutuola, the Yoruba writer, were regarded with horror by many Western-educated Africans, the more so when praise from European critics was suspected of patronizing Africans in their quaint ways.

Such negativism was qualified, however, for nationalists also experienced cultural pride and the need to contribute an African idiom to a greater world civilization. Sierra Leone produced a number of writers on African themes while in Ghana, the University College was a center for performance and research in traditional music, dance, and theater. Similar developments were apparent in Nigeria. In 1957, *Black Orpheus*, the Ibadan-based literary review, began its vigorous support of modern African artistic and literary expression, giving early public attention to such individuals as the playwright Wole Soyinka, Christopher Okigbo the Ibo poet, and the painter and stage director Demas Nwoko. It was at this time that the novelists Cyprian Ekwensi and Chinua Achebe embarked on literary careers, in Achebe's case, as he later explained, expressly designed to generate a cultural pride among his own people.

An Independent African Civilization

In time the negritude movement came under criticism among francophone Africans, as its shortcomings clarified and its novelty faded. Concurrently, in English-speaking Africa, skepticism toward negritude was tempered by the growing interest in traditional culture. Looking back, therefore, the debate over the merits of negritude seems largely illusory. Hindsight suggests that the moment of independence brought Africans from all compass points together in a unity of purpose—how to convert political freedom into economic affluence, how to assert an idiomatic African personality in the world, reflecting a genuinely African culture.

Indeed, this cultural affirmation had begun long before the independence era, early stirrings dating back to the dark years between the two world wars when colonialism attained its high water mark, insisting upon cultural as well as political domination. If the concept of assimilation had brought forth the reaction of negritude in the overseas territories controlled by France, British cultural insouciance caused an analogous response among Britain's colonials. The early negritude movement was marked by the names of Senghor and Césaire, but also by the Antilian poet Léon Damas, Dr. J. Price-Mars of Haiti, the Senegalese writers, Birago Diop and Ousmane Socé, or the Fulani scholar, Amadou Hampaté Ba, among others.

Similarly, there was no dearth of activity in the British areas. Take, for example, Apolo Kagwa collecting traditional histories among the Baganda, Jomo Kenyatta's anthropological study of his native Kikuyu, *Facing Mount Kenya*, the early hortatory writings of Nnamdi Azikiwe of Nigeria, or those tracts dealing with Akan history and culture by J. B. Danquah of the Gold Coast. Significantly these were all prominent political figures, but there were others whose concerns were more exclusively cultural. In Nigeria a talented young artist, Ben Enwonwu, began searching for an African expression in his work. Among the Gold Coasters the physician, Oku Ampofo, engaged in a similar activity. For music there were the composers Fela Sowande of Nigeria and Ephraim Amu from the Transvolta region of the Gold Coast.

The career of Amu is illustrative. Mission trained and headed for a conventional career as schoolteacher and Presbyterian catechist, he was early diverted by an interest in traditional music. Amu began to collect songs and instruments that were falling into disuse, replaced by Western models and hymnals. He noticed that the Sunday congregations remained silent for the most part during the hymns, for, as Amu surmised, the people were unfamiliar both with the imported words and the music. Secretly the young man composed and rehearsed a hymn based upon local modes, then presented it one Sunday to the unrestrained delight of the congregation.

That was in 1928, an early manifestation of cultural nationalism too far ahead of its time, for it was deemed sacrilegious, if not subversive, by the church fathers, and Amu was dismissed from his teaching post when he persisted in his activities. The end of one career was the beginning of another, however, for Amu was in fact on the leading edge of the search for an African culture that came to characterize the years following the Second World War. In time he was able to step up his efforts in collecting and composition, first at Achimota College and eventually with the Institute of African Studies of the University of Ghana. Many years later, honored on his retirement, Amu could look back with satisfaction on a body of work that had done much to establish a genuinely African culture in the world.

It was significant that Amu's career was closely associated with education for, as African political independence drew near, the new national universities came to play a crucial role, both in training for leadership and in the continuing search for an African cultural expression. It was the universities that lent encouragement to creative writing, both for itself and for an African theater. The imaginative experiments in theater by Efua Sutherland were eventually based at the University of Ghana, while much of the theatrical activity in Nigeria—many of the plays of Wole Soyinka and his fellow dramatist, J. P. Clark, for example—originated in the university programs at Ibadan. The universities, moreover, established special institutes for the study of indigenous culture, Islamic civilization, and African social and economic problems. Finally, it was the universities that took a leading part in promoting research and instruction in African history.

With independence, African history had assumed growing importance as a source of past endeavor to secure present achievement. During the colonial era the African past had been largely ignored, regarded as irrelevant, even nonexistent, while instruction focused on the virtues of European civilization. The new universities were able to change all that, generating a serious concern for Africa's own culture and past, in the process introducing new concepts and techniques to meet the special problems of people whose history by and large lacked written sources. The study of oral traditions came in for particular attention, pioneered by a number of individuals, both European and African, but in this context best represented in 1967 by the Kenya scholar, B. A. Ogot, with his *History of the Southern Luo*.

Ogot's study was monographic and intensive in contradistinction to a series of panoramic surveys of the African past produced by the Senegalese historian, Cheikh Anta Diop, particularly his *Nations Nègres et Culture* published in 1954. Extensive in range, Diop's thesis was daring and controversial in concept, for he sought to show that the diversity of modern African societies came from an ancient cultural unity that originated in Egypt. More than that, Diop insisted, Egypt's civilization was no less than the source for Graeco-Roman culture which in turn was the foundation of modern Western civilization.

Here was African cultural assertion with a vengeance, not to be followed to its extremes by others who nevertheless were able to break fresh ground in pursuing the imperatives of the new discipline of African history. There were, for example, the historians based at the university in Ibadan, Nigeria, a group brought together by K.O. Dike who was responsible for many of the advances in historical scholarship that marked the two decades following the conclusion of the Second World War. In 1956 Dike published his doctoral thesis dealing with nineteenth century commercial activities in the Niger River delta. Some years earlier he had joined the history faculty of the then University College at Ibadan, rising in 1956 to become professor and chairman from which position he was able to launch a number of projects that eventually established the Ibadan department as the most productive and imaginative of all the centers in Africa engaged in historical research and teaching.

Under Dike's direction there were initial changes in the syllabus and systematic recruitment of talented undergraduates for advanced study abroad in preparation for their eventual return to join the ranks of the Ibadan department. A national archives for Nigeria was created at Dike's insistence; at the same time he founded the Historical Society of Nigeria with its own journal, an instrument for the encouragement of local history both among scholars and the public at large. Those sent abroad were set to work on Africa-related doctoral theses, most of which were eventually published in the Ibadan University Series that Dike had arranged with the British publishing house of Longmans.

In 1960 Dike was appointed principal of the newly independent national University of Ibadan, the history department left in capable hands while Dike turned to related matters of a wider scope. While the department went about the business of reforming the teaching curriculum to take account of new research in African materials, Dike was able to found an Institute of African Studies, a department of Arabic and Islamic civilization, and the Scheme for the Study of Benin History and Culture which attempted an interdisciplinary examination of a particular region by combining the work of historians, ethnographers, archaeologists, and specialists in African traditional art. All in all Dike inaugurated a broad range of programs that soon gained the ultimate accolade of imitation by other universities. More than that, his work had established a secure base for the study of an African past.

Europe and the African Personality

In their exertions to demonstrate a genuine African civilization, the proponents of negritude as well as individuals like Ephraim Amu and K.O. Dike were also assaulting European assumptions of Western sophistication and African barbarism. It was indeed an existential question—did an African culture of merit exist, or was it, as was so many times said, the primitive creation of backward peoples? Political freedom could not be expected to succeed in isolation. There had to be a concurrent declaration of cultural independence.

There were two problems involved. The first was the obvious—to demonstrate an authentic African culture different from that of Europe but equal in its own way. The second rested in the fact that Africa had already absorbed much of Europe's civilization. Did this adulterate, even destroy, what was essentially African? In practice the two problems merged. To assert an African cultural uniqueness was to deny European influences, but if they were already there, embedded in the matrix of African life, how could they be acknowledged without Africa becoming overwhelmed and assimilated? Where should the line be drawn between Africa and Europe, between what was acceptable and what was not?

These issues gained a full hearing at the First International Congress of Black Writers and Artists held in Paris in 1956 under the sponsorship of the black cultural revue, *Présence Africaine*. The journal's editor, Alioune Diop, had organized the conference to bring together leading African and Afro-American intellectuals for the very purpose of affirming the civilization of blacks. There were many participants and speakers, much debate and lively exchanges, but the essential question of the congress was contained in two addresses—one by the Martiniquan poet, Aimé Césaire, the other offered by Richard Wright of the United States. Both were literary figures of international reputation, their views eagerly awaited by the assembled delegates.

Césaire's address was both forceful and adroit. It was colonialism, not blackness, that the delegates shared, he argued, a colonialism that had sought to deprive them of their humanity and crush their common culture. If this were achieved, he warned, those who had suffered under colonialism would be permanently wounded, the death of their indigenous culture brought about by political domination, for culture could not survive without the support of a concurrent political expression. Through its machinery of subjugation, Césaire concluded, colonialism had created a cultural anarchy and this could only lead to barbarism.

Here were words designed to appeal to the sympathies of those present— just what the delegates wanted to hear. Nevertheless Richard Wright was nonplused for he had planned an address far different in objective, one that dealt more directly with the basic issue of Europe's influence, good or bad, on an African civilization. Ringing changes on the evils of colonialism and racial prejudice was not the point, Wright insisted. These were plain enough. Should therefore the West be rejected out of hand, its merits of no consequence to Africa? What about concepts like rational thought and pragmatic action, artistic autonomy and experimental science, intellectual freedom and man as an end in himself? Should we turn our backs on such ideas as well as the technology that had made colonialism possible, Wright wanted to know? ''I . . . say 'Bravo' to the consequences of Western plundering . . . that created . . . the possible rise of rational societies. . . . Thank you, Mr. White Man, for freeing me from the rot of my irrational traditions and customs, though you are still the victim of your own.'' It took some courage to raise these matters before an unsympathetic audience, yet Wright persisted. During subsequent discussions at the congress, the differences between Richard Wright and Aimé Césaire were not so much resolved as papered over, for the problem of how to reconcile the two civilizations was bound to persist, extending far beyond the deliberations at Paris, confounding Africans in latter-day twentieth

century as it had confounded them one hundred years earlier in the days of
Edward Blyden and Africanus Horton.

One reconciliation of the apparently antithetical worlds of Africa and Europe
was to be found in the negritude of Léopold Senghor, in his "Civilization
of the Universal" that attempted to balance European rationalism against
African intuition. While Senghor's ideas had appeal for many Africans, they
encountered sharp criticism from others, from Marxists who felt negritude
to be an abandonment of proletariat aspirations, from realists who resisted
what they regarded as rose-tented images of an idyllic past that had never
existed.

In particular two leading exponents of African culture emerged to challenge
the postulates of negritude, Frantz Fanon and Wole Soyinka. Indeed, for Fanon
this was an emotional upheaval because he had initially been a fervent supporter
of negritude. While serving with the Free French forces during the Second
World War, he tells us, he had looked into the white man's eyes to discover
that he was not, as he had always thought, simply a man among men, a French-
man, though dark. No. He was a *black man*, an inferior being, "battered
down by tom-toms, cannibalism, intellectual deficiency, fetishism, racial
defects, slave-ships. . . . " Such an existential characterization was at first
shattering. But Fanon found himself rescued for a time by negritude with
its assertion of racial dignity and achievement. Then he encountered Sartre's
"Black Orpheus," urging him to abandon his negritude with its antiracist
racism in order that he might embrace a common humanity. Disillusioned,
Fanon turned from negritude, eventually to develop a doctrine of violence
as the only catharsis by which the oppressed of the world could shed their
sense of inferiority and lift up their heads in a positive affirmation of culture
and humanity.

Soyinka's attack on negritude was both general and specific. His general
reservation suggested the absurdity of a black man obliged to assert his obvious
blackness, while the specific critique aimed at the false syllogism contained
in Senghor's analysis of differing black and white racial characteristics. In
"Black Orpheus" Sartre had established the dialectic of white racism, opposed
by black antiracist racism, and resolved in the synthesis of universal brotherhood. Senghor elaborated on this progression. European thought is analytical,
he argued, while the African thinks intuitively. Neither is better nor worse;
they are just different. Thus, Senghor concluded, each contributes its share
to the perfect whole of a universal civilization.

Such an analysis is insupportable, said Soyinka. By implication Senghor
denies the African the capacity for logical thought, adopting a Western racist
slur based upon unconvincing pseudoanthropological assertions from Europe
propelled by the dialectics of Marx and Hegel. Without basis in fact, ignoring
the character of intellectual processes in Africa, Soyinka continued, Senghor's
reasoning also disregards the metaphysical unity of the African's psychic
existence, a continuum through time from the ancestors to the yet unborn.

As a validation of African civilization, said Soyinka, Senghor's negritude argues only by sufferance from Europe, its conclusions groundless.

Attacking negritude, Soyinka was nonetheless as intense in defense of African culture as its most ardent supporters. His writings have been infused with the essence of an idiomatic African world view that establishes social proprieties and moral behavior, and enables people to identify themselves and their gods through sacred rites, far removed from any European cosmology. The Western mind, says Soyinka puts emotions, intuitions, scientific observations, and phenomena into compartments, isolating one from the other, thereby complicating efforts to achieve a harmonious world view. The African, by contrast, sees the cosmos as a seamless whole embracing people and their gods, embodying past, present, and future. Soyinka points to the theater as an apt metaphor of this distinction between fragmented West and communal Africa. In the Western stage, he points out, the proscenium separates the action from fee-paying strangers. The African theater combines performer and bystander as equal parts of the action.

The attacks on negritude, multiplying during the early independence years, were accompanied by a resurgence of interest in Europe, in European technology and economic planning, but also in ideologies, Marxist socialism, for example, which was widely regarded as the appropriate path toward development of new, self-directing societies. This European orientation was also reflected in the activities of a school of young African philosophers whose work drew increasing attention during the 1980s. A leading exponent was Paulin Hountondji who published a controversial volume, *Sur la Philosophie Africaine*, in 1977. Like experimental science, said Hountondji, philosophy is a tool, a technique, that owes no geographic or racial allegiance. African philosophy, therefore, is merely the stuff of philosophical method as discussed among Africans in Africa. It most certainly is not the study of traditional African cosmologies; that is the province of the ethnographer. Genuine philosophy in Africa, Hountondji continued, must therefore begin with what had already been developed in the West, principles and concepts to be assimilated and carried forward by philosophers in Africa, their work available in turn for application equally in all corners of the globe.

Such views were a flat contradiction of negritude which had endorsed analyses of African cosmologies like Father Placide Tempel's *Bantu Philosophy*, a study of the metaphysical system of the Luba people, or the work of Abbé Kagamé of Rwanda who also argued a distinctive African mentality. If Hountondji and others of like mind seem a latter-day version of assimilation, their objective was nonetheless the strengthening of the fabric of African society. Similar, though not so didactic, are the views of the Nigerian designer, Demas Nwoko. Clearly, says Nwoko, Africa cannot progress in the modern world without absorbing and utilizing the most advanced machines already developed in the West. There is no going back to traditional African technologies. Africa must have the best in machinery, design, and process.

But these must always be made to meet an African, not a foreign, condition. If the solution is of African origin — types of building design, for example — let us use it. If the technology is foreign, the only criterion is that it meet a genuinely African need. Nwoko is categorical, the solution must be an African solution.

Thus the debate has continued, its ebb and flow determined more by momentary fashion than any fundamental change of position or new discovery. What does seem predictable, however, is that whatever the future may bring, the African personality will continue to be an amalgam, drawing inspiration from the West to be assimilated into the essential Africa.

The Victims

No less an African ideologue than Cheikh Anta Diop had long argued that today's diverse African societies are in fact a unity, all descended from their ancient heritage in pharaonic Egypt. Others, more pragmatic in view, echoed Diop, at least to the extent of pointing out the advantages that would accrue to an African continent united in facing the complexities of the modern world. Thus Kwame Nkrumah organized international conferences to deal with Africa-wide problems even before most Africans had achieved independence, later leading the movement that resulted in the creation of the Organization of African Unity (OAU) in 1963. Unity of action could not match unity of purpose, however, and over the ensuing decades the OAU found itself, more often than not, facing internal, intra-African conflicts it seemed powerless to resolve.

During the 1960s there was the chronic instability within the former Belgian Congo colony as well as the civil war in Nigeria. The 1970s brought the quarrel between Algeria and Morocco over the Saharan territory relinquished by Spain, the invasion of Zaire's Shaba (formerly Katanga) province by Katangans based in Angola, a shooting war between Ethiopia and Somalia, and the growing confrontation in the Sahara between Libya and Chad. Added to this were the Tanzanian invasion of Uganda that brought the downfall of Idi Amin's infamous regime in 1978-1979, and the civil war waged in Angola by the UNITA forces of Jonas Savimbi. By 1983, the twentieth anniversary of the OAU founding, there was little cause for satisfaction among nations that, if anything, were more quarrelsome than ever.

Through the 1980s African unrest intensified. While the Angolan war continued without letup and the Eritrean separatist struggle against Ethiopia gained strength in longevity, the dispute over the former Spanish Sahara resolved itself into a savage conflict between Morocco and the Algerian-backed Popular Front for the Liberation of Saguia Hamra and Rio de Oro (POLISARIO). Concurrently the RENAMO guerrillas emerged in

Mozambique to spread death and devastation, while long standing civil strife in Chad and the Sudan seemed to defy all efforts at solution.

This chronic and often savage warfare, frustrating to the OAU and vexing to poor nations searching for political and economic well-being, brought the full force of its fury, not on governments but on the people of Africa. Perhaps the most widespread suffering has come in the Sudan, beset by periodic drought and ravaged by decades of civil war. Up to 1988 more than 800,000 Sudanese had fled their country, most to Ethiopia, a dubious surcease considering that country's parlous condition, itself racked by famine and civil war that has created over a half million Ethiopian refugees. In 1988 alone at least 260,000 Sudanese perished from warfare or disrupted food production and distribution. While many villagers sought haven in other lands, internal refugees were far more numerous, some one million from the southern provinces journeying to Khartoum to take residence in camps of appalling conditions, starving and under attack by unsympathetic authorities.

Similar circumstances prevailed elsewhere. Lethal attacks by RENAMO forces have reportedly caused 100,000 civilian fatalities and created 1.6 million refugees, more than 600,000 of whom have taken flight to Malawi, a serious burden for that crowded, impecunious country. More than 50,000 refugees from Burundi entered Rwanda following ethnic violence between Tutsi and Hutu in August 1988. That same year 450,000 Somalis left their homeland for Ethiopia to avoid internal conflict. Namibians by tens of thousands moved to Angola in search of refuge while like numbers of Angolans abandoned their villages, moving to sanctuary in Zaire, even to South Africa.

These recent atrocities were readily matched by those from the past. With the rise of Idi Amin, Uganda had become a land where terror reigned as reports reaching the outside world told of army purges, individual murders, and massacres of villages or ethnic groups. Amin's 1971 coup was the lesser violence; having taken power, he was obliged to consolidate his control, particularly in the face of Obote's Lango supporters, a process that involved liquidation of political or tribal opponents, beginning with the army itself. As the months wore on, the purges intensified, the army first ravaging its own ranks, then turning on the country to brutalize the population into submission. Firm figures were hard to come by. After numerous counter coups and attempts on Amin's life, waves of systematic repression up to the end of 1977 were said to have claimed as many as 300,000 victims, with 100,000 regarded as a conservative reckoning.

For Uganda, the very vagueness of statistics heightened the aura of fear in a beautiful, remote land where a once happy people were frightened into silence. In Rwanda and Burundi, remoteness also made difficult the confirmation of heavy loss of life that marked periodic civil strife in those states during the 1960s and 1970s; in Equatorial Guinea, reports of official violence and repression persisted for over a decade, surviving both the country's physical isolation and the government's firm exclusion of the Western press. Refugees, diplomats, and others nonetheless revealed a grim picture of imprisonment and death for dissenters, with upwards of 200,000 killed, exiled, or subjected to forced labor between the time that the former Spanish colony gained independence in 1968 and 1979 when the reign of terror was terminated by an army coup.

While large numbers of refugees have been uprooted as the result of military strifes, still others have been obliged to move through pressure of economic dislocation, victims of policy by governments whose hand is forced by their own people. Although immigrants are frequently a productive factor in the economy, their status as strangers makes them unpopular, especially if they are skillful in turning a profit or occupy jobs which otherwise, it is thought, would belong to friends, relatives, or other local citizens. In 1958 some 25,000 Togolese and Dahomean workers were forced to leave the Ivory Coast when violence erupted in Abidjan over competition for much-prized white-collar jobs. Some years later President Houphouet-Boigny was obliged to revoke the dual citizenship offered to Upper Volta and other members of the Entente because of opposition within the Ivory Coast. In 1964 Zaire expelled thirty thousand citizens of Burundi and Brazzaville Congo Republic, and during 1971 President Mobutu deported large numbers of Senegalese and other West Africans regarded as economically superfluous.

During 1972 the deportation of Uganda's fifty thousand Asian residents caused great hardship and was accompanied by widespread press coverage, stimulated in part by General Amin's flamboyant style and partly by the fact that most of the emigres found refuge outside Africa, chiefly in Britain. There were other, far more severe, economically motivated evacuations of refugees, however. One of the more painful repatriations occurred in 1969 when the Busia government in Ghana ordered the expulsion of all foreign Africans lacking proper credentials. Local unemployment exceeding five hundred thousand in a country of eight million compelled this action which resulted in an exodus of as many as two hundred thousand, mostly Nigerians, over a two-week period. Fourteen years later, in 1983, the tide was reversed, as the Nigerian government, beset by recession and slumping oil sales, yielded to public pressure and abruptly expelled large numbers of foreign workers. Most were Ghanaian in origin and all were compelled to leave on two-weeks notice; estimates varied upward from a minimum of 500,000 who choked the docks and roads that led to an uncertain future.

Others have on occasion encountered official displeasure leading to imprisonment or enforced exile, particularly for articulate critics of government, intellectuals, and members of the press. Not surprisingly the Amin regime grievously weakened Uganda's university, but teachers have also been harassed in less bloodthirsty environments. In their time, Nkrumah and the Convention People's Party constantly feuded with university faculty and students and later, in 1975, the government of General Acheampong briefly imprisoned a prominent poet, Kofi Awoonor, for alleged subversion. In Nigeria, Wole

Soyinka was confined without charge or trial during the Nigerian civil war; in 1977, the Kenyan government detained the novelist Ngugi wa Thiong'o and shut down a play he had written, presumably because of its critical political commentary.

Official suspicion of the press, both domestic and foreign, well reflects governmental instinct for survival. In many countries of Africa, as in other parts of the world,the press is regarded as part of the developmental apparatus, its primary function to educate and motivate. Censorship has therefore become common, and foreign journalists have come under increasing official surveillance. The argument has been advanced that Western reporters and news agencies tend to distort Third World news; hence, governments should control all news media, limiting press reports exclusively to official versions.

Withall, actions of censorship have been a minor tremor to the great upheavals of death, destruction, and displacement that have plagued Africa's people. Statistics, though impersonal, often provide the most vivid account. In 1979 it was estimated that there were some two million refugees in Africa. A decade later the figure had doubled; put otherwise, one of every one hundred twenty-five Africans was a refugee, fully one-third of the world total of 12 million.

The African Woman—A Quest for Social Justice

Warfare and population displacement in Africa have borne down most severely on women and children, an ironic twist in a continent where both have been so valued through the ages. Traditionally women and their offspring have been prized and accumulated as wealth in societies where survival as well as status lay in numbers and their productivity. Though generalization is risky, a typical community contained a nucleus of male relatives with control over land—or cattle in the case of pastoralists—maintaining unity and authority through female links. Daughters were sent to outside villages as marriage partners, thus providing both labor and progeny for a husband, and eventual reciprocity for a father. In this manner women were placed in a weakened position with few rights and many obligations both in the fields and at the hearth. Elders, controlling sisters and nieces, were able to rely on female labor for their ease, keeping a firm hold over young males by regulating prospects of future wives. The important members of these communities were senior males with dominance over dependent wives, slaves, clients, or others who had no strong ties of local kinship.

Despite their economic and social importance, therefore, women in traditional African society were securely under male control, a situation that until recently had changed little. Where the rural farming village remained typical, African women were weighed down by heavy labor and preoccupied with child bearing and rearing, with little time for self-improvement, let alone self-awareness. Since independence, the situation has altered somewhat, perhaps more in direction than in substance. Increasing urban population, the growth of industry, a worldwide movement for the liberation of women culminating in the United Nations Decade for Women, 1975-1985, and government action within Africa have all contributed to a measure of improvement.

Thus far the greatest changes have occurred in legal and procedural matters most readily achieved through direct action by governments. The right to vote and hold office, equal access to education, health care programs that look to women's needs beyond their reproductive function, better economic advance through employment or entrepreneurial activity have been given legislative and administrative sanction. Difficulties arise, however, in realizing these legal opportunities, particularly when they run contrary to custom or encounter widespread ignorance among African women concerning the specific details of their own rights.

Senegal, for example, is a secular state with a family code largely borrowed from French civil law. It is also an overwhelmingly Muslim nation where the role of women has been heavily circumscribed by Quranic injunction. Much improvement has been effected in such matters as marriage, inheritance, and divorce, but discrimination still exists while ignorance of the law and social pressure insure that many women do not take advantage of their rights, particularly on the countryside. Elsewhere in Africa, the gap between the law and its enforcement remains the main obstacle to genuine reform in lands long accustomed to perceptions of female inequality.

Ecological Imperatives

The African environment has writ large in Africa's history, but the process has been reciprocal as Africans have learned to accommodate and, increasingly, to alter their surroundings, not always with salutary results. Illustrations abound, but none more eloquent than the major intervals of drought that have punctuated the decades of independence.

Shortages of water culminating in periodic drought have been endemic to Africa over many millennia, and these cycles of normalcy have done much to shape events. Recent research suggests, for example that drought may have been a factor in the religious upheavals that erupted across the West African savanna late in the eighteenth century. Similarly, Bantu migrations, perhaps initially set in motion by climatic urgencies, were continually affected by the search for water, leading on occasion to such aberrations as the cannibalistic Jaga who burst into Kongo and Angola in the sixteenth century. The droughts that descended on Africa, first from 1968 to 1973 and again during the 1980s, however, bore down with a particular intensity, for they were complicated by conditions that had not been encountered in Africa during precolonial times.

The problem begins with Africa's exploding population, brought about initially during the colonial era by improved public health facilities matched against ancient customs that dictated fertile wives and many children. In the delicately balanced ecology of the West and Central African Sahel, the traditional ratio of cattle and people to territory was overturned. When drought struck, pastoralists could not survive as formerly by conserving reduced herds and moving to moister latitudes. The alternative was starvation and migration, whole villages wiped out, survivors resorting to a scratched out existence in a dusty patch of garden, or, more often, joining the thousands who gravitated to refugee camps on the outskirts of urban centers like Nouakchott in Mauritania, living not in hope but on international relief.

As usual the statistics are appalling. During the drought of the 1970s, as many as a quarter million perished in the savanna states along with 3.5 million of their cattle. Millions were displaced, 250,000 refugees in Mauritania alone, a desert country of former nomads, now 85 percent of its population living poverty-stricken in cities. The 1984-1985 drought produced comparable figures that included afflicted countries in southern Africa as well as the Sahel from Senegal to the Sudan and Ethiopia. In the state of Niger three million or more, almost half of the total population, were affected, Tuareg and Fulani herds wiped out, their owners impoverished. Of Mozambique's 15 million population, fully four million faced starvation or severe food shortages. In Angola the figure was 690,000, while up to 10 million in the Sahel were forced to abandon their homes in search of food. By 1984, 150 million Africans had been driven to the brink of starvation. When the drought ended in 1985 it left behind more than one million dead.

Such massive casualties were not entirely the result of unchecked birth rates acting on an overburdened land. With Ethiopia and the Sudan both engaged in civil war, there is evidence that populations were forcibly moved and famine relief supplies manipulated for military gain. In Mozambique RENAMO rebels routinely disrupted agriculture and appropriated cattle, forcing villagers into relief camps. Nonetheless critics also point to numerous governmental policies that greatly intensified the disastrous effects of drought. On independence African governments greatly stepped up the pace of industrialization, at the same time penalizing agriculture with relative neglect, withholding funds for development, and pegging food prices at artificially low levels to accommodate growing urban populations. The result was a decline in agricultural production along with a black market that limited supplies as populations rose, forcing governments to import food that had to be bought with scarce foreign currency. When the droughts struck there was too little for too many, again largely at the expense of the farmer. As one outside observer remarked, "Governments recognize that if the people in the cities go hungry, they rise up in revolt, but if the farmers go hungry, they just die of starvation."

Drought's end left more than the dead and the starving, as misperception and mismanagement combined to perpetuate misery. To their credit the nations of the world contributed generously in famine relief through the United Nations and other agencies, but much of the relief never achieved its purpose through inefficient organization, inadequate storage and transport facilities, as well as corruption and profiteering. Even well-meaning and proficient technical assistance had effects often quite opposite to their intended purpose. Wells bored in the savanna brought immediate relief for people and cattle, but adequate water encouraged herd populations which grew beyond the capacity of the land to feed them, overgrazing robbed the dry terrain of its plant cover resulting in ever-widening desertification, and many of the wells were soon out of order for lack of parts or the technical knowledge needed to run the pumps. Human population grew as well, intensifying the search for food and water, and depriving the Sahel of its trees which were increasingly cut for firewood. Even the use of dung for fuel had its drawback, for it took from the fields much needed fertilizer.

The attack on trees was even more devastating in the forest where logging became a big business, making heavy inroads on the equatorial rain forest. Like the recent losses through an increase of animal poaching for hides, rhino horn, and elephant ivory, the forest is a dwindling resource difficult or impossible to replace, its destruction even more serious than the immediate elimination of precious timber. Scientists have recently identified high levels of ozone and acid rain over the rain forests of Africa and South America, encouraging speculation that deforestation is contributing to the so-called greenhouse effect. In this event fires used to clear land release carbon dioxide and other gases normally absorbed by vegetation, but with deforestation the gases ascend to pollute the upper atmosphere and contaminate the moisture of clouds. Highly acid rain causes plant and tree damage, while the buildup of gases in the ozone layer traps heat rising from the surface of the earth, much as is achieved in a greenhouse, contributing, in the opinion of some experts, to the sharp rise in global temperatures over the past decade.

To this dismal account must be added one final misery—the appearance of the Acquired Immune Deficiency Syndrome, or AIDS, virus. Some studies suggest that the virus has long resided in Africa at low levels of infection, but this ecological balance has been upset recently by rapid social change including mass migrations. People moving in large numbers from village to town have cast off many traditional restraints, drawn into sexual promiscuity among other things, a major conduit for the transmission of AIDS from person to person. Incidence of infection has struck hardest at a band of countries, chiefly in east-central Africa. In the Central African Republic, Zaire, Rwanda, Burundi, Uganda, Zambia, and Tanzania, the infection rate is about five percent in the cities, seemingly far less a problem than such scourges as measles, malaria, tuberculosis, or tetanus, but a disease without cure and a potential burden that could easily overwhelm fragile health facilities. Thus another plague has come to beset hard-pressed African nations struggling to gain some measure of the prosperity, health, and happiness that was the promise of independence.

Free Markets and Democratic Politics

In 1986 Joachim Chissano succeeded Samora Machel as president of
Mozambique after the latter's death in a plane crash. Chissano inherited a nation
stricken by drought and harassed by ten years of bitter guerrilla warfare. He
also inherited a stagnant economy that had been crippled by years of unrealistic and inefficient economic planning. Immediate and radical action was called
for and it was initiated by Chissano when he persuaded the ruling Mozambique
Liberation Front to consider fundamental democratic reforms for his government and to arrange an end to hostilities with the RENAMO rebels. The imperative was economic rehabilitation, the move toward a free market that would
produce the goods and services necessary to national prosperity. The means
were political — first of all a much needed peace through negotiation; second,
introduction of constitutional guarantees that would allow democracy to flourish
and create a government that was both representative and responsible.

The concept of economic progress through political reform was no idea
limited to apostate Marxists in Mozambique. Africa had become a continent
of collapsing economies characterized by inflation and mounting foreign debt,
scarce consumer goods and black markets, low productivity and adverse trade
balances, declining foreign investment, weak infrastructure, bureaucratic inertia
and corruption. The need for reform had become increasingly evident, and
was triggering ever more insistent public demands for political action, a
movement away from anachronistic socialist states and inefficient single party
regimes toward some form of popular government broadly representative and
directing economies based on free markets. While parallelling similar developments among the ailing Marxist regimes in eastern Europe, the basic impulse
appeared to be domestic, an African response to an African problem.

There were many examples. By 1990, a military regime in Nigeria had
created political parties preparatory to a return of civilian government. In
Gabon, Togo, Congo, and Benin, public unrest forced moves toward multiparty
elections and constitutional reform. While the single party government of Kenya
held out against repeated demands for political pluralism, multiparty politics
were promised in Zaire, with Zimbabwe and Zambia probably to follow.
Before its fall, even the heavily Marxist regime in Ethiopia had begun quietly
to remove portraits and other political symbols from the streets and to abandon
centralized economic planning in favor of a free market. Other single party
governments were more circumspect, content with modest electoral changes
or shifts in cabinet personnel as in Ivory Coast and Niger, but the overall
movement was clear.

Nevertheless, it was an open question as to how fundamental or lasting
these reforms might prove. The prospective changes in South Africa toward
a multiracial state faced the complications of ethnic rivalries among Africans,
and there was speculation as to whether political reform elsewhere was genuine
or perhaps no more than superficial and temporary cosmetic change.

Suggestions for Further Reading

A recent work dealing with cultural independence in Africa is Robert W. July, *An African Voice* (Durham, NC: Duke University Press, 1987). Material may also be found in the writings of African leaders, representative examples cited in the suggested readings for Chapter 23. For Sartre, see his *Black Orpheus* (Paris: Presence Africaine. n.d.). For Fanon, *The Wretched of the Earth* (New York: Grove Press, 1966) and *Black Skin, White Masks* (New York: Grove Press, 1967) should be consulted along with Irene L. Gendzier, *Frantz Fanon: A Critical Study* (New York: Pantheon, 1973). Studies of Senghor's thought include I. L. Markovitz, *Léopold Sédar Senghor and the Politics of Negritude* (New York: Atheneum, 1969) and J. L. Hymans, *Léopold Sédar Senghor* (Edinburgh: Edinburgh University Press, 1971). For the political ideas of Wole Soyinka, see R. W. July, ''The Artist's Credo: The Political Philosophy of Wole Soyinka,'' *Journal of Modern African Studies*, Vol. 19, No. 3, 1981.

For a comprehensive survey of African writing there is O. R. Dathorne, *The Black Mind: A History of African Literature* (Minneapolis: University of Minnesota Press, 1974). Literary trends and African culture are discussed in two provocative analyses — Abiola Irele, *The African Experience in Literature and Ideology* (London: Heinemann, 1981); and Lewis Nkosi, *Tasks and Masks: Themes and Styles of African Literature* (Harlow, Essex: Longman, 1981). Also to be consulted is Peter Benson, *Black Orpheus, Transition, and Modern Cultural Awakening in Africa* (Berkeley: University of California Press, 1986).

The work of African historians active since the Second World War may be seen in representative journals like those of the historical societies of Nigeria, Ghana, and Kenya, as well as in longer studies, many available through series published by Longman. Selections from Cheikh Anta Diop's *Nations Nègres et Culture* and other of his works have been translated by Mercer Cook under the title *The African Origin of Civilization* (New York: Lawrence Hill, 1974). More recently other of his writings have been reissued in translation by Lawrence Hill, Third World, and Africa World (1987).

There is much information available on the subject of refugees in Africa. The best place to begin is with the annual surveys and other reports of the U.S. Committee for Refugees. Similarly ecological problems have been widely reported upon, but see in particular the annual reports, *State of the World* (New York: W. W. Norton) of the Worldwatch Institute.

Much the same may be said for the subject of woman in Africa; however, two special sources may be noted — articles contained in *Africa Report*, March-April, 1985, Vol. 30, No. 2; and the Summer, 1989 issue of the African Studies Association publication, *Issue, A Journal of Opinion*, Vol. XVII, No. 2.

Index

Aba, Nigeria, 369

Aba Island, eastern Sudan, 197, 198; *map*, 190

ABAKO (*Alliance des Ba-Kongo*), 450, 451

Abbas I, Egyptian ruler, 193

Abbud, General Ibrahim, eastern Sudan, 439, 507

Abdallahi ibn Muhammad (*Khalifa*), 198, 200-201

Abd al-Qadir, eastern Sudan *shaikh*, 191

Abd al-Rahman al-Mahdi, eastern Sudan leader, 358, 359, 439

Abd al-Salem, and Sokoto jihad, 170

Abdullahi, Fulani leader, 170

Abdullahi Arabs, eastern Sudan, 90

Abeokuta, Nigeria, 108, 233, 235, 236, 241, 295, 303, 369; *maps*, 95, 237

Aberdares Mountains, Kenya, 460

Abidjan, Ivory Coast, 545

Abiodun, Oyo Yoruba king, 103, 235

Abolition, slavery, 216, 227, 230, 272, 355, 398; slave trade, 225, 226, 232, 272, 355, 398

Abolition Act, 1833, Britain, 227

Abomey, Dahomey, 108, 236; *maps*, 95, 237

Aborigines' Rights Protection Society, Gold Coast, 307, 308

Abuja, Nigeria, 506

Abyssinia, 36, 82; *maps*, 6, 27. *See also* Ethiopia

Accra, Ghana, 110; *maps*, 95, 168, 237

Acheampong, Colonel I.K., Ghana leader, 500, 501, 502, 545

Achebe, Chinua, African writer, 433, 536

Achimota College, Ghana, 375, 538

Acholi, people, East Africa, 341, 456; *map*, 342

Action Group, Nigerian political party, 433, 444, 445

Adal, Muslim Ethiopian state, 84, 85; *map*, 87

Adamawa, region, 170; *map*, 168

Adandozan, Dahomean king, 108

Adaptability, human, 10, 11-12

Addis Adaba, Ethiopia, 284, 285, 438

Aden, Gulf of, 70; *maps*, 27, 75, 87, 274

Adeniyi Jones, C.C., Nigerian nationalist, 372

Administrative justice, 293, 370

Adoula, Cyril, Congo (Zaire) leader, 452

Adowa, battle, Ethiopia, 277, 285, 437; *maps*, 190, 274

Adrar, region, 35; *map*, 34

Adulis, Axum port, 38, 40, 70; *maps*, 27, 75

Afar and Issa, people, 465, 466

Afonja, Yoruba leader, 235, 303

Afonso, Kongo king, 135

Africa, independent, agriculture, 473-76, 483-84; mining, 476-77; industry, 477-80; economic cooperation, 484-85; theories of modernization, 469-73; and foreign aid, 477; and political stability, 543-46; and military coups, 495, 499-503, 505; and cultural emancipation, 533-43

Africa, response and resistance to European influences, 144-49, 277-81; in West Africa, 145, 147-48, 229-35, 239-44, 288-90, 304-8; and trade, 147, 148-50, 278-79; traditional societies, 146, 280, 288-89;

Westernized elite, 146, 158, 228, 229-35, 289-90, 294-300, 336, 364; in Egypt, 160-64, 357-58; in eastern Sudan, 197; in South Africa, 144, 222-23, 280, 325, 326-27; in Central Africa, 280, 281, 334, 336; to colonial occupation, 277-81, 351-52; in Ethiopia, 282-83, 285-86; in East Africa, 144, 278, 281, 348-51; in Belgian Congo, 388-91; in French Equatorial Africa, 395-96

African Lakes Company, Nyasaland, 333

African Marxists and Marxism, 469-70, 496, 514-15, 518, 541, 550

African Mineworkers' Union, Northern Rhodesia, 419

African Mine Workers Union, South Africa, 412

African Morning Post, Accra, 433

African National Congress (ANC), South Africa, 327, 410, 411, 412, 433, 526, 527, 528, 529; Southern Rhodesia, 462; Northern Rhodesia, 421, 423, 424, 461; Nyasaland, 421, 422, 462

African National Council, Zimbabwe political party, 517

"African personality," 433, 536, 537

African protest, South Africa, and political rights, 326-27; pass laws, 413; direct action and civil disobedience, 411, 412-13, 526-31

African response to colonial control, 181, 277-81, 288-90, 304-5, 306-8, 349-51, 352, 362, 369, 389-90, 391, 395-96, 399-400, 421-24

African socialism, 469-70, 489

African Students' Association of the United States and Canada, 441

Afrikaans language, 216, 408

Afrikander Bond, South Africa, 317, 321

Afrikaner (Boer), people, 321, 407, 408, 409, 525, 530

Afro-Asiatic language group, 15, 20, 22, 65; *map*, 21

Afro-Shirazi Party (ASP), 455

Agaja, Dahomean king, 107

Agau, people, Ethiopia, 15, 83, 84, 88

Agbebe, Majola, African nationalist, 433

Age grades, 97-98; Ibo, 96; in Sudanic states, 56; Ngoni, 209; among Kikuyu, 127; and Shakan revolution, 205

Agonglo, Dahomean king, 108

Agriculture, African, 8, 12-16, 31, 118, 330, 385, 430, 481, 483-84, 548; in Egypt, 13, 16-17, 161-62; in Ethiopia, 13, 37; in West Africa, 13, 45, 47, 67, 68, 98-100, 101; in East Africa, 122, 128-29, 258, 341, 343, 344, 459; and South African Boers, 140; and Europe, 145-46, 228; among Bantu, 114, 116, 118, 120; in eastern Sudan, 192, 356; and modernization, 440, 447, 473-76, 483, 548

Ahaggar, region, 5, 42, 43; *maps*, 6, 34

Ahijo, Ahmadu, Cameroun president, 502-3

Ahmad, Kanem-Bornu king, 177

Ahmad Abu Widan, Egyptian Sudan governor, 191, 192

Ahmad ibn Ghazi (Ahmad Gran), jihad leader, Ethiopia, 85, 86, 88

Ahmadu, son of *al-Hajj* Umar, 176, 181, 281

Ahmadu II, Masina, 174

Ahmadu III, Masina, 174, 175

Ahmadu Lobbo, Masina, 173, 174

Ahmose, Egyptian pharaoh, 28

AIDS (Acquired Immune Deficiency Syndrome), 549

Ain Farah, Darfur, *map*, 87

Air, region, western Sahara, 66; *map*, 46

Aja, states and people, West Africa, 107; *map*, 95

Ajasa, Kitoyi, Nigerian leader, 289, 371

Akan, language and people, West Africa, 96-97, 108-9

Akassa, Niger Delta, 243; *maps*, 237, 274

Akidas, German East African officials, 351

Akim Abuakwa, Gold Coast, 373

Akosombo, Ghana, 480

Akuffo, General S.W.K., Ghana leader, 500, 502

Akure man, 93

Akwamu, Akan state, 110, 149; *map*, 95

Akwapim, Akan state, 110, 236; *maps*, 95, 237

Akyem, Akan state, 110; *map*, 95

al-Azhari, Ismail, eastern Sudanese leader, 358, 438-39, 507

Albert, Lake. *See* Mobutu, Lake

Algeria, region and state, 392, 465, 469, 499; *maps*, 274, 275, 457

al-Hajj Ahmad, Muslim scholar, 68

Ali, Kanem-Bornu king, 178

Ali Abd al-Latif, eastern Sudan nationalist, 358

Ali Ghaji, Kanem-Bornu king, 66

Ali Khurshid, Egyptian Sudan governor, 191

Alkalawa, Gobir, 170; *map*, 168

Allada, city-state, West Africa, 107; *map*, 95

All-African Convention, South Africa, 412

All-African Peoples' Conference, Accra, 450, 460

Almoravids, Berber group, 59

Alodia (Alwa), 88; *map*, 87

Aluyi, people, Central Africa, 211; *map*, 208. *See also* Lozi

Alvarez, Father Francisco, Portuguese missionary, 82, 85

Alwa, eastern Sudan state, 88, 89, 90; *map*, 87

Amanitare, Kushite queen, 32

Amda Seyon, Ethiopian king, 84

Amenemet II, Egyptian pharaoh, 26

Amenhotep III, Egyptian pharaoh, 28

American Colonization Society, 228, 301

Americo-Liberians, 301, 379, 380, 381, 499

Amhara, Ethiopian region, 40, 83, 84, 85, 88, 281; *maps*, 27, 87

Amharic, Ethiopian language, 83

Amin, General Idi, Ugandan president, 503, 543, 544

Amina, Hausa queen, 69

Ampofo, Oku, Ghanaian artist, 537

Amu, Ephraim, Ghanaian composer, 537-38, 539

Anglo-Congolese agreement of 1894, 384

Anglo-Portuguese treaty of 1884, 264, 265

Angola, region, 137, 152, 271, 511; and Portuguese colonialism, 137, 291, 396-97, 399, 400, 513-14; African resistance, 399-400; civil war, 511, 515-16, 543; *maps*, 117, 136, 247, 274, 275, 393, 457

Ankole, state, East Africa, 341, 456, 503; *map*, 342

Ankrah, Lieutenant General J. A., Ghana officer, 501

Annuak, Nilote people, 194; *map*, 190

Ansar, Mahdist followers, 198, 507

Anti-Slavery and Aborigines' Protection Society, Britain, 386, 434

Anti-Slavery patrol, British, 228, 233, 266

Apartheid, South Africa, 139, 310, 401-7, 408, 409, 525, 526, 529-31; petty apartheid, 402, 407, 525; grand apartheid, 402, 406, 407; legislation, 403, 404, 410, 411

Apolo Kagwa, Baganda leader, 340, 341, 537

Aquatic civilization, Sahara, 14-15, 16, 22

Arabia, 37, 39; *map*, 87

Arabs (and Swahili), 40, 44, 73, 391; in East Africa, 73, 159, 209, 249-52, 253, 254, 256, 339, 354-56, 455; in Egypt and eastern Sudan, 89-90, 188, 189, 194, 195; in Central Africa, 254, 334; in eastern Congo, 257-58, 272, 384

Aragon, Iberia, 132; *map*, 136

Arguin Island, West Africa, 133, 138, 172; *map*, 136

Arma, Moroccans, 165

Armies, African, 103, 104, 107, 109, 110, 111, 151, 162-63, 180, 182, 186, 199, 203-5, 207, 212, 213, 214, 254, 285, 437-38, 500-503, 504, 505, 506-7, 508-9

Aro Chuku oracle, Iboland, 147; and slave trade, 147

Arqamani (Ergamenes), Kushite king, 32

Arusha, Tanzania, *map*, 342

Arusha Declaration, 470

Arussi, Ethiopian region, 284

Asante, people and kingdom, West Africa, 51, 109-11, 149, 236, 238, 242, 280, 442; and Golden Stool, 109; and coastal trade, 109, 148, 149; government, 109, 111; British war of 1873-1874, 242, 267; *maps*, 21, 95, 136, 168, 237, 274

Ashiqqa party, eastern Sudan, 358, 438

Ashmun, Yehudi, Liberian official, 228-29

Ashraf, Mahdist group, eastern Sudan, 200

Asians, in South Africa, 325, 402, 404, 525, 526, 527; in East Africa, 343, 345, 355, 545; in Mozambique, 97, 397

Askia, Songhai dynasty, 62

Asmara, Eritrea, 277; *map*, 274

Aspelta, Kushite king, 31

Assab, Eritrea, 283

Assegai, spear, South Africa, 204, 212, 214, 218

Assimilados, Portuguese Africa, 399

Assimilation, in Zululand, 205; and Ngoni, 207, 209; Kololo and Lozi, 211; Ndebele, 211, 212; Basuto, 214, 362-63, 368; French colonial doctrine and policy, 225-26, 229-30, 289-90, 293-94, 446, 448, 537; in British West Africa, 228, 231-32, 290, 371; in Senegal, 230, 292-93, 305; in Liberia, 301; in South Africa, 321, 407; in Southern Rhodesia, 330; in French Equatorial Africa, 395; in Portuguese areas, 398-99; and southern Sudan, 439

Assin, Akan state, 236, 242; *maps*, 95, 237

Association, French colonial doctrine, 293, 363, 367, 368, 448; parallel development, Rhodesia, 417, 419

Association of Natives of French Equatorial Africa, 395

Assyrians, 29-30

Asurbanipal, Assyrian king, 30

Aswan, Egypt, 24, 32, 188; *maps*, 28, 87

Atbara River, eastern Sudan, 30; *maps*, 27, 87, 190

Atlantic Charter, 436

Atlas Mountains, Morocco, 4, 35; *maps*, 6, 34

Attahiro I, Sultan of Sokoto, 305

Attoh-Ahuma, S.R.B., African nationalist, 433

Australopithecines, hominids, 9

Awdaghost, West Africa, 48, 49, 53, 54, 58; *map*, 34

Awolowo, Obafemi, Nigerian nationalist leader, 433, 445

Awoonor, Kofi, Ghanaian writer, 545

Axim, Gold Coast, 143; *maps*, 27, 75, 136

Axum, kingdom, Abyssinia, 36-41, 70, 82; overruns Kush, 32; and Christianity, 39-40; and Indian Ocean trade, 70; *map*, 27

Azande, people, eastern Sudan, 194; *maps*, 21, 190

Azikiwe, Nnamdi, Nigerian nationalist leader, 372, 433-34, 443-44, 445, 469, 537

Azores, 133

Baako, Kofi, Ghana nationalist, 442

Ba, Amadou Hampaté, Muslim scholar, 537

Babadinga, General Ibrahim, Nigerian head of state, 507

Bab el Mandeb, straits, 37, 39, 70; *maps*, 27, 75

Badagry, West Africa, 233; *map*, 237

Badi, Funj king, 186

Baganda, people, East Africa, 126, 339-43, 454, 455-56; *maps*, 21, 342

Bagirmi, state, central Sudan, 178, 183, 391, 392; *maps*, 21, 168, 393

Bahr al-Ghazal, region and Nile tributary, 183, 186, 193, 194, 195, 196, 201, 384, 507; *maps*, 190, 274

Bahr al-Jebel (Upper White Nile), 194; *map*, 190

Bahutu, Bantu people, East Africa, 453, 500, 509, 510

Bai Bureh, Sierra Leone chieftain, 303

Baikie, W. B., British explorer, 241

Baker, Josephine, 534

Baker, Samuel, British explorer, 196, 259

Bakongo, Congo people, 395

Bakungu, Baganda chiefs, 340

Balali, Congo people, 395

Balewa, Sir Abubakar Tafawa, Nigerian political leader, 445

Bali (Bale), Muslim Ethiopian state and region, 84, 85, 284; *map*, 87

Ballets Africains, Guinea, 535

Bamako, Mali, 447, 449

Bamara, people, West Africa, 61, 64, 165, 173, 175; *map*, 168

Bambata, Zulu leader, 326

Bambuhu (Bure), West Africa region, 51; *map*, 168

Banana, 72, 73, 100, 120

Banda, Dr. H. K., Malawi president, 422, 424, 462

Banda, West Africa region, 110; *map*, 95

Bangala, Congo, 272; *map*, 274

Bangweulu, Lake, Zambia, 248; *maps*, 117, 247

Banning, South Africa, 528, 529

Bantu Authorities Act, South Africa, 403

Bantu Education Act, 1953, South Africa, 404

Bantu language group, 73, 120, 404; *map*, 21

Bantu migration, 20, 22, 80, 116-19, 124-25, 202, 203, 547

Bantu Philosophy, 542

Bantu speakers and people, 20, 22, 71, 73, 79, 118, 159, 245, 383-84, 391; governments, 124-25; and culture, 119-22, 124-28; in South Africa, 159, 202, 310; *map*, 21

Bantustans, South Africa, 402, 403-4, 413-14, 415, 416, 524

Banyans, Indian bankers, 250

Baqqara, people, eastern Sudan, 188, 198, 200; *map*, 190

Baqt, treaty, 89

Baraka, Islam, 189, 197

Barbary peninsula, Senegal, 291

Barghash, Sayyid, Sultan of Zanzibar, 251, 252

Bari, people, eastern Sudan, 123, 194; *map*, 190

Baringo, Lake, Kenya, 11

Barley, 16, 37, 43

Barotseland, Zambia, 332-33, 461; *map*, 335

Barre, Siad, Somali head of state, 511

Barth, Heinrich, explorer, 172, 232

Basuto, people, South Africa, 212-14, 221, 465

Basutoland, South Africa, 212-14, 217, 221, 312, 403, 414, 415; *maps*, 219, 275, 320, 335

Bateke, Congo people, 391-92

Bathurst (Banjul), Gambia, 369, 375

Batouala, 534

Bauchi, Nigerian region, 171; *map*, 168

Baule, people, West Africa, 96, 447; *map*, 45

Bawa, Gobir king, 169

Bayajidda, Hausa mythical figure, 68

Beauttah, James, Kikuyu nationalist, 349

Bechuanaland, South Africa, 317, 403, 414, 415, 465; *maps*, 274, 275, 320

Bedouin, Arabs, 25, 44

Beecroft, John, British consul, 240, 241

Begemder, Ethiopian region, 85; *map*, 87

Behanzin, Dahomean king, 302

Beja, people, eastern Sudan, 39, 40, 199; *maps*, 21, 27, 190

Bekwai, Asante state, 109

Belgian Congo, 201, 384-91; colonial philosophy, 387; concessionaires, 387; direct administration, 387-88, 390-91; missions, 388-89; and independence, 390, 391, 450-53; *maps*, 275, 342, 393

Bello, Sir Ahmadu, Nigerian political leader, 445

Bemba, Central African Bantu, 253, 257, 334; *maps*, 117, 208, 247

Bena, people, Tanzania, 251; *map*, 247

Ben Bella, Ahmad, Algerian leader, 499

Benguela, Angola, 396; *map*, 393

Benin, kingdom, 104-6, 539; art of, 94; government, 104-6; European impact, 105-6, 145; demise, 106; *map*, 136

Benin City, Nigeria, 106, 279; *maps*, 95, 136, 168, 237, 274

Benin (Dahomey), modern state, 500, 550; *map*, 457

Benin River, Nigeria, 279; *map*, 274

Benue River, Nigeria, 243; *maps*, 46, 237, 274

Berber, eastern Sudan, 188, 189; *map*, 190

Berbers, North African language and people, 15, 20, 36, 43, 44, 49, 50, 51, 54, 58; *map*, 21

Berenice, Egypt, 70; *map*, 75

Berlin Act, 265, 270

Berlin Conference, 252, 263-65

Beti, Mongo, African writer, 433

Beyla, region, West Africa, 179; *map*, 168

Biafra, state, 504, 505

Biko, Steve, South African Bantu nationalist, 527, 528

Bilad al-Sudan, 45

Bini (Edo), people, Nigeria, 104

Bipedalism, 9-10

Biram, Hausa state, 68; *map*, 46

Bisa, Central African Bantu, 248, 249, 253; *maps*, 117, 247

Bismarck, Otto von, 264-65, 268, 273

Bissandugu, Samori empire, 181, 182; *map*, 168

Bito, Luo dynasty, 125

Biya, Paul, Cameroun president, 502-3

Black Circuit Court, South Africa, 215

Black Consciousness movement, 527

Black Orpheus, and Jean-Paul Sartre, 534, 541; literary review, 536

Black Peoples Convention, 527

"Black Spots," South Africa, 403, 406

Blanco, Cape, West Africa, 133; *map*, 136

Blantyre, Malawi, 336; *map*, 335

Bloc Démocratique Sénégalais (BDS), 447-48

Bloemfontein, South Africa, 221; *maps*, 219, 320

Bloemfontein Convention, South Africa, 221, 312

Blood River, battle, South Africa, 218

Blue Nile, 36, 90; *maps*, 6, 27, 87, 190

Blyden, Edward W., West African nationalist, 297-300; racial theories, 297-99, 401; and African culture, 298; supports segregation, 299; West African

university, 299; and independent churches, 300; influence, 300

Boers (*trekboers*), South Africa, 206, 212, 214-18, 281; character and attitudes, 214-15, 218, 222, 316, 317; dislike of British rule, 215-16, 218, 321, 407; and Bantu, 212, 216, 217-18, 220, 221-23, 310

Boer War, 1899-1902, 319, 321

Boganda, Barthélémy, Ubangi-Chari political figure, 449

Boilat, Abbé, Senegal mulatto, 230, 289

Bojador, Cape, West Africa, 133; *map*, 136

Bokassa, Jean-Bedel, political leader, Central African Republic, 503

Bonds of 1844, Gold Coast, 242

Bongo, B.-A., Gabon president, 497

Bonny, Niger Delta, 147, 240, 241, 243; *maps*, 136, 237, 274

Booth, Joseph, British evangelist, 336

Bophuthatswana, Bantustan, South Africa, 404, 524

Boran, people, East Africa, 346; *map*, 342

Borana, Ethiopian region, 284

Bordeaux, France, 240, 292, 367

Borgu, Nigerian region, 276; *map*, 95

Bornu, region and state, West Africa, 49, 55, 66, 67, 170, 175, 176-78, 183, 391; *maps*, 34, 46, 393. *See also* Kanem-Bornu

Botha, Louis, Boer leader, 407, 408

Botha, P.W., South African prime minister, 321, 524-25, 526

Botsio, Kojo, Ghana nationalist, 442

Botswana, state, South Africa, 465; *map*, 457

Boumedienne, Houri, Algerian leader, 499

Bourbon (later Réunion) Island), 81

Brakna Moors, 267; *map*, 274

Brand, J.H., Orange Free State president, 317

Brandenburg, 143

Brass, Niger Delta, 147, 241, 243, 280; *maps*, 136, 237, 274

Brava, Somalia, 77; *map*, 75

Brazza, Pierre Savorgnan de, French

explorer, 264, 266, 269, 391-92, 394

Brazzaville, Congo, 392, 395, 396; *maps*, 274, 393

Brazzaville Conference, 1944, 396, 436, 446

Brazil, 138

Brew, James H., Gold Coast leader, 306

Brière de l'Isle, Senegal governor, 266

Britain, 226; in Yorubaland, 241, 304; in Benin, 302-3; on Gold Coast, 238, 242, 306-8, 372-74, 440-42; in South Africa, 142, 206, 215-16, 220-21, 273, 311-12, 314, 319, 326, 407, 408, 414-15, 526; in West Africa, 143, 181, 240-44, 290, 305-6, 363-64, 368-74; in central Sudan, 183, 392; in eastern Sudan, 201, 276-77, 356-57, 438, 439; in Zanzibar, 251-52, 355; in Congo, 264, 265; and Egypt, 163, 270, 356-57; in East Africa, 273, 340-41, 344-48, 350, 353-54, 453-61; in Somalia, 277; in Ethiopia, 282-83; in Sierra Leone, 302, 303, 369; in Central Africa, 330-31, 336, 417, 419, 424, 463-64, 516-19; after Second World war, 436; in Nigeria, 303-4, 369-72, 504-5; and economic aid, 443

British Cameroons, U.N. trust territory, 450

British East Africa (Kenya), 343, 345, 453-61; *map*, 275

British Kaffararia, South Africa, 322

British Somaliland, 465; *map*, 275

British South African Company, 273, 328, 332, 333, 336, 461

Broederbond, South Africa, 408, 530

Brussels Conference for Abolition of the Slave Trade, 384

Buddu, state, East Africa, 126; *map*, 117

Buganda, state, East Africa, 126-27, 253, 258-59, 278, 339-41, 503; government, 126-27, 258, 340; trade, 251, 259; economy, 258, 259; society, 259, 339-40, 455, 456; *maps*, 117, 247, 274, 342

Buganda Agreement 1900, 340

Buhari, General Muhammad, Nigerian head of state, 506-7

Bulala, central Sudanic people, 66; *map*, 46

Bulawayo, 114; *map*, 320

Bulom, Sierra Leone region, 94

Bunyoro, state, East Africa, 124, 125-26, 253, 259, 278, 456, 503; government, 125-26, 341; *maps*, 117, 247, 274, 342

Bure, West African region, 51, 181; *map*, 168

Burgers, T., Orange Free State president, 313

Burkina Faso (Upper Volta), state, 502; *map*, 457

Burton, Richard, British explorer, 243

Buruli, state, East Africa, 126; *map*, 117

Burundi, state and region, East Africa, 125, 353, 453; civil strife, 497, 499, 510, 544; *maps*, 247, 457

Bushmanoid population, 19, 20; *map*, 21

Busia, Kofi, Ghana prime minister, 501

Busoga, state, East Africa, 126, 456; *maps*, 117, 247, 342

Butha Buthe, Basutoland, 213; *map*, 219

Buthelezi Gatsha, Kwazulu leader, 404, 414, 524, 527-28

Buxton, T. F., British philanthropist, 232, 233

Buyoya, Pierre, Barundi head of state, 510

C-group people, eastern Sudan, 25

Cabinda, Angola, 515; *maps*, 275, 393, 457

Cabral, Amilcar, Guinea-Bissau leader, 514

Caderneta, Portuguese Africa, 399

Caillié, René, French explorer, 232

Calabar, Nigeria, 371

Caledon River, South Africa, 220; *map*, 320

Calicut, India, 134

Camel, in Africa, 36, 44, 49, 50

Cameron, Sir Donald, British colonial governor, 353-54, 370

Cameroon, Mount, 5, 33; *maps*, 34, 168

Cameroun, state, 351, 502; German protectorate, 265; U.N. trust territory, 447; independence, 450; *maps*, 274, 275, 393, 457

Campaoré, Blaise, Upper Volta head of state, 502

Cão, Diogo, Portuguese explorer, 133

Cape to Cairo axis, 276, 315, 318

Cape Coast, Ghana, 231, 306

Cape Colony, South Africa, 220, 313, 317; early society, 139-40, 142; *maps*, 141, 219, 274

Cape Coloureds, people, South Africa, 144, 402, 404, 521, 525, 526, 527

Cape Province, South Africa, 408, 409, 410, 411; *map*, 320

Cape Town, South Africa, 139, 140, 142, 158, 214, 527, 528; *maps*, 141, 208, 219, 320, 335

Cape Verde, 92, 133

Cape Verde, archipelago, modern state, 514

Capitalism, African, 162, 471-72, 489-90, 550

Carnavon, Lord, British political figure, 312, 313, 314

Carr, Henry, Nigerian leader, 371

Carter, Sir Gilbert, Lagos governor, 304

Carter, Land Commission, Kenya, 348

Carthage, North Africa, 32, 35, 36; *map*, 34

Casely Hayford, J. E., Gold Coast leader, 306, 373-74, 433; and National Congress of British West Africa, 362, 374-76

Casement, Roger, British consul, Congo, 386

Castes, Wolof and Serer, 97

Castile, Iberia, 132; *map*, 136

Cataracts, Nile, 5, 25, 26, 28, 30, 187, 188; *map*, 190

Cattle culture, 43, 57, 120, 128-29, 188, 214

Caucasoids, 42

Caulkers, mulatto chiefs, West Africa, 145

Cayor, Wolof kingdom, 238-39; region, 240, 431; *map*, 237

Central Africa, 113-16, 207, 209-10, 245, 276, 383-84, 419, 461-64

Central African Federation (Rhodesia and Nyasaland), 421

Central African Republic, 499, 503; *map*, 457

Central Sudanic (Chari-Nile) languages, 22, 122, 123

Césaire, Aimé, and negritude, 533, 540

Cetewayo, Zulu king, 206, 323

Ceuta, Morocco, 133; *map*, 136

Chad, Lake, 65, 66, 392; *maps*, 6, 34, 46, 168, 274, 393

Chad, state and region, 392, 496; French colony, 392; civil war, 500, 510-11, 543, 544; *map*, 393

Chadic languages, 22, 65; *map*, 21

Chagga, eastern Bantu, 352; *maps*, 117, 342

Chamberlain, Joseph, British political figure, 318

Champion, Allison, Zulu leader, 411

Changamire, state, Central Africa, 78, 114, 115, 207; *maps*, 219, 247

Chari-Nile languages, *map*, 21

Chari River, Cameroun/Chad, 194

Chiefly authority, 97, 305-6, 308, 363, 364, 369, 373-74, 376, 387-88, 432

Chilembwe, John, Nyasa churchman, 336, 421, 429

China, 74

Chinese, in East Africa, 73; in South Africa, 319, 325

Chipembere, Henry, Nyasaland nationalist, 422

Chissano, Joachim, Mozambique President, 550

Chiume, M.W.K., Nyasaland nationalist, 422

Chokwe, Congo people, 254, 255; *maps*, 117, 247

Christianity, Coptic, 39, 89, 106; Ethiopian, 38, 39, 40, 83-84, 86, 88, 281, 282, 498; and eastern Sudan, 88-90, 439; Portugal and Kongo, 135; in Senegal, 146; in British West Africa, 228, 231, 232-233, 243-44,

295, 429; and Buganda, 339, 456; and African churches, 295, 299-300, 326, 334, 336, 389-90; in Belgian Congo, 388-90
Church Missionary Society (CMS), 228, 232, 233, 241, 243-44, 259, 294
Chwezi, Hima clan, 125
Ciskei, South Africa 404, 524; *map*, 320
Cities, 240, 348, 405, 482, 483; western and central Sudan, 53-55; Benin City, 106; West African coast, 291-92, 293; East African coast, 73-74, 76; and African independence, 431-32, 443
Citizenship, French 293, 365, 366, 368, 395, 446
Civilizations, Africa, 546-47; Egyptian, 16-19, 24-26, 28-29; Saharan, 42-44; in western and central Sudan, 45, 47, 51-58, 60-62, 64-67, 178-79, 291; East African coast, 124; Ethiopian, 37-41, 508-9; eastern Sudan, 194, 439, 507; West African forest, 93-102, 145-48, 148-49, 152-53, 225, 301; Mutapa and Changamire, 113-16; Bantu, 116-22, 123-28, 205-6, 209, 210, 211, 212, 213-14, 222-23, 254-55, 328, 329, 350-1, 388-89, 453, 470; Luba-Lunda, 246; Nilotic, 123-24, 128-29; and Islam, 52-53, 60-61, 62, 63, 67, 243; Westernized, 228, 230, 231-33, 240, 242, 294, 295, 296, 348-49, 373, 388-89, 430, 547; and Felix Eboue, 396; and present day, 474, 533-43
Civil wars, 504-11, 543-45; Cameroun, 504; Sudan, 89, 507-8; Chad, 504, 510-11; Burundi, 504, 509-10; Rwanda, 504, 509-10; Ethiopia, 86, 504; Biafra, 504, 505; Eritrea, 504, 508, 509; Nigeria, 235-36, 477, 504-5; Angola, 400, 511, 515-16; Algeria, 448; Congo, 452-53, 504; Rhodesia, 517-19
Ciwere, Ngoni section, 209; *maps*, 208, 247
Clapperton, H., British explorer, 171, 232
Clark, J. P., Nigerian writer, 538
Clarkson, Thomas, British abolitionist, 226

Clevelands, mulatto chiefs, West Africa, 145
Climate, African, 3-4, 16; Mediterranean, 4, 19; and agriculture, 16, 203; in South Africa, 203
Cloves, 250, 251
Cobalt, 476
Cocoa, 351, 440, 443, 447, 472
Coffee 267, 344, 351, 353, 419, 447, 472, 473
Cohen, Sir Andrew, Uganda governor, 455
Colonial administration, 266-67, 338-39, 361-65, 379, 380-81, 436, 465; in Uganda, 340-41, 455-56; in Kenya, 344-48, 350; in German East Africa, 351-53; in Tanganyika, 351-54, 454; in Zanzibar, 355, 455; in eastern Sudan, 356-57; in French territories, 305, 362-63, 365, 367, 368, 377, 378, 392, 394, 396; in British areas, 305-6, 311-12, 314, 363-64, 368-74, 375-76, 414-15, 440-42, 443-45, 458, 459-60; in Senegal, 290-94; and Leopold II, 384-86; in Belgian Congo, 386-89, 390-91, 450-51; Portuguese, 396-400
Colonial Council, Senegal, 367
Colonial Development and Welfare Acts, 443
Colonial Exposition, Paris, 534
Colonial Office, British, and "trustee-ship," 417, 418, 419
Colonialism, European, 429, 431, 432, 435-36, 450, 540
Common Man's Charter, Uganda, 503
Common Market (European Economic Community — E.E.C.), 477
Communications, 8; by river, 8, 24-26, 28; in savanna, 8, 47-48; in desert, 35-36, 44, 48-49, 50-51; in forest, 123
Communism, 447; in South Africa, 411-12, 413
CONAKAT (Confédération des Associations Tribales du Katanga), 450
Condominium, Anglo-Egyptian, 356-57, 358; *map*, 275
Congo, Republic of (Brazzaville), 497, 550; *map*, 457
Congo, Republic of (Kinshasa). *See* Zaire

Congo basin, 263, 264, 265, 272, 391; eastern, 257, 272

Congo Independent State, 254, 255, 257, 258, 265, 269, 270; atrocities, 385-86; concessionaires, 385; *maps*, 275, 335

Congo Reform Association, 386

Congo River (Zaire River), 5, 263, 264, 265, 384, 385; *maps*, 6, 7, 117, 247, 335, 393

Congress of South African Trade Unions, 529

Conny, John, Gold Coast chieftain, 148

Conservative Party, South Africa, 531

Convention People's Party (CPP), Ghana, 441-42, 493-94, 497

Copper, 8, 17, 19, 65, 416, 418, 476

Copper Belt, Zambia, 418, 419, 421, 423

Corruption, 481, 499; in Ghana, 493-95, 502; in Nigeria, 505, 506

Coryndon, R. T., British South Africa Company official, 332

Costa da Mina, West Africa, 133

Cotonou, Dahomey, 271; *map*, 274

Cotton, 13-14, 45, 68, 71, 162, 267, 341, 351, 356, 357, 419, 443, 473

Coussey Committee, Gold Coast, 441, 442

Covilhã, Pero da, Portuguese explorer, 27, 85, 134

Cowries, 49, 150

Creoles, Sierra Leone, 231-22, 294, 296

Cromer, Lord, British colonial officer, 356

Crown Lands Ordinance, Kenya, 348

Crowther, Bishop S. A., African clergyman, 233-34, 242-44, 294-95, 429; and Niger missions, 233-34, 243

Crusades, 131, 132

Cuba, 509, 515, 516, 522

Cushitic languages and speakers, 15, 20, 37, 38, 84, 85, 122-24; *map*, 21

Cyrenaica, North Africa, 277; *map*, 274

Dacko, David, political leader, Central African Republic, 503

Daddah, Mokhtar Ould, Mauritanian president, 500

Dadié, Bernard, Ivory Coast writer, 535

da Gama, Vasco, Portuguese explorer, 77, 134

Dagomba, West Africa state, 111; *map*, 95

Dahomey, kingdom, West Africa, 107-8, 111, 230, 235, 236, 449, 496, 500; and slave trade, 107, 236; government, 107; economy, 107, 108, 236; last days, 236, 302; as French colony, 271, 276, 302; and independent state, 449; and military coups, 499; *maps*, 95, 136, 168, 237, 457

Dajjal, Islamic Antichrist, 197

Dakar, Senegal, 239, 240, 291, 365, 431, 449; *map*, 237

Damara, people, Namibia, 521

Damas, Léon, West Indian poet, 537

Dan, West African people, 96

Danaqla, people, eastern Sudan, 188, 195, 196, 197, 198, 200; *map*, 190

Danes, 238

Danquah, J. B., Gold Coast nationalist, 374, 441, 537

Darfur, region, eastern Sudan, 186, 188; *maps*, 27, 34, 87, 190

Dark Child, The, 535

"Dash," 149

Daud, Songhai king, 63

Daura, Hausa state, 68; *maps*, 46, 168

Davies, H. O., Nigerian nationalist, 443

Debt, foreign, 482, 487-89

de Gaulle, General Charles, 446, 449, 450, 497

de.Klerk, F. W., South African president, 529-30, 531

Degel, Gobir, 169; *map*, 168

Degradados, Angola, 396

Delagoa Bay, Mozambique, 206, 207, 317; *maps*, 219, 320, 393

Delamere, Lord T. P., Kenya, 344

Delgado, Cape, Mozambique, 80; *maps*, 75, 117

Democratic Party, Uganda, 456

Dendi, West African region, 64; *map*, 46

Denham, Major D., British explorer, 232

Denkyira, Akan state, 110, 149, 236, 242; *maps*, 95, 237

Department of Bantu Administration and Development, South Africa, 403-4

Department of Native Affairs, South Africa, 404

Dergue, Ethiopia, 509

Desert 4, 42-44, 48-49, 391; *maps,* 6, 7

Dhanis, Francis, Belgian soldier, 273

Dia, Mamadou, Senegalese leader, 496

Diagne, Blaise, Senegalese parliamentary deputy, 294, 362, 365-68, 377-78, 434, 435, 447

Diamonds, 8, 312-13, 416, 476

Diara, ancient Ghana, 63; *map,* 46

Dias, Bartolomeu, Portuguese explorer, 77, 134

Difaqane, 205

Diggers' Republic, South Africa, 313

Dike, K. O., Nigerian historian, 538-39

Dingane, Zulu king, 206, 217, 218

Dingiswayo, southern Bantu leader, 203, 204, 205

Dinguiray, Guinea, 175; *map,* 168

Dinka, Nilotes, eastern Sudan, 123, 193, 194, 195; *maps,* 21, 190

Diop, Alioune, Senegalese editor, 535

Diop, Birago, Senegalese writer, 537

Diop, Cheikh Anta, Senegalese historian, 535, 538, 543

Diop, David, African poet, 535-36

Diouf, Abdou, Senegal president, 502

Diouf, Galandou, Senegalese parliamentary deputy, 367, 368

Direct rule, 363, 364

Dirma, West Africa, 64; *map,* 46

Disraeli, Benjamin, 314

Divine kingship, in Egypt, 18, 24, 106; in Kanem-Bornu, 65, 178; among Wolof and Serer, 97; in Central Africa, 115, 122; and Bunyoro, 126

Djibouti, Republic of, 466

Djibouti, Somalia, 285, 465; *maps,* 274, 457

Doaro, Muslim Ethiopian state, 84, 85; *map,* 87

Docemo, Lagos royal family, 370

Dodowa (Katamansu), battle, Gold Coast, 236; *map,* 237

Doe, Samuel, Liberian head of state, 500, 511

Dogali, battle, Ethiopia, 283

Domesticated animals, 16

Dominion Party, Southern Rhodesia, 421, 424, 463

Dongola Reach, eastern Sudan, 26, 28; *map,* 27

Dowa, Malawi, 209

Drakensberg Mountains, South Africa, 4, 202, 203; *maps,* 6, 219

Drought, 45, 166, 203, 482-83, 508, 547-48

Du Bois, W. E. B., American black leader, 434; and pan-African congresses, 362, 377-78

Dunama, Kanem-Bornu king, 177, 178

D'Urban, Benjamin, Cape Colony governor, 216

Durban, Natal, 527, 528; *map,* 335

Dutch, 148, 238, 242; in South Africa, 138-40, 142

Dwane, James M., South African churchman, 326

Dyula Mandinka traders, 48, 51, 102, 179; expansionism, 179-80

East Africa, 20, 35, 38, 134, 250; high plains, 5, 10, 245; European occupation, 273

East African Association, Nairobi, 349, 350, 433

East African coast, 20, 38, 70-74; civilization, 70-74; trade, 70-71, 72, 73, 76; and Portugal, 76-79, 80; Omani Arabs, 80-82

East African Community (E.A.C.), 485

East African High Commission, 454

East Africa Protectorate (later Kenya), 343, 345

East India Company, Dutch, 138, 139, 214, 215

Eboué, Félix, French-African administrator, 396, 446

Ebrohimi, Itsekiri center, 280; *map,* 274

Ecole William Ponty, Dakar, 433

Economic Community for West Africa (ECOWAS), 485

Economic development, 364-65, 443, 469-73, 481-86, 548, 550; and West African missions, 232-33; in Uganda, 341, 343, 503; in Kenya, 344, 458-59, 471; in German East Africa and Tanganyika, 352-53; in Egypt, 356; in eastern Sudan, 357; Gabon, 448, 476, 477; Liberia, 476, 477; Belgian Congo, 387, 388, 452; French West Africa, 447; French Equatorial Africa, 394; in Portuguese Africa, 397-99; in South Africa, 325-26; Southern Rhodesia, 331; in Nyasaland, 419; and environment, 473-74; in Zambia, 476; in Ghana, 440, 469-70, 476, 501; and agriculture, 473-76, 483-84; and minerals, 476-77; and industry, 477-80; and pan-Africanism, 484-85; theories of, 469-73, 489-90; and foreign aid, 477, 487-89; in Ivory Coast, 491-93; and Zaire, 452, 476

Economic growth, self-contained, 470

Economy, national, Ghana, 440, 470, 476, 480, 481, 488, 490, 545; Nigeria, 443, 477, 481, 488, 506, 545; French West Africa, 447; Zaire, 452, 475, 481, 486, 488; Kenya, 458-59, 471, 475; Uganda, 458, 475; Chad, 477; Gabon, 476, 477; Ivory Coast, 471-72, 475, 481, 487; Liberia, 476, 479; Mali, 470, 475, 477; Guinea, 470, 476; Malawi, 477; Niger, 476; Senegal, 431, 449, 476; Togo, 476; Tanzania, 470, 477, 486; Zambia, 479, 488

Edo (Bini), people, Nigeria, 103, 104

"Educated Africans," 362, 364, 365-68, 375, 376, 429-30, 432-33, 459; in Nigeria, 369-72; in Gold Coast, 372-74, 440-41; in French Equatorial Africa, 395; in Congo, 388-89, 390, 450-53

Education, 299; European, 352, 375, 396, 399, 429-30, 443, 446; in South Africa, 404-5; and independence, 440, 458

Edusei, Krobo, Ghana nationalist, 442

Efik, Nigerian people, 147; map, 136

Egba, Yoruba people, Nigeria, 108, 236, 241, 280, 295, 304, 369; maps, 237, 274

Egba United Board of Management, 295

Egbado, Yoruba people, 236; map, 237

Egbe Omo Oduduwa, Yoruba association, 433, 444

Egga, Nigeria, 243; map, 237

Egypt, 24-29, 71, 259, 359, 507, 538; predynastic, 16-19; early civilization, 16-19, 24-29; early influence on eastern Sudan, 24-32, 89; connection with Axum and Ethiopia, 37, 38, 283; government, 17-18; and modernization, 160-64, 356; occupation of Sudan, 89, 185-87, 191-93, 195-97, 438-39; and the Mahdi, 199; European occupation, 270; and Condominium, 356-57; independence movement, 357; economy, 16-19, 24-26, 28, 356; maps, 27, 190, 274, 275, 457

Ehangbuda, Benin king, 106

Eighteenth Dynasty, Egypt, 28

Ekiti, Yoruba people, Nigeria, 304; map, 237

Ekwensi, Cyprian, Nigerian writer, 536

Eleko controversy, Lagos, 370-71

El Fasher, Darfur, 25; maps, 27, 34

Elisabethville (Lubumbashi), Congo, 393, 450

Elmina, Ghana, 133, 138, 143, 242; map, 136

El Obeid, Kordofan, 188, 199; map, 190

Ensete, Ethiopian plant, 13

Entente, West African states, 449, 485

Enugu, Nigeria, 445

Environment, African, 3-8, 52, 92-93, 94, 123-24, 128-29, 134, 187-88, 202-3, 213, 245-46, 547-49; and natural selection, 10, 11, 12, 19; and specialization, 11, 19-20; and population movements, 64-65, 93-94, 116,

118, 124, 202-3, 213, 405, 406; and development, 473-74, 482-83

Enwonwu, Ben, Nigerian artist, 537

Equatoria, eastern Sudan province, 196, 507; *map*, 190

Equatorial Guinea, 544-45; *map*, 457

Ergamenes (Arqamani), Kushite king, 32

Eritrea, region, 277, 285, 437, 438, 504, 508, 509; *maps*, 190, 274, 275

Esarhaddon, Assyrian king, 29-30

Ethiope River, Nigeria, 279; *map*, 274

Ethiopia, 36-41, 82-88, 277, 281-86, 392, 437-38, 500, 550; geography, 36-37; civilization, 37-38, 40-41, 83-84, 86, 87; and Judaic culture, 37-38, 83-84; and European contacts, 38, 82, 84-85, 144, 282-83, 285-86; and eastern Sudan, 200, 283; and modernization, 282-83, 285-86, 437; and independence, 438; and civil war, 500, 504, 508-9; *maps*, 87, 190, 274, 275, 342, 457

Ethiopian (Monophysite) Church, 39, 86, 88, 281, 282

Ethiopian highlands, 4

Ethiopian People's Revolutionary Party, 509

Ethnic divisiveness ("tribalism" and regionalism). *See* "Tribalism"

European colonial expansion, 131-32, 137-38, 338-39; and African response, 144-48; and Portugal, 132-37, 145; Netherlands, 137-42; French, 146-47, 266, 270, 302; and Leopold II, 265; Berlin Conference, 263-65; British, 142, 266, 270, 276, 302-4; and African partition, 265-70; and Germany, 264-65, 268-69, 271, 273; and Egypt, 270; in East Africa, 273, 339-40; and Italy, 277, 283-85; in West Africa, 145, 302-4; in Ethiopia, 285; and African independence, 429-34

European Economic Community (E.E.C.). *See* Common Market

European influences in Africa, 144-49, 160-61, 196, 199-200, 201, 224-26,

228, 231-33, 429-32, 434-35, 473, 486, 535, 542-43; in West Africa, 105-6, 109, 111, 149, 158, 175, 181-83, 230, 231-33, 238, 242, 243-44, 288-90, 536, 537; and trade, 115, 225, 226, 473; and slave trade, 108, 151-53, 224-25, 226; in East Africa, 76-79, 115, 343-46, 458; in Egypt, 160-61, 163; in South Africa, 142, 206, 214-18, 220-21, 222-23; in Ethiopia, 144, 282-83, 285-86; in Belgian Congo, 386-91

Europeans, anti-African prejudice, 140, 142, 144, 363, 417, 420; sense of cultural superiority, 140, 142, 214, 243, 344-45, 388-89, 398-99, 409, 539; in South Africa, 140, 142, 214, 310, 311, 407, 409

Evolution, human, 8-12

Ewe, people and states, West Africa, 442, 491; *map*, 95

Ewedo, Benin king, 105

Eweka, Benin king, 104, 105

Ewuare, Benin king, 105

Existentialism, 534, 541

Extension of University Education Act, South Africa, 404

Ezana, Axumite king, 32, 33, 39; and Christianity, 39

Ezzidio, John, Sierra Leone creole, 231

Facing Mount Kenya, 471, 537

Faidherbe, L. L. C., Senegal governor, 239-40, 266, 271, 290, 291, 293

Falasha, Ethiopian Jews, 38

Falémé, River, Senegal, 51; *map*, 237

Fanon, Frantz, 535, 541

Fante, Gold Coast people and states, 110-11, 236, 238; *maps*, 95, 237

Fante Confederation, 235, 238, 242, 267

Faras, Nubia, 89; *map*, 87

Fashoda, eastern Sudan, 201, 276, 392; *map*, 190, 274

Fasiladas, Ethiopian king, 86

Fatajar, Muslim Ethiopian state, 85; *map*, 87

Fazari, al-, Arab astronomer, 56

Federation of Rhodesia and Nyasaland (Central African Federation), 419-24, 463; African opposition, 420; European opposition, 421

Female circumcision, Kenya, 350-51

Fernando Po, Equatorial Guinea, 133, 465; *maps*, 136, 274, 457

Ferry, Jules, French premier, 242, 269

Fezzan, North African region, 35, 36, 49, 172; *map*, 34

Field, Winston, Southern Rhodesian politician, 421, 463

Fifth Cataract, Nile, *maps*, 27, 190

Fiftieth Ordinance, South Africa, 215, 216

"Fingoes" (Mfengu), South African people, 322

Fire, developed in Africa, 10-11

Firearms, 150-51, 175, 180, 198, 212, 214, 284; and East African interior, 252-55, 256, 259

Firestone, Harvey S., American businessman, 380

First Cataract, Nile, 25; *maps*, 27, 190

First International Congress of Black Writers and Artists, Paris, 540

Fischer, Abraham, Boer leader, 321

Fish River, South Africa, 142, 202, 216; *maps*, 141, 208, 219, 320

Fodeba, Keita, Guinean politician, 535

Fonio, West African millet, 13

Force Publique, Congo army, 501

Forminière, Belgian Congo, 390

Fort Hall (Muranga), Kenya, 460

Fort Jameson, Zambia, 209

Fort Jesus, Mombasa, 78, 80

Fourah Bay College, Freetown, 233, 234

Four Communes, Senegal, 292, 293, 294, 305, 365, 368, 446

Fourth Cataract, Nile, 28; *map*, 27, 190

Fourth Dynasty, Egypt, 24-25

France, in West Africa, 143, 175, 176, 181, 182, 225-26, 239-40, 268, 269, 270, 276, 289-90, 302, 362-63, 446-50; in Senegal, 225-26, 229-30, 238-39, 290-94; in Egypt, 160-61, 270; in central Sudan, 183, 276, 384; in eastern Sudan, 201; in Dahomey, 236, 302; and Congo, 264-65, 272, 498; and North Africa, 277; in

Somalia, 269, 285, 465, 466; in Equatorial Africa, 384, 391-95, 396; after Second World War, 446-50; and economic aid, 471-72, 477; and former colonies, 495, 496-97, 503

Franchise, South Africa, 321, 322, 323, 326, 408, 409, 410; French territories, 292, 365, 446; Kenya, 460; Northern Rhodesia; 461; British West Africa, 371-72, 374, 445; Liberia, 381

Franco-Prussian War, 264, 268

Free French, 396, 446

Freetown, Sierra Leone, 93, 143, 158, 182, 227, 228, 231-32, 233, 294, 296, 369; *maps*, 136, 168, 274

French community, 449, 450

French Equatorial Africa, 384, 390, 391-96, 446, 448, 449; concessionaires, 392, 394; atrocities, 394-95; and Free French, 396; *map*, 275

French League for the Defense of the Rights of Man, 395

French Revolution, 158, 225-26, 239

French Somaliland, 465; *map*, 275

French Union, 436, 446, 447, 448

French West Africa, 366, 367, 446, 448; *map*, 275

Frere, Sir Bartle, British colonial administrator, 314, 323

Front for the Liberation of Mozambique (FRELIMO), 514, 515

Front for the Liberation of Zimbabwe, 517

Frumentius, Syrian monk, 39

Fufu, 100

Fulani, West African people, 22, 52, 64, 106, 167, 235, 303, 304, 548; in Hausaland, 67, 166, 170-72, 505; and Islam, 167, 169-72; in Masina, 173, 174; and Kanem-Bornu, 67, 176-77; *maps*, 46, 168

Funj, state and people, eastern Sudan, 90, 186, 188; *map*, 87

Futa Jalon, region, West Africa, 5, 93, 167, 175; *map*, 168

Futa Toro, region, Senegal, 167, 175; *map*, 168

Ga, people, Ghana, 110; *map*, 95

Gabon, region and state, 230, 391, 392,

496, 550; economy, 448, 476, 477;
    maps, 274, 393, 457
Gades, Iberia, 33; map, 34
Galawdewos, Ethiopian king, 85
Galla, people, Ethiopia, 85, 86, 281, 284;
    Wello Galla, 284; map, 21
Galla Confederation, Ethiopia, 284
Gallinas, Sierra Leone region, 302
Gambia, state and region, 92, 93, 238,
    368-69, 465, 502; maps, 274, 275,
    457
Gambia River, West Africa, 238; maps,
    6, 46, 95, 136, 168, 237, 274
Gangara (Wangara), West Africa, 51;
    map, 46
Gao, Songhai empire, 48, 49, 53, 54, 55,
    60, 61; maps, 46, 95, 168
Garamantian, people, North Africa, 35, 36
Gardafui, Cape, 71; map, 27
Gareng, John, Southern Sudanese leader,
    508
Garvey, Marcus, American Black (West
    Indian) leader, 378, 379, 401, 434
Gaza, Bantu kingdom, 207; map, 219
Gazankulu, Zulu "homeland," South
    Africa, 404
Gazargamu, Bornu, 66, 177; maps, 46,
    168
Gbedemah, K. A., Ghana political leader,
    442
Gedi, Kenya, 74; map, 75
Ge'ez, Ethiopian language, 37, 40, 83
General Council, Senegal, 367
Gentil, E., French officer, 392
Geography, African, 3-5, 8; and history,
    3, 116, 118, 121, 202-3; East African
    coast, 70-71; eastern Sudan, 187-88;
    South Africa 282-83
Germa, North Africa, 35; map, 34
German East Africa, 351-53; map, 275
German East African Company, 351
Germany, in central Sudan, 183, 392; and
    African partition, 264-65, 268-69,
    271; in East Africa, 273, 281, 351-53;
    and South Africa, 273, 521
Gesuiwerdes, South Africa, 408
Gezira, region, eastern Sudan, 89, 90,

186, 357, 475; maps, 87, 190
Gezo, Dahomean king, 108, 236
Ghademes, North Africa, 35; map, 34
Ghana, savanna kingdom, 45, 51, 52, 53,
    54, 58-59; map, 46
Ghana, modern state, 442-43, 450,
    493-95, 500; economy, 469-70, 476,
    486, 488, 490, 494, 501; map, 457
Ghana, The Autobiography of Kwame
    Nkrumah, 493
Ghat, North Africa, 172
Gibraltar, 33
Gichuru, James, Kikuyu leader, 460
Gide, André, French writer, 394, 534
Gisu, people, East Africa, 341, 456; map,
    342
Githaka, Kikuyu land, 347-48
Gizenga, Antoine, Congo (Zaire) political
    figure, 451
Gladstone, William E., British prime mini-
    ster, 314
Glele, Dahomean king, 236
Glen Gray Act 1894, 324
Glottochronology, 119
Glover, J. H., Lagos governor, 241, 280
Goa and Goans, 79, 397, 513
Gobir, Hausa state, 68, 69, 167, 170, 171;
    maps, 46, 168
Gojjam, Ethiopian region, 83, 85, 88, 282;
    map, 87
Gold, 8, 26, 28, 29, 35, 38, 60; in West
    Africa, 49, 51-52, 58, 60; in Central
    Africa, 114, 115; in East Africa, 77,
    78; in South Africa, 315-16, 476, 523,
    525
Gold Coast, West Africa, 133, 143, 148,
    236, 238, 242, 267, 306-8; British
    colony, 242, 306-8, 372-74; and
    independence, 439-43; maps, 136,
    237, 274, 275
Gold Coast Leader, 376
Gold trade, 26, 28, 29, 35, 38, 49-50,
    50-52, 58, 72, 76, 77, 78, 114, 115,
    149, 246, 383
Golden stool, Asante, 109
Goldie, George Taubman, British mer-
    chant, 242, 268, 271

Gomes, Fernão, Portuguese merchant, 133

Gondar, Ethiopia, 86, 88, 282; *maps*, 87, 190

Gondokoro, eastern Sudan, 193; *map*, 190

Good Hope, Cape of, 77, 134; *maps*, 6, 136, 141

Gordon, Charles George, administrator in eastern Sudan, 183, 196, 199-200, 259

Gordon Memorial College, Khartoum, 358

Gorée Island, Senegal, 138, 143, 146, 225, 291, 292, 365; *map*, 136

Gorowa, Cushitic people, 123

Goukouni, Woddeye, Chad political figure, 511

Governments, African, precolonial, in western and central Sudan, 56-65, 67, 69; independent, 489-90, 492-99, 501-11, 548, 550; instability, 543-46

Gowon, General Yakubu, Nigerian head of state, 500, 504, 505

Gqokoli Hill, battle, South Africa, 205

Graaf-Reinet, South Africa, 142; *map*, 141

Graduates' General Congress, eastern Sudan party, 358, 438

Grain Coast, West Africa, 228

Granada, Iberia, 132; *map*, 136

Grand Bassam, Ivory Coast, 230; *map*, 168

Grant, A. G., Gold Coast nationalist, 440

Grant, William, Sierra Leone creole, 231, 294

Great Lakes, East Africa, 125, 159, 339, 343, 346

Great Trek, South Africa, 206, 216-18, 311, 322; *map*, 208

Great Zimbabwe, 113, 114

Grey, Sir George, Cape Colony governor, 312

Giots, praise singers, 238

Griqua, states and people, 212, 214, 217, 220, 322; *map*, 219

Griqualand West, South Africa, 220, 313, 314; *map*, 320

Grobler Treaty, Transvaal, 316, 328

Groundnuts, 290-91, 351, 353, 419, 431, 443, 447, 475, 497

Group Areas Act, 1950, South Africa, 403, 529

Guadeloupe, West Indies, 229

Guardafui, Cape, Somalia, 71, 277; *maps*, 27, 75

Guari, Hausaland, 171; *map*, 168

Guerrillas, 514-18, 522, 523, 525

Guet N'Dar, Senegal, 291

Guèye, Lamine, Senegal nationalist, 368, 435, 447

Guinea, Gulf of, 92; *map*, 6

Guinea, state and region, 5, 92, 179, 302, 449, 495-96; and French, 276, 302; independence, 449; economy, 469-70, 476; *maps*, 136, 237, 274, 457

Guinea-Bissau, West Africa, 92, 514-15; *map*, 457

Guinea coast, West Africa, 3, 145, 271

Gum, 49, 192, 229, 239, 267, 290

Gurage, Ethiopian region, 284

Guro, West African people, 96; *map*, 95

Gwandu, Hausaland, 170; *map*, 168

Gwangara, Ngoni section, 209; *maps*, 208, 247

Gyaman, region, West Africa, 100, 111; *map*, 95

Habitants, Senegal, 146

Habré, Hissen, Chad political leader, 511

Hadya, Muslim Ethiopian state, 84; *map*, 87

Hamdallahi, Masina, 173; *map*, 168

Hand ax, 10, 11

Hanga, state, East Africa, 278, 346; *map*, 274. *See also* Wanga

Hanno, Carthage admiral, 33

Harar, Muslim Ethiopian state, 85, 284; *map*, 87

Haratin, people, Sahara, 43

Harkhuf, Egyptian governor, 25

Harlem Renaissance, 533, 535

Hasan bin Omari, of Kilwa, 352

Hatshepsut, Egyptian queen, 28, 38, 70

Hausa, West African people and states, 67-69, 170, 505; *map*, 21

Hausaland, West Africa, 67-69, 166, 167,

171; *maps*, 46, 168

Hehe, people, East Africa, 251, 253, 281, 352; *maps*, 247, 342

Hellenistic civilization, and Kush, 31; and Axum, 40

Hennessy, J. Pope, Sierra Leone governor, 267

Henry, Prince of Portugal, 77, 133

Herero, people, Namibia, 415, 520, 521; *map*, 247

Herodotus, 33, 35, 49, 51, 144

Hertzog, J. B. M., Boer leader, 321, 407, 408, 410, 412

Het Volk, Boer political party, 321

Hicks, William, British soldier, 199

High Commission Territories, British, 414, 465; dependence on South Africa, 414-15; and political independence, 465

Hijra, Islam, 170, 173, 175, 198

Hill, S. J., Sierra Leone governor, 268

Hima, people, East Africa, 123, 125; *map*, 117

Hinda, people, East Africa, 125

History, African, 57-58, 60, 62, 538-39

History of the Southern Luo, 538

Hlubi, people, South Africa, 210, 213; *map*, 219

Hoe, 13, 37, 45

Hofmeyr, Jan, Boer leader, 317, 319, 321

Hoja, East African coast, 77; *map*, 75

Holle, Paul, Senegal mulatto, 175, 230, 289, 429

Hombori Mountains, West Africa, 62; *map*, 46

"Homelands," South Africa, 402, 403, 404, 405, 406, 413, 414, 416, 521, 524, 525, 526, 531

Hominids, African origins, 8-12

Homo erectus, 10-11

Homo habilis, 9-10

Homo sapiens, 12

"Horn," East Africa, 38, 70

Horses, in Africa, 36, 50

Horton, J. A. B., West African creole leader, 234-35, 242

"Hottentots." *See* Khoikhoi

Hountondji, Paulin, African philosopher, 542

Houphouet-Boigny, Felix, Ivory Coast president, 447, 448, 449, 471, 487, 496

House of Commons, Report of Select Committee on West Africa, 241, 266

House system, Niger Delta, 147-48

Housing, in ancient Egypt, 16, 17, 19; in East Africa, 74; in West Africa, 99

Huggins, Godfrey, Rhodesia Federation prime minister, 417, 420, 421

Huguenots, in Cape Colony, 139

"Human Investment," Guinea, 470

Humanitarianism, 215, 226-28, 266, 429

Hume, Kanem-Bornu king, 66

Hunter-gatherer economy, 12, 13, 16, 22

Hut tax war, Sierra Leone, 303

Hyksos, 28, 36

Ibadan, Nigeria, 236, 241, 303, 304; *map*, 237

Iberian peninsula, 33, 132; *map*, 136

Ibi, Nigeria, 271; *map*, 274

Ibibio State Union, Nigeria, 444

Ibn Battuta, Moroccan traveler, 47, 50, 55, 60, 144

Ibo, West African people, 96, 147, 231, 443, 505

Iboland, West Africa, 102, 147; *maps*, 95, 136

Ibrahim, Kanem-Bornu king, 178

Ibrahim Nagwamatse, Emire of Kontagora, 172

Idris Aloma, Kanem-Bornu king, 67

Idria Katakarmabi, Kanem-Bornu king, 66

Ifat, Muslim Ethiopian state, 84, 85; *map*, 87

Ife, Yorubaland, 94, 103, 236; *maps*, 95, 237

Igbebe, Nigeria, 243; *map*, 237

Igbo Ukwa, Iboland, 102

Ijebu, Yoruba people, Nigeria, 236, 304; *map*, 237

Ijesha, Yoruba people, Nigeria, 304; *map*, 237

Ijo, Nigerian people, 147; *map*, 136

Ikoli, Ernest, Nigerian nationalist, 443

Ikorodu, Nigeria, 241; *map*, 237

Ila, people, Zambia, 461

Ile de France (Later Mauritius), Indian Ocean, 81

Ilorin, Yorubaland, 171, 235; *maps*, 168, 237

Imbangala, people, Angola, 135; *map*, 247

Imperial British East Africa Company, 339, 340

Independence movements, African, 235, 239, 436, 448; in Egypt, 37; in eastern Sudan, 438-39; in Gold Coast, 439-43; Ethiopian, 437-38; in Nigeria, 443-45; in French areas, 446-50, 448, 449-50; in Congo, 450-53; in Tanganyika, 454-55; in Zanzibar, 455; in Uganda, 455-56; in Kenya, 458-61; in Zambia, 461-62; in Malawi, 462; in Rhodesia, 462-64; and African culture, 468-69; and Guinea-Bissau, 514-15

Independent church movement, in West Africa, 295, 300; in South Africa, 326; in Nyasaland, 334, 336; in Congo, 389-90, 395-96, 497; in Zambia, 497

India, 71, 74, 78, 82; influence on Kush culture, 31; and international trade, 74, 78, 82

Indian Ocean, 70, 71, 77, 81, 134, 250; *maps*, 117, 208, 219, 247

Indigénat, administrative justice, 367, 395, 446

Indirect rule, 333, 363-64, 387-88; in Natal, 323; in Buganda and Uganda, 340-41; in German East Africa, 351; and Tanganyikan mandate, 353; in eastern Sudan, 358; in Gold Coast, 306; under Félix Eboué, 396; and South African Bantustans, 405; and chiefly authority, 306, 363, 387-88; in Nigeria, 305, 369, 370

Indonesia, 73, 74

Induna, military leader, southern Bantu, 205, 212

Industrial and Commercial Workers' Union (ICU), South Africa, 411

Industrial Conciliation Act, 1934, Southern Rhodesia, 417-18

Industrialization, in Egypt, 162, 163; in South Africa, 223; in Ghana, 479, 494; and modernization, 476-80

"Influx control," South Africa, 406, 528

Ingombe Ilede, Central Africa, 121

Inkatha, Zulu political group, 528, 529

Internal Security Act, South Africa, 529

International Association of the Congo, 258, 263, 264, 269, 270

International Association for the Exploration and Civilization of Central Africa (International African Association), 269

International Bank for Reconstruction and Development. *See* World Bank

International Court of Justice, and Namibia (South-West Africa), 415, 416

International Labor Organization, 367

International Monetary Fund, 488

Intertropical Convergence zone, 3, 4

Iraqw, Cushitic people, Tanganyika, 123

Iringa, region, Tanganyika, 281; *map*, 274

Iron, and Assyrians, 29; and Meroe, 31, 33; in West Africa, 33, 36, 45, 118, 476; in North Africa, 36; and East African coast, 72; sub-Equatorial Africa, 118, 120, 476; and modernization, 476

Irrigation, 192; in Egypt, 16, 18; in Ethiopia, 37

Isandhlwana, battle, South Africa, 314; *map*, 320

Islam, 52-53, 57, 64, 160, 163, 176, 183; in ancient Mali, 59-60; and Songhai, 62, 64; in Kanem-Bornu, 65, 67, 176-79; in Hausaland, 68, 160, 167, 169-72; on East African coast, 73; and East African interior, 339; and Ethiopia, 40, 82, 85, 88; and Samori, 180-82; in West Africa, 52-53, 57, 64, 165-67, 172-76, 238, 293; in eastern Sudan, 188, 189, 197-200, 439, 507

Ismail, Egyptian general, 187; conquers eastern Sudan, 186
Ismail, Egyptian khedive, 162, 195-96, 259, 270
Italian Somaliland, 437, 465; *map*, 275
Italy, and European expansionism, 277, 283-85, 437-38
Itsekiri, people, Nigeria Delta, 279; *map*, 274
Ivory trade, 19, 25, 26, 28, 35, 38, 70, 71, 72, 76, 246, 267, 351; in eastern Sudan, 193, 194, 195; in East Africa and Congo, 159, 252, 259, 383, 385, 392
Ivory Coast, region and state, West Africa, 230, 302, 496, 545, 550; and French, 230, 276, 302, 447, 449; economy, 447, 448, 471-73, 481, 487, 488, 545; *maps*, 274, 457

Ja'alayyin, people, eastern Sudan, 188, 195, 198, 200; *map*, 190
Jabavu, D.D.T., South African Bantu nationalist, 412
Jabavu, John T., Xhosa nationalist, 326-27, 410, 412
Jackson, T. H., Nigerian nationalist, 370, 371
Jaga (Imbangala), people, Congo, 79, 119, 135; *map*, 117
Jaja, king of Opobo, Nigeria, 279
Jallaba, traders, eastern Sudan, 195, 196, 198
James, C. L. R., West Indian nationalist, 441
Jameson, L. S., Rhodes lieutenant, 327, 329; and raid, 318-19
Jam'iyyar Mutanen Arewa (Northern Peoples' Congress), Nigeria, 444
Jenne, Mali, 50, 56, 61, 64, 179; *maps*, 46, 168
Jere, people, South Africa, 207
Jesuits, in Ethiopia, 86, 144
Jihad, Muslim holy war, 53, 59, 63, 160, 166, 167, 179, 180, 181; and Fulani, 69, 176-77, 235, 236; Sokoto, 167, 169-72; Masina, 172-74; Tokolor,

174-76; and the Mahdi, 198-200
Jihadiyya, eastern Sudan, 198
Joalland, Lieutenant, French officer, 392
Job reservation, South Africa, 407, 413
Johannesburg, South Africa, 315, 317, 412, 528; *map*, 320
John I, Portuguese king, 133
John II, Portuguese king, 133
Johnson, G. W., West African nationalist, 295
Johnson, James, West African nationalist, 295, 429, 433
Johnson, Samuel, Yoruba historian, 304
Johnston, Harry, British colonial officer, 276, 279, 315, 333-34, 340
Jonathan, Chief Lebua, Lesotho prime minister, 465
Jones, Sir Glyn, Nyasaland governor, 462
Jos Plateau, Nigeria, 5, 118; *map*, 6
Juaben, Asante state, 109
Juba River, Somalia, 71; *maps*, 75, 117, 274
Judar Pasha, Moroccan soldier, 64
Jumbes, German East Africa officials, 351

Kaarta, Bambara state, West Africa, 61, 64, 165, 173, 175; *map*, 168
Kabaka Yekka (KY), Baganda political party, 456
Kadali, Clements, African nationalist, 411
Kaduna, Nigeria, 445
Kaffa, Ethiopian region, 284
"Kaffir" wars, South Africa, 222, 322
Kafue dam site, Northern Rhodesia, 423
Kagamé, Abbé, Rwandan writer, 542
Kagera River, Lake Victoria, 126; *map*, 117
Kalahari Desert, 4, 11, 14, 119, 202, 210; *maps*, 6, 7, 117
Kalenjin, Nilotes, 123
Kamba, people, Kenya, 251, 253, 281, 343, 461; *map*, 247, 274, 342
Kampala, Uganda, 431; *map*, 342
Kanajeje, Hausa king, 69
Kanbalu Island, East African coast, 73
Kanem-Bornu, savanna kingdom, 45, 64-68, 69; and al-Kanemi, 176-78;

decline, 67, 179-80; *maps*, 46, 168

Kanembu, people, Lake Chad, 170, 177; *map*, 21

Kanemi, al-, Kanembu leader, 170, 176-78; and Sokoto jihad, 176-77

Kangaba, Mali empire, *map*, 46

Kangethe, Joseph, Kikuyu nationalist, 350

Kaniaga, Mali empire, 59; *map*, 46

Kankan, Samori empire, 181; *map*, 168

Kano, Hausa city-state, 53, 68, 170, 171, 172, 445; *map*, 168

Kanuri, people, Lake Chad, 65, 391; *maps*, 21, 46, 393

Kapwepwe, S., Zambian nationalist, 423

Karamojong, Nilotic people, East Africa, *maps*, 117, 342

Kariba Dam, Zambezi River, 423

Karifa-Smart, John, Sierra Leone nationalist, 435

Kariuki, Jesse, Kikuyu nationalist, 349, 350

Karnak, Egypt, 30; *map*, 27

Karume, Abeid, Zanzibar political figure, 455

Kasai, river and region, 255, 385; *maps*, 117, 247, 274, 393

Kasanje, Angola, 248; *map*, 247

Kasavubu, Joseph, Congolese political figure, 450-52

Kasongo, eastern Congo, 257; *map*, 247

Kassa (Tewodros), Ethiopian prince, 281-82

Kasse, region, Sierra Leone, 303

Katamansu (Dodowa), battle, Gold Coast, 236, 238; *map*, 237

Katanga, Zaire (Congo), region, 254, 272, 273, 384, 385, 390, 418, 452, 498, 543; *maps*, 117, 247, 274, 335, 393

Katanga Company, 385

Kateregga, Buganda king, 126

Katikiro, Buganda chief minister, 340

Katsina, Hausa city-state, 55, 68, 170; 46, 168

Kaunda, Kenneth, Zambia president, 423, 424, 461, 469, 497

Kavirondo Gulf, Lake Victoria, 124; *map*, 274

Kazembe, Lunda king and state, 246, 248, 249, 253, 254; *map*, 247

Kebbi, kingdom, West Africa, 69, 169, 170, 171; *maps*, 46, 168

Kei River, South Africa, 216, 322; *maps*, 141, 219, 320

Keiskamma River, South Africa, 216, 322; *maps*, 219, 320

Keita, Fodeba, Guinean leader, 535

Keita, Modibo, Mali political leader, 449, 469, 499

Kennedy, Sir Arthur, Sierra Leone governor, 267

Kenya, Mount, East Africa, 5, 127, 253, 460; *maps*, 6, 117, 247

Kenya, region and state, 345, 346, 422, 497, 500, 502, 550; independence, 458-61; economy, 344, 345, 471; *maps*, 275, 393, 457

Kenya African Democratic Union (KADU), political party, 461

Kenya African National Union (KANU), political party, 460, 497

Kenya African Union (KAU), political party, 459, 460

Kenya People's Union (KPU), political party, 498

Kenyapithecus, 8

Kenya Teacher Training College, 351

Kenyatta Jomo, Kenya president, 350, 351, 459, 460, 461, 471, 498, 537

Kerma, Kush, 25, 26; *map*, 27

Ketu, Yoruba state, 108, 302; *map*, 95

Khalifa Abdullahi, Mahdist leader, 200-201

Khama, Seretse, Botswana president, 465

Khartoum, eastern Sudan, 28, 30, 36, 199; *maps*, 190, 274

Khatmiyya, Muslim brotherhood, 358, 439, 507

Khoikhoi ("Hottentots"), people, South Africa, 19, 20, 139, 140, 142, 144, 158, 202, 212, 215, 402, 410, 520, 521; *maps*, 21, 136

Khoisan language group, 19, 20; *map*, 21

Kiambu, Kenya region, 349; *map*, 342

Kigoma, Tanzania, 352; *map*, 342

Kikuyu, Kenya Bantu, 127-28, 251, 253, 281, 343, 344, 347-48, 458, 459-60, 461; government, 127-28; culture, 127-28, 347-48; political protest, 349-51; and Mau Mau, 348, 459-60; *maps*, 247, 274, 342

Kikuyu Association, 349

Kikuyu Central Association (KCA), Kenyan political group, 350, 351, 433, 459

Kikuyu Provincial Association, 350

Kilimanjaro, Mount, East Africa, 5, 72, 253, 468; *maps*, 6, 117, 247

Kilwa, island and city, East African coast, 74, 76, 77, 80, 81, 248, 253, 352; *maps*, 75, 117, 247, 342

Kimbangu, Simon, African evangelist and cult, 389-90, 395, 433

Kimberley, Cape Colony, 313, 315; *map*, 320

Kimbundu, people, Angola, 514

King, Charles, Liberian president, 380

Kings, African, 97; and peripatetic court, 62, 126

Kipande, Kenyan identification card, 349

Kipsigis, Nilotes, 123

Kirk, John, British consul, 252, 257

Kisale, Lake, Katanga, 118; *map*, 117

Kisangani (Stanleyville), Zaire (Congo), 385; *map*, 393

Kitawali (Watchtower) movement, Zaire, 390, 498

Kitchener, General H. H., in eastern Sudan, 201, 277, 392

Kivu, Lake, Zaire/Uganda, 125; *maps*, 117, 297, 274, 342

Ki-Zerbo, Joseph, Voltaic historian, 535

Kizimkazi Mosque, Zanzibar, 74

Kokofu, Asante state, 109

Kola nuts, 49, 68, 100, 109, 180

Kololo, people, South Africa, 210-11; *map*, 208

Kong, city-state, West Africa, 181, 182; *map*, 168

Kongo, state, 134-37, 152; *maps*, 117, 136, 247

Kontagora, state, West Africa, 172; *map*, 168

Kordofan, region, eastern Sudan, 31, 118, 186, 188, 195; *maps*, 27, 87

Kordofanian language, 20; *maps*, 21, 190

Kosoko, Lagos king, 241

Kotal Kunta, Kebbi king, 69

Kpengla, Dahomean king, 108

Krio, Freetown dialect, 232

Kruger, Paul, Boer leader, 314, 316, 317, 318, 407

Kubai, Fred, Kenya nationalist, 459

Kubayh, Darfur, 188; *map*, 190

Kukawa, Bornu, 177, 178, 183; *map*, 168

Kukiya, Songhai, 61; *map*, 46

Kumasi, Ghana, 109; Asante state 109; *maps*, 95, 237, 274

Kumbi Saleh, ancient Ghana, 53, 54, 58, 59; *maps*, 34, 46

Kunta Arabs, West Africa, 169, 173

Kurgus, Kush, 28; *map*, 27

Kurti, eastern Sudan, 188; *map*, 190

Kuseri, battle, Chari River, 183, 392; *maps*, 168, 393

Kush, kingdom (Meroe), 22, 26, 28, 29-33; controls Egypt, 29-30; civilization, 29-33; destroyed by Axumites, 32, 39; influence of, 22, 31, 32-33; *map*, 27

Kwango River, Congo region, *maps*, 117, 136

Kwazulu, Bantustan, South Africa, 404, 414, 527

Kwilu River, Congo region, 255; *map*, 247

Labor, African, 101, 364, 443, 479; and South Africa, 323, 324-26, 397-98, 405, 406, 407, 408, 410, 411, 412, 415, 416, 525, 528; in Rhodesia, 329, 330; East Africa, 344-45, 354, 458-59; and forced labor, 293, 354, 380, 385-86, 388, 396, 397, 398, 446; atrocities, 385-86, 394-95; in Liberia, 380, 381; French Congo, 392, 394, 395; Belgian Congo, 385-86, 388; in Mozambique, 397-98; in Angola, 398; in Central Africa, 329, 330, 331, 417-18

Labour Party, Britain, 346, 434, 436, 459

Lacerda, Francisco de, Portuguese explorer, 249

Lagos, Nigeria, 105, 241, 445; British colony, 241, 271, 369-72; and Nigerian nationalism, 369-72; *maps*, 168, 237, 274

Lagos Weekly Record, 370

Laird, Macgregor, British shipbuilder, 241

Lalibela, Ethiopian king and capital, 83, 84; *map*, 87

Lamu, island, East Africa, 71, 76, 77, 80; *map*, 75

Lamy, Major L., French officer, 392

Land, in precolonial societies, 96, 307-308; hunger, Boers and Bantu, 203, 216, 218, 222, 322; and colonial policy, 215, 307-8; South African policy, 215, 314, 323-24; in Southern Rhodesia, 329, 330, 417; in Buganda, 340; and Kenya, 344, 345, 346, 347-48, 349, 459, 460; in Belgian Congo, 385; in French Equatorial Africa, 392, 394; and modernization, 475

Land Apportionment Act, Southern Rhodesia, 324, 331, 417, 463

Lander, Richard and John, British explorers, 232

Langalibalele, Hlubi leader, 323

Lango (Langi), people, East Africa, 341, 456, 503, 544; *map*, 342

Languages, African, 15, 19-22, 31, 103, 118, 119-20, 194

Lasta, Ethiopian region, 84, 85; *map*, 87

Lat-Dior, Cayor king, 238-39, 240

Laterite, 8

Lavigerie, Cardinal, White Fathers, 272

Laye, Camera, African author, 535

League for the Defense of the Rights of Man, 395

League of Nations, Tanganyikan mandate, 353-54; Ruanda-Urundi mandate, 353; and pan-Africanism, 377; International Labor Organization, 367; and Liberia, 380; and South-West Africa, 415; and Ethiopia, 437, 438

Leakey, Louis, paleontologist, 9

Leakey, Mary, 9

Leakey, Richard, *Homo* origins, 9-10

Lebna Dengel, Ethiopian king, 85

Legislative Council, 375; in Sierra Leone, 296, 369; in Southern Rhodesia, 331; in Kenya, 345, 346, 458, 459; in Zanzibar, 355, in Gambia, 368-69; in Nigeria, 371-72, 432, 444; in Gold Coast, 307, 372, 374, 432; in Northern Rhodesia, 336, 418; in Tanganyika, 454

Lenshina Mulenga, Alice, Independent church leader, 497

Leo Africanus, Moorish historian, 55

Leopard's Kopje, Zimbabwe, 114

Leopold II, Belgian king, 254, 263, 264, 265, 269-70; and Congo Independent State, 265, 269, 272-73, 384-86, 387, 388

Leopold II, Lake, Belgian Congo, 385, 396; *map*, 393

Leopoldville (Kinshasa), Belgian Congo, 272, 399, 450, 451; *maps*, 274, 393

Lesotho, state, 465, 523; *map*, 457

Lewanika, Lozi king, 332-3

Lewis, Sir Samuel, Sierra Leone creole, 296-97, 369, 429

Liberia, 92, 228-29, 276, 300-302, 379-81, 498-99, 500, 511; independence, 229; and American black settlers, 228, 229, 301; and indigenous population, 228, 277, 301; and Marcus Garvey, 379; and U.S. government, 276, 477; and forced labor, 380; economy, 476, 477; *maps*, 274, 275, 457

Liberia College, 297

Liberia Herald, 297

Liberto, freed slave, Portuguese Africa, 398

Libreville, Gabon, 391, 395; *maps*, 168, 393

Libya, state, 465, 500, 511; *maps*, 275, 393, 457

Lij Jasu, Ethiopian emperor, 437

Limann, Hilla, Ghana head of state, 502

Limpopo River, southern Africa, 113, 202, 327, 328; *maps*, 6, 117, 208,

219, 247, 320, 335
Lindi, Tanzania, 352; *map*, 342
Lineage, in Sudanic states, 54, 57
Lion Temple, Naga, Kush, 31-32
Lisbon, Portugal, 138; *map*, 136
Litham, Tuareg veil, 43
Livingstone, David, British missionary, 211
Lobengula, Ndebele king, 212, 281, 316, 378-79
Lobi, region, West Africa, 51; *map*, 46
Lochner, F.E., Rhodes' agent, 332; Lochner Concession, 332, 333
Locke, John, and slavery, 226
Loi-cadre, French Africa, 448, 495
Lokoja, Nigeria, 241, 243, 271; *maps*, 168, 237, 274
Lomani River, Congo region, 257; *maps*, 247, 393
London Convention, 315
London Missionary Society, 215
Loti, Pierre, French writer, 291
Lourenco Marques (Maputo), Mozambique, 398; *maps*, 320, 335, 393
Lower Egypt, 16, 17, 30
Lozi, people, Central Africa, 211, 246; *map*, 208
Lualaba River, Congo region, 257, 384; *maps*, 117, 208, 247, 274, 393
Luanda, Angola, 137, 396, 398, 399, 514, 515; *maps*, 136, 247, 393
Luapula River, Congo region, *map*, 247
Luba, Congo people and state, 246; *maps*, 21, 117, 247
Lubumbashi (Elisabethville), Congo (Zaire), 450; *map* 393
Lugala, Tanganyika, 352; *map*, 342
Lugard, Sir Frederick, British Colonial administrator, 276, 305, 339, 363, 370, 371, 417
Lukiko, Baganda legislature, 340, 456
Lulua River, Congo region, *map*, 247
Lumpa Church, independent sect, 497
Lumumba, Patrice, Congolese nationalist, 450-52
Lunda, Congo people and state, 246, 248,

249; government, 246; *maps*, 21, 117, 247
Lungu, people, Congo region, 257; *map*, 247
Luo, language and people, East Africa, 22, 123, 126, 194, 346, 349, 460, 461; *maps*, 117, 243, 342
Luthuli, Albert, South African Bantu nationalist, 413
Luyia, people, East Africa, 346, 349; *map*, 247, 342
Luxor, Egypt, 28; *map*, 27
Ly, Abdoulaye, Senegalese historian, 535

Maasai, East African Nilotes, 123, 124, 251, 253, 343, 344, 346, 347, 348; *maps*, 21, 117, 247, 342
Ma Ba, Muslim leader, Senegal, 238
Maban, language group, *map*, 21
Macarthy, Charles, British West African governor, 238, 267
Macaulay, Herbert, Nigerian nationalist, 370-72, 432, 433, 443, 444
Macaulay, Zachary, Sierra Leone governor, 227
Machel, Samora, Mozambique president, 515
Machemba, Yao leader, 352
Maclean, George, British Gold Coast official, 238, 267
Macleod, Ian, British colonial official, 424
Macpherson Constitution, Nigeria, 444
Madagascar, 73, 81, 139, 269, 397; *maps*, 75, 274, 275
Madeira, island, 133, 145; *map*, 136
Mafeking, Southern Africa, 317; *map*, 320
Mafia Island, Tanzania, 76, 80; *map*, 75
Magdala, Ethiopia, 283
Maghili, al-, Muslim scholar, 63, 68, 172
Maghrib, North Africa, 49, 100; *map*, 46
Mahdi (Muhammad Ahmad), eastern Sudan, 183 197-200; early career, 197; character, 198; jihad, 198-200
Mahdi, al-, Sadiq, Sudanese head of state, 508
Mahdist revolution, 197-200, 358; background, 195-97

Mahdist state, 200-201, 356

Mahdiyya, Muslim reformers, 170, 507

Mahu Bey Urfali, Egyptian Sudan governor, 191

Maji Maji rising, 352

Majid, Sultan of Zanzibar, 252

Makanjira, Yao leader, 334

Makoko, Bateke king, Congo region, 392

Makonde, people, Tanganyika, 352; *map*, 342

Makouria, kingdom, Nubia, 88, 89, 90; *map*, 87

Malagasy, people and language, 73

Malan, D. F., Afrikaner leader, 408-9

Malange, Angola, 399; *map*, 393

Malawi, Commonwealth of, 209, 502; independence, 424, 462; economy, 477; *maps*, 247, 457

Malawi, kingdom (Maravi), 79, 248, 253; *map*, 247

Malawi, Lake (Nyasa), 5, 79, 207, 248; *maps*, 6, 7, 117, 208, 247, 274, 342

Malawi Congress Party, 422, 424, 462

Mali, modern state, 449, 469, 496; economy, 469-70; military coup, 499; *map*, 457

Mali, savanna kingdom, 45, 51, 52, 53, 59-61, 144; *map*, 46

Mali Federation, 449

Malindi, Kenya, 72, 74, 76, 79, 80; *map*, 75

Mamadu Lamine, Sarakole Muslim leader, 281

Mamluks, Egypt, 89, 160, 161, 185

Mampon, Asante state, 109

Mamprussi, state, West Africa, 166; *map*, 95, 168

Manda Island, East African coast, 80; *map*, 75

Mandela, Nelson, South African Bantu leader, 413, 526, 528, 529, 530

Mandinka, people, West Africa, 48, 175, 180; *maps*, 21, 46

Mani Koura, Mali empire, *map*, 46

Manilla, currency, 150

Manioc (cassava), 100, 146

Mankessim, Ghana, 110; *map*, 95

Mano River, Sierra Leone, 302

Mansfield, Lord, British jurist, 226

Manua Sera, Nyamwezi leader, 251, 256

Mapupo, Ngoni center, 207; *map*, 208

Maran, René, West Indian writer, 534

Marchand, Captain J. B., French officer, 276, 392

Markets, African, 38, 48, 49, 51, 72, 102, 147, 189, 291, 484, 486, 487, 489, 550

Maroons, Sierra Leone settlers, 227

Martinique, West Indies, 229

Maseko, Ngoni leader, 209, 334; *map*, 208, 247, 335

Masina, western savanna state, 64, 166; and Fulani jihad, 172-74, 175, 176; and al-Hajj Umar, 175; *maps*, 46, 168

Mashonaland, Rhodesia, 207, 276; *maps*, 219, 274, 335

Massawa, Eritrea, 85, 86, 277, 283; *maps*, 87, 274

Masters and Servants Act, South Africa, 411

Matabeleland, Rhodesia, 211, 212, 276, 329; *maps*, 219, 274, 335

Matadi, Zaire, 384; *map*, 393

Matanzima, Kaiser, Transkei prime minister, 404, 413-14, 524

Matope, Rozwi king, 115

Matswa, André, African nationalist, 395, 396

Mau Mau, Kenya, 437, 459-60

Mauritania, state, 35, 465, 500, 548; *map*, 457

Mazrui family, Mombasa, 81, 250, 343

Mba, Léon, Gabon president, 497

Mbadiwe, Ozoumba, Nigerian nationalist, 435

Mbari, Kikuyu lineage, 127, 347

Mboya, Tom, Kenya political leader, 460, 498

Medina, Senegal, 175, 240; *map*, 168

Mediterranean Africa, 33-36, 42

Mehu, Dahomean official, 107

Mekambo, iron deposits, Gabon, 476

Mema, West Africa, 62

Memphis, Egypt, 30

Mende, people, West Africa, 96, 98; *map*, 95

Mendez, Alphonso, Portuguese missionary, 86

Menelik I, Ethiopian king, 38, 84

Menelik II, Ethiopian emperor, 277, 283-86, 437; and Ethiopian expansionism, 284; and modernization, 285-86

Mengisto, Haile Mariam, Ethiopian political leader, 509, 511

Mensah Sarbah, John, Gold Coast leader, 306-8; on Gold Coast indigenous institutions, 307; and colonial rule, 306-7; and *Fanti National Constitution*, 307; on land alienation, 307-8

Mercantilism, 137-38, 143, 399, 447

Meroe, Kush, 28, 30, 31; described, 31-32; influence 31, 32-33; language, 31; *maps*, 27, 87

Meru, eastern Bantu people, 124

Mesurado, Cape, Liberia, 228

Metemma (al-Qallabat), battle, Ethiopia, 283; *map*, 190

Métis, (mulattoes), Senegal, 146, 230

Mfecane, 159, 205, 207, 210, 211, 218

Mfengu (''Fingos''), South African people, 322

Micombero, Captain Michel, Burundi leader, 510

Middle Congo, French, 392; *map*, 393

Middle East, 13, 15, 17, 22, 37, 38, 132, 161, 162, 163

Middle Kingdom, Egypt, 25-26, 28

Migan, Dahomean official, 107

Military coups, 495, 499-503, 505

Millet, cereal, 13, 37, 43, 45, 120

Mills, T. Hutton, Gold Coast leader, 306

Milner, Sir Alfred, Cape Colony governor, 319, 321, 402, 407

Milo, Niger tributary, 180; *map*, 168

Mines and Work Act, 1911, South Africa, 410

Mines and Work Amendment Act, South Africa, 410-11

Mining, 51, 115, 316, 325

Mirghani, al-, Sayyid Ali, eastern Sudan leader, 358, 439

Mirambo, Nyamwezi leader, 251, 255-56, 257, 278

Missionaries, European, 333, 350-51,

352, 429, 439; in Kongo, 135; South Africa, 214, 215; West Africa, 228, 233-34, 242-44; Buganda, 259, 339; Belgian Congo, 388-89

Missionaries' Road, southern Africa, 317

Mkwawa, Hehe leader, 281

Mlozi, Zanzibari trader, 334

Mma Ntatisi, Tlokwa queen, 213

Mobutu, Sese Seko, Zaire president, 452-53, 498, 499

Mobutu, Lake (Albert), Zaire/Uganda, *maps*, 117, 190, 247

Modernization, 135, 157-58, 430-32; in Egypt, 160-64, 356; and eastern Sudan, 192; in West Africa, 158, 232-33, 440, 443; in Ethiopia, 282-83, 285-86, 437; and South Africa, 313, 315-16, 523; French territories, 447; in East Africa, 341, 348-49; and agriculture, 473-76; and mining, 476-77; and industry, 477-80; and conflicting theories, 469-73;

Moffat Treaty, Ndebele, 328

Mogadishu, Somalia, 74, 76, 77; *map*, 75

Mohenjo-Daro, Indus River valley, 14

Moi, Daniel Arap, Kenyan president, 461, 500

Mokone, M. M., South African churchman, 326

Molteno, J. C., Cape Colony prime minister, 313, 314

Mombasa, island and city, East Africa, 72, 76, 77, 78, 79, 80, 250, 343, 348, 459; *maps*, 75, 247, 342

Mombera, Ngoni leader, 209, 334; *maps*, 208, 247, 335

Monckton Commission, Northern Rhodesia, 424

Mondlane, Eduardo, Mozambique nationalist, 515

Monomotapa, 76, 115. *See also* Mwene Mutapa; Mutapa kingdom

Monrovia, Liberia 380; *maps*, 168, 237

Montesquieu, C. L., on slavery, 226

Moors, 132, 230; Brakna, 267; Trarza, 240, 267

Morel, E. D., British reformer, 386

Morice, Captain, French trader, 81
Morocco, region and state, 35, 58, 63-64,
    277, 465, 498, 511; independence,
    448; maps, 46, 136, 274, 457
Moshi, Tanzania 353; map, 342
Moshoeshoe, Basuto leader, 213-14, 221,
    280, 312, 465; statesmanship, 213-14
Moshoeshoe, Lesotho king, 465
Mossi, people and kingdom, West Africa,
    56, 61, 63, 165; maps, 46, 168
Mount, Cape, West Africa, 145; map, 136
Mouvement National Congolais (MNC),
    450
Mouvement Populaire de la Révolution
    (MPR), 497
Mozambique, region and state, 72, 77, 80,
    81, 249, 271, 331, 333, 516, 548,
    550; island, 80; and Portuguese
    colonialism, 77, 271, 333, 397-98,
    514, 515; maps, 247, 274, 275, 320,
    335, 393, 457
Mpadi, Simon, African evangelist, 390
Mpande, Zulu king, 206, 218
Mpezeni, Ngoni leader, 209, 334; maps,
    208, 247, 335
Mpondo, people, South Africa, 322
Msiri, Katangan leader, 254, 273
Mthethwa, people, South Africa, 203,
    204, 205; map, 219
Mugabe, Robert, Zimbabwean president,
    518, 519, 520
Muhammad Ahmad (Mahdi), 197-200
Muhammad Ali, 90, 160-64, 174;
    establishes Egyptian rule, 161; occu-
    pation of Sudan, 185-87, 191, 193;
    Egyptian modernization, 160-64
Muhammad Bello, Sultan of Sokoto, 169,
    170-71, 175, 177
Muhammad ibn Ahmad, Muslim scholar,
    68
Muhammad Rimfa, Hausa king, 68
Muhammad Said, Egyptian ruler, 193
Muhammad Sharif, Muslim scholar, 197
Muhammad Toure, Songhai king, 52, 53,
    55, 62-63, 172
Mulattoes, in Senegal, 146, 230, 292, 293,
    365

Mulele, Pierre, Zaire rebel leader, 453
Mulenga, Alice Lenshina, 497
Mumia, Hanga king, 278, 346
Murtala Muhammad, Nigerian head of
    state, 500, 505
Musa, Mali king, 52, 55, 60
Muscat, Arabia, 78, 80, 82, 250; map, 75
Mutapa kingdom, 115; civilization,
    115-16; trade, 115; and Portuguese,
    115; map, 117
Mutesa I, Buganda king, 259, 278, 339
Mutesa II, Buganda king, 455-56
Mutota, Rozwi king, 115
Muzorewa, Bishop Abel, Zimbabwe-
    Rhodesian leader, 517
Mwanga, Buganda king, 339, 340
Mwata Yamvo, Lunda king and state, 246,
    248, 249, 255; map, 247
Mwena Mutapa (Monomotapa), royal title,
    76, 115
Mweru, Lake, Zaire/Zambia, 333; maps,
    6, 117, 208, 247, 335, 342
Mzililikazi, Ndebele king, 211-12
Mzinga Mkuwu, Kongo king, 135

Nafata, Gobir king, 169
Naga, Meroe, 31, 32
Nairobi, Kenya, 345, 348, 349, 459, 460;
    map, 342
Nama, people, Namibia, 521
Namib desert, 4, 119, 202; maps, 6, 7
Namibia (South-West Africa), 516,
    520-22, 544; name adopted, 416, 520;
    people of, 520-21; domestic policy,
    521-22; and United Nations Organi-
    zation, 520, 521, 522; SWAPO
    recognized, 522; map, 457
Nana, Itsekiri leader, 279-80
Nandi, East African Nilotes, 251, 281,
    343, 346; maps, 247, 342
Napata, Kush, 28, 30; map, 27
Napier, Sir Robert, British soldier, 283
Napoleon I, 160
Nasser, Colonel G. A., Egyptian
    president, 499
Natal, South Africa, 206, 217-18, 220,
    311, 317; maps, 219, 274, 320

National Congress of British West Africa, 362, 374-76, 433

National Council of Nigeria and the Cameroons (NCNC), political party 444-45

National Liberation Council, Ghana, 501

National Liberation Movement, political party, Ghana, 442

National Party, South Africa, 401, 408, 409, 524, 531

National Party of Nigeria (NPN), 506

National Redemption Council, Ghana, 501

National Union for the Total Independence of Angola (UNITA), 511, 514, 515, 516, 523, 543

National Unionist Party (NUP), Sudan, 507

Nationalism, 365-74, 374-76, 381, 431, 433-34, 436-37, 455, 485; Afrikaner, 140, 317, 321, 407, 408, 409, 524; Egyptian, 163, 357; and Samori, 182; Zulu, 205; Basuto, 214; Ngoni, 210; and Mirambo, 255; and African churches, 300, 326, 336; in Kenya, 349-51, 458-61; in eastern Sudan, 357-59, 439; in Senegal, 365-68; in Nigeria, 369-72, 443-45; and Gold Coast, 372-74, 440-43; in Congo (Zaire), 433, 450-53; South African Africans, 409-14, 526-29; in Central Africa, 421-24, 462-64; in French Africa, 446-50; in Tanganyika, 354, 454-55; in Zambia, 461-62

Nations Nègres et Culture, 538

Native Administration Act, South Africa, 411

Native Administration Ordinance, Gold Coast, 373

Native Authority Ordinance, Tanganyika, 353

Native Labour (Settlement of Disputes) Act, 1953, South Africa, 403

Native Representation Act, South Africa, 411

Native Urban Areas Act, South Africa, 410

Natives Registration Ordinance, Kenya, 344

Natives' Land Act, South Africa, 324, 410, 529

Natives' Representation Council, South Africa, 412

N'Dar Tout, Senegal, 291

Ndebele (Matabele), people, South and Central Africa, 115, 211-12, 214, 217, 328-29, 519-20; maps, 208, 335

Ndwandwe, people, South Africa, 203, 205; map, 219

Negritude, 289, 433, 448, 533-36, 537, 541, 542

Negroids, 16, 20, 42, 43, 45, 72, 188; in West Africa, 20

Nembe, Niger Delta state, 280; map, 274

Neocolonialism, 469, 489

Netekamani, Kushite king, 32

Neto, Agostinho, Angolan president, 514, 515

New Kingdom, Egypt, 28-29

Newspapers, 546; and African nationalism, 433-4

Ngala, Ronald, Kenya political leader, 461

Ngoni, people, Central Africa, 115, 159, 207, 209-10, 245, 253, 334, 352; divisions, 209-10; maps, 208, 247, 335, 342

Ngugi wa Thiong'o, Kenyan writer, 546

Nguni speakers, South Africa, 79, 158, 202, 203, 207; map, 208

Ngwane, people, South Africa, 203; map, 219

Niani, Mali empire, 60; map, 46

Nicol, George, Sierra Leone clergyman, 294

Niger, state 449, 500, 550; map, 393

Niger Coast Protectorate, 303

Niger-Congo languages (Niger-Kordofanian), 20, 65, 103, 118; map, 21

Niger Delta, 5, 103, 147-48, 240, 241, 279; society, 47-48; maps, 237, 274

Niger Districts Protectorate, 271

Niger Expedition, 221, 233

Niger Missions, CMS, 242-44

Niger River, 5, 61, 62, 64, 181, 241, 243, 263, 265, 271; maps, 6, 7, 34, 46, 95, 136, 168, 237, 274

Nigeria state, 103, 271, 505-7; as British

colony, 363, 369-72; northern protectorate, 305, 363, 364; western region,
305; eastern region, 305, 364; and
African nationalism, 369-72; federa-
tion, 370, 443, 445; independence,
443-45, 450; economy, 477, 484,
488; civil war, 235-36, 477, 499,
504-5; *maps*, 275, 393, 457
Nigerian National Democratic Party
(NNDP), 371, 433
Nigerian Pioneer, 371
Nigerian Youth Movement, 372, 443
Nile Delta, 16, 30
Nile River, 5, 13, 16, 17, 18, 36;
cataracts, 5, 8, 16, 24, 30, 36, 190;
maps, 7, 27, 34, 75, 87, 136, 190, 274
Nile Valley, 14, 15, 17, 36, 88-89
Nilo-Saharan languages, 20, 31, 118, 122;
Central Sudanic branch, 122, 123
Nilotes, people, 20, 22, 122-24, 128-29,
194; and government, 128-29
Nimba, Mount, Liberia and Guinea, 476
Nimeiry, al-, General Gaafar, Sudan
leader, 507-8
Nkomo, Joshua, Zimbabwean nationalist,
462, 463, 464, 517, 518, 519, 520
Nkrumah, Kwame, Ghanaian nationalist
leader, 435, 441-43, 493-95, 499,
501, 536, 545; and Gold Coast
independence, 441-43, 468, 469; and
modernization, 469, 470; and pan-
Africanism, 495, 543
Nkumbula, Harry, Zambian African
nationalist, 423, 424, 461
Noba, people, Kush, 32
Nobatia, kingdom, Nubia, 88, 89; *map*, 87
Nok culture, Nigeria, 33, 94
North Africa, 33-36, 49, 67; and European
penetration, 270, 277
Northern Peoples' Congress (NPC),
Nigerian political party, 444, 445
Northern People's Party, Ghana, 442
Northern Rhodesia (Zambia), 336,
418-19; and "partnership," 418; and
federation, 420, 423-24; and African
nationalism, 421-22, 423-24;
independence, 461-62; *maps*, 275,
335, 342, 393

Northern Rhodesian African Congress,
421, 423
Nova Scotians, Sierra Leone settlers, 227,
228
Nsama, Tabwa people leader, eastern
Congo, 257
Nsuta, Asante state, 109
Nuba Hills, eastern Sudan, 193, 194; *map*,
190
Nubia, region and kingdom, eastern
Sudan, 24-26, 28, 29-33, 89-90;
maps, 27, 190
Nubian (Nuba) people, eastern Sudan, 188
Nuer, Nilotes, eastern Sudan, 123, 194;
map, 190
Nujoma, Sam, Namibian president, 522
Nupe, people and kingdom, West Africa,
103, 171, 231; *maps*, 46, 95, 168
Nutrition, 47, 99
Nwoko, Demas, Nigerian artist, 536,
542-43
Nyamwezi, people, East Africa, 209, 248,
255-56, 257, 278, 352; as traders,
248-49, 251, 252; *maps*, 247, 274,
342
Nyangwe, eastern Congo, 257; *map*, 247
Nyanza, Kenyan region, 349, 461; *map*,
342
Nyasa, Lake. *See* Lake Malawi
Nyasaland, 333, 419; and federation, 420,
422; and African nationalism, 421,
422; independence, 462; *maps*, 275,
335, 342, 393
Nyasaland African Congress, 421, 422
Nyerere, Julius K., Tanzanian president,
454-55, 468; and state planning, 470,
486
Nyeri, Kenya, 460
Nyika, region, East Africa, 72
Nzinga, Anna, Angola queen, 137

Oathing, Kenya, 459-60
Obasanjo, Olasegun, Nigerian head of
state, 505
Obiri, Yeboa, Asante king, 109
Obote, Milton, Ugandan president, 456,
503, 544
Odinga, Oginga, Kenya Luo leader, 460,
498

Oduduwa, mythical Yoruba ruler, 103
Ofori Atta, Nana, Gold Coast leader, 373
Ogaden, Ethiopian region, 284
Ogot, B. A., Kenyan historian, 538
Ogowe River, Gabon, 391; *map*, 393
Ogun River, Nigeria, 93; *map*, 237
Oil Rivers (Niger Delta), 241; *map*, 274
Oil Rivers Protectorate, 280; *map*, 274
Okigbo, Christopher, Nigerian writer, 536
Old Calabar, Nigeria, 147, 240, 241; *maps*, 136, 237
Old Kingdom, Egypt, 24-25
Olomu, Itsekiri leader, 279
Olympio, Sylvanus, Togo president, 499
Oman, Arabia, 80-82; *map*, 75
Omani Arabs, 78, 250; in East Africa, 80-81, 250-52
Omdurman, eastern Sudan, 200, 201; *maps*, 190, 274
Onitsha, Nigeria, 243; *map*, 237
Opobo, Niger Delta state, 279; *map*, 274
Opoku Ware, Asante king, 110, 111
Opone, Somalia, 71; *map*, 75
Orange Free State, South Africa, 220, 221, 312, 313, 314, 317, 319; *maps*, 274, 320
Orange River, South Africa, 119; *maps*, 6, 117, 141, 208, 219, 274, 320, 335
Orange River Sovereignty, South Africa, 220, 221, 311
Oranje Unie, Boer political party, 321
Oranmiyan, Yoruba king, 104
Organization of African Unity (OAU), 487, 515, 543
Organization of Petroleum Exporting Countries (OPEC), 485-86, 488
Organization of Senegal River States (OERS), 485
Originaires, Senegal, 293, 365, 446
Osagyfo, Kwame Nkrumah, 494
Osei Bonsu, Asante king, 109, 110
Osei Kwame, Asante king, 111
Osei Kwando, Asante king, 111
Osei Tutu, Asante king, 109, 110
Ovambo, people, Namibia, 416, 520, 521, 522
Ovamboland, Namibia, 416, 521; *map*, 335
Ovenramwen, Benin king, 303
Ovimbundu, Angolan people, 255, 514, 515; *map*, 247
Owu, Yorubaland, 235; *map*, 237
Oyo, Yoruba kingdom, 103, 104, 107, 108, 235, 303; Old Oyo, 235, 303; government, 103, 104; *maps*, 95, 237
Oyoko clan, Asante, 109
Oyo Mesi, Yoruba council, 104, 235

Padmore, George, Nkrumah adviser, 441
Paez, Pedro, Portuguese missionary, 86
Palm and palm oil, 14, 100, 120, 267, 351, 443
Palmas, Cape, Liberia, 92, 93; *maps*, 95, 136, 168
Pan-African movement, 376-78, 470, 495; and National Congress of British West Africa, 374-76; objectives, 376-77; early congresses, 377-78; Fifth Congress, 378, 436, 441-42; and economic cooperation, 484-85
Pan-Africanist Congress (PAC), South Africa, 413, 526, 527, 529
Pangani River, Tanzania, 72; *map*, 75
Pan-Ibo Federal Union, 444
"Parallel development," Southern Rhodesia, 417, 419
Park, Mungo, British explorer, 232
Parti Démocratique de Guinée (PDG), 495, 497
Parti Démocratique de la Côte d'Ivoire (PDCI), 447, 496
Parti Solidaire Africain (PSA), Congo (Zaire), 451
"Partnership," racial, in Central Africa, 418, 419, 463; in French colonies, 446; in Tanganyika, 454; in Kenya, 458, 460
Passfield, Lord (Sidney J. Webb), 418
Pass laws, Southern Africa, 215, 330, 403, 407, 413, 525, 528
Pastoralism, 4, 15, 548
Pate Island, Kenya, 76, 77, 80, 81; *map*, 75
Patriotic Front, Zimbabwe, 518, 519

Peasant, Egyptian, 17, 18, 160, 162

Pedi, people, South Africa, 314

Pellegrin, Gabriel, Senegalese mulatto, 230

Pemba Island, Zanzibar, 73, 76, 80; *map*, 75

Pepi II, Egyptian pharaoh, 25

Periplus of the Erythraean Sea, 70-71, 72, 120

Perpetual kinship, Lunda, 246

Persia, 70, 72, 73

Peters, Carl, German explorer, 267, 273

Petits blancs, French Africa, 447

Petroleum, 476, 477, 505, 506, 515, 516, 517

Philip, John, British missionary, 215

Philip II, Spanish king, 137

Phoenecians, 33

Piankhy, Kushite king, 29

Pillars of Hercules (Gibraltar), 33; *map*, 34

Plaatje, Sol T., South African Bantu nationalist, 327, 410

Plow, 37

Pointe Noire, Congo-Brazzaville, 395

Pokot, Nilotes, East Africa, 123

POLISARIO. *See* Popular Front for the Liberation of Saguia Hamra and Rio de Oro

Political cohesion, 491-92; and environment, 8, 57-58; in ancient Egypt, 17-19; in Ethiopia, 40, 88; in western and central Sudan, 56-58, 62, 63, 64, 66, 67, 69, 165, 178-79; in West African forest, 96-98; and Old Oyo, 103-4; in Benin, 105, 106; in Dahomey, 107, 108; and Asante, 109, 111; and Mutapa kingdom, 114, 115; among Bantu and Nilotes, 121, 124-25, 126-27; among Luba and Lunda, 246; and Zulu, 159, 205-6; Ngoni influence, 209; and Muhammad Ali, 161; Basuto, 213-14; and Mirambo, 256; Ndebele, 212, 328-29; in modern Ghana, 442-43; and Nigeria, 443-45; in French Union, 448-50; in Uganda, 455-56; in eastern

Sudan, 507-8; in Congo (Zaire), 451-53, 498

Pombeiros, Portuguese African traders, 248, 249

Pondoland (Mpondu), South Africa, 206, 218, 323; *maps*, 219, 320

Popular Front for the Liberation of Saguia Hamra and Rio de Oro (POLISARIO), 465, 511, 543

Popular Movement for the Liberation of Angola (MPLA), 399, 513, 515

Population, 12, 19-22, 153, 383, 416, 479, 481-82, 483, 507, 510, 521; in Egypt, 18, 162; in Liberia, 229, 301, 379; and Sierra Leone, 231; in Senegal, 291; Southern Rhodesia, 330, 331, 418, 517; Northern Rhodesia, 336, 418; Kenya, 346; French West Africa, 367; in Belgian Congo, 388; in French Congo, 391; in Angola, 396-97; in South Africa, 203, 214, 218, 405, 406; in Nyasaland, 419; in Namibia, 521

Population Registration Act, South Africa, 403, 529

Poqo, South Africa, 413, 527

Poro, secret society, West Africa, 98

Port Elizabeth, South Africa, 410, 528; *map*, 320

Port Natal, South Africa, 206, 220; *map*, 219

Porto Novo, Dahomey, 271

Portugal, 132-37, 246, 249, 264, 265, 383-84, 398-400, 513-15, 516, 517, 522; and East African coast, 76-78, 80; and Ethiopia, 82, 144; and West Africa, 105-6, 133; and Mutapa state, 115; imperial expansion, 132-37, 144-45, 333, 383-84; and Kongo, 135; in Angola, 137, 246, 384, 396-97, 515-16; in Mozambique, 246, 384, 397-98, 515; in Guinea, 514-15; *map*, 136

Portuguese Guinea, 98, 145, 146, 271; and Guinea-Bissau, 514; *map*, 274

Positional succession, Lunda, 246

Potgieter, Andries, Boer leader, 217, 220

Pottery, 120, 121
Pra River, Ghana, 110; *maps*, 95, 237
Pratt, W. H., Sierra Leone creole, 231
Prazos, Mozambique, 397
Prempeh, Asante king, 280
Présence Africaine, review, 433, 535
Prester, John, 82, 84, 134, 135
Pretoria, Transvaal, 315; *map*, 320
Pretoria Convention, 315
Pretorius, Andries, Boer leader, 218, 316
Pretorius, Marthinus, Boer leader, 316-17
Preventive Dentention Act, Ghana, 493-94
Principe, island, 514
Promotion of Bantu Self-Government Act,
    1959, South Africa, 403
Province of Freedom, Sierra Leone, 227
Provincial councils, Gold Coast, 373
Ptolemy, Claudius, geographer, 72, 120
Punt, region, Somali "horn," 28, 38, 70;
    map, 27
Pygmoids, 19-20

Qaddafi, Muammar al, 500, 511
Qadir, Kordofan, 198; *map*, 190
Qadiriyya, Muslim brotherhood, 167,
    169, 172, 176
Qallabat, al- (Metemma), battle, 283;
    map, 190
Qarri, eastern Sudan, 188; *map*, 190
Quaker, James, Sierra Leone creole, 294
Queen Adelaide Province, 216; *map*, 219
Quinine, 241
Quz Rajab, eastern Sudan, 188; *map*, 190

Raba, Nigeria, 171; *map*, 168
Rabih Fadlullah, Sudanese conqueror,
    179, 182-83; 392
Racial discrimination, 140, 142, 432, 435,
    541; in South Africa, 140, 142, 158,
    311, 322, 403; in West Africa, 243,
    293; in Central Africa, 330-31,
    416-18, 419, 420, 421, 423, 462; in
    East Africa, 344-45, 346-47, 348,
    355; in Belgian Congo, 389, 390-91;
    in French Equatorial Africa, 395; in
    Portuguese Africa, 399
Racial policies, in South Africa, 322, 323,
    324, 325-26, 401-7, 410-11; in
    Southern Rhodesia, 330-31, 416-18,
    420; in Northern Rhodesia, 418-19,
    420, 462; in Kenya, 344-45; in
    Belgian Congo, 389, 390-91; in
    Portuguese Africa, 399
Railroads, 317, 343, 352, 384, 395, 431,
    525
Rainfall, African, 3-4, 8, 166, 482; in
    Congo basin, 3; in desert, 45; in East
    Africa, 4, 128; in Ethiopian highlands,
    4; in South Africa, 4; *map*, 7
Rain forest, 4, 45, 92-94, 391; *map*, 7
Rainy, William, Sierra Leone creole, 294
Ramapithecus, 8, 9, 10
Randle, John, Nigerian leader, 371
Rano, Huasa city-state, 68; *map*, 46
Rassemblement Démocratique Africain
    (RDA), French Africa, 447, 495
Ras Tafari (Haile Selassie), 437
Rawlings, J.J., Ghana head of state, 490,
    500, 502
"Recaptives," Liberated African slaves,
    228, 231
Red Sea, 5, 37, 70; *maps*, 6, 27, 34, 75,
    87, 190, 274, 393
Red Sea Hills, 15, 25, 199; *map*, 190
Refugees, African, 544-46, 548
Rehoboth Bastars, people, Namibia, 521
RENAMO (Mozambiquan National
    Resistance), 516, 543-44, 548, 550
Republic of South Africa, 409
Republic of the Congo, 400, 452-53
Reservation of Separate Amenities Act,
    South Africa, 403
Reserves, South Africa, 322, 323, 402,
    415; Rhodesia, 330, 417; Kenya, 348
"Resettlement," South Africa, 406, 528
Resident Natives Ordinance, Kenya, 324,
    345
Retief, Piet, Boer Leader, 217-18
Réunion Island, Indian Ocean, 81, 229,
    397
Rhapta, East African coast, 71, 72
Rhodes, Cecil, British empire builder,
    273, 276, 315, 318-19, 324, 327-28,
    332, 333, 384

Rhodesia, region, 334, 414; northwestern, 334; northeastern, 334; *map*, 335

Rhodesia, state, 464, 516-19

Rhodesia Party, 464

Rhodesian Front, Southern Rhodesia, 424, 463-64, 517

Rice, 13, 92

Richards, Sir Arthur, Nigerian governor, 444

Riebeeck, Jan van, and South Africa, 139

Rift Valley, East Africa, 5, 122, 123, 344, 346; *map*, 117

Rinderpest, 330, 343

Rio Muni, Equatorial Guinea, 465; *maps*, 393, 457

Rivonia trial, 413, 526

Roberto, Holden, Angolan leader, 513, 514, 515

Roberts, Joseph J., Liberian president, 301

Robinson, Sir Hercules, British South African administrator, 328

Roman influences in Africa, 32, 35

Rovuma River, East Africa, 273; *maps*, 75, 247, 274, 335

Round Table Conference, and Belgian Congo, 451

Royal African Company, British, 143, 150

Royal Niger Company, 271, 280

Royal seclusion, in Benin, 105; and Zimbabwe, 115; in Kanem-Bornu, 65, 178

Roye, Edward J., Liberian president, 301

Rozwi, Mutapa rulers, 115

Ruanda-Urundi, Belgian mandate, 353, 453; *maps*, 275, 342, 393

Rubber, 351; in Belgian Congo, 385; in French Congo, 391, 392

Rubusana, Walter, South African Bantu nationalist, 326

Rudd Concession, Ndebele, 328

Rudolf, Lake (Lake Turkana), East Africa, 5, 128; *maps*, 6, 117, 247, 342

Rufiji River, Tanzania, 72; *map*, 75, 247

Rufisque, Senegal, 291, 293, 365

Ruga-ruga, irregulars, East Africa, 256

Rwanda, state, East Africa, 253, 353, 453, 497, 500, 509-10, 544; *maps*, 247, 457

Saad Zaghlul, Egyptian nationalist, 357

Sabaean, language and people, 37

Sahara Desert, 4, 11, 17, 42-44, 48-49, 116; *map*, 34

Saharan language group; *map*, 21

Sahel, desert edge, 44-45, 482

Sahili, al-, Muslim architect, 60

Sahle Selassie, King of Shoa, 283

Said, Sayyid, Zanzibar ruler, 81, 82, 249-51

Saif, ibn Dhi Yazan, Kanuri leader, 65

Saifawa dynasty, Kanem-Bornu, 65, 67, 178

Saint-Louis, Senegal, 143, 146, 158, 175, 225, 238, 239, 240, 291, 365; *maps*, 136, 168, 237

Sakura, Mali King, 60

Salazar, General Antonio, Portuguese prime minister, 399, 513, 514

Salim Qapudan, Turkish explorer, 193

Salisbury, Lord, British political figure, 266

Salisbury (Harare), Rhodesia, 327, 329; *map*, 335

Salmon, C. S., Gold Coast official, 267

Salt trade, 49, 50-51, 149, 180

Sammaniyya, Muslim brotherhood, 197

Samori Toure, Mandinka empire builder, 179-82, 183, 281; early career, 179-80; statemaking, 181, 182; relations with Europeans, 180-81, 182, 271; character and achievements, 179, 181-82; *map*, 274

San ("Bushmen"), people, Southern African, 19, 20, 142, 144, 158, 202-3; *maps*, 21, 136

Sande, secret society, West Africa, 98

Sand River Convention, South Africa, 221, 312

Sanga, people, Katanga, 254

Sangha River, Congo-Brazzaville, 272; *map*, 274

Sangu, people, Tanzania, 251, 253; *map*, 247

Sanhaja Berbers, 58; *map*, 46

Sankara, Thomas, Upper Volta head of state, 502

Sankore Mosque, Timbuktu, 55

Santos, dos, J. E., Angolan president,

516, 522

Sanusiyya, Muslim reformers, 170

São Jorge da Mina, West Africa, 138; map, 136

São Tomé Island, 135, 138, 398; maps, 136, 274, 393

São Tomé and Principe, state, 514; map, 457

Sapara Williams, C. A., Nigerian leader, 371

Sarbah, John, Gold Coast leader, 306

Sarraut, Albert, French colonial official, 364

Sarsa Dengel, Ethiopian king, 86

Sartre, Jean-Paul, 534

Savanna, 4, 45, 47, 391; map, 7

Savimbi, Jonas, Angolan political figure, 514, 515, 516, 523, 543

Sebetwane, Kololo leader, 210, 211

Second Cataract, Nile, 26, 30; maps, 27, 190

Secret Societies, West Africa, 98

Sefwi, Akan state, 111; map, 95

Segeju, eastern Bantu, 79, 80; map, 117

Segu, Bambara state, 61, 64, 165, 166, 173, 175; map, 168

Selassie, Haile, Ethiopian Emperor, 437-38, 508, 509

Seme, Dr. Pixley, South African Bantu nationalist, 327, 410

Semitic languages and people, 15, 22, 37, 83

Semna, Nubia, 25, 26; map, 27

Sena, Mozambique, 79; maps, 75, 117, 247

Senegal, state and region, 92, 229-30, 393, 449, 496, 497, 502; and France, 229-30, 365; and parliamentary deputy, 292, 365-68; and representative government, 292, 365-66; and Blaise Diagne, 365-68; independence, 449; economy, 448, 476; maps, 95, 237, 457

Senegal River, 5, 229, 238, 239, 291; maps, 6, 34, 46, 95, 136, 168, 327, 274

Senegambia, region, 92; map, 95

Senghor, Léopold S., Senegal president,

289, 433, 447, 448, 496, 497, 502, 534, 535

Sennar, Funj capital, 90, 186, 188; maps, 87, 190

Senufo, people, West Africa, 96, 180; map, 95

Serer, people, Senegal, 97, 238; map, 95

Sesuto, Bantu language, 211

Settlers, European, in Rhodesia and Nyasaland, 327, 329, 336, 417, 418, 419, 420, 421, 422-23, 437, 462-63, 517, 519; in East Africa, 343-46, 353, 437, 454, 458, 459; in Portuguese Africa, 396-97

Sey, J. W., Gold Coast leader, 306

Shaba, Zaire, 498, 543

Shagari, Shehu, Nigerian president, 506

Shaka, Zulu king, 119, 202; character and early life, 204, 206; military reforms, 204-5; conquests, 205, 206; political reforms, 205-6; assassination, 206

Shakiyya, people, eastern Sudan, 186; map, 190

Shari'a, Islamic law, 169

Sharp, Granville, British philanthropist, 226, 227

Sharpe, Alfred, British colonial agent, 333

Sharpeville massacre, South Africa, 413, 527, 528

Sheba, Queen, 38, 39, 84

Shendi, eastern Sudan, 186, 188, 189; map, 190

Shepstone, Theophilus, Natal official, 323

Sherbro Estuary, Sierra Leone, 146; map, 136

Sherbro Island, Sierra Leone, 33; maps, 34, 136

Sherkarer, Kushite king, 32

Shilluk, Nilotes, eastern Sudan, 90, 123, 188, 193, 194; map, 190

Shirazi, people, East African coast, 73

Shire River and region, Malawi, 210, 419; maps, 208, 274, 335

Shoa, Ethiopian region, 40, 83, 88, 281, 284; maps, 27, 87

Shona, people, Central Africa, 114, 115, 519-20, 524; maps, 21, 335

Shungwaya, region, East Africa, 80; map, 117

Sidama, people, Ethiopia, 84

Sidama, Ethiopian region, 84, 284

Sierra Leone, state and region, West Africa, 92, 227, 228, 233, 302, 303, 369, 465, 499, 536; economy, 476; *maps,* 95, 136, 274, 275, 457

Signares, Senegal, 146

Sijilmasa, Morocco, 44, 49; *map,* 46

Sikasso, West Africa, 180; *map,* 168

Siki, Nyamwezi leader, 281, 352

Sikonyela, Tlokwa leader, 213

Singh, Makhan, Kenyan nationalist, 459

Single-party government, 455, 456, 492-99

Sisal, 344, 351

Sisulu, Walter, South African Bantu nationalist, 413, 529

Sithole, Ndabaningi, Rhodesian African nationalist, 464, 517, 518

Sixth Dynasty, Egypt, 25

Slave Coast, West Africa, 152; *map,* 274

Slave trade, 28, 71, 81-82, 138, 143, 224-25, 228, 246, 267; Egypt and Kush, 28, 29; Trans-Saharan, 35, 49, 50, 67, 172; in East Africa, 71, 72, 76, 81-82, 159, 252-53, 259, 397; eastern Sudan, 187, 189, 193-95; West Africa, 65, 67, 68, 103, 104, 107, 108, 143, 145, 151-53, 181, 182, 236; volume, 151-52; in Kongo, 135, 137, 152; in Angola, 137, 152, 397; and Britain, 143; abolition of, 108, 143, 152, 225, 227, 238, 398; in Congo region, 248, 254, 255, 383

Slavery, abolition, 215, 216, 227, 230, 398, 437

Slavery, Africa, domestic, 97, 145, 152-53, 172, 228, 363; in South Africa, 139, 140, 142; in West Africa, 145, 147-48, 172, 228, 380; in East Africa, 192, 252

Small Scarcies River, Sierra Leone, 303

Smith, Harry, Cape Colony governor, 220, 311

Smith, Ian, Rhodesian prime minister, 463, 464, 516, 517, 518, 519

Smuts, Jan, Boer leader, 321, 407, 408, 410

So, people, central Sudan, 66

Soba, Alwa (Alodia), capital, 89; *map,* 87

Sobat River, eastern Sudan, 194; *map,* 190

Sobhuza, southern Bantu leader, 203, 205

Sobukwe, Robert, South African Bantu nationalist, 413, 527-28

Socé, Ousmane, Senegalese writer, 433, 537

Sofa, Samori regulars, 182

Sofala, Mozambique, 76, 77, 78; *maps,* 75, 117

Sokoto, city and Fulani state, 170, 171, 175; *map,* 168

Solanke, Ladipo, Nigerian nationalist, 435

Solomonid Dynasty, Ethiopia, 84, 88

Somali, people, 346, 544

Somalia, region and state, 28, 71, 72, 269, 285, 392, 465, 500; Italian penetration, 277; economy, 477; *maps,* 75, 274, 457

Somerset, James, freed slave, Britain, 226, 227

Songhai, people, West Africa, 45, 173; *maps,* 21, 168

Songhai, savanna kingdom, 53, 61-64; origins, 61; administration, 62, 63; decline, 58, 64; *maps,* 46

Soninke, people, West Africa, 52, 54, 58, 173; *maps,* 46, 168

Sorghum, West Africa, 13, 45

"Sorting," African trade, 150

Soshangane, Gaza king, 205, 207

Soso, people, upper Niger, 54, 59, 60

Sotho speakers, South Africa, 202; *map,* 208

Soudan, French West Africa, 449

South Africa, region and state, 202-6, 401-14, 522-31; and Dutch, 137-42; and British, 206, 276; and unification, 312-22; and racial policies, 322-23, 424-26, 401-7, 408, 409; pass laws, 215, 407, 525, 528; treason trial, 412-13; and High Commission territories, 414, 415, 525-26; industrialization, 315-16, 325, 523; and independent Africa, 515-16, 522-23, 525; and Rhodesia, 517, 523; and Namibia (South-West Africa), 415-16, 521-22, 523; *maps,* 141, 219, 320, 457

South Africa Act, 1909, 414

South African Communist Party, 412

South African Indian Congress, 412
South African Native National Congress
   (African National Congress), 327
South African Party, 321, 408
South African Republic (Transvaal), 220,
   313; *map*, 320
South African Students Organization
   (SASO), 527
Southern Cushites, 122, 123
Southern Rhodesia, 331, 336; and
   "native" policy, 416-18; and land
   policy, 417; self-governing colony,
   331, 417; and federation, 422; and
   African nationalism, 421; and
   independence, 462-64; *maps*, 275,
   320, 335, 393
Southern Sudan (of eastern Sudan),
   environment and people, 193-94; and
   slave trade, 195; *map*, 190
South-West Africa (Namibia), 403,
   415-16; German protectorate, 265,
   273, 317, 415; South African mandate, 415; independence, 521-22;
   maps, 274, 275, 320, 335, 393. *See
   also* Namibia
South-West People's Organization
   (SWAPO), 522
Soviet Union, 436, 509, 511, 515, 516,
   522
Sowande, Fela, Nigerian composer, 537
Soweto, South Africa, 524, 527, 528
Soyinka, Wole, Nigerian writer, 536, 538,
   541-42, 545-46
Spain, 137-38, 277, 465
Spanish Sahara, 465, 511, 543
Spear of the Nation, South Africa, 413,
   527
Specialization, technological, and eco-
   nomic, 11, 12, 17, 18, 102, 121, 124
Speke, J. H., British explorer, 258
Stack, Sir Lee, British colonial official,
   357
Stanley, H. M., American explorer, 258,
   259, 264, 269
Stanley Falls, Congo (Zaire), 257; *maps*,
   247, 274
Stanley Pool, Congo (Zaire) River,

Kinshasa, 384, 392; *map*, 393
Stanleyville (Kisangi), Belgian Congo,
   385, 451; *map*, 393
Stateless societies, 96, 97, 128-29, 347
Stel, Simon van der, 139
Stel, Willem van der, 139
Stellenbosch, South Africa, 139; *map*, 141
Stephen, James, British abolitionist, 226
Strijdom, J. G., Afrikaner leader, 409
Strikes, South Africa, 408, 410, 411, 412,
   413, 528
Suakin, eastern Sudan, 188, 199,*map*, 190
Sudan, Anglo-Egyptian (eastern), 356-59,
   507-8, 544; and independence,
   438-39; and Egypt, 356-57, 438; and
   the south, 439; economy, 357; poli-
   tical stability, 507-8, 544; *maps*, 274,
   275, 342, 393
Sudan, Democratic Republic of, 507-8
Sudan, region, 35, 52-56, 56-58; central,
   52-56; 56-58; eastern, 28, 29, 32,
   88-89, 185-93; southern, 193-201,
   507; western, 52-56, 56-58; and
   African imperial administration,
   56-58; *map*, 34
Sudan People's Liberation Movement, 508
Sudd, Nile River, 31, 186, 188, 193;
   maps, 27, 190
Suez Canal, 270
Sufism, saint worship, Islam, 167, 169,
   189, 191
Sulb, Kush, 28, *map*, 27
Sulaiman, Zeriba chief, eastern Sudan,
   196
Sultan bin Seif, Omani ruler, 80
Sumaguru Kante, Soso leader, 59
Suna, Buganda king, 259
Sunday River, South Africa, 142; *map*,
   141
Sundiata, Mali king, 56, 59, 60
Sunni Ali, Songhai king, 53, 55, 57, 61,
   62, 63
Sur la Philosophie Africaine, 542
Susenyos, Ethiopian king, 86
Susu, people, Futa Jalon, *map*, 168
Sutherland, Efua, Ghanaian dramatist, 538
Swahili, language, people, and culture, 73,

120, 249, 250, 383

Swazi, people, South Africa, 159, 205; *map*, 208

Swaziland, 318, 323, 403, 414, 415, 465; *maps*, 219, 275, 320, 335, 457

Sweden, 143

Swellendam, South Africa, 142; *map*, 141

Swollen shoot virus, cocoa, 440

Sylvester Williams, Henry, West Indian pan-Africanist, 377

Table Bay, South Africa, 138; *map*, 136

Tabora, Tanzania, 250, 251, 256; *maps*, 247, 274, 342

Tabwa, people, eastern Congo, 257; *map*, 247

Taggada, central Sudan, 55; *map*, 46

Taghaza, Sahara, 50-51, 60, 63; *map*, 46

Taharqa, Kushite king, 30

Tana, Lake, Ethiopia, 36, 85; *maps*, 27, 87, 190

Tana River, East Africa, 72; *maps*, 75, 117, 274

Tanganyika, Lake, East Africa, 5, 125, 207, 248, 257; *maps*, 6, 7, 117, 208, 247, 274, 335

Tanganyika, region and state, 74, 353-54; independence, 454-55; *maps*, 335, 342, 393, 457

Tanganyika African National Union (TANU), 454-55, 497

Tanis, Egypt, 30; *map*, 27

Tanzania, state, 455, 502; economy, 470, 486-87; *map*, 457

Tawfiq, khedive of Egypt, 270

Taxation, colonial, 351, 362, 363, 369, 376, 381, 388; and African custom, 303, 307, 332, 388; and labor policy, 325, 330, 344, 349, 385, 388, 392

Tea, 267

Teda, people, Tibesti, 35, 36, 43, 44, 57, 67; *map*, 34

Teff, Ethiopian cereal, 13, 37

Tekrur, state and region, West Africa, 60, 133; *maps*, 46, 136

Tema, Ghana, 480

Tempel, Placide, 542

Territory of Afars and Issas, 465

Teso, people, East Africa, 341, 456; *map*, 342

Tete, Mozambique, 79, 249; *maps*, 75, 117, 247

Tetela, people, eastern Congo (Zaire), 257; *map*, 247

Tewodros (Theodore), Ethiopian king, and modernization, 282-83

Thaba Bosiu, Basutoland, 213, 214; *map*, 219

Thaba Nhu, South Africa, 217; *maps*, 208, 219

Thebes, Egypt, 29, 30; *map*, 27

Thembu, people, South Africa, 222, 322; *map*, 219

Theodore (Tewodros), Ethiopian king, 282-83

Third Cataract, Nile River, 26, 90; *maps*, 27, 190

Thornton, Henry, British abolitionist, 226, 227

Three Points, Cape, Gold Coast, 148; *map*, 136

Thuku, Harry, Kikuyu nationalist, 349-50, 429

Thutmose I, Egyptian pharaoh, 28, 29

Thys, Albert, Belgian businessman, 384

Thysville, Lower Congo (Zaire), 389; *map*, 393

Tibesti, Saharan region, 5, 35, 42, 43, 391; *maps*, 6, 34, 393

Tigre, Ethiopian region, 39, 40, 85, 88, 281, 282, 283, 509; *maps*, 27, 87

Tijani, al-, Muslim reformer, 174

Tijaniyya, Muslim brotherhood, 174, 176

Tile, Nehemiah, South African Churchman, 326

Timber, 472, 473, 476

Timbuktu, West Africa, 44, 49, 53, 54, 55, 60, 61, 173; *maps*, 34, 46, 95, 136, 168

Tippu Tip, Swahili trader, 251, 252, 255, 256-58, 272

Tirailleurs Sénégalais, riflemen, 240

Tiv, people, West Africa, 96; *map*, 95

Tlokwa, people, South Africa, 210, 213,

217; *map*, 219

Todd, Garfield, Southern Rhodesia prime minister, 463

Togo, state, West Africa, 499, 550; German protectorate, 265, 351; U.N. trust territory, 448; independence, 450; economy, 476; *maps*, 274, 275, 457

Tokolor, people, and Muslim state, West Africa, 174, 176, 230, 271; *al-Hajj* Umar jihad, 176; Muslim state, 176, 181, 271; *maps*, 168, 274

Tolbert, W.R., Liberian president, 499, 500

Tombalbaye, N., Chad president, 500, 510

Tomlinson Commission, South Africa, 402-3

Tondibi, battle, Songhai, 64; *map*, 46

Tonga, people, Zambia, 334, 461; *map*, 335

Tool making, 9-10, 11

Toro, state, East Africa, 341, 456, 503; *map*, 342

Torodbe, Fulani Muslim clerics, 167

Torwa, Central Africa, 114, 115; *map*, 117

Touré, Sekou, Guinea president, 449, 469, 495-96

Trade, African, 38, 47-50, 102, 135, 165, 171-72, 229-30; Egypt and Kush, 5, 6, 8, 24; Egypt and Axum, 38; trans-Saharan, 35, 36, 48-50, 57, 58, 64, 68, 171-72, 179; silent trade, 51; East African and Indian Ocean, 38, 70-72, 76, 114, 121, 134, 185, 249-51, 339; West African forest, 48, 102, 109, 147, 148-49, 239-40; Central Africa, 135, 248, 249; eastern Sudan, 189

Trade, international, 63, 138, 165, 245, 246, 249-51, 263, 267, 268, 278-79, 313; Egyptian, 17, 24-26, 28; Indian Ocean, 70-72, 114, 134, 249; and Axum, 38, 39, 40, 70; and West Africa, 47-50, 63, 149-50, 165, 171-72, 179, 239-40, 240-41, 243; and Zimbabwe and Mutapa, 114, 115;

and eastern Sudan, 188, 189

"Trade ounce," 150

Trade routes, trans-Saharan, 35, 47-50; in Egypt and eastern Sudan, 188-89; in East Africa and Congo basin, 248, 249-51, 255-56, 257; *maps*, 27, 34, 247

Transkei, South Africa, 322, 404, 524; *map*, 320

Transorangia, South Africa, 217; *map*, 219

Transvaal, South Africa, 118, 211, 312, 313, 314-16, 317, 319; *maps*, 219, 274, 320, 335

Trarza Moors, Mauritania, 240, 267; *map*, 274

Travail obligatoire, 470

Treason trial, South Africa, 412-13

Treaty of London, 163

Trekboer, Dutch frontiersman, South Africa, 140

Treurnicht, Andries, South African politician, 531

"Tribalism" (regionalism), 349-50, 443-45, 450-53, 454, 456, 458, 460-461, 464, 491-92, 497, 500, 504-505, 506, 509-510, 519-20, 528, 529, 550

Tripoli, North Africa, 49, 63, 171; *map*, 46

Tripolitania, region, North Africa, 277; *map*, 274

True Whig Party, Liberia, 301, 379, 498

Trusteeship, 353, 417, 418, 419

Tshombe, Moise, Congo (Zaire) political figure, 450, 452-53, 498

Tswana, people, South Africa, 202, 312, 524; *map*, 208

Tuareg, people, Sahara, 43-44, 57, 61, 64, 67, 391, 482, 483, 548; *maps*, 21, 46

Tubman, William V.S., Liberian president, 381, 499

Tubu (Teda), people, Tibesti, 35; *map*, 34

Tugela River, South Africa, 206; *maps*, 208, 219, 320

Tunis, North Africa, 49; *map*, 46

Tunisia, region and state, North Africa, 269, 448; independence, 448; *maps*, 275, 457

Turkana (Rudolf), Lake, 5, 128; *maps*, 6, 117, 190, 247, 342

Turkana, Nilotes, East Africa, 123, 128-29, 347; *maps*, 117, 342

Turks, Ottoman, 78, 86

Turnhalle Alliance, Namibia, 522, 523

Tushki, battle, Egypt, 200, 201; *map*, 190

Tuta, Ngoni section, 209; *map*, 208

Tutsi, people, Rwanda/Burundi, 123, 125, 453, 509, 510; *map*, 117

Tutu, Bishop Desmond, South Africa, 528

Tutuola, Amos, Nigerian writer, 536

Twenty-fifth Dynasty, Egypt, 29

Twining, Sir Edward, Tanganyikan governor, 454

"Two pyramids," Southern Rhodesia, 417

Tyeddo, Cayor soldiers, Senegal, 239

Ubangi-Chari, French colony, 392, 449; *map*, 393

Ubangi River, Congo-Brazzaville, 272, 391, 392, *maps*, 274, 393

Uccaili (Wichali), treaty, Ethiopia, 285

Uganda, region and state, East Africa, 339-43, 497, 503, 543, 544; and British control, 339-43; independence, 455-56; *maps*, 275, 342, 393, 457

Uganda National Congress, political party, 456

Uganda People's Congress (UPC), political party, 456

Uganda People's Union, political party, 456

Uitlanders, South Africa, 315, 318

Ujamaa, Tanzania, 470, 487

Ujiji, Tanganyika, 250, 251, 256; *map*, 208, 247

Uli, Mali king, 60

Ulundi, battle, South Africa, 314, 323; *map*, 320

Umar, *al-Hajj*, Tokolor empire builder, 174-76, 230, 240

Umar, Kanem-Bornu leader, 178

Umar ibn Idris, Kanem-Bornu king, 66

Umma party, eastern Sudan, 358, 438, 439, 507

Unemployment, 407, 479, 482, 483, 485, 495, 545

Unification, South Africa, 312-16, 316-21, 322, 326

Unilateral Declaration of Independence (UDI), Rhodesia, 462, 464, 516, 517, 519

Union Minière de Haut-Katanga, 385, 390

Union of South Africa, 321, 322; *maps*, 275, 335

Union of Soviet Socialist Republics (U.S.S.R.). *See* Soviet Union

Union of the Peoples of Angola (UPA), 399, 513, 515

Union Soudanaise (US), 496

UNITA. *See* National Union for the Total Independence of Angola

United African Company (Royal Niger Company), 271

United Democratic Front, South Africa, 529

United Federal Party, Rhodesia Federation, 421, 424, 463

United Gold Coast Convention (UGCC), political party, 440-41, 442

United National Independence Party (UNIP), Zambia, 423, 424, 461, 497

United Nations, 436, 447, 448, 465, 511, 516; and South-West Africa (Namibia), 415-16, 520, 521, 522; and Eritrea, 438; and Congo, 452; and Tanganyika, 454; and Rhodesia, 516

United Party, South Africa, 408, 409

United States, 436, 511, 515, 522, 526; and Liberia, 228-29, 302, 379-80; Berlin Conference, 263; and racial issues, 435, 526, 529; foreign aid, 477

United Tanganyika Party, 454

Universal Negro Improvement Association, 379

Universities, 294, 299, 390, 404, 545; in West Africa, 294, 299, 536, 538, 539

Unyamwezi, region, East Africa, 248, 251; *map*, 247

Unyanyembe, Nyamwezi trade center, 250, 251, 256; *map*, 247

Upper Egypt, 16, 17, 29

Upper Nile, province, 507
Upper Volta (Burkina Faso), state, 449,
    496, 499, 500, 502; *map*, 457
Urabi Pasha, Egyptian colonel, 270
Urabist revolt, Egypt, 199, 270
Urambo, Mirambo capital, 256; *map*, 247
Uranium, 8, 476, 477
Urban Areas Act, South Africa, 403
Urbanism, 12, 483; in Egypt, 17; in South
    Africa, 324-25, 405; in Kenya, 348;
    and African independence, 431-32
Usuman dan Fodio (*Shehu*), Muslim
    reformer, 68, 69, 177; and Sokoto
    jihad, 167, 169-70, 172
Uzama, Benin chiefs, 105

Vaal River, South Africa, 217, 220; *maps*,
    141, 208, 219, 320, 335
Van Vollenhoven, J., French colonial
    governor-general, 362
Venda, South African "homeland," 404,
    524
Venn, Henry, British philanthropist, 232,
    234, 243
Verde, Cape, Senegal, 92, 238; *maps*, 6,
    95, 136, 168, 237
Verwoerd, Dr. Hendrik, South African
    prime minister, 401, 402, 403, 409
Vet River, South Africa, 220; *map*, 219
Victoria, Lake, East Africa, 5, 125, 248,
    343; *maps*, 6, 7, 117, 208, 247, 335,
    342
Victoria Falls, Zambezi River, 5, 210;
    maps, 208, 335
Volta River, West Africa, 93, 108; *maps*,
    46, 95, 168, 237; Black Volta, 51,
    108; *maps*, 46, 95, 168; industrial
    complex, 476, 480
Voluntary associations, 433, 459
Vorster, John, South African prime
    minister, 409, 517
Voyage au Congo, 394, 534

Wadai, kingdom, central Sudan, 178, 179,
    391; *maps*, 46, 168, 393
Wadi Halfa, eastern Sudan, 187, 200;
    maps, 27, 190
Wafd, Egyptian nationalist party, 357
Wagadugu, Mossi state, 165; *map*, 168

Wahabiyya, Muslim reformers, 174, 185
Walata, western Sudan, 48, 53, 54, 59;
    maps, 34, 46
Wallaga, Ethiopian region, 284
Walo, region, Senegal, *maps*, 95, 237
Wanga, state, East Africa, 278, 346; *map*,
    342. *See also* Hanga
Wangara, people and region, West Africa,
    48, 51, 58, 60; *map*, 46
Warden, H. D., British South African
    official, 221
Wargala, North Africa, 49
Warri River, Nigeria, 279; *map*, 274
Waruhiu, Chief, Kikuyu leader, 460
Wassa, Akan state, 236; *maps*, 95, 237
Wassulu, West African region, 181; *map*,
    168
Waterboer, Griqua leader, 312
Watson Commission, Gold Coast, 441
Webb, Stanley J. (Lord Passfield), 418
Welensky, Roy, Rhodesian Federation
    prime minister, 420, 421, 422, 423,
    424, 463, 464
West Africa, 20, 32-33, 92; savanna
    civilization, 45, 47, 52-55, 56-58;
    trans-Saharan trade, 48-52, 57-58;
    forest civilization, 92-102; internal
    trade, 47-48; slave trade, 107, 133,
    143, 147, 152, 153, 226; European
    trade, 133, 149-51; and Westerniza-
    tion, 145-49, 158; and partition, 266,
    267, 268, 271, 276; French territories,
    290-94, 365-68; British territories,
    294-97, 305-8, 368-74
West African Customs Union, 485
West African Economic Community, 485
West African forest, 45, 92, 93, 94
West African Pilot, Lagos, 433
West African Students' Union, Britain,
    435
West Indies, British, 226-27; French, 229,
    533
West Indies Company, French, 143
Wet, C. R. de, Boer leader, 321
Wet and dry phases, Sahara, 17, 42-43,
    93, 116
Wheat, 16, 37, 43
White Fathers, missionaries, 272
White Flag League, eastern Sudan, 358

Whitehead, Sir Edgar, Southern Rhodesia prime minister, 463
White Highlands, Kenya, 344, 345, 347, 349, 459, 460, 475
White mercenaries, Congo (Zaire), 452, 453
White Nile, 36, 194, 196; *maps*, 6, 87, 190, 247, 342
Whydah, Dahomey, 107, 230; *map*, 168
Wichali (Ucciali), treaty, Ethiopia, 285
Wilberforce, William, British abolitionist, 226, 228
Winburg, South Africa, 220; *map*, 219
Windhoek, Namibia, 521
Witwatersrand, Transvaal, 316; *map*, 320
Wodehouse, Sir P., Cape Colony governor, 312
Wolof, Senegal people, 47, 146, 238; *maps*, 21, 95, 237
Women, 98, 102, 107, 121, 125, 212, 388, 394, 403, 405, 406, 412, 546-47, 548; status in western and central Sudan, 47, 54, 65, 97, 146, 547; traders, 102; among Wolof and Serer, 97; and female circumcision, 350-51
World Bank (International Bank for Reconstruction and Development), 487, 488, 489
World War, First, 361-62, 366, 370, 408, 435; Second, 435-36, 438, 473
Wright, Richard, Black American writer, 540
Writing, in Egypt, 18; in Meroe, 31; in Ethiopia, 37; in West Africa, 52

Xhosa, South African people, 142, 158, 202, 216, 222, 322, 404, 524, 528, 529; *map*, 219

Yam, 13, 99-100, 120
Yao, people, East Africa, 248, 249, 251, 252, 253, 334, 352; *maps*, 21, 335, 342
Yatenga, Mossi State, 165; *map*, 168
Yeke, Congo people, 254; *map*, 247
Yekuno Amlak, Ethiopian king, 84
Yemen, Arabia, 37, 73; *maps*, 27, 75, 87
Yemenites, in Ethiopia, 37, 38, 83

Yohannes IV, Ethiopian king, 200, 283, 284
Yoruba, West African people, 96, 103-4, 235-36, 302, 444; and civil wars, 104, 108, 235-36, 242, 303-4; *map*, 21
Yorubaland, West Africa, 104, 171, 224, 241; *maps*, 95, 168, 237
Young Gabon, society, 395
Young Kavirondo Association, 349, 350
Young Kikuyu Association, 349
Young Senegalese, 294, 365
Yunfa, Gobir king, 170

Za, Songhai dynasty, 61
Za Dengel, Ethiopian king, 86
Zagawa, central Sudan people, 65
Zagwe dynasty, Ethiopia, 83, 84
Zaire (Congo-Kinshasa), economy, 452, 476, 486, 488, 545; political stability, 451-53, 497, 499, 543, 550; *map*, 457
Zaire river. *See* Congo River
Zambezi River, Central Africa, 5, 71, 72, 78, 79, 114, 115, 119, 207, 210, 423; *maps*, 6, 7, 75, 117, 208, 219, 247, 274, 335
Zambia, state, Central Africa, 423, 502, 550; independence, 461-62; economy, 476, 488; and Rhodesia, 477; *map*, 457
Zambia African National Congress, 423
Zambia, Hausa state, 169; *map*, 168
Zanj, East African coast, 73
Zanzibar, East Africa, 71, 74, 76, 77, 82, 248, 257, 343, 455; Omani domination, 81, 82, 250-52; British control, 273, 343; independence, 455; *maps*, 75, 247, 274, 275, 342, 457
Zanzibar National Party (ZNP), 455
Zanzibar and Pemba People's Party (ZPPP), 455
Zara Yakob, Ethiopian king, 84
Zaria (Zazzau), Hausa city-state, 55, 68, 170, 171; *maps*, 46, 168
Zaudita, Ethiopian empress, 437
Zeribas, eastern Sudan, 195, 196
Zimba, people, East Africa, 79-80; *map*, 117
Zimbabwe, Central Africa, 78, 113; Great

Zimbabwe, 113-14; *maps*, 117, 219
Zimbabwe, modern state, 488, 519-20,
  550; *map*, 457
Zimbabwe African National Union
  (ZANU), political party, 464, 517
Zimbabwe African People's Union
  (ZAPU), political party, 462, 464,
  517, 519, 520
Zinder, region, Central Sudan, 178; *map*,
  168
Zong, slave ship, 225

Zubair, al-, Rahma Mansur Pasha, eastern
  Sudan, 183, 195, 196, 198
Zula, people and state, South Africa, 119,
  158, 204-6, 213, 217, 314, 323, 414,
  527, 528; *maps*, 21, 208, 219
Zululand, South Africa, 203, 314, 323;
  maps, 219, 320
Zuurveld, South Africa region, 142; *map*,
  141
Zwagendaba, Ngoni leader, 205, 207, 209
Zwide, southern Bantu leader, 203, 205